Second Edition

FOUNDATIONS OF ADDICTIONS COUNSELING

David Capuzzi

Johns Hopkins University

Walden University

Professor Emeritus, Portland State University

Mark D. Stauffer

Oregon State University

Walden University

PEARSON

Boston Columbus Indianapolis New York San Francisco Upper Saddle River
Amsterdam Cape Town Dubai London Madrid Milan Munich Paris Montreal Toronto
Delhi Mexico City São Paulo Sydney Hong Kong Seoul Singapore Taipei Tokyo

Vice President and Editor in Chief: Jeffery W. Johnston
Senior Acquisitions Editor: Meredith D. Fossel
Editorial Assistant: Nancy Holstein
Vice President, Director of Marketing: Margaret Waples
Senior Marketing Manager: Christopher Barry
Senior Managing Editor: Pamela Bennett
Senior Project Manager: Mary M. Irvin
Senior Operations Supervisor: Matt Ottenweller
Senior Art Director: Diane Lorenzo

Cover Designer: Candace Rowley
Cover Art: Fotolia
Full-Service Project Management: S4Carlisle Publishing Services, Inc.
Composition: S4Carlisle Publishing Services, Inc.
Printer/Binder: Courier
Cover Printer: Courier
Text Font: Minion

Every effort has been made to provide accurate and current Internet information in this book. However, the Internet and information posted on it are constantly changing, so it is inevitable that some of the Internet addresses listed in this textbook will change.

Library of Congress Cataloging-in-Publication Data
Foundations of addictions counseling / [edited by] David Capuzzi, Mark D. Stauffer.
    p. cm.
  Includes bibliographical references and index.
  ISBN 978-0-13-705778-8 (alk. paper)
  1. Drug abuse counseling.   I. Capuzzi, Dave.   II. Stauffer, Mark D.
  RC564.F69 2011
  362.29'186—dc22

                                2010043247

10 9 8 7 6 5 4 3 2 1

www.pearsonhighered.com

ISBN 10:   0-13-705778-4
ISBN 13: 978-0-13-705778-8

PREFACE

Whether you are entering the field of addictions counseling or are a counselor who wants to be prepared for the screening, assessment, and treatment of addiction in your practice, this text provides a foundational basis. *Foundations of Addictions Counseling* addresses real-life clinical concerns while providing the necessary information to keep up to date with field trends. It also addresses the evolving standards of professional organizations, accrediting bodies, licensure boards, and graduate programs and departments. Counselors in school, mental health, rehabilitation, hospital, private practice, and a variety of other settings must be thoroughly prepared to support clients in their quest to be healthy and unimpaired. As the addictions profession has matured, more and more emphasis has been placed on the importance of preparing counselors to work holistically and synthesize knowledge domains from mental health, developmental, and addiction perspectives. The authors provide this knowledge in support of your work on behalf of various clients and diverse communities.

Counselors can expect some of their clients to want to address concerns connected with the use of substances and the development of addictive behavior. This book draws on the specialized knowledge for each contributed chapter. It is written for use in graduate-level preparation programs for counselors. Because of the clarity of the writing and the use of case studies, it may also be adopted in some undergraduate and community college courses. Requirements of the Council for the Accreditation of Counseling and Related Educational Programs (CACREP) and other certification associations have led most university programs in counselor education to require an addictions course for all students, regardless of specialization (school, community, rehabilitation, couples, marriage and family, student personnel, etc.). Addictions counseling is also being offered for CADC I and II certifications, which require undergraduate coursework related to addictions counseling.

NEW TO THIS EDITION

- A new chapter dedicated to process addictions
- Cross-cultural addictions counseling chapter on engaging ethnic diversity
- Broadening knowledge of addictions counseling for specific settings, with coverage of prevention programs in college settings
- Additional case studies to further illustrate points and enliven class discussion
- Informational sidebars to encourage the visual learner and reader contemplation
- Integration of updated and current research from the field's peer-reviewed journals
- Instructor's manual that includes journal, groupwork, and experiential exercises for the online as well as face-to-face classroom.

It is our hope that this second edition of *Foundations of Addictions Counseling* will provide the beginning student counselor with the basics needed for follow-up courses and supervised practice in the arena of addictions counseling.

Although the text addresses the history, theories, and research related to addictions counseling, at least half of the book's emphasis is on techniques and skills needed by the practitioner.

In addition, guidelines for addictions counseling in family, rehabilitation, and school settings are addressed; as are topics connected with cross-cultural counseling and addictions. Some of the topics that make the book engaging and of high interest to readers:

- Concrete reference to assessment tools
- Outpatient and inpatient treatment
- Maintenance and relapse prevention
- Counseling with addicted/recovering clients
- Counseling couples and families that are coping with addictions issues
- Addictions prevention programs for children, adolescents, and college students

Writers experienced in addictions counseling were asked to contribute so that the reader is provided with not only theory and research but also with those applications so pertinent to the role of the practicing, licensed, and certified addictions counselor. This book also reflects the view of the editors that counselors must be prepared in a holistic manner, since addiction issues are so often the reason clients seek the assistance of a professional counselor.

The book is unique in both format and content. The contributing authors' format provides state-of-the-art information by experts nationally recognized for their expertise, research, and publications related to addictions counseling. The content looks at areas not always addressed in introductory texts. Examples include chapters on professional issues in addictions counseling, process addictions, and gender and addictions counseling. Chapters focused on addictions counseling with gay, lesbian, and bisexual clients; on engaging ethnic diversity; and on pharmacotherapy provide perspectives often overlooked in texts of this kind. The format and content enhance readability and interest and should engage and motivate graduate students in counseling and aligned professions as well as those enrolled in lower division courses.

The book is designed for students taking a preliminary course in addictions counseling. It presents a comprehensive overview of the foundations of addictions counseling, the skills and techniques needed for addictions counseling, and addictions counseling in specific settings. As editors, we know that one text cannot adequately address all the complex and holistic factors involved in assisting clients who present with issues related to addictive behavior. We have, however, attempted to provide our readers with a broad perspective based on current professional literature and the rapidly changing world we live in at this juncture of the new millennium. The following overview highlights the major features of the text.

OVERVIEW

The format for the co-edited textbook is based on the contributions of authors who are recognized for their expertise, research, and publications. With few exceptions, each chapter contains case studies illustrating practical applications of the concepts presented. Most chapters refer the reader to Web sites containing supplemental information. Students will find it helpful to use the study material on the Web site maintained by Pearson Publishing. Professors may want to make use of the PowerPoints developed for each chapter, as well as the test manual that can be used to develop quizzes and exams on the book's content.

The text is divided into the following four parts: (1) Introduction to Addictions Counseling; (2) The Treatment of Addictions; (3) Addictions in Family Therapy, Rehabilitation, and School Settings; and (4) Cross-Cultural Counseling in Addictions.

PART 1 Introduction to Addictions Counseling (Chapters 1 through 6), begins with information on the historical perspectives and etiological models that serve as the foundation for current approaches to addictions counseling, and provides the reader with the contextual background needed to assimilate subsequent chapters. Chapters focused on substance and process addictions, professional issues, an introduction to assessment, and assessment and diagnosis of addictions are included as well.

PART 2 The Treatment of Addictions (Chapters 7 through 13), presents information about motivational interviewing, other psychotherapeutic approaches, co-occurring disorders, group work, pharmacotherapy, 12-step programs, and maintenance and relapse prevention. All chapters provide overviews and introduce readers to the skills and techniques used in the addictions counseling process.

PART 3 Addictions in Family Therapy, Rehabilitation, and School Settings (Chapters 14 through 16), presents information relative to addiction and families; persons with disabilities; and children, adolescents, and college students. These chapters highlight information that has relevance and application to diverse contexts.

PART 4 Cross-Cultural Counseling in Addictions (Chapters 17 through 19), discusses ethnic diversity; gender and addictions; and gay, lesbian, and bisexual affirmative addictions treatment.

ACKNOWLEDGMENTS

We would like to thank the 30 authors who contributed their expertise, knowledge, and experience in the development of this textbook. We would also like to thank our families, who provided us with the freedom and encouragement to make this endeavor possible. Our thanks are also directed to members of the Pearson production team for their encouragement and assistance with copyediting and, ultimately, the publication of the book.

Special thanks are extended to Cass Dykeman, professor of Counselor Education at Oregon State University, for his suggestions on content areas included in this book. Thanks to his input, readers of *Foundations of Addictions Counseling* will benefit from a more comprehensive overview of counseling with clients experiencing addictions issues.

We would like to thank the reviewers of our manuscript for their comments and insights: Wendy Bianchini, Montana State University; Connie Brewer, California State University, Long Beach, California State University, Fullerton, and Cypress College; Steven Dinsmore, Wayne State College; Carol Rankin, California State University, Fresno; Caroline Reid, Eastern Kentucky University; and Rita Schellenberg, Old Dominion University.

CONTRIBUTORS

MEET THE EDITORS

David Capuzzi, Ph.D., NCC, LPC, is a professor emeritus at Portland State University, senior faculty associate in the Department of Counseling and Human Services at Johns Hopkins University, and a member of the core faculty in the Ph.D. in Counselor Education and Supervision in the School of Counseling and Social Service at Walden University. Previously, he served as an affiliate professor in the Department of Counselor Education, Counseling Psychology, and Rehabilitation Services at Pennsylvania State University. He is past President of the American Counseling Association (ACA), formerly the American Association for Counseling and Development.

From 1980 to 1984, Dr. Capuzzi was editor of *The School Counselor*. He has authored a number of textbook chapters and monographs on preventing adolescent suicide and is coeditor and author with Dr. Larry Golden of *Helping Families Help Children: Family Interventions with School Related Problems* (1986) and *Preventing Adolescent Suicide* (1988). He co-authored and edited with Douglas R. Gross *Youth at Risk: A Prevention Resource for Counselors, Teachers, and Parents* (1989, 1996, 2000, 2004, and 2008); *Introduction to the Counseling Profession* (1991, 1997, 2001, 2005, and 2009); *Introduction to Group Work* (1992, 1998, 2002, 2006, and 2010); and *Counseling and Psychotherapy: Theories and Interventions* (1995, 1999, 2003, 2007, and 2011). Other texts are *Approaches to Group Work: A Handbook for Practitioners* (2003), *Suicide Across the Life Span* (2006), and *Sexuality Issues in Counseling,* the last co-authored and edited with Larry Burlew. He has authored or co-authored articles in a number of ACA-related journals.

A frequent speaker and keynoter at professional conferences and institutes, Dr. Capuzzi has also consulted with a variety of school districts and community agencies interested in initiating prevention and intervention strategies for adolescents at risk for suicide. He has facilitated the development of suicide prevention, crisis management, and postvention programs in communities throughout the United States; provides training on the topics of youth at risk and grief and loss; and serves as an invited adjunct faculty member at other universities as time permits.

An ACA fellow, he is the first recipient of ACA's Kitty Cole Human Rights Award and also a recipient of the Leona Tyler Award in Oregon. In 2010, he received ACA's Gilbert and Kathleen Wrenn Award for a Humanitarian and Caring Person.

Mark D. Stauffer, Ph.D., NCC, received his doctoral degree from Oregon State University Department of Teacher and Counselor Education. He specialized in couples, marriage, and family counseling during his graduate work in the Counselor Education Program at Portland State University, where he received his master's degree. He was a Chi Sigma Iota International fellow.

Dr. Stauffer has worked in the Portland, Oregon metro area at crises centers and other non-profit organizations working with addictions-affected individuals, couples, and families. He is a contributing instructor at Oregon State University's Department of Teacher and Counselor Education and at Walden University's School of Counseling and Social Service.

He has studied and trained in the Zen tradition, and presents locally and nationally on meditation and mindfulness-based therapies in counseling. He has co-edited two other textbooks in the counseling field with Dr. David Capuzzi: *Introduction to Group Work* (2010); and *Career Counseling: Foundations, Perspectives, and Applications* (2006).

MEET THE AUTHORS

Lisa Langfuss Aasheim, Ph.D., NCC, ACS, is the Coordinator of the School Counseling Program and the Director of the Community Counseling Training Clinic at Portland State University. She specializes in Clinical Supervision and has spent over a decade working with drug affected individuals and families in various settings. Currently, she teaches Master's, Doctoral, and post-Graduate level courses focusing on Clinical Supervision, Addictions Counseling, and Counselor Education. She provides trainings for counselors, social workers, and helping professionals throughout the Pacific Northwest in topics such as Motivational Interviewing, The Therapeutic Alliance, Agency Dynamics, and Relational Change Strategies in Agency Work.

Vanessa Alleyne, Ph.D., is Associate Professor & Coordinator of the Addiction Studies Program at Montclair State University in New Jersey. She teaches courses in all areas of addictions and other areas, including counseling children & adolescents, clinical practica, and counseling theories. Her research interests include examining racial identity and motivation for treatment among African American substance abusers; forensic evaluation; chemical dependency and treatment of incarcerated women; and group processes. Her clinical career in counseling psychology has spanned many venues, including hospital based addiction treatment programs; male and female forensic settings; counseling battered women and their children in New York city shelters; and psychological consulting for Headstart. She currently heads the Institutional Review Board for Urban Pathways, Inc., one of New York City's largest social services programs, which provides assistance to nearly ten thousand homeless men and women each year.

Senait Alem Bairu, M.A., recently graduated from the Educational Psychology and Guidance Program at the University of Texas at El Paso. She received her Bachelor's Degree in Child and Youth Care from the University of the Frasier Valley in British Columbia, Canada. While finishing her degree she completed several internships with various agencies that developed her experience in the mental health field. She has varied work experience related to children and youth, including substance abuse issues, sexual trauma, physical and emotional abuse, and gang violence. Most recently she has been working as a graduate research assistant at the University of Texas at El Paso researching such topics as language barriers in counseling efficacy and racial biases in the judicial system.

Malachy Bishop, Ph.D., CRC, is a professor in the Rehabilitation Counseling Program in the Department of Special Education and Rehabilitation Counseling at the University of Kentucky. He completed his doctoral study in Rehabilitation Psychology at the University of Wisconsin–Madison. His research interests include quality of life, adaptation to chronic illness and disability, and the psychological and social aspects of chronic neurological conditions. He has authored over 50 peer-reviewed articles, 14 book chapters, and a co-edited book.

Cynthia A. Briggs, Ph.D., NCC, LPC, is a fourth-year assistant professor of Counselor Education at Winona State University in Minnesota. She also serves as the Addictions Counseling Program Coordinator, developing and implementing a certificate program for graduate students of addictions counseling. Her research interests include addiction issues, veterans, and women's health. She is co-author of the landmark text *Women, Girls, and Addiction: Celebrating the Feminine in Addiction Treatment and Recovery,* published in 2009 by Routledge. In addition, she writes a regular blog entitled The Sophia Project *(www.drcyndibriggs.wordpress.com),* focused on women's health and wholeness.

Jennifer Burris, M.A., is a doctoral student in the Department of Special Education and Rehabilitation Counseling at the University of Kentucky. She received her bachelor's degree from Washington University in St. Louis and her master's degree from Maryville University. She has worked as a teacher in general education and support in special education. Her research interests include self-efficacy and minority populations.

Stephanie A. Calmes, M.A., is a Doctoral Graduate Assistant in the Department of Counselor Education & School Psychology at the University of Toledo. She is a Licensed Professional Clinical Counselor (PCC) in the state of Ohio, a Licensed Chemical Dependency Counselor-III (LCDC-III), and a National Certified Counselor (NCC). Her research interests include chemical dependency counseling and supervision, dual diagnosis, multiple relationships, and stigma. Stephanie has experience working in dual diagnosis treatment, as well as in both outpatient and residential chemical dependency treatment programs. Stephanie is the current (2009–2010) secretary for the Ohio Association for Counselor Education and Supervision (OACES) and president of the Alpha Omega chapter of Chi Sigma Iota.

Pamela A. Cingel, Ph.D., earned her Ph.D. from the University of Toledo in 1992. She has been a full-time counselor educator and psychology instructor for 20 years. She has over 16 years of clinical experience as a counselor. She was the manager of an inpatient chemical dependency unit for adolescents and provided clinical supervision to various community agencies. She is currently a Professor and Director of the Psychology Program as well as Director of Faculty and Student Research Center at St. Thomas University in Miami, Florida. Her research interests include emotional intelligence, adolescents, and gender studies.

Reverend Professor Christopher C. H. Cook, MD, FRCPsych, is a Professorial Research Fellow in the Department of Theology & Religion at Durham University, England. He trained at St George's Hospital Medical School, London, and has worked in the psychiatry of substance misuse for 24 years. He was Professor of the Psychiatry of Alcohol Misuse at the University of Kent from 1997 to 2003. He was ordained as an Anglican priest in Canterbury Cathedral in 2001. He is interested in spirituality, theology, and health, and his publications include *Alcohol, Addiction and Christian Ethics* (Cook, CCH, Cambridge University Press, 2006).

Cass Dykeman, Ph.D., NCC, NCSC, MAC, is an associate professor of counselor education at Oregon State University. He is a Master Addictions Counselor (MAC), National Certified Counselor (NCC), and National Certified School Counselor (NCSC). Dr. Dykeman received a master's in counseling from the University of Washington and a doctorate in counselor education from the University of Virginia. He served as principal investigator for a 1.5 million federal school-to-work research project. In addition, he is the author of numerous books, book chapters, and scholarly journal articles. Dr. Dykeman is past President of both the Washington State Association for Counselor Education and Supervision and the Western Association for Counselor Education and Supervision. He is also past chairperson of the School Counseling Interest Network of the Association for Counselor Education and Supervision. His current research interests include psychopharmacology and addictions counseling.

Ellyn Joan (EJ) Essic, Ph.D., LPC, is the 2009-2010 President of the International Addiction and Offender Counselors Division of ACA. She received a master's degree in 1987 from Wake Forest University and a doctorate from the University of North Carolina–Greensboro in 1999 in Counselor

Education. She is a practitioner with 24 years of counseling experience in addictions, interpersonal violence, trauma, gender issues, and stress management. She recently retired as the Clinical Director of a large alcohol and drug treatment program located in rural Alaska. She has taught counselor educators and others over the years in a number of university settings, and has presented nationally and internationally on native issues, domestic violence and addiction, and other topics. She currently lives in Palmer, Alaska and is training as a Disaster Relief worker for the American Red Cross.

Holly Fetter, Ph.D., is an associate professor in the Counselor Education Department at Canisius College in Buffalo, New York. Originally from the state of Washington, Dr. Fetter earned her bachelor's degree from Washington State University, her master's degree in counselor education from Portland State University, and her Ph.D. in counselor education from the University of New Orleans where she was a recipient of a Positive Mental Health Fellowship. Her research and writing interests focus on wellness issues related to law enforcement.

Abbé Finn, Ph.D., is the Associate Dean for Graduate Programs in the College of Education and teaches in the Counseling Program at Florida Gulf Coast University. She is a graduate of the University of New Orleans Counselor Education Program. She has worked extensively in the mental health field, with individuals as well as groups in counseling. Before joining the university faculty full time, she was an Employee Assistance Counselor with United States Postal Service employees. Dr. Finn specialized in working with groups in crisis response, survivors of childhood sexual trauma, and with clients in addiction recovery.

Scott E. Gillig, Ph.D., earned his Ph.D. from the University of Toledo in 1988. He has been a full-time counselor educator for 20 years, with an additional five years of part-time university teaching. He has over 20 years of clinical experience as a counselor. He has worked with chemically dependent adolescents and adults in a dual diagnosis chemical dependency treatment residential unit. He is currently a Professor and Coordinator of the Educational Leadership Doctoral Program at St. Thomas University in Miami, Florida. He teaches both master's and doctoral courses. His research interests include counseling outcomes, depression, chemical dependency, treatment planning, and student mentoring.

Melinda Haley, Ph.D., received her doctorate in counseling psychology from New Mexico State University in Las Cruces, New Mexico and is currently an Assistant Professor at the University of Texas, El Paso. Melinda has written numerous book chapters and multimedia presentations on diverse topics related to counseling and psychology. She has extensive applied experience working with adults, adolescents, children, inmates, domestic violence offenders, and culturally diverse populations in the areas of assessment, diagnosis, treatment planning, crisis management, and intervention. Melinda's research interests include multicultural issues in counseling, personality development over the lifespan, personality disorders, the psychology of criminal and serial offenders, trauma and posttraumatic stress disorder, bias and racism, and social justice issues.

Debra A. Harley, Ph.D., CRC, is a professor and chair of the Department of Special Education and Rehabilitation Counseling at the University of Kentucky. She completed her doctoral study at Southern Illinois University–Carbondale in Special Education and Rehabilitation. She is past editor of the Journal of Applied Rehabilitation Counseling and the Journal of Rehabilitation Administration. She is co-editor of a book on contemporary mental health issues among African Americans. Her research interests include substance abuse, cultural diversity, and gender issues.

Emeline P. Hollander, M.A., NCC, LPC, is currently the Director of Counseling Services at Greensboro College in Greensboro, North Carolina She earned her master's degree in community counseling from Wake Forest University. Prior experience includes being a staff counselor at Wake Forest University Counseling Center, working with college students in the areas of personal and career counseling and crisis response. She is the former Web site editor of the International Association of Addictions and Offender Counselors. Her clinical interests include working with adolescents and adults in the areas of process addiction, career, grief and loss, and relationships issues.

Misty K. Hook, Ph.D. was a professor of psychology for five years at Texas Woman's University where she taught counseling and family psychology courses. She is currently a psychologist in private practice, working with families, couples, and individuals. Dr. Hook received a master's in counseling psychology from the University of Kansas and a doctorate in counseling psychology from Ball State University. She is a co-founder of the Mothering Caucus for the Association for Women in Psychology. In addition, Dr. Hook continues to research issues concerning families and has written many book chapters, columns, and scholarly journal articles. Her current research and practice work includes mothering issues, divorced families, addictions counseling, public policy, and mind/body balance.

Adrianne L. Johnson, Ph.D., is an Assistant Professor of Mental Health counseling in the Counseling and Psychological Services Department at the State University of New York at Oswego. She earned her Doctorate in Counselor Education from the University of Arkansas in 2007, and currently works both as a Counselor Educator and as a Mental Health Practitioner in community mental health. She is active in various organizations committed to mental health advocacy, and strongly promotes excellence in counseling education. Dr. Johnson's research interests and professional experience include higher education leadership, community mental health counseling, multicultural counseling, and substance abuse.

Pamela S. Lassiter, Ph.D., received her Ph.D. in Counseling from Georgia State University in 2004. She has been an assistant professor and coordinator of the Substance Abuse Certificate Program at the University of North Carolina at Charlotte since 2004. She has 25 years of work experience as a counselor, clinical supervisor, and administrator in substance abuse treatment and community mental health. Her areas of research include multicultural counseling, gay and lesbian issues in counseling, GLBT parenting issues, substance abuse counseling, and women's issues. She is past President of the International Association of Addictions and Offender Counseling (IAAOC) where she served as an officer for five years. She is the 2008 recipient of the Dr. Mary Thomas Burke Mentoring Award, given by the North Carolina Association of Spiritual, Ethical, and Religious Values in Counseling; and the 2005 recipient of the JoAnna White Founder's Award, given by the Chi Epsilon Chapter of Chi Sigma Iota International.

John M. Laux, Ph.D., received his Ph.D. in Counseling Psychology from the University of Akron. John is a Licensed Professional Clinical Counselor (with supervisory endorsement), a Licensed Independent Chemical Dependency Counselor, and a Psychologist (all in Ohio). His areas of clinical and research interest include substance dependence, personality disorders, counselor education, and personality assessment. He has clinical experience in a variety of treatment settings including the Cincinnati VAMC, a community mental health center, a campus counseling center, and an inpatient chemical dependence treatment center. Dr. Laux has been published in numerous journals and he currently serves on the editorial board of the *Journal of Addictions and Offender Counseling.*

Rochelle Moss, Ph.D., is currently an assistant professor in the Department of Counseling at Henderson State University in Arkadelphia, Arkansas. She taught previously at the University of Mississippi and at Texas A & M University–Commerce. She was employed as a school counselor for 15 years, and has worked in private practice for the past 10 years. She is a Licensed Professional Counselor and Supervisor in the state of Arkansas and has worked extensively with adolescents, young adults, and college athletes as well as cancer patients and their families. Dr. Moss is an active member of the American Counseling Association, American School Counselor Association, Association of Counselor Education and Supervision, and is President-Elect of the Arkansas Association of Counselor Education and Supervision. Her research interests include eating disorders, body image, addictive behaviors, and effective strategies for counseling adolescents.

Cynthia J. Osborn, Ph.D., is Professor of Counseling and Human Development Services at Kent State University in Kent, Ohio, where she routinely teaches the addictions courses offered. She is licensed in Ohio as a Professional Clinical Counselor (PCC) and a Chemical Dependency Counselor (LCDC-III), and is a member of the Motivational Interviewing Network of Trainers (MINT). Her clinical background is in substance abuse counseling, primarily servicing a population with co-occurring disorders (i.e., mental health and substance use concerns). Her research, publications, and presentations have focused on solution-focused counseling, counseling supervision, motivational interviewing, college alcohol use, and leadership in the counseling profession.

Dilani M. Perera-Diltz, Ph.D., NCC, is currently a Counselor Educator at Cleveland State University, Ohio. She is licensed in Ohio as a Professional Clinical Counselor (PCC), Licensed Independent Chemical Dependency Counselor (LICDC), and a School Counselor (provisional). She has worked in a variety of settings as a chemical dependency and mental health counselor. Her research interests include addictions, trauma, and school counselor issues.

Jane E. Rheineck, Ph.D., NCC, is currently an Assistant Professor in Counseling, Adult and Higher Education at Northern Illinois University. Prior to her work as a counselor educator, Dr. Rheineck worked as a crisis counselor in Student Affairs and a mental health counselor with children and adolescents in a variety of settings that included inpatient residential treatment, outpatient, and schools.

Jennifer L. Rogers, M.A., NCC, is a doctoral student and University Fellow at Syracuse University. She earned her master's in counseling from Wake Forest University. She has clinical experience in intensive outpatient, university mental health, and primary care settings, including performing alcohol screenings and brief counseling interventions with trauma patients at Wake Forest University Baptist Medical Center.

Donna S. Sheperis, Ph.D., earned her Ph.D. in Counselor Education from the University of Mississippi. A Core Faculty member in the Mental Health Counseling Program of Walden University, Dr. Sheperis is a Licensed Professional Counselor, National Certified Counselor, and Approved Clinical Supervisor with 20 years of experience in community counseling settings. In addition to teaching, her professional experiences include providing vocational preparation for individuals with developmental disabilities; working with children and adolescents in residential group home settings; serving as the adult outpatient services coordinator in a community mental health setting; operating a behavioral assessment private practice; and supervising students in a university counseling center. Her primary areas of interest include mental health and coping, counselor development, ethics, and supervision.

Laura R. Simpson, Ph.D., LPC, NCC, ACS, is Core Faculty for Counselor Education and Supervision with Walden University. Dr. Simpson is a Licensed Professional Counselor, National Certified Counselor, and Approved Clinical Supervisor, as well as the founder of Lotus Counseling & Consultation. Dr. Simpson currently serves on the Mississippi Licensed Professional Counselors Board of Examiners. She has presented research at a variety of state, regional, and national conferences and serves on the executive board for the Mississippi Counseling Association and the Mississippi Licensed Professional Counselor Association. Dr. Simpson has published numerous scholarly writings within professional journals and counseling textbooks. Her primary areas of interest include counselor wellness and secondary trauma, spirituality, crisis response, cultural diversity, and supervision.

Anneliese A. Singh, Ph.D., LPC, is an Assistant Professor in the Department of Counseling and Human Development Services at the University of Georgia. She received her doctorate in counseling psychology from Georgia State University in 2007. Her clinical, research, and advocacy interests include: LGBTQQ youth; Asian American/Pacific Islander counseling and psychology; multicultural counseling and social justice training; qualitative methodology with historically marginalized groups (e.g., people of color, LGBTQQ, immigrants); feminist theory and practice; and empowerment interventions with survivors of trauma. Dr. Singh is a past President of the Association of Lesbian, Gay, Bisexual, and Transgender Issues in Counseling (ALGBTIC) where her Presidential Initiatives included the development of counseling competencies for working with transgender clients; supporting queer people of color; and ensuring safe schools for LGBTQQ youth. She is a founder of the Georgia Safe Schools Coalition, an organization that works at the intersection of heterosexism, racism, sexism, and other oppressions to create safe school environments in Georgia. She is the recipient of the 2007 Ramesh and Vijaya Bakshi Community Change Award and the 2008 O'Hana award from Counselors for Social Justice of the American Counseling Association for her organizing work with LGBTQQ youth.

Jason Vasquez, Ph.D., received his doctorate in counseling psychology from New Mexico State University in Las Cruces, New Mexico. He is currently a Staff Psychologist at Student Counseling Services at Illinois State University and a Visiting Assistant Professor at Illinois Wesleyan University in Bloomington–Normal, IL. Jason has written book chapters and presented at numerous local, regional, and national conferences on topics related to counseling and diversity. He has extensive experience working with individuals throughout the age spectrum, college students, domestic violence offenders, and other diverse populations. Jason's research interests and expertise have focused on Asian American and Latino populations in the areas of ethnic identity development, racial identity development, acculturation, perceived discrimination, and subjective well-being. His clinical interests and expertise is in ethnic minority student development, men's issues, depression, obsessive compulsive and other anxiety disorders, interpersonal conflicts, alcohol abuse, and college transition issues.

Laura J. Veach, Ph.D., LPC, LCAS, CCS, NCC, received her Ph.D. in Counselor Education from the University of New Orleans, her master's in counseling from Wake Forest University, and is an associate professor in the Department of Counseling at the University of North Carolina at Charlotte, North Carolina, with a primary focus on counselor education in addictions. With her research, she also has a joint faculty appointment as associate professor in the Department of Surgical Sciences at the Wake Forest University School of Medicine in Winston-Salem, North Carolina. She serves as co-principal investigator with the Level I Trauma Center there for the Robert Wood Johnson Foundation Grant, The

Teachable Moment, researching best practices with alcohol screening and brief counseling interventions in a prospective clinical trial comparing two counseling interventions. She specializes in addictions and substance abuse counseling and has over 25 years of clinical, management, and start-up experience in counseling settings.

She also provides clinical services for the Red Cross, with specialized training in Disaster Mental Health response and served in Louisiana and at Virginia Tech. She previously taught for 12 years in the Department of Counseling at Wake Forest University. Dr. Veach was the 2006 President of the International Association of Addictions and Offender Counseling (IAAOC). She was awarded the IAAOC Counselor Educator Award in March 2007, the WFU Graduate Faculty Award for excellence in teaching at Wake Forest University in May 2007, the ACA Counselor Education Advocacy Award in March 2008, and in North Carolina was named the 2010 recipient of the Dr. Mary Thomas Burke Professional Award (The Mentoring Award).

BRIEF CONTENTS

CONTENTS

Chapter 1

History and Etiological Models of Addiction

David Capuzzi
Walden University, Johns Hopkins University
Mark D. Stauffer
Oregon State University, Walden University

The history of addictions counseling, a specialization within the profession of counseling, follows a pattern of evolution similar to that witnessed in many of the helping professions (social work, psychology, nursing, medicine). Early practitioners had more limited education and supervision, were not licensed by regulatory boards, did not have well-defined codes of ethics upon which to base professional judgments, may not have been aware of the values and needs of diverse populations, and did not have access to a body of research that helped define best practices and treatment plans (Hogan, Gabrielsen, Luna, & Grothaus, 2003).

It is interesting to watch the evolution of a profession and specializations within a profession. For example, in the late 1950s, the profession of counseling was energized by the availability of federal funds to prepare counselors. The impetus for the U.S. Government to provide funds for both graduate students and university departments was Russia's launching of Sputnik. School counselors were needed to help prepare students for academic success especially in math and science so the U.S. could "catch up" with its "competitors."

As noted by Fisher and Harrison (2000), in earlier times, barbers who also did "bloodletting" practiced medicine, individuals who were skilled at listening to others and making suggestions for problem resolution became known as healers, and those who could read and write and were skilled at helping others do so became teachers with very little formal education or preparation to work with others in such a capacity. Fifty years ago nursing degrees were conferred without completing a baccalaureate (today a baccalaureate is minimal and a masters degree is rapidly becoming the standard), a teacher could become a school counselor with 12 to 18 credits of coursework (today a two-year masters is the norm), and twenty years ago an addictions counselor was an alcoholic or addict in recovery who used their prior experience with drugs as the basis for the addictions counseling done with clients.

Until the mid-1970s licensure for counselors did not exist and those wishing to become counselors could often do so with less than a master's degree. In 1976 Virginia became the first state to license counselors and outline a set of requirements that had to be met in order to obtain a license as a counselor. It took 33 years for all 50 states to pass licensure laws for counselors; this achievement took place in 2009 when the state of California passed its licensure law for counselors.

The purpose of this chapter is threefold: first, to provide an overview of the history of substance abuse prevention in the United States; second, to describe the most common models for explaining the etiology of addiction; and third, to provide an overview and relate the discussion of the history of prevention and the models for understanding the etiology of addiction to the content of the text.

APPROACHES TO THE PREVENTION OF ADDICTION IN THE UNITED STATES

Alcoholic beverages have been a part of this nation's past since the landing of the Pilgrims. Early colonists had a high regard for alcohol because it was regarded as a healthy substance with preventive and curative capabilities, rather than an intoxicant. Alcohol played a central role in promoting a sense of conviviality and community until, as time passed, the production and consumption of alcohol caused enough concern to precipitate several versions of the "temperance" movement (Center for Substance Abuse Prevention, 1993). The first of these began in the early 1800s, when clergymen took the position that alcohol could corrupt both mind and body and asked people to take a pledge to refrain from the use of distilled spirits.

In 1784 Dr. Benjamin Rush argued that alcoholism was a disease and his writings marked the initial development of the temperance movement. By 1810, Dr. Rush called for the creation of a "sober house" for the care of what he called the "confirmed drunkard."

The temperance movement's initial goal was the replacement of excessive drinking with more moderate and socially approved levels of drinking. Between 1825 and 1850, thinking about the use of alcohol began to change from temperance-as-moderation to temperance-as-abstinence (White, 1998). Six artisans and workingmen started the "Washingtonian Total Abstinence Society" in a Baltimore tavern on April 2, 1840. Members went to taverns to recruit members and, in just a few years, precipitated a movement that inducted several hundred thousand members. The Washingtonians were key in shaping future self-help groups because they introduced the concept of sharing experiences in closed, alcoholics-only meetings. Another version of the temperance movement occurred later in the 1800s with the emergence of the Women's Christian Temperance Movement and the mobilization of efforts to close down saloons. Societies such as the Daughters of Rechab, the Daughters of Temperance, and the Sisters of Sumaria are examples of such groups. (Readers are referred to White's discussion of religious conversion as a remedy for alcoholism for more details about the influence of religion in America on the temperance movement.) These movements contributed to the growing momentum to curtail alcohol consumption, leading to the passage of the Volstead Act and prohibition in 1920. Even though Prohibition was successful in reducing per capita consumption of alcohol, the law created such social turmoil and defiance that it was repealed in 1933.

Shortly after the passage of the Volstead Act in 1920, "speakeasies" sprang up all over the country in defiance of prohibition. The locations of these establishments were spread by word of mouth and people were admitted to "imbibe and party" only if they knew the password. Local police departments were kept busy identifying the locations of speakeasies and made raids and arrests whenever possible. Often the police were paid off so that raids did not take place and patrons would feel more comfortable in such establishments.

Following the repeal of Prohibition, all states restricted the sale of alcoholic beverages in some way or another in order to prevent or reduce alcohol-related problems. In general, however, public policies and the alcoholic beverage industry took the position that the problems connected with the use of alcohol existed because of the people who used it and not because of the beverage itself. This view of alcoholism became the dominant view for quite some time and, until recently, influenced, many of the prevention and early treatment approaches used in this country.

Paralleling the development of attitudes and laws for the use of alcohol, the nonmedical use of drugs other than alcohol can be traced back to the early colonization and settlement of the United States. Like alcohol, attitudes toward the use of certain drugs, and the laws passed declaring them legal or illegal, have changed over time and often have had racial/ethnic or class associations based on prejudice and inaccurate information. Prohibition was in part a response to the drinking patterns of European immigrants who became viewed as the lower class. Cocaine and opium were legal during the 19th century and favored by the middle and upper class, but cocaine became illegal when it was associated with African Americans following the Reconstruction era in the United States. The use of opium was first restricted in California during the latter part of the 19th century when it became associated with Chinese immigrant workers. Marijuana was legal until the 1930s when it became associated with Mexican immigrants. LSD, legal in the 1950s, became illegal in 1967 when it became associated with the counterculture.

It is interesting to witness the varying attitudes and laws concerning the use of marijuana. Many view marijuana as a "gateway" drug and also disapprove of the medical use of marijuana; others think that marijuana use should be legalized, that access should be unlimited, and use should be monitored only by the individual consumer.

It is interesting to note that it was not until the end of the 19th century (Center for Substance Abuse Prevention, 1993) that concern arose with respect to the use of drugs in patent medicines and products sold over the counter (cocaine, opium, and morphine were common ingredients in many potions). Until 1903, believe it or not, cocaine was an ingredient in some soft drinks. Heroin was even used in the 19th century as a nonaddicting treatment for morphine addiction and alcoholism. Gradually, states began to pass control and prescription laws and, in 1906, the United States Congress passed the Pure Food and Drug Act designed to control addiction by requiring labels on drugs contained in products, including opium, morphine, and heroin. The Harrison Act of 1914 resulted in the taxation of opium and coca products, with registration and record keeping requirements.

Current drug laws in the United States are derived from the 1970 Controlled Substance Act (Center for Substance Abuse Prevention, 1993), under which drugs are classified according to their medical use, potential for abuse, and possibility of creating dependence. Increases in per capita consumption of alcohol and illegal drugs raised public concern so that by 1971 the National Institute on Alcohol Abuse and Alcoholism (NIAAA) was established; by 1974, the National Institute on Drug Abuse (NIDA) had also been created. Both of these institutes conducted research and had strong prevention components as part of their mission. To further prevention efforts, the Anti-Drug Abuse Prevention Act of 1986 created the United States Office for Substance Abuse Prevention (OSAP). This office consolidated alcohol and other drug prevention initiatives under the Alcohol, Drug Abuse, and Mental Health Administration (ADAMA). ADAMA mandated that states set aside 20% of their alcohol and drug funds for prevention efforts, while the remaining 80% could be used for treatment programs. In 1992, OSAP was changed to the Center for Substance Abuse Prevention (CSAP) and became part of the new Substance Abuse and Mental Health Services Administration (SAMSHA) and retained its major program areas. The research institutes of NIAAA and NIDA were then transferred to the National Institute of Health (NIH). The Office of National Drug Control Policy (ONDCP) was also a significant development when it was established through the passage of the Anti-Drug Abuse Act of 1988. It focused on dismantling drug trafficking organizations, on helping people to stop using drugs, on preventing the use of drugs in the first place, and on preventing minors from abusing drugs.

Time passed and Congress declared that the United States would be drug free by 1995; that "declaration" has not been fulfilled. Since the mid-1990s, there have been efforts to control the recreational and nonmedical use of prescription drugs and to restrict the flow of drugs into the country. In 2005, Congress budgeted $6.63 billion for U.S. government agencies directly focused upon the restriction of illicit drug use. However, as noted later in this text, 13–18 metric tons of heroin is consumed yearly in the United States (Department of Health and Human Services, [DHHS] 2004). There has been an attempt to restrict importation by strengthening the borders and confiscating illegal substances before they enter the United States. There has also been an attempt to reduce importation. The U.S. government uses foreign aid to pressure drug-producing countries to stop cultivating, producing, and processing illegal substances. Some foreign aid is tied to judicial reforms, anti-drug programs, and agricultural subsidies to grow legal produce (DHHS, 2004).

In an attempt to reduce drug supplies, the government has incarcerated drug suppliers. Legislators have mandated strict enforcement of mandatory sentences, resulting in a greater increase in prison populations. As a result, the arrest rate of juveniles for drug-related crimes has doubled in the past 10 years, while arrest rates for other crimes has declined by 13%. A small minority of these offenders (2 out of every 1,000) will be offered Juvenile Drug Court (JDC) diversionary programs as an option to prison sentences (CASA, 2004).

During the last few years, there has been much media attention focused on the drug cartels in Mexico and the drug wars adjacent to the U.S. border near El Paso, Texas. In April of 2010, the Governor of Arizona signed into law legislation authorizing the police to stop anyone suspected of being an illegal immigrant and demand proof of citizenship.

CURRENT POLICIES INFLUENCING PREVENTION

A number of policies that currently influence the prevention of addiction should be noted (McNeese & DiNitto, 2005) and are listed below.

- All states in the United States set a minimum age for the legal consumption of alcohol and enact penalties for retailers who knowingly sell alcohol to minors and underage customers. Some states penalize retailers even when a falsified identification is used to purchase liquor.
- Even though the Twenty-First Amendment repealed prohibition, the "dry" option is still open to individual states, and some states, mainly in the South, do have dry counties.

Even though a few states still have "dry" counties, residents of those counties can often consume alcohol in restaurants that allow patrons to enter the establishment with a bottle of alcohol, usually wrapped or "bagged." The restaurant then charges a fee for opening the bottle and allowing the liquor to be served. In addition, some counties allow liquor stores to be located just outside the county line perhaps on a waterway accessed by a short walk across a connecting boardwalk or foot bridge.

- Many state governments influence the price of alcohol through taxation and through the administration of state-owned liquor stores.
- Besides taxation and the operation of state-owned liquor stores, government can attempt to regulate consumption by controlling its distribution. It accomplishes this through adopting policies regulating the number, size, location, and hours of business for outlets as well as regulating advertising.
- Perhaps no other area of alcohol policy has been as emotionally charged as the setting of the minimum legal age for consuming alcoholic beverages. Most states have adopted the age of 21 as the minimum legal age for unrestricted purchase of alcohol. This is a point of contention among many, since 18 is the eligible age for military service.
- In most states, driving an automobile while legally intoxicated (a B.A.C. of 0.08 to 0.10) is a crime. Penalties can range from suspension of the driver's license to a mandatory jail sentence, depending on the frequency of convictions.
- Insurance and liability laws can also be used to influence lower consumption of alcohol since those drivers with DUI convictions may face higher insurance premiums or may be unable to purchase insurance. In addition, in a majority of states, commercial establishments that serve alcoholic beverages are civilly liable to those who experience harm as a result of an intoxicated person's behavior.
- Public policies regarding the use of illicit drugs have not reached the same level of specificity as those regulating the use of alcohol (and, for that matter, tobacco). Since Ronald Reagan's election in 1981, federal policy has been more concerned with preventing recreational use of drugs than with helping habitual users. The approach chosen by the George H. Bush administration was one of zero tolerance. The administration did increase treatment funding by about 50%. Simultaneously, it continued to focus its attention on casual, middle-class drug use rather than with addiction or habitual use. In 1992, presidential candidates George H. Bush and Bill Clinton rarely mentioned the drug issue except as related to adolescent drug use. In 2000, the major issue in the campaign of George W. Bush was whether Mr. Bush had ever used cocaine. The administration of George W. Bush made very few changes in drug policy.
- Of major significance is the fact that SAMHSA was reauthorized in the year 2000 (Bazelon Center for Mental Health Law, 2000). That reauthorization created a number of new programs, including funding for integrated treatment programs for co-occurring disorders for individuals with mental illness as well as substance abuse disorders.

MODELS FOR EXPLAINING THE ETIOLOGY OF ADDICTION

Substance use and abuse has been linked to a variety of societal issues and problems (crime and violence, violence against women, child abuse, difficulties with mental health, risks during pregnancy, sexual risk-taking, fatal injury, etc.). Given the impact the abuse of substances can have on society in general and the toll they often exact on individuals and families, it seems reasonable to attempt to understand the etiology or causes of addiction so that diagnosis and treatment plans can be as efficacious as possible. There are numerous models for explaining the etiology of addiction (McNeese & Di Nitto, 2005); these models are not always mutually exclusive and none is presented as the one correct way of understanding the phenomena of addiction. The Moral, Psychological, Family, Disease, Biological, Socio-cultural, and some Multi-causal models are described in the subsections that follow.

The Moral Model

The moral model is based on beliefs or judgments of what is right or wrong, acceptable or unacceptable. Those who advance this model do not accept that there is any biological basis for addiction; they believe that there is something morally wrong with people who use drugs heavily.

The moral model explains addiction as a consequence of personal choice, and individuals engaging in addictive behaviors are viewed as capable of making alternative choices. This model has been adopted by certain religious groups and the legal system in many states (see the history section above). For example, in states in which violators are not assessed for chemical dependency and in which there is no diversion to treatment, the moral model guides the emphasis on "punishment." In addition, in communities in which there are strong religious beliefs, religious intervention might be seen as the only route to changing behavior. The moral model for explaining the etiology of addiction focuses on the sinfulness inherent in human nature. Since it is difficult to establish the sinful nature of human beings through empirically based research, this model has been generally discredited by present day scholars. It is interesting to note, however, that the concept of addiction as sin or moral weakness continues to influence many public policies connected with alcohol and drug abuse (McNeese & DiNitto, 2005). This may be part of the reason why needle/syringe exchange programs have so often been opposed in the United States.

Although the study of the etiology of alcoholism and other addictions has made great strides in moving beyond the moral model, alcoholics are not immune to social stigma, and other types of addiction have yet to be widely viewed as something other than a choice. But as we move further away from the idea that addiction is the result of moral failure, we move closer to providing effective treatment and support for all those who suffer.

Psychological Models

Another explanation of the reasons people crave alcohol and other mind-altering drugs has to do with the mind and emotions. Several different psychological models explain the etiology of alcoholism and drug addiction, including cognitive-behavioral, learning, psychodynamic, and personality models.

COGNITIVE-BEHAVIORAL MODELS.   Cognitive-behavioral models suggest a variety of motivations and reinforcers for taking drugs. One explanation suggests that people take drugs to experience variety (Weil & Rosen, 1993). Drug use might be associated with experiences such as self-exploration, religious insights, altering moods, escaping boredom or despair, enhancing creativity, performance, sensory experience or pleasure, and so on (Lindgren, Mullins, Neighbors, & Blayney, 2010). If we assume that people enjoy variety, then it can be understood why they repeat actions that they enjoy (positive reinforcement).

> The use of mind-altering drugs received additional media attention in the 1960s, when "flower children" sang and danced in the streets of San Francisco and other cities and sometimes lived together in communities they created. Much press was given to the use of drugs to enhance sensory experience in connection with some of the encounter groups led by facilitators in southern California.

The desire to experience pleasure is another explanation connected with the cognitive-behavioral model. Alcohol and other drugs are chemical surrogates of natural reinforcers such as food and sex. Social drinkers and alcoholics often report using alcohol to relax even though studies show that alcohol causes people to become more depressed, anxious, and nervous (NIAAA, 1996).

Dependent behavior with respect to the use of alcohol and other drugs is maintained by the degree of reinforcement the person perceives as occurring; alcohol and other drugs may be perceived as being more powerful reinforcers than natural reinforcers and set the stage for addiction. As time passes, the brain adapts to the presence of the drug or alcohol and the person experiences unpleasant withdrawal symptoms (i.e., anxiety, agitation, tremors, increased blood pressure, and seizures). To avoid such unpleasant symptoms, the person consumes the substance anew (negative reinforcement) and a repetitive cycle is established. In an interesting review of the literature on the etiology of addiction (Lubman, Yucel, & Pantelis, 2004), it was proposed that, in chemically addicted individuals, maladaptive behaviors and high relapse rates may be conceptualized as compulsive in nature. The apparent loss of control over drug-related behaviors suggests that individuals who are addicted are unable to control the reward system in their lives and that addiction may also be considered a disorder of compulsive behavior very similar to Obsessive-Compulsive Disorder.

LEARNING MODELS.   Learning models are closely related to and overlap somewhat the explanations provided by cognitive-behavioral models. Learning theory assumes that alcohol or drug use results in a decrease in uncomfortable psychological states such as anxiety, stress, or tension, thus providing positive reinforcement to the user. This learned response continues until physical dependence develops and, like the explanation provided within the context of cognitive-behavioral models, the aversion of withdrawal symptoms becomes a reason and motivation for continued use. Learning models provide helpful guidelines for treatment planning because, as pointed out by Bandura (1969), what has been learned can be unlearned; the earlier intervention occurs the better since there will be fewer behaviors to unlearn.

PSYCHODYNAMIC MODELS.   Psychodynamic models link addiction to ego deficiencies, inadequate parenting, attachment disorders, hostility, homosexuality, masturbation, etc. As noted by numerous researchers and clinicians, such models are difficult to substantiate through research since they deal with concepts that are difficult to operationalize and with events that occurred many years prior to the development of addictive behavior. A major problem with psychodynamic models is the fact that the difficulties linked to early childhood development are not specific to alcoholism or addiction but are reported by nonaddicted adults with a variety of other psychological problems (McNeese & DiNitto, 2005). Nevertheless, current thinking relative to the use of psychodynamic models as a potential explanation for the etiology of addiction has the following beliefs in common (Dodgen & Shea, 2000):

1. Substance abuse can be viewed as symptomatic of a more basic psychopathology.
2. Difficulty with an individual's regulation of affect can be seen as a core problem or difficulty.
3. Disturbed object relations may be central to the development of substance abuse. Readers are referred to chapter 12 of *Slaying the dragon: The history of addiction treatment in America* by William L. White (1998) for a more extensive discussion of psychodynamic models in the context of the etiology of addiction.

PERSONALITY THEORY MODELS.   These theories make the assumption that certain personality traits predispose the individual to drug use (An "alcoholic personality" is often described by traits such as dependent, immature, impulsive, highly emotional, having low frustration tolerance, unable to express anger, confused about their sex role orientation, etc.) (Catanzaro, 1967; Schuckit, 1986).

Although many tests have been constructed that attempt to identify the personality traits of a drug-addicted person, none have consistently distinguished the traits of the addicted individual from those of the nonaddicted individual. One of the subscales of the Minnesota Multiphasic Personality Inventory does differentiate alcoholics from the general population, but it may be detecting only the results of years of alcoholic abuse rather than underlying personality traits (MacAndrew, 1979). The consensus among those who work in the addictions counseling arena seems to be that personality traits are not of much importance in explaining addiction because an individual can become drug dependent irrespective of personality traits (Raistrick & Davidson, 1985).

Family Models

As noted in Chapter 14, during the infancy of the field of addictions counseling, addictions counselors were used to working only with the addict. Family members were excluded. However, it soon became clear that family members were influential in motivating the addict to get sober or, conversely, in preventing the addict from making serious changes.

There are at least three models of family-based approaches to understanding the development of substance abuse (Dodgen & Shea, 2000).

BEHAVIORAL. A major theme of the behavioral model is that, within the context of the family, there is a member (or members) who reinforces the behavior of the abusing family member. A spouse or significant other, for example, may make excuses for the family member or even prefer the behavior of the abusing family member when he or she is under the influence of alcohol or another drug. Some family members may not know how to relate to a particular family member when he or she is not "under the influence."

FAMILY SYSTEMS. Many studies have demonstrated the role of the family in the etiology of drug abuse (Baron, AbolMagd, Erfan, & El Rakhawy, 2010). As noted in Chapter 14, the family systems model focuses on the way roles in families interrelate (Tafa & Baiocco, 2009). Some family members may feel threatened if the person with the abuse problem shows signs of wanting to recover, since caretaker roles, for example, would no longer be necessary within the family system if the member began behaving more responsibly. The possibility of adjusting roles could be so anxiety producing that members of the family begin resisting all attempts of the "identified patient" to shift relationships and change familiar patterns of day-to-day living within the family system.

FAMILY DISEASE. This model is based on the idea that the entire family has a disorder or disease and must all enter counseling or therapy for improvement to occur within the addicted family member. This is very different from approaches to family counseling in which the counselor is willing to work with whichever family members will come to the sessions, even though every family member is not present.

The Disease Model

E. M. Jellinek (1960) is generally credited with introducing this controversial and initially popular model of addiction in the late 1930s and early 1940s (Stein & Foltz, 2009). However, it is interesting to note that, as early as the later part of the 18th century, the teachings and writings of Benjamin Rush, the Surgeon General of George Washington's revolutionary armies, actually precipitated the birth of the American disease concept of alcoholism as an addiction (White, 1998).

In the context of this model, addiction is viewed as a primary disease rather than being secondary to another condition (reference the discussion, earlier in this chapter, of Psychological Models). Jellinek's disease model was originally applied to alcoholism but has been generalized to addiction to other drugs. In conjunction with his work, Jellinek also described the progressive stages of the disease of alcoholism and the symptoms that are connected with each stage. These stages (prodromal, middle or crucial, and chronic) were thought to be progressive and not reversible. Consistent with this concept of irreversibility is the belief that addictive disease is chronic and incurable. Once the individual has this disease, according to the model, it never goes away and there is no treatment method that will enable the individual to use again without the high probability that the addict will revert to problematic use of the drug of choice. One implication of this philosophy is that the goal for an addict must be abstinence. This is the position taken by Alcoholics Anonymous (Fisher & Harrison, 2005). In addition, the idea that addiction is both chronic and incurable is the reason that addicts who are maintaining sobriety refer to themselves as "recovering" rather than as "recovered."

> The vocabulary of *recovery* was first used by AA in 1939 and is significant because we use the term *recovery* in the context of disease or illness rather than in connection with moral failure or character deficits. This reinforces the disease model to explain the etiology of addiction.

Interestingly, although Jellinek's disease model of addiction has received wide acceptance, the research from which he derived his conclusions has been questioned. Jellinek's data was gathered from questionnaires. Of the 158 questionnaires distributed, 60 were discarded; no questionnaires from women were used. Questions about the original research, leading to the conceptualization of the "disease" model have led to controversy. On the one hand, the articulation of addiction as a disease removes the moral stigma attached to addiction and replaces it with an emphasis on treatment of an illness, results in treatment coverage by insurance carriers, and sometimes encourages the individual to seek assistance much like that requested for diabetes, hypertension, or high cholesterol. On the other hand, the progressive, irreversible progression of addiction through stages does not always occur as predicted and the disease concept may promote the idea, for some individuals, that one is powerless over the disease, not responsible for behavior, may relapse after treatment, or may engage in criminal behavior to support the "habit."

Biological Models

Biophysiological and genetic theories assume that addicts are constitutionally predisposed to develop dependence on drugs. These theories or models support a medical model of addiction, apply disease terminology, and often place the responsibility for treatment under the purview of physicians, nurses, and other medical personnel. Usually, biological explanations branch into genetic and neurobiological discussions.

GENETIC MODELS.   Although genetic factors have never really been established as a definitive cause of alcoholism, the statistical associations between genetic factors and alcohol abuse are very strong. For example, it has been established that adopted children more closely resemble their biological parents than their adoptive parents when it comes to their use of alcohol (Dodgen & Shea, 2000; Goodwin, Hill, Powell, & Viamontes, 1973); alcoholism occurs more frequently in some families than others (Cotton, 1979); concurrent alcoholism rates are higher in monozygotic twin pairs than in dizygotic pairs (Kaij, 1960); and children of alcoholics can be as much as seven times more likely to be addicted than children whose parents are not alcoholic (Koopmans & Boomsina, 1995). Because of such data, some genetic theorists have posited that an inherited metabolic defect may interact with environmental elements and lead, in time, to alcoholism. Some research points to an impaired production of enzymes within the body; other lines of inquiry point to the inheritance of genetic traits resulting in a deficiency of vitamins (probably the vitamin B complex) which leads to a craving for alcohol as well as the accompanying cellular or metabolic changes (Tarter & Schneider, 1976).

There have been numerous additional lines of inquiry that have attempted to establish a genetic marker that predisposes a person toward alcoholism or other addictions (Bevilacqua & Goldman, 2010). Studies that examined polymorphisms in gene products and DNA, the D2 receptor gene, and even color blindness as factors have all been conducted and then more or less discounted. Genetic research on addiction shows potential but is a complex activity given the fact that each individual carries genes located on 23 pairs of chromosomes. Currently, the Human Genome Project, which is supported by the National Institutes of Health and the U.S. Department of Energy, are conducting some promising studies (NIAA, 2000).

NEUROBIOLOGICAL MODELS.   Neurobiological models are complex and have to do with the neurotransmitters which serve as the chemical messengers of our brain (Kranzler & Li, 2008; Wilcox, Gonzales, & Miller, 1998). Almost all addictive drugs, as far as we know, seem to have primary transmitter targets for their actions. The area of the brain in which addiction occurs is the limbic system or the emotional part of the brain. The limbic part of the brain refers to an inner margin of the brain just outside the cerebral ventricles and the activity of the transmitter dopamine in the limbic system is key in the development of addiction. As a person begins to use a drug, changes in brain chemistry in the limbic system begin to occur and lead to addiction. Current thinking is that these changes can also be reversed by the introduction of other drugs in concert with counseling and psychotherapy.

Sociocultural Models

Sociocultural models have been formulated by making observations of the differences and similarities between cultural groups and subgroups. As noted by Goode (1972), the social context of drug use strongly influences drug definitions, drug effects, drug-related behavior, and the drug experience. These are contextual models and can only be understood in relation to the social phenomena surrounding drug use. A person's likelihood of using drugs, according to these models, the way he or she behaves, and the way abuse and addiction are defined are all influenced by the sociocultural system surrounding the individual.

SUPRACULTURAL MODELS.   The classic work of Bales (1946) provided some hypotheses connecting culture, social organization, and the use of alcohol. He believed that cultures that create guilt, suppress aggression and sexual tension, and that support the use of alcohol to relieve those tensions will probably have high rates of alcoholism. Bales also hypothesized that the culture's collective attitude toward alcohol use could influence the rate of alcoholism. Interestingly, he categorized these attitudes as favoring: (1) abstinence, (2) ritual use connected with religious practices, (3) convivial drinking in a social setting, and (4) utilitarian drinking (drinking for personal reasons). The fourth attitude (utilitarian) in a culture that produces high levels of tension is the most likely to lead to high levels of alcoholism; the other three lessen the probability of high alcoholism rates. Another important aspect of Bale's thinking is the degree to which the culture offers alternatives to alcohol use to relieve tension and to provide a substitute means of satisfaction.

A culture that emphasizes upward economic or social mobility will frustrate individuals who are unable to achieve at such high levels and increase the possibility of high alcoholism rates.

In 1974, Bacon theorized that in cultures that combine a lack of indulgence of children with demanding attitudes toward achievement and negative attitudes toward dependent behavior in adults, high rates of alcoholism were likely to exist. An additional important factor in supracultural models is the degree of consensus in the culture regarding alcohol and drug use. In cultures in which there is little agreement, a higher rate of alcoholism and other drug use can be expected. Cultural ambivalence regarding the use of alcohol and drugs can result in the weakening of social controls allowing the individual to avoid being looked upon in an unfavorable manner.

CULTURE-SPECIFIC MODELS.   Culture-specific models of addiction are simultaneously fascinating and hampered by the possibilities inherent in promoting stereotypes and overgeneralizing about the characteristics of those who "seem" to fit the specific culture under consideration. For example, there are many similarities between the French and Italian cultures since both cultures are profoundly Catholic and both support wineries and have populations that consume alcohol quite freely (Levin, 1989). The French drink both wine and spirits, with meals and without, at home as well as away from the family. They often consider it bad manners to refuse a drink and the attitudes toward drinking too much are usually quite liberal. The Italians drink mostly wine, with meals, and at home and strongly disapprove of public misconduct due to the overconsumption of wine. They do not pressure others into accepting a drink.

In some Italian-American Families children over the age of about 10 can drink wine with dinner but are admonished never to drink large amounts of wine; wine is to be enjoyed in social situations but never to be consumed in excess. As a result, these children usually become adults who drink wine in moderation and never have problems caused by too much consumption of alcoholic beverages.

As the reader might expect from prior discussion, the rate of alcoholism in France is much more problematic than in Italy. Although the authors would agree that the prevailing customs and attitudes relating to the consumption of alcohol in a specific culture can provide insight and have usefulness as a possible explanation of the etiology of addiction in the culture under consideration, readers should be cautious about cultural stereotyping and make every attempt to address diversity issues in counseling as outlined in the current version of the Code of Ethics of the American Counseling Association (ACA) as well as the ACA guidelines for culturally competent counseling practices. (See the ACA Web site at www.counseling.org).

SUBCULTURAL MODELS.   It should also be briefly noted that there have been many investigations of both sociological and environmental causes of addiction and alcoholism at the sub-cultural level. Factors related to age, gender, ethnicity, socioeconomic class, religion, and family background can create different patterns within specific cultural groups (McNeese & DiNitto, 2005: White, 1998) and can be identified as additional reasons why counselors and other members of the helping professions must vigilantly protect the rights of clients to be seen and heard for who they really are rather than who they are assumed to be.

Multi-causal Models

At this point in your reading you may be wondering which of these etiological models or explanations of addiction is the correct model. As you may have already surmised, although all of these models are helpful and important information for counselors beginning their studies in addiction counseling, no single model adequately explains why some individuals become addicted to a substance and others do not. An important advance in the study of addiction is the realization that addiction is probably not caused by a single factor and the most likely models for increasing our understanding and our development of treatment options are multivariate (Buu et al., 2009; McNeese & DiNitto, 2005; Stevens & Smith, 2005). Even though there may be some similarities in all addicted individuals, the etiology and motivation for the use of drugs varies from person to person. For some individuals, there may be a genetic predisposition or some kind of a physiological reason for use and later addiction to a drug. For others, addiction may be a result of an irregularity or disturbance of some kind in their personal development without a known genetic predisposition or physiological dysfunction. The possible debate over which model is the correct model is valuable only because it assists the practitioner to see the importance of adopting an interdisciplinary or multi-causal model.

An interesting example of a multi-causal model that has been proposed is the *Syndrome Model* of addiction (Shaffer et al., 2004). This model suggests that the current research pertaining to excessive eating, gambling, sexual behaviors, shopping, substance abuse, etc., does not adequately capture the origin, nature, and processes of addiction. The researchers believe that the current view of addiction is very similar to the view held during the early days of AIDS awareness, when rare diseases were not recognized as opportunistic infections of an underlying immune deficiency syndrome. The *Syndrome Model* of addiction suggests that there are multiple and inter-acting antecedents of addiction that can be organized in at least three primary areas: (1) shared neurobiological antecedents, (2) shared psychosocial antecedents, and (3) shared experiences and consequences. Another promising example of a multi-causal model is the *Integral Model* (Amodia, Cano, & Eliason, 2005). This integral approach examines substance abuse etiology and treatment from a four-quadrant perspective adapted from the work of Ken Wilbur. It also incorporates concepts from integrative medicine and transpersonal psychology. Readers are referred to the references cited above for more complete information about both the *Syndrome* and *Integral Models.*

The multi-causal model is similar to the public health model recently adopted by health care and other human service professionals. This model conceptualizes the problem of addiction as an interaction among three factors: the "agent" or drug, the "host" or person, and the "environment" which may be comprised of a number of entities. When the agent or drug interacts with the host, it is important to realize that there are a variety of factors within the host, including the person's genetic composition, cognitive structure and expectations about drug experiences, family background, and personality traits, that must be taken into consideration as a treatment plan is developed. Environmental factors that need to be considered include social, political, cultural, and economic variables. When a counselor or therapist uses a multi-causal model to guide the diagnosis and treatment planning process, the complex interaction of a variety of variables must be taken into consideration.

Summary and Some Final Notations

This chapter provided an overview of the historical evolution of approaches to the prevention of addiction in the United States. It chronicled the movement from the rudimentary and unregulated approaches of early practitioners to the more carefully regulated, credentialed, and evidence based methods in use today. The social and political influences on attitudes toward the use of drugs for both recreational and medical purposes were also addressed. A brief review of the federal government's role in funding agencies focused on the prevention of drug abuse as well as the provision of treatment for addicted individuals provided the background for some of the current policies influencing the prevention of addiction. Descriptions of the moral, psychological, family, disease, biological, socio-cultural and multi-causal models for understanding the etiology of addiction provided the reader with the background to understand topics covered in subsequent chapters of the text.

In addition to the first chapter on history and etiological models of addiction, Part I of our text, *Introduction to Addictions Counseling,* includes chapters on substance and process addictions, professional issues, interviewing clients, and assessment and diagnosis of addiction. These introductory chapters provide the background for Part II, *The Treatment of Addictions,* which provides a thorough examination of current treatment modalities. The seven chapters in this section address motivational interviewing, psychotherapeutic approaches, co-occuring disorders and addictions treatment, group work and addictions, pharmacological treatment of addictions, 12-step facilitation of treatment, and maintenance and relapse prevention. Part III, *Addictions in Family*

Therapy, Rehabilitation, and School Settings, provides the reader with needed perspective regarding variations in treatment modalities so necessary for competent counseling in specific settings. The chapters in this section discuss interventions with couples and families, persons with disabilities and addictions, and prevention programs for children, adolescents, and college settings. Part IV, *Cross-Cultural Counseling in Addictions* addresses ethnic diversity; gender and addictions; and gay-, lesbian- and bisexual-affirmative addiction treatment.

Although it is impossible to include every conceivable topic that would be helpful to a counselor or therapist beginning the study of addictions counseling in a single text, we believe the information in this book is comprehensive enough in scope and sufficiently detailed to provide an excellent foundation for follow up courses as well as supervised practicum and internship experiences for those wishing to develop a specialization in addictions counseling.

Useful Web Sites

The following Web sites provide additional information relating to the chapter topics:

CLEARINGHOUSES:

National Clearinghouse for Alcohol and Drug Information
1-800-729-6686
http://www.health.org

National Mental Health Information Center
1-800-889-2647
http://www.mentalhealth.org

FUNDING OPPORTUNITIES

NIMH
http://www.nimh.nih.gov/

NIDA Extramural Affairs
http://www.drugabuse.gov/funding/

NIAAA
http://www.niaaa.nih.gov/

NIH Grants and Funding Opportunities
http://grants.nih.gov/grants/index.cfm

Enhancing Practice Improvement in Community-Based Care for Prevention and Treatment of Drug Abuse or Co-occurring Drug Abuse and Mental Disorders
http://grants.nih.gov/grants/guide/rfa-files/RFA-DA-06-001.html

NIH Grants for Mental Health, Addiction Research
http://www.jointogether.org/sa/news/funding/reader/
    0%2C1854%2C575039%2C00.html

HRSA
http://www.hrsa.gov/grants/default.htm

FUNDING SOURCES FOR PREVENTION PROGRAMS

The Catalog of Federal Domestic Assistance (CFDA)
http://www.cfda.gov/
A database of all Federal programs available to State and local governments (including the District of Columbia); federally recognized Indian tribal governments; territories (and possessions) of the United States; domestic public, quasi-public, and private profit and nonprofit organizations and institutions; specialized groups; and individuals.

Federal Register (FR)

http://www.gpoaccess.gov/fr/index.html

The Federal Register is the official daily publication for all Federal agency funding notices. The bound version can be viewed at a local or university library.

The Foundation Center

http://www.fdncenter.org/

The Foundation Center's mission is to support and improve institutional philanthropy by promoting public understanding of the field and helping grantseekers succeed.

Foundations & Grantmakers Directory

http://www.foundations.org/grantmakers.html

This directory lists foundations and grantmakers by name.

Grant Search and Information

http://www.silcom.com/~paladin/grants.html

This Web page, sponsored by the Paladin Group, offers grant-related information.

The Grantsmanship Center

http://www.tgcigrantproposals.com

This resource is designed to help nonprofit organizations and government agencies write better grant proposals and develop better programs.

GrantsNet

http://www.hhs.gov/grantsnet

GrantsNet is a tool for finding and exchanging information about U.S. Department of Health and Human Services and other selected Federal grant programs.

GrantsWeb

http://www.msue.msu.edu/msue/resources/grantweb.html

A starting point for accessing grant-related information and resources on the Internet.

GuideStar

http://www.guidestar.org/

GuideStar is a free information service on the programs and finances of more than 600,000 charities and nonprofit organizations. The database of nonprofit organizations is searchable by several different criteria. The site also offers news on philanthropy and other resources for donors and volunteers.

The Research Assistant

http://www.theresearchassistant.com/funding/index.asp

Resources for new and minority drug abuse researchers.

The Robert Wood Johnson Foundation (RWJF)

http://www.rwjf.org/index.jsp

RWJF, the largest U.S. foundation devoted to improving the health and health care of all Americans, funds grantees through both multisite national programs and single-site projects.

U.S. Department of Education (DOE)

http://www.ed.gov/topics/topics.jsp?&top=Grants+%26+ Contracts

DOE only posts those grants currently open for competition at this site.

U.S. Department of Housing and Urban Development

http://www.hud.gov/grants/index.cfm

References

Amodia, D. S., Cano, C., & Eliason, M. J. (2005). An integral approach to substance abuse. *Journal of Psychoactive Drugs, 37*(4), 363–371.

Bacon, M. K. (1974). The dependency-conflict hypothesis and the frequency of drunkenness. *Quarterly Journal of Studies on Alcohol, 40,* 863–876.

Bales, B. F. (1946). Cultural differences in rates of alcoholism. *Quarterly Journal of Studies on Alcohol, 6,* 480–499.

Bandura, A. (1969). *Principles of behavior modification.* New York: Holt, Rinehart, and Winston.

Baron, D., AbolMagd, S., Erfan, S., & El Rakhawy, M. (2010). Personality of mothers of substance-dependent patients. *Journal of Multidisciplinary Healthcare, 3,* 29–32.

Bazelon Center for Mental Health Law (2000). Legislative Update: 2000 SAMHSA reauthorization. Retrieved January 2006 from *http://www.bazelon.org/takeaction/ alerts/10-17-00samhsa.htm*

Bevilacqua, L., & Goldman, D. (2010). Geonomics of addiction. *Current Psychiatry Reviews, 6,* a22–134.

Buu, A., DiPiazza, C., Wang, J., Puttler, L. I., Fitzgerald, H. E., & Zucker, R. A. (2009). *Journal of Studies of Alcohol and Drugs, 70,* 489–498.

CASA: National Center on Addiction and Substance Abuse at Columbia University. (2004). Criminal neglect: Substance abuse, juvenile justice and the children left behind. New York City: Author.

Catanzaro, P. (1967). Psychiatric aspects of alcoholism. In D. J. Pittman (Ed.), *Alcoholism.* New York: Harper and Row.

Center for Substance Abuse Prevention (1993). *Prevention primer: An encyclopedia of alcohol, tobacco and other drug prevention terms.* (DHHS Publication No. SMA 2060). Rockville, MD: National Clearing House for Alcohol and Drug Information.

Cotton, N. A. (1979). The familial incidence of alcoholism. *Journal of Studies on Alcohol, 40,* 89–116.

DHHS. (2004). *National Drug Control Strategy.* Washington, DC: Government Printing Office.

Dodgen, C. E., & Shea, W. M. (2000). *Substance use disorders: Assessment and treatment.* San Diego: Academic Press.

Fisher, G. L., & Harrison, T. C. (2000). *Substance abuse: Information for school counselors, social workers, therapists and counselors* (2nd ed.). Boston: Allyn and Bacon.

Fisher, G. L., & Harrison, T. C. (2005). *Substance abuse: Information for school counselors, social workers, therapists and counselors* (3rd ed.). Boston: Allyn and Bacon.

Goode, E. (1972). *Drugs in American Society.* New York: Alfred A. Knopf.

Goodwin, D. W., Hill, S., Powell, B., & Viamontes, J. (1973). The effect of alcohol on short-term memory in alcoholics. *British Journal of Psychiatry, 122,* 93–94.

Hogan, J. A., Gabrielsen, K. R., Luna, N., & Grothaus, D. (2003). *Substance abuse prevention: The intersection of science and practice.* Boston: Allyn and Bacon.

Jellinek, E. M. (1960). *The disease concept of alcoholism.* New Haven, CT: Hillhouse Press.

Kaij, L. (1960). *Alcoholism in twins: Studies on the etiology and sequels of abuse of alcohol.* Stockholm, Sweden: Almquist and Wiskell.

Koopmans, J. R., & Boomsina, D. L. (1995). *Familiar resemblances in alcohol use: Genetic or cultural transmission.* Amsterdam, The Netherlands: Department of Psychonomics, Vriji Univeriteit.

Kranzler, H. R., & Li, T. (2008). What is addiction? *Alcohol Research and Health, 31,* 93–95.

Levin, J. D. (1989). *Alcoholism: A bio-social approach.* New York: Hemisphere.

Lindgren, K. P., Mullins, P. M., Neighbors, C., & Blayney, J. A. (2010). Curiosity killed the cocktail? Curiosity, sensation-seeking, and alcohol-related problems in college women. *Addictive Behaviors, 35,* 513–516.

Lubman, D. L., Yucel, M., & Pantelis, C. (2004). Addiction, a condition of compulsive behaviour? Neuroimaging and neuropsychological evidence of inhibitory dysregulation. *Society for the Study of Addiction, 99,* 1491–1502.

MacAndrew, C. (1979). On the possibility of the psychometric detection of persons who are prone to the abuse of alcohol and other substances. *Journal of Addictive Behaviors, 4,* 11–20.

McNeese, C. A., & DiNitto, D. M. (2005). *Chemical dependency: A Systems Approach* (3rd ed.). Boston: Allyn and Bacon.

National Institute on Alcohol Abuse and Alcoholism (NIAAA). (1996). *Alcohol Alert* (no. 33). Washington, DC: U.S. Government Printing Office.

National Institute on Alcohol Abuse and Alcoholism (NIAAA). (2000). *Tenth Special Report on alcohol and health to the U. S. Congress.* Washington, DC: U.S. Government Printing Office.

Raistrick, D., & Davidson, R. (1985). *Alcoholism and drug addiction.* New York: Churchill and Livingstone.

Schuckit, M. A. (1986). Etiological theories on alcoholism. In N. J. Estes & M. E. Heinemann (Eds.), *Alcoholism; Development, consequences, and interventions* (3rd ed., pp. 15–30). St. Louis, MO: C. V. Mosby.

Shaffer, H. J., LaPlante, D. A., LaBrie, R. A., Kidman, R. C., Donato, A. N., & Stanton, M. V. (2004). Toward a syndrome model of addiction: Multiple expressions, common etiology. *Harvard Review of Psychiatry, 12,* 367–374.

Stein, D. B., & Foltz, R. (2009). The need to operationally define "disease" in psychiatry and psychology. *Ethical Human Psychology and Psychiatry, 11,* 120–141.

Stevens, P., & Smith, R. L. (Eds.). (2005). *Substance abuse counseling: Theory and practice.* Upper Saddle River, NJ: Merrill/Prentice Hall.

Tafa, M., & Baiocco, R. (2009). Addictive behavior and family functioning during adolescence. *The American Journal of Family Therapy, 37,* 388–395.

Tarter, R. E., & Schneider, D. U. (1976). Models and theories of alcoholism. In R. E. Tarter & A. A. Sugarmen (Eds.), *Alcoholism: Interdisciplinary approaches to an enduring problem.* Reading, MA: Addison-Wesley.

Weil, A., & Rosen, W. (1993). *Alcoholism: The nutritional approach.* Austin: The University of Texas Press.

White, W. L. (1998). *Slaying the dragon: The history of addiction treatment and recovery in America.* Bloomington, IL: Chestnut Health Systems.

Wilcox, R. E., Gonzales, R. A., & Miller, J. D. (1998). Introduction to neurotransmitters, receptors, signal transduction and second messengers. In C. H. Nemeroff & A. E. Schatzberg (Eds.), *Textbook of Psychopharmacology* (pp. 3–36). Washington, DC: American Psychiatric Press.

Chapter 2

Substance Addictions

Laura J. Veach
University of North Carolina at Charlotte
Wake Forest University School of Medicine
Jennifer L. Rogers
Syracuse University

E. J. Essic
Past-President of International Association
of Addictions & Offender Counselors

Current estimates indicate that the extent of addiction disorders, with the exclusion of tobacco addiction, involve approximately 32 million Americans (James & Gilliland, 2005). The American Psychiatric Association (APA, 2000) estimates that in any given year approximately 5% of the population meet diagnostic criteria for alcohol dependence, 1.2% for cannabis abuse or dependence, and approximately 0.2% for cocaine abuse or dependence. Throughout history, humans have used drugs to achieve desired changes of experiences; even ancient warriors "fortified themselves with alcohol before battle to boost their courage and decrease sensitivity to pain" (Weil & Rosen, 1983, p. 20). For some people, the ingestion of chemicals results in substance, or ingestive, addiction which will be discussed at length in this chapter. For others, engaging in certain behaviors or processes, such as gambling, triggers process addiction which will be reviewed in Chapter 3. The term 'addiction' will be used to best incorporate the many features involved in the addictive process which may additionally involve physical dependence. Recent emphasis among addiction specialists highlights the clarity provided by the term 'addiction' rather than 'dependency' or 'habit': "By emphasizing the behavioral aspects of compulsive substance use, addiction captures the chronic, relapsing, and compulsive nature of substance use that occurs despite the associated negative consequences" (Kranzler & Li, 2008, p. 93).

To better inform and prepare counselors, this chapter provides comprehensive information about the neurobiological and physiological factors regarding addiction. Tolerance and withdrawal aspects will also be reviewed. In addition, we also examine substances of addiction. First, we will discuss biological factors.

NEUROBIOLOGY AND THE PHYSIOLOGY OF ADDICTION

Records indicate that people sought help for drinking problems in Egypt approximately 5,000 years ago (White, 1998). Even though substantial research has taken place in the ensuing years, there remain many questions regarding addiction. Research continues to provide more information regarding the biology and treatment of addiction. However, most addiction experts agree that "alcoholism and other addictions are complex, multiply-determined disorders in which biological and environmental factors interact to enhance personal vulnerability" (White, 1998, p. 289). Addiction is the result of many heterogenous factors involving various combinations of genetic, environmental, social, and psychological influences (Kranzler & Li, 2008). In essence, many questions remain regarding a clear biological understanding of addiction; to date there is no one single biological factor or explanation of addiction. Yet it is increasingly clear in neuroscience that "addictive behaviors are not the same as enhanced habits" (Yin, 2008, p. 342).

The organ of the body perhaps most researched in addiction is the brain. This research is referred to as *neurobiology*. There are more than 100 billion neurons, or nerve cells, in the brain, with at least 40,000 connections, or synapses, for every neuron (Amen, 2005). Neurobiology is complex considering one sample of brain material approximately "the size of a grain of sand contains a hundred thousand neurons and one billion synapses, all 'talking' to one another" (Amen, 2005, p. 20). It is thought that our neurons age with us over time but the synapses, as chemical messengers exchange information, change depending on the experiences of our bodies and our neurons (Taylor, 2006). Injuries to our brains, such as a stroke, cause permanent changes to neurons and synapses; it is thought that recovery in the brain often involves *brain plasticity,* the brain's ability to "repair, replace, and retrain its neural circuitry" (Taylor, 2006, p. 35).

Addiction hijacks the brain, contributing to permanent damage and many changes in the connections between neurons (Amen, 2005; Lubman, Yücel, & Pantelis, 2004). It has been likened to "Trojan horses that sneak into the nerve cells and take control" (Moyers & Ketcham, 2006, p. 278). Compelling neurobiology studies have uncovered a better understanding of the brain and its complex functions pertaining to addiction. The National Institute on Drug Abuse (NIDA), a key leader in addiction research, clearly notes that addiction is a brain disease and can be successfully treated (NIDA, 2008). Researchers have identified specific areas within the brain most prone to the effects of euphoria-producing connections, chemicals, or processes. These areas have been studied closely to try and ascertain how the addictive cycle is triggered. Many addiction experts agree that the neurobiology of addiction is complex and remains challenging, even as we better understand how the brain changes with the onset of addiction.

Neuroscience of the Twelve Steps

Addiction is considered to be a chronic, or lifelong, disease by both the medical establishment and programs like Alcoholics Anonymous. There is increasing neuroscientific data suggesting that twelve-step programs may help addicts achieve and maintain sobriety by protecting and enhancing the prefrontal cortex of the brain (Schnabel, 2009). The prefrontal cortex—which controls complex activities like self-monitoring, social thinking, abstract thought, and moral behavior—seems to be impaired in persons struggling with addiction. The processes of attending meetings (involving social interaction) and "working the steps" (involving abstract thought and moral behavior) may strengthen the prefrontal cortex to allow for abstinence (self-monitoring). According to Nora Volkow, director of the National Institute on Drug Abuse, "A lot of the treatment programs out there are targeting these systems without necessarily knowing that they are doing it."

Source: Schnabel, J. (2009). Neuroscience: Rethinking rehab. *Nature, 458* (7234), 25–27.

A basic overview of the neurobiology of addiction includes information about the key areas of the brain most involved in the addictive cycle, together comprising "the reward pathway." Several parts of the limbic system in the brain, as illustrated in Figure 2.1, show the ventral tegmental area (VTA), nucleus accumbens, and the prefrontal cortex, thought to make up the reward pathway (NIDA, 2005). Stimuli activate these particular areas of the brain to produce pleasurable sensations. Chemical messengers, called *neurotransmitters*, play critical roles in transmitting information between neurons through synapses. The communication that occurs between the neurons at the synapse, a specialized gap, measures between 20 to 50 nanometers and happens within milliseconds (Lovinger, 2008). The neurotransmitters involved in pleasurable sensations include an important one, dopamine (Lubman et al., 2004). Curiously, dopamine

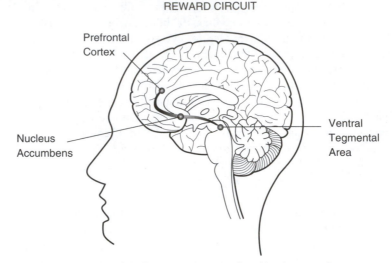

FIGURE 2.1   Reward Pathway   *Source:* National Institute on Drug Abuse. (2005). *Mind over Matter, Teacher's Guide.* Retrieved from http://teens.drugabuse.gov/mom/teachguide/MOMTeacherGuide.pdf

is "made by very few cells in the brain and acts mainly within a subset of brain regions . . . and [yet] seems to have a disproportionately large impact on brain function" (Lovinger, 2008, p. 204). In Figure 2.2, an illustration shows how cocaine, for example, interferes with the normal action of dopamine by blocking the removal, or reuptake, of this important neurotransmitter (NIDA, 2005). The resulting increase of dopamine at the neurons, brain cells, and overstimulation of neuroreceptors, or receiving neurons, leads to pleasurable euphoria. An addict incurs an abundance of several powerful neurotransmitters, such as dopamine, and seeks to continue reexperiencing those euphoric sensations; thus, in the brain, addiction primarily involves the dopaminergic transmission and reward pathway (Lovinger, 2008; Lubman et al., 2004; NIDA, 2008). Other important neurotransmitters, such as gamma-amino butyric acid (GABA) and glutamate, are identified in current research as significant when examining the brain's response to alcohol (Spirito, 2009). It is believed that advanced research will unlock more keys to understand GABA's special role in particular features of alcohol intoxication, such as uncoordinated motor activity (stumbling, unsteady movements), anti-anxiety properties, and alcohol withdrawal complications (Lovinger, 2008). Glutamate, the predominant excitatory neurotransmitter in the brain, functions in many key aspects of the brain's operations such as learning and memory; alcohol's memory-impairing actions are thus better understood since, as only one of many of its effects on glutamate, it interferes with the actions of this key neurotransmitter (Lovinger, 2008).

Neuroimaging technology used in brain research allows researchers to test and assess living brain activity (Oscar-Berman & Marinkovic, 2004; Taylor, 2006). One such technique, positron emission tomography (PET), has further aided researchers by allowing them to visualize the effects of addictive chemicals and how brain activity differs between those using and those not using mood-altering substances.

In addition to understanding the role of the reward pathway in the addicted brain, neurobiology research is also investigating the complex hallmark of addiction pertaining to loss of control: continued drug use despite significant adverse consequences. Scientists have identified two frontal areas of the brain, the anterior cingulated cortex (ACC) and the orbitofrontal cortex (OFC)

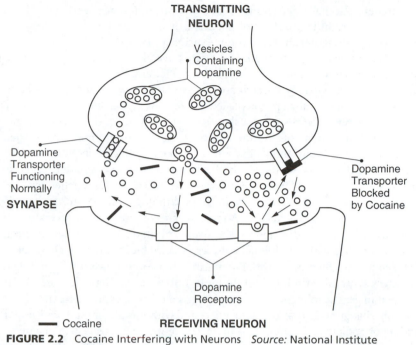

FIGURE 2.2 Cocaine Interfering with Neurons *Source:* National Institute on Drug Abuse. (2005). *Mind over Matter, Teacher's Guide.* Retrieved from http://teens.drugabuse.gov/mom/teachguide/MOMTeacherGuide.pdf

for this important neurological area of study; these areas are thought to be key components of another aspect of the brain, the inhibitory pathway. Lubman and colleagues, for example, assert that in the use of neuroimaging studies investigating disorders involving compulsive patterns of behavior, including addiction, " . . . compulsive behaviour, as seen in both intractable addiction and OCD [obsessive-compulsive disorder], requires dysfunction within two highly interconnected cortical systems (ACC and OFC) critically involved in self-regulation (i.e., the *inhibitory* system)" (2004, p. 1497). Additional areas of intense study that address the compulsive nature of addiction and continued use despite adverse consequences (i.e., an inability to stop using even after major family, job, or integrity losses) involve another part of the brain, the cortico-basal ganglia network. Within this network lies the dorsal striatum (Yin, 2008) where substantial excitatory and inhibitory neurotransmitters work that are primarily involved in controlling behavior. Yin notes "it is possible that all addictive drugs, including alcohol, can affect the capacity for change (i.e., plasticity) in the cortico-basal ganglia networks, thereby altering normal learning processes that are critical for selecting and controlling actions" (p. 323). This emphasis on brain circuitry alteration can assist counselors to improve their understanding and empathy when the addict will not 'just learn to stop' as compulsive using or drinking continues; critical research suggests the brain is physically damaged and less capable of unlearning.

At present, it is significant that researchers can now study, with neuroimaging equipment, the effect of drugs on the brain's functioning, both while under the influence of drugs and long after the drug has been eliminated from the body. One neuropsychiatrist using scanning equipment for a number of years in addiction treatment notes that alcoholics, notably, "have some of the worst brains of all" (Amen, 2005, p. 81) and estimates indicate about half of approximately 20 million alcoholics have brain damage to some degree (Oscar-Berman & Marinkovic,

2004). Researchers also have determined that some brain damage seen in alcoholics suggests more damage to the right hemisphere of the brain than the left hemisphere (Oscar-Berman & Marinkovic, 2004) and significant brain volume shrinkage (Crews, 2008; Sullivan & Pfefferbaum, 2005). Also, "depending on age, the brain of the detoxified alcoholic can appear as ravaged as that of a patient with Alzheimer's disease . . . " (Sullivan & Pfefferbaum, p. 583).

Cutting-edge neurobiology research now suggests that new brain cells may be created from the division of neural stem cells, a process called *neurogenesis*. When alcohol's effects on neurogenesis were studied, Crews (2008) noted a significant disruption in this process. New promising approaches in the treatment of cocaine addiction, for example, may involve neurosurgical procedures such as, deep brain stimulation, currently in use with certain patients with Parkinson's disease. Rouaud et al. (2009) examined the effect of deep brain stimulation in the subthalamic nucleus of rats and found evidence of a decrease in motivation for further cocaine. Extensive research with PET scans and other neuroimaging technology will add to the knowledge of the causes, effects, and treatment of addiction. An exciting area of research, due to vast amounts of data produced in alcohol and other drug research being used to sift through substantial research findings and better compare data with multiple laboratories, is called bioinformatics, also referred to as data mining (Hitzemann & Oberbeck, 2008). Bioinformatics involves powerful computing resources to help researchers synthesize findings; for example, one tool, the GeneNetwork (Williams & Lu, 2008), is related to genetic influences, with work focused on gene expression arrays.

Other physiological factors, such as tolerance and withdrawal symptoms, are important to our understanding of addiction. Tolerance, the brain and central nervous system's neuroadaptation to continual surges of neurotransmitters, has often been misunderstood (NIDA, 2008). Many drinkers, including those who binge drink, mistakenly believe that they are somehow less at risk of addiction if they demonstrate greater tolerance. For example, heavy drinkers may brag that they "can drink others under the table" and show little impairment. In fact, studies indicate that a high metabolic and pharmacodynamic tolerance yields a greater risk for alcohol dependency—the body is already doing something different in metabolizing a neurotoxin (NIAAA, 2005; van Wormer & Davis, 2003). When the body becomes more efficient in processing and eliminating a mood-altering substance the term *metabolic tolerance* is accurate; when the central nervous system is less impaired by the drug the accurate term is *pharmacodynamic tolerance* (Doweiko, 2002). Thus, those who drink heavily are at higher risk for developing substance use disorders and display pharmacodynamic tolerance. Tolerance is one of the first signs of physical dependency (Doweiko, 2009) and the counselor is well advised to address binge drinking or drug-abusing patterns earlier rather than later. There is increasing evidence to support complex molecular and genetic influences pertaining to alcohol tolerance as molecular scientists conduct extensive laboratory research into the neural mechanisms involved in tolerance and addiction (Lovinger, 2008; Pietrzykowski & Treistman, 2008).

Tolerance helps explain why approximately 11% of the drinking population consumes over 50% of the alcohol in this country (Knapp, 1996; van Wormer & Davis, 2003). It takes increasing amounts of mood-altering chemicals or processes to achieve the desired effect when tolerance develops. For example, ongoing research focused on increasing trends of risky drinking patterns of college athletes. Researchers noted that nearly 60 percent (59.4%) of those surveyed reported patterns of heavy drinking, consuming at least five or more drinks at any one sitting (National Collegiate Athletic Association [NCAA], 2006). Of importance is the finding that slightly more than 18 percent of the athletes who drink report drinking 10 or more drinks at any one drinking occasion, thus demonstrating markedly increased tolerance (NCAA, 2006).

To further illustrate this let us look at a sample case. Susan is a 20-year-old college student athlete. Now in her junior year, she is a strong competitor on her college swim team. Susan began drinking in her freshman year of college and would feel euphoric effects after one drink. With continued drinking, perhaps on weekends, Susan noticed after 3 months that she could have four drinks and experience minimal euphoria, so she increased her intake to achieve the desired effect. In this example, Susan found that having five or six drinks during any one drinking episode was not unusual for her, yet for a female, four or more drinks per drinking episode is defined as abusive drinking. Binge drinking is defined for males as five or more drinks; for females as four or more in any one drinking episode (National Institute on Alcohol Abuse and Alcoholism [NIAAA], 2004; Watson, 2002). With continued drinking over multiple years, Susan saw her tolerance increase. She now reports drinking at least six drinks on any one occasion, with minimal effects.

Because of a recent arrest for Driving Under the Influence (DUI), Susan goes to a counselor. The counselor should note that heavy alcohol use in women increases the chances of osteoporosis (NIAAA, 2005), a major condition for the physically active individual. The counselor should also understand that recent research indicates that women have a greater incidence of complications from alcohol use, and experience more physical damage with less alcohol in a shorter time frame than males (Miller, 2004; NIAAA, 2005). Even though some studies show cardiovascular benefits with no more than one drink daily, for women there is also evidence that such daily consumption may increase breast cancer risks (NIAAA, 2005). It is important for the beginning counselor to also attend to issues regarding tolerance and possible physical withdrawal from drugs, especially alcohol. Fortunately, Susan agrees to continue counseling to address her drinking issues. How will you determine whether Susan is a risky drinker or alcohol dependent? What counseling approach do you think would be most helpful for this athlete? How would you gauge your rapport and empathy with her? What will you do if she continues risky drinking?

Substance withdrawal refers to the physiological changes that occur when a substance leaves the body. These changes, depending on their severity, can provide evidence that pharmaco-dynamic tolerance is present. Most withdrawal symptoms, which are usually the opposite of the drug effects, can begin within 4 hours of last use and may continue for varying lengths of time, usually 3–7 days, depending on the substance, degree of physical dependence, genetic factors, and overall health of the person (Doweiko, 2002). At its most benign, a hangover after an episode of heavy drinking is one example of substance withdrawal. In its more complicated progression, withdrawal, depending on the drug use, can manifest as mild to extreme tremors; nausea or vomiting; mood disturbances such as pronounced anxiety, depressed mood, and increased irritability, or *anhedonia*; neurological disturbances such as delusions, headaches, sleep disturbance, mild to severe seizures, or delirium tremens involving visual, auditory, or tactile hallucinations; physiological conditions such as diarrhea, goose bumps, fever, or rhinitis; and cardiac complications including elevated blood pressure, pulse, and cardiac arrhthymias (Doweiko, 2009; van Wormer & Davis, 2003). Complicated alcohol withdrawal, for example, is one of the most serious life-threatening types of withdrawal and nearly 15% of alcohol-dependent individuals can have withdrawal seizures if not medically detoxified.

SUBSTANCES OF ADDICTION

There are a number of chemical substances with addictive properties. To better understand these substances, they are classified into the following categories: depressants, stimulants, cannabinoids, hallucinogens, and opioids. Table 2.1 shows commonly abused illicit and prescription drugs, the Drug Enforcement Agency Schedule regulating drugs, route of administration, drug effects, and health risks in a chart prepared by the National Institute on Drug Abuse (NIDA, 2003). History shows a pattern of increasing concentration levels to better achieve maximum euphoric effects.

TABLE 2.1 *Commonly Abused Drugs, National Institute on Drug Abuse*

COMMONLY ABUSED DRUGS
Visit NIDA at www.drugabuse.gov

NIDA — NATIONAL INSTITUTE ON DRUG ABUSE

Substances: Category and Name	Examples of *Commercial* and Street Names	DEA Schedule*/ How Administered**	*Intoxication Effects/Potential Health Consequences*
Cannabinoids			*euphoria, slowed thinking and reaction time, confusion, impaired balance and coordination/cough, frequent respiratory infections; impaired memory and learning; increased heart rate, anxiety, panic attacks; tolerance, addiction*
hashish	boom, chronic, gangster, hash, hash oil, hemp	I/swallowed, smoked	
marijuana	blunt, dope, ganja, grass, herb, joints, Mary Jane, pot, reefer, sinsemilla, skunk, weed	I/swallowed, smoked	
Depressants			*reduced anxiety, feeling of well-being; lowered inhibitions; slowed pulse and breathing; lowered blood pressure, poor concentration/fatigue; confusion; impaired coordination, memory, judgment; addiction; respiratory depression and arrest, death*
barbiturates	*Amytal, Nembutal, Seconal, Phenobarbital:* barbs, reds, red birds, phennies, tooies, yellows, yellow jackets	II, III, V/injected, swallowed	
benzodiazepines (other than flunitrazepam)***	*Ativan, Halcion, Librium, Valium, Xanax:* candy, downers, sleeping pills, tranks	IV/swallowed, injected	*Also, for barbiturates—sedation, drowsiness/depression, unusual excitement, fever, irritability, poor judgment, slurred speech, dizziness, life-threatening withdrawal*
flunitrazepam***	*Rohypnol:* forget-me pill, Mexican Valium, R2, Roche, roofies, roofinol, rope, rophies	IV/swallowed, snorted	*for benzodiazepines—sedation, drowsiness/dizziness*
GHB***	gamma-hydroxybutyrate: G, Georgia home boy, grievous bodily harm, liquid ecstasy	I/swallowed	*for flunitrazepam—visual and gastrointestinal disturbances, urinary retention, memory loss for the time under the drug's effects*
methaqualone	*Quaalude, Sopor, Parest:* ludes, mandrex, quad, quay	I/injected, swallowed	*for GHB—drowsiness, nausea/vomiting, headache, loss of consciousness, loss of reflexes, seizures, coma, death*
			for methaqualone—euphoria/depression, poor reflexes, slurred speech, coma
Dissociative Anesthetics			*increased heart rate and blood pressure, impaired motor function/memory loss; numbness, nausea/vomiting*
ketamine	*Ketalar SV:* cat Valiums, K, Special K, vitamin K	III/injected, snorted, smoked	*Also, for ketamine—at high doses, delirium, depression, respiratory depression and arrest*
PCP and analogs	*phencyclidine:* angel dust, boat, hog, love boat, peace pill	I, II/injected, swallowed, smoked	*for PCP and analogs—possible decrease in blood pressure and heart rate, panic, aggression, violence/loss of appetite, depression*
Hallucinogens			*altered states of perception and feeling; nausea; persisting perception disorder (flashbacks)*
LSD	*lysergic acid diethylamide:* acid, blotter, boomers, cubes, microdot, yellow sunshines	I/swallowed, absorbed through mouth tissues	*Also, for LSD and mescaline—increased body temperature, heart rate, blood pressure, loss of appetite, sleeplessness, numbness, weakness, tremors*
mescaline	buttons, cactus, mesc, peyote	I/swallowed, smoked	*for LSD—persistent mental disorders*
psilocybin	magic mushroom, purple passion, shrooms	I/swallowed	*for psilocybin—nervousness, paranoia*
Opioids and Morphine Derivatives			*pain relief, euphoria, drowsiness/nausea, constipation, confusion, sedation, respiratory depression and arrest, tolerance, addiction, unconsciousness, coma, death*
codeine	*Empirin with Codeine, Fiorinal with Codeine, Robitussin A-C, Tylenol with Codeine:* Captain Cody, Cody, schoolboy; (with glutethimide) doors & fours, loads, pancakes and syrup	II, III, IV, V/injected, swallowed	
fentanyl and fentanyl analogs	*Actiq, Duragesic, Sublimaze:* Apache, China girl, China white, dance fever, friend, goodfella, jackpot, murder 8, TNT, Tango and Cash	I, II/injected, smoked, snorted	*Also, for codeine—less analgesia, sedation, and respiratory depression than morphine*
heroin	*diacetylmorphine:* brown sugar, dope, H, horse, junk, skag, skunk, smack, white horse	I/injected, smoked, snorted	*for heroin—staggering gait*
morphine	*Roxanol, Duramorph:* M, Miss Emma, monkey, white stuff	II, III/injected, swallowed, smoked	
opium	*laudanum, paregoric:* big O, black stuff, block, gum, hop	II, III, V/swallowed, smoked	
oxycodone HCL	*OxyContin:* Oxy, O.C., killer	II/swallowed, snorted, injected	
hydrocodone bitartrate, acetaminophen	*Vicodin:* vike, Watson-387	II/swallowed	
Stimulants			*increased heart rate, blood pressure, metabolism; feelings of exhilaration, energy, increased mental alertness/rapid or irregular heart beat; reduced appetite, weight loss, heart failure, nervousness, insomnia*
amphetamine	*Biphetamine, Dexedrine:* bennies, black beauties, crosses, hearts, LA turnaround, speed, truck drivers, uppers	II/injected, swallowed, smoked, snorted	*Also, for amphetamine—rapid breathing/tremor, loss of coordination; irritability, anxiousness, restlessness, delirium, panic, paranoia, impulsive behavior, aggressiveness, tolerance, addiction, psychosis*
cocaine	*Cocaine hydrochloride:* blow, bump, C, candy, Charlie, coke, crack, flake, rock, snow, toot	II/injected, smoked, snorted	*for cocaine—increased temperature/chest pain, respiratory failure, nausea, abdominal pain, strokes, seizures, headaches, malnutrition, panic attacks*

*Schedule I and II drugs have a high potential for abuse. They require greater storage security and have a quota on manufacturing, among other restrictions. Schedule I drugs are available for research only and have no approved medical use. Schedule II drugs are available only by prescription (unrefillable) and require a form for ordering. Schedule III and IV drugs are available by prescription, may have five refills in 6 months, and may be ordered orally. Some Schedule V drugs are available over the counter.

**Taking drugs by injection can increase the risk of infection through needle contamination with staphylococci, HIV, hepatitis, and other organisms.

***Associated with sexual assaults.

Substances: Category and Name	Examples of *Commercial* and Street Names	DEA Schedule*/ How Administered**	*Intoxication Effects*/Potential Health Consequences
Stimulants (continued)			
MDMA (methyl-enedioxymeth-amphetamine)	Adam, clarity, ecstasy, Eve, lover's speed, peace, STP, X, XTC	I/swallowed	for MDMA—*mild hallucinogenic effects, increased tactile sensitivity, empathic feelings/impaired memory and learning*, hyperthermia, cardiac toxicity, renal failure, liver toxicity
methamphetamine	*Desoxyn*: chalk, crank, crystal, fire, glass, go fast, ice, meth, speed	II/injected, swallowed, smoked, snorted	for methamphetamine—*aggression, violence, psychotic behavior/memory loss*, cardiac and neurological damage; impaired memory and learning, tolerance, addiction
methylphenidate (safe and effective for treatment of ADHD)	*Ritalin*: JIF, MPH, R-ball, Skippy, the smart drug, vitamin R	II/injected, swallowed, snorted	
nicotine	cigarettes, cigars, smokeless tobacco, snuff, spit tobacco, bid's, chew	not scheduled/smoked, snorted, taken in snuff and spit tobacco	for nicotine—additional effects attributable to tobacco exposure: adverse pregnancy outcomes; chronic lung disease, cardiovascular disease, stroke, cancer; tolerance, addiction
Other Compounds			
anabolic steroids	*Anadrol, Oxandrin, Durabolin, Depo-Testosterone, Equipoise*: roids, juice	III/injected, swallowed, applied to skin	no intoxication effects/hypertension, blood clotting and cholesterol changes, liver cysts and cancer, kidney cancer, hostility and aggression, acne; in adolescents, premature stoppage of growth; in males, prostate cancer, reduced sperm production, shrunken testicles, breast enlargement; in females, menstrual irregularities, development of beard and other masculine characteristics
Dextromethorphan (DXM)	Found in some cough and cold medications; Robotripping, Robo, Triple C	not scheduled/swallowed	*Dissociative effects, distorted visual perceptions to complete dissociative effects/for effects at higher doses see 'dissociative anesthetics'*
inhalants	Solvents *(paint thinners, gasoline, glues)*; gases *(butane, propane, aerosol propellants; nitrous oxide)*; nitrites *(isoamyl, isobutyl, cyclohexyl)*: laughing gas, poppers, snappers, whippets	not scheduled/inhaled through nose or mouth	stimulation, loss of inhibition; headache, nausea or vomiting; slurred speech, loss of motor coordination; wheezing/unconsciousness, cramps, weight loss, muscle weakness, depression, memory impairment, damage to cardiovascular and nervous systems, sudden death

U.S. Teens Who Have Ever Used Illicit Drugs or Cigarettes
Source: University of Michigan, *Monitoring the Future Study*, 2006.

U.S. Population (Aged 12 and Over) Who Have Ever Used Illicit Drugs, Cigarettes, or Prescription Drugs for Non-Medical Purposes
Source: SAMHSA, *National Survey on Drug Use and Health*, 2005.

Order NIDA publications from NCADI:
1-800-729-6686
or TDD: 1-800-487-4889

Principles of Drug Addiction Treatment

More than three decades of scientific research have yielded 13 fundamental principles that characterize effective drug abuse treatment. These principles are detailed in NIDA's *Principles of Drug Addiction Treatment: A Research-Based Guide.*

1. **No single treatment is appropriate for all individuals.** Matching treatment settings, interventions, and services to each patient's problems and needs is critical.

2. **Treatment needs to be readily available.** Treatment applicants can be lost if treatment is not immediately available or readily accessible.

3. **Effective treatment attends to multiple needs of the individual, not just his or her drug use.** Treatment must address the individual's drug use and associated medical, psychological, social, vocational, and legal problems.

4. **At different times during treatment, a patient may develop a need for medical services, family therapy, vocational rehabilitation, and social and legal services.**

5. **Remaining in treatment for an adequate period of time is critical for treatment effectiveness.** The time depends on an individual's needs. For most patients, the threshold of significant improvement is reached at about 3 months in treatment. Additional treatment can produce further progress. Programs should include strategies to prevent patients from leaving treatment prematurely.

6. **Individual and/or group counseling and other behavioral therapies are critical components of effective treatment for addiction.** In therapy, patients address motivation, build skills to resist drug use, replace drug-using activities with constructive and rewarding nondrug-using activities, and improve problem-solving abilities. Behavioral therapy also facilitates interpersonal relationships.

7. **Medications are an important element of treatment for many patients, especially when combined with counseling and other behavioral therapies.** Buprenorphine, methadone, and levo-alpha-acetylmethodol (LAAM) help persons addicted to opiates stabilize their lives and reduce their drug use. Naltrexone is effective for some opiate addicts and some patients with co-occurring

alcohol dependence. Nicotine patches or gum, or an oral medication, such as bupropion, can help persons addicted to nicotine.

8. **Addicted or drug-abusing individuals with coexisting mental disorders should have both disorders treated in an integrated way.**

9. **Medical detoxification is only the first stage of addiction treatment and by itself does little to change long-term drug use.** Medical detoxification manages the acute physical symptoms of withdrawal. For some individuals it is a precursor to effective drug addiction treatment.

10. **Treatment does not need to be voluntary to be effective.** Sanctions or enticements in the family, employment setting, or criminal justice system can significantly increase treatment entry, retention, and success.

11. **Possible drug use during treatment must be monitored continuously.** Monitoring a patient's drug and alcohol use during treatment, such as through urinalysis, can help the patient withstand urges to use drugs. Such monitoring also can provide early evidence of drug use so that treatment can be adjusted.

12. **Treatment programs should provide assessment for HIV/AIDS, hepatitis B and C, tuberculosis and other infectious diseases, and counseling to help patients modify or change behaviors that place them or others at risk of infection.** Counseling can help patients avoid high-risk behavior and help people who are already infected manage their illness.

13. **Recovery from drug addiction can be a long-term process and frequently requires multiple episodes of treatment.** As with other chronic illnesses, relapses to drug use can occur during or after successful treatment episodes. Participation in self-help support programs during and following treatment often helps maintain abstinence.

Source: National Institute on Drug Abuse. (2007). *Commonly abused drugs*. Retrieved from http://www.drugabuse.gov

Depressants

ALCOHOL.   It is important to understand the most commonly abused substances that jeopardize the health and well-being of an individual. By far, the most abused mood-altering substance today is ethanol, or ethyl alcohol, with approximately 129 million people in the United States over age 12 identifying themselves as current drinkers in 2008 (Substance Abuse and Mental Health Services Administration [SAMHSA], 2009). Note the alcohol consumption per capita values displayed in Table 2.2. The Centers for Disease Control and Prevention (CDC) note that excessive drinking is the primary risk factor leading to injury, and a major cause of death, ranking third in the United States. This translates to one preventable death every 7 minutes (CDC, 2009). Alcohol is "humanity's oldest domesticated drug" (Siegal & Inciardi, 2004, p. 78) and no one is immune from its potential for addiction. Regarding its effects and attraction, Knapp writes that alcohol is "the drink of deception: alcohol gives you power and robs you of it in equal measure" (1996, p. 95).

Alcohol has certainly been evident in anthropological records for centuries, although it is not clear how it was first discovered. Historians generally believe it was about 10,000 years ago, after berries or fruits left too long in the sun began fermenting, resulting in a crude version of wine (Erickson, 2001; Siegal & Inciardi, 2004). Distilling alcohol to get higher potency began around 800 A.D. in Arabia. Jabir ibn Hayyan, otherwise known as Geber, in searching for an alchemy formula, burned impurities in wine and thus discovered distilled spirits (Spicer, 1993). Distillation, however, was not popular until the thirteenth century, when a university professor in France, Arnauld de Villeneuve, promoted this new type of alcohol as a cure for diseases (Spicer, 1993).

Alcohol is classified as a depressant to the central nervous system (CNS). As such it often was used as an anesthetic or sleep aid. Drinking to achieve relaxation and euphoria contributed

TABLE 2.2 Apparent Per Capita Alcohol Consumption: National, State, and Regional Trends, 1977–2007

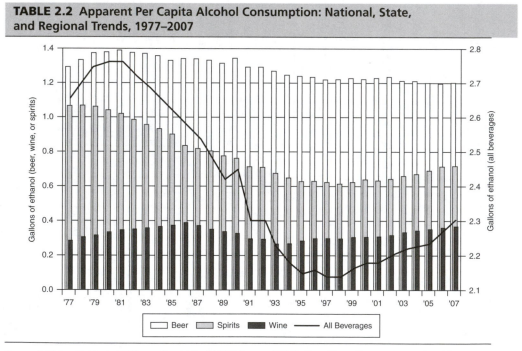

Source: LaVallee, Robin A., Williams, Gerald D., & Yi, Hsiao-ye. (2009). *Surveillance Report #87.* Retrieved from http://pubs.niaaa.nih.gov/publications/survelliance87/CONS07.htm

to the reputation of alcohol also as a desirable social lubricant due to its disinhibition and relaxation features. However, alcohol is also a powerful neurotoxin and alcoholism leads to critical areas of damage to key executive brain functioning with a "profound untoward effect on the cerebrum and cerebellum" (Sullivan & Pfefferbaum, 2005, p. 590).

Many addiction specialists and addiction counselor educators emphasize that the critical ingredient in alcohol is ethanol, whether a person consumes beer, wine, or distilled liquor. It is important for those counselors working with clients discussing information about alcohol use to address the common misconception that some alcoholic beverages are safer or less addicting than others. Some individuals have rationalized that since beer, for example, is only 5% ethanol it is less harmful, hence less addicting. What is important to understand is that "the same quantity of alcohol is consumed if someone drinks either a 12-ounce can or bottle of beer, a three- to four-ounce glass of wine, or a mixed drink made with one and one-half ounces of distilled spirits" (Siegal & Inciardi, 2004, p. 75). Although the overall sizes of the drinks vary, the amount of ethanol is equivalent; and it is ethanol that is the significant addicting agent in alcoholic beverages.

To better determine the potency of ethanol, the term "proof" is used to indicate the beverage's strength or, in other words, the percentage of pure ethanol in the beverage. Using the standard formula one roughly doubles the percentage of ethanol to determine potency; for example, wine is generally around 7% alcohol equating to 14 proof; the same is true for over-the-counter cough and cold preparations containing alcohol, such as popular brands which may be 20% alcohol, or surprisingly, 40 proof. Conversely, to determine the percentage of ethyl alcohol in a beverage one can divide by half the designated proof, for example, 151-proof rum is 75.5% ethanol.

Physiologically, when alcoholic beverages are consumed, ethanol is readily absorbed into the bloodstream through the lining of the stomach and small intestine, so its mood-altering effects are usually felt within 20 minutes. The effect of ethanol can be moderated by a variety of factors such as food in the stomach, total body weight, gender, and the response to alcohol (tolerance). There are notable gender differences. Researchers have established that women achieve higher blood alcohol content (BAC) levels when consuming the exact same amount of alcohol as males (NIAAA, 2005; Oscar-Berman & Marinkovic, 2004). Explanations of this difference point out that women experience higher alcohol concentrations due to lower dilution rates, since women have less water weight per pound than men (NIAAA, 2005). Because several researchers noted women show more severe consequences, faster progression through the stages of alcohol dependency, and higher blood alcohol concentrations, the term 'telescoping' is often used when describing women's responses to alcohol (Gilbertson, Prather, & Nixon, 2008). Questions remain whether this telescoping effect is due to gender differences as neuroscientists using neuroimaging have observed micro- and macrostructural brain damage differences between male and female alcoholics (Gilbertson, Prather, & Nixon). Gender issues pertaining to substances are also discussed in greater detail in Chapter 18.

The effects of alcohol are experienced biologically for as long as the ethanol remains in the body. The liver is the major organ responsible for eliminating, or detoxifying, alcohol. The main job of the liver is to metabolize or excrete toxins, processing ethanol as a toxin to the system (Doweiko, 2009), hence the appropriate term, *intoxicated*. The liver processes ethanol at relatively the same speed and rate for most people. Myths of drinking pots of hot coffee or taking frequent cold showers do not speed the rate at which the liver metabolizes ethanol (van Wormer & Davis, 2003). No substance exists that can accelerate the rate of breakdown of ethanol (Siegal & Inciardi, 2004). Of particular note to the counselor regarding ethanol-metabolizing rates are the number of young people who die each year as a direct result of alcohol poisoning (Falkowski, 2000). Often those with little experience drinking alcohol do not understand that overintoxication can be fatal. Since death due to overintoxication occurs infrequently, awareness of this danger is often limited, so it is important that counselors stress the risk one takes when consuming large quantities of alcohol quickly. Respiratory arrest or aspiration of vomit have been the leading fatal factors in recent high-profile deaths of inexperienced young college drinkers after imbibing large quantities of alcohol in a short time period (Falkowski, 2000).

An additional important concept for the counselor to understand is the method of measuring the amount of alcohol in one's body. To determine the amount of alcohol in the bloodstream, a blood alcohol concentration (BAC) is often measured either by a breathalyzer or a blood sample. There are a number of portable, easy-to-use breathalyzer instruments available for measuring BAC. Ordinarily a BAC level is best obtained within 12 hours after drinking as the ethanol may be eliminated from the body after this time period. The relatively short elimination time for alcohol is one of the main reasons a breathalyzer is the preferred measuring method, as opposed to a urine drug screen, the preferred method for measuring other drug levels.

Hospital emergency rooms and trauma units are the most likely setting to obtain blood samples for alcohol levels, often due to alcohol-related injuries such as falls, burns, and motor vehicle crashes. The National Highway Traffic Safety Administration (NHTSA) estimates that a person is injured every 2 minutes in an alcohol-related crash in the United States (2007). Healthcare costs are extensive when trauma injury, such as injuries received in a motor vehicle crash, are alcohol-related. Alcohol screening for risky drinking and brief counseling intervention (ASBI) studies in trauma settings have recently demonstrated such efficacy that the American College of Surgeons' Standards now require ASBI services in all Level I Trauma Centers in the United States (ACS, 2006). This innovative policy mandates that Level I Trauma Centers use the "teachable moment" generated by traumatic alcohol-related injury (approximately 50% of trauma patients) as a gateway to effective prevention of future alcohol abuse, especially with underage and young adult drinkers, and to decrease or delay the onset of alcohol use disorders (SAMHSA, 2007). Nationally, many Level 1 and 2 hospital trauma centers are increasing routine alcohol screenings and brief counseling interventions in concentrated efforts to reduce trauma recidivism and impact risky drinking patterns (SAMHSA, 2007; Schermer, 2005). The use of an evidence-based screening tool, such as a positive finding of binge drinking, is used to help identify risky drinkers (SAMHSA, 2007). This new prevention strategy indicates that a brief counseling intervention has a powerful impact that facilitates changes in future behavior (Dunn et al., 2008; Leontiva et al., 2009; Toumbourou et al., 2007) and reduces hospital trauma recidivism by 50% (Crawford et al., 2004; Gentilello et al., 1999). One study examining youth aged 12–18 admitted to a hospital with major injuries found that alcohol counseling during their hospitalization reduced alcohol consumption in addition to further injury (Dunn et al., 2008). By far, those deemed risky drinkers (approximately 30% of drinkers) have a favorable response to ASBI, may delay or prevent alcohol dependency by changing risky drinking patterns, and improve their overall health. More than 50% of alcohol-impaired drivers involved in a fatal automobile crash have a BAC at or above .16 (National Highway Traffic Safety Administration [NHTSA], 2004). Currently all 50 states and the District of Columbia have enacted .08 BAC laws stating that any driver with a BAC at or above .08 would be charged with operating a vehicle illegally, commonly referred to as Driving Under the Influence (DUI) (NHTSA, 2009). Drivers aged 21 to 25 were reporting driving under influence (26.1%) at more than twice the average rate in the United States (12.4%; 30.9 million individuals) (SAMHSA, 2009).

Employers are also affected by alcohol-related trauma: The total cost to employers related to automobile crashes where at least one driver was alcohol-impaired is more than $9 billion annually and of that total, $3.1 billion is directly related to alcohol impairment on the job (NHTSA, 2004). Recent data further indicated that in 2008, 56.2% of whites aged 12 and above reported current alcohol use, followed by 43.3% of persons identified as American Indians or Alaska Natives, 43.2% for persons of Hispanic descent, 41.9% of African-Americans, and 37% of persons identified as Asian (SAMHSA, 2009). The SAMHSA data further showed the highest rate of binge drinking patterns were noted in the Hispanic population (25.6%).

Youth are not immune to alcohol-related trauma. Toumbourou et al. (2007) examined current studies regarding patterns of alcohol use worldwide and noted "hazardous alcohol use alone has been estimated to cause 31.5% of all deaths in 15–29 year old men in the developed world and 86% of the 3.6 million substance-related deaths of 15–29 year old men and women worldwide" (p. 1391). Their findings also show that harmful use and abuse rather than dependence make up the majority of problems in substance use among adolescents. Miller, Levy, Spicer, and Taylor (2006) calculated that in the United States, alcohol use by minors accounted for approximately 16% of all alcohol sales in 2001. Their findings further illustrated cost by calculating that 3,170 deaths, 2 million other harmful events, $5.4 billion in medical costs, $14.9 billion from loss of work or other resources, for a total cost of $41.6 billion in lost quality of living, were all attributed to underage drinking. The findings noted that alcohol-related violent acts and motor vehicle crashes were primary factors in the cost analysis. The CDC also identified patterns of alcohol use among high school students (9th–12th graders) in their biannual Youth Risk Behavior Surveillance Survey (YRBSS); in 2007 three-fourths (75%) of students reported consuming one or more alcoholic beverages in their lifetime with slightly over one-fourth (26%) indicating a pattern of heavy drinking as defined by five or more drinks during any one drinking occasion on at least one day in the month preceding the survey (2009). On closer examination, it is of particular note that just under half (40.4%) of male 12th graders indulged in binge drinking in the month prior to the survey, far exceeding the next highest percentage of binge drinkers (26.1%) who were 18–24 years of age (CDC, 2009). Further comparison data indicate, for example, that less than a tenth (7.8%) of those aged 55–64 reported similar binge drinking patterns (CDC, 2009). College students aged 18 to 22 were found to have the highest binge drinking rates (40.5%) with approximately 16 percent deemed heavy drinkers (SAMSHA, 2009).

Case Study.   In an informal survey done by a student reporter for the high school newspaper, it was reported that almost 20% of the student body used either cigarettes or smokeless tobacco (which were viewed as much safer than cigarettes). While the numbers for most illicit drug use was low, one in 15 students reported recreational use of prescription drugs ranging from OxyContin to Ritalin. Almost 70% of the 300 students surveyed reported alcohol use within the past 6 months, with 41% reporting semi-regular binge drinking (30% of 11th and 12th graders and 11% of 9th and 10th graders).

What major issues should the school counselor and faculty be concerned about, and how might they go about effectively addressing these issues? Which behaviors offer the highest risks and why? Which behaviors, and with whom, would you address first? Discuss how you think these students compare to national averages, including illicit drug use.

In summary, alcohol abuse, addiction, and risky drinking create significant problems for many people. The addiction counselor benefits from increased knowledge and awareness about the most commonly abused substance, alcohol, which impacts far more individuals in a negative way than any other mood-altering chemical substance.

Addiction, Mental Health, & Childhood Trauma

In a recent study examining traumatic childhood events among persons diagnosed with both substance use and mental health disorders who were being treated in an in-patient setting, 65.9% of the 402 participants reported emotional abuse and neglect during their childhood (Wu, Schairer, Dellor, & Grella, 2010). Physical abuse was reported by 49.3%, 48% reported sexual abuse, and 56% reported family violence. The severity of childhood traumatic events were scored on a 6-point scale. Each unit increase in severity of trauma increased the risk of lifetime alcohol dependence by 18% and tobacco use by 16%. As has been found in previous research, there is strong correlation between substance use, mental health diagnoses, and childhood trauma, suggesting the ecological complexity of substance abuse.

Source: Wu, N.S., Schairer, L.C., Dellor, E., & Grella, C. (2010). Childhood trauma and health outcomes in adults with comorbid substance abuse and mental health disorders. *Addictive Behaviors, 35*(1), 68–71.

Case Study.   Because several members of Ellen's family, including both parents, were alcoholic, she abstained from alcohol until she was 29, when she began drinking socially. Six years later, her drinking began affecting her job. An increasing pattern of absenteeism, tardiness, and attitude problems resulted in a confrontation with her boss, who required she get an assessment and follow any recommendation made. The results indicated a high degree of tolerance, and a multitude of social and physical problems related to her drinking. She insists that she drinks only wine, not hard liquor, does not drink every day, and never before evening, so she is certain that alcohol is not a problem.

What areas of her life need more exploration? What kinds of data and counseling techniques might a counselor utilize in order to help break through Ellen's denial and increase her motivation to address the issues alcohol is causing in her life?

The *Teachable Moment*, focused on Alcohol Screening, Brief Counseling Interventions, and policy implications in a Level I Trauma Center at Wake Forest University Baptist Medical Center in North Carolina, is a three-year prospective clinical trial research study funded by the Substance Abuse Policy Research Program of The Robert Wood Johnson Foundation. Principal Investigator: **Mary Claire O'Brien**, MD; Co-Investigators: **Laura J. Veach**, PhD and **Beth Reboussin**, PhD.

Janeé R. Avent *(Counseling Intern, 2nd year Counseling student, UNC-Greensboro)*: One of the most stressful times for a counseling graduate student is finding an internship site. As always, I chose to embark on something that was both new and seemingly quite challenging. I selected a new internship in the Trauma Center of Wake Forest University Baptist Medical Center. I did not know what to expect coming into this internship. I had limited counseling experience and had never worked in a hospital setting.

This learning experience has been both challenging and rewarding. Challenging in that it is never an easy task to walk unexpectedly into a client's hospital room in the trauma center to talk with them about their alcohol use. Challenging in that it is difficult to ask concerned family members to step out of the room while I talk with their loved one in confidence about risky drinking. There is also a personal emotional challenge that comes with witnessing someone in such physical and affective pain concurrently.

Nonetheless, for every measure of challenge, there is an even greater sense of reward. It is so easy to view oneself as the expert, but it never ceases to amaze me how much the clients teach me; they teach me about strength, determination, and humility. Many are willing to be vulnerable and discuss personal issues surrounding alcohol and related injuries because they are willing to do whatever is necessary to make healthy changes in their lifestyles. Even the clients that are not ready to discuss change remind me that I am here to plant a seed and hopefully one day that seed will grow.

Due to the support and respect I receive from the entire Trauma community, this experience has been very rewarding. The learning curve has been very steep and there has been a significant amount to process at one time, it has been manageable because of the trust and reassurance I gain from the Trauma surgeons and staff, my clinical supervisors, and the Teachable Moment research team. If internship is the time when one is shaping their clinical approach and is preparing for their future career in counseling, then I can only be excited about the possibilities that exist not only for me but for the counseling profession. There are new opportunities that unfold every day, and I have the ability to work with populations that I had not anticipated, but I have come to appreciate and greatly enjoy.

I look forward to my continued work on the research study for the remainder of my graduate studies. I know that the learning has really just started for me. I am excited about the expansion of alcohol screenings and brief interventions and the contributions that counselors can make to the clients and the medical profession. This is only the beginning and I am grateful that I am granted the opportunity to learn from the "Teachable Moment."

Janeé R. Avent is a graduate of the Counseling and Educational Development program at the University of North Carolina at Greensboro. She was the Counseling Intern for the Trauma Service and Burn Unit of Wake Forest Baptist Medical Center June 2009–May 2010.

SEDATIVES/HYPNOTICS.   Another classification of drugs that depress the central nervous system (CNS) is sedative/hypnotic drugs. The most common drugs in this group are benzodiazepines, barbiturates, and nonbarbiturates. Currently, benzodiazepines, sometimes referred to as tranquilizers, are frequently prescribed for a wide range of symptoms ranging from sleeplessness, anxiety, and muscular strain, to seizures (Doweiko, 2009; Erickson, 2001) and are of particular risk for women. For instance, findings show women are 55% more likely to be prescribed benzodiazepines than men (NIDA, 2005). With their discovery in the 1960s, many heralded them as a much safer alternative to barbiturates with the belief that no addictive potential existed. Decades later researchers found that benzodiazepines, such as Valium (diazepam) or Xanax (alprazolam), are highly addictive with long-term use and often have serious withdrawal complications requiring medical detoxification. Researchers also note that benzodiazepines, even taken as prescribed by a physician, are toxic to the brain as evidenced with brain scanning techniques showing " . . . an overall diminished or dehydrated pattern of activity, just as with drugs of abuse" (Amen, 2005, p. 79). Benzodiazepines are often prescribed as the initial drug for treating anxiety despite research showing limited effectiveness with long-term use, in part due to tolerance issues. Short-term use (4–8 weeks) may show maximum effect for anxiety but other medications, such as antidepressants with anti-anxiety actions, are far more effective for long-term anxiety management without the addictive potential as seen with benzodiazepines (Doweiko, 2009).

Concerns about benzodiazepine abuse and addiction are growing. For example, trend analyses note a 41% increase (from 71,609 to 100,784) in benzodiazepine-related emergency department visits between 1995 and 2002 (Crane & Lemanski, 2004). Addiction treatment admissions in which tranquilizers were the primary drug of addiction climbed 79% over a 10-year period, 1992 to 2002 (SAMHSA, 2005). For women, it is a particularly troublesome pattern when "men lead women in numbers of addicts for every substance except prescription medications" (Briggs & Pepperell, 2009, p. 20).

Another concern about benzodiazepines is their potential for use as a "date-rape" drug. Rohypnol (flunitrazepam), a benzodiazepine with amnesiac properties which is approximately 10 times more potent than Valium, has been used in sexual assault crimes (Falkowski, 2000).

CNS depressants also include barbiturates, such as Tuinal (amobarbital with secobarbital) or Nembutal (pentobarbital). Barbiturates use was most prevalent during the 1950s through the

1970s when, at that time, they were second only to alcohol as a drug of abuse (Erickson, 2001). Barbiturates are fast-acting. Within the brain, neurotransmitters and depolarizing activity decreases thereby further depressing the CNS, thus making barbiturates dangerous in their potential for lethal overdose, especially if combined with other CNS depressants (Erickson, 2001).

Nonbarbiturates include drugs such as Quaalude (methaqualone) and have much the same physiological profile as barbiturates. Because of accidental overdosing dangers associated with both barbiturates and nonbarbiturates their use, fortunately, has declined.

Case Study.   Daphne, a 35-year-old African-American married mother of two, has struggled with anxiety since she was young, but has done well and graduated with an MS in nursing two years ago. This year she was hired to teach nursing students in a hospital program. Due to her anxiety, her MD prescribed Valium. She loves her job, but feels that the stress of being "on stage" can only be managed with the help of her medication. For six months, her MD continued to prescribe the sedative, but has refused to prescribe it any longer because she is demanding more and stronger dosages in order to cope. Daphne has come to you in hopes of convincing the psychiatrist in your practice to prescribe Valium for her.

What are the issues here, and how would you address them? If she continues to work with you, what kind of treatment plan would you create with her, and what are some of the modalities you might employ?

Stimulants

TOBACCO.   The primary mood-altering substance in tobacco products is nicotine, a mild stimulant. It is believed that the indigenous people of the Americas used tobacco long before the first white Europeans arrived (Doweiko, 2002). The resulting history and expansion of the use of tobacco has had profound effects. Tobacco addiction is associated with the deaths of 100 million people in the 20th century (NIDA, 2008). It is important to examine trends among youth since substantial prevention efforts have been implemented to reduce tobacco use. In 2008, adolescents aged 12 to 17 showed a declining trend of tobacco use since 2002, decreasing from 15.2% to 11.4% with most of that decline attributed to decreasing cigarette use (SAMHSA, 2009). However, slightly over one-fifth of adults continue to smoke despite evidence of serious health risks associated with smoking (Stevens, 2009).

Cigarette use is associated with those addicted to other substances. In 2008, one survey found that heavy alcohol intake was associated with tobacco use; 58 percent of heavy drinkers also smoked cigarettes in the same month (SAMHSA, 2009).

In an effort to find the benefits of nicotine without the dangers associated with becoming a smoker, some rationalized that chew or smokeless tobacco might be less dangerous to one's health; adolescent trends have remained relatively stable, with approximately 2% of 12 to 17 year olds reporting monthly use of smokeless tobacco (SAMHSA, 2009). More evidence indicates that smokeless tobacco, for example, carries significant health risk for hypertension, coronary artery disease, oral cancer, oral lesions, and tumors (Doweiko, 2002; Prentice, 2003; The Higher Education Center for Alcohol and Other Drug Prevention, 2002). Medications such as Bupropion, Varenicline, and nicotine replacement aids are increasingly utilized to treat tobacco addiction (NIDA, 2008).

Case Study.   Many studies have shown a high concurrent use of cigarettes with alcohol and other substance use. Many treatment centers have instituted no-smoking policies, believing that in addition to the risks posed by nicotine addiction, continued tobacco use may heighten the likelihood of relapse for recovering alcoholics and drug addicts. Others believe that forcing a nicotine-dependent person to stop smoking when he or she is in substance-abuse treatment may cause them to drop out of treatment, thus lessening the chances of recovery from the primary addiction. A new treatment center, ChangeNOW, is totally smoke-free.

When consulting with this new treatment center, what conceptual views would you support and why? How would you address these issues with both the counselors you are consulting with (several of whom smoke) and with a new client, a heavy smoker, who really wants a referral from you to this new facility?

EPHEDRINE, AMPHETAMINES, AMPHETAMINE-LIKE MEDICATIONS. Other types of stimulants include ephedrine, amphetamines, and amphetamine-like medications (Ritalin). Unlike many other mood-altering substances that are primarily used for the euphoria produced by the drug, amphetamines are often used for the euphoric experience and to enhance productivity. Although, as Weil and Rosen point out, "instead of automatically improving physical and mental performance, stimulants sometimes just make people do poor work faster" (1983, p. 38).

Abuse of Prescription Stimulants by Young People

Researchers identified 21 studies representing a total of 113,104 subjects in a recent systemic review of the medical literature examining the prevalence of nonprescribed stimulant medication use among children and young adults (Willens et al., 2008). According to the research, 5–9% of grade school and high school students reported taking nonprescribed stimulant medications (i.e., Ritalin, Adderall) in the last year. The reported rates among college-age persons ranged from 5–35%. Among those people who had a prescription for stimulants, 16–29% had been asked to give, trade, or sell their medications. Reasons stated for using nonprescribed stimulants included improving alertness and concentration, experimenting, and "getting high." Persons at the highest risk for misusing and diverting stimulants included whites, members of fraternities and sororities, individuals with lower grade point averages, those prescribed immediate-release compared to extended-release preparations, and individuals who reported ADHD symptoms.

Source: Wilens, T., Adler, L., Adams, J., Sgambati, S., Rotrosen, J., Sawtelle, R., Utzinger, L., & Fusillo, S. (2008). Misuse and Diversion of Stimulants Prescribed for ADHD: A Systematic Review of the Literature. *Journal of the American Academy of Child and Adolescent Psychiatry, 47*(1), 21–31.

Ancient Chinese medicine began using plants containing ephedrine over 5,000 years ago; more recent medical refinement resulted in extensive use in the United States after 1930 for problems mainly affecting the respiratory system. The legal ban in 2004 of ephedrine (Hall, 2004) was a result of a drug fraught with significant side effects. Almost 70 years ago efforts to find a synthetic alternative to ephedrine with fewer side effects (such as anxiety) and better outcomes resulted in the pharmaceutical development of amphetamines.

Several addiction experts note that "speed" (a slang term for amphetamines) was used extensively by military personnel during wartime in the 1940s to improve endurance and alertness (Doweiko, 2002; Miller, 2004; Weil & Rosen, 1983). In the 1950s it was injected as a treatment to stop heroin addiction (Miller, 2004). Amphetamine use in the 1960s and 1970s spiraled, with "approximately 10 billion amphetamine tablets manufactured in the United States in the year 1970" (Doweiko, 2009, p. 118). With such extensive amphetamine use, many of the negative side effects such as agitation with severe anxiety, cardiovascular damage, paranoia, severe depression, drug-induced psychosis, and withdrawal-induced suicidal ideation were discovered. Warnings about the abuse and addiction potential of speed were commonplace in the early 1970s since "amphetamines had acquired a reputation as known killers"

(Doweiko, 2002, p. 137). Overall, the illicit use of amphetamines has been problematic, highlighted by increasing methamphetamine-related episodes; NIDA (2004) documented a 30% increase in hospital emergencies between 1999 and 2000. Current research shows an increasing overall usage rate of amphetamines in athletes (4.1%) with alarming trends, for example, of greater use of stimulants by female than male athletes and higher rates of use in white athletes (NCCA, 2006).

Methamphetamine is often the preferred stimulant of abuse and can be taken by mouth, snorted, smoked or, most problematically, injected. Recovering amphetamine addicts show continued slower physical movement and impaired memory even after ceasing any methamphetamine use for 9 months and researchers are further concerned that addicts may have an increased risk for other neurodegenerative diseases (Zickler, 2002). The methamphetamine manufacturer cautions in the *Physician's Desk Reference* (PDR) "methamphetamine has a high potential for abuse . . . may lead to drug dependence" (PDR, 2002, p. 440). Tolerance to methamphetamine develops quickly, which can exacerbate the addictive cycle. Often, end-stage addiction includes intravenous administration and severe withdrawal, intense craving patterns, brain damage, and often, significant cardiac complications (NIDA, 2008). Encouraging data from 2008 show the rates of monthly use of methamphetamine decreased over 50% between 2006 and 2008 in the United States (SAMHSA, 2009).

Alternatives to pharmaceutically-produced amphetamines are illicit amphetamines; one example is a form of methamphetamine known as "ice" and more recently, methcathinone or "Kat." Both Kat and ice produce stimulant effects and have many of the same risks and side effects as amphetamines; because of the lowered cost associated with illicit amphetamines— averaging $15 per gram—combined with the relative ease of manufacturing the drug, illegal methamphetamine labs remain a significant concern in many communities (Stevens, 2009). One report, in an effort to educate individuals to better detect illegal methamphetamine-making labs, stressed that a variety of toxic chemicals are often present such as lye, rock salt, lithium batteries, pool acid, iodine, antifreeze, paint thinner, lighter fluid, and are detectable during manufacturing particularly with items "such as phosphine, ether, ammonia, battery acid, and acetone, [because they] have distinctive smells . . . phosphine smells like garlic, sulfur smells like rotten eggs, ammonia smells like cat urine, and acetone smells like nail polish remover" (Scott, 2002, p. 29). Efforts to reduce the illegal manufacture of methamphetamine are having a positive effect in the United States but children and individuals remain at risk from the toxic chemical spills and explosions associated with such labs.

Other stimulants of particular focus for the counselor are amphetamine-like stimulants, such as Ritalin or its generic name, methylphenidate. For a number of years methylphenidate has been used extensively for the treatment of attention-deficit/hyperactivity disorder (ADHD). Its main action in the brain involves blocking dopamine reuptake, which results in behavior changes of improved concentration and tracking of information (Doweiko, 2006). Ritalin also exhibits side effects that include weight and appetite loss, insomnia, nausea, hypertension, anemia, or perseveration (Doweiko, 2006). There is considerable research examining long-term effects of this drug. Newer research points to complications such as: liver damage, decreasing seizure thresholds, growth hormone disruption, cardiac arrhythmias, and heart tissue damage in some individuals (Breggin & Cohen, 2007; Doweiko, 2009). Unfortunately, more reports indicate Ritalin is also being abused by illegally diverting the drug to individuals without a prescription. Breggin & Cohen (2007) further point out that Ritalin (methylphenidate) and other amphetamines (dextroamphetamine, dexamphetamine [Adderall], methamphetamine [Desoxyn], often prescribed for young people in the treatment of ADHD, were required by the Federal Drug Administration in 2006 to be labeled with a warning against prescribing them to individuals with heart problems, due to increasing reports of sudden death in children and adults prescribed these stimulants. Continued research into the long term effects of Ritalin and other stimulants prescribed for ADHD remains a needed priority.

Case Study.   Bailey, 21, is a gay biracial single male and has been through treatment four times for his methamphetamine addiction, the last one a seven-day program followed by a four week IOP. After this last attempt, he was able to stay clean for only two weeks before relapsing, despite being highly motivated. While high, he was arrested for stealing $34 from a convenience store. He was referred to drug court and the judge has agreed to give him one last try at treatment before incarcerating him.

What treatment level, modalities, length, and aftercare plans do you think would be most likely to help Bailey attain and maintain sobriety? Discuss the difficulties a meth addict faces in maintaining recovery that differ from those of many other substances. What, if any, other, issues might the counselor want to consider?

COCAINE.   Cocaine is also classified as a stimulant, as is crack cocaine, the smokeable, concentrated form of cocaine. History shows, as with many mood-altering drugs, increasing efforts to produce more concentrated forms of the drug to achieve maximum euphoric effect. Note in Table 2.3 the history of methods used to increase the concentration of cocaine (Inaba & Cohen, 2007). Current trends show a steady decline in use of cocaine since the mid-1990s. For example, a 2002 report indicated 2% of athletes surveyed reported cocaine use in the recent year as compared to 5% usage in 1989, a significant declining trend (The Higher Education Center for Alcohol and Other Drug Prevention, 2002).

TABLE 2.3 History of Cocaine: Methods to Increase Potency

Time Period	Methods to Increase the Potency of Cocaine	Time for Euphoric Effect to Reach Brain
Peru, 1450s	Chew Coca leaf with charred oyster shells (slow absorption rate).	20–30 minutes
Europe & United States, 1900s	Snort powder cocaine (snuff); increased absorption rate via mucosa in nasal passages via snorting.	3–5 minutes
	Liquify cocaine in liquid products claiming improved health such as tonics or 'soft' drinks, such as Coca-Cola.	15–30 minutes
	Injecting cocaine either intravenously (IV) or intramuscularly (IM); increased absorption rapidly with intense euphoric effect.	30 seconds (IV) 3–5 minutes (IM)
United States, 1970s	Smoking cocaine known as "freebasing" (complicated mixing of highly flammable ethyl ether with cocaine to produce more concentrated form of cocaine via heating in a pipe). Addiction potential appeared in diagnostic literature.	5–8 seconds
United States, 1980s	Smoking "crack" cocaine, readily packaged concentrated form of cocaine in smokeable form (simple and expedient path to intoxication peak). Highest risk for addiction because of most rapid delivery and easily concealed packaging also led to ease of sales and distribution resulting in crack epidemic.	5–8 seconds

Source: Inaba, D. S., & Cohen, W. E. (2007). *Uppers, downers, all-arounders* (6th ed.). Medford, OR: CNS Productions, Inc.

Epidemics of cocaine abuse and addiction occurred in the late 1800s and again in the early 1900s which helped lead to its prohibition of use with legislation of the Harrison Act of 1914 (Doweiko, 2009). By the late 1970s many stimulant abusers and addicts were seeking a safer alternative to amphetamines; hence the rise in cocaine use began again. This time a new, more powerful form of cocaine, crack, was synthesized and its distribution was rampant throughout all socioeconomic strata in the 1980s and early 1990s (Stevens, 2009). Since smoking a substance is the fastest route into the bloodstream, usually in approximately 4 seconds, intense cravings accompany the pattern of abuse and increasing doses are often sought by the user. Addiction can develop quickly. In one addict's account, the initial experience with crack is aptly described as an all-encompassing experience: "In seconds my brain exploded. . . . My heart felt as if it would explode with light, with love. Nothing else mattered except reaching that peak of rapture over and over again" (Moyers & Ketchum, 2006, p. 101–102). Many celebrities and professional athletes were featured in media segments about their cocaine and crack addictions while many prevention specialists organized to combat the deleterious consequences of cocaine abuse and dependency. At one time it was believed that cocaine users were only at risk for habituation or psychological dependence; however, it is now clear that physical dependence can occur, as evidenced by tolerance and withdrawal symptomatology (American Psychiatric Association [APA], 2000). Cocaine's effect on the brain involves many of the same brain regions in the reward pathway, particularly sexual desire, complicating recovery efforts, again because of intense cravings. One writer who struggled in recovery from crack addiction, described the cravings which led to yet one more relapse, after a three-year abstinence, as "a 'physiological imperative' . . . evoking a howling internal torment that overrides the need for food, for water, for sleep, for love" (Moyers & Ketcham, 2006, p. 278).

In summary, stimulant drugs often result in a strong potential for abuse and dependency, with physical and psychological complications thwarting recovery efforts.

Case Study.   Bette is a 34-year-old Latina woman with two children aged 10 and 4. She began using cocaine recreationally with friends a few months ago. She has become rapidly dependent on the drug and is now using rock cocaine as well. She vanished from home for four days after emptying the family bank account of $14,000. She reports wanting to stop but has tried three previous times (two of them short in-patient stays) to quit and has relapsed within a few days each time. Explain what is happening in terms of addiction theory and discuss the components of a treatment plan that could be developed as an effective intervention.

Cannabinoids

Marijuana, possibly one of the most controversial illicit drugs, is in a drug class all by itself. Marijuana "is an ancient drug, used since prehistoric times in parts of the Old World" (Weil & Rosen, 1983, p. 113) and often it acts like a stimulant; at other times it is similar to a depressant and it resembles a mild psychedelic drug. It is in its own classification as a cannabinoid because of its many unique properties. It is considered to be the most commonly abused illegal drug (NIDA, 2008). Recent attention has focused on legalizing marijuana for restricted medical use and reclassifying it so it can be legally prescribed for certain medical conditions (Stevens, 2009). The latest data trends indicated that those aged 50 and older are showing increased use of illicit drugs. For example, in 2002 1.9% of those aged 55–59 reported illicit drug use whereas in 2008 that percentage increased to 5% (SAMHSA, 2009).

For a number of years, experts questioned whether one could develop a dependency on marijuana; however, by 1983 experts in drug issues noted that tolerance, withdrawal, and dependence occurred with regular marijuana use. It became increasingly clear that the pattern of dependency is different: "at its worst marijuana dependence consists of chain smoking, from the moment of getting up in the morning to the time of falling asleep . . . but dramatic withdrawal syndromes don't occur . . . and craving for the drug is not nearly as intense as for tobacco, alcohol, or narcotics" (Weil & Rosen, 1983, p. 119). Diagnostic categories for marijuana dependence are included as a substance use disorder in the widely accepted diagnostic manual of mental disorders (APA, 2000).

The negative physical effects of smoking marijuana on a frequent basis are seen with the reduced lung capacity estimated between 15% and 40% (Prentice, 2003). Other concerns include lowered testosterone levels, increased exercising pulse rates upwards of 20%, and decreased muscle strength (Prentice, 2003). Brain changes, especially in short-term memory functioning, the capacity to learn, and focused attention are also associated with negative effects of continued marijuana abuse (NIDA, 2008). Also, newer analyses note an association between the use of marijuana and psychosis-related complications. One recent in-depth examination, using sibling pair analysis of over 3,000 individuals since birth, found at the 21-year follow-up significant patterns that support mounting evidence that "longer duration since first cannabis use was associated with multiple psychosis-related outcomes in young adults" (McGrath et al., 2010, p. E5). These psychosis-related outcomes include diagnoses of schizophrenia, persistent delusional disorder, or acute psychotic disorders, for example; these diagnoses were seen at a much higher rate in those individuals who reported at least 6 years of marijuana use. These outcomes could not be better explained by factors such as family mental illness, environmental concerns, or genetics (McGrath et al., 2010). Promising new research will continue to yield a better understanding of the unique properties and health effects of marijuana.

Hallucinogens and Other Psychedelics

Another classification of commonly abused drugs includes hallucinogens. Examples of hallucinogens include lysergic acid derivatives (LSD) or psilocybin; indole-type hallucinogens; and phencyclidine (PCP), a phenylethylamine-type hallucinogen, also referred to as a dissociative anesthetic. Hallucinogens range in their effect on the brain; for example, LSD alters the neurotransmitter serotonin and PCP blocks major neurotransmission reuptake and disrupts neuro-electrical impulses (Erickson, 2001). Currently 1.1 million people were identified as hallucinogen users within the recent month they were surveyed (SAMHSA, 2009).

Other psychoactive drugs which are not technically hallucinogens but have perception-altering properties—psychedelics—include MDMA (Ecstasy). The most popular psychedelic of the 1990s, MDMA, also designated as 3,4 methylenedioxymethamphetamine, is a synthesized psychoactive drug with stimulant properties and its chemical makeup is a "synthetic compound related to both mescaline and the amphetamines" (Inciardi & McElrath, 2004, p. 286).

Hallucinogens and other psychedelic drugs may often be used with other addictive drugs, but are not regarded as having physiologically addicting properties such as tolerance or withdrawal syndromes. Psychological dependency, however, has been noted with hallucinogens and other psychedelics. Complications from traumatic experiences and emotions are noted as unpredictable responses to hallucinogens (NIDA, 2008).

Opioids

Opium is "the parent of all narcotic drugs" (Weil & Rosen, 1983, p. 80) and contains 20 different drugs, the primary one being morphine. Opioids, derivatives of opium compounds, are abused because of their ability to affect the brain's reward pathway so dramatically and produce a longer-lasting euphoria that includes initial sensations compared often to orgasm, followed by drowsy bliss-like states (Doweiko, 2006). Morphine was used extensively in the Civil War and the resulting addictive patterns became known as "soldier's disease" (Stevens, 2009).

Heroin, more potent than morphine, was not extracted from opium until 1895 and heralded because it reduced the side effects associated with morphine (Stevens, 2009). In the United States, for decades many prevention and addiction specialists focused on heroin abuse and addiction due to its highly addictive nature and potency.

Intravenous injection is the preferred route of administration in heroin addiction; however, recent trends indicate an increase in the use of heroin by snorting and smoking, possibly due to higher grade potency in recent years and heightened awareness of HIV infection risks (Dziegielewski & Suris, 2005). One addict's case example describes the heroin addictive cycle aptly as " . . . a shot of heroin and all that pain and suffering gets instantly traded in for rainbows, warm sunshine, and laughter. . . . [F]ear of withdrawal combined with the easy access of high purity heroin is what keeps so many addicted" (Dziegielewski & Suris, p. 155).

Long-term efforts to recover from heroin addiction may include use of a slower-acting opioid, such as methadone, to assist the heroin addict in harm-reduction. After three decades of methadone maintenance programs, methadone is generally regarded as effective in harm reduction and heroin addiction treatment (Dziegielewski & Suris, 2005). A newer, slow-acting synthetic opiate, buprenorphine, is also gaining in use as an alternative to methadone (Doweiko, 2009) and is used in treating opioid addiction (NIDA, 2008). One study by Horton et al. (2009) stressed that even past use of heroin, found in as many as 1 in 4 of those seeking residential substance abuse treatment, indicates a greater tendency for riskier behaviors, poorer outcomes, and higher relapse potential, possibly related to clinical dissociation patterns. Horton and colleagues encourage better screening for dissociative disorders among clients with a history of heroin use in addition to continued research.

OxyContin is the trade name for one synthetic opioid that has received extensive media attention due to its abuse potential and addictive features. Recent information, for example, indicates that in 2001 more than 7.2 million prescriptions were written for OxyContin resulting in sales of $1.45 billion, increasing the next year to sales of $1.59 billion (Inciardi & Goode, 2004). From 1994 to 2002 NIDA (2005) noted a 450% increase in oxycodone-related medical emergencies. The continued search for other pain management medications in lieu of opioids because of their serious addictive properties remains important. Overall, addiction specialists view opiate abuse and addiction with significant concern. More research is needed to better understand the neurobiology of opiate addiction to develop more effective treatment resources.

CASE STUDY.   Injured in an accident, Peter, a 23-year-old separated white male, was hospitalized for several weeks and given morphine for pain. Upon discharge, OxyContin was prescribed. Two months after release, Peter continues to describe high levels of pain. He has seen his MD twice to request more and stronger dosages of OxyContin. Today he made a third appointment and his estranged wife called the physician to discuss her concerns over Peter's continued pain, as well as his changing behavior, including irritability, work absenteeism, and his often appearing groggy. Peter told her that he is having flashbacks about the accident and that the medication seems to help alleviate these as well as lessening his physical pain.

As a counselor, discuss how you and the doctor can help Peter deal with his emotional and physical issues. Discuss the complications of the addictive and medical issues present, and how addiction theory and practice can be put to use in this example.

Summary and Some Final Notations

Most current research and treatment approaches point to the multiple genetic and environmental factors in attempting to better understand all addictions, and emphasize treating the whole person (Center for Substance Abuse Treatment [CSAT], 2008). Although promising genetic research into addiction (Conner et al., 2005) has been conducted in the previous decade, researchers have not yet defined a single physiological or neurobiological marker as the key link to predicting or diagnosing addiction (Doweiko, 2006; White, 1998).

In Chapter 2, the reader was provided information to better inform and prepare oneself as an effective counselor. Comprehensive information about the neurobiology and physiological factors regarding addiction indicate how much progress has been made in our understanding of addiction. In addition, various substances of addiction were examined. Finally, it is important to conclude that continued evidence-based research remains key for providing effective addictions counseling.

Useful Web Sites

The following Web sites provide additional information relating to the chapter topics:

Al-Anon and Alateen
http://www.al-anon.org/

Alcoholics Anonymous World Services, Inc.
http://www.alcoholics-anonymous.org/

Center for Substance Abuse Treatment (CSAT)
http://www.samhsa.gov

Cocaine Anonymous World Services, Inc.
http://www.ca.org/

Genetic Bioinformatics
http://genenetwork.org

Information on the links between HIV/AIDS and Drug Use
http://HIV.drugabuse.gov

Motivational Interviewing Information
http://www.motivationalinterview.org/

Narcotics Anonymous
http://www.na.org/

National Clearinghouse for Alcohol and Drug Information (NCADI)
http://ncadi.samhsa.gov/

National Council on Alcoholism and Drug Dependence, Inc. (NCADD)
http://www.ncadd.org

National Institute on Alcohol Abuse and Alcoholism (NIAAA)
http://www.niaaa.nih.gov

National Institute on Drug Abuse (NIDA)
http://www.nida.nih.gov

NIDA for Teens—The Science Behind Drug Abuse
http://www.teens.drugabuse.gov

Office of National Drug Control Policy (ONDCP)
http://www.whitehousedrugpolicy.gov

Screening and Brief Interventions
http://sbirt.samhsa.gov

Substance Abuse and Mental Health Services Administration (SAMSHA), Department of Health and Human Services
http://www.samhsa.gov/

References

Amen, D. G. (2005). *Making a good brain great: The Amen clinic program for achieving and sustaining optimal mental performance.* New York: Harmony Books.

American College of Surgeons. (2006). *Resources for optimal care of the injured patient: 2006.* Chicago, IL: Author.

American Psychiatric Association (APA). (2000). *Diagnostic and statistical manual of mental disorders* (4th ed., Text Rev.). Washington, DC: Author.

Breggin, P. R., & Cohen, D. (2007). *Your drug may be your problem: How and why to stop taking psychiatric medications* (Rev. ed.). Philadelphia, PA: Da Capo Press.

Briggs, C. A., & Pepperell, J. L. (2009). *Women, girls, and addiction: Celebrating the feminine in counseling treatment and recovery.* New York: Routledge.

The Centers for Disease Control and Prevention (CDC). (2009).*The issue: Excessive drinking and injuries.* Retrieved from *http://www.cdc.gov/InjuryResponse/alcohol-screening/*

Center for Substance Abuse Treatment (CSAT). (2008). *Managing depressive symptoms in substance abuse clients during early recovery. Treatment Improvement Protocol (TIP) Series 48* DHHS Publication No. SMA 08–4353. Rockville, MD: SAMHSA.

Conner, B. T., Noble, E. T., Berman, S. M., Oskaragoz, T., Ritchie, T., Antolin, T., & Sheen, C. (2005). DRD2 genotypes and substance use in adolescent children of alcoholics. *Drug and Alcohol Dependence, 79,* 379–387.

Crane, E. H., & Lemanski, N. (2004). *Benzodiazepines in drug abuse-related emergency department visits: 1995–2002, The DAWN Report.* Rockville, MD: Office of Applied Studies, Substance Abuse & Mental Health Services Administration.

Crawford, M. J., Patton, R., Touquet, R., Drummond, C., Byford, S., Barrett, B., . . . Henry, J. A. (2004). Screening and referral for brief intervention of alcohol-misusing patients in an emergency department: A pragmatic randomized controlled trial. *Lancet, 364,* 1334–1339.

Crews, F. T. (2008). Alcohol-related neurodegeneration and recovery. *Alcohol Research & Health, 31*(3), 377–388.

Doweiko, H. E. (2002). *Concepts of chemical dependency* (5th ed.). Pacific Grove, CA: Brooks/Cole.

Doweiko, H. E. (2006). *Concepts of chemical dependency* (6th ed.). Belmont, CA: Thomson Brooks/Cole.

Doweiko, H. E. (2009). *Concepts of chemical dependency* (7th ed.). Belmont, CA: Thomson Brooks/Cole.

Dunn, C., Rivara, F. P., Donovan, D., Fan, M. Y., Russo, J., Jurkovich, G., & Zatzick, D. (2008). Predicting adolescent alcohol drinking patterns after major injury. *The Journal of Trauma: Injury, Infection, and Critical Care, 65*(3), 736–740.

Dziegielewski, S. F., & Suris, N. (2005). Heroin and other opiates. In S. F. Dziegielewski (Ed.), *Understanding substance addictions: Assessment and intervention* (pp. 150–173). Chicago: Lyceum Books, Inc.

Erickson, S. (2001). Etiological theories of substance abuse. In P. Stevens & R. L. Smith (Eds.), *Substance abuse counseling: Theory and practice* (2nd ed., pp. 77–112). Upper Saddle River, NJ: Prentice-Hall.

Falkowski, C. L. (2000). *Dangerous drugs: An easy-to-use reference for parents and professionals.* Center City, MN: Hazelden.

Gentilello. L., Rivara, F., Donovan, D., Jurkovich, G. J., Daranciang, E., Dunn, C. W., . . . Ries, R. R. (1999). Alcohol interventions in a trauma center as a means of reducing the risk of injury recurrence. *Annals of Surgery, 230,* 473–483.

Gilbertson, R., Prather, R., & Nixon, S. J. (2008). The role of selected factors in the development and consequences of alcohol dependency. *Alcohol Research & Health, 31,* 389–399.

Hall, J. (2004, May 18). Ephedrine ban has holes. *The Free Lance-Star.* Retrieved from *http://www.freelancestar.com/News/FLS/2004/052004/05182004/1360590*

The Higher Education Center for Alcohol and Other Drug Prevention. (2002, February). *College athletes and alcohol and other drug use.* Newton, MA: Education Development Center, Inc. Retrieved from *http://www.edc.org/hec/pubs/factsheets/fact_sheet3.html*

Hitzemann, R., & Oberbeck, D. (2008). Strategies to study the neuroscience of alcoholism: Introduction. *Alcohol Health & Research, 31,* 231–232.

Horton, E. G., Diaz, N., Peluso, P. R., Mullaney, D., Weiner, M., & McIlveen, J. W. (2009). Relationships between trauma, posttraumatic stress disorder symptoms, dissociative symptoms, and lifetime heroin use among individuals who abuse substances in residential treatment. *Journal of Addictions & Offender Counseling, 29,* 81–95.

Inaba, D. S., & Cohen, W. E. (2007). *Uppers, downers, all-arounders*(6th ed.). Medford, OR: CNS Productions, Inc.

Inciardi, J. A., & Goode, J. L. (2004). OxyContin: Miracle medicine or problem drug? In J. C. Inciardi & K. McElrath (Eds.), *The American drug scene* (4th ed., pp. 163–173). Los Angeles: Roxbury Publishing.

Inciardi, J. A., & McElrath, K. (Eds.). (2004). *The American drug scene* (4th ed.). Los Angeles: Roxbury Publishing.

James, R. K., & Gilliland, B. E. (2005). *Crisis intervention strategies.* Belmont, CA: Thomson Brooks/Cole.

Knapp, C. (1996). *Drinking: A love story.* New York: Dell Publishing.

Kranzler, H. R., & Li, T-K. (2008). What is addiction? *Alcohol Research & Health, 31,* 93–95.

LaVallee, Robin A., Williams, Gerald D., & Yi, Hsiao-ye. (2009). *Surveillance Report #87.* Retrieved from *http://pubs.niaaa.nih.gov/publications/survelliance87/CONS07.htm*

Leontiva, L., Horn, K., Helmkamp, J., Furbee, M., Jarrett,T., & Williams, J. (2009). Counselors' reflections on the administration of screening and brief intervention for alcohol problems in the emergency department and 3-month follow-up outcome. *Journal of Critical Care, 24,* 273–279.

Lovinger, D. M. (2008). Communication networks in the brain: Neurons, receptors, neurotransmitters and alcohol. *Alcohol Research & Health, 31,* 196–214.

Lubman, D. I., Yücel, M., & Pantelis, C. (2004). Addiction, a condition of compulsive behaviour? Neuroimaging and neuropsychological evidence of inhibitory dysregulation. *Addiction, 99*, 1491–1502.

McGrath, J., Welham, J., Scott, J., Varghese, D., Degenhardt, L., Hayatbakhsh, M. R., . . . Najman, J. M. (2010). Association between cannabis use and psychosis-related outcomes using sibling pair analysis in a cohort of young adults. *Archives of General Psychiatry, 67*, E1–E8. doi:10.1001/archgenpsychiatry.2010.6

Miller, M. A. (2004). History and epidemiology of amphetamine abuse in the United States. In J. C. Inciardi & K. McElrath (Eds.), *The American Drug Scene* (4th ed., pp. 252–266). Los Angeles: Roxbury Publishing.

Miller, T. R., Levy, D. T., Spicer, R. S., & Taylor, D. M. (2006). Societal costs of underage drinking. *Journal of Studies on Alcohol, 67*, 519–528.

Moyers, W. C., & Ketcham, K. (2006). *Broken: My story of addiction and redemption.* New York, NY: Penguin Books Ltd.

National Collegiate Athletic Association (NCAA). (2001). *NCAA study of substance use habits of college student-athletes.* Indianapolis, IN: Author.

National Collegiate Athletic Association (NCAA). (2006). *NCAA study of substance use of college student-athletes.* Indianapolis, IN: Author. Retrieved from *http://www.ncaa.org*

National Highway Traffic Safety Administration (NHTSA). (2004). *The economic burden of traffic crashes on employers*, posted January 15, 2004. Retrieved from *http://www.nhtsa.dot.gov/people/injury/airbags/EconomicBurden/index.html*

National Highway Traffic Safety Administration (NHTSA). (2009). *U.S. Transportation Secretary Ray LaHood announces intensive holiday drunk and impaired driving crackdown & advertising blitz*, posted December 7, 2009. Retrieved from *http://www.nhtsa.gov/portal/site/nhtsa/template.MAXIMIZE/menuitem.f2217bee37fb*

National Institute on Alcohol Abuse and Alcoholism (NIAAA). (2005). *Alcohol: A women's health issue* (NIH Publication No. 03–4956). Rockville, MD: NIAAA.

National Institute on Drug Abuse. (2004). Methamphetamine abuse and addiction. *Research Report Series.* Retrieved from *http://www.drugabuse.gov/ResearchReports/Methamph/methamph2*

National Institute on Drug Abuse (NIDA). (2005). Prescription drugs: Abuse and addiction. *Research Report Series.* Retrieved from *http://www.drugabuse.gov/ResearchReports/Prescription/prescription.html*

National Institute on Drug Abuse (NIDA). (2006). *Medical consequences of drug abuse.* Retrieved from *http://www.drugabuse.gov/consequences/*

National Institute on Drug Abuse (NIDA). (2007). *Commonly abused drugs.* Retrieved from *http://www.drugabuse.gov/DrugPages/DrugsofAbuse.html*

National Institute on Drug Abuse (NIDA). (2008). *Drugs, brains, and behavior: The science of addiction* (NIH Pub No. 08–5605). Retrieved from *www.nida.nih.gov/scienceofaddiction*

Oscar-Berman, M., & Marinkovic, K. (2004). *Alcoholism and the brain: An overview.* Retrieved from *http://www.pubs.niaaa.nih.gov/publications/arh27–2/125–133.htm*

Physician's Desk Reference (56th ed.). (2002). Montvale, NJ: Thomson PDR.

Pietrzykowski, A. Z., & Treistman, S. N. (2008). The molecular basis of tolerance. *Alcohol Research & Health, 31*(4), 298–309.

Prentice, W. E. (2003). *Arnheim's principles of athletic training: A competency-based approach* (11th ed.). New York: McGraw Hill.

Rouaud, T., Lardeux, S., Panayotis, N., Paleressompoulle, D., Cador, M., & Baunez, C. (2009). Reducing the desire for cocaine with subthalamic nucleus deep brain stimulation. *Proceedings of the National Academy of Sciences, 107*(3), 1196–1200. Retrieved from *http://www.pnas.org/cgi/doi/10.1073/pnas.0908189107*

Schermer, C. R. (2005). Feasibility of alcohol screening and brief intervention. *The Journal of Trauma: Injury, Infection, and Critical Care, 59*(3), S119–S123.

Schnabel, J. (2009). Neuroscience: Rethinking rehab. *Nature, 458*(7234), 25–27.

Scott, M. S. (2002). Clandestine drug labs. *Problem-Oriented Guides for Police, No 16.* Washington, DC: U.S. Department of Justice.

Siegal, H. A., & Inciardi, J. A. (2004). A brief history of alcohol. In J. C. Inciardi & K. McElrath (Eds.), *The American drug scene* (4th ed., pp. 74–79). Los Angeles: Roxbury Publishing.

Spicer, J. (1993). *The Minnesota Model: The evolution of the multi-disciplinary approach to addiction recovery.* Center City, MN: Hazelden Educational Materials.

Spirito, A. (2009). Alcohol Education Inventor–Revised: What every mental health professional should know about alcohol. *Journal of Substance Abuse Treatment, 37*, 41–53.

Stevens, P. (2009). Introduction to substance abuse counseling. In P. Stevens & R. L. Smith (Eds.), *Substance abuse counseling* (4th ed., pp. 1–30). Upper Saddle River, NJ: Pearson Education, Inc.

Substance Abuse and Mental Health Services Administration (SAMHSA). (2003). Overview of findings from the 2002

National Survey on Drug Use and Health. (NHSDA Series H-21, DHHS Publication No. SMA 03–3774). Rockville, MD: Office of Applied Studies, Substance Abuse and Mental Health Services Administration.

Substance Abuse and Mental Health Services Administration (SAMHSA). (2005). Characteristics of primary tranquilizer admissions: 2002. *The DASIS Report*. Rockville, MD: Office of Applied Studies, Substance Abuse and Mental Health Services Administration. Retrieved from *http://www .oas.samhsa.gov/2k5/tranquilizerTX/tranquilizerTX.htm*

Substance Abuse and Mental Health Services Administration (SAMHSA). (2007). *Alcohol screening and brief intervention for trauma patients: Committee on Trauma quick guide* (DHHS Publication No.(SMA 07–4266). Rockville, MD: SAMHSA.

Substance Abuse and Mental Health Services Administration (SAMHSA), (October 15, 2009). *The NSDUH Report: Trends in tobacco use among adolescents: 2002 to 2008*. Rockville, MD: Office of Applied Studies.

Substance Abuse and Mental Health Services Administration (SAMHSA). (2009). *Results from the 2008 National Survey on Drug Use and Health: National Findings* (NSDUH Series H-36, HHS Publication No. SMA 09–4434). Rockville, MD: Office of Applied Studies.

Sullivan, E. V., & Pfefferbaum, A. (2005). Neurocircuitry in alcoholism: A substrate of disruption and repair. [Electronic version]. *Psychopharmacology, 180*, 583–594.

Taylor, J. B. (2006). *My stroke of insight: A brain scientist's personal journey*. New York: Viking.

Toumbourou, J. W., Stockwell, T., Neighbors, C., Marlatt, G. A., Sturge, J. & Rehm, J., (2007). Interventions to reduce harm associated with adolescent substance use. *The Lancet, 369*, 1391–1401.

van Wormer, K., & Davis, D. R. (2003). *Addiction treatment: A strengths perspective*. Pacific Grove, CA: Brooks/Cole.

Watson, J. C. (2002). Assessing the potential for alcohol-related issues among college student-athletes. *Athletic Insight, 4*(3). Retrieved from *http://www.athleticinsight .com/Vol4Iss3/AlcoholAssessment.htm*

Weil, A., & Rosen, W. (1983). *Chocolate to morphine*. Boston: Houghton Mifflin.

White, W. L. (1998). *Slaying the dragon: The history of addiction treatment and recovery in America*. Bloomington, IL: Chestnut Health Systems.

Wilens, T., Adler, L., Adams, J., Sgambati, S., Rotrosen, J., Sawtelle, R., . . . Fusillo, S. (2008). Misuse and Diversion of Stimulants Prescribed for ADHD: A Systematic Review of the Literature. *Journal of the American Academy of Child and Adolescent Psychiatry, 47*(1), 21–31.

Williams, R. W., & Lu, L. (2008). Integrative genetic analyses of alcohol dependence using the GeneNetwork Web resources. *Alcohol Research & Health, 31*, 275–277.

Wu, N. S., Schairer, L. C., Dellor, E., & Grella, C. (2010). Childhood trauma and health outcomes in adults with comorbid substance abuse and mental health disorders. *Addictive Behaviors, 35*(1), 68–71.

Yin, H. H. (2008). From action to habits: Neuroadaptations leading to dependence. *Alcohol Research & Health, 31*, 340–344.

Zickler, P. (2002). Methamphetamine abuse linked to impaired cognitive and motor skills despite recovery of dopamine transporters. *NIDA Research Findings, 17*(1), 4–6.

Chapter 3

Process Addictions

Laura J. Veach
University of North Carolina at Charlotte
Wake Forest University School of Medicine
Emeline P. Hollander
Greensboro College

Jennifer L. Rogers
Syracuse University
E. J. Essic
Past-President of International Association
of Addictions & Offender Counselors

Addiction may be further defined in terms of ingestive or process addictions. Chemical dependence is classified as an ingestive addiction due to the taking-in of mood-altering chemicals, like alcohol or other drugs (AOD); whereas process addictions encompass behavior patterns (for example, gambling or sexual addictions). Addiction specialists rarely debate that addiction is a bio-psychosocial disease, but many continue to challenge the nature of addiction with questions about substance versus process addictions.

The term "process" addiction—an addiction to a behavior, process, or action—is still contentiously debated. It was not until the 1970s and 1980s that the addiction field began to formally discuss the idea that a behavior could be diagnosed as an addictive disorder. Past research on addiction focused on the presence of physical dependence to the substance or behavior as demonstrated by tolerance and withdrawal, but current research claims physical dependence is no longer necessary to diagnose an addiction to a substance or behavior (Hagedorn & Juhnke, 2005). In fact, the *DSM-IV-TR* explicitly states that "neither tolerance nor withdrawal is necessary or sufficient for a diagnosis of Substance Dependence" (APA, 2000, p.194). Yet researchers and experts continue to debate whether a behavior can be diagnosed under the same criteria as a substance-use disorder. Several addiction specialists, including the International Association of Addictions and Offender Counselors Committee on Process Addictions, currently advocate for the forthcoming *DSM 5th edition* to include diagnostic categories of addictive disorders which include subtypes for gambling, sex, spending, work, exercise, Internet, and eating (Hagedorn, 2009). However, at present there remains a lack of agreement on a common terminology throughout the multidisciplinary field of addictions counseling (Kranzler & Li, 2008).

According to Buck and Amos (2000), counselors assess substance addiction according to the four following criteria: (1) preoccupation with the substance or activity, (2) withdrawal signs after not engaging with the activity or substance, (3) increased tolerance for the substance or activity in order to receive the same effect, and (4) continued use of the substance or involvement in the activity despite negative consequences. Many would argue that these same criteria can be used to assess whether an individual has an addiction to a process or behavior as well. Hagedorn outlines clinical criteria for diagnosing an addictive disorder that include similar criteria to substance dependence criteria but can be universally applied to all addictive disorders (2009). Hagedorn and Juhnke (2005) cite a need for a universal definition of an addictive disorder to "[create a] common clinical language, a legitimization of the disorder for the purposes of third-party reimbursement, and a step toward a standardized treatment protocol" (p. 70). Further, it is critical for the counselor to distinguish a process addiction from, for example, an undesirable social behavior or social taboo. A person struggling with an addiction, whether it be process or substance, is engaging in behaviors with key features of obsessive, compulsive, and significant life (career, relationship, health) impairment whereas someone engaging in a social taboo is quite different. Violating a social taboo, such as discussion of sexual practices in social settings or eating certain foods, may lead to awkward silences and social regrets, but is not addiction. If, however, an individual experiences euphoria while compulsively and obsessively discussing sexual practices in social settings, even after an ongoing pattern of adverse consequences related to this behavior (for example, arguments with spouse/partner or disciplinary action by an employer), then the counselor would be advised to evaluate further for an addictive pattern. An addiction, when one accepts the inherent nature of this disorder, results in marked impairment or functioning accompanied by a continuance of the behavior despite serious adverse consequences, thereby eliminating it from being merely a social habit or taboo. Addiction is a far more complex disorder leading to clinically significant impairment and process addictions warrant further discussion.

The debate continues as to whether behavioral addictions, such as sexual addiction, should be classified as an addictive disorder. As a result, the concept of what we classify and diagnose as an addiction is still evolving. Whether we are speaking of a process or substance addiction, addictions interfere with people's ability to truly know themselves, their spirituality, and the world around them (Schaef, 1990). In this chapter we will discuss five of the most prominent and researched process addictions to date: sex, gambling, working, compulsive buying, and food.

It is important to note that frequently, addiction to one substance or process is accompanied or replaced by addiction to another substance or process (e.g., a female with an eating disorder is also struggling with substance abuse or dependence; a male recovering from a sexual addiction develops a gambling addiction). Comorbid or multiple addictions are quite common whether a person is suffering from a substance or a process addiction (National Association of Anorexia Nervosa and Associated Eating Disorders [ANAD], 2010; Fassel & Schaef, 1989; Grilo, Sinha, & O'Malley, 2002; Hagedorn, 2009; Hagedorn & Juhnke, 2005; Mitchell et al., 2001). As Schaef aptly points out, "the addiction changes behavior, distorts reality and fosters self-centeredness . . . [and] no one has only one addiction. As addicts begin recovering from their primary addiction and achieve some sobriety, other addictions emerge" (1990, p. 18).

The prevalence of process addictions is not clearly known since currently there is a lack of agreement as to what precise criteria can be used to define the various types of process addictions. Some believe that process addictions are rampant in our society. According to the Illinois Institute for Addiction Recovery, in the general population 5% to 10% are addicted to the Internet, 8% to 10% to chemicals or alcohol, 1.5% to 3% to gambling, 1% to 3% to food, 5% to sex, and 2% to 8% to spending (Zamora, 2003). As an example of projected prevalence, Hagedorn (2009) extrapolated various data and reported that each sexual addiction treatment center in operation would need to serve 1.08 million persons struggling with sexual addiction; for gambling addiction, there is one treatment facility for every 250,000 individuals suffering; and, for those struggling with Internet addiction, one treatment facility exists per 2.9 million clients. Similar to substance addiction, warning signs of process addiction can include a greater sense of isolation, less social interaction, less attention to personal hygiene, increased legal difficulties, changes in eating and sleeping patterns, increased irritability, and wariness of changing compulsive behavior (Zamora, 2003).

SEXUAL ADDICTION

Experts in the field of addiction did not really start talking about sex addiction until the early 1980s, when Patrick Carnes introduced the idea that a behavior, rather than a drug, could be an addiction (Schneider, 2004). The prevalence of sexual addiction is estimated to range from 17 to 37 million Americans, more than the combined number of pathological gamblers and individuals with eating disorders (Hagedorn & Juhnke, 2005). An estimated 40% to 50% of sexual addicts are women (Ferree, 2002, as cited in Seegers, 2003). The incidence of sexual addiction is on the rise because of increased affordability, easy access to sexual materials, and anonymity of the Internet (Hagedorn & Juhnke, 2005). Love, or relationship, addiction pertains to different behaviors and often may involve the spouse or partner of addicts, but is not focused primarily on compulsive sexual behaviors, and thus is excluded from this section on sexual addiction. More information can be found in materials related to codependency (Co-Dependents Anonymous, Inc., 1995; S-Anon, 2010).

There are varying definitions of sexual addiction. Sexaholics Anonymous (SA) defines a "sexaholic" as someone who is addicted to lust. The sexaholic can no longer determine what is right or wrong, has lost control, lost the power of choice, and is not free to stop sexual behavior despite adverse consequences, such as threats of job or family loss (Sexaholics Anonymous Inc., 2010). Common characteristics of male and female sexaholics include marked isolation, prevalent guilt, marked depression, and a deep feeling of emptiness. Typical behaviors of a sexaholic include compulsively fantasizing about sexual desires; remaining in harmful codependent relationships; engaging in compulsive masturbation; obsessive and compulsive use of pornography, including on the Internet; repeatedly engaging in promiscuous sexual relationships; conducting adulterous affairs; and compulsively pursuing exhibitionism or sexually abusive relationships, regardless of legal, career, or family consequences (Sexaholics Anonymous Inc., 2010).

According to Sex Addicts Anonymous (SAA), sex addicts report that their unhealthy use of sex has a progressive downward path. For some it may begin with masturbation, pornography, or a relationship, but progresses in an obsessive and compulsive pattern to increasingly dangerous behaviors and greater risks (Sex Addicts Anonymous, 2005). Cybersex, another term often referenced when discussing sex addiction, involves "Internet-related sexually oriented chat rooms, message boards, and pornography" (Long, Burnett, & Thomas, 2006, p. 218). Long, Burnett, and Thomas (2006) further identify pornography and telephone sex with dependence patterns.

Denial is the undertone of all addictions. Sexual addiction can be the primary, secondary, or simultaneous disorder along with other substance or process addictions such as chemical dependency, eating disorders, work addiction, compulsive buying, or compulsive gambling. Additionally, sexual addiction often coexists with other psychiatric issues such as depression, anxiety, personality disorder, relationship issues, or bipolar disorder (Seegers, 2003). For example, increased buying, spending, and sexual behaviors often accelerate during manic episodes but do not warrant a diagnosis of sex addiction. Conversely, in some cases, without adequate knowledge about addiction, a client may be misdiagnosed with bipolar disorder when the primary focus of clinical attention is a process addiction. Differential diagnoses add complications since sex addiction can resemble other disorders, for example, a manic or hypomanic episode with hypersexual behaviors. It is recommended that counselors evaluate carefully and obtain adequate psychosocial history before making a final diagnosis. There are few empirical studies regarding the comorbidity of sexual addiction and another psychiatric disorder or addiction (Miller, 2005). Zapf, Greiner and Carroll (2008) found relational anxiety and avoidance behaviors were more prevalent in sexually addicted men in their recent study, noting "sexually addicted men are nearly 50% less likely to relate to their partners in a secure manner than nonaddicted men . . ." (p. 169). More research is needed to investigate sexually impulsive and out of control behaviors (Bancroft & Vukadinovic, 2004).

Parkinson's Disease and Impulse Control

Parkinson's disease is a disorder of the central nervous system. It is a degenerative condition that usually impairs a person's speech, motor skills, and other functions. Persons suffering from Parkinson's disease may experience tremors, joint stiffness, and a decline in the executive functioning of the brain. A relationship between Parkinson's disease and impulse control disorders is currently being examined by researchers (Ceravolo, Frosini, Rossi, & Bonuccelli, 2010). Dopamine receptor agonists, a type of drug used to treat Parkinson's, is associated with compulsive gambling, sex, eating, and shopping. Changes in medication doses usually results in improvement in these behaviors.

As of now there are no diagnostic criteria or classifications for sexual addiction (APA, 2000) in the *Diagnostic and Statistical Manual of Mental Disorders* (*DSM-IV-TR*). There are, however, *DSM-IV-TR* diagnoses for sexual disorders that can involve harm to others such as voyeurism, pedophilia, sexual sadism, sexual masochism, and exhibitionism (APA, 2000). Patrick Carnes has compiled ten categories of addictive sexual disorders. These ten disorder categories include: fantasy sex, seductive role sex, anonymous sex, paying for sex, trading sex, voyeuristic sex, exhibitionist sex, intrusive sex, pain exchange, and exploitive sex (Seegers, 2003). Often treatment for sexual addictions involve many treatment approaches used in substance addictions, such as cognitive behavioral therapy; however, additional biological approaches, such as hormonal therapy involving antiandrogens or certain libido-inhibiting antidepressants, may also be used (Long, Burnett, & Thomas, 2006).

Case Study

Kevin's AA sponsor has insisted he come talk with you about his "sex addiction." He reports being highly sexed and sleeping with several women in the program "just as any other healthy male might." Upon deeper exploration, he reports having slept with over 500 women in the last two years and that when he is not able to have regular and frequent sexual contact, he gets depressed and really wants to drink. He is proud of his sexual prowess and feels that his behavior is to be envied rather than a source of concern. He says that he thinks sex is a much healthier outlet than drinking, and that it is fun, not an addiction.

Discuss whether Kevin's behaviors seem addictive and why. What red flags do you see? Discuss how he may fit on the addiction spectrum. Conceptually, what is happening? What theories/methods might you employ in his treatment? What leads you to differentiate Kevin's behavior as addictive rather than in the normal range of healthy sexual behavior?

GAMBLING ADDICTION

Gambling continues to rise with the increase in casinos, lotteries, and Internet gambling sites (Buck & Amos, 2000; Suissa, 2007). There is evidence that gambling can be traced back thousands of years with Egyptian evidence of shell games dating from 2500 B.C. (Suissa, 2007). According to the *DSM-IV-TR*, the lifetime prevalence rate of adult pathological gambling ranges from 0.4% to 3.4% (APA, 2000). The prevalence rate for adolescents and college students is higher, ranging from 2.8% to 8% (APA).

Internet Addiction

There is debate in the field as to whether compulsive use of the Internet will eventually be acknowledged as a process addiction. Because of the prevalence of Internet use in the general population, symptoms of problematic use may be mischaracterized as legitimate computer use; researchers suggest that appropriate diagnostic criteria for the disorder may be similar to those used to identify pathological gambling (Young, 2009). The overuse of Massively Multiplayer Online Role Playing Games (MMORPGs) is growing worldwide, especially among college students, and researchers are exploring means by which to both operationalize the phenomenon and predict problematic use (Hsu, Wen, & Wu, 2009). This growing area of addictions research will perhaps stretch conceptualizations of addictions in the 21st century.

Source: Hsu, S., Wen, M., & Wu, M. (2009). Exploring user experiences as predictors of MMORPG addiction. *Computers & Education, 53*(3), 990–999. doi:10.1016/j.compedu.2009.05.016

Source: Young, K. (2009). Internet addiction: Diagnosis and treatment considerations. *Journal of Contemporary Psychotherapy, 39*(4), 241–246. doi:10.1007/s10879-009-9120-x

The term "gambling addiction" is debated, and some argue that "it is a complex multifactorial psychosocial phenomenon" (Suissa, 2007, p. 97). Pathological gambling is designated as an impulse control disorder in the *DSM-IV-TR* (APA, 2000). Criteria were first published in 1980 (Suissa, 2007) and now include many of the same elements in any addiction: increased preoccupation with gambling and betting; money problems due to overspending; repeated attempts to stop or reduce gambling; and feelings of exhilaration experienced when gambling (APA, 2000). Pathological gamblers do not ingest a substance to experience their "high," and yet researchers have found that pathological gambling is related to neuroadaptation, or tolerance and withdrawal symptoms (Shaffer & Kidman, 2003). Men evidence more gambling-related problems and comorbidities, although research indicates the trends show an increasing number of women involved in gambling (Rainone, Marel, Gallati, & Gargon, 2007; van Wormer & Davis, 2003).

Similar to most addictions, some warning signs of pathological gambling are easy to identify while others are well hidden by the individual. Signs of gambling addiction can include: "secretiveness and excessive time with phone calls and Internet access, unaccounted time away from work or home, unexplained preoccupation, increased debt and worry over finances, extravagant expenditures, and increased alcohol, drug consumption or both" (Buck & Amos, 2000, p. 5). Other risky behaviors, such as binge drinking or other drug use, are often associated with gambling, further complicating treatment (National Council on Problem Gambling [NCPG], 2009). For 2008, NCPG's data indicate costs of $6.8 billion related to gambling when factoring in bankruptcies, job loss, and criminal justice actions. Early intervention and treatment is urged by NCPG. Other national data is lacking but an involved household survey in New York yielded important trends concerning the need for intervention and treatment. One finding indicated 67% of adults within the state had engaged in one or more gambling activity within the past year, and of those, approximately 5% reported problem gambling symptoms that could benefit from addiction counseling services (Rainone, Marel, Gallati, & Gargon, 2007). As knowledge about the prevalence of gambling addiction improves, more is also known about cultural considerations. Further, some helping professionals in the United States are recognizing gambling addiction as a hidden problem within Asian-American communities. One study found gambling problems at rates five times greater in Asian-American AOD clients than in the general AOD population (University of California Los Angeles Center for Community Partnerships [UCLACCP], 2008). A recent report suggests Asian-Americans may choose gambling as a leisure activity but more problematic within the community are those affected by gambling addiction (UCLACCP, 2008). Literature and outreach videos have been prepared with a specific focus on Mandarin, Cantonese, and Vietnamese communities in the United States, to separate moderate gambling social activity from serious problem gambling (Massachusetts Council on Compulsive Gambling, National Problem Gambling Awareness Week 2009 [NPGAW2009], 2009).

Other helpful approaches advocate adaption of a harm reduction model with an emphasis on self-empowerment (Suissa, 2007). The number of Gamblers Anonymous (GA) meetings have increased since their beginnings in 1957 (Suissa, 2007). Gambling addictions continue to create significant financial, family, and legal problems and continued research is needed. Counselors benefit from specialized counseling training and may also want to investigate national certification in this area as outlined by NCPG (2009).

Case Study

Marilyn reports that the major difficulty in her marriage is due to Du Nguyen's constant gambling. Family savings are gone, and the couple is three months behind on mortgage payments. Du Nguyen, embarrassed for seeking counseling, says that he has tried stopping because he is worried about his marriage. He says he wants to quit and feels shameful and guilty, but when faced with an opportunity to bet on sports or horses, his impulses overcome his reason. He has tried a number of unsuccessful strategies to control himself, and he wants help in order to save his marriage. He says he wants to understand his urges and be able to control them.

How can you help this couple understand the addiction process? What resources can you draw on to help them? What modalities might you use in working with them? How will you approach Du Nguyen's desire to "control" his gambling addiction?

WORK ADDICTION

While the term "workaholism" is commonly used, there is no recognized diagnosis in current diagnostic manuals such as the *DSM-IV TR* (APA, 2000). There is little data available on the actual prevalence of workaholism. Additionally, the oftentimes secretive nature of the addiction, as well as the societal acceptance and even reward of workaholism, limits the availability of accurate data. According to Bonebright, Clay, and Ankenmann (2000), Oates first coined the term "workaholism" more than 25 years ago and since then many researchers define workaholism differently. Seybold and Salamone (1994) describe workaholism as an excessive commitment to work that results in the neglect of important aspects of life. "In the narrowest sense, workaholism is an addiction to action; but the action takes many forms . . . the type of action may vary, but the process is the same: You leave yourself" (Fassel, 1990, p. 4). Chamberlain and Zhang (2009) describe work addiction as a dependence on work despite adverse consequences, with their research focusing on areas of increased somatic complaints, psychological symptoms, and poor self-acceptance.

The primary characteristics workaholics include "multiple addictions, denial, self-esteem problems, external referencing, inability to relax, and obsessiveness" (Fassel, 1990, p. 27), as well as out-of-control behavior and an escape from personal issues or relationship intimacy (Buck & Amos, 2000). These characteristics can be the result of a need to control one's life, an overly competitive drive to succeed, being raised by a workaholic parent or role model, and low self-esteem or self-image (Buck & Amos, 2000). In Figure 3.1, the stages of work addiction are examined utilizing a biopsychosocial approach depicting the progressive nature of addiction.

Work Addiction Stages	Symptoms	Organizational Response
Early Stage *Timespan: 5–8 years on average*	*Bio:* Stress-related symptoms first noticed: frequent headaches, generalized anxiety (especially pertaining to work), digestive problems, minimal sleep problems, or mild irritability. *Psycho:* Increased hours thinking about or being at work, seeking additional projects/assignments, greater emphasis being placed on external recognition, decreased ability to self-validate, e.g., ("I did a good job, I can stop now and continue this tomorrow"), increased self-criticism ("I should do more, spend more time at the office; I'm afraid I'm not working hard enough; It's got to be done better"). *Social:* Late arrival at home or social events due to increased work activity; increasing work at home or at social events via cell phone, texting, or Internet communication; increasing heated discussions with partner about time spent on work.	Promotions, recognition from peers & management, increased pay, bonuses, increased workload/assignments, favorable job reviews & evaluations.
Middle Stage *Timespan: 8–12 years on average*	*Bio:* Increased stress-related symptoms; Sleep disorders: Insomnia/hypersomnia; pronounced weight loss/gain, or weight fluctuations; increased use of medications for sleep, anxiety, depression, increased use of mood-altering chemicals or processes (e.g. extramarital affairs, sexual promiscuity, gambling) to achieve pleasure or relaxation due to frequent tension and increased difficulty relaxing. *Psycho:* Increasing hours spent on work (both on and off site), perfectionism increasing, decreased tolerance of mistakes (self or colleagues), preoccupation with work products, projects, or outcomes. *Social:* Less leisure pursuits and/or decreased time spent in established leisure outlets, greater identity associated with workplace, title, or role; work-family conflicts experienced, minimal marital/partner separation may occur; intermittent experiences of significant job dissatisfaction leading to geographic escape from 'this demanding job' to new locations.	Promotions, greater responsibilities assigned, management opportunities, possible relocation, increased travel, increased recognition and community service encouraged; job changes, seeking advancement, & may be due to varying productivity or employer/supervisee conflicts.
Late Stage *Timespan: 10–15 years on average*	*Bio:* Stress-related physical complications such as cardiac events, e.g., heart attack or stroke, brought on by poor physical care with inability to successfully manage intense stress; probable activation of co-occurring addiction to mood-altering chemicals or processes (pathological gambler, alcoholism, or food addict). *Psycho:* Working continually or "bingeing" resulting in sustained work activity with *reduced* accomplishment; less productivity but more time spent on work; greater job dissatisfaction; increased agitation; workplace conflicts increasing; complaints by co-workers/supervisees; poor risk-taking with job assignments. *Social:* Minimal leisure activity; increased strife with work-family conflicts, impending divorce or estranged, poor communication with family/loved ones, withdrawn from family and social events.	Varied: Possible advancement due to long history of products OR demotions, RIF, job termination;mandatory supervisory referral to Executive Coach or Employee Assistance Program Counselor.

FIGURE 3.1 Stages of Work Addiction, Biopsychosocial Model, L. J. Veach

Workaholics do things in excess. They keep a frenetic pace and do not feel satisfied with themselves unless they are always doing something. As a result, workaholics tend to have more than one addiction. Often they smoke, drink, or do drugs as a way to cope with stress. They may have strict eating and exercise regimes in order to have enough energy to sustain such a fast-paced lifestyle. These efforts to cope help hide what is truly going on and prolong the individual's denial (Fassel & Schaef, 1989). Family, friends, and coworkers are thought to also experience negative effects of workaholism (Bonebright et al., 2000; Chamberlain & Zhang, 2009).

Operationalizing "Workaholism"

New research conducted in Japan and the Netherlands assessed the validity of new scales to measure two aspects of work addiction: working excessively hard and working compulsively. Workaholics who worked excessively hard and compulsively showed a high risk of burnout. While more research in this area is needed, the hypothesized two-factor construct fit the data in both countries and may prove a valuable means by which to better understand this process addiction.

Source: Schaufeli, W. B., Shimazu, A., Taris, T. W. (2009). Being driven to work excessively hard: The evaluation of a two-factor measure of Workaholism in the Netherlands and Japan. *Cross-Cultural Research, 43*(4), 320–348.

A compounding problem of workaholism is that our fast-paced, performance-driven society readily supports, encourages, and rewards it (Fassel, 1990). In fact, many people are self-proclaimed workaholics. A common myth of the workaholic is that since they work longer hours they are more productive; research, however, indicates otherwise (Bonebright et al., 2000; Fassel & Schaef, 1989). Workaholics tend to be less productive than the more relaxed worker who keeps regular hours. The irony is that the workaholic's perfectionist tendencies and inability to delegate tasks to others can reduce efficiency and flexibility and decrease progress in the workplace (Bonebright et al., 2000). Numerous studies suggest that there is a relationship between workaholism and many difficulties (Brady, Vodanovich, & Rotunda, 2008; Bonebright et al., 2000; Chamberlain & Zhang, 2009). Although it is difficult to pinpoint accurate numbers, the estimated cost of stress-related issues to companies is $150 million per year. These costs include workers' compensation for stress, burn-out, hiring and retraining new employees, and legal fees when companies get sued by employees for stress-related illnesses (Fassel & Schaef, 1989).

Bonebright, Clay, and Ankenmann (2000) claim there are three "causal explanations" for why individuals choose to dedicate so many hours to their work. First, they truly find enjoyment and satisfaction in their work. Second, they have an uncontrollable desire to work, even if they do not enjoy the task. Third, they receive a euphoric high from accumulating the rewards of their hard work. Eventually, their desire to receive these accolades, the workaholic's euphoria, interferes with their health, relationships, family, and other activities, which is indicative of the addictive cycle.

Research supports that workaholics compared to nonworkaholics have greater anxiety, stress, anger, and depression. Likewise, workaholics perceive themselves as having more job stress, perfectionism, anxiety, health complaints, and less willingness to delegate job responsibilities to others (Robinson, 1998). In their recent work, Chamberlain and Zhang reported significant findings, namely that workaholism negatively affects physical health, psychological well-being, and self-acceptance. These researchers also noted that adult children of workaholics were predominantly self-described workaholics, suggesting the parent's work addiction is often mirrored in their children. It is of particular concern with the reported low self-acceptance patterns of workaholics that "this nonaccepting attitude toward oneself could transfer to being overly critical and demanding of others" (Chamberlain & Zhang, 2009, p.167). Brady, Vodanovich, and Rotunda (2008) added empirical knowledge with an extensive study examining workaholism and work-family conflict, job satisfaction, and leisure among university faculty and staff in one sample along with employees in various community work settings in a different sample. These researchers noted that in both samples: first, high workaholism scores were significant predictors of heightened work-family conflict; next, higher drive scores, or ambition-driven behaviors, led to lower job satisfaction findings, particularly in the university employees; and finally, less enjoyment of leisure was significantly found in workaholics (2008). Lastly, studies indicate that an individual's work addiction, as is true with other addictions, has a severe impact on others, producing marital conflict, dysfunction within the family, and strained social relationships (Brady, Vodanovich, & Rotunda, 2008; Robinson, 1998). Children of workaholics may be prone to developing workaholic tendencies of poor self-acceptance, increased physical complaints or full-blown workaholism as a result of being raised in a workaholic family environment (Chamberlain & Zhang, 2009; Robinson, 1998). Treatment considerations may need to stress family counseling, self-talk, and reviewing with clients their individual reinforcement patterns, as outlined by Chamberlain and Zhang. More research is needed in the area of diagnosing and effectively treating work addiction, as well as closer examination of the stages of work addiction in order to assess whether, as with other addictions, the adverse consequences of workaholism are progressive. Many researchers emphasize the need to examine the cost of workaholism to organizations, especially when higher incidences of hypercritical, inefficient, negative, and overcontrolling behaviors or increased complaints by supervisees occur (Brady, Vodanovich, & Rotunda, 2008; Vodanovich & Piotrowski, 2006).

Case Study

Bryant, a married 48-year-old African-American male, is an associate professor at a mid-sized university. Recently, he has been experiencing marital discord and his only child, a 15-year-old son, has been experiencing pronounced anxiety accompanied by panic attacks at school. Bryant has recently been considering the offer of a promotion into university administration as an Associate Provost. He has an active research agenda, numerous textbooks and publications, and his professional service has received outstanding reviews in his field. He knows he is spending less and less time with his family and on leisure activities, and had a negative encounter with a colleague where he lost his temper, but believes he deserves this next step up since he has worked so hard. He wonders if he should pursue this prestigious offer and seeks career counseling with you, his Employee Assistance Program Counselor. What particular areas would you address? How would you begin to explore workaholism?

COMPULSIVE BUYING

The estimated incidence of compulsive buying ranges from 1% to 10% of the U.S population (Lee & Mysyk, 2004). Since most of the data on compulsive buyers come from self-selected samples it is difficult to know the true prevalence of this disorder. Compulsive shopping, uncontrolled buying, addictive buying, addictive consumption, shopaholism, and spendaholism are all names for compulsive buying (Lee & Mysyk, 2004). Compulsive buying has been described as a condition caused by chronic failures at self-regulation that becomes self-reinforcing over time, as persons move through antecedent, internal/external trigger, buying, and post-purchase phases

(Kellet, 2009). Sometimes referred to as oniomania, it is often comorbid with substance use, eating and impulse control disorders, and mood disorders (Tavares, Lobo, Fuentes, & Black, 2008). In clinical samples, women make up 80% of subjects.

Compulsive buying has been defined as consistent, repetitive purchasing that becomes the first response to negative or stressful life events or feelings. Compulsive buyers try to fill the meaninglessness, unhappiness, and void in their lives by purchasing items to relieve these negative feelings. Compulsive buying takes a toll on the individual, family, and society and it can lead to "overspending, indebtedness, and bankruptcy" (Lee & Mysyk, 2004, p. 1710).

Lee and Mysyk (2004) examine the larger social context of what it means to be a compulsive buyer in today's society. They point out that it is important to keep in mind, when examining and diagnosing a compulsive buyer, that we live in a consumer-driven society fueled by powerful messages to spend. These messages tell us that buying things will enhance our self-esteem, make us happy, and increase social status. Additionally, counselors should be wary of pharmacological interventions, and that strategies such as teaching individuals how to resist these powerful messages and examine the social forces at work may be more useful. Lee and Mysyk (2004) do not rationalize the behavior of compulsive buyers, but do point out that the social forces behind purchasing in our society, including the media, the state of the economy, and easy access to credit, can also fuel the compulsive buyer. Psychosocial (Tavares et al., 2008) and cognitive behavioral (Kellet, 2009; Tavares et al., 2008) treatment modalities have been suggested by the literature. It is important to continue to gather data regarding prevalence and patterns associated with compulsive buying in order to better understand this process addiction.

Case Study

Gina is a recovering alcoholic whose husband died last year. She has struggled with depression and has withdrawn from most normal activities, including meetings. She began watching and ordering from one of the shopping networks a few months ago. Over the last two months her daughter has become increasingly concerned and brought her in for counseling because Gina has spent almost $10,000 on items she does not use or need. Sometimes, Gina admits, she may not even want the item but feels good when she orders from her "family at the shopping network." She is angry at being confronted and says that it is her money and her choice. Considering information about process addictions and spending, and Gina's circumstances, do you consider this behavior problematic? Addictive? Discuss what you think may be happening for Gina, the danger signals you see, and how you would approach counseling with her.

FOOD ADDICTION AND DISORDERED EATING

Some addiction experts claim that—similar to alcohol or drugs—food can be addictive (Avena, Rada, & Hoebel, 2008; Baker, 1995; Gearhardt, Corbin, & Brownell, 2009b; Gearhardt, Corbin, & Brownell, 2009a; Gold, Graham, Cocores, & Nixon, 2009; Sheppard, 1993; von Deneen, Gold, & Liu, 2009), while others continue to debate the issue (von Ranson, McGue, & Iacono, 2003). Experts who claim that eating disorders (including anorexia, bulimia, and binge eating) are addictions argue that individuals suffering with these disorders often share common traits with those addicted to alcohol or drugs, such as obsession, compulsion, denial, tolerance, withdrawal symptoms, and cravings (Overeaters Anonymous, Inc., 2006; Sheppard, 1993). Researchers are exploring the possible addictive qualities of certain types of foods, including foods with high fat and/or sugar content (Gold et al., 2009). For example, sugar releases opioids and dopamines in the brain, causing neurochemical changes and suggesting possible addictive qualities (Avena et al, 2008). The role of hormones and genes that may be related to whether or not a person is likely to develop addictive eating patterns are also being investigated (von Deneen et al., 2009). Gold et al. (2009) assert that our nation's obesity epidemic alone suggests that certain foods may promote a loss of control and continued use despite negative consequences, which are among the diagnostic criterion for substance abuse and dependence. The existence of 12-step recovery programs for disordered eating, modeled after Alcoholics Anonymous' Twelve Steps and Traditions, perhaps indicates growing support among both the population and professionals for the treatment of eating disorders as addictions (von Ranson et al., 2003). Such programs include Overeaters Anonymous, Inc., Food Addicts in Recovery Anonymous, Anorexics Anonymous, and Bulimics Anonymous.

The debate about whether eating disorders are addictions continues as researchers learn more about the causes and best treatment for eating disorders and food addiction. There is still a great deal to learn about the causes of eating disorders. What is known is that eating disorders are complex, involving long-term psychological, behavioral, emotional, interpersonal, familial, biological, spiritual, and social factors (ANAD, 2010; NEDA, 2002). In fact, although people with eating disorders are preoccupied with food, appearance, and weight, they also often struggle with issues of control, acceptance, and self-esteem. Regardless of the potential causes of eating disorders, they can create a self-perpetuating cycle of physical and emotional abuse that requires professional help.

Anorexia nervosa is typified by compulsive self-starvation and excessive weight loss. Some of the symptoms can include refusal to maintain a normal body weight for height, body type, age, and activity level; intense fear of weight gain; loss of menstrual periods; continuing to feel "fat" despite extreme weight loss; extreme obsessive concern with body weight and shape (NEDA, 2002). The National Association of Anorexia Nervosa and Associated Eating Disorders [ANAD], (2010) states that symptoms of anorexia nervosa include weighing 15% below what is expected for age and height. An individual with anorexia nervosa may have a low tolerance for change and new situations, may fear growing up and taking charge of their own life, and be overly dependent on parents and family. Dieting may represent avoidance of and ineffective attempts at coping with the demands of new stages of life (ANAD, 2010).

Bulimia nervosa is typified by a compulsive cycle of binge eating and then purging. An individual with bulimia eats a large amount of food in a short period of time and then gets rid of the food and calories through vomiting, laxative abuse, or excessive exercise. Some of the symptoms of bulimia include repeated cycles of bingeing and purging, frequent dieting, extreme concern with body weight and shape, and feeling out of control during a binge, as well as eating beyond the point of fullness. Impulse control can be a problem for those with bulimia and lack of control may also extend to risky behaviors such as shoplifting, sexual adventurousness, and alcohol and other drug abuse (ANAD, 2010).

Binge eating disorder is differentiated from bulimia nervosa in that there are episodes of uncontrollable, impulsive bingeing but there is no purging. An individual with binge eating disorder engages in random fasting and diets and feels extreme shame and self-hatred after bingeing. Individuals with binge eating disorder tend to eat rapidly and secretly, and be depressed and obese. Other eating disorders include a combination of symptoms from anorexia, bulimia, and binge eating disorders but the symptoms are not severe enough to be considered a clinical disorder (NEDA, 2002).

Case Study

Maggie is an 18-year-old college freshman. During high school, she was an honor roll student and athlete, participating on the soccer and swim teams. Maggie is very driven to succeed at college, and is feeling the strains of being in a new place with high academic standards. She began to gravitate to comforting favorite foods in the cafeteria, such as pizza, French fries, and soft serve ice cream. She soon began to notice that her clothes were getting tight. Maggie became very scared of gaining the "freshman fifteen" and started working out and eating more healthfully. After she lost the few pounds she had gained, however, she decided she could stand to lose a few more. She began getting up at 6 A.M. to fit in a long gym workout before class, and began to make rules about which foods in the cafeteria she was allowed to eat. Maggie comes to see you at the university counseling center because she is "stressed" and "anxious." During your assessment, you notice that she is very thin, and you learn that she has lost 20 pounds since she began what she describes as "just eating better and working out to be healthier."

What are the most important concerns to focus on first as her counselor? How would you begin to explore your concerns about her eating patterns, or would you? What levels of care might you consider: outpatient, intensive outpatient, and/or residential? Explain.

According to the *DSM-IV-TR* the lifetime prevalence rate of anorexia nervosa among females is 0.5% and one-tenth of that for men (APA, 2000). In the last 20 years the occurrence of anorexia nervosa has increased. The lifetime prevalence of bulimia nervosa among women is 1% to 3% and the prevalence for men is roughly one-tenth of that of females (APA, 2000). According to ANAD (2010) 1% of female adolescents suffer from anorexia nervosa and 1% to 4% of women suffer from bulimia nervosa during their life. Ten percent of individuals suffering from anorexia and bulimia are male (ANAD, 2010). The National Eating Disorders Association (NEDA) reports roughly 25 million are struggling with binge eating disorder (2002). Due to the fact that physicians are not required to report eating disorders to a health agency, and because the nature of the disorder is secretive, we only have rough estimates of how many people in this country are affected by eating disorders (ANAD, 2010; NEDA, 2002).

Summary and Some Final Notations

In summary, "to recognize the underlying addictive process is to acknowledge that society itself operates addictively; its institutions perpetuate the addictive process. It does not merely encourage addictions; it regards them as normal" (Schaef, 1990, p. 18). This chapter provides counselors with comprehensive introductory information about process addictions. It is imperative that counselors continue their education about the new scientific discoveries as well as the intricate and complex issues surrounding addiction.

Useful Web Sites

The following Web Sites provide additional information relating to the chapter topics:

Anorexia Nervosa and Related Eating Disorders, Inc.
http://www.anad.org/

Eating Disorder Awareness and Education
http://www.anorexicsanonymous.com

CoDependents Anonymous
http://www.codependents.org

Food Addicts in Recovery Anonymous
http://www.foodaddicts.org

Gamblers Anonymous
http://www.GamblersAnonymous.org

Gambling, National Council on Problem Gambling
http://www.ncpgambling.org

National Eating Disorders Association
http://www.nationaleatingdisorders.org

Overeaters Anonymous
http://www.oa.org

S-Anon (for family and friends of sexually addicted people)
http://www.sanon.org

Sex Addicts Anonymous
http://www.saa-recovery.org

Sexaholics Anonymous
http://www.sa.org

Sex and Love Addicts Anonymous
http://www.slaafws.org

References

American Psychiatric Association (APA). (2000). *Diagnostic and statistical manual of mental disorders* (4th ed., text revision). Washington, DC: Author.

Avena, N. M., Rada, P., & Hoebel, B. G. (2008). Evidence for sugar addiction: Behavioral and neurochemical effects of intermittent, excessive sugar intake. *Neuroscience & Biobehavioral Reviews, 32*(1), 20–39. doi:10.1016/j.neubiorev.2007.04.019

Baker, L. (1995). Food addiction deserves to be taken just as seriously as alcoholism. *Addiction Letter 11*(7), 1–2.

Bancroft, J., & Vukadinovic, Z. (2004). Sexual addiction, sexual compulsivity, sexual impulsivity, or what? Toward a theoretical model. *The Journal of Sex Research, 41*, 225–234.

Bonebright, C. A., Clay, D. L., & Ankenmann, R. D. (2000). The relationship of workaholism with work-life conflict, life satisfaction, and purpose in life. *Journal of Counseling Psychology, 47*, 469–477.

Brady, B. R., Vodanovich, S. J., Rotunda, R. (2008). The impact of workaholism on work-family conflict, job satisfaction, and perception of leisure activities. *The Psychologist-Manager Journal, 11*, 241–263. doi:10.1080/10887150802371781

Buck, T., & Amos, S. (2000). *Related addictive disorders* (Report No. CG030040). U.S. Department of Education, Office of Educational Research and Improvement. (ERIC Document Reproduction Service No. ED440345)

Ceravolo, R., Frosini, D., Rossi, C., & Bonuccelli, U. (2010). Impulse control disorders in Parkinson's disease: Definition, epidemiology, risk factors, neurobiology and management. *Parkinsonism and Related Disorders, 15*(SUPPL 4), S111–S115.

Chamberlain, C. M., & Zhang, N. (2009). Workaholism: Health and self-acceptance. *Journal of Counseling & Development, 87*, 159–169.

Co-Dependents Anonymous, Inc. (1995). *Co-Dependents Anonymous*, Dallas, TX: CoDA Resource Publishing.

Fassel, D. (1990). *Working ourselves to death.* New York: HarperCollins.

Fassel, D., & Schaef, A. W. (1989, January). The high cost of workaholism. *Business & Health, 38*(5).

Gearhardt, A. N., Corbin, W. R., & Brownell, K. D. (2009a). Food addiction: An examination of the diagnostic criteria for dependence. *Journal of Addiction Medicine, 3*(1), 1–7. doi:10.1097/ADM.0b013e318193c993

Gearhardt, A. N., Corbin, W. R., & Brownell, K. D. (2009b). Preliminary validation of the Yale food addiction scale. *Appetite, 52*(2), 430–436. doi:10.1016/ j.appet.2008.12.003

Gold, M. S., Graham, N. A., Cocores, J. A., & Nixon, S. J. (2009). Food addiction? *Journal of Addiction Medicine, 3*(1), 42–45. doi:10.1097/ADM.0b013e318199cd20

Grilo, C. M., Sinha, R., & O'Malley, S. S. (2002). Eating disorders and alcohol use disorders. *Alcohol Research & Health, 26*(2), 151–160.

Hagedorn, W. B. (2005). Sexual addiction as a precursor to chemical addiction. In V. A. Kelly & G. A. Juhnke (Eds.), *Critical incidents in addictions counseling* (pp. 25–33). Alexandria, VA: American Counseling Association.

Hagedorn, W. B. (2009). The call for a new *Diagnostic and Statistical Manual of Mental Disorders* diagnosis: Addictive disorders. *Journal of Addictions & Offender Counseling, 29*, 110–127.

Hagedorn, W. B., & Juhnke, G. A. (2005). Treating the sexually addicted client: Establishing a need for increased counselor awareness. *Journal of Addictions & Offender Counseling, 25*, 66–86.

Hsu, S., Wen, M., & Wu, M. (2009). Exploring user experiences as predictors of MMORPG addiction. Computers & Education, 53(3), 990–999. doi:10.1016/j.compedu.2009.05.016

Kranzler, H. R., & Li, T-K. (2008). What is addiction? *Alcohol Research & Health, 31*, 93–95.

Kellett, Stephen. (2009). Compulsive buying: A cognitive-behavioural model. *Clinical Psychology Psychotherapy, 16*(2), 83.

Lee, S., & Mysyk, A. (2004). The medicalization of compulsive buying. *Social Science & Medicine, 58*, 1709–1718.

Long, L. L., Burnett, J. A., & Thomas, R. V. (2006). *Sexuality counseling: An integrative approach.* Upper Saddle River, NJ: Pearson Education, Inc.

Manisses Communication Group Inc. (2004, January 5). People with eating disorders likely to abuse alcohol, drugs. *Alcoholism & Drug Abuse Weekly,* 3–5.

Massachusetts Council on Compulsive Gambling, National Problem Gambling Awareness Week 2009 [NPGAW2009]). (2009, February 27). MCCG Asian awareness Cantonese, Mandarin and Vietnamese [Video file]. Retrieved from *http://www.youtube.com/watch?v=NWTDtZ2vBE& feature 5channel*

Miller, G. (2005). *Learning the language of addiction counseling.* Hoboken, NJ: John Wiley & Sons.

Mitchell, J. E., Redlin, J., Wonderlich, S., Crosby, R., Faber, R., Miltenberger, R., Smith, J., . . . Lancaster, K. (2001). The relationship between compulsive buying and eating disorders. Retrieved from *http://www.interscience.wiley.com*

National Assocation of Anorexia Nervosa and Associated Eating Disorders (ANAD). (2010). Eating disorder statistics. Retrieved from *www.anad.org*

National Council on Problem Gambling (NCPG). (2009, April 7). National Council on Problem Gambling [Web log post]. Retrieved from *http://dialogue.samhsa.gov/ samhsa_communications_dia/national-council-on-problem-gambling.html*

National Eating Disorders Association (NEDA). (2002). Retrieved from *http://www.nationaleatingdisorders.org*

Overeaters Anonymous, Inc. (2006). The twelve steps of overeaters anonymous. Retrieved from *http://www.oa .org/twelve_steps.html*

Rainone, G., Marel, R., Gallati, R. J., & Gargon, N. (2007). *Gambling behaviors and problem gambling among adults in New York state: Initial findings from the 2006 OASAS household survey.* New York State Office of Alcoholism and State Services. Retrieved from *http://www.oasas .state.ny.us/gambling/documents/gamblingHH110107.pdf*

Robinson, B. E. (1998). The workaholic family: A clinical perspective. *The American Journal of Family Therapy, 26,* 65–75.

Schaef, A. W. (1990, January 3–10). Is the church an addictive organization? *The Christian Century, 107* (1), 18–21.

Schaufeli, W. B., Shimazu, A., Taris, T. W. (2009). Being driven to work excessively hard: The evaluation of a two-factor measure of Workaholism in the Netherlands and Japan. *Cross-Cultural Research, 43*(4), 320–348.

Schneider, J. P. (2004). Sexual addiction & compulsivity: Twenty years of the field, ten years of the journal [Editorial]. *Sexual Addiction & Compulsivity, 11,* 3–5.

Seegers, J. A. (2003). The prevalence of sexual addiction symptoms on the college campus. *Sexual Addiction & Compulsivity, 10,* 247–258.

S-Anon. (2010). What is S-Anon? Retrieved from *http:// www.sanon.org/sanondef.htm*

Sex Addicts Anonymous. (2005). What is sexual addiction? Retrieved from *http://www.sexaa.org/addict.htm*

Sexaholics Anonymous Inc. (2010). What is a sexaholic and what is sexual sobriety? Retrieved from *http:// www.sa.org/sexaholic.php*

Shaffer, H. J., & Kidman, R. (2003). Shifting perspectives on gambling and addiction. *Journal of Gambling Studies, 19*(1), 1–6.

Seybold, K. C., & Salamone, P. R. (1994). Understanding workaholism: A review of causes and counseling approaches. *Journal of Counseling & Development 73*(1), 4–10. Shaffer, H. J., & Kidman, R. (2003). Shifting perspectives on gambling and addiction. *Journal of Gambling Studies, 19*(1), 1–6.

Sheppard, K. (1993). *Food Addiction: The Body Knows* (rev. ed.). Deerfield Beach, FL: Health Communications, Inc.

Suissa, A. J. (2007). Gambling addiction as a pathology: Some markers for empowerment. *Journal of Addictions Nursing, 18,* 93–101. doi: 10.1080/10884600701334952

Tavares, H., Lobo, D. S. S., Fuentes, D., & Black, D. W. (2008). Compulsive buying disorder: A review and a case vignette. [Compras compulsivas: Uma revisão e um relato de caso] *Revista Brasileira De Psiquiatria, 30*(SUPPL 1), S16–S23.

University of California Los Angeles Center for Community Partnerships (UCLACCP). (2008). *Asian gambling: Interview with Dr. Timothy Fong.* Retrieved from *http://www.la.ucla.edu/profiles/fong/shtml*

van Wormer, K., & Davis, D. R. (2003). *Addiction treatment: A strengths perspective.* Pacific Grove, CA: Brooks/Cole.

Vodanovich, S. J., & Piotrowski, C. (2006). Workaholism: A critical but neglected factor in O.D. *Organizational Development Journal, 24,* 55–60.

von Deneen, K. M., Gold, M. S., & Liu, Y. (2009). Food addiction and cues in Prader-Willi syndrome. *Journal of Addiction Medicine, 3*(1), 19–25. doi:10.1097/ADM . 0b013e31819a6e5f

von Ranson, K. M., McGue, M., & Iacono, W. G. (2003). Disordered eating and substance use in an epidemiological sample: II. Associations within families. *Psychology of Addictive Behaviors, 17*(3). Retrieved from PsychARTICLES database.

Young, K. (2009). Internet addiction: Diagnosis and treatment considerations. *Journal of Contemporary Psychotherapy, 39*(4), 241–246. doi:10.1007/s10879-009-9120-x

Zamora, D. (2003). *Internet to sex: Defining addiction.* WebMD. Retrieved from *http://my.webmd.com/content/ Article/76/90153.htm*

Zapf, J. L., Greiner, J., & Carroll, J. (2008). Attachment styles and male sex addiction. *Sexual Addiction & Compulsivity, 15,* 158–175. doi: 10.1080/10720160802 035832

Chapter 4

Important Professional Issues in Addictions Counseling

Melinda Haley
University of Texas at El Paso
Jason Vasquez
Illinois State University

Senait Alem Bairu
University of Texas at El Paso

Professional issues in addictions counseling are those topics that must be attended to for the ethical, legal, and competent treatment of individuals suffering from addictions and substance abuse. There are many issues that could be discussed within such an extensive topic—in fact, entire books have been written on many of the topics covered in this chapter alone. However, due to space and practical constraints, the discussion will focus on two broad areas related to addictions counseling: professional issues pertaining to counselors and treatment and research issues.

These are difficult subjects to write about because addictions counselors, though united in the professional treatment of clients with addictions or substance abuse problems, may differ both in professional affiliation and ethical code. To add to this diversity, states have different laws regulating the addictions profession. Therefore, every attempt has been made to point out both differences and similarities where applicable. It is the responsibility of each and every addiction professional to know, understand, and practice under the specific state and federal laws, and the specific ethical codes of the credentialing agency through which they have obtained their certification or licensing.

One unique aspect of the addictions field is that it is multidimensional and multidisciplinary. Those providing treatment for individuals with addictions or other substance abuse issues can be physicians, psychiatrists, psychologists, social workers, clergy, family therapists, or addictions counselors (Burrow-Sanchez, Lopez, & Slagle, 2008). While some might consider this a drawback, others find the diversity within the field essential (Madden et al., 2008; Mangrum & Spence, 2008). Because so many professions are involved in treating people with addiction or dependence, there are many titles for these individuals, such as addictions counselors, substance abuse and dependence counselors, chemical dependency counselors, alcohol and other drug (AOD) counselors, and so on. In order to be consistent, the terms used to describe this profession within this chapter will be addiction(s) counselor, or counselor. However, it should be recognized that not all clients treated by these counselors have a problem with addiction. Some clients may be classified as substance abusing, but not necessarily addicted.

PROFESSIONAL ISSUES PERTAINING TO COUNSELORS

Addictions counselors have responsibilities to clients, the addictions field, other professionals, the public, and their employers (Brown & Srebalus, 2003). This section on professional issues pertaining to addictions counselors will review topics related to counselor competence and credentialing.

Counselor Competence

We are all limited in our practice as counselors. No one person is fully competent in all areas of mental health care, or in addictions counseling. It is up to the addictions counselor to recognize his or her limitations with respect to the types of services he or she can offer. This section will review counselor competence within the following issues: (a) comorbidity; (b) special populations; (c) clinical knowledge of polysubstance abuse and dependence; (d) knowledge of theory, treatment, and recovery models; (e) multiculturalism; (f) education; (g) counselors in recovery; (h) self-care; (i) research-based practice; and (j) continuing education.

COMORBIDITY.   According to Ferdinandi and Hui Li (2007), the most common comorbid condition is the dual diagnosis of a substance abuse disorder and a mental illness (e.g., a psychiatric condition described in the DSM-IV-TR). The high incidence of co-occurring psychiatric and substance use disorders has been well documented in the literature (Mangrum & Spence, 2008). Treating clients with a comorbid condition offers a unique challenge to the competency of the addictions counselor; especially cases where he or she does not have training or experience working with individuals with a particular mental disorder. According to the National Association of Addiction Professionals Code of Ethics (NAADAC, 2008), addictions counselors are mandated to avoid practicing in areas that are outside their level of competence.

Within the scope of the comorbid conditions, there are many variables that may impact the prognosis and etiology of the conditions (Ilomäki et al., 2008). Addictions counselors need to be aware all of the issues impacting the comorbid condition (Mueser & Drake, 2007). Ethically, the addictions counselor needs to get supervision or refer the client to a mental health specialist for treatment of the mental health condition. It would be unethical to practice outside the scope of the counselor's competency and treat this client without supervision for the mental health issue.

A psychiatric disorder (e.g., anxiety, depression, bipolar disorder) can cause a person to desire to self-medicate, thus increasing their substance use. The substance use issue may continue during or after the treatment of the psychiatric disorder (Schuckit, 2006). In addition, some substances that are abused can mimic the symptoms of certain psychiatric disorders. For example, methamphetamine use can produce a paranoid psychosis that is often misdiagnosed for schizophrenia or paranoid schizophrenia in individuals who do not have schizophrenia (Yui, Kajii, & Nishikawa, 2006). Therefore, it is very important when diagnosing a client for any disorder to also assess for substance use and how that use may impact the disorder or mimic symptoms. In some cases, such as in methamphetamine abuse, individuals may be misdiagnosed due to the similarity of the pattern of psychosis to that of a person suffering from schizophrenia.

SPECIFIC POPULATIONS.   While it is beyond the scope of this chapter to outline every specific population that might struggle with addictions concerns, one unique population that has garnered increased attention by addiction professionals in recent years has been minors (e.g., adolescents and children) seeking treatment for substance abuse or addictions. There are a number of legal and ethical questions that arise when working with minors. For example, counselors need to recognize that though they may be competent to work with adults, this competency does not extend to working with adolescents or children unless the counselor has received training specific to this population (Howard, Stubbs, & Arcuri, 2007; Sussman, Skara, & Ames, 2008). Kaczmarek (2000) would take this issue further and say that a counselor trained in working with children does not necessarily have the competency for working with adolescents. Both have unique developmental and treatments issues as well as ethical and legal considerations (Bukstein, 2009).

In addition to the issue of competence in provision of services, counselors also have to consider whether or not the child or adolescent with whom they are working can legally provide consent for their own treatment; especially if they are attempting to access services without the knowledge of their parents. The age at which minors can legally enter into financial, service, or relationship contracts varies from state to state. Also, the legal mandates for working with youth may vary as well. Under Federal Law (42 C.F.R. §2.14), a minor of 12 years of age or older has the legal authority to sign into treatment and execute written consent to disclose confidential information without the parent's or guardian's consent. However, the fact that minors can sign into legal agreements and consent to treatment poses an ethical dilemma for addictions counselors.

For example, what if a minor discloses to an addictions counselor a pattern of ongoing alcohol and other drug use that clearly endangers the youth to him- or herself or others? Under NAADAC's code of ethics (2008), addictions counselors are obligated to protect their clients from harm brought on by themselves or others. Therefore, if facts are revealed relative to the potential harm to the life or physical well-being of the minor, counselors are mandated both by law and ethics to act in their client's best interest; even if that means the counselor breaks confidentiality. From an ethical perspective, counselors should get supervised experience when working with special populations with whom he or she has no prior experience, because there may be numerous ethical, legal, treatment issues, and other considerations specific to these groups. For an excellent review of the ethical and legal considerations when working with adolescents and children in treatment for alcohol and other substance abuse problems see Bukstein (1994) and Kaminer and Bukstein (2008).

CLINICAL KNOWLEDGE OF POLYSUBSTANCE ABUSE AND DEPENDENCE. According to a report by the National Institute on Drug Abuse (NIDA, 2004) there continues to be a high incidence rate of multidrug use in the United States, especially among adolescents and young adults. Given this trend, it is extremely important that counselors and other mental health professionals have the clinical knowledge necessary to treat individuals dealing with polysubstance abuse and dependence. Yet, despite this critical need, there remains a lack of training among counselors and others to deal with this population. For example, Bina and Colleagues (2008) found that masters of social work (MSW) had a lack of training in the area of substance abuse treatment, which is often negatively correlated with the social worker's knowledge, attitudes, and effectiveness in working with individuals with substance abuse disorders. In their study, they surveyed MSW graduates regarding their perceived knowledge of a number of key content areas of substance abuse, including polysubstance abuse, and found that a majority of the participants had limited expertise in these areas and rated themselves as lacking in preparation to treat individuals with these concerns. Counselors and other helping professionals need to be knowledgeable about polysubstance use and how it affects the client and treatment issues. According to NAADAC's code of ethics (2008), professionals need to strive for a better understanding of addictive disorders and seek training in areas that are beyond their area of competence.

KNOWLEDGE OF THEORY, TREATMENT, AND RECOVERY MODELS. The counselor also needs to be knowledgeable about the differing theories of addiction and treatment (Dowieko, 2006). One theory that has garnered increased attention among addictions professionals over the course of the past 20 years has been Prochaska and DiClemente's (1984) Transtheoretical Model of Change (TTM). This model is one of the leading approaches for explaining and intervening across a wide variety of health related behaviors, such as smoking cessation (Huber & Mahajan, 2008), alcohol abuse (Prochaska et al., 2004), dieting (Wells & Wells, 2007), and substance abuse

(Barber, 1995). In terms of theoretical underpinnings, the TTM posits four central concepts essential for client behavior change: (a) Stages of Change (e.g., Precontemplation, Contemplation, Preparation, Action, and Maintenance); (b) Processes of Change (e.g., cognitive, behavioral, and affective activities that facilitate change); (c) Self-Efficacy (e.g., client's confidence in making changes); and (d) Decisional Balance (e.g., advantages and disadvantages of change) (Prochaska et al., 2004). For an excellent overview of other theories, treatment, and recovery models, see Dowieko (2006).

Prochaska and DiClemente's Transtheoretical Model of Behavior Change

Stage of Change	Description of Typical Client Attitudes and Behaviors	Counseling Techniques
Pre-Contemplation	"I don't have a problem. I can stop whenever I want to." Client has no plans to quit at this time. They tend to avoid reading or thinking about their risk-taking behaviors.	Help the client explore the benefits and consequences of using. Do the consequences outweigh the benefits? This stage is about raising the client's awareness and helping them self-evaluate their use without judgment or confrontation. The purpose is to create dissonance and help the client acknowledge the down side of using and tip the balance to the contemplation stage.
Contemplation	"Well maybe I have a problem. I'll think about that." Client is considering the option of changing, but may feel ambivalent or scared of change.	Help the client explore the pros and cons of their use and the pros and cons of changing. How has using impacted their relationships, job performance, participation in hobbies, etc.? The key is to allow the client to lead and self-explore. The purpose is to help the client acknowledge that he or she does have a problem and tip the balance toward the preparation stage.
Preparation	"Okay, I have a problem, but I don't know what to do about it. I need to look at my options." Client is planning on quitting within the next 30 days and has begun to take some action toward their goal.	Help the client explore resources and options. Identify barriers and help identify strategies to overcome them. Teach skill development to prepare client for change and encourage small steps.
Action	"I have a problem, I know what to do about it, and I'm going to do it." Client is in the active process of change and has begun to make significant changes in their lifestyle.	Teach positive coping skills to replace reliance on substances. Help client identify triggers and develop strategies to overcome them. Provide support and continued resource exploration.
Maintenance	"I beat my problem. I'm doing good. I no longer use!" Client has been sober for at least six months and is developing confidence in their ability to change.	Help client find internal rewards for success and reinforce positive behaviors. Discuss signs of relapse and develop strategies for prevention. Discuss coping skills in case of relapse.
Relapse	"I blew it. I can't believe that happened to me." Client has relapsed and may either be discouraged or determined. He or she will regress back to an earlier stage of change (e.g., contemplation, preparation, or action).	Evaluate and help the client self-explore his or her relapse triggers. Help the client identify strategies to prevent the issue(s) from occurring in the future. Reassess barriers and supports. Reassess coping strategies. Discuss that relapse is often a part of recovery.

Source: Prochaska, Fava, Norman, & Reading, 1998.

BOUNDARY VIOLATION ISSUES.   The relationship between the client and the counselor is vital to the recovery process. Because individuals entering into the rehabilitation process are essentially admitting that they cannot change on their own, it is essential that providers of professional assistance be not only knowledgeable, but able to form strong interpersonal relationships with others (Gottdiener, 2008). According to Rogers (1961), counselors who are most effective at connecting with their clients often exhibit the following characteristics: (a) warmth, (b) dependability, (c) consistency, (d) unconditional positive regard, (e) empathy, (f) non-judgmental understanding, and (g) a belief that individuals strive toward self-actualization. Counselors who embody these characteristics tend to most strongly impact a client's motivation toward change and to influence the client's ability to: (a) to trust the counselor, (b) depend on the therapist, (c) be open with the therapist, and (d) to accept external help (Bell, Montoya, Atkinson, 1997; Cooper, 2009). Therefore, it makes sense that therapists with strong interpersonal skills would be best suited for helping individuals in recovery change.

Given the inequity of power and the intensity of the client-counselor relationship, one legal and ethical problem that may arise within the milieu of treatment is boundary violations (Gottdiener, 2008). There are many examples of what can constitute a boundary violation. Historically these have been in the areas of "role, time, place and space, money, gifts, services, clothing, language, self-disclosure, and physical contact, (p. 639) (Pope & Keith-Spiegel, 2008). However, the most serious boundary violation is of a sexual nature.

For example, what if while working for agency treating individuals with substance abuse problems, it becomes known that a colleague is sexually involved with a former client? While the ethical prohibition against exploitive relationships with clients is consistent across the helping professions, there often is an avoidance of, and variance in, the degree of sexual activity between therapists and former clients, as well as a lack of consistent definition of when, if ever, a client ceases to become a client. According to NAADAC (2008), addictions counselors are prohibited from entering into sexual relationships with both current and former clients.

Other types of boundary issues are often examined on a case by case basis and can be impacted by numerous variables (e.g., theoretical orientation, rural vs. urban community, counselor gender, client gender, clinical context, professional context, and cultural context), as well as many other factors (Pope & Keith-Spiegel, 2008). Pope and Keith-Spiegel (2008) argue that not all boundary crossings are detrimental to a client and some, in fact, can be therapeutic. They offer suggestions for making decisions about crossing boundaries. A summary of these can be found on Table 4.1, but for a detailed discussion on this issue please refer to the article by these authors. The underlying message these authors provide, however, is that boundaries are never crossed lightly or without much thought and contemplation. Boundary crossing should be considered every bit as carefully as an ethical dilemma.

MULTICULTURALISM.   Given both social and demographic changes among African-American, Latino, Asian-Pacific Islanders, Southeast Asian, and Middle Eastern populations, addictions counselors need to be cognizant of cultural differences and how they might affect the assessment and treatment of addiction disorders in culturally different clients. However, neither the professional substance abuse research literature, nor many credentialing bodies, places much emphasis on multicultural competence among practitioners (Lassiter & Chang, 2006). In fact, one major criticism of contemporary models of substance abuse treatment is that they are essentially "culturally blind" in that they often fail to take into account cultural variables, such as beliefs, values, norms, and behaviors (Castro & Hernandez-Alarcon, 2002). For example, cultural variables that might impact the treatment relationship among culturally different clients in treatment for addictions include: acculturation (Zenmore, Mulia, Ye, Borges, & Greenfield, 2008), cultural identity

TABLE 4.1 Boundary Crossing Decision-Making Guidelines
1. Evaluate what the positive and negative consequences would be to each person/agency involved if the boundary was crossed.
2. Check for historical and current research on the particular boundary you are considering and contemplate recommendations.
3. Consult all applicable ethics codes, laws, local legislation etc., for rulings on the boundary.
4. Also, consult with others in the field. Ask your colleagues their opinion on the boundary and whether crossing it could be therapeutic.
5. Monitor your emotions for any signs of uneasiness, guilt, or regret. This may be a sign to you that this is a boundary you should not have crossed.
6. Discuss the boundary with your client, preferably beforehand, and get his or her thoughts and informed consent on the possible boundary crossing.
7. Refer the client if there are any factors that might cause harm to either you or the client.
8. Document, document, document the entire process (e.g., your theoretical orientation, prescribed use of the boundary crossing, who you consulted, what the ethics code and law says about that particular boundary etc.).

Source: Pope & Keith-Spiegel, 2008.

(Rastogi & Wadha, 2006), spirituality (Wong & Longshore, 2008), and gender roles (Quintero, Lilliott, & Willging, 2007).

Perron, Gotham, and Cho (2008) suggest that substance abuse among African-American youth may be linked to economic deprivation, racism, and stress. Chong and Lopez (2000) found that for Native Americans, modeling variables, relationship problems, and peer pressure can be factors in substance abuse and relapse. For Latinos, acculturation stress, language barriers, low self-esteem, lack of education, the daily stress of living, and exposure to substance use are primarily the predisposing factors (Alvarez, Leonard, Olson, Ferrari, & Davis, 2007; Zenmore, Mulia, Ye, Borges, & Greenfield, 2008). Therefore, addictions counselors need education in multicultural factors affecting the substance use and dependence in these populations. Hence, in order to practice within one's own scope of competence, counselors need to be able to provide culturally appropriate services for all clients (Livingston et al., 2008). If multicultural competency is not emphasized within an addiction counselor's training program, then he or she is ethically and morally obligated to seek out such training elsewhere. Otherwise, he or she can do great harm to the culturally different client.

EDUCATION. Substance abuse and addiction continue to be a widespread problem in this country, and there are few indications that the level of severity or numbers of individuals struggling with these problems will drastically decrease in the near future (Salyers, Ritchie, Cochrane, & Roseman, 2006). As a result, there remains a critical need for competent addictions professionals. However, recently there has been some concern about how adequately trained professionally licensed counselors are in providing services for clients struggling with substance abuse and addictions issues (Salyers et al., 2006; Cardosa, Chan, Pruett, & Tansey, 2006).

These concerns arise in light of the fact that some addictions counselors can receive certification without formal graduate training in counseling (Burrow-Sanchez & Lopez, 2009; Mangrum & Spence, 2008). In fact, there are a variety of ways in which addictions counselors can receive education in the area of substance abuse and addictions. These include conferences, lectures, on-the-job training, role playing, seminars, short courses, and workshops (Bina et al., 2008).

These counselors could be considered as practicing without the level of competency required of other counselors (Toriello & Benshoff, 2003). What level of competency can such a counselor claim? At what point should the addictions counselor with a high school diploma or an associate's degree refer a client? According to Salyers and colleagues (2006), one way for counselors to develop the necessary clinical skills to work with individuals with substance abuse and addictions problems is through clinical practicum and internship settings with this population under continuing supervision. They also pointed out the necessity for coursework and postgraduate experiences. Finally, they argued for the need to develop (1) Council of Counseling and Related Education Programs (CACREP) program area in substance abuse, (2) a common core curriculum across the substance abuse program area, and (3) infusion of substance abuse issues across all core program areas mandated by CACREP.

COUNSELORS IN RECOVERY.   Crabb and Linton (2007) note that there are often two types of counselors in the addictions field: those who have never been addicted, and those who are currently in recovery. It is estimated that one-third of all addiction counselors are in recovery at any given time (Field Grapples with Sobriety, 2006). In the addictions literature regarding ethics, one concern addressed by numerous researchers is dual relationships (Doyle, 2005; Hecksher, 2007). One unique dual relationship that concerns addictions professionals may occur when an addictions counselor is in recovery. Although most ethical and legal codes deal with sexual and nonsexual dual relationships, there are very few guidelines for counselors in recovery.

Perhaps as a way to mitigate this concern, the Alcoholics Anonymous Guidelines (2008) for AA members employed in the alcoholism field, specifies that counselors in recovery should have at least 3–5 years of abstinence before working as an addictions counselor. However, there are no mechanisms in place within the field to enforce this recommendation (Field Grapples With Sobriety, 2006). Although the AA guidelines are geared toward those in recovery from alcohol, they can be extended to recovery from all mind altering substances.

Alcoholics Anonymous

Alcoholics Anonymous (AA) is a voluntary support group located in 180 countries for individuals who wish to stop drinking alcohol. Its companion group for those who abuse other drugs is Narcotics Anonymous. AA was founded in 1935 by a New York stockbroker and an Ohio surgeon and it is estimated there are currently over 2 million members worldwide. The only requirement for membership is the desire to stop drinking or using other substances. There are no fees or costs associated with membership and AA is self-supporting through member donations. The philosophy behind AA is that alcoholism is an illness that cannot be cured, but can be controlled through hard work and perseverance "one day at a time." Therefore, one is always in "recovery" unless one has relapsed. The goal is to help one another through fellowship, understanding, and by working the 12-steps and 12-traditions. Each step and tradition helps the individual make changes to behaviors, beliefs, and emotions so he or she can obtain sobriety and good health.

Source: Alcoholics Anonymous, 1972.

According to Hecksher (2007), there has recently been a growth in the number of counselors hired in recovery in treatment centers around the country. What are the ethical implications if an addictions counselor should happen to have a relapse while engaged in counseling work? How does that affect that counselor's clients, who are struggling to maintain their own sobriety? Some counselors have sponsored their own clients for AA (Bissell & Royce, 1994). What are the ethical implications associated with that course of action? These are not easy questions to answer and reflect the growing controversy regarding the amount of formal training acquired by current addictions counselors or other professionals providing addictions treatment (Fahy, 2007). Crabb and Linton (2007) assert that one failing of addiction counselors who are themselves in recovery is that they often lack the training, skills, and techniques to be effective as addictions counselors and often uphold their "in recovery" status as their primary credential.

In terms of counselors in recovery, there are two other key issues impacting this population. These include: (a) counter-transference issues, and (b) self-disclosure. As indicated in a previous section of this chapter, the ability of the addictions counselor to develop a strong therapeutic relationship with their clients is essential for behavior change. However, in developing a helping relationship with a client, a primary ethical concern, especially for counselors in recovery, is counter-transference. In 1995, NAADAC conducted a survey and found that 58% of its membership was in recovery (as cited in Doyle, 2005). Given this high percentage, what are the implications if an addictions counselor is working with someone who may be struggling with the same addiction that the counselor, or a member of the counselor's family, is recovering from? Given their own history of struggles with addiction, counselors in recovery may be able to empathize with clients in rehabilitation at a higher level than those who don't have a history of addiction. However, according to White (2008), counselors with their own history of addiction may be tempted to "expect or try to cultivate in their clients the same type of rational control over alcohol and other drug (AOD) consumption that has worked successfully in the counselor's life" (p. 520). This may either help or hinder the recovery process. In order to minimize the potential negative effects of counter-transference, counselors in recovery need to maintain regular supervision, especially when working with clients who suffer from similar addictions.

There are several reasons why a counselor may disclose his or her own struggles with addictions. For instance, in order to enhance client engagement, counter resistance, minimize shame and isolation, engender hope, and illustrate a particular problem-solving strategy a counselor may self-disclose. However, volunteering such information also comes at the risk of losing clinical focus and establishing an inappropriate level of intimacy within the therapeutic relationship (White, 2008). Therefore, when disclosing such information, it is suggested that counselors proceed with caution and be mindful of the timing, duration, and appropriateness of the disclosure.

COUNSELORS WHO HAVE NEVER BEEN USERS.   For some addictions professionals who have never had an AOD history, working with clients struggling with addictions can be challenging and frustrating; especially if the client's behavior continues to be self-destructive. Counselors may unconsciously stigmatize these clients by making assumptions based on media images and stereotypes. Because AOD use and addiction-related lifestyles may have the potential to conflict with the counselor's values as a member of his or her culture, it can result in possible negative feelings towards the client. This may have deleterious consequence, such as the loss of the counselor's capacity for empathy as well as possible early client termination. It is suggested that counselors evaluate their own past and current relationships with AODs, their role in the decision to do work in the field of addictions, and the degree of congruence/incongruence between those relationships and one's responsibilities as an addictions professional (White, 2008). It is also important to note that one does not have to have a history of AOD use to become an effective addictions professional and that other factors, such as counselor credibility, educational preparation, and clinical experience, may impact their ability to work with this population (White, 2008).

Many researchers note differences in preferred treatment methods, belief systems, fundamental ethnical standards, and procedures between nonusing and past-using addiction counselors

(Crabb & Linton, 2007; Hollander, Bauer, Herlihy, & McCollum, 2006). Crabb and Linton (2007) also note that there may be different personality traits between these two groups that may affect the therapeutic environment. However, they also cite research that concludes that clients have no clear preference between counselors of these two groups.

SELF-CARE.   Another professional issue faced by addiction counselors is the issue of postsecondary trauma and self-care. It is becoming increasingly recognized in the field that substance abuse work incurs stress and trauma for those that work with this population. This stress is also known as "burnout," "compassion fatigue," or "vicarious trauma" (Fahy, 2007). The stress involved in working with the addicted varies with the setting and individual, but addictions counselors often endure poor working conditions due to a lack of resources, lack of support from administrators, high treatment demands from managed care and the criminal justice system, high turnover rate of employees, high chronicity of the treatment population, and lack of commitment from those being treated. This stress can be especially detrimental for counselors who are themselves in recovery (Fahy, 2007; McNulty, Oser, Johnson, Knudsen, & Roman, 2007).

While self-care is essential for any type of counselor, it is especially so for the addictions counselor. Self-care can include such activities as (a) taking time for oneself daily, (b) counseling for the treatment provider, (c) taking periodic sabbaticals, (d) acquiring supervision, (e) maintaining a sense of humor, (f) engaging in regular exercise, (g) maintaining loving relationships, (h) eating a healthy diet, (i) engaging in relaxation and massage, and so forth (Fahy, 2007; Roysircar, 2009). Burnout is a serious condition that can cause detriment to both counselor and client. It is important that addictions counselors take care of themselves so they can take proper care of their clients.

RESEARCH-BASED PRACTICE.   Over the course of the past two decades, an important focus in the provision of mental health services has been the implementation of evidenced based practices (Fahy, 2007). Evidence-based practices are interventions for which empirical verification exists to suggest that these interventions improve client outcomes; and which are developed through clinical trials, consensus reviews, and expert opinions. The American Psychological Association has further defined evidence-based practice as "practice based on evidence" that "must consider the best available research, use clinical expertise, and consider client contextual variables (p. 403)" (Wilson, Armoutliev, & Yakunina, 2009). In the field of addictions, there are a number of scientifically based treatment approaches. These include: (a) cognitive-behavioral therapy, (b) community reinforcement approaches, (c) motivational enhancement therapy, (d) the twelve-step approach, (e) contingency management techniques, (f) pharmacological interventions, and (g) systems treatment (Morgenstern & McKay, 2007; NIDA, 2004). However, a number of concerns exist about the implementation of evidence-based practices in the field of addictions, such as the role of ethical values in shaping practice, limitations of supporting evidence, and absence of scientific evidence for some approaches (Drake et al., 2001).

In addition, some addictions professionals have voiced concerns that, within this rapidly changing world of addictions counseling, even graduate training might not be enough, based on the belief that training programs are not keeping up with developments in the clinical world and are not grounded in the scientific evidence regarding treatment (Foley, Garland, Stimmel, & Merino, 2000; Hoge, Jacobs, Belitsky, & Migdole, 2002). Many in the field assert that practice should be based on recent research findings, rather than on what has been done in the past (Moore et al., 2004; Crabb & Linton, 2007). Scott (2000) found the apparent disconnect between research and practice disturbing, especially when one considers relapse rates are 50% to 90%. Ethical practice mandates that practitioners base their practice on research and empirical findings, not on faith. Scott states that one barrier to integration of theory, research, and practice in the addictions field is also a unique attribute of the field: the reliance on a strong tradition of using personal experience with addictions in counseling work with addicted clients. However, the stance of "It worked for me, so it will work for everyone" is not necessarily what is best for the client (Field Grapples With Sobriety, 2006).

Other investigators of the apparent separation between research and practical application find several reasons for this disconnect, such as: (a) managed care consolidating service with fiscal concerns, (b) researchers who are not practitioners and are therefore disconnected from practical application, (c) new treatment approaches that may be impractical in terms of cost or are not well received by staff and clients, (d) the cost in terms of time and money, both of which are in limited supply with community treatment agencies, of keeping up with the latest research findings, and (e) limited resources for training, technical assistance, and consultation (Fahy, 2007; Moore et al., 2004).

Cardosa and colleagues (2006) posited that because a vast majority of training programs are not offering courses and clinical rotations in the area of substance abuse treatment, leadership in professional associations, such as the American Counseling Association, should consider at least providing some in-service training for its members in empirically supported substance abuse treatment as a way of filling that critical gap in training. Otherwise, if counselors are not utilizing current research in their practice with clients struggling with substance abuse issues, what does this say about their level of competence in working with this population?

CONTINUING EDUCATION.   Addictions counseling is a rapidly changing area of treatment. Counselors need to keep abreast of new developments and research that impact their understanding, competency, and treatment provision. This represents a significant dilemma for counselors who, while ethically responsible for knowledge of the latest research, work in an agency that does not place the same value on current knowledge in the field. Continuing education (e.g., conferences, workshops, and classes) is a major factor in helping addictions professionals develop the skills necessary to effectively meet the needs of individuals struggling with addictions (Pulvermacher, 2007). According to Fahy (2007), in addition to supervision and wellness programs, continuing education is a critical component to preventing compassion fatigue, burnout, and secondary traumatic stress. In terms of skill development, researchers have found that even a half day spent participating in a continuing education program that incorporated active learning for practicing clinicians improved the use of brief intervention and screening for alcohol and other drugs. This change was found to last as long as five years after the class was taken (Saitz, Sullivan, & Samet, 2000). Therefore, continuing education can be used to enhance treatment and assessment by addictions counselors and partially bridge the gap between research and practice, assuming, of course, that the continuing education program utilizes the current research.

Credentialing

Most healthcare professions in this country employ a combination of legal mechanisms, such as credentialing, licensure, inspections, and safety standards, to manage the organization, delivery, and quality of services provided to individuals in their care. The following section will provide an overview of licensure, certification, and accreditation as it pertains to training in addictions counseling. According to Chriqui, Terry-McElrath, McBride, Edison, and VanderWaal (2007), licensure is often regarded as a minimal standard and is generally granted after determining that an individual or organization has met a desired criteria, generally through passing an examination. In contrast, certification for individuals and accreditation for organizations are considered the optimal industry standards.

CERTIFICATION.   Many states now require some type of certification or licensure for addictions counselors to practice (Addictions Counseling, 2010; Kurita & Guydish, 2007). Certification assures the general public that the profession is regulating its members and that practitioners have met the basic qualifications of competency for the profession (National Institute on Alcohol Abuse and Alcoholism, 1982). However, there is no unified national standard for credentialing of addictions counselors (Knudsen, Gallon, & Gabriel, 2006; Mustaine, West, & Wyrick, 2003). In fact, there are many agencies that offer drug and alcohol counseling certification.

The International Association for Addictions and Offender Counselors (IAAOC), a division of the American Counseling Association (ACA) working in conjunction with the National Board for Certified Counselors (NBCC), have developed standards and a program for the certification of master's-level addictions counselors (MACs). One requirement for the MAC credential is a passing score on the Examination for Master Addictions Counselors (EMAC) (Master Addiction Counselor Credential, 2010). For more information on MAC criteria for credentialing, see Table 4.2.

TABLE 4.2 Master Addiction Counselor Criteria for Certification

Criteria for the MAC credential includes:

1. The counselor must pass the National Certified Counselor (NCC) exam prior to applying for MAC certification.

2. A counselor must receive a minimum of 36 months of supervision, 24 of which must occur after date of graduation from an advanced degree in counseling.

3. Supervision must be from a master's level (or higher) professional in counseling, psychology, psychiatry, marriage and family therapy, or social work, and cannot be related to the counselor applying for certification.

4. A master's level (or higher) colleague who is not related to the counselor must also endorse the applicant seeking certification. He or she must attest that he or she believes the applicant is an ethical counselor. This colleague cannot be the counselor's supervisor and must be a professional in counseling, psychology, psychiatry, marriage and family therapy, or social work.

5. A counselor seeking MAC certification must have a minimum of 36 months of experience as an addictions counselor with at least 24 months occurring after graduation from an advanced degree. This experience must have entailed at least 20 hours per week over those 36 months.

6. To qualify for the MAC credential, a counselor must have a minimum of 12 semester (or 18 quarter) hours of graduate level coursework in addictions counseling. These credits must include courses in drug terminology, theories of addictions, and treatment methods. These credits must be from a regionally accredited college or university. The applicant can use up to 6 semester (or 9 quarter) hours in group counseling and/or family counseling toward the total number of credits required in addictions.

7. Post-graduate counselors who wish to add the credential, but did not have addictions coursework in their graduate program, may use continuing education (CE) hours in addictions at the substitution rate of 500 CE hours per 12 semester hours (or 42 CE hours per every one semester hour).

8. Counselors must also pass the Examination for Master Addictions Counselors (EMAC). This is a 100-item, multiple choice exam and covers the content area for assessment, treatment planning and implementation, prevention, group and family counseling, general drug terminology, specific drug information, theories of addiction, medical and psychological aspects of addiction, and treatment of addictions.

Source: Master Addictions Counselor Credential, 2010.

Other national organizations, such as the International Certification Reciprocity Consortium (ICRC), the National Association of Alcoholism and Drug Abuse Counselors (NAADAC), the National Institute on Alcohol Abuse and Alcoholism (NIAAA), the Commission on Rehabilitation Counselor Certification (CRCC) and the American Psychological Association (APA), have also developed certification for addictions counselors (Manisses Communications Group, 2005b).

In addition, each credentialing body has different requirements for certification. These requirements vary across the different certifying agencies, and from state to state, but generally each has three broad goals in mind. These goals are: (a) to define a core set of counselor job tasks, (b) to define a core knowledge base of skills that reflect the competencies expected in the alcohol and drug counseling profession, and (c) to use assessment measures of competency for individuals seeking credentialing (NIAAA, 1982).

However, many credentialing agencies and states differ in opinion regarding just how many competencies are needed. Mustaine and colleagues (2003) report that a survey of different states found varying minimum training requirements needed for certification. These requirements ranged from 1.5 to 3 years of experience, 0 to 810 hours of training, 0 to 1,000 hours of practicum, 0 to 300 hours of training in counseling, and 0 to 540 hours of training in drug and alcohol issues. Many credentialing bodies (e.g., NBCC, CRCC) also require a master's degree in counseling before certification as an addictions counselor can be obtained, while others do not (Salyers et al., 2006). The NAADAC surveyed hundreds of counselors and came up with a list of 188 core areas of knowledge and skills and 91 core tasks needed to effectively counsel a person with addictions (Page & Bailey, 1995).

Consequently, addictions counselors face different sets of credentialing criteria depending on the state of practice and the different credentialing bodies issuing certification (Knudsen et al., 2006). One example of the core tasks and skills required for credentialing can be seen from the example of the NAADAC. Their core tasks and skills fall into the general categories of assessment, treatment planning, client orientation, case consultation, confidentiality, individual, group, and family counseling, crisis intervention, discharge planning, follow-up activities, referral, client advocacy, and personal and professional growth activities (NAADAC, 2008).

Some credentialing organizations also have different levels of certification. For example, the International Certification Reciprocity Consortium (IC & RC), a national organization of certifying boards providing reciprocity of certification nationally and within different states, has three levels of certification: (a) Certified Addictions Counselor, (b) Certified Drug Counselor, and (c) Alcohol and Drug Counselor. Each level has different requirements in terms of training, education, and supervised experience, and the higher the level of certification, the higher the level of requirements (IC & RC, 2010).

Generally, each certifying body also requires some form of written exam applicants must pass before certification is complete. The IC & RC has a national exam used by many states. Those agencies that certify differing levels of counselors (e.g., IC & RC and NAADAC) also have different tests for each level of certification. The NAADAC exam covers the content areas of pharmacology of psychoactive substances, counseling practice, theoretical bases, and professional issues. For an overview of the NAADAC exam content areas see Table 4.3.

In acknowledgement of the various and differing levels of certification and requirements thereof, Mustaine and colleagues (2003) questioned the minimum preparation standards for the counseling profession in addictions counseling. They challenge the idea that addictions counselors can achieve their education through seminars and workshops, rather than through formal education that uses criteria for evaluating competency. They question whether or not "professionals of experience," and "professionals of education," really share the same competency in the

TABLE 4.3 NAADAC Exam Content Areas

Topic	Information Covered
Pharmacology of Psychoactive Substances	This area includes information on specific categories of drugs, physiological effects, psychological effects, withdrawal symptoms, drug interactions, and treatment applications.
Counseling Practice	This area includes information concerning client evaluations, treatment planning, counseling, patient care, patient management, education, continuing care, special issues, and special populations.
Theoretical Bases	This area includes information concerning behavioral, cognitive, and analytical theories of addiction, human growth and development, family, and addiction.
Professional Issues	This area includes information concerning law and regulation, professional behavior, and ethics.

Source: NAADAC, 2008.

addictions field. Mustaine and colleagues further question the vast differences in training and found that 30% of addictions counselors only had a high school diploma.

Scott (2000) believes this dichotomy in the profession regarding the requirement that (a) an addictions counselor must be a recovering addict or a codependent, or (b) must have a minimum of a master's degree in addictions or a related field (e.g., counseling, social work, psychology) is splitting the field and causing dissent from within. While each group brings positive attributes to the profession, the addictions field is complicated and addictions counselors must have knowledge and training in chemical and behavioral addictions, relapse prevention, goal setting, neuropsychological processes in addiction, assessment and individualized treatment planning, family counseling for substance-abusing clients, and 12-step principles (Dowieko, 2006; Von Steen, Vacc, & Strickland, 2002). To address these variations, Hoge, Huey, and O'Connell (2004) offer 16 recommended best practices to standardize training. These suggested best practices can be seen in Table 4.4.

A call to the profession has been made to nationally standardize these credentialing requirements (Hoge et al., 2004; Mustaine et al., 2003; Salyers et al., 2006). Realization of this goal is getting closer, especially with the merger of the National Certification Commission (NCC) and the International Certification and Reciprocity Consortium (IC & RC), as well as membership organizations such as the NAADAC, the Association for Addiction Professionals (AAP), and the Society of Credentialed Addiction Professionals (SCAP). These associations have agreed to "unification through merger," which will hopefully serve to standardize the credentialing of addictions counselors from state to state (Manisses Communications Group, 2005a).

LICENSURE. Licensure is the most rigorous form of professional regulation. The movement to license addictions counselors is not as advanced as that of certification. As of 2003, only six states had licensure for addictions counselors. Unlike certification, which can be granted nationally (e.g., national certified counselor), state law establishes licensure, and each state determines the requirements for licensure. In general, to be licensed as an addictions counselor a person must pass an exam of competency and then engage in a certain number of hours of postgraduate supervised practice (Magnuson, Norem, Wilcoxon, 2002).

The purpose of post-graduation supervised hours prior to licensure is to ensure that: (a) counselors continue in their professional development, (b) the work of less experienced counselors is

TABLE 4.4 Sixteen Recommended Best Practices

1. Education and training should be competency-based
2. Continuing education should be a requirement
3. Practice guidelines should be used as teaching tools
4. Students should develop competency with manualized therapies
5. Teaching methods should be evidence-based
6. Curricula should be routinely updated to address the values, knowledge, and skills essential for practice in contemporary health systems
7. Skill development should include clinical, management, and administrative components
8. Training should develop an understanding of all competing paradigms of service delivery and the forces that shape healthcare (e.g., scientific, professional, economic, and social)
9. Students should train in programs and settings in which they are likely to practice
10. Training sites should incorporate diversity and interdisciplinary practice, and allow for student tracking of patients throughout the continuum of care
11. The term "workforce" should be better defined and all aspects of the "workforce" should receive consistent training
12. Training should be offered to culturally diverse groups
13. Clients and family members should be engaged as teachers of the "workforce" in terms of the understanding the experience of addiction
14. Teachers and supervisors in the training of addictions counselors should be experienced in providing such treatment and should be currently involved in the delivery of such health care
15. The faculty in training programs should be composed of many disciplines involved in the treatment of addictions as a diversity of approaches is needed in the delivery of behavioral health care
16. Training programs should reward faculty for teaching excellence to promote more attention to training rather than clinical or research pursuits that have historically led to greater compensation

Source: Hoge, Huey, & O'Connell, 2004.

monitored to protect client welfare, (c) the new counselor is following the legal, ethical, and professional guidelines of the profession, and (d) applicants for licensure are practicing at the appropriate levels of competence to practice autonomously (Magnuson et al., 2002).

Different states have different requirements for licensure. We will discuss one example, from the state of Colorado. First, Colorado certifies three different levels of counselors. Those who have been certified as a level three certified addictions counselor (CAD) may be eligible for the Licensed Addictions Counselor (LAC) credential if the following requirements are met: (a) applicants must hold a current CAD III issued in the state of Colorado and be in good standing, (b) applicants must have a master's degree in the social sciences or an equivalent program, (c) applicants must pass either the NAADAC MAC exam or the ICRC exam after graduating from a master's or doctoral program, and within the last five years prior to licensure application, and (d) as of July 1, 2004, all applicants for a certification, license, or upgrade are required by Colorado Statute to pass a mail-in Jurisprudence Examination (Addictions Counselors Licensure, 2010). In Colorado, master's programs that are eligible for addictions licenses are quite broad and include the fields of anthropology, counseling (e.g., community counseling, marriage and family counseling, rehabilitation counseling), psychology (e.g., counseling psychology, human psychology, educational psychology), sociology, social work, psychiatric nursing, and behavioral studies (Addictions Counselors Licensure, 2010).

ACCREDITATION.   Accreditation applies to the specific counselor education program within colleges and universities that educate and train addictions counselors. It does not apply to individual counselors in the way that licensure and certification does. Accreditation procedures are intended to ensure the quality and standardization of graduate education for the academic preparation of addictions counselors (Magnuson et al., 2002).

In the accreditation process, professional organizations specify standards for the training of professionals. For example, accreditation standards usually dictate student-to-faculty ratio to ensure students will get a certain degree of individualized attention. Accreditation standards also specify the critical content and experiential components of the graduate program, to ensure the knowledge base and competency of graduating students. Accrediting bodies evaluate graduate and training programs to ensure students within these programs are receiving education in line with these standards and criteria (Peterson & Nisenholz, 1999). Programs that meet or exceed the specified standards are then accredited.

Different educational programs (e.g., rehabilitation versus community counseling) will have different accreditation agencies, just as different organizations offer credentialing for addictions counselors. Examples of accrediting bodies include the Council for Accreditation of Counseling and Related Educational Programs (CACREP) for community counseling graduate programs; the Council on Rehabilitation Education (CORE) for rehabilitation counseling graduate programs; the American Psychological Association (APA) for psychology graduate programs; and the American Association for Marriage and Family Therapy (AAMFT) for family counseling graduate programs. Typical accredited master's degree programs include a minimum of 2 years of full-time study, including 600 hours of supervised clinical internship experience (Bureau of Labor Statistics, 2009).

TREATMENT AND RESEARCH ISSUES

There are many treatment issues relating to clients with addictions that could be discussed. This section will focus on topics relating to managed care and treatment funding and measuring outcomes and efficacy of treatment.

Managed Care and Treatment Funding

The advent of managed care has changed the way health care provisions are administered in this country (Cohen, Marecek, & Gillham, 2006). Managed care refers to any type of intervention aimed at the financing of health care, and focused on elimination of unnecessary and inappropriate care and reduction of costs (Beattie, McDaniel, & Bond, 2006). While the managed care system has been successful in lessening short-term costs, many consider that it has been at the price of long-term consequences for clients and practitioners (Jansson, Svikis, Velez, Fitzgerald, & Jones, 2007). There are many ethical concerns discussed in the literature specifically regarding managed care. The core of these concerns regard cost-containment practices of setting session limits, restricting provider availability, and issues relating to conflict of interest, confidentiality, informed consent, client abandonment, pressures to breach fiduciary responsibilities, and implementing mandatory *Diagnostic and Statistical Manual of Mental Disorders (DSM)* diagnostic procedures (Haley & Carrier, 2009).

Managed care is even changing what services and interventions are offered. For example, even though the managed care system, instituted by the Health Maintenance Organization Act of 1973, was focused on prevention as a cost-reducing measure, Robinson, Haaz, Petrica, Hillsberg, and Kennedy (2004) assert that managed care has not been interested in providing prevention for substance abuse issues. Robinson and colleagues further state that any goal of integrating substance abuse prevention into the managed care rubric has been a challenge. The focus under many managed care programs has been on treating substance abuse issues after they have already occurred, rather than on preventing or minimizing these issues in the first place (Brown et al., 2001).

In addition, in order to be treated under managed care, substance abuse conditions must be diagnosed and a *Diagnostic and Statistical Manual of Mental Disorders (DSM)* diagnosis given (Cohen et al., 2006). This labels an individual as a substance abuser or as someone who is substance dependent (Robinson et al., 2004). This can have far-reaching ramifications for the individual. In terms of intervention, counselors are at the mercy of utilization review boards that scrutinize traditional counseling procedures. As a result of this scrutiny, most long-time counseling methods have been replaced by time-limited approaches and managed care utilization reviews can deny coverage for prescribed treatments (Cohen et al., 2006; Field Wins, 2009; Whittinghill, Whittinghill, & Loesch, 2000).

Some researchers have suggested that primary care providers under the managed care system are not referring individuals with substance abuse issues for treatment. It is further asserted that managed care organizations have eliminated, or limited, substance abuse coverage due to rising costs and high relapse rates (Scott et al., 2004). Managed care organizations might even put a limit on the lifetime amount of substance abuse treatment a person can use (Fisher & Harrison, 2005). This can lead to decreased health services in an attempt to reduce costs. This makes undertreatment an ethical issue and a concern for practitioners (Cohen et al., 2006). In addition, researchers of managed care have found that managed care organizations can demand practices that are unethical for mental health practitioners (Walfish & Barnett, 2009).

Under this system, an individual needing substance abuse treatment must first pass through a "gatekeeper," usually his or her primary health care provider. This physician must refer the client for treatment. If such a referral is given, the individual must use a preferred provider accepted by the organization in order to have the treatment covered, which limits consumer choice. Treatment usually must be brief, measurable, and its efficacy backed by research (Hoge et al., 2002; Merta, 2001). Group therapy is one of the most popular treatments as it is less expensive than individual therapy, but again limits individual care (Haley & Carrier, 2009).

Bissell and Royce (1994) identified a growing concern by the National Counsel on Alcoholism and Drug Dependence (NCADD) and other field organizations that treatment decisions are being made by phone and often by a clerk in an insurance company. These crucial decisions are being made by individuals who have no clinical training in addictions counseling and who probably will never see the client. Another concern is that individuals other than the provider have access to confidential information regarding the client (Haley & Carrier, 2009).

Yet another concern has been that managed care companies, under utilization review, can supersede the recommendations of substance abuse providers and deny coverage in the name of cost containment (Harrow et al., 2006). However, one recent development in Pennsylvania may change the practice of utilization review for substance abuse treatment under managed care. The Pennsylvania Supreme Court recently ruled that "managed care may not apply utilization review to override a physician's or psychologist's judgment on appropriate treatment (p. 3)." In other words, if a physician or psychologist believes inpatient care is necessary, a managed care company cannot deny such care and force the client to settle for outpatient care. Other states are considering such legislation or already have similar laws or statutes on their books (Field Wins, 2009). This may change the managed care climate as we have known it.

However, other concerns remain. Because not all addictions counselors are licensed it is difficult, if not impossible, for these counselors to get reimbursed from managed care organizations or other third-party payers. This further limits consumer choice and ability of addictions counselors to work in the managed care system (Fisher & Harrison, 2005; Mustaine et al., 2003). Therefore, there may be preferred providers providing treatment who are not specifically trained in addictions counseling (Fisher & Harrison, 2005).

Some researchers suggest that studies regarding quality of care for persons with behavioral health problems and who have been treated within managed care have been limited (Bachman, Tobias, Master, Scavron, & Tierney, 2008; Beattie et al., 2006; Larson, Zhang, Smith, & Kasten, 2005). Studies conducted recently have provided mixed results. Some have found that being enrolled in Medicaid or another managed care company was a positive experience in terms of satisfaction in services, access to alcohol and drug counseling, and joint mental health/addictions counseling (Beattie, et al., 2006; Bigelow, McFarland, McCamant, Deck, & Gabriel, 2004; Larson et al., 2005) and that clients within managed care programs showed more or as much improvement as did clients in standard fee-for-services care (Beattie et al., 2006; Harrow et al., 2006; Witbrodt et al., 2007). However, enrollment in a behavioral health care carve-out program rather than fee-for-service, Medicaid, or public funding, did not have an impact on consumer satisfaction or had mixed results (Larson et al, 2005; Shepard, Daley, Ritter, Hodgkin, & Beinecke, 2002).

Other data is controversial. For example, Larson and colleagues (2005) report that a study conducted by the state of Oregon found increased access to substance abuse treatment after the state moved to managed care, while other studies have shown no difference in access or outcomes due to managed care. Fisher and Harrison (2005) suggest addictions and other counselors advocate for substance abuse and mental health parity for the clients under the managed care system. This means that the managed care company would be required to provide both substance abuse and mental health services, just as they offer medical services (Chi, Sterling, & Weisner, 2006). Preventive services for substance abuse and dependence would be included, just as for medical conditions. Walfish and Barnett (2009) argue that there are both positive and negative factors within the managed-care model of providing services and that counselors should examine their style of practice to find the best fit.

Measuring Outcomes and Efficacy of Treatment

Within the last couple of decades there has been an outcry for evidence-based practice and a call for providers to employ treatments supported by controlled research (Eaves, Emens, & Sheperis, 2008; Lilja, Giota, Hamilton, & Larsson, 2007). Professional associations and governmental agencies have issued practice guidelines and treatment algorithms which support selected treatments or levels of care for specific conditions (Hoge et al., 2002; Simotis, Jacobucci, & Houston, 2006). Even so, there has been some criticism regarding conducting outcome research and studies of efficacy of treatment, in both prevention and remedial efforts (Lilja et al., 2007; Springer et al., 2004). There have also been concerns that there is not enough research evidence to support the validity of these practice guidelines or whether they really have an impact on client outcomes (Lilja et al., 2007; Stuart et al., 2002). Therefore, it is clear that more effective outcome research is needed to support empirically-based interventions. Many organizations are moving in this direction. For example, evidence-based practice in psychology has been written into the guidelines of the APA in 2006 to promote cultural sensitivity in service delivery, enhance communication, and advocate for best practices and benefits for clients (La Roche & Christopher, 2009).

A REVIEW OF RECENT RESEARCH.   Many research studies and meta-analyses of several prevention programs found promising results regarding why some programs are more effective than others.
Their findings indicate, at least for adolescent programs, that the following components were
effective in prevention of drug and alcohol abuse: (a) interactive methods of delivery were more likely
to produce intended outcomes than noninteractive methods, (b) smaller programs tended to be
more effective than large programs, (c) system-wide interventions (e.g., those that incorporate
students, parents, teachers, families, community) were more effective than those only targeting students, (d), programs lasting at least 10 hours were more effective than those of shorter duration and
(e) programs that emphasized comprehensive behavioral life skills and social influences were more
effective than those that did not (Lilja et al., 2007; Tobler & Stratton, 1997: Tobler et al., 2000).

Timko, Sempel, and Moos (2003) reported that research using randomized trials of standard versus intensive treatment on the variables of drug outcomes and life functioning indices
indicated comparable improvement for clients in both types of programs. They suggested that
higher staff-to-client ratios made a difference in client outcomes because more individualized
attention was given to each client. They also suggested that cognitive-behavioral theories and
interventions provided better outcomes than did psychodynamic theories and interventions.

Machado's (2005) review of the research found that some treatments worked better than
others, and much of a program's success was based on idiographic characteristics unique to the
program. For example, in some programs it was found that client outcomes were better for clients
with less severe psychiatric problems than those with severe ones. Some research showed that
stable clients do better in short, inexpensive programs than clients with more serious conditions.
Other research found that staff qualifications, competency, confidence and rapport with clients
were the most important ingredient (Lilja et al., 2007; Machado, 2005). It has been suggested that
combining or sequencing treatments may give better outcomes. Therefore, new research might
explore theory-based therapeutic models for combined treatment (McCaul & Monti, 2003).

For many years it was believed that matching clients to treatments based on their characteristics would make them more successful in treatment. However, a study called Project MATCH,
which was supported by the National Institute on Alcohol Abuse and Alcoholism (NIAAA) found
that matching did not significantly improve or alter client outcomes (Morgenstern & McKay,
2007; NIAAA, 1997).

PROBLEMS WITH OUTCOME RESEARCH.   The problem with outcome research lies with
methodological issues that restrict the interpretation and generalization of results across
different treatment settings (Lilja et al., 2007; Machado, 2005). For example, problems exist in
applying research findings from one program to another, as each uses different outcome
measures, methodology, and research designs to ascertain effectiveness (Springer et al., 2004).
Further problems are defined in terms that many such studies: (a) use treatment retention as a
proxy measure for post discharge treatment outcomes; (b) generally use short-term outcomes,
predictors for which may be different from long-term outcomes; (c) use homogeneous samples
that may overlook some predictors; (d) often restrict the range of baseline measures to only
static predictors or to measures of prior substance use; (e) rely heavily on single-item predictors,
which affect reliability of the measures and replication of the findings; and (f) have not
extended predictor selection beyond bivariate analyses (Barber et al., 2006; Lilja et al., 2007;
Staines et al., 2003).

Another problem in outcome research identified by Whittinghill and colleagues (2000) is that
the theoretical constructs upon which traditional substance abuse counseling strategies were
formulated are not easily stated in behavioral terms. Many are based on philosophical and not

empirical arguments, thus making outcomes difficult to measure in concrete terms. As one can see, conducting outcome research that would be applicable to all clients and settings is daunting at best.

An ethical dilemma associated with one method of effective outcome research is that a control group is needed to compare the results of those who received treatment to those who did not (Fisher & Harrison, 2005; Lilja et al., 2007). There can be inherent ethical and practical issues involved in the random assignment of clients to treatments (or to no treatment). This further complicates the ability to provide outcome research. Morgenstern and McKay (2007) assert that research in the addiction field is limited by the use of the "psychotherapy technology model" and the medical research paradigm which has guided addictions treatment research. They advocate researchers exploring other alternatives and methods of research in order to fully understand which treatment variables are effective.

SUGGESTIONS FOR FUTURE RESEARCH.   In order to adequately conduct outcome research that can be compared across programs, researchers must (a) use both qualitative and quantitative research, (b) use common classification that enables comparison between programs and program components, (c) include only programs with drug use measures, and (d) work with a large set of programs when conducting meta-analyses (Koenig & Crisp, 2008; Tobler & Stratton, 1997).

Merta (2001) and Lilja and Colleagues (2007) conducted literature reviews, which suggested that evaluations should: (a) be both summative and formative, (b) take multiple forms and use multiple measures, (c) incorporate relapse prevention, (d) test each module of a program separately in order to assess its effects (e) test each program in different social conditions, and (f) incorporate four different measures (a baseline measurement, a measurement during counseling, a measurement immediately after counseling, and a measurement of long-term gains sometime after counseling has ended).

Client variables must also be taken into consideration when evaluating client outcomes (Lilja et al., 2007). These include variables of age, gender, duration of use, types of substances used, life problems experienced, social systems, whether treatment was voluntary or mandatory, client physical and mental health, legal problems due to use, level of education, and income (Lilja et al., 2007). It is also important to look at treatment setting (e.g., private, for-profit, public, nonprofit, inpatient, or outpatient) (Fisher & Harrison, 2005; Koenig & Crisp, 2008).

In addition, client success criteria need to be standardized. Do different programs measure client success differently? Is success defined as a client completing the program? Is it defined as being sober or abstinent for a number of months or years? Or is success defined as the reduction of life problems associated with substance use? Machado (2005) conducted a review of the recent research literature and found that outcome expectations should center on (a) client reduction of alcohol and drug use, (b) improved personal and social functioning, and (c) public health improvement. Machado's review found that, while the evidence largely supports that addictions treatment is effective in each of these target areas, not all programs are equally effective. Similarly Bergmark (2008) reviewed the COMBINE study published in 2006 which tested treatment outcomes of combining pharmacology and behavioral interventions with clients dealing with alcohol dependency and concluded that further research is necessary not only on interventions, but on the professionals conducting the various treatments.

It is clear that more research is needed and questions must be answered regarding program effectiveness. More research is also needed in how the addictions field can implement these findings across programs to initiate an industry-wide standard of care. With continuing outcome research, it is hoped that the addictions field will be able to implement evidence-based interventions and devise best practice guidelines in order to provide the best care to clients and the community.

Summary and Some Final Notations

There is much involved in the ethical, legal, and competent practice of addictions counseling. The issues explored within this chapter were those related to counselor competency, certification, licensure, accreditation, managed care and treatment funding, and outcome measurement and efficacy of treatment.

Useful Web Sites

Readers wanting more information on chapter topics are directed to the following Web sites:

Alcoholics Anonymous
www.aa.org

Avoiding Exploitive Dual Relationships: A Decision-Making Model
http://kspope.com/dual/gottlieb.php

Commission on Rehabilitation Counselor Certification
http://www.crccertification.com/

Ethical Decision-Making and Dual Relationships
http://kspope.com/dual/younggren.php

International Association for Addictions and Offender Counselors (IAAOC)
http://www.iaaoc.org/

International Certification Reciprocity Consortium (IC & RC)
http://www.icrcaoda.org/

Narcotics Anonymous
www.na.org

National Association of Alcoholism and Drug Abuse Counselors (NAADAC)
http://naadac.org/

National Board for Certified Counselors (NBCC)
http://www.nbcc.org/

National Institute on Alcohol Abuse and Alcoholism (NIAAA)
http://www.niaaa.nih.gov/

National Institute on Drug Abuse
http://www.nida.nih.gov/

Nonsexual Multiple Relationships: A Practical Decision-Making Model for Clinicians
http://kspope.com/site/multiple-relationships.php

SAMHSA's National Registry of Evidence-based Programs and Practices (NREPP)
http://www.nrepp.samhsa.gov/

Substance Abuse and Mental Health Services Administration
http://www.samhsa.gov/index.aspx

Understanding HIPAA Privacy
http://www.hhs.gov/ocr/privacy/hipaa/understanding/index.html

References

Addictions counseling: Five steps to becoming a certified addictions counselor. (2010). Retrieved Jan, 1, 2010 from *http://degreedirectory.org/articles/Addictions_Counseling_5_Steps_to_Becoming_a_Certified_Addictions_Counselor.html*

Addictions Counselors Licensure Information for the State of Colorado (2010). *Frequently asked questions.* Retrieved Jan. 2, 2010, from *http://www.dora.state.co.us/mental-health/faqs.htm#CACfaqs.*

Alcoholics Anonymous. (1972). A brief guide to Alcoholics Anonymous. Retrieved Jan. 3, 2010 from *http://www.aa.org/pdf/products/p-42_abriefguidetoaa.pdf*

Alcoholics Anonymous Guidelines (2008). Retrieved Dec. 9, 2009 from *http://www.aa.org/en_pdfs/mg-10_foraamembers.pdf*

Alterman, A. I., Randall, M., & McLellan, T. (2000). Comparison of outcomes by gender and for fee-for-service versus managed care: A study of nine community programs. *Journal of Substance Abuse Treatment, 19*, 127–134.

Alvarez, J., Leonard, J. A., Olson, B. D., Ferrari, J. R., & Davis, M. I. (2007). Substance abuse prevalence and treatment among Latinos and Latinas. *Journal of Ethnicity in Substance Abuse, 6*(2), 115–141.

Bachman, S. S., Tobias, C., Master, R. J., Scavron, J., & Tierney, K. (2008). A managed care model for Latino adults with chronic illness and disability: Results of the Brightwood Health Center intervention. *Journal of Disability Policy Studies, 18*(4), 197–204.

Barber, J. G. (1995). Working with resistant drug abusers. *Social Work, 40*(1), 17–23.

Barber, J. P., Gallop, R., Crits-Christoph, P., Frank, A., Thase, M., Weiss, R. D., & Gibbons, M. B. C. (2006). The role of therapist adherence, therapist competence, and alliance in predicting outcome of individual drug counseling: Results from the National Institute Drug Abuse Collaborative Cocaine Treatment Study. *Psychotherapy Research, 16*(2), 229–240.

Beattie, M., McDaniel, P., & Bond, J. (2006). Public sector managed care: A comparative evaluation of substance abuse treatment in three counties. *Addiction, 101,* 857–872.

Bell, D. C., Montoya, I. D., & Atkinson, J. S. (1997). Therapeutic connection and client progress in drug treatment. *Journal of Clinical Psychology, 53*(3), 215–224.

Bergmark, A. (2008). On treatment mechanisms: What can we learn from the COMBINE study? *Addiction, 103*(5), 703–705.

Bigelow, D. A., McFarland, B. H., McCamant, L. B., Deck, D. D., & Gabriel, R. M. (2004). Effect of managed care on access to mental health services among Medicaid enrollees receiving substance treatment. *Psychiatric Services, 55*(7), 775–779.

Bina, R., Hall, D. M. H., Mollete, A., Smith-Osborne, A., Yum, J., Sowbel, L., & Jani J. (2008). Substance abuse training and perceived knowledge: Predictors of perceived preparedness to work in substance abuse. *Journal of Social Work Education, 44*(3), 7–20.

Bissell, L., & Royce, J. E. (1994). *Ethics for addiction professionals* (2nd ed). Center City, MN: Hazelden Information and Education.

Brown, D., & Srebalus, D. J. (2003). *Introduction to the counseling profession.* Boston: Allyn & Bacon.

Brown, R. L., Marcus, M., Amodeo, M., Graham, A., Madden, T., Schoener, E., MacLane, E., Baeder, D., Gonzalez-Willis, A., & Kahn, R. (2001). Abstracts of the AMERSA national conference, November, 2000: Empirical studies special program. *Substance Abuse, 22*(2), 127–152.

Bukstein, O. (1994). Treatment of adolescent alcohol abuse and dependence. *Alcohol Health and Research World, 18,* 297–301.

Bukstein, O. (2009). Substance use disorders and ADHD. *CNS Spectrums, 14*(7-Supplement No. 6), 10–12.

Bureau of Labor Statistics, U.S. Department of Labor. (2009, Dec, 17). Counselors. *Occupational Handbook,* 2010–2011 Edition. Retrieved Jan. 2, 2010 from *http://stats.bls.gov/oco/ocos067.htm*

Burrow-Sanchez, J. J., & Lopez, A. L. (2009). Identifying substance abuse issue in high schools: A national survey of high school counselors. *Journal of Counseling and Development, 87,* 72–79.

Burrow-Sanchez, J. J., Lopez, A. L., & Slagle, C. P. (2008). Perceived competence in addressing student substance abuse: a national survey of middle school counselors. *Journal of School Health, 78*(5), 280–286.

Cardosa, E. D. S., Chan, F., Pruett, S. R., & Tansey, T. N. (2006). Substance abuse assessment and treatment: The current training and practice of APA Division 22 members. *Rehabilitation Psychology, 51*(2), 175–178.

Castro, F. G., & Hernandez-Alarcon, E. (2002). Integrating into drug abuse prevention and treatment with racial/ethnic minorities. *Journal of Drug Issues, 32,* 783–810.

Chi, F. W., Sterling, S., & Weisner, C. (2006). Adolescents with co-occurring substance use and mental conditions in a private managed care health plan: Prevalence, patient characteristics, and treatment initiation and engagement. *American Journal on Addictions, 15,* 67–79.

Chong, J., & Lopez, D. (2000). Predictors of relapse for Native American Indian women after substance abuse treatment. *The Journal of the National Center for American Indian and Native American Programs, 14*(3), 24–48.

Chriqui, J. F., Terry-McElrath, Y., McBride, D. C., Edison, S. S., & VanderWaal, C. J. (2007). Does state certification or licensure influence outpatient substance abuse treatment program practices? *Journal of Behavioral Health Services & Research, 34*(3), 309–328.

Cohen, J., Marecek, J., & Gillham, J. (2006). Is three a crowd? Clients, clinicians, and managed care. *American Journal of Orthopsychiatry, 76*(2), 251–259.

Cooper, M. (2009). Welcoming the other: Actualizing the humanistic ethic at the core of counseling psychology practice. Invited Paper: Keynote Speaker, Conference 2009. *Counseling Psychology Review, 24*(3–4), 119–129.

Crabb, A. C., & Linton, J. M. (2007). A qualitative study of recovering and nonrecovering substance abuse counselors' belief systems. *Journal of Addictions and Offender Counseling, 28,* 4–20.

Doweiko, H. E. (2006). *Concepts of chemical dependency* (6th ed.). Pacific Grove, CA: Brooks/Cole.

Doyle, K. (2005). Substance abuse counselors in recovery: Implications for the ethical issue of dual relationships. *Journal of Counseling & Development, 75,* 428–432.

Drake, R. E., Goldman, H. H., Leff, H. S., Lehman, A. F., Dixon, L., Mueser, K. T., & Torrey, W. C. (2001). Implementing evidenced based practices in routine mental health settings. *Psychiatric Services, 52*(2), 179–182.

Eaves, S., Emens, R., & Sheperis, C. (2008). Counselors in the managed care era: The efficacy of the data-based problem solver. *Journal of Professional Counseling: Practice, Theory, and Research, 36*(2), 1–12.

Fahy, A. (2007). The unbearable fatigue of compassion: Notes from a substance abuse counselor who dreams of working at Starbucks. *Clinical Social Work Journal, 35*, 19–205.

Ferdinandi, A. D., & Hui Li, M. (2007). Counseling persons with comorbid disorders: A quantitative comparison of counselor active rehabilitation service and standard rehabilitation counseling approaches. *Journal of Humanistic Counseling, Education, and Development, 46*, 228–241.

Field grapples with sobriety time for counselors in recovery. (2006, Dec. 11). *Alcoholism & Drug Abuse Weekly*, 3–4.

Field wins in final legal battle against utilization review in Pa. (2009, June 8). *Alcoholism & Drug Abuse Weekly*, 3–4.

Fisher, G. L., & Harrison, T. C. (2005). *Substance abuse: Information for school counselors, social workers, therapists, and counselors* (3rd ed.). Needham Heights, MA: Allyn & Bacon.

Foley, M. E., Garland, E., Stimmel, B., & Merino, R. (2000). Innovative clinical addiction research training track in preventative medicine. *Substance Abuse, 21*(2), 111–119.

Gottdiener, W. H. (2008). Sexual boundary violations in residential drug-free therapeutic community treatment. *International Journal of Applied Psychoanalytic Studies, 5* (4), 257–272.

Haley, M., & Carrier, J. W. (2009). Psychotherapy groups. In D. Capuzzi, D. Gross, & M. Stauffer (Eds.) *Introduction to group work, 5th ed.* Denver Colorado: Love Publishing Company.

Harrow, B. S., Tompkins, C. P., Mitchell, P.D., Smith, K.W., Soldz, S., Kasten, L., & Fleming, K. (2006). The impact of publicly funded managed care on adolescent substance abuse treatment outcomes. The *American Journal of Drug and Alcohol Abuse, 32*, 379–398.

Hecksher, D. (2007). Former substance abusers working as counselors: A dual relationship. *Substance Use & Misuse, 42*, 1253–1268.

Hoge, M. A., Huey, L. Y., & O'Connell, M. J. (2004). Best practices in behavioral health workforce education and training. *Administration and Policy in Mental Health, 32*(2), 90–106.

Hoge, M. A., Jacobs, S., Belitsky, R., & Migdole, S. (2002). Graduate education and training for contemporary behavioral health practice. *Administration and Policy in Mental Health, 29*(4–5), 335–357.

Hollander, J. K., Bauer, S., Herlihy, B., & McCollum, V. (2006). Beliefs of board certified substance abuse counselors regarding multiple relationships. *Journal of Mental Health Counseling, 28* (1), 84–94.

Howard, J., Stubbs, M., & Arcuri, A. (2007). Comorbidity: Coexisting substance use and mental disorders in young people. *Clinical Psychologist, 11*(3), 88–97.

Huber, G. L., & Mahajan, V. K. (2008). Successful smoking cessation. *Disease Management & Health Outcomes, 16*(5), 335–343.

Ilomäki, R., Södervall, J., Ilomäki, E., Hakko, H., Räsänen, P., & The STUDY-70 Workgroup. (2008). Drug-dependent boys are more depressed compared to girls: A comorbidity study of substance dependence and mental disorders. *European Addiction Research, 14*, 161–168.

International Certification Reciprocity Consortium (IC&RC). (2010). *Credentialing*. Retrieved Jan. 2, 1010 from *http://www.icrcaoda.org/credentialing.asp*.

Jansson, L. M., Svikis, D. S., Velez, M., Fitzgerald, E., & Jones, H. (2007). The impact of managed care on drug-dependent pregnant and postpartum women and their children. *Substance Use & Misuse, 42*, 961–974.

Kaczmarek, P. (2000). Ethical and legal complexities inherent in professional roles with child and adolescent clients. *Counseling and Human Development, 33*(1), 1–24.

Kaminer, Y., & Bukstein, O. (2008). *Adolescent substance abuse: Psychiatric comorbidity and high risk behaviors.* New York, NY. New York: Taylor & Francis.

Knudsen, J. R. W., Gallon, S. L., & Gabriel, R. M. (2006). Relating substance abuse counselor background to the provision of clinical tasks. *Journal of Psychoactive Drugs, 38*(4), 473–481.

Koenig, T. L., & Crisp, C. (2008). Ethical issues in practice with older women who misuse substances. *Substance Use & Misuse, 43*, 1045–1061.

Kurita, K., & Guydish, J. (2007). Substance abuse counselor certification in California: How is nicotine addiction addressed? *Journal of Psychoactive Drugs, 39*(4), 473–477.

La Roche, M. J., & Christopher, S. (2009). Changing paradigms from empirically supported treatment to evidence based practice: A cultural perspective. *Professional Psychology: Research and practice, 40*(4), 396–402.

Larson, M. J., Zhang, A., Smith, K., & Kasten, L. (2005). Access to services: Multiple perspectives from adults with substance abuse disorders in Massachusetts. *Administration and Policy in Mental Health, 32*(4), 356–371.

Lassiter, P. S., & Chang, C. Y. (2006). Perceived multicultural competency of certified substance abuse counselors. *Journal of Addictions & Offender Counseling, 26*, 73–83.

Lilja, J., Giota, J., Hamilton, D., & Larsson, S. (2007). An example of international drug politics—The development and distribution of substance prevention programs directed at adolescents. *Substance Use & Misuse, 42*, 317–342.

Livingston, J., Holley, J., Eaton, S., Cliette, G., Savory, M., & Smith, N. (2008). Cultural competence in mental health practice. *Best Practices in Mental Health, 4*(2), 1–14.

Machado, M. P. (2005). Substance abuse treatment, what do we know? *European Journal of Health Economics, 50,* 53–64.

Madden, T. E., Graham, A. V., Lala, S., Strausner, A., Saunders, L. A., Schoener, E., Henry, R., Marcus, M. T., & Brown, R. L. (2008). Interdisciplinary benefits in project MAINSTREAM: A promising health professions educational model to address global substance abuse. *Journal of Interprofessional Care, 20*(6), 655–664.

Magnuson, S., Norem, K., & Wilcoxon, S. A. (2002). Clinical supervision for licensure: A consumer's guide. *Journal of Humanistic Counseling, Education, and Development, 41*(1), 52–60.

Mangrum, L. F., & Spence, R. T. (2008). Counselor and client characteristics in mental health versus substance abuse treatment settings providing services for co-occurring disorders. *Community Mental Health, 44,* 155–169.

Manisses Communications Group. (2005a). NAADAC and IC & RC take next step toward unification. *Alcoholism and Drug Abuse Weekly, 17*(25), 3–5.

Manisses Communications Group. (2005b). NAADAC directory of education and training. *Behavioral Healthcare Tomorrow, 14*(2), S72–83.

Master Addictions Counselor Credential. (2010). Retrieved Jan. 2, 2010, from *http://www.nbcc.org/AssetManagerFiles/apps/mac-app_T10.pdf*

McCaul, M. E., & Monti, P. M. (2003). Research priorities for alcoholism treatment. In M. Galanter, H. Begleiter, D. Lagressa, & J. P. Allen, (Eds.), *Recent developments in alcoholism, vol. 1: Research on alcoholism treatment* (pp. 405–414). New York: Kluwer Academic Publishers.

McNulty, T. L., Oser, C. B., Johnson, J. A., Knudsen, H. K., & Roman, P. M. (2007). Counselor turnover in substance abuse treatment centers: An organizational-level analysis. *Sociological Inquiry, 77*(2), 166–193.

Merta, R. J. (2001). Addictions counseling. *Counseling and Human Development, 33*(5), 1–27.

Moore, K. A., Peters, R. H., Hills, H. A., LeVasseur, J. B., Rich, A. R., Hunt, W. M., Young, M. S., & Valente, T. W. (2004). Characteristics of opinion leaders in substance abuse treatment agencies. *American Journal of Drug and Alcohol Abuse, 30*(1), 187–204.

Morgenstern, J., & McKay, J. R. (2007). Rethinking the paradigms that inform behavioral treatment research for substance use disorders. *Addictions, 102,* 1377–1389.

Mueser, K., T., & Drake, R. E. (2007). Comorbidity: What have we learned and where are we going? *Clinical Psychology: Science and Practice, 15,* 64–69.

Mustaine, B. L., West, P. L., & Wyrick. B. K. (2003). Substance abuse counselor certification requirements: Is it time for a change? *Journal of Addictions and Offender Counseling, 23*(2), 99–107.

National Association of Addiction Professionals Code of Ethics (NAADAC). (2008). *Guide to Certification.* Alexandria, VA: NAADAC.

National Institute of Drug Abuse (NIDA). (2004). *Nationwide trends.* Bethesda, MD: National Institute on Drug Abuse & National Institute of Health.

National Institute on Alcohol Abuse and Alcoholism (NIAAA). (1982, May). Development of model professional standards for counselor credentialing: A contract report. Rockville, MD: U.S. Department of Health and Human Services: Public Health Service, Alcohol, Drug Abuse, and Mental Health Administration.

National Institute on Alcohol Abuse and Alcoholism (NIAAA). (1997). Matching alcoholism treatments to client heterogeneity: Project match posttreatment drinking outcomes. *Journal of Studies on Alcohol, 58,* 7–29.

Page, R. C., & Bailey, J. B. (1995). Addictions counseling certification: An emerging counseling specialty. *Journal of Counseling and Development, 74*(2), 167–172.

Perron, B. E., Gotham, H. J., & Cho, D. (2008). Victimization among African American adolescents in substance abuse treatment. *Journal of Psychoactive Drugs, 40*(1), 67–75.

Peterson, J. V., & Nisenholz, B. (1999). *Orientation to counseling,* (4th ed.). Boston: Allyn & Bacon.

Pope, K. S., & Keith-Spiegel, P. (2008). A practical approach to boundaries in psychotherapy: Making decisions, bypassing blunders, and mending fences. *Journal of Clinical Psychology: In Session, 64*(5), 638–652.

Prochaska, J. M., Prochaska, J. O., Cohen, F. C., Gomes, S. O., Laforge, R. G., & Eastwood, A. L. (2004). The transtheoretical model of change for multi-level interventions for alcohol abuse on campus. *Journal of Drug & Alcohol Education, 47,* 34–50.

Prochaska, J. O., & DiClemente, C. C. (1984). *The transtheoretical approach: Crossing traditional boundaries of therapy.* Melbourne, FL: Krieger.

Prochaska, J. O., Fava, J. L., Norman, G. J., & Reading, C. A. (1998). Smoking cessation and stress management: Applications of the transtheoretical model of behavior change. *Homeostatis, 38,* 216–233.

Pulvermacher, A. (2007). Process improvement education with professionals in the addiction treatment field. *Adult Learning,* 22–23.

Quintero, G. A., Lilliott, E., & Willging, C. (2007). Substance abuse treatment provider's views of culture: Implications for behavioral health care in rural settings. *Qualitative Health Research, 17*(9), 1253–1267.

Rastogi, M., & Wadha, S. (2006). Substance abuse among Asian Indians in the United States: A consideration of cultural factors in etiology and treatment. *Substance Use & Misuse, 41,* 1239–1249.

Robinson, J. H., Haaz, E. J., Petrica, S. C., Hillsberg, B. S., & Kennedy, N. J. (2004). Managed care and prevention of mental health and substance abuse problems: Opportunities for growth through collaboration in the new millennium. *The Journal of Primary Prevention, 24*(3), 355–373.

Rogers, C. (1961). *On becoming a person: A therapist's view of therapy.* London, England, U.K.: Constable.

Roysircar, G. (2009). The big picture of advocacy: Counselor, heal society and thyself. *Journal of Counseling and Development, 8,* 288–294.

Saitz, R., Sullivan, L. M., & Samet, J. H. (2000). Training community-based clinicians in screening and brief interventions for substance abuse problems: Translating evidence into practice. *Substance Abuse, 21*(1), 21–31.

Salyers, K. M., Ritchie, M. H., Cochrane, W. S., & Roseman, C. P. (2006). Inclusion of substance abuse training in CACREP-accredited programs. *Journal of Addictions and Offender Counseling, 27,* 47–58.

Schuckit, M. A. (2006). Comorbidity between substance use disorders and psychiatric conditions. *Addiction, 101*(Suppl. 1), 76–88.

Scott, C. G. (2000). Ethical issues in addiction counseling. *Rehabilitation Counseling Bulletin, 43*(4), 209–214.

Scott, M., Parthasarathy, S., Kohn, C., Hinman, A., Sterling, S., & Weisner, C. (2004). Adolescents with substance diagnoses in an HMO: Factors associated with medical provider referrals to substance abuse and mental health treatment. *Mental Health Services Research, 6*(1), 46–60.

Shepard, D. S., Daley, M., Ritter, G. A., Hodgkin, D., & Beinecke, R. H. (2002). Managed care and the quality of substance abuse treatment. *The Journal of Mental Health Policy and Economics, 5*(4), 163–174.

Simotis, L., Jacobucci, R., & Houston, H. (2006). Novice, seasoned and veteran counselors' views of addiction treatment manuals: The influence of counselor characteristics on manual usefulness. *Journal of Psychoactive Drugs, 38*(4), 483–491.

Springer, J. F., Sale, E., Hermann, J., Sambrano, S., Kasim, R., & Nistler, M. (2004). Characteristics of effective substance abuse prevention programs for high-risk youth. *The Journal of Primary Prevention, 25*(2), 170–194.

Staines, G., Magura, S., Rosenblum, A., Fong, C., Kosanke, N., Foote, J., & Deluca, A. (2003). Predictors of drinking outcomes among alcoholics. *American Journal of Drug and Alcohol Abuse, 29*(1), 203–219.

Stuart, G. W., Rush, A. J., & Morris, J. A. (2002). Practice guidelines in mental health and addiction services: Contributions from the American college of mental health administration. *Administration and Policy in Mental Health, 30*(1), 21–33.

Sussman, S., Skara, S., & Ames, S. L. (2008). Substance abuse among adolescents. *Substance Use & Misuse, 43,* 1802–1828.

Timko, C., Sempel, J. M., & Moos, R. H. (2003). Models of standard and intensive outpatient care in substance abuse and psychiatric treatment. *Administration and Policy in Mental Health, 30*(5), 417–436.

Tobler, N. S., Roona, M. R., Ochshorn, P., Marshall, D. G., Streke, A. V., & Stackpole, K. M. (2000). School-based adolescent drug prevention programs: 1998 meta-analysis. *The Journal of Primary Prevention, 20,* 275–336.

Tobler, N. S., & Stratton, H. H. (1997). Effectiveness of school-based drug prevention programs: A meta-analysis of the research. *The Journal of Primary Prevention, 18,* 71–128.

Toriello, P. J., & Benshoff, J. J. (2003). Substance abuse counselors and ethical dilemmas: The influence of recovery and education level. *Journal of Addictions and Offender Counseling, 23*(2), 83–98.

Von Steen, P. G., Vacc, N. A., & Strickland, I. M. (2002). The treatment of substance-abusing clients in multiservice mental health agencies: A practice analysis. *Journal of Addictions and Offender Counseling, 22*(2), 61–82.

Walfish, S., & Barnett, J. E. (2009). To managed care or not to managed care. *Financial success in mental health practice: Essential tools and strategies for practitioners* (pp. 183–195). Washington, DC, US: American Psychological Association.

Wells, K. M., & Wells, T. D. (2007). Preventing relapse after weight loss. *American Medical Athletic Association Journal,* Spring Issue, 5–16.

White, W. L. (2008). Alcohol, tobacco, and other drug use by addictions professionals: Historical reflections and suggested guidelines. *Alcoholism Treatment Quarterly, 26*(4), 500–535.

Whittinghill, D., Whittinghill, L. R., & Loesch, L. C. (2000). The benefits of a self-efficacy approach to substance abuse counseling in the era of managed care. *Journal of Addictions and Offender Counseling, 20*(2), 64–74.

Wilson, J. L., Armoutliev, E., & Yakunina E. (2009). Practicing psychologists' reflections on evidence-based practice in psychology. *Professional Psychology: Research and Practice, 40*(4), 403–409.

Witbrodt, J., Bond, J., Kaskutas, L. A., Weisner, C., Jaeger, G., Pating, D., & Moore, C. (2007). Day hospital and residential addiction treatment: Randomized and nonrandomized managed care clients. *Journal of Consulting and Clinical Psychology, 75*(6), 947–959.

Wong, E. C., & Longshore, D. (2008). Ethnic identity, spirituality, and self-efficacy influences on treatment among Hispanic American methadone maintenance clients. *Journal of Ethnicity in Substance Abuse, 7*(3), 328–340.

Yui, K., Kajii, Y., & Nishikawa, T. (2006). Neurobiological and molecular bases of methamphetamine-induced behavioral sensitization and spontaneous recurrence of methamphetamine psychosis and its implication in schizophrenia. *Current Psychiatry Reviews, 2*(3), 381–393.

Zenmore, S. E., Mulia, N., Ye, Y., Borges, G., & Greenfield, T. K. (2008). Gender, acculturation, and other barriers to alcohol treatment utilization among Latinos in three national alcohol surveys. *Journal of Substance Abuse Treatment, 36,* 446–456.

Chapter 5

Introduction to Assessment

Mark D. Stauffer
Oregon State University, Walden University
Holly Fetter
Canisius College

David Capuzzi
Walden University, Johns Hopkins University

"I would like to get my life back together," Janelle told her counselor matter-of-factly. "It's been a hard two years since my divorce and I . . . I am probably drinking too much. I know I'm drinking too much . . . at least for me." Silence occurred as their eyes briefly met, and the counselor actively listened, providing a nonverbal presence. "I've just been kinda crazy . . . crying all the time . . . angry the rest. I'm just not as strong as I thought I was . . . or .:. as I normally am . . . I guess I just need some extra help." Janelle smiled uncomfortably and then said, "Don't get me wrong. I'm not really crazy." Mikia, replied in a warm and openly inquisitive tone, "Are you concerned about how I will view you as you share about your life and who you are?" Janelle hesitated before responding, "Yes." Her voice was vulnerable, yet clear. "Yes, I don't want to have to go to a meeting and say I'm a drunk for the rest of my whole life. I don't want to be put in a box . . . and . . . and . . . I don't want to be given a label like those other people. I am a strong person . . . maybe too strong! I just need to get back to myself."

Screening and Assessment is a critical first step in addictions treatment. As this opening session between Janelle and her counselor conveys, assessment, done correctly, can be a window into a person's life. Though often associated with "testing," assessment also includes clinical interviewing. If counselors are not trained in, experienced with, and competent in assessment, then clients will have unnoticed, marginalized, and thus untreated addiction. Many readers of this chapter may not be employed as addictions counselors nor planning to specialize in addictions counseling but will still want to know what to do when a client presents with addiction-related problems. Learning about the knowledge and skills base one must acquire to become competent as an addictions counselor is an important first step.

This is the first of two chapters in our text that focus on assessment. As we wrote this chapter, our intent was to provide an overview of the important aspects of addictions assessment, from a holistic perspective. Janelle wanted to be viewed for who she was, to be seen and accepted. Professional helpers can keep the possibilities open when they suspend judgment. One finding of Strupp's (1993) research on the therapeutic relationship was that immediate negative evaluations of clients by therapists lead to poorer outcomes. Helpers can make assessment an art form and a dance of life when we allow our view to come from an "I don't know" frame of mind. This should be seen as an introduction to addictions assessment that will benefit and inform continued learning and practice. Some instruments related to important content matter and interviewing will be discussed in this chapter; however, a more thorough examination of specific instruments used for screening and assessment will be undertaken in Chapter 6.

PHILOSOPHICAL FOUNDATIONS OF ADDICTIONS COUNSELING

Although the history, theory, and research base that informs addictions counseling is unique and different from that of other fields—for example, developmental psychology or school counseling—we believe that addictions counselors draw on similar holistic, developmental, contextual, and multicultural approaches. Our theoretical orientation as helpers affects how we work with clients. Our actions should be informed by aspirations and guiding principles. We anecdotally present a few ideas as a philosophical foundation for the assessment of clients: (1) the client and counselor must have some level of hope; (2) assets, strengths, and well being are as important as problems, challenges and unpleasant realities; (3) change occurs for the whole person (i.e., intrapersonal, interpersonal, ecological, cultural systems) rather than to part of a person; (4) client change is a process that is encouraged by intrinsic motivation even when social pressure has initiated treatment; (5) a collaborative relationship between client and counselor is essential and requires the client to take responsibility for change in his or her life; (6) counselors and their clients collaborate with and use the assets of a multidisciplinary team; and, (7) assessment may lead to advocacy.

Hope

Effective counselors encourage a sense of hope in clients, because hope is seen as a condition of successful psychotherapy (Babits, 2001; Moltu, Binder, & Nielsen, 2010; Shabad, 2001). This is also true in addictions treatment (see Sowards, O'Boyle, & Weissman, 2006). Would you work with a client if you felt you had no chance for success of any kind? Will clients be motivated to engage in recovery without hope? There are many definitions in the literature ranging from the spiritual to the mundane, e.g., behavioral coping mechanisms (see Bergin & Walsh, 2005). Dufault and Martocchio (1985) stated that hope is "characterized by a confident yet uncertain expectation of achieving a future good, which, to the hoping person, is realistically possible and personally significant" (p. 380). With some clients, especially those with treatment refractory conditions, i.e., "non-responders," we may have little hope for change or even maintenance of current status. Yet, an effective counselor must believe and cultivate what is possible. We must be good at suspending judgment that impedes growth. A good assessment should tap into what is most essential to the client's positive change beliefs.

Hope can be seen in a dichotomous way: adaptive and beneficial or maladaptive and dysfunctional. Adaptive hope manifests as proper coping skills, healthy transitions, resiliency, and acceptance. In a study examining the self-identification of those with serious mental illnesses in recovery, Buckley-Walker, Crowe, and Caputi (2010) concluded that "the more meaning, hope and direction people have, the more likely they will be able to problem solve/plan and be more actively involved in managing their own recovery" (p. 224). Conversely, maladaptive hope rests on fantasies and an underlying insistence that reality should be or should have been a certain way. Maladaptive hope impinges on normal functioning and growth and prevents a person from "engaging in life as it presents itself" (Bergin & Walsh, 2005, p. 9).

Strength-Based Approaches

Assessment includes the identification of strengths and accomplishments (Lappalainen, Savolainen, Kuorelahti, & Epstein, 2009; Substance and Mental Health Services Administration (SAMSHA), 1998a). For example, it should entail those strategies or methods that worked in the past. Strength-based approaches encourage a more holistic attitude, emphasize hopeful elements, and facilitate the development of a more comprehensive treatment plan. Cheon (2008) stated that, "The strengths perspective assumes that all consumers have positive capabilities and the capacity for success" (p. 769). Counselors assist clients to use assets and strengths while not avoiding difficult problems, challenges, and unpleasant realities. So interviewing clients is best done with a nonjudgmental orientation marked by curiosity and a matter-of-fact quality demonstrated both verbally and nonverbally. It also should take into account the specific strengths of a client's family and social support system (McIntyre, 2004; SAMSHA, 1998b).

"Strength-based assessment is defined as the measurement of those emotional and behavioral skills, competencies, and characteristics that create a sense of personal accomplishment, contribute to satisfying relationships with family members, peers, and adults, enhance one's ability to deal with adversity and stress, and promote one's personal, social and academic development."

Source: Lappalainen, Savolainen, Kuorelahti & Epstein, 2009, pp. 746–747.

A Whole Person Approach

This chapter examines assessment of the "whole" person, because those who are assessed and successfully treated for an impairing addiction will most likely draw on various internal and external resources in recovery, and change aspects of lifestyle and identity seemingly unrelated to identified addictions. Diagnostic tools and structured assessment measures have definite strengths for the helping professions, yet client strengths and contextual factors can mistakenly be overlooked by professionals when pathology is overemphasized.

The *Diagnostic and Statistical Manual* (DSM-IV-TR), now in its fourth edition and soon to appear in a revised fifth edition, is the gold standard for classifying mental health pathology in the United States (APA, 2000). For a look at potential revisions go to APA's DSM-V development site at: *http://www.dsm5.org/ProposedRevisions/Pages/Substance-RelatedDisorders.aspx.* The field of addictions relies heavily on the DSM's criteria and nomenclature for addiction-related disorders, with some marked advantages. First and foremost, it increases reliability in research, nomenclature, and clinical applications. Professionals across location and discipline can understand that certain terminology means roughly certain symptoms are occurring. Many less-noticed benefits exist as well, for example, allowing individuals and families to normalize disorders that had been previously viewed as resulting from moral inappropriateness or character failure. The DSM is also the best source currently available for classifying mental health disorders. Though similar, The ICD-10 should also be explored for its differences, as well as because of its use in other countries. For further discussion of the history and comparative nature of DSM and ICD classification systems see Saunders (2006).

The DSM has limitations, many of which are described in the preface to the manual itself. At the level of cautious examination, Berger and Luckman (1967), as well as Goffman (1961), reminded the profession that disorders are a social construct. Diagnostic terminology can unintentionally be turned into pejorative or misconstrued labels, leading to narrow views of individuals. Furthermore, the DSM categorizes disorders as specific and distinct when actually they may exist on a continuum. Although it is tempting to isolate and target problems, dysfunction affects and is affected by physical, social, cultural, emotional, spiritual, and psychological factors. Diagnosis using the DSM as a guide has a vital place in best practices for clients. It is mentioned in this section because of its importance to the field as well as its potential to be misunderstood or misused by professionals and lay people alike. When misused it often negatively impacts the holistic view of clients by increasing the use of stigmatizing labels.

Motivation

Counselors who are skilled at helping clients see the benefit of making changes in their lives precipitate the most efficacious outcomes when they encourage client motivation. We refer to motivation as both internal and external. Often clients enter treatment because of legal social controls, formal social controls (e.g. employer mandated) and informal social controls (e.g. friends, family, spouses) (Wild, 2006). Though the element of coercion or pressure may have brought a client to an assessment, a competent assessor will try to gauge these pressures and determine what intrinsic motivation exists. In a study of 300 clients seeking substance abuse treatment, Wild, Cunningham, and Ryan (2006), found that social pressures and legal referral to enter treatment, quit, and/or cut down did not affect client treatment engagement upon entry. Internal motivation may feel like pressure as well when it stems from negative self-perceptions (Tims, Leukefeld, & Platt, 2001). External pressure (i.e., saving a marriage, staying out of jail, keeping one's job) may be motivating reasons to enter treatment; however, intrinsic motivation is emphasized for greater change.

Client Collaboration in Addictions Counseling

Counselors make clear that the therapeutic process requires effort by the client for successful recovery. Ideally, clients must "work" in each counseling session and are responsible and empowered to achieve the necessary day-to-day work between sessions. Finn and Tonsager (1997) suggested a collaborative model in which counselors and clients share and explore assessment results. Whether it is a simple intake form or a more intensive assessment instrument, being on the same team is important. Many agencies will start with a self-report intake that is later followed up in person. As an example of collaboration a counselor might open with, "Janelle, I have read over the form you filled out. I want to go over it with you so that I can hear from you directly about your life. This also helps me know that my interpretation of what you wrote is what you mean." Clients are more likely to be involved and invested in the assessment process if they are treated as collaborators and it fits with their goals. Clients involved in the assessment process are more likely to give more accurate and important information, because motivation and trust levels are higher (Sattler, 1998).

Multidisciplinary Approach

Quite often, the counselor and client work in concert with other helping professionals and healthcare providers in the context of a comprehensive treatment plan. A client may gain the most from having their family therapist, addictions counselor, rehabilitation counselor and parole officer working together toward his or her desired recovery outcomes. Turning one's life around takes effort and the best outcomes often occur when clients have access to and assistance from linked professional and community supports (SAMHSA, 1996.) For example, Saitz, et al. (2005), concluded that formally linking patients during detoxification to primary medical care services improved levels of addiction severity.

Advocacy

Assessment also provides information about areas for which clients may need an advocate (Graham, Timney, Bois, & Wedgerfield, 1995). Whether in an addictions, mental health, school, or vocational rehabilitation context, an assessment may lead to client advocacy. Lewis, Lewis, Daniels and D'Andrea (2003) suggested that a client may need to be advocated for (direct advocacy) or on behalf of (indirect advocacy). A question an assessor should ask is, "In what ways does my client need advocacy?"

THE ROLE OF AN ADDICTIONS ASSESSOR

Assessment is more successful when the relevancy of the information obtained increases. Professional helpers gather information based on the role and function of their work. So, assessment goals will be different for a clinical psychiatrist, a nurse, a social worker, a nutrition specialist, a couples counselor, and a group counselor in the juvenile justice system (Sattler, 1998). SAMHSA (1998b) listed five basic objectives for the assessment of persons with substance abuse and dependence problems. See following sidebar. One might also add that the role of an assessor is to create documents useful to treatment and continuity of care. Continuity of care refers to how treatment providers (counselor, clinic, health system) are able to assist a client over time through continued contact and involvement, by coordinating care among multiple providers and by connecting them with community resources.

Five Objectives for Assessment (SAMSHA, 1998b, p. 4)

1. To identify those who are experiencing problems related to substance abuse and/or have progressed to the stage of dependency
2. To assess the full spectrum of problems for which treatment may be needed
3. To plan appropriate interventions
4. To involve appropriate family members or significant others, as needed, in the individual's treatment
5. To evaluate the effectiveness of interventions implemented

POINTS TO REMEMBER ABOUT HUMAN ASSESSMENT MEASURES

Whether it is a formal or informal method of evaluation, there are a few points to consider ensuring that an assessment is being carried out in an ethical and supportive manner.

Protect Client Welfare and Information

A client's welfare is of primary importance throughout the assessment process. Informed consent must be gained for assessment in the same way that it must be for counseling services. Counselors only release assessment results to qualified professionals in a confidential manner (Remley & Herlihy, 2010).

Be Competent to Use a Given Assessment Instrument

Counselors must know the limits of their professional competence; this includes using and interpreting results of assessment instruments. Seek proper training and exert care in the use of assessments, including circumstances where technology or testing services are employed (ACA code of ethics, 2005, E.2).

Recognize Uniqueness and Diversity

Multicultural competency is an important part of a counselor's training and ongoing practice that extends into our best practices in the realm of addiction (Arredondo et al., 1996). Knowing how culture affects assessment of addiction is important (Straussner, 2001). Principle 1 of the ethics code of the National Association of Alcohol and Drug Abuse Counselors (NAACAD)

(2008) states that, "I shall affirm diversity among colleagues or clients regardless of age gender, sexual orientation, ethnic/racial background, religious/spiritual beliefs, marital status, political beliefs, or mental/physical disability" (p. 1). Cultural differences may lead to variations in how an assessment is selected, administered, interpreted, and reported. For example, Cunningham (1994) contributed this clear point: "The cultural beliefs of a group of people are directly related to how alcohol and other drug problems are defined. The very definition of health differs by ethnicities and cultures. Therefore, it is of critical importance to understand how the members of an ethnic group define alcohol and other drug problems; what is considered to be a positive outcome; and what they feel are appropriate ways to prevent these problems from occurring" (p. viii). The ACA (2005) Code of Ethics provides this important guideline: "Counselors recognize that culture affects the manner in which clients' problems are defined" (E.5.b). For more specific ethical guidelines refer to the Standards for Multicultural Assessment (Association for Assessment in Counseling, 2003.)

WATCH OUT FOR STEREOTYPES.   There are a few ways one can be fooled by and encourage stereotypes and stigmas. First, a counselor can miss identifying substance and process addictions because a client's appearance or behavior does not fit into the counselor's beliefs about "Addicts" (Freimuth, 2005). Second, clients often enter counseling with self-identified mental health problems and have unidentified addictions because they may be using without noticeable, current, or significant impairment. Third, results and diagnosis should not be misused by describing a person according to a pathology. Referring to a client by saying "Janelle is an addict" is different than saying, "Janelle's self-report of her alcohol use fits the criteria for a diagnosis of alcohol abuse." Test results are like the moon's reflection in the water; we know of the moon, but to point to the reflection and say, "that is the moon" falls short. Reverence for the mystery and unknown possibilities of each person is important. Using terms like "tendency" and "probability" as a practice may aid our suspension of judgment, allowing us to explore and experiment with the main goal of addictions counseling: to help our client who, like a mountain, may appear different depending on where one stands to view.

BE TRUE TO THE INITIAL DESIGN AND PURPOSE OF THE INSTRUMENT.   Counselors should use screening and assessment instruments in the way they were designed to be used. For example, was the tool made to screen for addiction or measure the severity of an addiction? Know what a measure can or cannot indicate. Counselors must ascertain whether or not the instrument selected for assessment purposes will provide the information needed for the development of a treatment plan and the process of counseling.

Keep Empathic Connection Alive

"Develop and maintain empathic connections with clients" when assessing (Finn & Tonsager, 1997, p. 378). Often initial interviews can feel mechanical, choppy, and disconnected from the client, not to mention unrelated to matters that feel most pressing. Maintain a therapeutic environment by explaining the nature of the interview process so the client can have a positive frame of reference for probing. Here is an example: "Janelle, I want to ask you some questions so that I can better get to know who you are; these questions help me understand the range of your life experience, which will make the counseling process more successful."

Use Multiple Methods

Utilizing multiple sources and methods in assessment will help the counselor gather a more useful body of evidence for treatment. A detailed interview helps the counselor know what areas need further inquiry. If too much or too little information is gathered it may cost both the client and counselor. For example, making a diagnosis on the basis of a screening device alone will be insufficient and unethical; gathering a lot of information on non-relevant topics may waste valuable time that could be used for treatment. To save resources and provide the best care, it is better to rely on several sources of information and utilize a multidisciplinary approach. As a short case example, Brian told his counselor he was "working hard" in treatment and maintaining his goals of "being clean." After a positive urinalysis test and further discussion with his counselor, it was clear that Brian had lapsed, but didn't want to vocalize his "failure" and "disappoint" his counselor. As multiple sources of information are gathered, discrepancies may arise that help shed light on what is occurring for the client. Resolve such discrepancies in collaboration with clients (SAMHSA, 2008).

Continue to Assess Over Time and in Relation to Stage of Treatment

Assessment is an ongoing process. Different types of information are gathered in context at different stages of change and recovery. For example, a client who is currently intoxicated or in withdrawal may be assessed for placement into the most appropriate care to monitor detoxification and manage withdrawal (Mee-Lee et al., 2001). In contrast, assessment of a client just leaving inpatient treatment might focus on the recovery environment and use related contextual factors (e.g., internal triggers, expectations related to use) that might help prevent relapse (Donovan & Marlatt, 2005).

Be Skilled When Communicating About Assessment Procedures and Results

Most clients have little understanding of psychological testing. Encourage client education at all stages of the assessment process. Counselors interpret or "translate" in easy to understand terminology. Results are also interpreted in the most accurate way possible while considering a client's explicit understanding. Counselors share with clients what an assessment clearly does and does not indicate (see Sattler, 1998, Chapter 1).

Explore results that are already known and accepted by the client's worldview and reality first, especially when clients are unsure or anxious. Assessments should support a feeling and belief that clients "do know" much about their inner and outer worlds. Finn and Tonsager (1997) noted that one motive for participation in the assessment process is *self-verification*. Self-verification occurs when one's reality and concept of self is affirmed.

Finally, clients may be more receptive to assessment results around addiction when it is done in conjunction with other non-addiction related information (e.g., health, career, family systems). So, the assessment process may be more productive when it connects to the breadth of a client's life and relates to his or her life goals, worldview, and values (Dimeff et al., 2000).

FLOW OF ADDICTIONS ASSESSMENT

Assessment starts the moment a client walks through the door or contacts the office for an appointment. It is part of an ongoing process and occurs before, during, and after treatment; therefore, assessment may help with referral, diagnosis, strength identification, or therapeutic outcome evaluations at any stage of change. There are several multistage models for assessment (see Allen & Mattson, 1993; Tarter, 1990). Screening is usually the first appraisal step and may

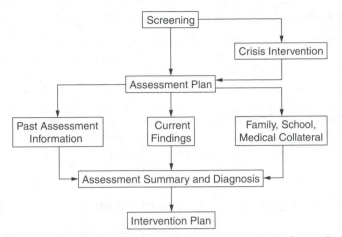

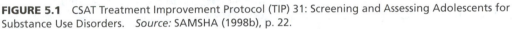

FIGURE 5.1 CSAT Treatment Improvement Protocol (TIP) 31: Screening and Assessing Adolescents for Substance Use Disorders. *Source:* SAMSHA (1998b), p. 22.

signify the need for immediate crisis intervention (see Figure 5.1). If screening does not indicate the need for crisis intervention, and indicates the need for more comprehensive assessment, then a plan for assessment is collaboratively made with the client. After a plan is created, a more comprehensive evaluation is initiated. The "multiple assessment approach" is preferred (SAMHSA, 1998b, p. 19). A comprehensive assessment will include multiple strategies to arrive at a summary of findings and hypotheses which will then direct intervention. With assessment comes a clearer picture for how intervention might occur.

An assessment may include referral to various treatment modalities: detoxification and stabilization, outpatient treatment, intensive outpatient treatment, partial hospitalization, outpatient programs, inpatient residential rehabilitation, or treatment groups (Johnson, 2003). The American Society of Addiction Medicine (ASAM) created a protocol, Patient Placement Criteria Second Volume Revised (PPC-2R), that is widely used to help place clients into an appropriate addictions treatment setting by assessing their level of care needs (Mee-Lee et al., 2001). The PPC was first created through consensus by a multidisciplinary team in the 1980s. Its main goal was to find a national set of criteria for placement to encourage "assessment-based, clinically driven and outcomes-oriented continuity of care" (Mee-Lee, 2005, p. 32). See Chapter 15, "Persons with Disabilities and Addictions," for a more in-depth look at this system.

Screening

Screening is often the first step in the evaluation process. Screening may be seen as a tool for spotting "red flags," a way to indicate that a more comprehensive assessment is needed (Kaminer, 2008). Screening is defined as "the process through which a counselor, client and available significant others determine the most appropriate initial course of action, given the client's needs and characteristics, and the available resources within the community" (SAMHSA, 1998a, p. 29). The process of screening leads the counselor to (1) rule out addiction, (2) request a more comprehensive assessment, or (3) refer for treatment with ongoing assessment. It may also make apparent imminent crises and the need for immediate intervention.

Crisis Intervention

An assessment may be temporarily delayed by impending crises that need to be responded to. Counselors should know what constitutes crises and what steps one should take for the most critical types of crises. Effective counselors know how to identify and intervene when suicidality, homicidality, life-threatening abuse, domestic violence, psychosis, and acute physical illness are present. Sometimes this means seeking immediate help from other professionals. This may involve crafting a more in-depth suicide intervention plan. Nonetheless, as a professional necessity, carefully log and record critical incidences for counselor and client safety, but also for self-reflecting on one's intervention as a counselor (Remley, & Herlihy, 2010).

OPERATIONALIZING ASSESSMENT INTERVIEWS

Gathering information becomes more successful as three qualities increase: reliability, validity, and relevancy. Reliability can be seen as the consistency of the assessment; a measure with high reliability will provide the same results when administered repeatedly. Validity is the correctness or accuracy of the information; a measure with high validity measures what it intends to measure (e.g., depression scale accurately measures depression and not anxiety.) Lastly, relevance in assessment is about collecting information efficiently and effectively; a relevant measure obtains the most essential data.

Structured, Semi-structured, and Unstructured Interviews

Assessment interviews can be placed on a continuum based on their structure. Here we will look at assessment interviews as falling into three categories: unstructured, semi-structured, and structured (see Sattler, 1998). These three types have advantages and disadvantages.

Unstructured interviews allow the client to more freely share experience, which may help build initial rapport with the counselor and allow resistance to be addressed. This format also allows the clinician to divert and probe into areas that arise during the interview. Both assessor and client can initiate discussion items and questions. The level or type of language of an unstructured interview can be adjusted to meet the knowledge, skills, and development of the client. One is also able to examine complicated processes, meanings behind behaviors, beliefs, in-depth examples, and the "rich" narrative of a client's story related to addiction and recovery. Time efficiency, the ability to generalize, and the potential to over-assess certain areas at the expense of others are limitations.

Semi-structured interviews provide a framework for addictions counselors to use while still allowing a sophisticated clinician to pursue areas of important client information and disclosure not addressed by a structured assessment tool. Often a designated list of open questions guides the interviewer. During a semi-structured exam, a counselor may be able to stop the content of a session to deal with resistance or increase rapport.

Structured interviews are instruments that optimize reliability and validity, with the intent of limiting assessor bias. Items are constructed with specific outcomes in mind (i.e., substance use identification), so wording of items are asked exactly as provided without interplay between counselor and client. This aids quantitative research. Language cannot be adjusted to increase clarity and comprehension. Structured interviews, in general, are time efficient, but may fall short when rapport problems or resistance arises. Structured interviews may need advanced training or certification specifically for the measure (Sattler, 1998).

Components of an Interview

A clinical interview takes into consideration many relevant components. Various protocols can be used to plan a course for information gathering. Here are ten steps that a counselor may want to follow when interviewing a client:

1. Review referral information
2. Obtain and review previous evaluations
3. Interview the client
4. Gather corroborating material (e.g., family interview)
5. Formulate hypothesis
6. Make recommendations
7. Create a report and other significant documents
8. Meet with the client over results
9. Meet with the support system of the client
10. Follow up on recommendations and referrals

Assessment Dimensions Related to Level of Care

Assessment often occurs in relationship to a client's treatment stage and level of care placement. Mee-Lee (2005) highlights six dimensions of assessment for determining level of care and treatment placement: (1) Acute Intoxication and Withdrawal Potential (e.g., detox and withdrawal management); (2) Biomedical Conditions and Complications (i.e., assess physical health conditions and their impact to addiction); (3) Emotional, Behavioral, and Cognitive Conditions and Complications (e.g., parasuicidal behavior, co-occuring disorders); (4) Readiness for Change (also readiness for treatment); (5) Relapse Prevention and Continued Use or Problem Potential (e.g., Contextual issues—internal and external cues, expectancy, triggers, treatment response); and (6) Recovery Environment (e.g., family, peers, work and vocation, legal, housing, financial, culture, transportation, child-care) (p. 2). Many of these areas of assessment will be highlighted in the following section.

GATHERING BACKGROUND AND CONTEXTUAL INFORMATION

Interviews and other assessment tools allow for an understanding of client strengths and weakness, as well as for a picture of the course, context, and current state of an addictive substance disorder or practice. As noted in Figure 5.1, we can compartmentalize information into three categories: previously gathered assessment information, current findings (i.e., information from the present assessment), and collateral information, (information that is gained from others besides the client, e.g., justice department, school, hospital, family) (SAMHSA, 1998b).

In compiling a comprehensive report, one obtains a variety of information. The first type of information for an addictions assessment is basic demographics (e.g., name, address, DOB) and other significant information. This should include essential healthcare contacts and insurance provider policy information. In a study of 36,081 injection drug users (IDUs), Chassler, Lundgren, and Lonsdale (2006) found that those with private health insurance were much more likely to seek more frequent treatment. The second type of information relates to client presentation and current functioning. A mental status exam is an example of a useful aid in examining presentation. A comprehensive assessment should also include information about current addictive behavior and use, past periods of addictive behavior and use, and contextual patterns of addiction such as internal triggers, expectations of use and consequences related to addiction (e.g. legal problems, medical complications)(Johnson, 2003).

Finally, the fourth category addresses treatment specific assessment information: past treatment experience, treatment outcome expectations, motivation for treatment, readiness for change, and current reasons for seeking counseling are examples of treatment specific assessment information (SAMHSA, 1998a, 1998b). Finally, an inventory of necessary and supportive information allows for a more holistic perspective. Included in this fourth category are psychosocial factors such as peer relationships, cultural contexts, family systems, and life skills (e.g., coping skills); and work, career, and spirituality.

Client Presentation and Functioning

Observing the presentation of a client provides information about overall functioning and can indicate long-term and current substance use. Presentation and functioning should be assessed on an ongoing basis. Performing a mental status exam (MSE) is one way to document client presentation and functioning. In a typical MSE, observations are made of five basic areas: sensory and cognitive function, thinking, perception, feeling and behavior, and physical appearance. Some kinds of information gathered in an MSE requires only observation, while others require some form of probing dialogue and questioning. There are many derivations of a mental status exam. See Figure 5.2 for an example of MSE categories. If you are new to doing MSEs, it may be a good practice to familiarize yourself with one by filling out elements of a mental status exam sheet after each counseling session, or after role plays or counseling videos. With practice, a counselor becomes habituated to observing these attributes.

Skilled counselors become accustomed to the physiological symptoms that are associated with addiction. How does a particular drug affect one's overall appearance (needle marks, abscesses, dilated pupils), behavior (staggered walking), speech (pressured, fast), attention (lacks focus)? We learn to screen for symptoms of use, withdrawal, and toxicity for different psychoactive substances which will affect functioning such as memory, attention, and executive functions (Lundqvist, 2005). This implies a familiarization with the effects of substances when used alone as well as in combination with other drugs (SAMHSA, 1998a). Inaba and Cohen's (2007) *Uppers, Downers and All Arounders: Physical and Mental Effects of Psychoactive Drugs* is an excellent text directed at drug presentation.

Examine the case below, which focuses on presentation. Use the MSE example in Figure 5.2 and your understanding of addictions to answer the following question: What elements of her mental status can you roughly determine about Tricia? Which elements might you want to rule out if you were counseling this client?

It was a scorching hot summer day. Tricia, a 22-year-old woman, had become homeless in the last year. She seemed a little disoriented as she slowly walked into the lobby for her scheduled first appointment with the counselor, who had just come out. She made eye contact and gave a candid and cordial greeting. Her eyelids were drooping slightly. Her pupils were constricted to the size of pinpoints. Her eyes did not appear to dilate as she moved out of the brightly lit lobby. Her clothes were well kept and she was well groomed. She didn't smell of smoke or alcohol. Tricia was wearing a long sleeved shirt with the logo of her favorite punk band on it. She seemed a bit tired, but commented on the hot day and how exhausted it made her feel. After making a joke about being homeless, she requested some time to get a drink and sit down for a minute, explaining that the heat had affected her. She reclined in the chair and dozed off briefly, only to revive a moment later for another sip. The counselor commented in a warm manner, "Looks like you could doze off right in that chair."

"I could use a nap," she replied. She paused, closing her eyes, then looked at the counselor with a slight smile. "I really wanted to talk about my housing situation, but maybe I am too tired today."

Category	Example or Sub-Category
Appearance	grooming, health, age, care/type of clothes
Behavior	psychomotor activity, posture, gait, eye contact
Attitude (in relation to examiner)	cooperative, aggressive, passive
Speech	tone (melancholic), articulation, volume (loud), rate (pressured, slow), language (lisp)
Affect (displayed reaction)	flat, labile, blunted, restricted; appropriate and inappropriate
Mood (underlying feeling state)	sad, euphoric, angry
Attention (arousal)	concentrated, focused, distractible
Form of thought (FOT)	rumination, word salad, tangential, blocking
Content of thought (COT)	fixations, irrational thought, suicidality, homicidality
Perception	hallucinations-false sensory perception, illusions-false perception of external object
Memory	remote memory, recent memory, immediate recall
Orientation	person, place and time, altered orientation usually starts effects in order of time, then place, then person
Intellectual Functioning	calculation, abstraction, knowledge, construction
Insight	emotional insight, intellectual insight
Judgment	appropriate for a situation, reasoning
Reading and writing	level, ability

FIGURE 5.2   Example of MSE Categories

CURRENT AND PAST USE AND ADDICTIVE BEHAVIORS.   A comprehensive assessment should include information about current and past use and addictive behaviors. Details of the last day, week, month, or two-year period can be useful in determining addiction severity, variability, and patterns. An in-depth interview will require time to explore common substance and process-related addictions. A more comprehensive interview might inquire about a list of commonly used substances. For example, the Composite International Diagnostic Interview (CIDI-Core) is used to document several types of substances used, duration, severity, amount used, methods used (e.g., inhaling, IV use), patterns of addiction (e.g., frequency, periods of abstinence, last use), preferred addiction or substance, motivation for change on each substance and process, associated beliefs and attributed meanings, as well as benefits and consequences (Robins, et al., 1989). Such an interview is structured to obtain an accurate picture of the daily addiction process or substance use of the client for treatment purposes.

Sometimes a history is gathered on a single substance or addiction. For example, the Time-Line Followback for Alcohol (TFLB-Alcohol) is used for determining a current use history of alcohol (Roy et al., 2008; Sobell & Sobell, 1992). The Alcohol TFLB provides a picture of the severity, variability, and extent of consumption over the past 7 days to 2 years depending on how far one wants to go back. A calendar and important dates such as holidays are used as memory aids (Sobell & Sobell). Roy et al. recommended that the Quick Drinking Screen (QDS) be used in place of the TFLB when detailed drinking data was not necessary or possible to obtain.

A counselor can also assign as homework a log to track ongoing use. The idea is for a client to track items such as the amounts, triggers, urges, circumstances, and concurrent thoughts and feelings for specific times of use. This method not only provides an excellent picture of the patterns of addiction, but allows the client to increase awareness through consistent self-monitoring. Such self-monitoring may also help to counteract the limitations of retrospective assessments. See NOVA Southeastern University's Center for Psychological Studies online resource at *http://www.nova.edu/gsc/online_files.html* for examples of such logs.

FIRST EXPOSURE AND SUBSEQUENT EXPOSURE.   Probing into the first exposure to and subsequent pattern of addiction may reveal key information about the nature of a person's addiction. Early onset may indicate problems in a client's development (Newcomb, 1997). Did the client begin to abuse alcohol after a traumatic event at age 31 or did he or she start using at age 12 at a neighbor's home? Early age onset of use of tobacco, alcohol, and other drugs is a risk factor for alcohol and drug abuse and dependence; subsequent use of other illicit drugs; high risk and delinquent behavior; and instability of employment (Jackson et al., 2002; Johnson & Mott, 2001).

THE CONTEXT OF USE AND ADDICTIVE BEHAVIOR.   Simply put, a contextual analysis ascertains the immediate environment within which use and process addictions occur. Knowing the proximal precipitants of addiction allows clinicians and clients to enhance awareness of the addictive process in both obvious and subtle ways, but also provides information valuable for preventing lapses and relapse (Donovan & Marlatt, 2005). See the following sidebar for items considered in a contextual analysis.

What you need to know for contextual analysis of substance use:

- Expectations of use (e.g., relaxation, better social interactions, sleeping better, etc.)
- Internal triggers for use (e.g., emotions, thoughts, withdrawal, craving, etc.)
- External triggers for use (e.g., people, places, seeing needles, music, etc.)
- Immediate reinforcers (e.g., escaping or feeling relaxed or high)
- Positive aspects of use (e.g., make friends, be "cool," feel good, etc.)
- Negative aspects of use (e.g., expense, hangover, interpersonal problems, etc.)

Source: Substance and Mental Health Services Administration. (2008). Integrated dual disorders treatment workbook. *CSAT Evidenced-based Practices*, Rockville: MD. Author.

INTERNAL AND EXTERNAL TRIGGERS.   Part of the contextual aspect of addiction assessment is the examination of internal and external triggers (SAMHSA, 2008), or cues, that are connected to neurological pathways of reward, memory, motivation, and control; and can induce lapses, relapse, and high risk behavior. Triggers encourage seeking, impulsive drug use, and strong craving. In order to prevent relapse, those in recovery must develop an awareness of and a fortifying response to their most salient triggers (Stippikohl et al., 2010).

NEGATIVE CONSEQUENCES AND POSITIVE ASPECTS.   Client observation and contemplation of adverse consequences and positive aspects of use can often be the catalyst for change. While consequences of addictive behaviors may coincide with the high-risk behaviors discussed below, they may also reflect less harmful but negative effects of addiction. Discrepancies between a client's goals, values, and feelings and the disadvantages of addiction provide good material for contemplation. It can be helpful to use an inventory that allows a client to place "pros and cons" side by side to contemplate choices and aid in decision making. Janis and Mann (1977) created a decisional balance sheet which is commonly used for this type of exercise. Often clients will experience physical dysfunction (blackouts, feeling ill), relationship problems (marital turmoil, divorce), intrapersonal consequences (low self-esteem, feelings of guilt or inadequacy), loss of resources (unpaid rent, debt to bookies, legal expenses, burned bridges within their support system, cost of a thousand packs of cigarettes after 3 years), unpleasant moods (lack of motivation, depression), social and legal problems (being fired/expelled, DUI charges, loss of friendships, missed opportunities), and loss of control (strong cravings, social alienation, blackouts and other embarrassing behavior (Johnson, 2003). Client awareness of negative consequences can precipitate increased readiness for change (Shealy, Murphy, Borsari, & Correia, 2007).

EXPECTANCY.   Along with the consequences and positive aspects of actual addiction, a key area to explore is a client's expectations or beliefs about the outcome of use (Grotmol et al., 2010). What are some of the perceived benefits of gambling, alcohol use, or "recreational" popping of prescription drugs? Expectations related to the perceived outcomes of using and/or quitting a substance or addictive process may be part of a contextual assessment. For example, the Alcohol Expectancy Questionnaire (AEQ) examines how a client might expect to gain certain effects as a result of alcohol consumption: sexual enhancement, positive global changes in experience, social and physical pleasure, ability to be assertive, arousal/interpersonal power, and relaxation/tension reduction (Brown, Christiansen, & Goldman, 1987). Another example of an expectancy questionnaire is the Alcohol and Drug Consequences Questionnaire (ADCQ) which has two subscales related to costs and benefits of quitting (Cunningham et al., 1997).

TREATMENT SPECIFIC ASSESSMENT INFORMATION

Readiness for Change

Motivation has been a focal point of much research in the field of substance addiction, due to the contributions of Miller and Rollnick (2002). One factor related to motivation is readiness for change, defined as a willingness to engage with the recovery process to alter one's life (Prochaska, DiClemente, & Norcross, 1992). The Readiness to Change Questionnaire (RTCQ) is one standardized assessment tool that can be used to better understand where a client might be at in the first three stages of change (Rollnick, Heather, Gold, & Hall, 1992). De Leon (1995) notes that those who are ready to change may often want to take measures that do not include treatment. For this reason, De Leon presented the term "readiness for treatment" to distinguish the difference. One instrument that assesses level of motivation to change is the Stages of Change Readiness and Treatment Eagerness Scales (SOCRATES) (Miller & Tonigan, 1996). Readiness for change constructs are used to help a counselor understand where a client is in the recovery process and how one might intervene at that stage. Stages of change will be highlighted in Chapter 7, "Motivational Interviewing."

Prior Treatment Related to Addiction

During an interview, counselors should find out if a client has experienced counseling and addictions treatment in the past. Basic information should be gathered: dates and location of treatment, modality of treatment, length of time in treatment, reasons for exiting and effect of treatment on use. If there have been previous treatment efforts, a release of information from the client may be requested, in order to help corroborate current findings.

Counselors should also be sensitive to the feelings clients have about past therapeutic relationships. Because the therapeutic alliance rests on rapport, a counselor may have to address treatment resistance if negative associations and beliefs exist about the addiction treatment process. Asking about prior counseling or treatment during the assessment may unveil important information about the client's fears and hopes and what has worked for him or her in the past. Client treatment expectancy is a contributing factor in therapeutic outcomes (see Asay & Lambert, 1999). Encouraging a client in this way not only cultivates rapport and but is fertile ground to discuss growth resulting from the interpersonal process of counseling.

Other Background Information

Understanding a client's lived experience helps to determine how distressed and impaired he or she actually is and what treatment modalities and strengths are available. In one study of clients seeking treatment, social stability was a factor in continued abstinence after an intensive outpatient program (Bottlender & Soyka, 2005). This chapter mentions several key psychosocial components related to the recovery environment; however, there are many others that influence addiction, including the realm of psychosocial disorders.

Family Systems and Peer Relationships

In addition to family transmission or heritable influences of substance disorders (Agrawal, & Lynskey, 2008), families and close peers influence the history, use, treatment, and recovery of clients (Tobler et al, 2000; Williams, 1987). They are often a significant factor in the recovery environment. Information can be taken about the lifestyle and addictive behaviors of family members and significant others, including spouses, cohabiting partners, housemates, and close peers. A counselor may directly interview a spouse, certain family members, and/or peers to gain collateral information (Miller, 1999). Adverse childhood events (ACEs) (i.e., childhood abuse, domestic violence, household dysfunction) are risk factors for addiction (Douglas et al., 2010). Dube et al. (2003) studied a cohort of 8613 participants and found that individuals with five or more ACEs reported greater levels of illicit drug use and addiction by 7–10 times. An in-depth inquiry into important client relationships may also shed light on how addiction is impacted by family roles, rituals, values, expectations, parenting styles, family grief and loss, power structures, pain and emotion management, boundaries, and communication in these relationships and relational systems. See Chapter 14 on interventions with families and couples for a more in depth look of this topic.

Peer influence and social networks and their relationship to and attitudes about addiction can increase risk or provide protection (Costenbader, Astone, & Latkin, 2006; Marlatt & Witkiewitz, 2009). Intimate and group relationships are often responsible for the initiation process into substance use (Draus & Carlson, 2006). Peers who use and offer drugs and engage in addictive behaviors place a person at higher risk for similar behavior. Likewise, peers that have attitudes and beliefs in opposition to substance use and addictive behaviors can be a protective factor (Chang, et al., 2006). These same peer groups and intimate relationships can aid or hinder the treatment and recovery process.

HIGH RISK BEHAVIOR.   High risk behavior is often seen in conjunction with addictive behaviors (Calsyn et al., 2010; Sexton, Carlson, Leukefeld, & Booth, 2006). High risk behaviors may include theft to procure drugs. Many stores have incorporated a policy of locking up batteries and cigarettes because of the large quantity of theft of these items, which are easy to sell on the street. Other drug-dependent persons resort to selling drugs to prevent withdrawal, which increases legal problems and safety risks.

High risk sex may also be a factor, whether unprotected sex when intoxicated, or prostitution for drugs or drug money (Gilchrist, Cameron, & Scoular, 2005). Driving and interpersonal violence may also be an ongoing risk of alcohol and drug use (Burke, 2005). Illicit IV drug use has serious associated health risks (e.g., HIV, Hepatitis B and C). Assessment explores whether or not IV drug use is done with clean needles, driving occurs during intoxication, or sexual activity and abuse happens as a result of intoxication or during blackouts. The assessment ascertains whether there are patterns of high risk behavior that should be addressed by some form of harm reduction intervention.

COPING SKILLS.   Assessing life skills, such as coping skills, assertive communication, social skills, problem solving, and self-efficacy, may also be part of a comprehensive assessment (Bowen et al., 2009; Tobler et al., 2000). Assessing a person's ability to cope with life stressors may be useful in choosing interventions related to relapse prevention (Anderson, Ramo, & Brown, 2006), because coping strategies help those in recovery deal with internal and external triggers (Cleveland & Harris, 2010). Coping strategies may include behavioral and cognitive strategies directed toward problem solving to eliminate or modify problem conditions. For example, "I plan my day so that I head directly to my AA and GA meetings, instead of hanging out after work where I might be tempted to drink and play video poker." Coping strategies that are cognitive in nature may help to perceptually control problematic experiences. Here successful coping may be found in the ways that individuals frame experience: "I experienced a lapse, but this is part of the recovery process and not the end of the world." Other strategies may be useful in helping a person eliminate, reduce, or manage emotional consequences by, for example, reducing, avoiding, or suppressing emotional stimuli (Pearlin & Schooler, 1978).

WORK AND VOCATION.   A client's career and life planning and the realities of "making a living" are important in the recovery process (Graham, 2006). Employment affects treatment outcomes and may be challenged by the treatment process. Vocation is relevant to every part of treatment (SAMHSA,1996). Consider, for example, the treatment choices available to a full-time employee who is the main income provider for a family of four. Will he or she be able to go to intensive inpatient treatment and still provide for the family?

The vocational component of a comprehensive assessment may look at current and past employment status, job satisfaction, employment skills, personal financial assets, employer benefits, employer programs related to addiction, client's feelings in relationship to his current employment position, how levels of treatment care affect employment needs, and employer knowledge. Other vocational information that may be important to an assessment include, but are not limited to: relapse triggers related to career and vocation, the presence of vocational resources within treatment programs, short-term goals and strategies for employment, necessary resources to make employment feasible (i.e., child care, transportation), and client knowledge of local employment and vocational services. For more specific information on the topic of vocation and addictions refer to SAMHSA's (2000) Treatment Intervention Protocol (TIP) 38 entitled *Integrating Substance Abuse Treatment and Vocational Services.*

SPIRITUALITY.   Considerable research has correlated spirituality to mental and physical health and overall well-being, thus meriting its inclusion into counseling (Bergin, 1988; Reinert & Bloomingdale, 1999). It has been found by millions to be important to recovery. Conner et al. (2009) found that treatment-seeking participants with high or increasing spirituality measurement scores had significantly fewer days of substance use (i.e., heroine, crack cocaine) than those with low or decreasing scores. Though this may be the case, spirituality is a factor that is often difficult to define, frequently misunderstood, and not assessed for by mental health professionals (Larson & Larson, 2003; Tisdell, 2000). Spirituality in addictions treatment may immediately bring to mind Alcoholics

Anonymous (AA) groups and a 12-step path to recovery. Furthermore, many clients connect their spirituality with a particular religion or traditional belief. Some clients may respond by saying, "I don't attend church" when asked about spirituality. Reframing may be necessary to address the idea that spirituality has many manifestations. Research literature suggests that clients want their counselors to address spirituality in counseling (Brown, 2004), including addictions related counseling (Goldfarb et al., 1996). Questions related to spirituality should consider that many definitions and paths exist. Is it appropriate to refer or recommend a client to a traditional AA meeting without discussing spirituality? Consider an atheist who does not identify with a "higher power." Spirituality can be an important avenue in the recovery process. The assessment can delve into how a person's religious and spiritual beliefs and practices might aid the client in treatment (Mackinnon, 2004).

Summary and Some Final Notations

Multistage assessment is an integral part of an addictions treatment and recovery process. Initial and ongoing assessment allows a counselor to build rapport and gather vital information about a client's lived experience and relationship to addiction and substance use disorder. There are many factors that contribute to a client's ability to make positive change. Due to the complexity of circumstances and unique differences of each individual and the systems within which they exist, assessment is best done in an orderly and relevant manner that allows a client to collaborate with a team of helpers to realize a better quality of life and sense of well-being.

Useful Web Sites

The following Web sites provide additional information relating to the chapter topics:

Association for Assessment in Counseling (AAC)
Standards for multicultural assessment link
http://aac.ncat.edu/resources.html

NIAAA—Information on Alcohol Measures
(i.e., TFLB, Form 90, QF measures)
http://pubs.niaaa.nih.gov/publications/Assesing%20Alcohol/ measures.htm

Substance Abuse and Mental Health Services Administration
List of free publication series
https://ncadistore.samhsa.gov/catalog/pubseries.aspx

SAMHSA Treatment Improvement Protocols
e.g., TIP 31 Teen Assessment, TIP 42 Co-occurring Disorders
https://ncadistore.samhsa.gov/catalog/results.aspx?h= publications&topic= 103

University of Washington University: Substance Use Screening & Assessment Instruments Database
http://lib.adai.washington.edu/instruments/glossary.htm

References

Agrawal, A., & Lynskey, M. (2008). Are there genetic influences on addiction? Evidence from family, adoption and twin studies. *Addiction, 103*(7), 1069–1081. doi:10.1111/j.1360–0443.2008.02213.x

Allen, J. P., & Mattson, M. E. (1993). Psychometric instruments to assist in alcoholism treatment planning. *Journal of Substance Abuse Treatment, 10,* 289–296.

American Counseling Association. (2005). *ACA code of ethics.* Alexandria, VA: Author.

American Psychiatric Association. (2000). *DSM-IV-TR: Diagnostic and statistical manual of mental disorders, text revised.* Washington, DC: Author.

Association for Assessment in Counseling. (2003). *Standards for multicultural assessment.* Alexandria, VA: American Counseling Association.

Anderson, K. G., Ramo, D. E., & Brown, S. A. (2006). Life stress, coping and comorbid youth: An examination of the stress-vulnerability model for substance relapse. *Journal of Psychoactive Drugs. 38*(3), 255–262.

Arredondo, P., Toporek, R., Brown, S. P., Jones, J., Locke, D. C., Sanchez, J., & Stadler, H. (1996). Operationalization of the multicultural counseling competencies. *Journal of Multicultural Counseling and Development, 24*, 42–78.

Asay, T. P., & Lambert, M. J. (1999). The Empirical case for the common factors in therapy: Quantitative findings. In M. A. Hubble, B. L. Duncan, and S. D. Miller (eds.) *The heart and soul of change: What works in therapy*, pp. 33–56. Washington, DC: American Psychological Association.

Babits, M. (2001). The phoenix juncture: Exploring the dimensions of hope in psychotherapy. *Clinical Social Work Journal, 29*(4), 341–350.

Berger, P. L., & Luckman, T. (1967). *The social construction of reality*. NY: Doubleday-Anchor.

Bergin, A. E. (1988). Three contributions of a spiritual perspective to counseling, psychotherapy, and behavior change. *Counseling and Values, 33*, 21–31.

Bergin, L., & Walsh, S. (2005). The role of hope in psychotherapy with older adults. *Aging and Mental Health, 9*(1), 7–15.

Bottlender, M., & Soyka, M. (2005). Efficacy of an intensive outpatient rehabilitation program in alcoholism: Predictors of outcome 6 months after treatment. *European Addiction Research, 11*(3), 132–137.

Bowen, S., Chawla, N., Collins, S., Witkiewitz, K., Hsu, S., Grow, J., et al. (2009). Mindfulness-based relapse prevention for substance use disorders: a pilot efficacy trial. *Substance Abuse: Official Publication of the Association For Medical Education and Research in Substance Abuse, 30*(4), 295–305.

Brown, S. A., Christiansen, B. A., & Goldman, M. S. (1987). The alcohol expectancy questionnaire: An instrument for the assessment of adolescent and adult alcohol expectancies. *Journal of Studies on Alcohol, 48*, 483–491.

Buckley-Walker, K., Crowe, T., & Caputi, P. (2010). Exploring identity within the recovery process of people with serious mental illnesses. *Psychiatric Rehabilitation Journal, 33*(3), 219–227.

Burke, P. J. (2005). Adolescent substance use: Brief interventions by emergency care providers. *Pediatric Emergency Care, 21*(11), 770–776.

Calsyn, D., Cousins, S., Hatch-Maillette, M., Forcehimes, A., Mandler, R., Doyle, S., et al. (2010). Sex under the influence of drugs or alcohol: Common for men in substance abuse treatment and associated with high-risk sexual behavior. *American Journal on Addictions, 19*(2), 119–127.

Chang, F. C., Lee, C. M., Lai, H. R., Chiang, J. T., Lee, P. H., & Chen, W. J. (2006). Social influences and self-efficacy as predictors of youth smoking initiation and cessation: A 3-year longitudinal study of vocational high school students in Taiwan. *Addiction, 101*(11), 1645–1655.

Chassler, D., Lundgren, L., & Lonsdale, J. (2006). What factors are associated with high-frequency drug treatment use among a racially and ethnically diverse population of injection drug users? *American Journal on Addictions, 15*(6), 440–449.

Cheon, J. (2008). Best practices in community-based prevention for youth substance reduction: towards strengths-based positive development policy. *Journal of Community Psychology, 36*(6), 761–779.

Cleveland, H., & Harris, K. (2010). The role of coping in moderating within-day associations between negative triggers and substance use cravings: A daily diary investigation. *Addictive Behaviors, 35*(1), 60–63.

Conner, B., Anglin, M., Annon, J., & Longshore, D. (2009). Effect of religiosity and spirituality on drug treatment outcomes. *Journal of Behavioral Health Services & Research, 36*(2), 189–198.

Costenbader, E. C., Astone, N. M., & Latkin, C. A. (2006). The dynamics of injection drug users' personal networks and HIV risk behaviors. *Addiction, 101*(7), 1003–1013.

Cunningham, M. S. (1994). Forward. In J. U. Gordon (Ed.), *Managing multiculturalism in substance abuse services* (p. vii-ix). Thousand Oaks: Sage Publications.

Cunningham, J. A., Sobell, L. C., Gavin, D. R., Sobell, M. B., & Breslin, F. C. (1997). Assessing motivation for change: Preliminary development and evaluation of a scale measuring the costs and benefits of changing alcohol or drug use. *Psychology of Addictive Behaviors, 11*(2), 107–114.

De Leon, G. (1995). Therapeutic communities for addictions: A theoretical framework. *International Journal of Addictions, 30*(12), 51–63.

Dimeff, L. A., Baer, J. S., Kivlahan, D. R., & Marlatt, G. A. (2000). Brief alcohol screening and intervention for college students (BASICS). *Substance Abuse, 21*(4), 283–285.

Donovan, D. M., & Marlatt, G. A. (Eds.). (2005). Relapse prevention: Maintenance strategies in the treatment of addictive behaviors (2nd Ed.). New York, NY: Guilford Press.

Douglas, K. R., Chan, G., Gelernter, J., Arias, A. J., Anton, R. F., Weiss, R. D., Brady, K., Poling, J., Farrer, L., & Kranzler, H. R. (2010). Adverse childhood events as risk factors for substance dependence: Partial mediation by mood and anxiety disorders. *Addictive Behaviors, 35*(1), 7–13.

Draus, P. J., & Carlson, R. G. (2006). Needles in the haystacks: The social context of initiation to heroin injection in rural Ohio. *Substance Use & Misuse, 41*(8), 1111–1124.

Dube, S. R., Felitti, V. J., Dong, M., Chapman, D. P., Giles, W. H., & Anda, R. F. (2003). Childhood abuse, neglect, and household dysfunction and the risk of illicit drug use: The adverse childhood experiences study. *Pediatrics, 111*(3), 564–572.

Dufault, K., & Martocchio, B.C. (1985). Hope: Its spheres and dimensions. *Nursing Clinics of North America, 20*(2), 379–391.

Finn, S. E., & Tonsager, M. E. (1997). Information-gathering and therapeutic models of assessment: Complementary paradigms. *Psychological Assessment, 9,* 374–385.

Freimuth, M. (2005). *Hidden addictions: Assessment practices for psychotherapists, counselors, and health care providers.* New York: Jason Aronson.

Gilchrist, G., Cameron, J., & Scoular, J. (2005). Crack and cocaine use among female prostitutes in Glasgow: Risky business. *Drugs: Education, Prevention & Policy, 12*(5), 381–391.

Goffman, E. (1961). *Asylums: Essays on the social situation of mental patients and other inmates.* NY: Anchor.

Goldfarb. L., Galanter. M., McDowell. D., Lifshutz. H., & Dermatis, H. (1996). Medical student and patient attitudes toward religions and spirituality in the recovery process. *American Journal of Drug and Alcohol Abuse, 22,* 549–561.

Graham, M. D. (2006). Addiction, the addict, and career: considerations for the employment counselor. *Journal of Employment Counseling, 43*(4), 168–178.

Graham, K., Timney, C. B., Bois, C., & Wedgerfield, K. (1995). Continuity of care in addictions treatment: The role of advocacy and coordination in case management. *American Journal of Drug & Alcohol Abuse, 21*(4), 433–451.

Grotmol, K., Vaglum, P., Ekeberg, Ø., Gude, T., Aasland, O., & Tyssen, R. (2010). Alcohol expectancy and hazardous drinking: A 6-year longitudinal and nationwide study of medical doctors. *European Addiction Research, 16*(1), 17–22.

Inaba, D. S., & Cohen, W. E. (2007). *Uppers, downers, all arounders: Physical and mental effects of psychoactive drugs* (6th ed.). Ashland, OR: CNS Publications, Inc.

Jackson, K. M., Sher, K. J., Cooper, M. L., & Wood, P. K. (2002). Adolescent alcohol and tobacco use: Onset, persistence and trajectories of use across two samples. *Addiction, 97*(5), 517–533.

Janis, I. L., and Mann, L. (1977). *Decision making: A psychological analysis of conflict, choice, and commitment.* NY: Free Press.

Johnson, S. L. (2003). *Therapist's guide to substance abuse and intervention.* San Diego, CA: Academic Press.

Johnson, T. P., & Mott, J. A. (2001). The reliability of self-reported age of onset of tobacco, alcohol and illicit drug use. *Addiction, 96*(8), 1187–1198.

Kaminer, Y. (2008). The teen addiction severity index around the globe: The tower of babel revisited. *Substance Abuse, 29*(3), 89–94.

Larson, D. B., & Larson, S. S. (2003). Spirituality's potential relevance to physical and emotional health: A brief review of quantitative research. *Journal of Psychology & Theology, 31*(1), 37–52.

Lappalainen, K., Savolainen, H., Kuorelahti, M., & Epstein, M. (2009). An international assessment of the emotional and behavioral strengths of youth. *Journal of Child & Family Studies, 18*(6), 746–753.

Lewis, J., Lewis, M. D., Daniels, J. A., & D'Andrea, M. A. (2003). *Community counseling: Empowerment strategies for a diverse society.* Pacific Grove, CA: Brooks/Cole.

Lundqvist, T., (2005). Cognitive consequences of cannabis use: Comparison with abuse of stimulants and heroin with regard to attention, memory and executive functions. *Pharmacology, Biochemistry & Behavior, 81*(2), 319–330.

Mackinnon, S. V. (2004). Spirituality: Its role in substance abuse, treatment and recovery. *DATA: The Brown University Digest of Addiction Theory & Application, 23*(7).

Marlatt, A., & Witkiewitz, K. (2009). [Commentary] Further exploring the interpersonal dynamics of relapse. *Addiction, 104*(8), 1291–1292.

Mee-Lee, D. (2005). ASAM's placement criteria: What's new? *Behavioral Health Management, 25*(3), 32–34.

Mee-Lee, D., Shulman, G. D., Fishman M., Gastfriend D. R., and Griffith J. H., eds. (2001). ASAM Patient Placement Criteria for the Treatment of Substance-Related Disorders, Second Edition-Revised (ASAM PPC-2R). Chevy Chase, MD: American Society of Addiction Medicine, Inc.

McIntyre, J. R. (2004). Family treatment of substance abuse. In S. L. A. Straussner (Ed.), *Clinical work with substance-abusing clients* (2nd ed., pp. 237–263). New York: Guilford Press.

Miller, G. A. (1999). *Learning the language of addiction counseling.* Allyn and Bacon.

Miller, W. R., & Rollnick, S. (2002). *Motivational interviewing: Preparing people for change* (2nd ed.). New York: Guilford Press.

Miller, W. R., & Tonigan, J. S. (1996). Assessing drinkers' motivation for change: The stages of change readiness and treatment eagerness scales (SOCRATES). *Psychology of Addictive Behaviors, 10,* 81–89.

Moltu, C., Binder, P., & Nielsen, G. (2010). Commitment under pressure: Experienced therapists' inner work during difficult therapeutic impasses. *Psychotherapy Research, 20*(3), 309–320.

National Association of Alcohol and Drug Abuse Counselors (2008). *NAACAD Code of Ethics.* Retrieved May 1,

2010 from http://naadac.org/documents/index.php?CategoryID=23

Newcomb, M. (1997). Psychosocial predictors and consequences of drug use: A developmental perspective within a prospective study. *Journal of Addictive Diseases, 16,* 51–89.

Pearlin, L., & Schooler, C. (1978). The structure of coping: Erratum. *Journal of Health & Social Behavior, 19*(2), 237.

Prochaska, J. O., DiClemente, C. C., & Norcross, J. C. (1992). In search of how people change: Applications to addictive behavior. *American Psychologist, 47,* 1102–1114.

Reinert, D. F., & Bloomingdale, J. R. (1999). Spiritual maturity and mental health: Implications for counselors. *Counseling & Values, 43*(3), 211–224.

Remley, T. P., & Herlihy, B. (2010). *Ethical, legal, and professional issues in counseling* (3rd ed.). Upper Saddle River, NJ: Pearson.

Robins, L. N., Wing, J., Wittchen, H. U., Helzer, J. E., Babor, T. F., Burke, J., Farmer, A., Jablensky, A., Pickens, R., Regier, D. A., Sartorius, N., & Towle, L. H. (1989). The composite international diagnostic interview: An epidemiologic instrument suitable for use in conjunction with different diagnostic systems and in different cultures. *Archives of General Psychiatry, 45,* 1069–1077.

Rollnick, S., Heather, N., Gold, R., & Hall, W. (1992). Development of the short "readiness to change" questionnaire for use in brief opportunistic interventions. *British Journal of Addictions, 87,* 743–754.

Roy, M., Dum, M., Sobell, L., Sobell, M., Simco, E., Manor, H., et al. (2008). Comparison of the Quick Drinking Screen and the Alcohol Timeline Followback with Outpatient Alcohol Abusers. *Substance Use & Misuse, 43*(14), 2116–2123.

Saitz, R., Horton, N., Larson, M., Winter, M., & Samet, J. (2005). Primary medical care and reductions in addiction severity: a prospective cohort study. *Addiction, 100*(1), 70–78.

Sattler, J. M. (1998). *Clinical and forensic interviewing of children and families: Guidelines for the mental health, education, pediatric and child maltreatment fields.* San Diego, CA: Author.

Saunders, J. (2006). Substance dependence and non-dependence in the diagnostic and statistical manual of mental disorders (DSM) and the international classification of diseases (ICD): Can an identical conceptualization be achieved? *Addiction, 101,* 48–58.

Sexton, R. L., Carlson, R. G., Leukefeld, C. G., & Booth, B. M. (2006). Methamphetamine use and adverse consequences in the rural southern United States: An ethnographic overview. *Journal of Psychoactive Drugs, 3*(38), 393–404.

Shabad, P. (2001). *Despair and the return of hope: Echoes of morning in psychotherapy.* Northvale, NJ: Jason Aronson, Inc.

Shealy, A. E., Murphy, J. G., Borsari, B., & Correia, C. J. (2007). Predictors of motivation to change alcohol use among referred college students. *Addictive Behaviors, 32*(10), 2358–2364.

Sobell, L. C., & Sobell, M. B. (1992). Timeline followback: A technique for assessing self-reported alcohol consumption. In R. Z. Litten & J. Allen (Eds.), *Measuring alcohol consumption: Psychosocial and biological methods* (pp. 41–72). New Jersey: Humana Press.

Stippekohl, B., Winkler, M., Mucha, R., Pauli, P., Walter, B., Vaitl, D., et al. (2010). Neural responses to BEGIN- and END-stimuli of the smoking ritual in nonsmokers, nondeprived smokers, and deprived smokers. *Neuropsychopharmacology: Official Publication of the American College of Neuropsychopharmacology, 35*(5), 1209–1225.

Substance and Mental Health Services Administration. (1996). *Substance abuse, disability and vocational rehabilitation.* Rockville: MD. Author.

Substance and Mental Health Services Administration. (1998a). Addiction counseling competencies: The knowledge, skills and attitudes of professional practice. *CSAT Treatment Improvement Protocol (TIP) 21,* Rockville: MD. Author.

Substance and Mental Health Services Administration. (1998b). Screening and assessing adolescents for substance use disorders. *CSAT Treatment Improvement Protocol (TIP) 31,* Rockville: MD. Author.

Substance and Mental Health Services Administration. (2000). Integrating substance abuse treatment and vocational services. *CSAT Treatment Intervention Protocol (TIP) 38,* Rockville: MD. Author.

Substance and Mental Health Services Administration. (2008). Integrated dual disorders treatment workbook. *CSAT Evidenced-based Practices,* Rockville: MD. Author.

Sowards, K. A., O'Boyle, K., & Weissman, M. (2006). Inspiring hope, envisioning alternatives: The importance of peer role models in a mandated treatment program for women. *Journal of Social Work Practice in the Addiction, 6*(4), 55–70.

Straussner, S. L. A. (2001). *Ethnocultural factors in substance abuse treatment.* New York: Guilford Press.

Strupp, H. H. (1993). Psychotherapy research: Evolution and current trends. In T. K. Fagan & G. R. VandenBos (Eds.), *Exploring applied psychology: Origins and critical analyses.* Washington, D.C.: American Psychological Association.

Tarter, R. E. (1990). Evaluation and treatment of adolescent substance abuse: A decision tree model. *American Journal of Drug and Alcohol Abuse, 16*(12), 1–46.

Tims, F. M., Leukefeld, C. G., & Platt, J. J. (2001). *Relapse and recovery in addictions*. London: Yale University Press.

Tisdell, E. J. (2000). Spirituality and emancipatory adult education in women adult educators for social change. *Adult Education Quarterly, 50*(4), 308–335.

Tobler, N. S., Roona, M. R., Ochshorn, P., Marshall, D. G., Streke, A. V., & Stackpole, K. M. (2000). School-based adolescent drug prevention programs: 1998 meta-analysis. *The Journal of Primary Prevention, 20,* 275–336.

Wild, T. C. (2006). Social control and coercion in addiction treatment: Towards evidence-based policy and practice. *Addiction, 101*(1), 40–49.

Wild, T. C., Cunningham, J. A., & Ryan, R. M. (2006). Social pressure, coercion, and client engagement at treatment entry: A self-determination theory perspective. *Addictive Behaviors, 31*(10), 1858–1872.

Williams, C. (1987). Child care practices in alcoholic families: Findings from a neighborhood detoxification program. *Alcohol Health and Research World, 94,* 74–77.

Chapter 6

Assessment and Diagnosis of Addictions

John M. Laux
The University of Toledo
Dilani M. Perera-Diltz
Cleveland State University

Stephanie A. Calmes
The University of Toledo

According to the Substance Abuse and Mental Health Services Administration (SAMHSA, 2007), approximately 5.4 million American adults meet criteria for both serious mental health and substance abuse or dependence disorders (SAMHSA). Due to the high co-morbidity between substance use disorders and other serious mental health disorders, counselors, regardless of their areas of specialty, can expect to provide services to clients who have substance use disorders. It is vital that counselors are aware of the signs and symptoms of substance use disorders and the ways they are detected and diagnosed (Laux, Newman, & Brown, 2004). Without this information, counselors risk misdiagnosis and mistreatment of their clients' presenting problems (Horrigan, Piazza, & Weinstein, 1996).

This chapter introduces the reader to many of the available substance abuse screens and assessments, providing the information needed to evaluate each instrument as well as the *Diagnostic and Statistical Manual* (*DSM IV-TR*) (American Psychiatric Association [APA], 2000) criteria used to reach a substance-use-related diagnosis.

By way of introduction, we present the case of Pedro, a hypothetical person whose life circumstances could easily place him before a counselor whose task it would be to help Pedro assess the role substances play in his life. We open with a review of Pedro's background and conclude the chapter with a discussion of Pedro's assessment.

Pedro is a 24-year-old single Mexican American male, and the oldest son of his first-generation American migrant farming parents. Pedro has three younger brothers who all looked up to him while growing up. The family was proud of Pedro the day he enlisted in the United States Army. He engaged in combat several times while in Iraq but was spared injury until the day the Humvee he was riding in ran over a roadside Improvised Explosive Devise. The vehicle's extra armor plating protected Pedro from the flying shrapnel; however, the explosion's shock waves caused him to suffer from symptoms consistent with a closed head injury. Also, the force of the explosion ruptured his ear drums, permanently impairing his hearing. Pedro was honorably discharged following a medical examination and returned to Northwest Ohio. He felt disconnected from the person he was before he left for military duty. He had difficulty falling asleep almost every night and found himself frequently thinking about what he had seen and experienced while in combat. He felt alone and isolated from his family, who had returned to Texas for the winter. To support himself, he accepted an offer to work as a manager at a local grocery store. He quickly found it difficult to motivate himself to go to work each day. His employer, a Vietnam-era veteran, felt obliged to continue Pedro's employment out of loyalty to a fellow soldier, but made no effort to hide the fact that Pedro's work was inadequate. He liked to complain to his subordinates about catching Pedro staring off into space and how he often came late and left early.

As time wore on, Pedro found himself spending more time at the Veterans of Foreign Wars (VFW) Post in the next town over. Initially, he would drive to the VFW after work in anticipation of the kinship he felt alongside others who had been in the service. After a while though, he noticed that his mind was focused more on the beer he drank than on those with whom he drank it. On more than one occasion, he found himself drinking until closing time. Over the course of the last month, Pedro took to sneaking a few bottles of beer in the storeroom before getting off work. He rationalized this behavior because he felt that he was underpaid for his services and drinking helped him both take the edge off and make the drive to the VFW a little easier to tolerate. Last week, Pedro crashed his car into a parked vehicle and landed in a ditch on the drive home from the VFW at 2:00 in the morning. He was found, passed out at the wheel, by a sheriff's deputy and transported to the local hospital. Although his car was totaled, he escaped the accident uninjured. He was cited for driving under the influence and for destruction of property.

Pedro retained an attorney who advised him that it might look good in the judge's eyes if he voluntarily subjected himself to a drug and alcohol assessment at the VA hospital in the state capital. Pedro seriously doubted that he had an alcohol problem but, upon his attorney's advice, he called his VA hospital and set up an appointment for an assessment. He followed through with his scheduled appointment and met with a chemical dependency counselor.

WHY USE STANDARDIZED ASSESSMENTS?

Counselors unfamiliar with assessment may believe that one's clinical judgment is all that is necessary to identify a substance abuser. This chapter does not subvert or replace clinical judgment. Rather, the benefits and limitations of standardized assessments are presented so that counselors can incorporate them as a part of the clinical decision-making process.

Standardized assessments provide data about clients relative to a normative population. This information is useful when working with resistant clients. Some clients compare their substance use to that of their friends or family members. Consequently, a client who argues that drinking 12 beers a day is normal in his family or his neighborhood, or is less than what he saw his father drink while growing up, may truly not understand that 12 beers a day is not "normal" alcohol consumption. Normative data may help to broaden the client's perspective on "normal drinking."

Normative data provides the benefit of objectivity. A resistant client may claim bias to reject a counselor's diagnosis using the following argument: "This is just your opinion. Who are you to pass judgment on me? You only get paid if you get people into treatment so of course you see me, and probably everyone else, as substance dependent." A counselor who explains that standardized assessments use the client's data, are scored in a standardized and objective method, and provide results about the person's use of substances relative to national data may not convince the client of the accuracy of the diagnosis, but can help demonstrate that the argument of bias is without merit.

A common belief is that substance abusers deny or minimize their substance use (APA, 2000). To counter client minimization, several standardized assessments employ indirect methods of screening. Indirect methods of screening ask questions that are not overtly related to substance abuse and therefore, conceptually, cannot be answered in a way to deny or minimize one's substance use.

Standardized assessments aid counselors in treatment planning. Imagine four different clients' responses to a screen. Client A's scores classify her as substance dependent. Client B scores

TABLE 6.1 Client Assessment Results and Recommendations

Client	A	B	C	D
Results	At or above substance dependence cutoff level	Below substance dependence cutoff level	Unusually high score	Below cutoff for substance use disorder but indicates drinking more than average
Recommendation	Referral to day-treatment	Referral to intensive out-patient treatment	Further evaluation for medical detoxification	Referral to education on substance dependence

just below the dependence cutoff. Client C scores higher than any client the counselor has assessed. Finally, client D's answers, while not indicative of a substance use disorder, do suggest he drinks more than the average person. These data provide the following treatment implications. Client A's score supports a diagnosis of substance dependence. Recommendations may include referral to a day treatment program. Client B's score supports a diagnosis of substance abuse. Client B may benefit from intensive outpatient treatment. Client C's presentation is so severe that a medical evaluation for detoxification treatment may be appropriate. Client D's data suggest that educational interventions may help the client evaluate the role substance use plays in his life. This information is summarized in Table 6.1.

PHILOSOPHICAL UNDERPINNING OF INSTRUMENT CONSTRUCTION

Substance use assessments are constructed using one of two methods, or a combination of the two. These are the logical and criterion keyed methods. Logically constructed instruments contain items that directly inquire about the amount, frequency, duration, and consequences of substance use. No attempt is made to hide or disguise the items' intent to assess substance abuse. Logically constructed instruments tend to have good internal consistency, construct validity stability across time, and content validity. However, because the items are transparent in nature, they may be subject to impression management.

The criterion-keyed method is used to circumvent defensiveness. Criterion-keyed scales are constructed by selecting a target group (the criterion group) that possesses the trait of interest and statistically comparing this target group with a group of persons known to be free of the target trait. Criterion-keyed items have no direct relationship with substance abuse. The only concern is selecting an item that statistically differentiates the two groups. Impression management is difficult because it is impossible to know which items are keyed toward indicating substance abuse. While criterion-keyed scales tend to have good criterion-related validity, they sometimes suffer from poor internal consistency, multiple underlying factor structures, and poor content validity.

The decision to use a criterion-keyed screen, a logically derived screen, or a screen that combines both approaches depends on the purpose of screening and the population of interest. Counselors concerned about detecting client dissimulation may feel more comfortable with a criterion-keyed screen. Counselors working with clients unlikely to attempt to "fake good" may opt for the logically derived method.

SCREENING, ASSESSMENT, AND DIAGNOSIS

The purpose of a screen is to determine if additional clinical attention is needed (Adger & Werner, 1994). A substance abuse screen provides an indicator of whether or not a problem *may* exist. A screen does not provide a diagnosis, but may point the clinician in the direction of an in-depth substance abuse assessment. Assessments tend to be more labor intensive than screens. The purpose of assessment is to investigate and discover data that will either confirm or rule out clinical hypotheses. Assessments are conducted in response to referral questions (Groth-Marnat, 2003). Diagnosis is the process of determining whether or not a person currently presents with symptoms sufficient to meet standardized and prescribed criteria. The final product of the diagnostic process is a multiaxial diagnostic categorization, which may include a rule of "no diagnosis." While the training and supervision criteria necessary to perform diagnosis vary between jurisdictions, the shared lexicon of mental and emotional disorders is the *DSM-IV-TR* (APA, 2000).

EVALUATING SUBSTANCE ABUSE SCREENS AND ASSESSMENTS

Piazza (2002) outlined five characteristics of a good screen. These are sensitivity, specificity, reliability, validity, and cost-efficiency. These concepts are explained here and used to evaluate, when possible, each of the screens in this chapter.

Sensitivity and Specificity

Sensitivity is the ratio of persons correctly screened "positive" for having a substance use disorder to those who actually have the disorder. For example, imagine that a group of 100 persons were administered the hypothetical "Accurate Alcohol Screen-A (AASA)." Of these 100, 50 were known to be alcohol dependent and 50 were not. If 45 of the 50 persons known to have alcohol dependence tested "positive," then the AASA's sensitivity would be .90. Conversely, *specificity* refers to the proportion of people that a screen accurately identifies as *not* having a substance use disorder. If the AASA's results suggested that 25 of the 50 nondependent people in our mock sample were "negative," then the AASA's specificity would be .50. These two concepts are often inversely related. A sensitive screen may lead counselors to errantly classify nondependent persons as "positive." The frequency at which a screen makes this error is referred to as the *false positive rate*. A screen with high specificity may inaccurately classify persons as "negative" who actually have a substance use problem. Such classifications are called *false negatives*. Figure 6.1 presents the four classification categories.

Ideally, a screen is able to both identify those who have the problem (high true positive) as well as rule out those who do not (high false negative). The setting determines the acceptable

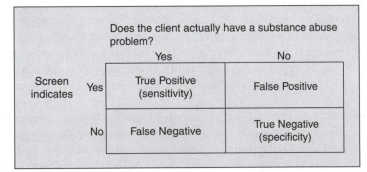

FIGURE 6.1 Sensitivity and Specificity

sensitivity and specificity rates. A researcher may tolerate a high false positive in order to increase the sample size; an agency with limited resources needs high specificity to reduce the number of referrals resulting in false negatives.

Reliability and Validity

Reliability is the consistency of a screen's results. A screen should not vary in its measurement, provided the construct being measured does not vary. A second type of reliability is called *internal consistency*. Internal consistency is the degree to which a screen's items vary together. If a scale's items all measure facets of the same construct, then they should all be answered in a consistent manner. When an instrument's total measurement is stable over time and its items vary together, the instrument is said to be reliable. Groth-Marnat (2003) noted that reliability estimates of states, such as substance abuse or dependence, are frequently lower than those of traits, such as intelligence. Groth-Marnat suggested that clinicians evaluate a screen's reliability in the context of other screens' estimates. According to Groth-Marnat (2003), reliability estimates of .70 or higher are optimal for trait-based screens.

High reliability is necessary but insufficient. A screen may produce consistent results across measurements but inaccurately measure the construct of interest. Validity is synonymous with accuracy. *Validity* is the degree to which a screen accurately represents the construct or criterion it was designed to measure. A screen is valid to the degree it has acceptable sensitivity and specificity. Piazza (2002) suggested that counselors consider validity estimates of .40 to be low and estimates of .90 to be high.

Cost-Efficiency

One way to evaluate a screen's cost is the direct costs associated with its purchase. Screens range in cost from several hundred dollars, when employed as part of a larger assessment battery, to those in the free domain. Less tangible are the human labor costs involved in administering, scoring, and interpreting a screen's results. Another important consideration is the implications of a screen's results. A low-cost or free screen with a high false positive rate may cause an agency to waste precious resources conducting unnecessary diagnostic assessment interviews. Conversely, a screen with poor sensitivity may cause an agency to misdiagnose and mistreat persons who truly need substance abuse services.

DIAGNOSIS

The *DSM-IV-TR* (APA, 2000) provides general criteria for substance abuse and dependence diagnoses, and provides specific criteria for the following substances: alcohol, amphetamines, caffeine, cannabis, hallucinogens, inhalants, nicotine, opioids, phencyclidine, sedatives/hypnotics or anxiolytics, polysubstance, and "other." Criteria are provided for intoxication, withdrawal, and intoxication-delirium for many of these substances.

This chapter focuses on those criteria spelled out for abuse and dependence. The reader is advised that while each of these substances shares the same general diagnostic criteria, the manifestations and associated behaviors of each vary greatly. The reader is advised to develop specific knowledge of the cultural, age, and gender features, and the prevalence of use, course, familiar pattern, and differential diagnoses associated with each substance.

Regardless of the substance, the *DSM-IV-TR* specifies that dependence is characterized by "a maladaptive pattern of substance use, leading to clinically significant impairment or distress, as manifested by three (or more) of the following, occurring at any time in the same 12-month period"

(APA, 2000, p. 197): (1) tolerance (defined as needing to consume increased amounts in order to obtain the desired effect or an experiencing of a reduction in impact while using the same amount of the substance as previously consumed); (2) withdrawal (experienced as maladaptive behavior accompanied by physiological and cognitive manifestations due to a reduction in consumption which cause significant distress or the continued use of a substance to avoid/relieve oneself from the same); (3) using more of a substance; (4) desire and/or attempts to cut down or quit without success; (5) the exertion of time and effort to obtain, use, or recover from use of the substance; and (6) social, work, or recreational consequences directly related to substance use, continued use despite knowledge of its persistent and recurrent negative physical or psychological consequences. Clinicians applying a diagnosis of dependence are required to specify whether or not the presenting symptoms are accompanied by physiological indicators (tolerance and/or withdrawal).

The criteria for substance abuse are similar to those required for a diagnosis of dependence. Specifically, the *DSM-IV-TR* defines substance abuse as "a maladaptive pattern of substance use leading to clinically significant impairment or distress, as manifested by one (or more) of the following, occurring within a 12-month period" (APA, 2000, p. 199): (1) major problems at work, school, or home due to continued substance use; (2) recurrent use in situations that are potentially physically hazardous; (3) recurrent legal problems associated with substance use; and (4) continued use despite continual and persistent social and/or personal problems associated with or exacerbated by the substance use. To qualify for a diagnosis of substance abuse, the person must have never met criteria for substance dependence.

See a copy of each test as you read this chapter! The reader may benefit from viewing each of these screens while reading through the chapter. To aid in this endeavor, we offer the following two Web sites, which provide a comprehensive list of screens.

http://www.utexas.edu/research/cswr/nida/instrumentListing.html
http://pubs.niaaa.nih.gov/publications/Assesing%20Alcohol/factsheets.htm

---

Counselors have a wide variety of substance abuse screens from which to choose. The Michigan Alcoholism Screening Test (MAST) (Selzer, 1971), CAGE (Ewing, 1984), and Substance Abuse Subtle Screening Inventory-3 (SASSI-3) (Miller, 1999) are the most often selected screening instruments (Juhnke, Vacc, Curtis, Coll, & Paredes, 2003). Other well-known and well-researched instruments include the Alcohol Use Disorders Identification Test (AUDIT) (Saunders, Aasland, Babor, de la Fuente, & Grant, 1993), the TWEAK (Russell et al., 1994), and the T-ACE (Sokol, Martier, & Ager, 1989). This chapter introduces and discusses a selected number of substance abuse screens and assessments. Self-administered screens are introduced first, followed by scales contained within the larger framework of personality assessments. The instrument section closes with discussions of a counselor-initiated comprehensive substance abuse assessment and screens used with pregnant women.

SELF-ADMINISTERED, STAND-ALONE SCREENING INSTRUMENTS

Substance Abuse Subtle Screening Inventory-3 (SASSI-3)

First published in 1985 by G. A. Miller, the SASSI uses the criterion keying and rational approaches. The current version (SASSI-3) requires about 17 minutes to complete, score, and interpret (Lazowski, Miller, Boye, & Miller, 1998). A Spanish version is available. The first half of

SASSI has 67 true/false questions that are unrelated to substance use. These items comprise eight empirically established scales: the Symptoms (SYM), Obvious Attributes (OAT), Subtle Attributes (SAT), Defensiveness (DEF), Supplemental Addiction Measure (SAM), Family vs. Control Subjects (FAM), and Correctional (COR) scales. The Random Answering Pattern (RAP) scale provides a measure of validity. A RAP raw score of two or more raises doubt about the results' validity (Miller, Roberts, Brooks, & Lazowski, 1997). Two subscales, the 12-item Face Valid Alcohol Scale (FVA) and the 14-item Face Valid Other Drug Scale (FVOD), were rationally developed and make up the second part of the test.

The SYM scale measures causes, consequences, and correlates of substance abuse. The OAT scale assesses clients' admission of substance abuse related limitations. The SAT scale provides an indirect indicator of substance abuse. The DEF scale measures clients' range of openness or defensiveness. High DEF scores could represent attempts to hide substance abuse, situational defensiveness, or pervasive defensiveness. The SAM scale helps clarify whether elevated DEF scores are due to general or situational defensiveness (low SAM) or defensiveness specific to substance use (high SAM).

The SASSI-3 is interpreted by using nine decision rules (Piazza, Martin, & Dildine, 2000). Four rules are based on clients' obvious recognition of abuse or dependence. Two are designed to circumvent defensiveness and/or denial. The remaining three combine data from the obvious and subtle scales. There is a "low probability of having a substance dependence disorder" (Miller, 1999, p. 10) if no rule is endorsed. One or more rule endorsements suggests a "high probability of having a substance dependence disorder" (Miller, p. 10).

The SASSI's FAM and COR scales, experimental in nature, do not contribute to the scoring system. The FAM scale's items measure traits present in persons who focus on others' problems rather than their own, and who may lack assertiveness. The COR scale contains items frequently endorsed by persons with a criminal history. FAM and COR scales interpretations should be highly tentative.

Recent survey data indicates that addictions counselors (Juhnke et al., 2003) view the SASSI-3 to be the most important and most frequently used screen. Gray (2001) reported excellent estimates of internal consistency for the face-valid scales but poor estimates for the indirect scales. Laux, Perera-Diltz, Smirnoff, and Salyers (2005) reported excellent internal consistency ($\alpha = .95$), unidimensional status, and acceptable item-to-scale correlations for the FVOD scale. Myerholtz and Rosenberg (1998) found the SASSI-3 to have acceptable temporal stability and moderate agreement with other instruments designed to assess similar constructs. Laux, Salyers, and Kotova (2005) concluded that the SASSI-3 outperformed the MAST, Mac-R, and CAGE in terms of one-week test-retest reliability, internal consistency, and factor structure in a college student sample. Lazowski et al. (1998) reported that the SASSI has a 95% rate of agreement with clinician's diagnoses. Swartz (1998) concluded that the SASSI-3 discriminates between moderate and severe substance dependence and less severe and no substance dependence. Despite the SASSI-3's popularity among clinicians, there is some question about the subtle scales' ability to provide unique diagnostic information over and above that provided by the obvious scales (Feldstein & Miller, 2007).

The SASSI-2A (Miller & Lazowski, 2001) is for 12- to 18-year-olds and requires a 4.4 grade reading level. The screen has 72 true-false questions and 28 face-valid questions about alcohol and other drug use and consequences. The SASSI-2A requires approximately 15 minutes to administer and score. Counselors should use the SASSI-2A with an 18-year-old client in high school and the SASSI-3 with an 18-year-old high school graduate. Rogers, Cashel, Johansen, Sewell, and Gonzalez (1997) reported the SASSI-A as useful for accurately identifying 75% of reporting users but as misclassifying approximately 66% of nonusers. Rogers et al. also reported a possible ethnic bias, with the SASSI-A demonstrating less efficiency in classifying Hispanic participants than Caucasian participants. Bauman, Merta, and Steiner (1999) concluded that the SASSI-A was able to differentiate between clinical and nonclinical at-risk groups, but questioned its validity as it "classified significantly more individuals as chemically dependent than did the clinicians" (p. 68). Sweet and Saules (2003) investigated the SASSI-A's validity in a sample of 490 adolescent offenders from a Michigan juvenile court. Their results were supportive for the FVOD and FVA scales. These researchers concluded that the subtle scales had poor construct validity, and that the subtle scales were better measures of conduct problems and emotional instability than substance abuse. Stein et al., (2005) noted that SASSI-A's construct validity was somewhat supported for use with juveniles in a correctional setting whose alcohol use levels were at 3 or above, but not useful for detecting drug use behavior. In a study summarizing available research on the SASSI, Feldstein and Miller (2007) concluded that very little empirical evidence supports the notion that SASSI scales are capable of screening for substance related disorders among non-reporters.

More information related to the SASSI, including free downloads and purchase information can be found at the following Web sites:

http://www.psychscreen.com/singletest/sassi.html
http://www.sassi.com/
https://www3.parinc.com/products/product.aspx?Productid=SASSI-3

The Michigan Alcoholism Screening Test (MAST)

The MAST (Selzer, 1971) has 25 true-false questions about alcohol use and can be completed in 10 to 15 minutes (Hedlund & Vieweg, 1984). Selzer assigned weights of 0, 1, 2, or 5 based on his view of each item's indicator of alcohol abuse. Individual item scores are summed and the following schema is used to interpret the results: 0–4, not alcohol dependent; 5–6, maybe alcohol dependent; 7 or more, alcohol dependent (Hedlund & Vieweg, 1984). The MAST is the "gold standard" of alcohol abuse screens (Martin, Liepman, & Young, 1990). Despite this reputation, the MAST is sometimes criticized based on the transparency of its items. Specifically, some (e.g., Friedrich & Loftsgard, 1978) suggest that MAST scores are more reflective of a willingness to self-identify as having alcohol-related problems than a pure measure of alcohol dependence. The MAST has been criticized as being vulnerable to client minimization (e.g., Stinnett, Benton, & Whitfill, 1991). Additionally, client denial about the scope and depth of alcohol-related problems may limit the MAST's accuracy (Shedler, Mayman, & Manis, 1993).

The MAST's original standardization sample was comprised of males convicted of driving under the influence (Selzer, 1971). Men and women experience the symptoms and consequences of alcohol dependence differently (e.g., Wilke, 1994). A screen constructed based on men's experience of alcohol abuse may not apply equally to women. The practice of interpreting MAST scores based on a total score presupposes that the instrument's items are homogenous and represent a single latent variable. Some suggest that the MAST consists of many different facets (e.g., Parsons, Wallbrown, & Myers, 1994). Others, however, (e.g., Thurber & Snow, 2001) report that the MAST does reflect a single latent variable of alcohol dependence. Laux, Newman, and Brown (2004) found that MAST scores were independent of client gender, age, education level, and income. Laux et al. (2004) also reported that the MAST was one-dimensional, and that low endorsement of certain items did not affect the screen's internal structure. However, Laux et al. found that MAST scores were susceptible to defensiveness. The MAST has a false positive rate of 33% (Jacobson, 1983) and an accuracy rate of 75% (Creager, 1989).

The MAST has been modified for use by special populations. A brief version, B-MAST, was published in 1972 (Pokorny, Miller, & Kaplan, 1972). The Adapted Short Michigan Alcoholism

Screening Test (ASMAST) for Fathers (F-SMAST) and Mothers (M-SMAST), with 13 items each, were published in 1992 (Crews & Sher, 1992) and are used with children of alcoholics to assess the father's and mother's history of alcohol use. Counselors working with the elderly may be interested in using the Michigan Alcoholism Screening Test-Geriatric Version (MAST-G) (Blow et al., 1992).

The questions and scoring rubric for the Michigan Alcoholism Screening Test are as follows:

1. Do you feel you are a normal drinker? ("normal" - drink as much or less than most other people)
2. Have you ever awakened the morning after some drinking the night before and found that you could not remember a part of the evening?
3. Does any near relative or close friend ever worry or complain about your drinking?
4. Can you stop drinking without difficulty after one or two drinks?
5. Do you ever feel guilty about your drinking?
6. Have you ever attended a meeting of Alcoholics Anonymous (AA)?
7. Have you ever gotten into physical fights when drinking?
8. Has drinking ever created problems between you and a near relative or close friend?
9. Has any family member or close friend gone to anyone for help about your drinking?
10. Have you ever lost friends because of your drinking?
11. Have you ever gotten into trouble at work because of drinking?
12. Have you ever lost a job because of drinking?
13. Have you ever neglected your obligations, your family, or your work for two or more days in a row because you were drinking?
14. Do you drink before noon fairly often?
15. Have you ever been told you have liver trouble such as cirrhosis?
16. After heavy drinking have you ever had delirium tremens (D.T.'s), severe shaking, visual or auditory (hearing) hallucinations?
17. Have you ever gone to anyone for help about your drinking?
18. Have you ever been hospitalized because of drinking?
19. Has your drinking ever resulted in your being hospitalized in a psychiatric ward?
20. Have you ever gone to any doctor, social worker, clergyman, or mental health clinic for help with any emotional problem in which drinking was part of the problem?
21. Have you been arrested more than once for driving under the influence of alcohol?
22. Have you ever been arrested, even for a few hours because of other behavior while drinking? (If Yes, how many times _____)

Scoring

Score one point for each YES answer except for on questions #1 and #4 (one point should be given for each NO answer on items #1 and #4)

Score	Possible Indication
0–2	No apparent problem
3–5	Early or middle problem drinker
6 or more	Problem drinker

Additional information about the MAST can be viewed at the following Web sites:

http://www.nccaringdental.com/michiganscreeningtest.htm
http://www.ncadd-sfv.org/symptoms/mast_test.html
http://www.ssc.wisc.edu/wlsresearch/pilot/P01-R01_info/aging_mind/Aging_AppB5_MAST-G.pdf

Source: The Michigan Alcoholism Screening Test (Selzer, 1971).

The CAGE

Ewing (1984) designed the CAGE for primary care physicians. Its brevity makes it easy to remember and administer (Piazza, 2002). The CAGE asks: have you ever felt the need to **c**ut down, been **a**nnoyed by other's criticism of your drinking, felt bad or **g**uilty about drinking, or used a drink in the morning (**e**ye opener). Two or more "yes" answers are suggestive of an alcohol use disorder. The CAGE's diagnostic accuracy rates range between 40% and 95% (Sokol et al., 1989). Lifetime CAGE sensitivity rates range from 60% to 95% (O'Connor & Schottenfeld, 1998). The CAGE screens for alcohol abuse only, and is not for use with other types of drug abuse. Due to its obvious nature, it is subject to manipulation. This screen does not specify current or past alcohol use. As such, the CAGE could misclassify persons whose alcohol dependence is currently in remission. Fleming (1993) reported false-positive rates in excess of 50%. Kitchens (1994) argued that the CAGE is better at screening for advanced stages of alcohol dependence but lacks the sensitivity to detect early stages of alcohol abuse.

The questions and scoring rubric for the CAGE are as follows:

C—Have you ever felt you should **Cut** down on your drinking?
A—Have people **Annoyed** you by criticizing your drinking?
G—Have you ever felt bad or **Guilty** about your drinking?
E—Have you ever had a drink first thing in the morning to steady your nerves or to get rid of a hangover (**Eye opener**)?

Scoring

Score one point for each YES answer.

Score	Possible Indication
0–1	No Apparent Problem
2 or more	Clinically Significant

Readers are encouraged to check out the following Web sites for additional information about the CAGE:

http://counsellingresource.com/quizzes/alcohol-cage/index.html
http://www.drugnet.bizland.com/assessment/cage.htm

Source: The CAGE Questionnaire (Ewing, 1984).

Alcohol Use Disorders Identification Test (AUDIT)

The AUDIT was developed by the World Health Organization (Hodgson et al., 2003). Its 10 items are divided into 3 subscales: 3 questions assess the quantity and frequency of alcohol use, 3 focus on alcohol dependence, and 4 tap into the negative consequences of alcohol use (Hodgson et al., 2003). Administration and scoring requires approximately 3 minutes. Fielling, Reid, and O'Connor (2000) reviewed six AUDIT sensitivity and specificity studies. The recommended cutoff of eight points produced a sensitivity score of .61 and a specificity rating of .90. The sensitivity and specificity ratings, respectively, adjusted to .40 and .96 when the cutoff score was raised to 11 points. Fielling et al. (2000) also investigated the sensitivity and specificity of the 8-point cutoff score in groups categorized as hazardous drinkers, harmful drinkers, and at-risk drinkers. The sensitivity and specificity data for each group, respectively, was .97 and .78, .95

and .85, and .51 and .96. Fielling et al. (2000) concluded that the AUDIT is more useful in detecting less severe alcohol consumption than alcohol abuse or dependence. The AUDIT has been translated into Turkish, Greek, Hindi, German, Dutch, Polish, Japanese, French, Portuguese, Spanish, Danish, Flemish, Bulgarian, Chinese, Italian, and Nigerian dialects (Babor, Higgins-Biddle, Saunders & Monteiro, 2001), but is not valid for use with the hearing impaired (Alexander, DiNitto, & Tidblom, 2005).

The AUDIT has been modified to produce three related substance abuse screens. These include the Fast Alcohol Screening Test (FAST), the AUDIT-C, and the AUDIT-3. The FAST consists of four questions (items 3, 5, 8, 10) from the original AUDIT. The FAST, administered in approximately 12 seconds, was developed for use in medical settings. The Spearman rank correlation between the AUDIT and the FAST is .79. Sensitivity and specificity of the FAST is reported to range from .89 to .95 and .84 to .90 respectively. According Hodgson et al. (2003), the FAST compares favorably to the AUDIT across age, gender, and clinical setting. The AUDIT-C was developed to provide primary and emergency care staff with a quick alcohol screen (Bush, Kivlahan, McDonell, Fihn, & Bradley, 1998). The AUDIT-C employs the first three questions of the AUDIT. High sensitivity (.81) and specificity (.86) estimates were reported in a female veteran sample (Bradley et al., 2003). Bush et al. (1998) reported sensitivity of .95 and specificity of .60. The AUDIT-C is reported to be more efficacious for hazardous drinking patterns than for alcohol use or dependence (Bush et al., 1998; Bradley et al., 2003).

The Alcohol Use Disorders Identification Test

The AUDIT manual contains an interviewer version and a self-report version of the audit. The manual can be downloaded from the World Health Organization at the following Web site:

http://whqlibdoc.who.int/hq/2001/WHO_MSD_MSB_01.6a.pdf

An online versions of the AUDIT is available at:

http://www.testandcalc.com/etc/tests/audit.asp

Alcohol Use Inventory (AUI)

The AUI is a 228-item tool that assesses clients' perceived benefits, styles, consequences, and concerns related to alcohol use (Horn, Wanberg, & Foster, 1990). The AUI is appropriate for use with persons 16 and older who have been admitted to an alcohol dependence treatment program. The AUI has 17 primary scales, 6 second-order scales, and a third-order general scale (Chang, Lapham, & Wanberg, 2001). Perceived benefits of alcohol use are measured by the Socialim (drinks to improve sociability), the Mentalim (drinks to improve mental functioning), the Mangmood (drinking to help manage moods), and the Maricope (drinking after having marital problems) scales. Styles of drinking are assessed by the Gregarus (social versus solo drinking), the Compulsv (compulsive drinking) and the Sustained (sustained versus periodic drinking) scales. The scales Lcontrol (loss of control over behavior when drinking), Rolemala (social role maladaption), Delirium (psychoperceptual withdrawal), Hangover (psychophysical withdrawal), and Mariprob (drinking causing marital problems) provide information about consequences of client drinking. Concerns about drinking are reported on the Quantity (quantity of daily use when drinking), the Guiltwor (guilt and worry associated with drinking), the Helpbefr (prior attempts to deal with drinking), the Receptiv (readiness for help) and the Awarenes (awareness of drinking problems) scales. The AUI requires approximately 35–60 minutes to complete, and is constructed at a sixth-grade reading level.

Alcohol Use Inventory

Further information on the AUI is available at the following Web sites:

http://www.cps.nova.edu/~cpphelp/AUI.html
http://pubs.niaaa.nih.gov/publications/Assesing%20Alcohol/InstrumentPDFs/15_AUI.pdf

SUBSTANCE ABUSE SCALES FOUND ON PERSONALITY ASSESSMENT INSTRUMENTS

Many of the most reputable personality assessment instruments include substance abuse scales. This section reviews the substance abuse screens found in the **Minnesota Multiphasic Personality Inventory-2** (MMPI-2; Butcher, Dahlstrom, Graham, Tellegen, & Kaemmer, 1989), the **Personality Assessment Inventory** (PAI; Morey, 1991), and the **Millon Clinical Multiaxial Inventory-III** (MCMI-III; Millon, Davis, & Millon, 1997). Note that unlike client-administered, stand-alone screening instruments, the following sections introduce only *components* of comprehensive personality assessment instruments. These scales cannot be administered independent of the entire battery of questions. The administration, scoring, and interpretation of these instruments require extensive training and credentialing. Finally, the ethical administration of a personality assessment frequently requires a clinical interview, 1–2 hours of the client's time to complete the battery, scoring time (which varies depending on the methods used), a comprehensive written report, and a feedback interview with the client. Use of the following personality assessments for the sole purpose of substance use screening is not recommended.

Minnesota Multiphasic Personality Inventory-2 (MMPI-2)

The MMPI (Butcher et al., 1989) is the most widely used personality assessment (Groth-Marnat, 2003). This tool has 567 true-false, criterion-keyed items that provide a wide range of data about an individual's overall psychological adjustment. The MMPI contains three scales designed to assess substance abuse: The MacAndrew Alcoholism Scale-Revised (MacAndrew, 1965), the Addiction Potential Scale (Weed, Butcher, McKenna, & Ben-Porath, 1992), and the Addiction Acknowledgement Scale (AAS). The following sections will address these scales in greater detail.

MMPI-2: THE MACANDREW ALCOHOLISM SCALE-REVISED (MAC-R). The Mac-R scale (MacAndrew, 1965) was constructed using the criterion-keying method. MacAndrew contrasted MMPI responses of 20 males diagnosed with alcohol dependence with those of 200 non-alcohol-dependent psychiatric patients. MacAndrew's analysis indicated that 49 non-alcohol-related items statistically differentiated these two groups. When the MMPI was revised in 1989, four of MacAndrew's original items were replaced with an equal number of items that discriminated between "alcoholic and nonalcoholic men" (sic) (Graham, 2000, p. 156) to form the Mac-Revised or Mac-R. Graham (2000) noted that high scores on the Mac-R "suggest the possibility of alcohol or other substance abuse problems" (p. 159).

The following rubric is generally accepted for interpreting Mac-R raw scores: 28 or more points are suggestive of substance abuse. Scores of 24 through 27, which are also suggestive of substance abuse, will produce false positives. Substance abusing persons are unlikely to produce scores less than 24.

The Mac-R's internal consistency estimates vary. While Butcher et al. (1989) reported alphas of .56 for men and .45 for women, Laux et al. (2004) reported an alpha of .88 for a mixed-gender outpatient sample, and Laux, Salyers, et al. (2005) reported an alpha of .82 in a college student sample. Estimates of the Mac-R's temporal stability have been fairly robust. For example, Laux, Salyers, et al. (2005), reported a 2-week stability coefficient of .97. Numerous studies (e.g., Hoffman, Loper, & Kammeier, 1974) indicate that Mac-R scores are stable over long-term treatment. Research into the Mac's factor structure (Weed, Butcher, & Ben-Porath, 1995) suggests the Mac-R measures cognitive impairment, school maladjustment, interpersonal competence, risk taking, extroversion and exhibitionism, and harmful habits.

Graham (2000) cautioned that persons with antisocial traits sometimes produce false positive Mac-R scores. Conversely, persons with schizophrenia or mood disorders who are also substance abusers may produce false-negative Mac-R scores. Also, Graham (2000) reported that African Americans are sometimes overpathologized by the Mac-R. Like many screens, the Mac-R is sensitive to substance abusing behaviors across the lifespan. Consequently, a person who previously abused substances but is now in recovery may produce a false-positive Mac-R score.

Finally, the Mac-R reportedly screens for substance abuse in general. Therefore, clinicians whose clients produce elevated Mac-R scores will have to conduct further inquiry to determine the use of exactly which substance(s) is (are) driving the elevation. For further Mac-R information see Craig's (2005) comprehensive review of the relevant literature.

MMPI-2: ADDICTION POTENTIAL SCALE (APS).   The APS (Weed, Butcher, McKenna, & Ben-Porath, 1992), a criterion-keyed scale, was designed to subtly assess adult personality traits thought to underlie the development of an addictive disorder (e.g., extroversion, excitement seeking, risk taking, self-doubts, and self-alienation). This scale's 39 items were selected based on their ability to discriminate persons who were dependent on alcohol or another drug from persons diagnosed with a non-substance-use-related psychiatric disorder, and from persons with no mental health diagnosis. T-scores of 60 or more indicate the need for additional substance abuse assessment (Graham, 2000).

Weed et al. (1992) reported one-week test-retest reliability estimates in the MMPI normative sample of .69 for men and .77 for women. Internal consistency estimates are available from a college student sample ($\alpha = .48$; Svanum, McGrew, & Ehrmann, 1994), and an Introductory Psychology class ($\alpha = .47$; Clements & Heintz, 2002). Sawrie and colleagues (1996) investigated the APS's underlying factor structure in inpatient substance dependent and psychiatric samples and found five factors: dissatisfaction with self, powerlessness/lack of self-efficacy, antisocial acting out, urgency, and risk taking/recklessness. Greene, Weed, Butcher, Arredondo, and Davis (1992) examined the APS's discriminative ability and found that it successfully distinguished between psychiatric and substance abusing samples.

The research investigating the APS's utility is mixed. While Green et al. (1992) concluded that the APS was a better measure of substance abuse than the Mac-R, Svanum et al. (1994) found that the APS was weakly correlated with substance abuse classifications produced by the computerized version of the Diagnostic Interview Schedule (DIS; Robins, Helzer, Croughan, & Ratcliff, 1981). Svanum et al. (1994) concluded that the APS possesses "at least uneven if not poor ability to identify substance dependence . . ." (p. 436). Clements and Heintz (2002) reported that the APS is less useful than direct measures of substance abuse. Clements and Heintz (2002) frankly doubted whether the APS is useful for substance abuse screening. Rouse, Butcher, and Miller (1999) offered a potential explanation for these findings when they noted that the APS's ability to discriminate between substance abusers and non-substance abusers is compromised in samples with high rates of emotional distress.

MMPI-2: ADDICTION ACKNOWLEDGMENT SCALE (AAS). The APS's 13 items directly meas-ure substance abuse. According to Weed et al. (1992), scores on the AAS represent "simple denial or acknowledgment of abuse problems" (p. 391). Scores on the AAS can be interpreted as a client's direct communication about his or her substance abuse status. High scores (T-scores greater than or equal to 60) represent open acknowledgment of substance abuse (Graham, 2000). Because the items are transparent, low scores may represent an absence of substance abuse; however, low scores could reflect interest in hiding one's substance abuse. Clinicians interpreting the AAS are cau-tioned that scores reflect a client's willingness to report substance abuse, and not the actuality of the abuse.

Weed et al. (1992) reported a coefficient alpha of .74 and a one-week test-retest coefficient of stability of .84 for females and .89 for males. Weed et al. (1992) reported that the AAS discrim-inated between a sample of substance abusers who scored the highest, non-clinical participants who scored the lowest, and psychiatric patients whose scores fell between these two groups. These findings were replicated by Greene et al. (1992) in a cross-validation study. Svanum et al. (1994) reported an alpha of .55 among a sample of college students and concluded that the AAS offered a "modest ability to detect substances dependent persons" (p 433). Svanum et al. (1994) suggested using a T-score cutoff of 59 to maximize sensitivity and minimize the false positive rate. Despite their findings of low internal consistency, Svanum et al. (1994) deemed the AAS to be the most useful of the MMPI-2 based substance abuse screens. Clements and Heintz (2002) calculated Cronbach's alpha in an introductory psychology college student sample and reported a value of .68. Clements and Heintz (2002) additionally compared the AAS to the APS and Mac-R and concluded that the AAS outperformed both. Using interviewer ratings as a criterion variable, Stein, Graham, Ben-Porath, and McNulty (1990) calculated the AAS's overall hit rate, sensitivity, specificity, and positive and negative predictive powers, for men and women separately, and compared them with those of the Mac-R and the APS. They concluded that the AAS is the best of MMPI-2 substance abuse screening scales. Rouse et al. (1999) agreed and declared the AAS to be the most efficacious of the MMPI-2's substance abuse scales.

Additional information about the MMPI-2 is available at:

http://psychcorp.pearsonassessments.com/ HAIWEB/Cultures/en-us/Productdetail.htm?Pid=MMPI-2" and *http://www.psychscreen.com/singletest/sam_mmpia.html*

Personality Assessment Inventory (PAI)

The PAI is an adult personality and psychopathology assessment. The PAI has 344 items that form 22 scales (Morey, 1991). Morey used both rational and empirical methods to assess a broad range of psychopathology, treatment-related variables, and interpersonal styles. The PAI contains one scale for assessing alcohol use (the Alcohol Problems Scale) and one for assessing drug use (the Drug Problems Scale). The following sections will provide greater detail about these two PAI scales.

PAI: ALCOHOL PROBLEMS SCALE (ALC). The ALC is a 12-item face-valid scale that measures both behaviors and experiences related to alcohol disorders (Ruiz, Dickinson, & Pincus, 2002). Schinka (1995) examined the ALC scales' reliability estimates in a sample of alcohol-dependent inpatient clients. Schinka's data produced an internal consistency alpha of .75 and a mean interitem correlation coefficient of .21. The PAI manual (Morey, 1991) reports that the ALC correlates ($r = .89$) with the MAST (Selzer, 1971). Morey (1991) also reports that ALC scores are related to personality traits generally associated with alcohol dependence (e.g., impulsivity, psychopathology, excitement seeking, and hostility). Parker, Daleiden, and Simpson (1999) reported that ALC scores were significantly related to the Addiction Severity Index's (ASI) (McLellan, Luborsky, O'Brien, & Woody, 1980), Alcohol Composite Score ($r = .49$), and ASI Interviewer Severity Ratings ($r = .44$).

PAI: DRUG PROBLEMS SCALE (DRG).   All DRG items are transparent in their nature. Schinka (1995) examined the DRG scales reliability estimates in a sample of alcohol-dependent inpatient clients. Schinka's data produced an internal consistency alpha of .92 and a mean interitem correlation coefficient of .49. Fals-Stewart (1996) investigated the DRG and ALC scales' characteristics in a nonclinical, forensic, and drug-treatment-seeking population. Fals-Stewart's results suggested that the ALC and DRG scales were subject to response management. Further, his results indicated that 31% of the nonclinical sample produced elevated scores on these scales despite not meeting current DSM criteria for substance abuse or dependence. These findings suggest that people can fake good on the DRG and ACL scales. In support of the DRG and ALC scales' discriminative ability, Schinka, Curtiss, and Mulloy (1994) reported that an alcohol-dependent-only group produced elevated scores on the ALC scale only, and not the DRG scale. A cocaine-dependent group produced elevated scores on the DRG scale only, and not the ALC scale. A third group comprised of both an alcohol- and cocaine-dependent subset and a polysubstance-dependent subset produced elevated DRG and ALC scales.

Further information about this scale, including free downloads, are offered at the following Web site:

http://www.psychscreen.com/singletest/pai.html

Millon Clinical Multiaxial Inventory-III (MCMI-III)

The MCMI-III's (Millon et al., 1997) 175 items provide a wide range of information about *DSM-IV* related personality disorders and clinical syndromes. The MCMI-III, valid for use with adults aged 18 and older, requires approximately 25 minutes to complete and provides information on 24 scales. The MCMI-III uses one scale to measures drug dependence (T) and one to measure alcohol dependence (B).

MCMI-III: DRUG DEPENDENCE (T).   According to the *MCMI-III Manual* (Millon et al., 1997), high scores on Scale T suggest that the client may have present or past problems with drug abuse, including difficulties with impulse management, acting within conventional social limits, and managing the consequences of one's behavior. Persons with high Scale T scores may have trouble organizing life's daily activities and may have difficulties with social, family, legal, and/or occupational life (Groth-Marnat, 2003). Many of Scale T's 14 items are indirect in nature. The *MCMI-III Manual* reports Scale T internal consistency and test-retest reliability estimates of .83 and .91, respectively, and a statistically significant correlation of .33 with the MAST (Selzer, 1971).

Calsyn, Saxon, and Daisy (1990) investigated Scale T's ability to discriminate between persons seeking drug treatment and psychiatric patients with no substance abuse history. Using the suggested cutoff level of 85 or higher, Scale T identified 19.7% of substance abusers. Scale T scores between 75 and 84 identified an additional 19.7% of the drug-abusing participants. 60% of the drug-abusing sample did not score high enough on Scale T for the MCMI to classify them as having a drug problem. Conversely, 12% of the nonusing psychiatric sample scored high enough on Scale T to be classified as having a substance use problem. Calsyn et al. (1990) concluded that the Scale T's 39.4% true positive rate and 60.6% false-negative rate should cause counselors to exercise caution when interpreting Scale T. This is in agreement with Marsh, Stile, Stoughton, and Trout-Landen's findings (1988) that only 49% of opioid-dependent persons scored higher than 74 on Scale T.

MCMI-III: ALCOHOL DEPENDENCE (B). High scores on the MCMI-III Scale B are likely indicative of persons who have a history of alcohol dependence, have attempted to overcome this issue with limited success, and have alcohol-related family and work complications. Scale B contains 15 items, many of which are indirect in nature. The *MCMI-III Manual* (Millon et al., 1997), reported Scale B internal consistency and stability estimates of .82 and .92, respectively, and a statistically significant correlation of .67 with the MAST (Selzer, 1971).

Further information about this scale, including free downloads of the PAI, are offered at the following Web site:

http://psychcorp.pearsonassessments.com/haiweb/cultures/en-us/productdetail.htm?pid=
PAg505&Community=CA_Psych_Settings_Military

COUNSELOR INITIATED COMPREHENSIVE SUBSTANCE ABUSE ASSESSMENT

Counselors interested in assessing their clients' use of alcohol or other drugs are not limited to a selection of standardized personality assessments and questionnaires. Diagnostic interviews can provide a rich source of data to help determine clarify clients' presenting issues. While some may elect to tailor their interviews to each individual client, others prefer a more standardized approach as a way to ensure that each client receives the same degree of inquiry. One standardized interview format available for this purpose is the Addiction Severity Index (McLellan et al. 1980), addressed in the following section.

The Addiction Severity Index (ASI)

The Addiction Severity Index (ASI) is now in its fifth edition (McLellan et al., 1980) and a sixth edition is expected soon. The ASI is in the public domain and there is no charge for its use. It was designed to serve as a generic tool with applicability across a wide variety of settings and is available in 17 languages. Leonhard, Mulvey, Gastfriend, and Shwartz (2000) describe the ASI as the standard assessment tool for alcohol and other addictions. The ASI is typically administered in an oral interview; however, a computerized version is available and Internet and automated telephone self-report versions were recently introduced. Estimated administration time is 60 minutes.

In addition to inquiring about demographic data, the ASI asks clients to answer a battery of questions about their medical history, employment background, alcohol and drug use, legal status, family history and social relationships, and psychiatric status. Clients answer these questions based on both their past 30 days and over the course of their life. At the end of each section, clients are asked to provide a self-rating scale from "not a problem at all" (0 points) to "extreme problem" (4 points). Likewise, counselors provide an interviewer rating scale ranging from "no real problem" (0–1 points) to "extreme problem" (8–9 points). The counselor severity ratings are estimates of the patient's need for additional treatment in each area. Counselors provide their rating based on the clients' symptom history, current situation, and the counselor's subjective judgment of the client's need for treatment in each area. The counselor also judges whether the client's self-rating is distorted due to misrepresentation or an inability to understand the questions. Composite scores are calculations of the client's problem severity during the past 30 days. Higher composite scores suggest a greater need for treatment in each respective area.

While ASI reliability and validity investigations are generally supportive (e.g., Butler et al., 2001; Leonhard et al., 2000; Moos, Finney, Ferderman, & Suchinsky, 2000; Rosen, Henson, Finney, & Moos, 2000), Makela's (2004) review of the empirical ASI literature, a total of 37 studies, led him to conclude that only three of the seven ASI composite scores demonstrated acceptable internal consistency reliability. Makela (2004) explained these findings by stating that the heterogeneous nature of the substance-abusing population is likely to provide inconsistent results from a homogenous screen such as the ASI. McClellan et al. (2004) found common ground with some of Makela's (2004) points but also countered that important articles were omitted from Makela's review.

A copy of the ASI is available at the following Web site:

http://www.densonline.org/ASICT.pdf
http://faculty.ugf.edu/jgretch/syllabi/adc_asi_form.pdf

ASI versions for Spanish speakers and persons of native American descent can be located here:

http://www.tresearch.org/resources/instruments.htm

INSTRUMENTS DESIGNED TO ASSESS ALCOHOL MISUSE DURING PREGNANCY

According to Bradley, Boyd-Wickizer, Powell, and Burman (1998) lifetime rates of alcohol abuse and dependence in women seen by primary care physicians range from 23% to 25%. Although women are more susceptible to medical complications from drinking, especially if pregnant, they are less likely to be detected with alcohol-related problems by healthcare providers (Bradley et al., 1998). Screening for women engaged in alcohol misuse during pregnancy is important due to the long-lasting impact of alcohol on children born to alcohol-misusing mothers.

Most existing alcohol screens were constructed based on male drinking patterns. Biological gender differences contribute to different effects of alcohol consumption, and about the effects of alcohol on the fetus contribute to different styles of drinking during pregnancy. Therefore, the adequacy of the currently available screens for use with pregnant women is questionable. One solution to accommodate these differences is to establish specific cutoff scores for pregnant women when using existing screens.

Because many women alter their alcohol consumption during pregnancy and deny or minimize the level of use, inquiries about alcohol use prior to pregnancy may produce more accurate information. This supposition is supported by the American College of Obstetricians and Gynecologists (ACOG) whose *Antepartum Record* (1989) presented the need for different screening methods for pregnant women. A movement to develop alcohol screening instruments for risky drinking by pregnant women grew due to these inadequacies in the existing screening instruments. To date, the literature features two such screens: the T-ACE, and the TWEAK. The following section will briefly address each.

T-ACE

The T-ACE was the first validated alcohol-risk screening instrument developed specifically for pregnant women. According to Chang (2001), the four-question T-ACE was developed based on the premise that women are less defensive when asked about tolerance to alcohol, rather than about the amount of alcohol consumed.

The T-ACE can be self-administered or administered by a counselor (Chang, 2001). The T-ACE includes a question each on tolerance (T), annoyance (A), efforts to cut down (C) and an eye-opener drink (E). The T-ACE can be administered in 1 minute and is scored on a 5-point scale by assigning 2 points for a positive "T," defined as a woman's self-report of needing more than 2 drinks to feel "high." The A, C, and E questions receive 1 point for affirmative answers. Two or more points indicate possible risk drinking during pregnancy (Chang, 2001). Using cutoff points of 1, 2, and 3, T-ACE sensitivity ratings of .83, .70, and .45, and specificity estimates of .75, .85, and .97 were reported by Russell et al. (1994) among a sample of African American women. In a diverse ethnic population, the sensitivity and specificity for risk drinking is reported as .92 and .38. When risk drinking was specified as less than 2 points, sensitivity decreased to 0.74 and specificity increased to 0.71.

The T-ACE is available at the following Web site:

http://pubs.niaaa.nih.gov/publications/arh25-3/204-209.htm

TWEAK

The TWEAK is a five-item instrument developed from questions from the MAST, CAGE, and T-ACE (Cherpitel, 1999). While not developed specifically to screen risk drinking in pregnant women, the TWEAK has been used almost exclusively for this purpose. The TWEAK includes a question each on Tolerance (from the T-ACE), concern (Worry) of friends and family (from the MAST), an eye-opener drink (from the CAGE), amnesia (from the MAST), and efforts to cut down (from the CAGE). The TWEAK is scored on a 7-point scale. A woman who reports consuming more than five drinks without falling asleep or passing out is awarded 2 points on the Tolerance question, as does a positive response to the Worry question. Affirmative answers to the last three questions (E, A, and K) receive 1 point each (Chang, 2001).

The TWEAK can be self-administered or administered by a counselor (Russell et al., 1994). Using cutoff points of 1, 2, and 3, sensitivity estimates of .87, .79, and .59 and specificity ratings of .72, .83, and .94 were reported by Russell et al. (1994) when the TWEAK was administered to a sample of African American women. Russell et al. (1994) also reported that the TWEAK is most sensitive in screening risk drinking prior to the fifteenth week of pregnancy, with an overall reported sensitivity and specificity of .78 and .84, respectively, during pregnancy. At a cutoff point of 3, Cherpitel (1999) reported that the TWEAK demonstrated higher sensitivity for males and higher specificity for females. The TWEAK's specificity and sensitivity rates were best for African Americans followed by European Americans, then Hispanic Americans. Cherpitel (1999) further concluded that the TWEAK is best used in emergency and primary care service settings. Bush et al. (1998) reported low sensitivity but excellent specificity for screening alcohol abuse or dependence and for hazardous drinking. Bradley et al. (1998) reviewed the literature on alcohol screening instruments for women and concluded that the TWEAK was the optimal instrument for identifying alcohol dependence in women.

Further information on the TWEAK including a copy of the instrument is available at the following Web sites:

> *http://pubs.niaaa.nih.gov/publications/Assesing%20Alcohol/InstrumentPDFs/74_TWEAK*
> *.pdf#search='TWEAK%20alcohol*
> *http://pubs.niaaa.nih.gov/publications/arh25-3/204-209.htm*

The following paragraph continues the case example presented at the beginning of this chapter. Pedro and the counselor met for approximately 2 hours, during which time he completed the MAST, SASSI-3, and the counselor-administered ASI. Pedro's responses to the MAST produced a score of 12. The SASSI-3 classified Pedro as likely substance dependent based on his elevated FVA scale score. The results of the ASI were consistent with the MAST and SASSI-3 but further suggested that Pedro receive a referral for a dual-diagnosis assessment to rule out additional psychological sequelae—post-traumatic stress disorder in particular. Pedro's counselor concluded that his presenting features supported the following *DSM-IV-TR* diagnoses:

Axis I:	309.9 Alcohol Dependence
	Rule out 309.81 Posttraumatic Stress Disorder
Axis II:	799.9 Deferred
Axis III:	None, by patient report
Axis IV:	Occupational Problems, Legal Problems
Axis V:	Current GAF: 55 Past year GAF: 70

Pedro was advised of the counselor's diagnosis and treatment recommendations. He decided to accept the recommendations to schedule an intake interview with the PTSD department and to place himself on the waiting list for inpatient alcohol dependence treatment. However, he felt it would be too embarrassing for him to attend Alcoholics Anonymous meetings in his community.

Olivia, a 17-year-old white Mennonite female, has been drinking alcohol since age 16. She drinks 4–5 beers a day plus "anything else she can get her hands on." She recently began experimenting with a variety of unknown drugs. Olivia reports no consequences related to her alcohol or drug use; however, while intoxicated, she did allow inappropriate photographs of herself to be posted on the Web. She says her parents are making a big deal out of nothing. Olivia's school suspended her because of the photos, as well as several alcohol-related incidents of misbehavior. In addition, she has been banned from attending her church. Both decisions please Olivia. She is verbally and physically abusive to her parents, who are deeply ashamed of her and are desperately seeking help. From the information provided in this chapter, what instrument may provide screening appropriate for Olivia's age and reporting behavior? What are some psychometrics of the instrument you choose that may confound the results?

Summary and Some Final Notations

Many standardized instruments are available to aid the diagnosis of substance abuse disorders. The benefits of using standardized assessment instruments include allowing clinicians to compare clients against a normative group, ensuring objectivity, the opportunity to counteract the confirmation bias mindset, and the opportunity to use objective data in clinical treatment planning and implementing of specific treatment interventions. For clarity, the benefits and limitations of the instruments discussed here are presented in Table 6.2.

Standardized assessment instruments are constructed using the logically derived method,

criterion keying method, or a combination of the two. When choosing an instrument it is important to examine its sensitivity, specificity, reliability, validity, and cost-efficiency, which are defined by Piazza (2002) as five characteristics of a good screen.

Screening instruments discussed in this chapter can be broadly categorized into two sections: stand-alone substance abuse screening instruments (e.g., ASI, AUI, AUDIT, CAGE, MAST, SASSI-A2, SASSI-3, T-ACE, TWEAK) and substance abuse scales found on personality assessment instruments (e.g., MMPI-2, MCMI, and PAI).

TABLE 6.2 Author's Rating of Abuse Screening and Assessment Instruments

Instrument	Strengths	Limitations
ASI		Requires training. Time consuming
AUDIT	Adequate sensitivity and specificity. Shorter versions available for quick screens	
AUI		Time consuming
CAGE	Face valid. Cost- and time-efficient. Adequate sensitivity and specificity	Not suitable for clients who are defensive about their use
MAST	Face valid. Cost- and time-efficient	Not suitable for clients who are defensive about their use
MCMI	Adequate reliability	Requires training. Not suitable for substance abuse screening only. Costs money. Time consuming
MMPI	Adequate reliability and validity	Requires training. Not suitable for substance abuse screening only. Costs money. Time consuming
PAI	Adequate reliability and validity	Requires training. Not suitable for substance abuse screening only. Costs money. Time consuming
SASSI-3	Adequate reliability and validity. Screening for adults. Includes face valid section and subtle screening for defensiveness	Requires training. Costs money
SASSI-2A	Screening for adolescents	Requires training. Costs money
T-ACE	Normed for pregnant clients. Adequate sensitivity and specificity	
TWEAK	Normed for pregnant clients. Adequate sensitivity and specificity	

Some of the stand-alone screens have different versions for special populations. For instance, MAST has a geriatric version and SASSI has an adolescent version. AUDIT and MAST have shorter versions (e.g., AUDIT C, FAST, and B-MAST) that could be administered when limited time is available for screening clients. TWEAK and T-ACE are specially used for screening for substance abuse disorders in pregnant women.

With the exception of the personality assessment instruments, most of the above-mentioned screening instruments could be administered and scored by clinicians without extensive training on the instrument. It is the recommendation of the authors that some of these instruments be included in the screening and assessment process of substance abuse disorders, along with clinical judgment, to provide clients with objective and accurate diagnosis.

Useful Web Sites

The following Web sites provide additional information relating to the chapter topics:

The Addiction Research Institute of the Center for Social Work Research at the University of Texas at Austin
*http://www.utexas.edu/research/cswr/nida/
    instrumentListing.html*
A compiled collection of instruments available online.

National Institute on Alcohol Abuse and Alcoholism
http://www.niaaa.nih.gov/
General information about alcohol abuse and dependency.

References

Adger, H., & Werner, M. J. (1994). The pediatrician. *Alcohol Health & Research World, 18*, 121–126.

Alexander, T., DiNitto, D., & Tidblom, I. (2005). Screening for alcohol and other drug use problems among the deaf. *Alcoholism Treatment Quarterly, 23*, 63–78.

American College of Obstetricians and Gynecologists. (1989). *ACOG Antepartum Record.* American College of Obstetricians and Gynecologists, Washington, DC.

American Psychiatric Association (APA). (2000). *Diagnostic and statistical manual of mental disorders* (4th ed., text revision). Washington, DC: Author.

Babor, T. F., Higgins-Biddle, J. C., Saunders, J. B., & Monteiro, M. G. (2001). *The Alcohol Use Disorders Identification Test: Guidelines for Use in Primary Care (2nd ed.).* Geneva, Switzerland: World Health Organization.

Bauman, S., Merta, R., & Steiner, R. (1999). Further validation of the adolescent form of the SASSI. *Journal of Child and Adolescent Substance Abuse, 9*, 51–71.

Blow, F. C., Brower, K. J., Schulenberg, J. E., Demo-Dananberg, L. M., Young, J. P., & Beresford, T. P. (1992). The Michigan Alcoholism Screening Test–Geriatric Version (MAST-G): A new elderly-specific screening instrument. *Alcoholism: Clinical and Experimental Research, 16*, 372.

Bradley, K. A., Boyd-Wickizer, J., Powell, S. H., & Burman, M. L. (1998). Alcohol screening questionnaires in women: A critical review. *Journal of the American Medical Association, 280*, 166–171.

Bradley, K. A., Bush, K. R., Epler, A. J., Dobie, D. J., Davis, T. M., Sporleder, J. L. et al. (2003). Two brief alcohol-screening tests from the alcohol use disorders identification test (AUDIT). *Archives of Internal Medicine, 163*, 821–829.

Bush, K. R., Kivlahan, D. R., McDonell, M. B., Fihn, S. D., & Bradley, K. A. (1998). The AUDIT alcohol consumption questions (AUDIT-C): An effective brief screening test for problem drinking. *Archives of Internal Medicine, 158*, 1789–1795.

Butcher, J. N., Dahlstrom, W. G., Graham, J. R., Tellegen, A., & Kaemmer, B. (1989). *Minnesota Multiphasic Personality Inventory-2 (MMPI-2): Manual for administration, scoring, and interpretation, revised.* Minneapolis: University of Minnesota Press.

Butler, S. F., Budman, S. H., Goldman, R. J., Newman, F. L., Beckley, K. E., Trottier, D., et al. (2001). Initial validation of a computer-administered Addiction Severity Index: The ASI-MV. *Psychology of Addictive Behaviors, 15*, 4–12.

Calsyn, D., Saxon, A., & Daisy, F. (1990). Validity of the MCMI Drug Abuse Scale with drug abusing and psychiatric samples. *Journal of Clinical Psychology, 46*, 244–246.

Chang, G. (2001). Alcohol-screening instruments for pregnant women. *Alcohol Research and Health, 25,* 204–209.

Chang, I., Lapham, S. C., & Wanberg, K. W. (2001). Alcohol Use Inventory: Screening and assessment of first-time driving-while-impaired offenders. I. Reliability and profiles. *Alcohol and Alcoholism, 36,* 112–121.

Cherpitel, C. J. (1999). Screening for alcohol problems in the U.S. general population: A comparison of the CAGE and TWEAK by gender, ethnicity, and service utilization. *Journal of Studies on Alcohol, 60,* 705–711.

Clements, R., & Heintz, J. M. (2002). Diagnostic accuracy and factor structure of the AAS and APS scales of the MMPI-2. *Journal of Personality Assessment, 79,* 564–582.

Craig, R. J. (2005). Assessing contemporary substance abusers with the MMPI Mac Andrews Alcoholism Scale: A review. *Substance Use & Misuse, 40,* 427–450.

Creager, C. (1989). SASSI test breaks through denial. *Professional Counselor, 4,* 65.

Crews, T. M., & Sher, K. J. (1992). Using adapted short MASTs for assessing parental alcoholism: Reliability and validity. *Alcoholism: Clinical and Experimental Research 16,* 576–584.

Ewing, J. A. (1984). Detecting alcoholism: The CAGE questionnaire. *Journal of the American Medical Association, 252,* 1905–1907.

Fals-Stewart, W. (1996). The ability of individuals with psychoactive substance use disorders to escape detection by the Personality Assessment Inventory. *Psychological Assessment, 8,* 60–68.

Feldstein, S. W., & Miller, W. R. (2007). Does subtle screening for substance abuse work? A review of the Substance Abuse Subtle Screening Inventory (SASSI). *Addiction, 102,* 41–50.

Fielling, D. A., Reid, C. M., & O'Connor, P. G. (2000). Screening for alcohol problems in primary care: A systematic review. *Archives of Internal Medicine, 160,* 1977–1989.

Fleming, M. F. (1993). Screening and brief invention for alcohol disorders. *Journal of Family Practice, 37,* 231–234.

Friedrich, W. N., & Loftsgard, S. O. (1978). A comparison of the MacAndrew Alcoholism Scale and the Michigan Alcoholism Screening Test in a sample of problem drinkers. *Journal of Studies on Alcohol, 39,* 1940–1944.

Graham, J. R. (2000). *MMPI-2: Assessing personality and psychopathology* (3rd ed.). New York: Oxford University Press.

Gray, B. T. (2001). A factor analytic study of the Substance Abuse Subtle Screening Inventory (SASSI). *Educational and Psychological Measurement, 61,* 102–118.

Greene, R. L., Weed, N. C., Butcher, J. N., Arredondo, R., & Davis, H. G. (1992). A cross-validation of MMPI-2 substance abuse scales. *Journal of Personality Assessment, 58,* 405–410.

Groth-Marnat, G. (2003). *Handbook of psychological assessment* (4th ed.). Hoboken, NJ: John Wiley & Sons.

Hedlund, J., & Vieweg, B. (1984). The Michigan Alcoholism Screening Test (MAST): A comprehensive review. *Journal of Operational Psychiatry, 15,* 55–64.

Hodgson, R. J., John, B., Abbasi, T., Hodgson, R. C., Waller, S., Thom, B., et al. (2003). Fast screening for alcohol misuse. *Addictive Behaviors, 28,* 1453–1463.

Hoffman, H., Loper, R. G., & Kammeier, M. L. (1974). Identifying future alcoholics with MMPI alcoholism scores. *Quarterly Journal of Studies on Alcohol, 35,* 490–498.

Horn, J., Wanberg, K. W., & Foster, M. (1990). Guide to the Alcohol Use Inventory (AUI). Minneapolis: National Computer Systems, Inc.

Horrigan, T. J., Piazza, N. J., & Weinstein, L. (1996). The Substance Abuse Subtle Screening Inventory is more cost effective and has better selectivity than urine toxicology for the detection of substance abuse in pregnancy. *Journal of Perinatology, 16,* 326–330.

Jacobson, G. R. (1983). Detection, assessment and diagnosis of alcoholism: Current techniques. In M. Galenter (Ed.), *Recent developments in alcoholism* (pp. 377–413). New York: Plenum Press.

Juhnke, G. A., Vacc, N. A., Curtis, R. C., Coll, K. M., & Paredes, D. M. (2003). Assessment instruments used by addictions counselors. *Journal of Addictions and Offender Counseling, 23,* 66–72.

Kitchens, J. M. (1994). Does this patient have an alcohol problem? *Journal of the American Medical Association, 272,* 1782–1787.

Laux, J. M., Newman, I., & Brown, R. (2004). The Michigan Alcoholism Screening Test (MAST): A psychometric investigation. *Measurement and Evaluation in Counseling and Development, 36,* 209–225.

Laux, J. M., Perera-Diltz, D., Smirnoff, J., & Salyers, K. M. (2005). The SASSI-3 Face-Valid Other Drug Scale: A psychometric investigation. *Journal of Addictions and Offender Counseling, 26,* 15–23.

Laux, J. M., Salyers, K. M., & Kotova, E. (2005). A psychometric evaluation of the SASSI-3 in a college sample. *Journal of College Counseling, 8,* 41–51.

Lazowski, L. E., Miller, F. G., Boye, M. W., & Miller, G. A. (1998). Efficacy of the Substance Abuse Subtle Screening Inventory-3 (SASSI-3) in identifying substance dependence disorders in clinical settings. *Journal of Personality Assessment, 71,* 114–128.

Leonhard, C., Mulvey, K., Gastfriend, D. R., & Shwartz, M. (2000). Addiction Severity Index: A field study of internal consistency and validity. *Journal of Substance Abuse Treatment, 18,* 129–135.

MacAndrew, C. (1965). The differentiation of male alcoholic outpatients from nonalcoholic psychiatric outpatients by means of the MMPI. *Quarterly Journal of the Study of Alcohol, 26,* 238–246.

Mäkelä, K. (2004). Studies of the reliability and validity of the Addiction Severity Index. *Addiction, 99,* 411–418.

Marsh, D. T., Stile, S. A., Stoughton, N. L., & Trout-Landen, B. L. (1988). Psychopathology of opiate addiction: Comparative data from the MMPI and MCMI. *American Journal of Drug and Alcohol Abuse, 14,* 17–27.

Martin, C. S., Liepman, M. R., & Young, C. M. (1990). The Michigan Alcoholism Screening Test: False positives in a college student population. *Alcoholism: Clinical and Experimental Research, 14,* 853–855.

McClellan, A. T., Cacciola, J. S., Alterman, A. I., Stenius, K., Butler, S. F., Greenfield, T. K., et al. (2004). Commentaries on Mäkelä. The ASI as a still developing instrument: Response to Mäkelä. *Addiction, 99,* 411–418.

McLellan, A. T., Luborsky, L., O'Brien, C. P., & Woody, G. E. (1980). An improved diagnostic instrument for substance abuse patients, The Addiction Severity Index. *Journal of Nervous and Mental Diseases, 168,* 26–33.

Miller, F. G., & Lazowski, L. E. (2001). *The adolescent SASSI-A2 manual: Identifying substance user disorders.* Springville, IN: The SASSI Institute.

Miller, G. A. (1985). *The Substance Abuse Subtle Screening Inventory (SASSI) manual.* Springville, IN: The SASSI Institute.

Miller, G.A. (1999). *The SASSI Manual: Substance Abuse Measures* (2nd ed.). Springville, IN: The SASSI Institute.

Miller, G. A., Roberts, J., Brooks, M. K., & Lazowski, L. E. (1997). *SASSI-3 user's guide.* Bloomington, IN: Baugh Enterprises.

Millon, T., Davis, R., & Millon, C. (1997). *Millon Clinical Multiaxial Inventory-III: MCMI-III Manual* (2nd ed.). Minneapolis: NCS Pearson, Inc.

Moos, R. H., Finney, J. W., Ferderman, E. B., & Suchinsky, R. (2000). Specialty mental health care improves patients' outcomes: Findings from nationwide program to monitor the quality of care for patients with substance use disorders. *Journal of Studies on Alcohol, 61,* 704–713.

Morey, L. C. (1991). *Personality Assessment Inventory—Professional Manual.* Odessa, FL.: Psychological Assessment Resources, Inc.

Myerholtz, L. E., & Rosenberg, H. (1998). Screening college students for alcohol problems: Psychometric assessment of the SASSI-2. *Journal of Studies on Alcohol, 59,* 439–445.

O'Connor, P. G., & Schottenfeld, R. S. (1998). Patients with alcohol problems. *The New England Journal of Medicine, 338,* 592–602.

Parker, J. D., Daleiden, E. L., & Simpson, C. A. (1999). Personality Assessment Inventory substance-use scales: Convergent and discriminant relations with the Addiction Severity Index in a residential chemical dependence treatment setting. *Psychological Assessment, 11,* 507–513.

Parsons, K. J., Wallbrown, F. H., & Myers, R. W. (1994). Michigan Alcoholism Screening Test: Evidence supporting general as well as specific factors. *Educational and Psychological Measurement, 54,* 530–536.

Piazza, N. J. (2002). Screening for alcohol and other substance use disorders. In R. S. Weiner (Ed.), *Pain management: a practical guide for clinicians* (3rd ed., pp. 825–832). Boca Raton, FL: CRC Press.

Piazza, N. J., Martin, N., & Dildine, R. (2000). Screening instruments for alcohol and other drug problems. *Journal of Mental Health Counseling, 22,* 218–227.

Pokorny, A. D., Miller, B. A., & Kaplan, H. B. (1972). The Brief MAST: A shortened version of the Michigan Alcoholism Screening Test. *American Journal of Psychiatry 129,* 342–345.

Robins, L. N., Helzer, J. E., Croughan, J., & Ratcliff, K. S. (1981). National Institute of Mental Health Diagnostic Interview Schedule: Its history, characteristics, and validity. *Archives of General Psychiatry, 38,* 381–389.

Rogers, R., Cashel, M. L., Johansen, J., Sewell, K. W., & Gonzalez, C. (1997). Evaluation of adolescent offenders with substance abuse: Validation of the SASSI with conduct-disordered youth. *Criminal Justice and Behavior, 24,* 114–128.

Rosen, C. S., Henson, B. R., Finney, J. W., & Moos, R. H. (2000). Consistency of self-administered and interview-based Addiction Severity Index composite scores. *Addiction, 95,* 419–425.

Rouse, S. V., Butcher, J. N., & Miller, K. B. (1999). Assessment of substance abuse in psychotherapy clients: The effectiveness of the MMPI-2 substance abuse scales. *Psychological Assessment, 11,* 101–107.

Ruiz, M. A., Dickinson, K. A., & Pincus, A. L. (2002). Concurrent validity of the Personality Assessment Inventory Alcohol Problem (ALC) scale in a college student sample. *Assessment, 9,* 261–270.

Russell, M., Martier, S. S., Sokol, R. J., Mudar, P., Bottoms, S., Jacobson, S., et al. (1994). Screening for pregnancy risk-drinking. *Alcoholism: Clinical and Experimental Research, 18,* 1156–1161.

Saunders, J. B., Aasland, O. G., Babor, T. F., de la Fuente, J. R., & Grant, M. (1993). Development of the Alcohol Use Disorders Identification Test (AUDIT): WHO Collaborative Project on Early Detection of Persons with Harmful Alcohol Consumption-II. *Addiction, 88,* 791–804.

Sawrie, S. M., Kabat, M. H., Dietz, C. B., Greene, R. L., Arrendondo, R., & Mann, A. W. (1996). Internal structure of the MMPI-2 Addiction Potential Scale in alcoholic and psychiatric inpatients. *Journal of Personality Assessment, 66,* 177–193.

Schinka, J. A. (1995). Personality Assessment Inventory scale characteristics and factor structure in the assessment of alcohol dependency. *Journal of Personality Assessment, 64,* 101–111.

Schinka, J. A., Curtiss, G., & Mulloy, J. M. (1994). Personality variables and self-medication in substance abuse. *Journal of Personality Assessment, 63,* 413–422.

Selzer, M. L. (1971). The Michigan Alcoholism Screening Test: The quest for a new diagnostic instrument. *American Journal of Psychiatry, 127,* 1653–1658.

Shedler, J., Mayman, M., & Manis, M. (1993). The illusion of mental health. *American Psychologist, 48,* 1117–1131.

Sokol, R. J., Martier, S. S., & Ager, J. W. (1989). The T-ACE questions: Practical prenatal detection of risk-drinking. *American Journal of Obstetrics and Gynecology, 160,* 863–870.

Stein, L. A. R., Graham, J. R., Ben-Porath, Y. S., & McNulty, J. L. (1990). Using the MMPI-2 to detect substance abuse in an outpatient mental health setting. *Psychological Assessment, 11,* 94–100.

Stein, L. A. R., Lebeau-Craven, R., Martin, R., Colby, S. M., Barnett, N. P., Golembeske, C., et al. (2005). Use of the adolescent SASSI in a juvenile correctional setting. *Assessment, 12,* 385–394.

Stinnett, R. E., Benton, S. L., & Whitfill, J. (1991). Simulation and dissimulation on alcoholism inventories: The ALCADD and the MAST. *Psychological Reports, 68,* 1360–1362.

Substance Abuse and Mental Health Services Administration (SAMHSA). (2007). *Advisory Council Report.* Rockville, MD: SAMHSA.

Svanum, S., McGrew, J., & Ehrmann, L. (1994). Validity of the substance abuse scales of the MMPI-2 in a college student sample. *Journal of Personality Assessment, 62,* 427–439.

Swartz, J. A. (1998). Adapting and using the Substance Abuse Subtle Screening Inventory-2 with criminal justice offenders. *Criminal Justice and Behaviors, 25,* 344–365.

Sweet, R. I., & Saules, K. K. (2003). Validity of the Substance Abuse Subtle Screening Inventory-Adolescent Version (SASSI-A). *Journal of Substance Abuse Treatment, 24,* 331–340.

Thurber, S., & Snow, M. (2001). Item characteristics of the Michigan Alcoholism Screening Test. *Journal of Clinical Psychology, 57,* 139–144.

Weed, N. C., Butcher, J. N., & Ben-Porath, Y. S. (1995). MMPI-2 measures of substance abuse. In J. N. Butcher & C. D. Spielberger (Eds.), *Recent Advances in Personality Assessment (Vol. 10)* (pp. 121–145). Hillsdale, NJ: Lawrence Erlbaum Associates.

Weed, N. C., Butcher, J. N., McKenna, T., & Ben-Porath, Y. S. (1992). New measures for assessing alcohol and drug abuse with the MMPI-2: The APS and AAS. *Journal of Personality Assessment, 58,* 389–404.

Wilke, D. (1994). Women and alcoholism: How a male-as-norm bias affects research, assessment, and treatment. *Health and Social Work, 19,* 29–35.

Chapter 7

Motivational Interviewing

Lisa Langfuss Aasheim
Portland State University

OVERVIEW: MOTIVATIONAL INTERVIEWING

Change is the central feature of any therapeutic interaction. Counselors work with clients to change feelings, attitudes, behaviors, perceptions, knowledge, skills, and behaviors. For decades, researchers have examined the change process and have attempted to find the mechanisms by which it occurs. In the 1980s, William Miller integrated his knowledge about the change process with ideas about how counselors can better enhance this process in their clients. These initial ideas paved the way for the emergence of motivational interviewing.

Motivational interviewing is a relationship-centered, client-centered system of change by which the counselor utilizes various techniques and interpersonal skills known to be effective agents of change. Motivational interviewing is not a theory of counseling; rather, it is a transtheoretical approach to the change process that encompasses both an attitude and set of techniques designed to elicit and enhance a client's internal change processes. This approach involves a spirit of collaborative communication and an interview-style format in which the counselor engages in a thoughtful exchange of questions and answers with a client in order to encourage and enhance motivation for change. Counselors using motivational interviewing embrace client autonomy and offer support and empathy to the client regardless of his or her place in the change process (Hettema, Steele & Miller, 2005). This system is based on the fluid and flexible Stages of Change Model (Prochaska, DiClemente, & Norcross, 1992). The central idea is that counselors engage clients in a voyage of discovery, during which clients discover their ambivalence about the change process, then resolve this ambivalence with activities designed to help them determine their own values and goals regarding the targets of change (in this case, whether to continue the use of substances or other addictive behaviors). Next, counselors work with clients to elicit motivation and enhance self-efficacy so that clients are more willing to commit to the change process. Once the client's commitment is fairly secure, counselors use a variety of techniques to help strengthen the commitment to change and support clients in continuing along the change trajectory.

In this chapter, counselors will learn about the Stages of Change Model. Second, the process of *change* and inherent *resistance* are explored. Third, readers will learn about the underlying principles of motivational interviewing, and fourth, will learn specific tools and techniques to employ when using motivational interviewing. Counselors will also learn about the varied forms of client resistance and how to manage resistance when it occurs in the therapeutic relationship. Finally, this chapter will focus on techniques that counselors can use to strengthen client commitment to change and, ultimately, maintain the desired change. This chapter concludes with a brief discussion of the advantages and disadvantages of motivational interviewing.

It is important for readers to note that motivational interviewing encompasses both an attitude (that the client is expert and that motivation comes from within), and a set of techniques and tools to facilitate change. Counselors must truly understand both the underlying principles and the techniques of change for motivational interviewing to truly be effective (Miller & Rollnick, 2002). In order to best understand motivational interviewing, readers must thoughtfully consider the nature and stages of the change process.

THE STAGES OF CHANGE MODEL

Making a permanent behavioral change is not usually an instantaneous act; rather, change is a process containing many stages leading up to and following the change itself. The Stages of Change Model provides counselors with a framework to better conceptualize and understand where clients are in this process (Prochaska & DiClemente, 1982). This model is transtheoretical, meaning that it can be used in addition to (and regardless of) a counselor's chosen theory or approach. The stages are nonlinear and may be conceptualized along a circle or wheel. Each stage represents a section of that wheel, and clients typically cycle around the wheel many times before achieving long-lasting change (Miller & Rollnick, 2002). That is, a client may begin the change process at any stage in the cycle and may either progress to the next stage or cycle back to prior stages. The process is quite fluid. Oftentimes, changes in activity level, motivation, or external circumstances may create a shift from one stage to another. The stages of change represented by this wheel are Precontemplation, Contemplation, Preparation, Action, Maintenance, and Relapse (Prochaska & DiClemente, 1982). It is important to note that Motivational Interviewing is not based on the stages of change model. Rather, the transtheoretical stages of change model explains how and why changes occur, while motivational interviewing focuses on increasing motivation for change (Miller & Rollnick, 2009).

Precontemplation is the earliest stage of the change process. In this stage clients have not considered changing their behavior, or they do not see why change is necessary. During this period individuals may deny having a problem behavior even though others (e.g., family, friends, physician, employer) are telling them otherwise. Precontemplators may even recognize they have a problem but may not believe they have the fortitude or willpower to change or overcome the behavior. Furthermore, precontemplators are typically unable to see or accept the negative consequences of their behaviors on themselves and/or others.

Case Study.　Jane has been drinking a glass of wine every evening for the past 12 years. In recent years, her consumption has increased to three glasses a night. She is able to keep a full-time job, raise two children, and manage her daily activities. Last week, she went to her physician and was informed that her liver is showing signs of damage and early stages of cirrhosis. Jane was told to stop drinking immediately. Jane's first reaction was, "I am not an alcoholic . . . I only drink a few glasses a day!" Further, liver problems run in her family, so she dismissed the problems as genetic, disregards what her physician has told her, and continues to drink several glasses of wine each night. She is unable to see her drinking as a problem and is not willing to stop at this time. Jane is precontemplative about change.

What techniques or questions might a counselor use to help increase Jane's motivation to cut down on her drinking without alienating Jane or losing her trust?

Contemplation is the next stage of change. In this stage, clients are open to the idea that perhaps their behavior is problematic. They are considering and mentally weighing the pros and cons of change, but are not yet ready to engage in actual change. Contemplators typically are thinking about change but do not act on those thoughts. This stage is characterized by marked ambivalence about the process.

Case Study. Jane's children begin to make comments about her drinking. Her son calls her a "stupid drunk" and her husband has demanded she cut back to one glass a night. Jane considers this but is terrified that she will be irritable, dizzy, and shaky like the last time she attempted to reduce drinking. Plus, how will she relax enough to be able to fall asleep? She continues to drink her typical amount each night, but begins to think about ways she can reduce her intake, and considers other ways of feeling relaxed instead of drinking. She does not intend to stop entirely but may eventually be willing to try to cut back to one glass a night to appease her family. What might a counselor say or do to honor Jane's initial thoughts about changing while addressing her hesitance about taking action (without coercing or trying to "convince" Jane to change)?

Jane is beginning to recognize that her drinking may be a bigger problem than she once thought. She realizes that when she reduces her consumption, she experiences some concerning and uncomfortable signs of withdrawal. She is considering decreasing her alcohol intake, but is not considering abstinence. She is contemplative about changing her target behavior and is considering reducing the amount of wine she drinks each night, but is not quite ready yet. She is considering the alternatives but is not quite ready to start behaving differently. Jane is on her way to the Preparation stage.

Preparation (previously referred to as *Determination*) is the stage when the client realizes that the behavior is having enough of a negative impact to warrant a change. The client is now ready to begin taking steps to actively change the target behavior. At this stage the client develops a specific plan. Oftentimes, clients will develop a change plan only after carefully examining their strengths, resources, and activities to determine what will help, and what may hinder, the change process (Solomon & Fioritti, 2002). The counselor, in this stage of change, plays a vital role in supporting change talk: that is, helping the client clarify and continue to articulate the value of potentially changing the target behavior (Mason, 2009).

Case Study. Jane speaks with her physician and gets a referral to a treatment center that specializes in problematic drinking. She makes an appointment to see a counselor after finding out that her insurance will cover treatment. She goes to the library and surfs the Internet to read material on alcohol dependence, and asks some family and friends for their assistance and emotional support. She selects her support team carefully as she does not want "support" from anyone who will ridicule her or make her feel inept. What might Jane's counselor say or do to help Jane feel the nonjudgmental support she is seeking at this pivotal stage of change?

Jane has created a change plan and has begun to act on her plan. She is now moving into the Action stage.

The *Action* stage is when the change plan is implemented. The counselor's role during this stage is to help the client remember why he or she decided that change was necessary. The client's role is to continue implementing the change plan and to call upon his or her support system for help as needed. This stage can be exciting for the client, counselor, and support system members who want to see the client's behavior change. However, it can also become overwhelming, as change affects multiple areas of a client's life. To help prevent the client from becoming overwhelmed or discouraged, counselors focus on increasing the client's self-efficacy (Miller & Rollnick, 2002).

Self-efficacy is a person's belief about his or her ability to accomplish a task (Bandura, 1993). According to self-efficacy theory, self-efficacy is a key predictor of performance (Tucker, Olson & Frusti, 2009). In this case, it is the addicted person's belief about whether or not he or she can reduce or eliminate the addictive substance, and the thoughts and behaviors associated with the addiction. Counselors practicing Motivational Interviewing will focus on enhancing self-efficacy throughout the entirety of the therapeutic relationship, but will focus even more specifically on a client's efficacy as action steps are taken.

Further, counselors with clients at this stage of change need to focus even more carefully on the quality of the therapeutic relationship and strength of the client-counselor alliance. Clients in these latter stages of change typically report stronger therapeutic alliances than clients at earlier stages and this factor appears to be quite crucial in helping a client maintain motivation to change (Emmerling & Whelton, 2009).

Case Study.   Before attending her first counseling session, Jane decides that she would like to cut back to half of a glass of wine a day. She is able to reduce to one glass (sometimes two), and is quite proud of her accomplishment. When Jane attends her first counseling session, she and her counselor discuss the plan to reduce to half a glass. Jane's counselor suggests that they enlist the help of her physician so that she is also under medical management to help with withdrawal effects. Jane's counselor asks her to discuss the support and strengths she has employed to be able to reduce her drinking thus far. The counselor helps Jane focus on her accomplishments to date, rather than on any setbacks or feelings of being overwhelmed she may be experiencing. Further, they will discuss the potential impact of continuing to drink even half a glass a day. Jane may decide it is a better idea to abstain entirely. What are the counselor's key duties at this stage in order to help Jane meet her goals?

Once the target behavior has changed and the action plan is complete, the client moves into the *Maintenance* stage of change. This stage is aptly named in that its sole focus is on maintaining the new, positive behaviors. Counselors at this stage will continually work with clients to maintain new behaviors in the face of cravings and relapse cues. Clients who engage in obsessive or catastrophic thinking in regards to their cravings may be more likely to relapse sooner rather than later (Nosen & Woody, 2009), so counselors focus regularly on addressing cravings and cues with clients.

Human tendency is to revert to an earlier stage of change and the target behavior is likely to return in times of stress or discouragement (Solomon & Fioritti, 2002). Counselors will view this as resistance and continue to engage the client in motivational interviewing. Relapses into former behaviors are viewed as a normal part of the change process, and their importance ought to be minimized. That is, rather than dwelling on the relapse as a "setback," clients can view it as an informative and typical event in the change process. The relapse is viewed as a signal that some additional action may need to be considered; the client and counselor can respond accordingly.

Case Study.   Jane has decided to fully abstain from drinking and is approaching six months of sobriety. She is actively using many of the techniques she learned in treatment and makes use of her sponsor and a support group. Jane has a strong sober support system and a recovery plan that details her steps to maintaining sobriety. Further, she has a relapse prevention plan and has listed the daily tasks she will engage in to actively prevent relapse. She is aware that she may relapse, but also has a plan in case that happens. She has shared these plans with her family and close friends so that she has extra support in times of need.

It is important to realize that the stages of change are not time-limited. That is, some stages may last only hours while others last for years. Sometimes a stage may be skipped altogether. Consider the following example:

John has been arrested for driving under the influence of an illegal substance. He subsequently lost his job, his girlfriend broke up with him, and his family feels disgraced. John wishes he never tried cocaine and wants to rid it from his life. Upon his release from jail, he decides immediately to enter treatment so as to break his cocaine addiction. In this case, John moves directly into the Preparation stage without spending time in the Contemplation stage. The Preparation stage is quite short-lived and he moves into Action as quickly as he can.

The stages of change are important in motivational interviewing because they help counselors determine the most appropriate techniques to use. Before using any motivational interviewing techniques, though, it is important that counselors fully understand the dynamics of change, the interpersonal nature of resistance, and the effect motivational interviewing can have on the change process.

CHANGE AND RESISTANCE

Change

Change is "the act, process, or result of altering or modifying" (American Heritage Dictionary, 2000). In the counseling process, "change" requires that clients make up their mind to do something differently, engage in different behaviors and thoughts, and then maintain the new, transformed state. Clients engaging in addictions counseling enter a quite complex process of change due to being both psychologically and physiologically affected by toxic and addictive substances. So, an addicted person's mind and body typically creates a physical, psychological, and neurological resistance to the removal of the coveted substance (Galanter & Kleber, 2004). This makes the addicted client's change process quite difficult, since, even when the addict decides that a change should occur, his or her body will likely continue to crave the substance of choice.

While counselors have an important job to facilitate and guide a client through change, it is necessary to remember that, typically, the change process belongs to the client. The client decides what behavior he or she would like to change, when that change will occur, and how quickly that change will take place. With addictions, the change process can be affected by the client's motivation as well as his body's recovery process as it is undoubtedly affected by the drug(s) of choice. Counselors need to acknowledge and honor the short- and long-term effects of addiction on the body systems, while taking great care not to use those effects as an excuse for complacency.

Resistance

Clients in all phases of the change cycle are likely to resist change at varying times. Resistance is described by Miller and Rollnick (2002) as an interpersonal exchange whereby a client appears to be working against change while a counselor may seem to be arguing for change. Resistance is often viewed as a client's desire to maintain the status quo by acting in opposition to the change process. However, motivational interviewing encourages counselors to approach resistance with welcoming arms. Counselors are encouraged to view resistance as a welcome signal that the therapeutic relationship is at a turning point. That is, the client is signaling the counselor that it is time to do something differently. The counselor, if attuned to this signal, will then switch direction and utilize another technique rather than continuing with the current approach. Rather than considering resistance as a problem with the client's motivation, it is viewed as an interpersonal strain between the counselor and client. The counselor's action in response to the resistance signals often determines what happens next in the counseling process. If the counselor continues to use the same technique that led to resistance, the client's resistance is likely to increase. If the counselor switches techniques and utilizes one of several "rolling with resistance" strategies (discussed later in this chapter), resistance is likely to decrease and the client's change process will continue (Miller & Rollnick, 2002).

Resistance can appear in a variety of ways throughout the change process. A client may appear to be resisting the initiation of a change process or may express a desire to stop pro-treatment behaviors. The techniques and principles of motivational interviewing provide counselors with the necessary tools to embrace, work with, and resolve resistance at any stage in the change process (e.g., Lewis & Osborn, 2004; Solomon & Fioritti, 2002).

MOTIVATIONAL INTERVIEWING: HELPING CLIENTS ACHIEVE CHANGE

Miller and Rollnick (2002) describe motivational interviewing (MI) as a "client-centered, directive method for enhancing intrinsic motivation to change by exploring and resolving ambivalence" (p. 25). Motivational interviewing is primarily used as a communication style that helps to facilitate change when clients are ambivalent about changing their behaviors. It is used as a collaborative tool between the client and the counselor that promotes self-efficacy and views resistance as part of the change cycle rather than as a personality defect or symptom of pathology. Rather than viewing a client as diseased or defective, clients' use is conceptualized in terms of the client's stage of change which the counselor is responsible for helping the client with. The counselor is responsible for employing MI tools that are effective at each stage of change. The change process is viewed as dynamic and fluid (Emmerling & Whelton, 2009), so counselors are flexible and adaptive in their work.

The change process is fluid and motivation can increase and decrease at any time. It is important for counselors to remember that they must assess a client's motivation to change at the beginning of each encounter. Further, counselors assess motivation ongoingly and will adjust their approach to be congruent with the client's motivation at any given time. Sometimes a client appears quite motivated, but when fear or anxiety set in, the motivation may decrease. It is necessary for a counselor to constantly monitor the client's experience and discuss these typical fluctuations as they occur.

William Miller created MI while working with psychology students who were asking provocative questions that he believed were facilitating change, yet did not necessarily fit in the realm of traditional psychotherapeutic approaches. Miller wrote an essay about his ideas called "Motivational Interviewing with Problem Drinkers" (Miller, 1983). In this article, he examined the means by which counselors can better facilitate change through the use of client-centered motivational enhancement. Over time he found these ideas were useful to practicing clinicians and decided to study the approach's process and outcomes. Motivational interviewing gained in popularity as outcome studies began to reveal the effectiveness of implementing it with substance-using clients (e.g., Miller, Sovereign, & Krege, 1988; Project MATCH Research Group, 1998).

Although motivational interviewing began as an approach to use when working with addiction, counselors, medical professionals, social workers, and other helping professionals now use it when working with a wide variety of problems, such as eating disorders, community health issues, couples counseling, criminal justice situations, HIV prevention, medication compliance, sexual health, and college binge drinking (Chanut, Brown, & Dongier, 2005; Gintner & Choate, 2003; Mason, 2009).

Motivational interviewing can be used in conjunction with a number of different counseling approaches and is not thought to be an approach to use on its own. It is not a theory of counseling, but a skill set used to engage people in counseling and the change process. Additionally, MI techniques are suitable for use through the entirety of the change process. Most important is the recognition that MI is more than merely a set of techniques. Instead, it should be conceptualized as a way of interpersonally relating to clients using collaboration, evocation, and autonomy (Miller & Rollnick, 2002).

A number of variables are considered to be important in the effective use of motivational interviewing. The counselor's individual style and use of techniques are important, as are the client's engagement, levels of resistance, intention, and experience of incongruence and discrepancy (Apodaca & Longabaugh, 2009). Clients whose counselors use MI are more likely to engage in change talk and commitment talk throughout the therapeutic process, which is predictive of better treatment outcomes (Amrhein, Miller, Yahne, Palmer & Fulcher, 2003: Apodaca & Longabaugh, 2009).

"Change talk" refers to statements or affective communications from the client that indicate a desire to make a change. A counselor's job is to detect change talk when it occurs and follow through on that change talk in a positive, reinforcing manner. Counselors use OARS to elicit change talk from clients. The "OARS" of MI are Open-Ended Questions, Affirmations, Reflective Listening, and Summaries. Counselors are intentional about what they choose to summarize and reflect upon and are careful to ensure the change talk stemmed from the client. Coercion and pressure from the counselor should be avoided at all times.

The Primary Principles of Motivational Interviewing

There are four pillars that guide the philosophy and subsequent counseling actions of motivational interviewing. These pillars inform counselors about how to relate to and act with clients engaged in any facet of the change process. The first pillar is *Expressing Empathy*. Empathy is the act of communicating to a client your understanding of his or her point of view with regard to his or her feelings, life experiences, and behaviors (Egan, 1998). According to the principles of MI, Expressing Empathy normalizes ambivalence and demonstrates that the counselor unconditionally accepts the client.

The second pillar is *Developing Discrepancy*. This activity is directive in nature and requires active listening and reflecting from the counselor. When a client is able to experience an internal discrepancy between his or her current behaviors and his or her values, beliefs, and goals, the change process can begin. This is due in large part to the underlying principle of *cognitive dissonance*. Simply stated, when there is a discrepancy between an individual's beliefs and behaviors, the individual will seek to reduce that inconsistency (Festinger, 1957). When a client reveals incongruence between beliefs (or attitudes) and behaviors, the counselor can help amplify the incongruency, thus highlighting ambivalence. Ambivalence is considered to be the catalyst to change, with the assumption that the client will seek to reduce the stress caused by cognitive dissonance. Motivational interviewers hope to help clients find consistency by engaging in behaviors that match their cognitive beliefs about how their life should be.

The third pillar is *Rolling with Resistance*. This means that a counselor must not argue for change; instead, the counselor will view resistance as a signal that the session should go in a different direction. The counselor will allow the resistance to exist and engage in methods that best address resistance (discussed later in the chapter).

The fourth and final principle of MI is to *Support Self-Efficacy*. It is crucial for clients to believe they have personal choice and control in changing their behavior. The client's idea that change is possible and that the counselor believes in his or her ability to change will increase self-efficacy.

These four pillars highlight the collaborative nature of the helping process, in which the client makes changes in their life without being coerced by external factors. They are instead internally motivated, which creates the perception of personal choice and is more likely to result in change.

Counselors should keep in mind the following guiding clinical principles when utilizing MI. First, counselors who use MI effectively increase change talk and decrease levels of client resistance more than counselors who use a confrontational or directive approach. Next, resistance talk (when clients argue against change) is inversely related to the degree of subsequent behavior change. Finally, the extent to which clients are able to verbalize commitment to change via change talk throughout the process is related to the degree of subsequent behavior change (Hettema, Steele, & Miller, 2005).

MOTIVATIONAL INTERVIEWING TECHNIQUES: EARLY IN THE CHANGE PROCESS

Five Techniques to Use Early and Often

The key book on motivational interviewing (Miller & Rollnick, 2002) provides descriptors of five early methods of motivation enhancement that counselors can use beginning from initial client contact and throughout all subsequent sessions. These five methods build a foundation for the tone of therapeutic work and immediately engage the client in enhancing his or her sense of importance, responsibility, and ownership of the treatment process. Several of these techniques are learned as counselors develop initial counseling skills: *asking open-ended questions*, *listening reflectively*, directly *affirming* the client's personhood and efforts, and *summarizing* the client's verbal expressions and exploration. The final method, *eliciting change talk*, is especially enhanced with counselors using motivational interviewing.

ASKING OPEN-ENDED QUESTIONS.   Counselors using motivational interviewing ask *open-ended questions* and try to avoid closed questions. Open-ended questions are inquiries that cannot be answered with a one-word response such as "yes" and "no," but instead require the client to provide more lengthy and thoughtful answers. The counselor may ask a client to "tell me about the times you use alcohol to relax" as opposed to asking "Do you ever use alcohol to relax?" Open-ended questions allow the client to explore aloud while the counselor provides encouragement and support.

In the early stages of motivational interviewing, it is the counselor's task to gather information and hear the client's goals. Questions designed to elicit this information will help build trust, develop rapport, and increase collaboration and consonance in the therapeutic relationship. Ideally, the counselor will ask an open-ended question and allow the client to speak uninhibited while the counselor responds with affirmations and encouragement so that the client may continue the verbal exploration. Counselors are cautioned against engaging in a back-and-forth question-and-answer session that may inhibit client exploration of ambivalence and intention. Counselors should also avoid closed questions that may be answered with a brief word or phrase as they provide limited options for the client, thus inhibiting exploration and sharing.

REFLECTIVE LISTENING.   Counselors using motivational interviewing understand the importance of *reflective listening*, as true reflective listening will help them provide answers that help move the client's change process along. Reflective listening is simply the act of repeating back to the client the content of his or her words in an unbiased, nonjudgmental manner. For example, if a client says, "I think it's fine to use marijuana. I have no idea why I got arrested for it!," the counselor may respond with "You're confused about why you were arrested when you feel you did nothing wrong."

Miller & Rollnick (2002) emphasize the importance of the counselor's response as crucial to the progress of the client's therapeutic work. Counselors who don't use reflective listening may respond in a manner that blocks the client's progress rather than demonstrating true listening and support. Imagine if, in the prior example, the counselor responded with "How could you not know why you were arrested? Marijuana's illegal!" The client's exploration process would likely be stifled and the therapeutic relationship strained. This is an example of a "block" in the change process.

Counselors are cautioned against engaging in any blocking behaviors. Some of these blocks include shaming, labeling, commanding, directing, threatening, warning, persuading with logic, lecturing, disagreeing, judging, criticizing, analyzing, consoling, sympathizing, questioning (probing), withdrawing, or changing the subject (Gordon, 1970; Miller & Rollnick, 2002). These responses are likely to be met with resistance or frustration, as the client may see them as attempts to change or reframe his thoughts and feelings. The counselor may use selective attention to decide which topics to reflect upon and which to pass over, yet it is essential that the client feel listened to and understood so that the client knows his or her feelings and goals will be honored throughout the change process.

AFFIRMATION.   It is important that a counselor support and *affirm* the client as exploration and sharing occurs. This may be done in a direct manner—for example, the counselor may say, "It seems that once you make a decision to change something, you give it your very best effort" or "That sounds like a great idea." The counselor is genuine and makes an effort to bring the client's strengths to the forefront. Affirmation is effective in enhancing the features and strengths that will assist the client greatly in his or her change process.

SUMMARIZATION.   Counselors using MI will make frequent use of *summary* statements. Summary statements recap what the client has spoken about and reinforce the content of what the client has shared thus far. Summaries are useful in ensuring the counselor understands the meaning of the client's exploration and lets him or her know that the counselor has been paying close attention. Additionally, summaries give the client a chance to hear their own words reflected back to them, thus prompting a response that leads to further exploration.

Miller and Rollnick (2002) discuss three types of summary statements that are particularly helpful in motivational interviewing. First, *collecting* summaries are short recaps designed to help the client maintain momentum. For example, the counselor who hears a client complain about the expense of cigarettes may respond with, "What are some additional reasons besides the expense of smoking that make you want to be a nonsmoker?"

Linking summaries use statements or ideas that the client came up with in the past (such as in prior therapeutic encounters) and relates those ideas to current information. These statements specifically address recurrent themes as presented in a series of sessions and are designed to highlight ambivalence. For example, a counselor might say, "You mentioned in our first session that you hate to be considered an addict, yet right now you would just prefer to stop caring about what people think of you rather than change the addiction. You don't want to be an addict yet you want to keep the addiction."

Transitional summaries are statements used to shift from one aspect of the therapeutic encounter to another. The counselor may use a transitional summary as a session wrap-up, or, in shifting from one topic of focus to another, to be certain the prior topic is fully discussed before moving on. Transitional summaries highlight the therapeutic alliance and make certain to reflect an understanding of the client's exploration and wishes. Summaries are not lectures nor are they one-sided; instead, clients should be encouraged to correct or add information that they feel is important.

ELICITING CHANGE TALK.   Motivational interviewing is a process that helps clients discover and examine their own reasons to change or not change. Motivational interviewers help clients by using *change talk;* that is, talk designed to prompt change rather than reinforce the benefits of the status quo. Eliciting change talk involves collaboration with the client, not confrontation.

The counselor's responsibility is to create a safe environment for the client so that the client can examine ambivalence. The client then decides upon a direction of change once the ambivalence has become uncomfortable enough to prompt change movement.

Several tools can be used to collaborate with clients and have them ask for change. One way is to ask open-ended questions. Another is the *Importance Ruler*, on which clients rate their ability to change their behavior on a scale from 1–10. Counselors then ask why the client chose that number rather than another one. The client's response helps reinforce the reasons to move toward change. The *Decisional Balance* can be used to help clients describe the positive and negative aspects of their behavior. During a decisional balance process, the counselor assists the client in fully exploring the pros and cons of change. A 2 by 2 table is often drawn, with four components: (1) the benefits of the status quo, (2) the costs of the status quo, (3) potential benefits of change and (4) potential costs of change (Miller & Rollnick, 2009). The counselor should help the client fully explore all components here and elaborate on their answers. This can be done by simply asking the client to "tell me more about that" or "describe that in more detail, please."

Querying Extremes involves asking questions that allow clients to look at the consequences of not changing, or imagining what life may look like if they did decide to change. When trying to assist in facilitating "change talk" it could be useful to have them look back at life before their problem behavior began or look forward to what they want their life to look like.

Looking Back or *Looking Forward* are techniques that can lead to clients developing their own discrepancies between the past, present, and future. For example, imagine if Jane's counselor asks her to remember a time when she was able to get through the day without wine. The counselor may also ask her to consider what life would be like if she had the confidence to get through a day without a glass of wine. The counselor might say, "Jane, how would you think and feel about yourself if you had non-alcohol ways of relaxing and coping with life?" or "How do you imagine your daughter would feel about you once you've had 10 years sober?" Any of these ideas can help clients facilitate change talk, especially when the client is precontemplative or contemplative about change.

THE ROLE OF RESISTANCE IN THE CHANGE PROCESS

The change process inevitably involves some client resistance. Resistance can affect the therapeutic relationship either positively or negatively, depending on the counselor's attitude and behaviors when resistance occurs. *Dissonance* is when the counselor and client are struggling with one another rather than working together in a truly collaborative effort toward similar goals (Miller & Rollnick, 2002). On the converse, counselor and client may be working *consonantly*, meaning that counselor and client are allied toward common goals and ideals. Consonance is the relational state that motivational interviewers strive for, and interruptions to this state (in the form of resistance) must be skillfully restored for the sake of an optimal working relationship. When a client demonstrates apparent resistance, it is important that the counselor interpret that as a signal of strain in the relationship (dissonance) rather than a pathology or attitudinal problem within the client.

The Many Forms of Resistance

Resistance behaviors may be divided into four process categories (Miller & Rollnick, 2002). One category, *arguing,* is when the client may appear hostile and argumentative, challenging the accuracy of the helper's statements and discounting the counselor's authority or credentials.

The next category, *interrupting,* is when the client takes on a defensive manner and may talk over the counselor or cut the counselor off. This is quite intentional in nature and is different than the client's typical conversational style.

A third category, *negating,* is seen when a client appears to be unwilling to acknowledge that there is a problem and/or appears to be resisting taking responsibility for the problems. This client will typically use excuse-making or blaming as a defense or may frequently disagree with potential solutions or suggestions. This client may also appear to have an illusion of invulnerability (Gerrard, Gibbons, & Warner, 1991) and may believe that the behavior is not putting him or her at risk for any potentially negative consequences. The client may appear uncooperative or intensely negative and counselors may find themselves experiencing countertransference in the form of negativity, helplessness, or anger toward these clients.

The fourth category of resistance behaviors is *ignoring.* A client may be using this form of resistance when he or she is not actively engaging in the helping conversation. The client may not be paying attention nor participating in the conversation, or not responding to prompts from the helper. The client may also be actively attempting to change the direction of the therapeutic conversation to a "safer" topic that is more amenable to the client yet off-topic and seemingly unrelated to the conversation at hand.

Counselors should be especially cautious of clients who change the subject to a "safer" topic when attempting to avoid (ignore) discussing the target behavior. Sometimes the change of subject is obvious and appears quite intentional. Other times, the change is subtle enough that a counselor may not recognize its occurrence. For instance, a client who is resistant to further discussion about decreasing heroin use may begin to discuss at length and with great emotion a troubled childhood and intense abuse. The counselor will undoubtedly feel tempted to change the course of counseling to address the childhood issues and may quickly lose sight of the initial conversation and original treatment focus.

Reducing Resistance

Counselors practicing motivational interviewing will reduce client resistance to the change process by maximizing *change talk* and reducing *resistance talk.*

To maximize change talk, counselors and clients will together examine the disadvantages of the current behaviors and patterns while examining the advantages of changing the target behavior. This may be done in the form of a pros and cons list, a decisional balance form that lists advantages of change in one column and disadvantages of change in another, or a verbal exchange where these factors are examined in-depth. Typically, it is helpful to discuss the client's intention to make a change and his or her feelings regarding the change (e.g., positive aspects, optimistic thoughts, and beliefs about the positive aspects of change).

At the same time, counselors will minimize resistance talk by decreasing the client's comfort with the status quo, challenging beliefs that the status quo is advantageous, and minimizing overall negativity about the change process. To accomplish this, counselors will utilize methods recommended in the practice of motivational interviewing while avoiding some potential hazards such as advocacy talk.

Advocacy talk occurs when a counselor reinforces or enhances resistance talk. Advocacy talk should be reduced because of its blocking effect on the change process. Some examples of advocacy talk include arguing for the client to make a change, playing the expert (recall that motivational interviewing assumes the client is the expert), blaming or criticizing the client, or being impatient or hurried during the therapeutic interaction. It is also especially concerning when the counselor puts his or her goals and ideas in the forefront, overriding the client's goals and intentions. Imagine that our client Jane has decided to reduce her drinking to one half glass of wine a day rather than two or three. Jane is not ready to eliminate her wine entirely. When Jane presents this plan to her counselor, the counselor responds with "You really should eliminate drinking altogether rather than cut back to half a glass a day. I've seen enough clients to know that you'll probably remain an alcoholic that way." Jane's plan for positive change has been blocked and diminished through the counselor's use of advocacy talk. More specifically, the counselor used criticism and arguing for change while assuming the expert stance.

In keeping with the collaborative spirit at the core of MI, counselors should be cautious when deciding to compare their clients with other clients or situations that they are aware of. While it is appropriate for a counselor to suggest remedies tried by others (once the client is at a solution-seeking stage), it is not appropriate for a counselor to suggest that a client will have the same outcome as others who use the same drug(s) of choice or have similar circumstances. Instead, the counselor focuses on the client's unique situation and elicits change talk from the client about how his or her own circumstances might change once the target behavior is adjusted.

Resistance is usually most apparent in the precontemplation and contemplation stages of change. Though it may be tempting to confront or argue with the client, this will usually lead to an increase in resistance and defensiveness. Instead, counselors using motivational interviewing will use a variety of *reflection responses* that are useful in working through resistance.

When a counselor uses reflection responses, the client does not have to become defensive and argumentative. Miller and Rollnick (2002) describe three types of reflection responses: Simple Reflection, Amplified Reflection, and Double-Sided Reflection. Consider the following examples of reflection responses to resistant statements:

Simple Reflection:

CLIENT: I don't know why my parents are making me come here. All my friends use pot.

COUNSELOR: It's hard to understand why your parents brought you here, when all your friends use pot.

Amplified Reflection:

CLIENT: My boss is interfering in my life by making me come here for treatment. I don't have a problem with alcohol.

COUNSELOR: Your boss' interference in your personal life is intolerable to you.

Double-Sided Reflection:

CLIENT: I can't believe my wife left me over my alcohol use. I don't know what her problem is—she should be in this room talking because she is the problem, not drinking.

INTERVIEWER: I hear you saying that you don't have a problem with drinking, but that maybe your relationship is the issue. It sounds like you care about your wife still since you are open to her coming to a session and maybe talking more about your relationship and the impact of your drinking.

Motivational interviewers will use the preceding reflections when encountering resistance. Some additional tools are also useful, include *Shifting Focus, Reframing*, and *Agreement with a Twist* (Miller & Rollnick, 2002).

Shifting Focus is used in order to talk around the feature of resistance rather than dealing with it in a straightforward manner. This is not avoiding the resistance, but instead taking a step away from the issue and refocusing on something with fewer barriers. The path to change does not need to take one giant leap over the wall, but can instead be comprised of taking on smaller walls as practice. For instance, a counselor who finds a client becoming argumentative whenever the counselor suggests reducing methamphetamine use may decide to engage the client in a conversation about his or her chronic underemployment. The client may find this a "safer" topic, but discussion about the client's repeated firings due to the aftereffects of drug binges may be an effective way to increase discomfort about the negative effects of the methamphetamine use.

Reframing entails restating what the client says, adding a new dimension to it. This may be done by adding educational information, creating or adding another meaning of the statement, or adding a different outlook. For instance, if a client says, "I've tried a hundred times to quit and each time I fail miserably," the counselor can respond with, "Yes, you are clearly determined and willing to get started in this process of change. Each attempt before has helped you get here now, to this moment, when your change process will get even further."

Combining a Reflection with a Reframe leads to the creation of another type of response, called *Agreeing with a Twist*. This is when the counselor agrees with the client's statement, then proposes a reframed outlook. For example, a counselor may say, "Yes, it may seem true that smoking cigarettes is considerably safer than your prior crack cocaine addiction. Given what you know about the dangers of smoking, do you think it's possible that cigarette smoking is more dangerous than not smoking any substances at all?"

The counselor needs to be aware of the many "traps" to avoid when encountering client resistance (Miller & Rollnick, 2002). The Question/Answer trap occurs when the counselor asks questions, the client provides answers, and the interview takes on the form of an interrogation or broken record rather than a thoughtful inquiry and exploration.

The confrontation/denial trap occurs when the counselor provides argument or suggestion for change and the client responds with reasons to maintain the status quo. Counselors must remember that motivational interviewing is not an attempt to coerce or convince a client to change; rather, it is intended to enhance motivation while allowing the client to make his or her own decision about the change (Miller & Rollnick, 2009).

The expert trap occurs when a counselor attempts to provide guidance or direction to a client without first laying the groundwork for such guidance. The counselor must thoroughly explore with the client his or her goals and intentions. They should resist the urge to provide guidance until after the client's motivation for change is strong (Miller & Rollnick, 2002).

The labeling trap indicates that a counselor has labeled a client as "addict" or "alcoholic," likely with the intent of urging along the change process. However, this is not in keeping with the spirit of MI and should be de-emphasized.

The blaming trap occurs as clients blame others for their problems. Miller and Rollnick (2002) espouse a "no-fault" policy which indicates that it is unnecessary to find fault or blame. It is not important to explore how the situation came to be, but only to determine the current problem, how much it bothers the client, and how to proceed in changing it.

The premature focus trap occurs when the counselor focuses too readily on a specific problem or component of a problem without careful exploration first. While MI is not Rogerian or Client-Centered therapy (Miller & Rollnick, 2009), it is necessary for the counselor to follow the client's lead to fully explore problems before identifying the target behavior that may be in need of change.

GUIDING THE CHANGE PROCESS: MORE MOTIVATIONAL INTERVIEWING TECHNIQUES

Enhancing Confidence

Clients are typically resistant to change because they either are not aware there is a problem (denial) or do not have the confidence to make the change in their life. Changing any behavior can be difficult and time consuming. It is important for counselors to remember that *enhancing confidence* is an important step in building self-efficacy, or belief in one's abilities to accomplish a given task (Bandura, 2001). While self-efficacy does not necessarily correlate with actual competence, higher self-efficacy does tend to help increase motivation to complete a task (Bandura, 2001; Greason & Cashwell, 2009).

Self-efficacy plays a vital role in helping build motivation toward change. A counselor may help a client build self-efficacy by assisting the client in finding small, manageable goals that a client can achieve in a short amount of time. These small goals help a client build self-efficacy and also lay the foundation for future change work. For instance, a client may decide that at some point in the future he would like to attend support groups and self-help meetings regularly. However, the client is not ready to attend his first meeting yet. The counselor may work with the client to create a small goal that leans in the direction of the larger goal, such as having the client look up a meeting schedule to consider the time and locations of various meetings.

Confidence is an internal process for clients and not something a counselor can create for them externally. However, there are strategies that counselors can use to enhance a client's confidence and self-efficacy. As mentioned earlier, the ruler approach could be used to first assess where the client's confidence level is at the present time. A counselor may ask, "On a scale from 1 to 10, with 10 being the most confident, what is your confidence level for changing your behavior?" Once the client has rated his or her confidence, a counselor can incorporate additional strategies to address confidence.

Some additional confidence-boosting strategies may include *reviewing past successes, examining personal strengths and supports*, and/or creating *hypothetical change*. *Reviewing past successes* involves counselors asking clients to discuss past successes (as determined by the client). The client then shares about the success and what he or she did to reach the goals. *Examining personal strengths and supports* involves the counselor and client together considering all of the supportive features and people that a client has access to, whether internal (e.g., sense of humor, determination) or external (e.g., supportive brother, support groups). *Creating hypothetical change* is encouraging the client to imagine what it would be like if their barriers were not an issue, or having the client look into the future and imagine what it would be like if they succeed in change. For instance, a counselor may say, "What will your average day be like when you are drug-free, employed, and living in your own home? Describe that day from start to finish. How will you feel and act?"

Strengthening Commitment

Once a client has the confidence to change, the next step is the commitment to change. Motivational interviewers use the *strengthening commitment* tool in this process. Strengthening commitment involves the counselor actively reiterating and highlighting what a client has accomplished since beginning the change process. This is a time that counselors may share advice with the client. As one of the key underlying philosophies of motivational interviewing states that the client is the expert in his or her own life, so giving unwanted advice becomes counterproductive. However, when the client has made the commitment to change and asks for advice or information about the process itself, counselors may give advice with the client's permission to do so. For example, a client may ask what to do next once he or she has made the decision to stop using drugs. The counselor may reply, "Well, you have many options. You could enter residential treatment, enter outpatient treatment, continue once-a-week counseling, or attend support groups. I think that outpatient intensive treatment would be a good place for you to begin."

Another way to strengthen a client's commitment is by using a Change Plan. A Change Plan, most useful when clients are in the Preparation or Action stage of change, is a collaborative project in which client and counselor develop a written plan of change. Miller and Rollnick (2002) suggest these four components when creating a Change Plan: (1) set goals, (2) consider change options, (3) arrive at or negotiate a plan, and (4) elicit a commitment. Counselors should ensure that client goals are attainable and not a set-up for failure. It is also important to be specific about how the goals are going to be accomplished. Counselors and clients should look at who is involved in the change process, what the change actions are, and when they will be completed. Obstacles to change may occur and it is necessary to plan for these proactively. It is also important to know what results the client is looking for once the plan is implemented and completed.

ADVANTAGES AND DISADVANTAGES OF MOTIVATIONAL INTERVIEWING

The advantages of motivational interviewing are plentiful. It allows clients, both mandated and voluntary, to discover their own reasons for making change. Motivational interviewing allows the impetus to change to emerge from within a client, thus honoring the his or her unique circumstances and worldview.

Motivational interviewing has been empirically validated by numerous studies that support its use with substance abuse and dependence, as well as with a variety of other mental health and medical issues (e.g., McCambridge & Strang, 2004; Moyers & Rollnick, 2002). A meta-analysis of 72 clinical trials utilizing MI describes the shorter term effects of MI use on certain populations across a wide range of problem areas (Hettema, Steele, & Miller, 2005).

However, motivational interviewing may not have the same effectiveness with severely mentally ill clients as it does with other clients due to barriers inherent in the severity of the illness (Ballack & DiClemente, 1999; Green, 1998). Ballack and DiClemente (1999) note that individuals with severe mental illness may not be motivated by the same reinforcers as most clients, thus rendering some MI techniques (e.g., affirmation) ineffective. Further, the impairment inherent in many severe mental illnesses may make the exploration process and cost-and-benefit analysis difficult at best. Imagine a client who has difficulty tracking in conversation and has flat affect, little ability to relate to others, and poor insight into his own ability to choose or not choose various behaviors. The counselor working with this client may have a difficult time practicing the early techniques for change, and may in fact not even be able to discover an adequate target behavior for change.

Additionally, it is important to note that motivational interviewing may not be sufficient in reaching all of a client's goals. A client may have some goals that revolve around making a behavioral or cognitive change, but would also prefer to do work that involves merely gaining support and additional information, rather than making a change. For instance, a client who comes to therapy to learn more about healthy communication with his or her partner may be better served by a psychoeducation group than an individualized change process involving motivational interviewing or other change techniques.

Summary and Some Final Notations

In this chapter, the process and stages of change were discussed as the foundation of motivational interviewing. Motivational interviewing is not a theory of counseling; rather, it is a transtheoretical approach to the change process that encompasses both an attitude and set of techniques designed to elicit and enhance a client's internal processes with regard to change. Readers learned about the foundational pillars of motivational interviewing: Expressing Empathy, Developing Discrepancy, Rolling with Resistance, and Supporting Self-Efficacy. Counselors learned that these four pillars serve as the foundational premise for the change process.

Next, counselors learned about the motivational interviewing techniques that are most effective in the early stages of engagement and retention. These techniques included: asking open-ended questions, listening reflectively, affirming the client's efforts, summarizing the client's expressions, and eliciting change talk. Counselors learned about client resistance and the many forms resistance can take, including arguing, interrupting, negating, and ignoring. Counselors also learned that resistance is not a client problem; instead, it is a welcome signal to the counselor that it is time to attempt a new technique rather than trying harder at what is not working. Counselors learned a number of techniques in this chapter to effectively roll with client resistance, including using Reflection, Shifting Focus, and Agreement with a Twist. Counselors also learned about the "traps" they may fall into while working with MI and are cautioned against working countertherapeutically.

Finally, readers learned additional techniques to enhance motivation and increase momentum in the change process. Counselors learned how to strengthen and renew a client's commitment to change, and learned about situations in which motivational interviewing may be disadvantageous and ineffective.

Useful Web Sites

The following Web sites provide additional information relating to the chapter topics:

The Addiction Technology Transfer Center
http://www.mid-attc.org/mi.htm

Motivational Interviewing Founder's Site
http://www.motivationalinterview.org/

Motivational Interviewing Guidelines
http://www.bhrm.org/guidelines/motiveint.pdf

Motivational Interviewing with a Corrections Population/ Lesson Plans
http://www.nicic.org/Library/019791

References

Amrhein, P. C., Miller, W. R., Yahne, C. E., Palmer, M., & Fulcher, L. (2003). Client commitment language during motivational interviewing predicts drug use outcomes. *Journal of Consulting & Clinical Psychology, 71*, 862–878.

Apodaca, T. R., & Longabaugh, R. (2009). Mechanisms of change in motivational interviewing: a review and preliminary evaluation of the evidence. *Addiction, 104*, 705–715.

Ballack, A. S., & DiClemente, C. C. (1999). Treating substance abuse among patients with schizophrenia. *Psychiatric Services, 50*(1), 75–80.

Bandura, A. (1993). Perceived self-efficacy in cognitive development and functioning. *Educational Psychologist, 28*, 117–148.

Bandura, A. (2001). Social cognitive theory: An agentive perspective. *Annual Review of Psychology, 52*, 1–26.

Chanut, F., Brown, T. G., & Dongier, M. (2005). Motivational interviewing and clinical psychiatry. *Canadian Journal of Psychiatry, 50*(9), 548–553.

Egan, G. (1998). *The skilled helper: a problem-management approach to helping* (6th ed.). Pacific Grove, CA: Brooks/Cole.

Emmerling, M. E., & Whelton, W. J. (2009). Stages of change and the working alliance in psychotherapy. *Psychotherapy Research, 19*(6), 687–698.

Festinger, L. (1957). *A theory of cognitive dissonance.* Stanford, CA : Stanford University Press.

Galanter, M., & Kleber, H. D. (2004). *Textbook of substance abuse treatment* (3rd ed.). Arlington, VA: American Psychiatric Publishing.

Gerrard, M., Gibbons, F. X., & Warner, T. D. (1991). Effects of reviewing risk-relevant behavior on perceived vulnerability among women marines. *Health Psychology, 10*, 173–179.

Gintner, G. G., & Choate, L. H. (2003). Stage-matched motivational interventions for college student binge-drinkers. *Journal of College Counseling, 6*(2), 99–113.

Gordon, T. (1970). *Parent effectiveness training.* New York: Wyden.

Greason, P. B., & Cashwell. C. S. (2009). Mindfulness and counseling self-efficacy: the mediating role of attention and empathy. *Counselor Education and Supervision, 49*, 2–19.

Green, M. F. (1998). Schizophrenia from a neurocognitive perspective: Probing the impenetrable darkness. Boston: Allyn & Bacon.

Hettema, J., Steele, J., & Miller, W. R. (2005). Motivational Interviewing. *Annual Review of Clinical Psychology, 1*, 91–111.

Lewis, T. F., & Osborn, C. J. (2004). Solution-focused counseling and motivational interviewing: A consideration of confluence. *Journal of Counseling & Development, 82*, 38–48.

Mason, M. J. (2009). Rogers redux: relevance and outcomes of motivational interviewing across behavioral problems. *Journal of Counseling & Development, 87*, 357–362.

McCambridge, J., & Strang, J. (2004). The efficacy of single-session motivational interviewing in reducing drug consumption and perceptions of drug-related risk and harm among young people: Results from a multi-site cluster randomized trial. *Addiction, 99*, 39–52.

Miller, W. R. (1983). Motivational interviewing with problem drinkers. *Behavioural Psychotherapy, 11*, 147–172.

Miller, W. R., & Rollnick, S. (2002). *Motivational interviewing: Preparing people for change* (2nd ed.). New York: Guilford Press.

Miller, W. R., & Rollnick, S. (2009). Ten things that motivational interviewing is not. *Behavioural and Cognitive Psychotherapy, 37*, 129–140.

Miller, W. R., Sovereign, R. G., & Krege, B. (1988). Motivational interviewing with problem drinkers: II. The drinker's check up as a preventive intervention. *Behavioral Psychotherapy, 16*, 251–268.

Moyers, T. B., & Rollnick, S. (2002). A motivational interviewing perspective on resistance in psychotherapy. *Psychotherapy in Practice, 58*(2), 185–193.

Nosen, E., & Woody, S. R. (2009). Applying lessons learned from obsessions: metacognitive processes in smoking cessation. *Cognitive Therapy Research, 33*, 241–254.

Prochaska, J. O., & DiClemente, C. C. (1982). Transtheoretical therapy: Toward a more integrative model of change. *Psychotherapy: Theory, Research and Practice, 19*, 276–288.

Prochaska, J. O., DiClemente, C. C., & Norcross, J. C. (1992). In search of how people change. *American Psychologist, 47*, 1102–1114.

Project MATCH Research Group. (1998). Therapist effects in three treatments for alcohol problems. *Psychotherapy Research, 8*, 455–474.

Solomon, J., & Fioritti, A. (2002). Motivational intervention as applied to systems change: The case of dual diagnosis. *Substance Abuse & Misuse, 37*(14), 1833–1851.

Tucker, S., Olson, M. E., & Frusti, D. K. (2009). Validity and reliability of the evidence-based practice self-efficacy scale. *Western Journal of Nursing Research, 31*(8), 1090–1091.

Chapter 8

Psychotherapeutic Approaches

Cynthia J. Osborn
Kent State University

COUNSELOR BELIEFS AND BEHAVIORS

Clinician attitudes significantly influence the acceptance and utilization of new or innovative therapeutic approaches (Levenson, Speed, & Budman, 1995). In addictions treatment, this is influenced in part by clinicians' understanding of addiction in general (Ogborne, Wild, Braun, & Newton-Taylor, 1998; Shaffer & Robbins, 1991), alcoholism in particular (Miller & Hester, 2003), and the purpose and intended outcome of treatment (e.g., abstinence; Caplehorn, Lumley, & Irwig, 1998).

Using cluster and discriminant analyses, Thombs and Osborn (2001) identified three distinct groups or types of chemical dependency counselors in Ohio ($N = 343$), based on participants' views of addiction and its treatment. "Uniform counselors" (56%) appeared to lend moderate support for moral and disease concepts of addiction, "multiform counselors" (29%) endorsed a broad range of beliefs about the nature of addiction and its treatment, and "client-directed counselors" (15%) were characterized as practitioners who recognized "heterogeneity among clients and consider[ed] counselor listening to be an essential aspect of treatment" (p. 454). Compared to the multiform counselors, client-centered counselors, among other characteristics, had greater confidence in their knowledge of *Diagnostic and Statistical Manual of Mental Disorders-IV* (*DSM-IV*; American Psychiatric Association, 1994) criteria, were more likely to hold a higher academic degree, and were more likely to be licensed as mental health counselors. This and other studies (e.g., Caplehorn et al., 1998; Moyers & Miller, 1993; Ogborne et al., 1998) suggests that addiction ideology (e.g., medical, humanitarian or empathic, moralistic) does affect the selection of treatment strategies.

Advances in medical technology have paved the way for more sophisticated research initiatives in the areas of human genetics, neurobiology, and behavior. Coherent synopses of these findings are available for professionals (e.g., W. R. Miller & Carroll, 2006) and laypersons alike (e.g., Interlandi, 2008), and have the potential to challenge longstanding and entrenched views of addiction, and drastically change how chemical dependence is treated.

Although W. R. Miller, Sorensen, Selzer, and Brigham (2006) noted a shift in how addiction is understood in the United States today, movement away from the "widespread" endorsement of substance dependence as a disease (Ogborne et al., 1998) to an understanding of addiction as a complex phenomenon is likely to be slow. This is true in light of the disease model's history as the "dominant" model of addiction in the United States (Morgenstern, Frey, McCrady, Labouvie, & Neighbors, 1996). Definitions of addiction as a disease do vary (see Thombs, 2006), but common elements include an acceptance of addiction (namely alcoholism) as a chronic, progressive, involuntary, irreversible, and potentially fatal illness, which has as its core criteria the loss of control over the intake of alcohol and physiological dependence. A single, standard, pre-determined form of treatment is often used, without regard for individual differences among clients. Lifetime abstinence is the unquestionable goal, and participation in Alcoholics Anonymous (AA) is strongly endorsed.

Many chemical dependency counselors may thus practice within the bounds of one model of addiction—likely the (ill-defined) disease model of addiction. Such a myopic perspective can have the effect of missing, ignoring, or even dismissing other, perhaps equally valid, explanations for a client's addiction and of an inability to appreciate or apply alternative treatment methods. Indeed, Tracy (2007) concluded her brief historical review of the disease concept in the United States by stating that "It may be time to embrace a more holistic view of disease and disability, to appreciate the multiplicity of factors . . . that affect what we consider 'healthy' and 'diseased'" (p. 91).

This chapter is intended to offer practitioners an array or menu of treatment approaches in their efforts to assist a variety of clients struggling with substance use concerns. Just as there is no one "alcoholic" or "drug addict," there is no one "tried and true" treatment approach. Miller and Hester's (2003) "informed eclecticism" model guides the content of this chapter in that (a) there is no single superior approach to treatment for all individuals, (b) treatment programs and systems should be constructed with a variety of approaches that have been shown to be effective, and (c) different types of individuals respond best to different treatment approaches. In addition, W. R. Miller and Hester strongly emphasize tailoring or customizing treatment to the unique needs and strengths of each individual client, thereby increasing treatment effectiveness and efficiency. Implicit in this model is the need for all helping professionals in the addictions field to be familiar with a multiplicity of interventions so as to select from and offer the most appropriate type (or combination of types) and level of care to those needing and deserving quality services. Attention is given in this chapter to the application of research-supported counseling approaches. A list of useful Web sites addressing topics discussed in this chapter (namely, cognitive-behavioral interventions, brief interventions, solution-focused counseling, and harm reduction) is provided.

EVIDENCE-BASED PRACTICES

As the mental health field has been challenged with implementing evidence-based practices (see Drake, Merrens, & Lynde, 2005; Goodheart, Kazdin, & Sternberg, 2006), so too has the substance abuse counseling/chemical dependency treatment field (P. M. Miller, 2009). As of January 2010, the Substance Abuse and Mental Health Services Administration's (SAMHSA) National Registry of Evidence-based Programs and Practices (NREPP; *http://www.nrepp.samhsa.gov*) listed 96 interventions for substance abuse prevention and treatment. Included are relapse prevention therapy, family behavior therapy, motivational interviewing (MI), motivational enhancement therapy (an adaptation of MI), multisystemic therapy, contingency management, Seeking Safety (treatment for co-occurring substance abuse and trauma), and several brief interventions (e.g., Brief Alcohol Screening and Intervention for College Students, BASICS).

Despite the proven record of many addiction treatments, however, adoption and implementation of these practices by facilities and practitioners providing direct service has been slow. W. R. Miller (1992) unabashedly stated that treatment programs have relied "to a surprising extent" on interventions "that have never been proven to be effective" (p. 99). Carroll (1998) described this tendency as "an inverse relationship between treatments with the highest level of empirical support and those most widely practiced" (p. 219). Such a gap was found in Herbeck,

Hser, and Teruya's (2008) survey of program administrators and front-line clinicians in California who reported recognizing certain interventions as efficacious, but not routinely implementing them.

Based on their extensive and exhaustive review of 363 controlled trials of 99 different alcoholism treatment modalities (involving 75,000 clients) through the year 2000, W. R. Miller, Wilbourne, and Hettema (2003) acknowledged little overlap between modalities with strong research support and "those components often employed in U.S. alcoholism treatment programs" today (p. 41). Due to both the methodological rigor employed and the strength of treatment outcome, 18 modalities were determined to be efficacious. These included brief intervention; motivation enhancement; community reinforcement; self-change manual; behavioral self-control training; social skills training; behavioral marital therapy and family therapy; a variety of pharmacologic interventions (e.g., Acamprosate, Naltrexone); and cognitive therapy. Results are comparable to two earlier reviews of 302 controlled clinical studies (W. R. Miller, Andrews, Wilbourne, & Bennett, 1998) and 361 controlled studies (W. R. Miller & Wilbourne, 2002) of treatments for alcohol problems through the year 1996 and 1998, respectively; that is, all treatment modalities demonstrating positive outcomes in earlier reviews maintained their treatment efficacy in W. R. Miller et al.'s (2003) review. This suggests that the efficacious modalities identified over the past 10 years or so for the treatment of alcohol problems are not anomalies or "flukes" but appear to represent credible and trustworthy approaches in addictions treatment.

COGNITIVE-BEHAVIORAL ASSUMPTIONS AND PRACTICES

As can be seen from W. R. Miller et al.'s (2003) review of alcoholism treatment approaches, cognitive-behavioral (CB) interventions are well represented among the most effective treatments. These include behavioral self-control training, community reinforcement, contingency management and behavior contracting, social skills training, and behavioral couples/family counseling. Additional research suggests that these and other CB approaches are also effective for treating other drug dependence (e.g., cocaine and opioids). Two approaches (contingency management and behavior contracting, and community reinforcement) are briefly discussed in this section, highlighting their incorporation into substance abuse counseling.

Assumptions of Cognitive-Behavioral (CB) Substance Abuse Counseling

1. Substance abuse involves complex cognitive and behavioral processes
2. Substance abuse and associated CB processes are, to a large extent, learned
3. Substance abuse and associated CB processes can be modified, particularly by means of CB counseling
4. A major goal of CB counseling for substance abuse is to teach coping skills to resist substance use and to reduce problems associated with substance abuse and dependence
5. CB counseling requires comprehensive case conceptualization that serves as the basis for selecting specific CB techniques
6. To be effective, CB counseling must be provided in the context of a warm, supportive, collaborative counseling relationship

Source: Najavits, Liese, & Harned, 2005.

As noted in the previous sidebar, cognitive-behavioral (CB) theories of substance abuse and dependence typically operate according to six assumptions (Najavits, Liese, & Harned, 2005).

The six CB assumptions convey the importance of the substance abuse counselor intentionally integrating and implementing a variety of technical skills and personal qualities (e.g., empathy). For example, in order to help or teach a client in the early phase of recovery from cocaine use specific ways to manage cravings (e.g., "ride the craving wave") and urges (e.g., "surf the urge"), the substance abuse counselor should not only have knowledge of the physiological effects of cocaine use and a comprehensive understanding of the client's substance use history (by having completed a thorough case conceptualization) but should also have an appreciation for the first-hand experiences of the client struggling to stay clean. That is, by abstaining from something important to him or her (e.g., a behavior, beverage, or food item) and entering into an actual "abstinence contract" while practicing as a counselor, the substance abuse counselor (whether recovering or not from chemical addiction) can acquire greater empathy for the client's subjective experiences. Graduate students ($N = 120$) enrolled in a substance abuse counseling course offered once per academic year (Osborn & Lewis, 2004) consistently reported that experiential assignments of trying to uphold an abstinence contract for the academic semester and attending 12-step self-help groups (e.g., AA) were valuable, possibly engendering greater empathy for persons struggling with substance use. As one student in the course noted,

> ". . . we get so involved in the role of counselor that we sometimes forget the client inside us. It can become habit to separate ourselves from our clients with a sense of self-righteousness that we do not have the problems they do." (p. 49).

Yet another student reflecting on the abstinence experience stated, "I don't know how many times I have said and heard others say to smokers, 'Just quit.' Now I have a sense of why that doesn't work" (p. 50). CB practices in substance abuse counseling, therefore, may not be confined to interventions used with clients; they might also include the substance abuse counselor's own personal practices. Experiential learning, which incorporates CB assumptions and practices, might be considered an activity shared by *both* the client and counselor while engaged in counseling.

Cognitive-Behavioral Interventions That Target Triggers

Najavits et al. (2005) described specific CB interventions that address coping skills and are grouped according to five factors or types of precursors (or triggers) to addictive behaviors. Due to the multiplicity of factors that contribute to problematic substance use, interventions can and often are implemented to address more than one type of trigger. *Social interventions* include certain lifestyle changes (e.g., exercise, meditation), enhancing one's sober social support (e.g., attending AA/NA meetings), and refusal skills (i.e., practicing verbal and nonverbal communication to avoid and turn down offers to use). One client I worked with requested that the guided imagery exercises we had engaged in during our weekly sessions (I had tailored a script designed for this particular client and facilitated—verbalized—the exercise) be audio taped so that he could participate in guided imagery outside of our sessions. One day when I left the counseling facility, I could see this client sitting on a nearby park bench, eyes closed, and earphones on. I surmised he might be listening to my voice, guiding him through relaxation and a new awareness of sobriety.

Cognitive-Behavioral Interventions

- Social – lifestyle changes, social skills training, interpersonal conflict management
- Environmental – living/geographic changes, cue exposure
- Emotional – to regulate both positive and negative emotions (e.g., distress tolerance, reframing, self-soothing)
- Cognitive – to modify automatic thoughts
- Physical – to introduce distractions from triggers, urges, and cravings to use

Source: (Najavits, Liese, & Harned, 2005)

Environmental interventions include cue exposure whereby environmental triggers associated with substance use (e.g., photos or videos of drug paraphernalia or persons using substances) are repeatedly viewed while being monitored so that automatic responses (e.g., cravings, urges to use) are diminished or even extinguished. Clients can also be advised to thoroughly clean their living space, one area or one room at a time, so as to reinforce their sense of control over their own personal or local environment. This practice could also symbolize a cleansing or purging of the "toxic self."

Emotional interventions are designed to regulate both positive and negative emotions so that neither serves as a trigger for relapse. Through cognitive strategies, clients may be taught to stay with the feeling while reviewing to themselves (preferably verbalizing out loud) the list of things they have already accomplished to stay sober (e.g., "Mark, you are reMARKable for having said, 'Let's take a time-out of 5 minutes to cool down before we talk about this some more'"). This practice is similar to the distress tolerance skills (e.g., self-soothing, one thing in the moment) taught in dialectical behavior therapy (Linehan, 1993a, 1993b). In self-soothing, clients are taught to focus on one of the five senses at a time, pausing to fully attend to, experience, or soak in the natural or non-substance-induced sensation (e.g., observing the contrast of green tree leaves against a bright blue sky) in order to withstand an urge or a craving to use. In addition, certain feelings can be reframed as positive protective devices, if not acted upon in destructive ways. For example, fear and anxiety can be understood as normal responses to a brand new reality or lifestyle, and regarded as the client's attempts to protect what is now valuable (i.e., sobriety). One reframe that I often use with clients is, "the compulsivity of addiction is the persistence of recovery," meaning that they didn't necessarily have to discard all aspects of "bad behavior"; rather, they could channel or redirect their frenetic energy into a "no-holds-barred" or "pull out all the stops" approach to recovery (e.g., continuing to attend AA meetings until they found their "home" fellowship).

Cognitive interventions are specifically intended to modify automatic thoughts and drug-related beliefs, as well as conditional assumptions and core beliefs. Rather than automatically thinking that only marijuana can help them get to sleep, clients can be taught to catch themselves from lighting up (perhaps by telling themselves out loud, "Hold off!" or "Wait!") and reviewing the written plan constructed with their counselor detailing alternative preparations for sleep (e.g., listening to relaxing music while depressing a stress ball). A list of cognitive comebacks to urges or cravings can be devised so that the client has an expanding toolbox of relapse prevention strategies. Such comebacks might resemble the externalization exercise (White & Epston, 1990) used in solution-focused counseling in which the client names the problem (e.g., "restless roamer," as one heroin addict described his struggle in finding "peace" in his life), is able to regard the problem as an external entity (i.e., "I am not the problem . . . 'restless roamer' is the problem"), and through conversation is able to keep the problem at a distance so as to diffuse its power over him. The client can be taught to confront the problem with comebacks such as, "You've led me astray!" and "I'm no longer following your twisted map!" and doing so out loud, with an amplified voice, while standing up. Using cognitive interventions, clients can also be taught to question the evidence regarding the seemingly infinite benefits of substance use, as well as the seemingly infinite detriments or negative assumptions about sobriety. Counselors can assist in stopping any circular reasoning by interjecting, "Okay, where's the evidence that this is true?" and "How do you *really* know that for sure?"

Physical interventions involve activities intended to distract the person's attention away from triggers and the consequent cravings and urges to use. Such activities include physical exercise (e.g., doing chores around the house, going for a walk), talking with someone (e.g., calling one's AA sponsor), breaking out into song, or snapping a rubber band worn on the wrist. In addition, clients can be reminded of the "insanity" of their active using days, recalling the "seemingly irrelevant decisions" made (see Marlatt & Donovan, 2005) and the negative physical consequences of their using. One I worked with, a blue-collar machinist who found his employment fulfilling because "I'm able to work on things that last," made the decision one morning to no longer drink. He said he was able to uphold this decision because "I was sick and tired of being sick and tired. I didn't want to lose this job." I recall commending this client on his decision and what I heard as his desire to work not only on large truck engines that would last, but on himself as well, so that *he* would last.

Contingency Management and Behavior Contracting

Specific CB approaches that have demonstrated efficacy in treating alcohol (Petry, Martin, Cooney, & Kranzler, 2000) and other drug dependence, namely cocaine and opioid dependence (Higgins & Silverman, 1999; Iguchi, Belding, Morral, Lamb, & Husband, 1997; Preston, Umbricht, Wong, & Epstein, 2001), have incorporated contingency management and behavior contracting (Higgins, Silverman, & Heil, 2008). These two approaches are based in part on the theory of behavioral economics, which posits that behavior is chosen because of the reward(s) it will provide, including monetary reward. Contingency management makes use of external incentives or tangible reinforcers (namely vouchers redeemable for goods and services, e.g., groceries, public transportation, movie theater tickets) contingent on the client meeting predetermined treatment goals, such as submitting drug-free urine specimens and arriving to counseling on time. Over time, clients may be awarded with an increasing number of vouchers or opportunities to win a prize (e.g., from a raffle or drawing) for not only submitting clean urine specimens, but also submitting documentation of having engaged in new and positive behaviors (e.g., going on a job interview, paying off court debts, bringing in a report card of improved school grades).

Contingency Management and Behavior Contracting

- Based on theory of behavior economics and operant conditioning
- Designed to shape and reinforce non-using behavior
- Clients and counselors agree (or contract) to participate in the systematic application of behavioral consequences
- Use of external incentives or tangible reinforcers (e.g., bus passes, vouchers redeemable for groceries or personal hygiene products), contingent upon changes in drug use and other therapeutic goals (e.g., attendance)

Source: Higgins, Silverman, & Heil, 2008.

Despite beneficial effects in research trials, it appears that contingency management practices have not been adopted by many practitioners due in part to the cost-prohibitive nature of the program. Counselors and agencies intent on offering helpful services, however, would be encouraged to pursue creative partnerships with local business representatives. These might include time-limited free access for agency clients on the local bus in exchange for free advertisement of the bus service on agency publications. In addition, as was done in Petry et al.'s (2000) study, local businesses could be approached to donate items (e.g., department store gift certificates) that would then be raffled off to clients who had upheld their contract.

Behavior contracting itself (apart from the use of vouchers) can be implemented with minimal or no cost to the counselor or agency. This practice might resemble treatment planning, but is typically not as comprehensive or expansive (i.e., the contract can focus on a specific task to accomplish in the next week) and can be done on a periodic basis. It is advised that the contracts be written (maybe even at times on a scrap piece of paper), the intended behavior clearly described, the targeted date of task completion specified, and both the incentive and the consequence for not abiding by the contract clarified. In addition, it should be signed by both the counselor and client, dated, and a copy provided to the client. Incentives for upholding the contract might include meeting with the counselor outside, on the grounds of the agency; having access to the agency's basketball court following a counseling session; an extended (by 5 minutes) smoke break during group counseling; and securing from the counselor a letter of reference for a job application. Particularly in residential treatment settings, behavior contracts are routinely used to encourage greater participation and cooperation among clients. Privileges for upholding one's contract might include telephone access to family members, being able to receive visitors on "Family Day," and being able to skip meal preparation and clean-up or other household chores for one day.

Community Reinforcement Approach

The community reinforcement approach (CRA) is a comprehensive biopsychosocial approach to the treatment of substance use disorders based on the premise that one's environment or community plays a critical role in reinforcing recovery efforts. CRA enlists community reinforcers (e.g., family, recreation, employment) to support change in an individual's substance use (Meyers, Villanueva, & Smith, 2005). Two reviews (Roozen et al., 2004; Smith, Meyers, & Miller, 2001) of studies conducted with the CRA in treating problematic alcohol and other drug use attest to its efficacy, particularly when combined with contingency management (e.g., use of vouchers as incentives).

Meyers et al. (2005) identified eight components of CRA, and although they conceded that each component is not necessarily used with every client, two are standard applications: functional analysis and treatment planning. After completing a functional analysis or thorough substance use assessment, including taking inventory of the client's external and internal motivations for substance use and its treatment, the focus of the CRA is to determine how environmental stimuli can be rearranged so that sobriety is supported and substance use is no longer tolerated or rewarded. Goals typically reflect the presence of something positive (e.g., maintaining employment, graduating from high school) rather than the absence of something negative (e.g., not drinking or drugging). Specific areas in the client's life considered in both assessment and treatment include social and recreational activities, employment, and family dynamics. Whenever possible, a significant other (e.g., life partner or spouse, girlfriend/boyfriend) is involved in treatment and regarded as an important ally in the construction and maintenance of a non-using and healthy lifestyle.

The CRA can be understood as a "package"; that is, "it contains a number of procedures that may or may not be used, depending on [the] client's specific needs" (Smith, Meyers, & Milford, 2003, p. 238). Indeed, the counselor can sift through many of the CB interventions already described in this chapter and then select those strategies that are most relevant for the client's current situation. These may include job skills training, social skills training, and couples counseling to address strains in communication. Careful attention is given to the ongoing assessment of external and internal triggers for substance use. Not only are attempts made to regulate environmental stimuli, but the counselor routinely inquires about the client's internal triggers (e.g., mood, beliefs, physical status). As a CB-oriented approach, the CRA is intended to equip the client with a variety of skills needed to not only effectively manage negative stimuli or triggers, but to also establish and maintain a lifestyle and environment that support and allow one's recovery to thrive.

A new version of CRA, Community Reinforcement and Family Training (CRAFT), is based on the principles of CRA but focuses on the environment (i.e., family members) of those persons with substance use problems who refuse to enter treatment (Meyers et al., 2005). Rather than working directly with the person with substance use problems, CRAFT enlists the assistance of a concerned significant other (CSO), such as a parent or a spouse, by training the CSO to interact with his or her loved one in new and more constructive ways. These would include not speaking with the family member when he or she is intoxicated (e.g., saying in a calm and measured voice, "I'm going to wait and talk with you about this in the morning, once you're sober") and allowing the family member to realize the natural consequences of his or her substance use (e.g., not bailing the family member out of jail). Although the goal of CRAFT is for the family member to enter treatment, it is designed to help CSOs take better care of themselves and to realize a sense of contentment on their own.

BRIEF INTERVENTIONS

Brief interventions for problematic drinking are not a homogeneous entity; rather, they are regarded as "a family of interventions varying in length, structure, targets of intervention, [and] personnel responsible for their delivery" (Heather, 1995, p. 287). However, W. R. Miller and Sanchez (1994) maintained that all brief interventions should include six elements, known by the mnemonic FRAMES. These shared elements are intended to fulfill the purposes of brief interventions, which Zweben and Fleming (1999) stated are to (a) increase one's awareness of the costs and consequences of substance use, (b) strengthen beliefs about one's ability to change (i.e., enhancing self-efficacy), (c) utilize natural helping systems to support positive change, (d) encourage the person to accept responsibility for change, and (e) promote a commitment to positive change.

FRAMES = Six Elements of Brief Interventions

- FEEDBACK of personal risk or impairment, delivered in nonjudgmental manner
- Emphasis on personal RESPONSIBILITY for change
- Providing clear ADVICE to change
- Offering MENU of alternative change options
- Therapist EMPATHY
- Facilitating client SELF-EFFICACY or optimism

Source: W. R. Miller & Sanchez, 1994.

The temporal nature of this service delivery certainly implies a shorter length of stay in treatment than what might be considered standard substance abuse counseling (i.e., detoxification followed by intensive outpatient individual and group counseling). "Brief" or "minimal" counseling can refer to one or two one-hour individual sessions, or structured and direct feedback provided in 5 to 30 minutes. Brief interventions are typically developed by specialists to be delivered by other professionals, and service settings vary from primary health care centers (e.g., hospital emergency rooms) to college campuses. Brief interventions conducted specifically with college students have included (a) an hour-long individual face-to-face motivational intervention with high-risk/binge drinkers (Borsari & Carey, 2000; Larimer et al., 2001; Marlatt et al., 1998; Murphy et al., 2001); (b) small group (e.g., fraternity house) review of assessment results (Larimer et al., 2001); (c) personalized mailed feedback of the student's reported substance use patterns (Collins, Carey, & Sliwinski, 2002; Walters, 2000; Walters, Bennett, & Miller, 2000); (d) computerized individual assessment and computer-generated feedback (Dimeff & McNeely, 2000; Neighbors, Larimer, & Lewis, 2004); and (e) combinations of these interventions.

Although believed to be underutilized by chemical dependency treatment professionals because they are thought to be reserved for those with less severe forms of substance use disorders, brief interventions should be delivered based on the recipient's stage of change (Vik, Culbertson, & Sellers, 2000) and targeted specifically to those who are relatively low on the readiness-to-change continuum (Maisto et al., 2001). Vik et al. (2000), however, noted that "Students contemplating change were the heaviest and most problematic drinkers" (p. 679). As a result, brief interventions for substance use problems should always be an option regardless of a client's level of substance dependence (Sanchez-Craig, 1990), and may be used to help prepare or cultivate one's readiness for more intensive or extensive services (W. R. Miller, 1992). Brief interventions for the substance dependent client can be ethically justified, therefore, particularly if the client would otherwise receive no help at all (Heather, 1995), including homeless adolescent substance users (Baer, Peterson, & Wells, 2004).

Studies report reduction in drinking as a result of participation in brief intervention, but no commensurate and significant reduction in *consequences* of drinking, such as missing college classes or engaging in risky sexual behaviors (Borsari & Carey, 2000; Collins et al., 2002; Murphy et al., 2001; Walters et al., 2000). Interventions should be devised, therefore, that will reduce drinking consequences, as well as consumption amounts and frequency. This may depend, among other things, on the counselor's ability to engage the student or client in a consideration of the potentially extensive and hazardous effects of one's substance use. Focused conversation on the person's use history, his or her current status and use patterns, comparisons with others in his or her peer group (e.g., age, gender, race/ethnicity), and the counselor's own informed perspective (from research findings and clinical wisdom) may at least help the client to think twice about the extent of future use.

SOLUTION-FOCUSED COUNSELING

Solution-focused counseling (SFC) was conceived and developed by de Shazer and colleagues (de Shazer, 1985, 1988; de Shazer et al., 1986; Molnar & de Shazer, 1987; O'Hanlon & Weiner-Davis, 1989) at the Brief Family Therapy Center (BFTC) in Milwaukee, Wisconsin, almost 40 years ago. It emerged as a form of brief or short-term psychotherapy with an emphasis on pragmatism (i.e., what works) and on mental health (rather than mental illness; Berg & S. D. Miller, 1992), thus representing an alternative to the problem-focused approaches that continue to prevail in both mental health practice and substance abuse treatment. SFC has its roots in the work of hypnotherapist Milton Erickson and family systems theory, and during its later years of development, in post-structural/post-modern or constructivist ideology (de Shazer & Berg, 1992).

The essence of SFC is its focus on the accomplishments, strengths, resources, and abilities of the client. That is, rather than prioritizing the problems and deficits that typically accompany a referral to counseling, the solution-focused practitioner solicits (from clients, family members, referral source, other treatment staff) and attends to those things in the client's life that have gone well and continue to go well. Indeed, SF counselors assume that clients want to change and that the solution, or at least part of it, is probably already taking place (Gingerich & Wabeke, 2001). This is not to say that presenting concerns are dismissed; rather, "exceptions" (de Shazer, 1988) to problem occurrence are given prominence so as to formulate with the client a solution or series of solutions so that formal treatment is no longer necessary. Such a focus exemplifies the clinician's confidence in the client's ability to make positive changes in his or her own life by accessing and utilizing strengths and resources. Positive change is not only regarded as possible, but inevitable (Berg & S. D. Miller, 1992), characterizing SFC as the "counseling of hope" (Nunnally, 1993).

Berg and S. D. Miller (1992) are credited with being the first to apply SFC to substance abuse treatment, specifically treatment for alcohol-related problems. Since then, many others have contributed to the conversation of integrating SFC within substance abuse treatment (Berg & Reuss, 1998; Chandler & Mason, 1995; de Shazer & Isebaert, 2003; Juhnke & Coker, 1997; Linton, 2005; Mason, Chandler, & Grasso, 1995; Osborn, 1997; Taleff, 1997). Additional contributions to the literature are needed to further support what S. D. Miller, Hubble, and Duncan (1996) described as SFC's suitability with a range of client concerns in a variety of treatment settings. Although SFC lacks a solid empirical research base (see reviews by Corcoran & Pillai, 2009; Gingerich & Eisengart, 2000; Kim, 2008), it remains a popular approach among mental health and substance abuse treatment providers. Indeed, Herbeck et al.'s (2008) survey of program administrators and staff members in California revealed that SFC was considered one of the more effective treatment approaches and used in more than half of participating sites despite the lack of compelling research findings. Herbeck et al. surmised SFC may be intuitively appealing to treatment providers because its "techniques and tools . . . fit particularly well with the complex needs of substance-abusing populations" (p. 708). Linton (2005) also noted that SFC can be integrated well with other interventions.

Encouragement from Research

Although not a study explicitly utilizing SF approaches, Iguchi et al.'s (1997) "shaping strategy" with 103 opioid dependent clients (63% male, 85% White) bears resemblance to several essential aspects of SFC and offers encouraging results for the use of SFC in substance abuse treatment. Clients were randomly assigned to one of three treatment groups: (a) standard treatment (ST; individual counseling with for take-home medication eligibility), (b) urinalysis-based reinforcement (UA; standard treatment plus opportunity to earn vouchers for each urine specimen testing free of unauthorized substances), and (c) treatment-plan-based reinforcement (TP). Vouchers were described to clients as "treatment assistance coupons" which could be redeemed only for expenses tied to a specific treatment plan goal, such as clothing appropriate for a job interview and transportation to counseling sessions.

In the TP group, counselors met weekly with clients to establish the following week's behavioral tasks and "were generally free to tailor tasks to suit the needs of individual participants" (p. 423); hence, the "shaping strategy" of TP. As opposed to the UA group, TP members earned vouchers for demonstrating their engagement in new and positive behaviors (e.g., contacting local computer training program), rather than their non-activity in or elimination of substance use (i.e., providing a "clean" urine specimen). That is, desirable behaviors were reinforced. In addition, if the client failed to earn vouchers for these tasks (e.g., not appearing for a scheduled counseling session), the counselor would be urged to establish an easier task (e.g., participating with the counselor in an abbreviated telephone conversation). When clients succeeded in earning vouchers, counselors were directed to gradually increase the difficulty of subsequent tasks, with the aim of achieving long-term treatment plan goals.

Primary results of Iguchi et al.'s (1997) study were that over the four 6-week evaluation periods, only TP clients demonstrated significant improvement in abstinence rates over time, and TP clients attended significantly more counseling sessions than clients in either of the other two groups. The authors interpreted these results to suggest that "the reinforcement of clearly defined behavioral tasks targeted toward long-term goals increases involvement in behaviors inconsistent with drug use among methadone maintenance patients" (p. 426). Overall, the TP program's encouraging outcomes indicate that a strengths-based, non-punitive, and collaborative form of treatment—an approach consistent with SFC—is appropriate and perhaps preferable to an approach where all clients receive the same type of care, are required to achieve abstinence, and are rewarded only for what they are *not* doing (i.e., using). Results such as these bode well for the continued integration of SFC in substance abuse treatment. Indeed, the design and implementation of the TP program appears to fulfill all seven of Berg and S. D. Miller's (1992) criteria of "well-formed" treatment goals: (a) saliency to the client; (b) small; (c) concrete, specific, and behavioral; (d) the presence rather than the absence of something; (e) a beginning rather than an end; (f) realistic and achievable within the context of the client's life; and (g) perceived as involving "hard work."

Related to personalized goal formulation, de Shazer and Isebaert (2003) studied nurse therapists and their patients who participated in a chemical dependency treatment program in Belgium that subscribed to an SF approach. The focus of treatment was on identifying exceptions to the presenting problem and honoring clients' preferences for therapy—that is, what patients wanted from treatment. Patients were allowed to choose a treatment goal of controlled drinking or abstinence, provided in an individual, couple, or family format. Approximately 10% of the clients who initially chose controlled drinking changed their goal to abstinence.

At 4-year follow-up (former patients contacted by telephone), 50% (*n* = 36) of the former patients reported being abstinent and 32% reported success at controlled drinking. de Shazer and Isabaert (2003) reported that only 19 of the 36 former clients who claimed abstinence had originally chosen abstinence as their goal; controlled drinking had been the choice of only 12.5% (*n* = 9) of those who were now claiming abstinence at follow-up. The authors stated that this result ". . . strongly suggests that having a choice of goals and the ability to change goals makes a big difference in patients' treatment success" (p. 49). In addition, such findings support the work of client-counselor collaboration in formulating treatment goals. Indeed, de Shazer and Isabaert noted that ". . . areas of choice allow the patients to cooperate with the treatment program" (p. 50). Rather than the counselor prescribing a goal (e.g., "Client will abstain from all mood- and mind-altering drugs"), SF counselors are encouraged to elicit from the client his or her preferred outcome and honor that choice as much as possible. This study suggests that clients may actually benefit in the long run by being active participants in counseling, empowered by having had their choices heard and respected. The authors concluded that:

> . . . at least some optimism is warranted. The situation is entirely changed once a second possible remedy to the alcohol problem is introduced. With two ways to approach the goal, failure at one only means that patients should try the other approach. . . . There is a big difference between choosing to drink and believing that you have no choice but to drink.[11] (p. 51)

Solution-Focused Integration

SFC has been used in combination with other counseling approaches, namely Adlerian therapy (Watts & Pietrzak, 2000), motivational interviewing (Lewis & Osborn, 2004); person-centered therapy (Cepeda & Davenport, 2006); existential therapy (Fernando, 2007); CB therapy and motivational interviewing (Corcoran, 2005); and creative arts therapy (Matto, Corcoran, & Fassler, 2003; Tyson & Baffour, 2004). A separate chapter of this book is devoted to motivational interviewing, and the specific practices of an integrated SFC and creative arts therapy approach appear to be particularly conducive for substance abuse counseling. Therefore, this latter combination is briefly highlighted.

Tyson and Baffour (2004) studied 108 adolescents ranging in age from 11 to 18 years (mean age of 15.29 years; 92.6% Caucasian, 67.5% female), who participated in an SF and strengths-based group treatment program on a child and adolescent unit of an acute-care psychiatric hospital (typical length of stay was 4 to 7 days). Just over 10% of the participants had a primary diagnosis of substance abuse (the 4th highest among 9 primary diagnoses assigned) and 24.1% had a secondary diagnosis of substance abuse (most frequent secondary diagnosis assigned, almost twice that of any other secondary diagnosis assigned). The focus of the study was on soliciting from the young patients their positive strengths for managing stress, with the assumption being that these internal resources would be useful in accentuating exceptions to the problem. That is, patients were asked to identify possible future crisis situations that would not require hospitalization as a result of their implementation of positive strengths (namely some type of expressive art that they alone identified).

Of those youth with a primary diagnosis of substance abuse, half identified "playing a musical instrument" as their arts-based strength (a statistically significant difference from those with a primary substance abuse diagnosis who did not identify with playing a musical instrument) that would be used to "stop the problem from pushing me around." None of the youth who reported that they initially "write poetry, journals, stories" as a means of dealing with their problems had a primary diagnosis of substance abuse. Tyson and Baffour (2004) concluded that youth with a primary diagnosis of substance abuse were more likely to play a musical instrument or sing in order to deal with an impending crisis. In terms of treatment, they stated, "For these youth, it might be appropriate and personally relevant to use some form of music (e.g., play musical instrument) in the context of treatment" (p. 223).

For both adolescents and adults struggling with substance use problems, the integration of SFC and art therapy may prove helpful. Matto et al. (2003) described the process of having clients draw a picture of their primary problem as a form of externalization or detachment from the problem. They stated that such an activity "introduces fluidity to problems . . . [so that] the oppressive nature of the problem is lifted . . ." (p. 266). In addition, depending on the skill of the counselor, solutions can be constructed in the very act of drawing. That is, clients can be encouraged to modify aspects of their art work (e.g., using another color, outlining some aspect of the drawing, erasing or removing something from the art work); this in itself conveys that solutions are constructed over time, in stages or increments (i.e., not necessarily one giant leap), and under the client's control. During this process, clients can be commended on changes made and can then be asked to draw their strengths, with the effect of making the strengths "more concrete and tangible [because of the] physical and emotional investment in the creative process" (p. 270).

SF Assumptions and Practices Useful in Substance Abuse Counseling

Several solution-focused (SF) assumptions guide the practice of SFC. Although clearly not exhaustive, the SF assumptions and practices presented in this section were selected in light of their feasibility to substance abuse counseling.

Assumptions of Solution-Focused Counseling

- Pragmatism and Parsimony
- Client-Counselor Collaboration
- Language of Hope
- Exceptions Facilitate Change
  - Past Exceptions
  - Recent and Recurrent Exceptions
  - Future Exceptions (e.g., Miracle Question)
- Notice the Difference
- Commendations

PRAGMATISM AND PARSIMONY.   Consistent with its origins as a brief or short-term therapy, SFC is known for its pragmatism and, as Berg and S. D. Miller (1992) highlight, its parsimony. Perhaps in conducting intentional counseling that addresses directly the client's presenting concerns and preferences (i.e., it is pragmatic), one is by default keeping the work simple or parsimonious. Conversely, simplicity may engender pragmatism. Regardless of the sequence, SFC resembles a brief intervention in its focus on helping the client get unstuck by not dwelling on the intricacies of the problem (e.g., the "reason" for the client's substance use). In many ways this is a respectful approach that avoids wasting the client's time gathering extensive historical data and prioritizes relief from pressing symptoms and concerns.

COLLABORATION IS KEY.   Solution-focused counseling (SFC) has been regarded as a means to further individualize care and to improve therapeutic partnerships with clients (Mason et al., 1995). The emphasis on or commitment to client-counselor collaboration is evident in SFC's proposition of three types of therapeutic *relationships* as opposed to three types of clients (Berg & S. D. Miller, 1992; Berg & Reuss, 1998). The *visitor-type relationship* describes the interaction that may ensue when the client believes there is not a problem and the counselor agrees, validates, or "goes along with" this perception, while at the same time offering to help the client in ways the client may be able to determine. The *complainant-type therapeutic relationship* typifies problem recognition and a shared understanding of the nature of the problem (e.g., on probation with the county municipal court for a repeated driving under the influence [DUI] charge), with the focus being on how the client can transition to seeing him- or herself as part of the solution (as opposed to looking to others for resolution, e.g., "Get my probation officer off my back"). Finally, the *customer-type relationship* involves joint construction of a solution plan or path that the client is able and willing to participate in and even take the lead on.

LANGUAGE OF HOPE.   Careful attention to the type of language and words used by clients is essential in the practice of counseling, as is counselor intentionality in the selection of words used with clients. This is particularly true for an SFC approach wherein words and language are thought to create reality and meaning. Given that the majority of clients in substance abuse treatment have not initiated services on their own (i.e., have been mandated by a court system or a social service agency and are thus considered "involuntary") and more than likely feel angry, demoralized, and fearful about being sent to counseling, skeptical about the need for treatment and its outcome, the specific words used by the counselor can have a significant effect on the client's amenability to and engagement in counseling. For example, use of the word "alcoholic" or "addict" to describe the counselor's assessment of the client may not initially engender cooperation and may actually further aggravate the client's frustration and reluctance to be in counseling. Gingerich and Wabeke (2001) articulated a SFC perspective on diagnostic labels by stating,

> . . . SFBT therapists eschew talk of diagnosis, disability, and pathology. Such talk, in spite of good intentions, frequently serves to confirm the client's view of himself or herself as someone who is disabled. Thus, unless there is reason to believe that diagnosing would lead to a needed medical intervention, the therapist steers conversation toward the client's desired scenario and what he or she can do to make that happen. (p. 35)

When conveying assessment results and the preliminary diagnosis from an SFC perspective, it is advisable for the counselor to refer to the substance use disorder as a *condition*, something the client *has*, rather than someone the client *is*. A focus on the condition rather than an insinuation of the person's worth (i.e., "you are the problem") can be viewed as an effort to externalize the problem, thus empowering the client to exert control over it rather than allowing it to continue to consume the client. Such externalization, however, may not be regarded as compatible with the disease concept of addiction.

Other examples of language usage in SFC that may be interpreted by the client as hopeful rather than disempowering or judgmental include the words "setbacks" rather than "relapses" (Berg & S. D. Miller, 1992), and "multiple episodes of sobriety" (Mason et al., 1995) rather than a sole or primary consideration of "multiple relapses" or referring to a client as "a chronic relapser." In addition, Berg and Reuss (1998) have made use of a "recovery checklist" (rather than a diagnostic or problem checklist) comprised of targeted positive behaviors for the client to engage in as part of his or her recovery. What may be regarded as a confrontational counseling style can be reframed as an "invitation for clarification," with the counselor beginning with, "Help me understand" (i.e., requesting clarification of two discrepant reports or stories, e.g., "I don't have a drinking problem" and a history of 3 DUIs). Although not originating from SFC, the "care map" (Chen et al., 2004) has been described as "a kind of algorithm outlining assessments and related treatment" (p. 857) specifically for children with asthma, and is developed by an interdisciplinary team in consultation with the child and his or her family. Although Chen et al. do not provide a specific example of such a "care map," the name itself suggests a positive, beneficent, and salutary approach that may have greater appeal for clients and providers alike than what is commonly referred to as a "treatment plan" (see Osborn, West, Kindsvatter, & Paez, 2008).

EXCEPTIONS FACILITATE CHANGE. An example of expeditious practice in SFC is the focus on exceptions to the problem rather than on the problem itself. Exceptions refer to occasions when the problem is not a problem or times when it could have happened (e.g., relapse) but did not. S. D. Miller (1992) characterized exceptions as problem "irregularit[ies]" (p. 2), further illustrating the notion that exceptions are changes or alterations to what the client may perceive as the "same old, same old" problem pattern. In order to help the client get unstuck from a "problem saturated story" (White & Epston, 1990), the counselor can inquire about exceptions in one or more of four areas (Nunnally, 1993): (a) the past, (b) recent nonproblem occurrences, (c) recurrent exceptions (i.e., instances that occur periodically, often without warning), and (d) occasions in the future when the client can imagine the problem no longer existing or being influential.

Past exceptions can be detected by inquiring about life before using or occasions when the negative consequences of one's use were not prominent or even existent. "Tell me about a time before cocaine came into the picture when you felt good about something you had done, even proud of yourself" is a means of shifting the client's perspective to a nonproblem time in the past when the client experienced positive emotions that were not drug-induced. If the client responds with "I don't know," the counselor should pursue with the follow-up, "Oh, take a moment to think back, maybe a time when you were in school, maybe when someone else pointed out something you had done well. Give it a shot." If the client is still not able to generate a past success story, the counselor can encourage the client to consider a hypothetical scenario such as, "If there had been a time when you felt good, even proud, of something you had done, when might that have been? What would you have hoped you would have been able to accomplish back then?"

Recent and recurrent exceptions, as with past exceptions, may not be in the client's awareness and so require the counselor's curiosity skills about recent events or experiences that can be interpreted as glimmers of a possible solution in the making. Reframing may also be necessary. For example, "Anton" was a young and quiet African American male who faithfully attended his counseling sessions but said he was only coming in because he "had to." "Okay, so you have to," his counselor acknowledged. "But you're here every week and on time, which is a miracle in itself compared to many other clients who come here. Tell me one thing that you've gotten out of our last few sessions that has brought you back for more." After a long pause and a brief sigh, with eyes downcast, Anton softly said, "I don't know, I guess I feel okay here, you know, like I'm not being hassled. You listen." Rather than wanting to take full credit for Anton's positive experience in counseling, his counselor followed up with: "Well, what's made it possible for you to trust this place, trust me, a White woman, and talk in here?" The intent of this question was to identify what may have been a new or recurrent exception to Anton's problem story (e.g., a change in thinking), an exception for which he could claim responsibility and credit, such as "I guess I need to lay off the weed so I can get through school this year. My auntie's been on me for months, but now I need to do something."

Perhaps the best known example for constructing *future exceptions* in SFC is the use of the "miracle question." de Shazer (1985) is credited with designing this creative question to encourage clients to visualize, and potentially make real, a future nonproblem period. By imagining and projecting themselves into a future situation in which the problem is no longer present, clients can view themselves as functioning satisfactorily (Molnar & de Shazer, 1987). The "script" for the miracle question might be worded as:

> "Suppose that tonight, while you are asleep, there is a miracle and the problem that brought you to counseling was solved. However, because you're asleep, you don't know that the miracle already happened. So, when you wake up tomorrow morning, what will be different that will tell you that this miracle has really taken place?"

Being the "Curious Columbos" (Selekman, 1993) and skillful inquirers that they are, SF counselors will ask the client for details of their miracle day—specific behaviors they will be engaging in, things other people will notice in them, things they will be thinking about, and feelings that will be prominent to them.

"Susan," a divorced Native American in her mid-30s, struggled with visualizing her nonproblem day. Not only had she been using alcohol problematically for the past 10–15 years, she also presented with symptoms of social phobia, and had been physically and sexually abused by her ex-husband. She was currently estranged from her immediate family members, including her teenage son, who had decided to live with Susan's father several hours away. Rather than continuing to press her for a description of her miracle morning, I contacted, with Susan's permission, her father and her son by mail, requesting that they complete a questionnaire I had devised containing specific questions that might elicit some "ingredients" to help Susan imagine and eventually make real at least one day that minimized or even was free of her problem.

The counseling session in which the returned and completed family questionnaires were shared with Susan remains vivid. Her father wrote that he was proud of his daughter's courage to finally leave her abusive husband and her son wrote that he was grateful for the love and protection his mother had shown him since he was little. Her son said he was doing well in school so that she would be proud of him. Susan was tearful throughout this counseling session as she heard the "testimony" of family members dear to her, testimonials to Susan's personal strengths and qualities (exceptions!) that she had not been able to recognize in herself for a long time. Following that session, Susan was able to use what she heard from her father and son to begin formulating her "miracle morning," in which she awakened with courage not to consume her usual alcohol "eye opener" and to talk to her neighbor instead, doing so without experiencing panic symptoms. She said this would be her way of continuing to love her son and to make both her son and father proud of her. Rehearsing this miracle morning was something that we did over the next few sessions, knowing that miracle construction would not take place in a day, but over time, in pieces or ripples, and with practice, feedback, support, and encouragement.

NOTICE THE DIFFERENCE.   It is critical that SF counselors are not only on the lookout for positive differences in or exceptions to client behaviors, but assist their clients (and the client's family members) to notice when these problem irregularities occur. One Appalachian client I had the privilege to work with over several months demonstrated the importance of this. "Ricky" was in his mid-30s, married and a father of two elementary school age daughters. He acknowledged being illiterate, experiencing discord in his marriage, consuming alcohol on a daily basis, and still grieving over the loss of his father (his "drinking buddy") 3 years earlier. Unemployed due to a physical disability, Ricky spent his time working in the garage on automobiles and motorcycles and secluding himself in a TV room he had fashioned for himself.

In one session, Ricky reported having maintained sobriety from alcohol for 4 consecutive days in the past week, a monumental effort given his long history of excessive alcohol use. After attempting to explore with Ricky how he was able to remain sober for 4 consecutive days (using SF coping questions), I asked about his return to drinking after 4 days: "What happened?" His response is still haunting and tugs at my empathic heart: "No one noticed." Without his genuine efforts to initiate sobriety being recognized by those most important to him, Ricky essentially gave up, perhaps asking himself, "What's the use?" Although he may have been able to identify for himself some benefits of his 4-day sobriety, at this very early stage of his recovery, Ricky needed the positive reinforcement of others (i.e., external motivators), particularly with the co-occurrence of depressive symptoms.

If I had this client case to work with again, I would have been more intentional about including Ricky's wife periodically in counseling (consistent with outcome research indicating the efficacy of behavioral marital therapy) or at least asking her on the telephone, "What have you noticed in Ricky this past week that's changed for the better?" (a question that presupposes positive change). I might have also challenged Ricky to engage in new and more positive behaviors that would be evident to his wife and daughters, things said or actions taken that would convince them he was making strides in attaining and maintaining abstinence. A target behavior could be reviewed and even practiced in counseling (e.g., "So when the girls get home from school, what will you do instead of working in the garage?" and "What will you say differently when your wife complains about you watching too much TV? Let's practice having you say it out loud.") and an assignment given such as,

"When you spend time with the girls this next week, and when you say something different to your wife, notice how they respond. Be on the lookout for changes you see and hear in them. We'll talk about this next week."

COMMENDATIONS.   Throughout the process of counseling, SF counselors look out for and notice positive differences—exceptions—in their clients. When sincere efforts or accomplishments are evident (e.g., attending one's first AA meeting), the counselor brings these to the client's attention through commendations or what are referred to in motivational interviewing as affirmations. Commendations or affirmations are not to be confused with well-intentioned, although less than substantive "cheers" that may be regarded by the client as disingenuous. In addition, accolades that do not specify a positive behavior the client has recently implemented (e.g., "You're doing a great job!") may fail to reinforce the specific positive behavior targeted as a client goal. Consistent with the hard work criterion of well-formed treatment goals in SFC, commendations should highlight the client's hard work. For example, "Ricky" would be commended for his 4 consecutive days of sobriety ("Despite really wanting to go out to the garage and drink, you didn't. You stayed inside and watched TV with the girls. I know this took a lot of effort on your part."), and "Susan" would be commended for not drinking in the morning before talking with her neighbor ("How did you manage to do that? How were you able to use your courage to actually go outside, knock on her door, and start a conversation with her? I am amazed and very proud of your hard work, Susan!").

HARM REDUCTION

Marlatt (1998), the most prominent voice of harm reduction in the addictions, has described this particular ideology and its practices according to five principles, assumptions, and values. Harm reduction can first be understood as a public health alternative to moral/criminal and disease models of drug use and addiction that, second, recognizes abstinence as an ideal outcome but accepts alternatives that reduce harm. This second principle implies that "prevention" is an approach intended to prevent, or at least reduce, the harmful effects of use, not use itself (Marlatt & Witkiewitz, 2002). The third principle or assumption of harm reduction is that it has emerged primarily at a local level and represents a "grass roots" approach based on addict advocacy, rather than originating as a federal "top-down" mandate. Fourth, harm reduction promotes low-threshold access to services (i.e., meeting the individual where he or she is, respecting the individual's initial goal as a means of engaging the person in services) as an alternative to traditional, "high-threshold" approaches (e.g., requiring abstinence as the initial treatment goal). Finally, harm reduction is based on the tenets of compassionate pragmatism (i.e., focusing on managing one's daily functioning) versus moralistic idealism.

From this preliminary description, it may be evident that harm reduction reflects cognitive-behavioral (CB) principles, embraces the FRAMES perspective of brief interventions, and bears resemblance to solution-focused (SF) counseling. Indeed, as a "low-threshold" entry into addiction services, harm reduction ". . . [accepts] the client's definition of the problem as the legitimate starting point for intervention . . . [so as] to join with that which motivates the client to seek help, meet the client's needs, and, around this motivation, facilitate a positive treatment alliance" (Tatarsky, 2003, p. 251). In addition, "Harm reduction approaches the participant as the expert of their story, respecting their solutions and pace" (Majoor & Rivera, 2003, p. 257), which echoes Walter and Peller's (2000) admonition that clinicians listen for and honor client preferences.

Consistent with one of the assumptions of SF counseling, harm reduction is a pragmatic approach to alcohol and drug use and related problems, which Kellogg (2003) described as having three purposes: staying alive, maintaining health, and/or getting better. Marlatt and Witkiewitz (2002) expanded on these in their listing of three core objectives of harm reduction: (a) reduce harmful consequences (to user, society) associated with alcohol/drug use; (b) provide alternatives to zero-tolerance approaches by incorporating using goals (abstinence or moderation) compatible with the needs of the individual; and (c) promote access to services by offering low-threshold alternatives to traditional substance use prevention and treatment. Thus, harm reduction counseling does not require abstinence as an initial treatment goal because, as W. R. Miller and Page (1991) argued, "abrupt attainment and maintenance of total abstention is the exception rather than the rule" (p. 231). In addition, as SF practitioners de Shazer and Isabaert (2003) noted,

> When a problem is believed to have only one remedy, failure in an attempt at that remedy is viewed as the individual's fault. Each subsequent failure demands that the individual increase his or her efforts at applying the remedy, that is, doing more of something that is not working. (p. 50)

Other routes to abstinence are therefore often considered in harm reduction, including Miller and Page's (1991) "warm turkey" approach. This alternative includes *sobriety sampling,* where the client attempts to abstain for a period of time (e.g., over a weekend), on an experimental basis, is intentional about taking mental or even written inventory of the experience (e.g., completing a self-monitoring card of cravings/urges, "close calls," emotional states, and any relapses), and then reports to his or her counselor at the next session how the trial period went. Another alternative to abstinence is *tapering down* (also described as "gradualism" and "abstinence eventually"; Kellogg, 2003), where the amount and frequency of consumption is gradually decreased, perhaps using a weekly or monthly calendar. This practice was used with a young adult male client whose marijuana use reportedly reduced and calmed his tactile hallucinations (i.e., sensation of bugs crawling over his body). Rather than require this client to abruptly abstain from the only "home-grown treatment" that so far had helped his co-occurring psychotic symptoms, we agreed that he would gradually reduce the number of marijuana joints he was smoking daily each week for the next month. A calendar was created on which the client was to mark the number of joints smoked each day and bring to each counseling session. This plan and practice was in place while we waited for his initial appointment with the psychiatrist for an evaluation. Similar in some ways to gradualism, a third alternative to abstinence is that of *trial moderation* which refers to a negotiated period of time when the client is allowed to try limiting his or her intake. Usually, however, this trial is commenced after a period of sobriety.

Despite the pragmatic and humanistic philosophy of harm reduction, many addiction counselors may not eagerly embrace its practices because they seemingly contradict long-held beliefs about addiction and its treatment (e.g., abstinence the only goal for the disease of addiction). Rosenberg and Phillips (2003) found that a majority of representatives (primarily clinical directors and program administrators) of drug and alcohol treatment agencies in the United States were receptive to implementing certain harm reduction strategies. Ten of 13 interventions listed were rated by a majority of respondents to the postal mail survey (51% return rate) as somewhat or completely acceptable, including education (63%), needle exchange (61%), and alternative therapies (e.g., acupuncture; 81%), as well as pharmacological interventions such as agents used in opiate detoxification (80%), postdetoxification (e.g., Naltrexone; 74%), and drug replacement (i.e., short-term use of methadone; 67%). Despite the rather high acceptability rates of these strategies, a majority of respondents indicated that the 13 harm reduction interventions listed were not available at their agency, primarily due to an incompatibility with agency philosophy and, to a lesser extent, lack of funding and staff resources. The use of nonabstinence as an intermediate treatment goal was reported by approximately a third of respondents as available at their agencies, whereas its use as a final goal for treatment was less available. Overall findings suggest that further education of staff about the legitimate benefits of harm reduction strategies (i.e., to promote a change in attitude or philosophy) would assist in the greater implementation of such interventions, along with parallel attitude changes in funding sources (e.g., federal government).

Similar to concerns raised with implementing brief interventions in alcohol and drug treatment, harm reduction may not be deemed appropriate by some practitioners because of what might be considered its "enabling" characteristics (i.e., viewed as encouragement to continue using). However, given that the vast majority of persons in the United States today with substance use problems do not receive treatment services (Substance Abuse and Mental Health Services Administration, SAMHSA, 2008), both brief interventions and a harm reduction approach appear well suited for reaching persons who may never obtain such services. Indeed, of the four most frequent reasons given for not pursuing services even when a need was recognized and an initial attempt made, two would be well-served by brief interventions and harm reduction: not ready to stop using (26.6%); and negative opinion from community/neighbors and negative effect on job (combined 15.9%). The remaining two reasons included cost or insurance barriers (35.9%) and other access barriers (e.g., transportation; 10.5%).

Pragmatic and humanistic counseling practices that respect the client's initial goal for treatment, emphasize client-counselor collaboration, and address harm reduction rather than substance use elimination only may very well benefit the 20.8 million persons in 2007 reported by SAMHSA (2008) who needed but did not receive treatment for a substance use problem. At the very least, these practices could "gently persuade" and engage persons in needed services and in so doing, might serve as "stepping stones" to more intensive services. As Tatarsky (2003) noted,

> Harm reduction practices are one way to begin an ambitious process of change, the endpoint of which cannot be foreseen at the outset. The goal is to support the client in going as far as [he or she] possibly can toward the harm reduction ideals of optimal health, self-sufficiency, self-actualization and satisfaction in the world of relationships. (pp. 250–251)

Summary and Some Final Notations

The counseling approaches described in this chapter share several common assumptions and practices and, when consulted or utilized in an intentional and collective fashion (e.g., adhering to W. R. Miller & Hester's, 2003, "informed eclecticism" model), may very well form a tapestry of a strengths-based and salutary counseling informed by theory and empirical research.

Indeed, harm reduction "suggests the need for an integrated treatment system with linkages across the spectrum of treatment modalities" (Tatarsky, 2003, p. 252), which serves as further indication of a healthy entanglement and useful network among cognitive-behavioral approaches, brief interventions, solution-focused counseling, and harm reduction.

Useful Web Sites

Following is a list of Web sites that can provide additional information relating to the topics presented and discussed in this chapter:

The Brief Family Therapy Center

http://www.brief-therapy.org

The "home" of solution-focused therapy/counseling, now offering primarily research and training services.

The Center on Alcoholism, Substance Abuse, and Addictions (CASAA)

http://www.casaa.unm.edu

Affiliated with the University of New Mexico, CASAA is devoted to conducting and disseminating research that informs substance abuse prevention and treatment (e.g., motivational interviewing, community reinforcement approach). Numerous assessment instruments are available free of charge and downloadable from the CASAA web site.

The Drinker's Check-up

http://www.drinkerscheckup.com

Developed by Dr. Reid Hester of Behavior Therapy Associates, The Drinker's Check-up is an on-line confidential service (exemplifying a brief intervention) intended to assess one's drinking patterns, provide feedback, and assist individuals in making decisions about their current drinking.

The Harm Reduction Coalition

http://www.harmreduction.org

A "national advocacy and capacity-building organization that promotes the health and dignity of individuals and communities impacted by drug use."

References

American Psychiatric Association. (1994). *Diagnostic and statistical manual of mental disorders* (4th ed.). Washington, DC: Author.

Baer, J. S., Peterson, P. L., & Wells, E. A. (2004). Rationale and design of a brief substance use intervention for homeless adolescents. *Addiction Research and Theory, 12*, 317–334.

Berg, I. K., & Miller, S. D. (1992). *Working with the problem drinker: A solution-focused approach.* New York: W. W. Norton.

Berg, I. K., & Reuss, N. H. (1998). *Solutions step by step: A substance abuse treatment manual.* New York: W. W. Norton.

Borsari, B., & Carey, K. B. (2000). Effects of a brief motivational intervention with college student drinkers. *Journal of Consulting and Clinical Psychology, 68*, 728–733.

Caplehorn, J. R. M., Lumley, T. S., & Irwig, L. (1998). Staff attitudes and retention of patients in methadone maintenance programs. *Drug and Alcohol Dependence, 52*, 57–61.

Carroll, K. M. (1998). Treating drug dependence: Recent advances and old truths. In W. R. Miller & N. Heather (Eds.), *Treating addictive behaviors* (2nd ed., pp. 217–229). New York: Plenum.

Cepeda, L. M., & Davenport, D. S. (2006). Person-centered therapy and solution-focused brief therapy: An integration of present and future awareness. *Psychotherapy: Theory, Research, Practice, Training, 43*, 1–12.

Chandler, M. C., & Mason, W. H. (1995). Solution-focused therapy: An alternative approach to addictions nursing. *Perspectives in Psychiatric Care, 31*, 8–13.

Chen, S. H., Yeh, K. W., Chen, S. H., Yen, D. C., Yin, T. J. C., & Huang, J. L. (2004). The development and establishment of a care map in children with asthma in Taiwan. *Journal of Asthma, 41*, 855–861.

Collins, S. E., Carey, K. B., & Sliwinski, M. J. (2002). Mailed personalized normative feedback as a brief intervention for at-risk college drinkers. *Journal of Studies on Alcohol, 63*, 559–567.

Corcoran, J. (2005). *Building strengths and skills: A collaborative approach to working with clients.* New York: Oxford University Press.

Corcoran, J., & Pillai, V. (2009). A review of the research on solution-focused therapy. *British Journal of Social Work, 39*, 234–242.

de Shazer, S. (1985). *Keys to solution in brief therapy.* New York: W. W. Norton.

de Shazer, S. (1988). *Clues: Investigating solutions in brief therapy.* New York: W. W. Norton.

de Shazer, S., & Berg, I. K. (1992). Doing therapy: A poststructural re-vision. *Journal of Marital and Family Therapy, 18*, 71–81.

de Shazer, S., Berg, I. K., Lipchik, E., Nunnally, E., Molnar, A., Gingerich, W., & Weiner-Davis, M. (1986). Brief therapy: Focused solution development. *Family Process, 25*, 207–221.

de Shazer, S., & Isebaert, L. (2003). The Bruges Model: A solution-focused approach to problem drinking. *Journal of Family Psychotherapy, 14*(4), 43–52.

Dimeff, L. A., & McNeely, M. (2000). Computer-enhanced primary care practitioner advice for high-risk college drinkers in a student primary health-care setting. *Cognitive and Behavioral Practice, 7,* 82–100.

Drake, R. E., Merrens, M. R., & Lynde, D. W. (Eds.). (2005). *Evidence-based mental health practice: A textbook.* New York: W. W. Norton.

Fernando, D. M. (2007). Existential theory and solution-focused strategies: Integration and application. *Journal of Mental Health Counseling, 29,* 226–241.

Gingerich, W. J., & Eisengart, S. (2000). Solution-focused brief therapy: A review of the outcome research. *Family Process, 39,* 477–498.

Gingerich, W. J., & Wabeke, T. (2001). A solution-focused approach to mental health intervention in school settings. *Children & Schools, 23,* 33–47.

Goodheart, C. D., Kazdin, A. E., & Sternberg, R. J. (2006). *Evidence-based psychotherapy: Where practice and research meet.* Washington, DC: American Psychological Association.

Heather, N. (1995). Brief intervention strategies. In R. K. Hester & W. R. Miller (Eds.), *Handbook of alcoholism treatment approaches: Effective alternatives* (2nd ed., pp. 105–122). Boston: Allyn and Bacon.

Herbeck, D. M., Hser, Y., & Teruya, C. (2008). Empirically supported substance abuse treatment approaches: A survey of treatment providers' perspectives and practices. *Addictive Behaviors, 33,* 699–712.

Higgins. S. T., Silverman, K., & Heil, S. H. (Eds.). (2008). *Contingency management in substance abuse treatment.* New York: Guilford.

Higgins, S. T., & Silverman, K. (Eds.). (1999). *Motivating behavior change among illicit-drug abusers: Research on contingency management interventions.* Washington, DC: American Psychological Association.

Iguchi, M. Y., Belding, M. A., Morral, A. R., Lamb, R. J., & Husband, S. D. (1997). Reinforcing operants other than abstinence in drug abuse treatment: An effective alternative for reducing drug use. *Journal of Counseling and Clinical Psychology, 65,* 421–428.

Interlandi, J. (2008, March 3). What addicts need. *Newsweek.*

Juhnke, G. A., & Coker, J. K. (1997). A solution-focused intervention with recovering, alcohol-dependent, single parent mothers and their children. *Journal of Addictions and Offender Counseling, 17,* 77–87.

Kellogg, S. H. (2003). On "gradualism" and the building of the harm reduction-abstinence continuum. *Journal of Substance Abuse Treatment, 25,* 241–247.

Kim, J. S. (2008). Examining the effectiveness of solution-focused brief therapy: A meta-analysis. *Research on Social Work Practice, 18,* 107–116.

Larimer, M. E., Turner, A. P., Anderson, B. K., Fader, J. S., Kilmer, J. R., Palmer, R. S., & Cronce, J. M. (2001). Evaluating a brief alcohol intervention with fraternities. *Journal of Studies on Alcohol, 62,* 370–380.

Levenson, H., Speed, J., & Budman, S. H. (1995). Therapists' experience, training, and skill in brief therapy: A bicoastal survey. *American Journal of Psychotherapy, 49,* 95–117.

Lewis, T. F., & Osborn, C. J. (2004). Solution-focused counseling and motivational interviewing: A consideration of confluence. *Journal of Counseling & Development, 82,* 38–48.

Linehan, M. M. (1993a). *Cognitive-behavioral treatment of borderline personality disorder.* New York: Guilford.

Linehan, M. M. (1993b). *Skills training manual for treating borderline personality disorder.* New York: Guilford.

Linton, J. M. (2005). Mental health counselors and substance abuse treatment: Advantages, difficulties, and practical issues to solution-focused interventions. *Journal of Mental Health Counseling, 27,* 297–310.

Maisto, S. A., Conigliaro, J., McNeil, M., Kraemer, K., Conigliaro, R. L., & Kelley, M. E. (2001). Effects of two types of brief intervention and readiness to change on alcohol use in hazardous drinkers. *Journal of Studies on Alcohol, 62,* 605–614.

Majoor, B., & Rivera, J. (2003). SACHR: An example of an integrated, harm reduction drug treatment program. *Journal of Substance Abuse Treatment, 25,* 257–262.

Marlatt, G. A. (1998). *Harm reduction: Pragmatic strategies for managing high-risk behaviors.* New York: Guilford.

Marlatt, G. A., & Donovan, D. M. (Eds.). (2005). *Relapse prevention: Maintenance strategies in the treatment of addictive behaviors* (2nd ed.). New York: Guilford.

Marlatt, G. A., Baer, J. S., Kivlahan, D. R., Dimeff, L. A., Larimer, M. E., Quigley, L. A., Somers, J. M., & Williams, E. (1998). Screening and brief intervention for high-risk college student drinkers: Results from a 2-year follow-up assessment. *Journal of Consulting and Clinical Psychology, 66,* 604–615.

Marlatt, G. A., Witkiewitz, K. (2002). Harm reduction approaches to alcohol use: Health promotion, prevention, and treatment. *Addictive Behaviors, 27,* 867–886.

Mason, W. H., Chandler, M. C., & Grasso, B. C. (1995). Solution based techniques applied to addictions: A clinic's experience in shifting paradigms. *Alcoholism Treatment Quarterly, 13*(4), 39–49.

Matto, H., Corcoran, J., & Fassler, A. (2003). Integrating solution-focused and art therapies for substance abuse treatment: Guidelines for practice. *The Arts in Psychotherapy, 30,* 265–272.

Meyers, R. J., Villanueva, M., & Smith, J. E. (2005). The community reinforcement approach: History and new directions. *Journal of Cognitive Psychotherapy, 19,* 247–260.

Miller, S. D. (1992). The symptoms of solution. *Journal of Strategic and Systemic Therapies, 11,* 1–11.

Miller, S. D., Hubble, M. A., & Duncan, B. L. (Eds.). (1996). *Handbook of solution-focused brief therapy.* San Francisco: Jossey-Bass.

Miller, W. R. (1992). The effectiveness of treatment for substance abuse: Reasons for optimism. *Journal of Substance Abuse Treatment, 9,* 93–102.

Miller, W. R., Andrews, N. R., Wilbourne, P., & Bennett, M. E. (1998). A wealth of alternatives: Effective treatments for alcohol problems. In W. R. Miller & N. Heather (Eds.), *Treating addictive behaviors* (2nd ed., pp. 203–216). New York: Plenum.

Miller, W. R., & Carroll, K. M. (Eds.). (2006). *Rethinking substance abuse: What the science shows, and what we should do about it.* New York: Guilford.

Miller, W. R., & Hester, R. K. (2003). Treating alcohol problems: Toward an informed eclecticism. In R. K. Hester & W. R. Miller (Eds.), *Handbook of alcoholism treatment approaches: Effective alternatives* (3rd ed., pp. 1–12). Boston: Allyn and Bacon.

Miller, W. R., & Page, A. C. (1991). Warm turkey: Other routes to abstinence. *Journal of Substance Abuse Treatment, 8,* 227–232.

Miller, W. R., & Sanchez, V. C. (1994). Motivating young adults for treatment and lifestyle change. In G. S. Howard & P. E. Nathan (Eds.), *Alcohol use and misuse by young adults* (pp. 55–81). Notre Dame, IN: University of Notre Dame Press.

Miller, W. R., Sorensen, J. L., Selzer, J. A., & Brigham, G. S. (2006). Disseminating evidence-based practices in substance abuse treatment: A review with suggestions. *Journal of Substance Abuse Treatment, 31,* 25–39.

Miller, W. R., & Wilbourne, P. L. (2002). Mesa Grande: A methodological analysis of clinical trials of treatments for alcohol use disorders. *Addiction, 97,* 265–277.

Miller, W. R., Wilbourne, P. L., Hettema, J. E. (2003). What works? A summary of alcohol treatment outcome research. In R. K. Hester & W. R. Miller (Eds.), *Handbook of alcoholism treatment approaches: Effective alternatives* (3rd ed., pp. 13–63). Boston: Allyn and Bacon.

Molnar, A., & de Shazer, S. (1987). Solution-focused therapy: Toward the identification of therapeutic tasks. *Journal of Marital and Family Therapy, 13,* 349–358.

Morgenstern, J., Frey, R. M., McCrady, B. S., Labouvie, E., & Neighbors, C. J. (1996). Examining mediators of change in traditional chemical dependency treatment. *Journal of Studies on Alcohol, 57,* 53–64.

Moyers, T. B., & Miller, W. R. (1993). Therapists' conceptualizations of alcoholism: Measurement and implications for treatment decisions. *Psychology of Addictive Behaviors, 7,* 238–245.

Murphy, J. G., Duchnick, J. J., Vuchinich, R. E., Davison, J. W., Karg, R. S., Olson, A. M., Smith, A. F., & Coffey, T. T. (2001). Relative efficacy of a brief motivational intervention for college student drinkers. *Psychology of Addictive Behaviors, 15,* 373–379.

Najavits, L. M., Liese, B. S., & Harned, M. S. (2005). Cognitive and behavioral therapies. In J. H. Lowinson, P. Ruiz, R. B. Millman, & J. G. Langrod (Eds.), *Substance abuse: A comprehensive textbook* (4th ed., pp. 723–732). Philadelphia, PA: Lippincott Williams & Wilkins.

Neighbors, C., Larimer, M. E., & Lewis, M. A. (2004). Targeting misperceptions of descriptive drinking norms: Efficacy of a computer delivered personalized normative feedback intervention. *Journal of Consulting and Clinical Psychology, 72,* 434–447.

Nunnally, E. (1993). Solution focused therapy. In R. A. Wells & V. J. Giannetti (Eds.), *Casebook of the brief psychotherapies* (pp. 271–286). New York: Plenum.

Ogborne, A. C., Wild, T. C., Braun, K., & Newton-Taylor, B. (1998). Measuring treatment process beliefs among staff of specialized addiction treatment services. *Journal of Substance Abuse Treatment, 15,* 301–312.

O'Hanlon, W., & Weiner-Davis, M. (1989). *In search of solutions: A new direction in psychotherapy.* New York: W. W. Norton.

Osborn, C. J. (1997). Does disease matter? Incorporating Solution-Focused Brief Therapy in alcoholism treatment. *Journal of Alcohol and Drug Education, 43,* 18–30.

Osborn, C. J., & Lewis, T. F. (2004). Experiential training in substance abuse counseling: Curricular design and instructional practices. *Journal of Teaching in the Addictions, 3*(2), 41–56.

Osborn, C. J., West, J. D., Kindsvatter, A., & Paez, S. B. (2008). Treatment planning as collaborative care map construction: Reframing clinical practice to promote client involvement. *Journal of Contemporary Psychotherapy, 38,* 169–176.

Petry, N. M., Martin, B., Cooney, J. L., & Kranzler, H. R. (2000). Give them prizes, and they will come: Contingency management for treatment of alcohol dependence. *Journal of Consulting and Clinical Psychology, 68,* 250–257.

Preston, K. L., Umbricht, A., Wong, C. J., & Epstein, D. H. (2001). Shaping cocaine abstinence by successive approximation. *Journal of Consulting and Clinical Psychology, 69,* 643–654.

Roozen, H. G., Boulogne, J. J., van Tulder, M. W., van den Brink, W., De Jong, C. A. J., & Kerkhof, A. J. F. M. (2004). A systematic review of the effectiveness of the community reinforcement approach in alcohol, cocaine, and opioid addiction. *Drug and Alcohol Dependence, 74,* 1–13.

Rosenberg, H., & Phillips, K. T. (2003). Acceptability and availability of harm-reduction interventions for drug abuse in American substance abuse treatment agencies. *Psychology of Addictive Behaviors, 17,* 203–210.

Sanchez-Craig, M. (1990). Brief didactic treatment for alcohol and drug-related problems: An approach based on client choice. *British Journal of Addiction, 85,* 169–177.

Selekman, M. D. (1993). *Pathways to change: Brief therapy solutions with difficult adolescents.* New York: Guilford.

Shaffer, H. J., & Robbins, M. (1991). Manufacturing multiple meanings of addiction: Time-limited realities. *Contemporary Family Therapy, 13,* 387–404.

Smith, J. E., Meyers, R. J., & Milford, J. L. (2003). Community reinforcement approach and community reinforcement and family training. In R. K. Hester & W. R. Miller (Eds.), *Handbook of alcoholism treatment approaches: Effective alternatives* (3rd ed., pp. 237–258). Boston: Allyn and Bacon.

Smith, J. E., Meyers, R. J., & Miller, W. R. (2001). The community reinforcement approach to the treatment of substance use disorders. *The American Journal on Addictions, 10*(Suppl.), 51–59.

Substance Abuse and Mental Health Services Administration. (2008). *Results from the 2007 National Survey on Drug Use and Health: National Findings* (Office of Applied Studies, NSDUH Series H-34, DHHS Publication No. SMA 08–4343). Rockville, MD.

Taleff, M. J. (1997). Solution-oriented and traditional approaches to alcohol and other drug treatment: Similarities and differences. *Alcoholism Treatment Quarterly, 15,* 65–73.

Tatarsky, A. (2003). Harm reduction psychotherapy: Extending the reach of traditional substance use treatment. *Journal of Substance Abuse Treatment, 25,* 249–256.

Thombs, D. L. (2006). *Introduction to addictive behaviors* (3rd ed.). New York: Guilford.

Thombs, D. L., & Osborn, C. J. (2001). A cluster analytic study of clinical orientations among chemical dependency counselors. *Journal of Counseling & Development, 79,* 450–458.

Tracy, S. W. (2007). Medicalizing alcoholism one hundred years ago. *Harvard Review of Psychiatry, 15,* 86–91.

Tyson, E. H., & Baffour, T. D. (2004). Arts-based strengths: A solution-focused intervention with adolescents in an acute-care psychiatric facility. *The Arts in Psychotherapy, 31,* 213–227.

Vik, P. W., Culbertson, K. A., & Sellers, K. (2000). Readiness to change drinking among heavy-drinking college students. *Journal of Studies on Alcohol, 61,* 674–680.

Walter, J. L., & Peller, J. E. (2000). *Recreating brief therapy: Preferences and possibilities.* New York: W. W. Norton.

Walters, S. T. (2000). In praise of feedback: An effective intervention for college students who are heavy drinkers. *Journal of American College Health, 48,* 235–238.

Walters, S. T., Bennett, M. E., & Miller, J. H. (2000). Reducing alcohol use in college students: A controlled trial of two brief interventions. *Journal of Drug Education, 30,* 361–372.

Watts, R. E., & Pietrzak, D. (2000). Adlerian "encouragement" and the therapeutic process of solution-focused brief therapy. *Journal of Counseling & Development, 78,* 442–447.

White, M., & Epston, D. (1990). *Narrative means to therapeutic ends.* New York: W. W. Norton.

Zweben, A., & Fleming, M. F. (1999). Brief interventions for alcohol and drug problems. In J. A. Tucker, D. M. Donovan, & G. A. Marlatt (Eds.), *Changing addictive behavior: Bridging clinical and public health strategies* (pp. 251–282). New York: Guilford.

Chapter 9

Co-Occurring Disorders and Addictions Treatment

Scott E. Gillig
St. Thomas University
Pamela A. Cingel
St. Thomas University

Research indicates that the comorbidity of addictive disorders and other mental health disorders is extensive and highly correlated (Brems & Namyniuk, 1999; Johnson, Brems, Wells, Theno, & Fisher, 2003; Schneider, 2005; Substance Abuse and Mental Health Services Administration [SAMHSA], 2005). This chapter addresses the history of how mental health systems have adapted to meet the needs of clients with multiple disorders. The prevalence of comorbidity is examined. Issues related to assessment, diagnosis, treatment, and care needs are addressed. Suggestions for a multidisciplinary team approach to treatment will be covered. The components of the counseling process will be reviewed and a case example showing co-occurring disorder (COD) assessment, diagnosis, and treatment planning will be presented.

HISTORY OF HOW MENTAL HEALTH SYSTEMS HAVE ADAPTED TO MEET THE NEEDS OF CLIENTS WITH MULTIPLE DISORDERS

Grella (2003) reported that those with co-occurring psychiatric problems usually have shorter stays in treatment, poorer treatment outcomes, and higher treatment costs than those with only one disorder. Because dual-diagnosed patients have diverse needs, their care requires flexible and integrated treatment methods and services. However, integrative treatment has historically been the exception rather than the rule. Most dual-diagnosed individuals have traditionally received either mental health or substance abuse treatment, rather than both simultaneously. Researchers have found that those working in substance abuse and mental health settings hold conflicting views about which treatment approaches work best for the dual-diagnosed (Grella, 2003). While both substance abuse and mental health professionals attributed the psychiatric symptoms of substance abusers to an underlying cause, it appears that substance abuse professionals more strongly supported strict policies on the necessity of abstinence, discharge criteria, confrontational, and self-help methods than did mental health professionals (Grella, 2003).

According to Sciacca (1997), confrontation was traditionally used to break down the defense system and denial of substance abusing clients. On the other hand, mental health clients were treated in a supportive, nonthreatening way to help them maintain their already unstable defenses. Prior to 1984, there were few, if any, treatments available to serve those clients\entering the mental health system who also presented with substance abuse issues that they denied and who were, thus, unmotivated for substance abuse treatment. Sciacca (1997) reports that dual-diagnosis treatment programs had their beginning in 1984 at a New York State outpatient psychiatric facility; the following year, such joint treatment programs were applied across multiple program sites in New York and throughout the country.

In 1984, Sciacca (1997) developed a non-confrontational approach with the aim of providing nonjudgmental acceptance of clients' symptoms and experiences related to both mental illness and substance disorders. Her method involves engaging clients in phase-by-phase interventions that move clients from denial to abstinence. The components of her approach include development of trust, exploring symptoms, exploring interaction effects that stem from substance abuse and mental health symptoms, working on client motivation, collaborating with the client to ameliorate symptoms, achievement of partial or full remission, and participation in an individualized maintenance routine for relapse prevention.

Helping professionals became progressively more aware of the link between substance abuse and mental disorders in the late 1970s and early 1980s. During the 1980s and 1990s, studies found that 50% to 75% of substance abuse clients had some type of co-occurring mental disorder while 20% to 50% of mental health clients had a co-occurring substance abuse disorder (SAMHSA, 2005). Besides its relationship to mental illness, substance abuse was found to drastically complicate treatment outcomes for those with mental illness. Those with mental illness coupled with substance abuse spent twice as many days in the hospital, had higher rates of HIV infection, more relapse, and higher suicide rates than those with mental illness alone (SAMHSA, 2005). Brems and Namyniuk (1999) emphasize the high financial and social costs associated with co-occurring disorders. Such costs include loss of productivity, difficulty keeping jobs, increased health care and hospitalization costs, less satisfying family relationships, poorer treatment outcomes, increased criminal and suicidal behavior, poor medication compliance, and faster relapse. Although substance abuse appeared to complicate mental health treatment, it was also found that treatment of clients with co-occurring mental illness and substance abuse disorders can be effective (SAMHSA, 2005).

PREVALENCE OF COMORBIDITY

New counselors working in the field of addiction treatment may wrongly assume that treating someone with an addiction is a straightforward process and that the identified addiction will be the sole focus of treatment. In practice, however, for a client to present with a single addiction, without a coexisting addiction or addictions, or a coexisting psychiatric disorder or disorders, would be the exception rather than the rule. According to Johnson et al. (2003) and Schneider (2005), comorbidity involves mental and emotional disorders that coincide with substance abuse within an individual.

Research suggests that the comorbidity of addictive disorders and other mental health disorders is prevalent and highly correlated (SAMHSA, 2005). For practical reasons, the term *co-occurring disorders* replaced the terms *dual disorders* or *dual diagnosis*. These latter terms, though used generally to refer to the combination of substance abuse and mental disorders, can be confusing in that they also refer to other combinations of disorders (such as mental disorders and learning disorders). Also, the terms imply that there are only two disorders occurring at the same time, when in fact there may be more than two. For example, an individual may have both major depressive disorder and panic disorder combined with alcohol dependence and cannabis abuse. In this chapter, *co-occurring disorders* refers to co-occurring substance use (abuse or dependence) and mental disorders that are not simply a cluster of symptoms resulting from one disorder (SAMHSA, 2005).

According to Von Steen, Vacc, and Strickland (2002), substance abuse treatment usually takes place in either specialized substance abuse treatment facilities or in community mental health centers. They report that about 25% to 30% of alcoholics experience depression and anxiety, respectively, while approximately 25% of all suicides are committed by individuals with chronic alcohol dependence.

"Rates of regular heavy drinking (five or more drinks for men or four or more for women in a single day, on 12 or more days during the past year) were also found to be high for respondents who had a past year major depression (9%) or specific phobia (8.3%). Respondents with lifetime antisocial, obsessive-compulsive, and paranoid personality disorders also showed regular heavy drinking patterns (8.7%, 8.9%, and 7%, respectively). In general, the national estimates for those adults with a co-occurring SUD and a mental disorder range from 5.2 million to 6.6 million." (Substance Abuse and Mental Health Services Administration [SAMHSA], 2009).

They report that counselor training programs need to offer increased coursework to prepare counselors to work in co-occurring settings. Based on their findings, they suggest that counselors in community and mental health counseling programs receive specific training in substance abuse assessment, 12-step work, family counseling for substance abusing clients, relapse prevention, and treatment planning for substance abuse clients.

Counselors should keep in mind that clients with COD often have cognitive limitations. Some of these limitations, which include difficulty concentrating, may improve during the initial weeks of treatment but some may become more obvious as part of a specific disorder (e.g., schizophrenia, attention-deficit disorder). Strategies to address these limitations can include more concrete communication, using simpler concepts, repeating concepts, and using multiple formats. Role-playing may be a useful technique and can include anything from practicing making a phone call to a sponsor to appropriate sharing in a group situation.

Since abstinence requires the development and utilization of a new set of recovery skills, clients with mental disorders and cognitive limitations usually have a harder time learning these new skills. That's why repetition and practice is especially important for these clients (SAMHSA, 2005).

The following case study provides an example on the use of repetition and skill building with a COD client.

In individual counseling sessions with Susan H., a 34-year-old Caucasian woman with bipolar disorder and alcohol dependence, the counselor observes that often she is forgetful about details of her recent past, including what has been said and agreed to in therapy. Conclusions the counselor thought were clear in one session seem to be fuzzy by the next. The counselor begins to start sessions with a brief review of the last session. He also allows time at the end of each session to review what has just happened. As Susan H. is having difficulty remembering appointment times and other responsibilities, he helps her devise a system of reminders in big letters on her refrigerator (SAMHSA, 2005).

While the above case of Susan illustrates a client with co-occurring diagnoses on Axis I, it is not uncommon to have a client with multiple diagnoses across several of the Axes such as the following case of Jeff G. This case involved a complex web of treatment issues: marital issues, family issues, sexual preference issues, religious orientation issues, early childhood abuse issues, clergy abuse issues, multiple physical illnesses, multiple chemical dependence and substance abuse issues, multiple psychiatric and personality disorder issues (such as those commonly found with co-occurring disorders such as major depression, borderline personality, disorder, and compulsive behaviors). According to APA (2000), major categories of mental disorders for COD schizophrenia and other psychotic disorders include anxiety disorders, mood disorders, somatoform disorders, dissociative disorders, eating disorders, sleep disorders, impulse-control disorders, sexual and gender identity disorders, adjustment disorders, and personality disorders. The Substance Abuse and Mental Health Services Administration (SAMHSA, 2009) has some excellent fact sheets related to co-occurring disorders. Links can be found at the end of the chapter.

CASE STUDY

Jeff, age 30, contacted Dr. Willis for individual counseling. During the intake session, he reported that issues from his family of origin were affecting his marriage. Jeff additionally complained that he had been feeling angry, anxious, bored, confused, depressed, fearful, and tense. He identified problems with family, sexual orientation, marriage, religion, procrastination, lack of motivation, and physical health to be of importance also. Jeff presented with a history of drug/alcohol abuse, impulsivity around sex, a pattern of unstable relationships, affective instability, feelings of boredom, and intense fear of abandonment. He complained that his in-laws are opposed to his being married to their daughter, especially in light of their discovery of his gay lifestyle. He also indicated his brother is currently in prison for rape. Jeff stated he was abused both emotionally and physically as a child by this older brother. Of importance is that Jeff initially experienced a conflict between the religion that he grew up with (Lutheran religion) and that to which he converted to please his wife (Jehovah Witness religion). His wife's religious support system was highly opposed to his gay experiences.

Jeff reported he began dating at 18 years of age. He indicated he has had difficulty trusting women. He reported being currently married to Nancy, 32, for two years and has been separated for approximately one year. He reported he told her of his homosexual orientation prior to marriage. Jeff initially expressed ambivalence about wanting to separate from his spouse until he resolved his family of origin issues. Jeff stated that he and his wife had previously been in therapy with Dr. Buford in a private practice off and on with apparent limited investment.

Jeff initially reported past use of marijuana for 14 years, cocaine use for 3 years, and alcohol use for 15 years. He reported that he rarely uses alcohol and does not use any other mind altering chemicals except for Zantac prescribed by his family doctor, Dr. Holland. Over the course of several sessions with Dr. Willis, it became evident that Jeff had lost control over his drinking on numerous occasions. It was also observed that when he is in a relationship, he tends to put on weight and discontinues having anonymous sex with partners he meets in bars, and limits his drinking and drugging (cocaine and marijuana). When he is not in a committed relationship, he loses weight and resumes drinking, drugging, and sexual acting out.

Dr. Willis met with Jeff and his wife for several couples counseling sessions. While Jeff initially lived with his wife and her two children at the onset of his counseling, as counseling went on, Jeff was very certain about both his gay identity and his desire to be separated and/or divorced from his wife. After becoming divorced, his ex-wife and children moved to another part of the state and maintained a separate residence there.

As part of his counseling treatment with Dr. Willis, Jeff was referred to an Adults Molested as Children program to help him address his child abuse issues. He did not follow through with this except for an initial visit. Then Jeff attempted several times to establish a gay support system on his own. Unfortunately, two of the individuals who he sought for support, attempted to seduce him. One was a paraprofessional and his actions were reported to the State Counseling Board. It was hypothesized that Jeff was reenacting a childhood dynamic of the time when his brother sexually molested him and his father failed to protect him. Jeff appeared to put Dr. Willis in the role of his father. He agreed with this interpretation and seemed to move forward in his counseling as a result of this insight. Though he refused to attend AA meetings, his counseling sessions with Dr. Willis involved attempts to help Jeff stop drinking and drugging. On a positive note, while in treatment with Dr. Willis, Jeff did follow through with his sessions and attended regularly. He reported at the time feeling more comfortable interacting with males as a result of his counseling. He reported himself not to be currently suicidal. Dr. Willis was planning to continue long-term counseling with this client who seemed to have the resources to improve. Unfortunately, Jeff impulsively terminated counseling without notifying Dr. Willis and moved out of state.

After moving out of state, Jeff contacted Dr. Willis by phone asking him for a referral. From his report, Jeff had entered an inpatient chemical dependency treatment program that offered him no aftercare plan or referrals. He had suffered two drug overdoses before entering chemical dependency treatment. He reported that during his inpatient chemical dependency treatment he was found to be infected with Hepatitis B.

Dr. Willis gave Jeff several referral options in his new location. According to reports by his new counselor, Dr. Brown, Jeff developed a profound clinical depression as indicated by a score of 36 on the Beck Depression Inventory and attempted suicide while in counseling. He was referred to a psychiatrist, Dr. Germaine, entered a treatment center for co-occurring disorders and was put on Prozac. Jeff responded quite well initially, but later showed hypomanic behavior, lost therapeutic motivation, and began to drink and frequent gay bars more often.

Dr. Willis was later contacted by phone by Jeff who indicated he was moving to another location to live with his sister. Jeff indicated he had appointments with both a therapist and a psychiatrist there.

A DSM IV-TR Diagnosis of the client is as follows:

AXIS I   309.81 – Post-traumatic Stress Disorder

303.90 – Alcohol Dependence
Cocaine Dependence
Marijuana Abuse

302.90 – Sexual Disorder, NOS (sexual addiction)

AXIS II 301.83 – Borderline Personality Disorder, primary

AXIS III Hepatitis B

AXIS IV 5, Extreme – marital separation, separation from stepchildren, loss of job, two overdoses, suicidal attempt, inpatient psychiatric hospitalization

AXIS V current – 35   past – 65

Treatment recommendations include having the client receive weekly individual counseling sessions, attending Alcoholics Anonymous, Drug Addicts Anonymous, Overeaters Anonymous, and Sex Addicts Anonymous meetings (as many as possible weekly), engaging in a gay support system, continuing with routine psychiatric treatment, obtaining employment, continuing to explore family of origin issues (i.e., sexual abuse, physical abuse), and be monitored for suicidal ideation on an ongoing basis.

Some of the innovations in treatment of co-occurring disorders include: the development of new models that stress the importance of knowledge of both mental health and substance abuse treatment when working with clients for whom both issues are present; the provision of a classification of treatment settings to assist in systematic planning, consultations, collaborations, and integration; and a reduction in the double stigma associated with both disorders through increased acceptance of substance abuse and mental health concerns as a standard part of health-care assessment (SAMHSA, 2005).

ASSESSMENT

According to Schneider (2005), all substance and behavioral dependencies have the following behaviors in common: compulsive use without control, continued use despite negative consequences, and obsession with using or obtaining the drug or behavior. Drug and alcohol abuse disorders, combined with mental health issues, can create a very complex clinical picture. The use of standardized testing instruments can be helpful for gaining clinical clarity with assessment of COD issues.

Juhnke, Vacc, Curtis, Coll, and Paredes (2003) surveyed master's-level addictions counselors (MACs) who hold National Certified Counselor (NCC) credentials and additionally specialize in treating addictions. They found that five assessment instruments were seen as most important to use and most often used by addictions counselors. These instruments include the Substance Abuse Subtle Screening Inventory (SASSI) (both the SASSI-3 and the SASSI Adolescent versions), the Beck Depression Inventory (BDI), the Minnesota Multiphasic Personality Inventory-2 (MMPI-2), the Addictions Severity Index (ASI), and the Michigan Alcoholism Screening Test (MAST). Interestingly, two of the five instruments, the BDI and the MMPI-2, are primarily used to detect mental and emotional disorders, rather than addictions per se.

Junhke et al. (2003) also found that while MACs mostly agree on the importance and relative frequency of use of these assessment instruments, counselors who specialize in addictions treatment use these instruments infrequently. Possible reasons cited for why counselors are not using assessment instruments more include: the belief that they can arrive at accurate diagnoses without the use of standardized assessment instruments, or that the use of such instruments could promote a pathology rather than a wellness focus; and the belief that they lack addictions-specific training in use of assessment instruments. Juhnke et al. (2003) have suggested that use of such assessment instruments could do much to enhance counselors' ability to assess clients with addiction issues.

Johnson et al. (2003) studied use of the Brief Symptom Inventory as a screening tool and found that 64% of 700 participants met the criteria for having co-occurring substance abuse and other psychiatric symptoms. Comorbid individuals were more apt to be homeless, unemployed, Caucasian, have a higher past arrest rate, more severe drug abuse, lower age of first drug use, and were more likely to have used various drugs more frequently than those without comorbidity (Johnson et al., 2003).

During the assessment process, counselors might ask, "Which came first, the addiction or the psychiatric problem?" It appears that either can be the case. According to Schneider (2005), abuse of addictive substances can initiate, exacerbate, mask, or mimic psychiatric problems. Similarly, psychiatric problems can make one more susceptible to addiction. Given alcohol's depressing and disinhibiting effects, many alcoholics are depressed and many have been diagnosed with antisocial personality disorder (Schneider, 2005). On the other hand, people who are depressed may self-medicate and get a temporary lift from drinking alcohol. A depressed person may also turn to cocaine or an amphetamine to get a lift since these are stimulants. However, withdrawal from these substances can result in increased depression and lack of energy. While children with attention-deficit/hyperactivity disorder (ADHD) are at higher risk of later substance abuse, treatment with stimulants such as Ritalin make substance abuse less likely to occur in the future (Schneider, 2005). The reason may be that these children were more closely monitored by their family physicians, who may of help in prevention of later substance abuse (Schneider, 2005). So the role of early intervention coupled with stimulant treatment for ADHD may have accounted for decrease in later substance abuse.

If a client has both an addictive disorder and a psychiatric disorder, there are several questions that a counselor should consider in addition to "Which one came first?" such as "Which one is primary?" and "Which one should be treated first?" Typically, symptoms like aggression and depression that stem from an addiction decrease once the person stops using the addicting substance. If this does not happen, it is likely that the psychiatric problem came first. Such an assumption can be strengthened by taking a thorough client history. When assessing a client with both a mental health problem and an addiction, the one that came first is usually primary and is important to address for relapse prevention. However, in either case, the addiction is typically dealt with first through detoxification and/or other medical intervention (Schneider, 2005).

To illustrate the importance of determining primacy and treatment importance, consider the assessment of a drug dependent gang member. If it were determined that this gang member also met diagnostic criteria for conduct disorder or antisocial personality disorder, it would be important to determine whether drug abuse and/or criminal activity started first and if either or both started before or after joining the gang. According to Duffy (2004), gang members use drugs more often and at higher levels than do non-gang members. It appears that being involved in gangs encourages involvement in drug abuse, drug trafficking, gun carrying, violence, and drug sales. "By its very nature, drug dependency opens the door to increased crime and violence. Addiction requires a steady stream of drugs and many addicted young gang members increase their criminal activities in order to obtain the drugs needed to support their habits. This is the vicious cycle of drug abuse leading to drug dependency leading to increased crime leading to increased drug use, and on and on." (Duffy, 2004, p. 6). If joining the gang opened the doorway for drug abuse, then exploring issues around gang membership should be considered very important for relapse prevention.

During assessment, effective COD counselors will also pay attention to compulsive behavioral patterns. Compulsive behaviors can interfere with treatment and can lead to relapse. This author recalls working with a 30-year-old male client who would drink alcohol excessively, overeat, and isolate himself and stay home when depressed. When his depression lifted, he would begin to lose weight, abuse cocaine, visit bars and nightclubs and have compulsive sex with multiple anonymous partners. The chemical addictions, behavioral compulsions, and mood disorder all needed to be addressed in order to assist this client. Some areas to assess for behavioral compulsions include: sex, work, shopping, relationships, eating, exercise, and gambling.

Cultural Issues Related to Assessment

The culture of the client is an important issue to address during the assessment phase. The number of minority, racial, and ethnic groups in the United States is on the rise (SAMHSA, 2005). Each geographic region has its own cultural blend, and counselors are advised to learn as much as possible about the cultures within their treatment populations. Especially during assessment, it is important that counselors understand the background of clients in addition to methods of communication, healing, and understanding of both mental disorders and substance abuse. Culturally effective counselors study the interpersonal interactions and expectations of family. For instance, in some groups, people may be inclined to somaticize symptoms of mental disorders, and clients from such cultures may assume the clinician will work to relieve their physical complaints. The same client may be insulted by too many probing, personal questions asked during assessment early in treatment and will prematurely self-terminate. Likewise, understanding the client's role in the family and its cultural impact is important (e.g., expectations of a daughter's responsibilities to her parents, protectiveness of the family toward the youngest child, and grandfather as patriarch) (SAMHSA, 2005).

Though counselors need to be attuned to the impact of culture on clients, overgeneralizing their views about clients based on culture is not helpful. It is possible that the level of acculturation and the particular experiences of an individual may result in that person identifying with the dominant culture, or even other cultures. For example, a person from China adopted by American parents at an early age may know little about the cultural norms in her country of origin. For such clients, it is still important to acknowledge the birth country and discover what this connection means to the client (SAMHSA, 2005).

Mental health issues can create perceived cultural constraints within clients. Brems and Namyniuk (1999) indicate that treating clients diagnosed with CODs tends to be more difficult as these clients perceive more treatment barriers than non-comorbid clients. The authors point to the importance of attending to comorbidity issues to increase client retention in treatment. They cited a study of 500 drug abusing or dependent patients by Ross, Glaser, and Germanson, who found that 68% had current and 84% had a past or current comorbid psychiatric diagnosis. It was further found that 73% had a current personality disorder, with 53% of patients having Cluster B diagnoses, 28% Cluster A diagnoses, and 24% Cluster C diagnoses.

According to SAMSHA (2005), counselors should be aware of cultural and ethnic bias in diagnosis. For example, there has been a tendency to overdiagnose African Americans as having paranoid personality disorders and women as being histrionic. Native Americans with spiritual visions have been misdiagnosed as delusional. Culturally sensitive counselors would refrain from over diagnosing Germans with obsessive-compulsive disorder or Latino/Hispanic people with histrionic disorder. In addition, it has been reported that African American, Latino/Hispanic, and Asian American clients are more inclined to self-report a lower level of functioning and to be seen by clinical staff as experiencing more serious and enduring symptomatology and as showing poorer psychosocial development (SAMSHA, 2005).

Researchers have also found that non-White clients tend to have less community resources available to them than White clients, and that clinicians have more difficulty linking them with needed services. The diagnostic criteria should be modulated by sensitivity to cultural differences in behavior and emotional expression and by an awareness of the clinician's own prejudices and stereotyping (SAMSHA, 2005).

In researching 192 ethnically diverse and substance using, pregnant women, Brems and Namyniuk (1999) found that more than 70% of the subjects had at least one DSM-IV diagnosis in addition to substance abuse disorder. Many clients had more than one such other diagnosis. On Axis 1, 24% had affective disorders, 15% anxiety disorders, 4% adjustment disorders, 3% psychotic disorders, 2% impulse control disorders, 2% eating disorders, 2% developmental disorders, and 2% other disorders. Axis II disorders were recorded for 24% of clients. Brems and Namyniuk (1999) found that comorbid clients had more pathology, higher suicide risk, and more drug usage that non-comorbid clients. They stress the importance of routinely assessing clients for comorbidity at all chemical treatment centers.

It is strongly recommended that culturally sensitive methods be used with clients with COD. Culturally sensitive counselors pay attention to cultural aspects of clients' lives while doing assessment, diagnosis, and treatment planning with people from diverse cultures. They respect culture and language as client strengths to be utilized in helping them. Such counselors make their helping models fit the culture of clients rather than expecting clients to change cultural values to fit their models. Culturally responsible counselors work to educate themselves about clients' cultures while working to reduce their own biases (SAMSHA, 2005).

TREATMENT AND CARE NEEDS

Certain COD treatment program elements appear to be essential according to experts who design such treatment. In order to be COD-qualified, these best practices should be present in both residential and outpatient programs: screening, assessment, referral, physical and mental health consultation, the presence of a prescribing on-site psychiatrist, availability of medication and medication oversight, psychoeducational classes that focus on mental health and substance abuse disorders including relapse prevention; on-site mental health and substance abuse groups; off-site dual recovery mutual self-help groups tailored to the special needs of a variety of people with COD; and family education and treatment (SAMSHA, 2005).

According to Johnson et al. (2003), those providing counseling services to clients with comorbidity must apply specialized techniques to deal with an increased probability of high-risk behaviors (e.g., sharing needles, unprotected sex, prostitution).

"Double Trouble in Recovery is a twelve-step fellowship of men and women who share their experience, strength and hope with each other so that they may solve their common problems and help others to recover from their particular addiction(s) and manage their mental disorder(s). DTR is designed to meet the needs of the dually-diagnosed, and is clearly for those having addictive substance problems as well as having been diagnosed with a psychiatric disorders" (Double Trouble in Recovery, 2009).

Comorbid clients often have inadequate social support and recovery support systems, unstable relationships, insufficient housing, are at higher risk for sexually transmitted diseases, and may be unemployed. Individuals presenting with comorbidity require careful treatment planning that addresses both substance abuse and mental health issues. Such treatment includes psychoeducational interventions and relapse prevention that address the role of high-risk behaviors in maintaining their substance abuse.

Chartas and Culbreth (2001) indicate that while there is a positive correlation between substance abuse and domestic violence, no cause-and-effect relationship has been demonstrated. They further indicate that those counselors involved primarily with substance abuse treatment differ in their case conceptualizations from those who specialize in working with domestic violence alone. Domestic violence counselors tend to hold the view that intoxication may lead to loss of control of hostile impulses or may serve as an excuse to attack rather than provide a reason for attack. On the other hand, substance abuse counselors often view battering as a symptom of addiction (Chartas and Culbreth, 2001).

This philosophical schism between substance abuse counselors and domestic violence counselors could impede the helping of clients when the two issues co-occur. For example, Chartas and Culbreth (2001) state that domestic violence counselors tend to be parental in their approach with chemically dependent domestic violence perpetrators and assume that batterers are using their chemical abuse to justify their battering. Therefore, these counselors tend to utilize reinforcement and punishment as therapeutic techniques. On the other hand, chemical dependence counselors would be more likely to see chemical dependence as a disease, with domestic violence as a consequence or symptom of that disease and treat the co-disordered perpetrators accordingly. Similarly, chemically dependent victims of domestic violence tend to be perceived and treated differently by domestic violence counselors and addictions professionals. Such paradigm inconsistencies, especially when they manifest within multidisciplinary treatment teams or between professionals who work with the same clients, can lead to mixed messages that contribute to client confusion and reduction of treatment effectiveness.

An effort to eliminate client confusion regarding co-occurring treatment is the recent creation of a policy called the "No Wrong Door Policy." The goal of this policy is to treat individuals for all their problems at the same time, whether they are initially seeking treatment for a mental health problem or a substance abuse problem. Without such a policy, if an individual initiated treatment for their substance abuse addiction at a treatment center exclusively focused on addiction, the mental health problem might not be addressed. This policy emphasizes the need for multiple agencies to coordinate services (mental health and addiction) and serve clients through one entry process overseen by one agency. Such a policy also helps eliminate duplication of services and ensures that clients get the support they need (Armor-Garb, 2004).

Most recently, in studies using both control and treatment groups, confrontation as a therapeutic technique has been found to be ineffective for clients diagnosed with substance abuse disorders. Several studies have found damaging effects of confrontation such as higher relapse and dropout rates (Miller and White, 2008).

Coexisting psychiatric disorders, such as major depression, can interfere with a client's ability to pay attention or concentrate sufficiently to benefit from addiction treatment (Schneider, 2005). It has been the present co-author's (Gillig's) experience that a chemically dependent client must be coached to use Alcoholic Anonymous (AA) effectively.

CASE STUDY

The following demonstrates how counselors could coach and prep a co-occurring disorder client for an AA meeting.

> Juan, a 35-year-old with schizophrenia, talks about seeing pink elephants in therapy and tends to speak of this among family and friends. However, his counselor anticipates that at AA meetings, Juan may be ridiculed by other members, scapegoated by the group, and may thus not benefit from the healing effects of the group. Essentially, Juan's schizophrenia makes him part of a unique culture not common to the AA group in general. Juan's therapist has advised him to only talk about the pink elephants in individual therapy, but to be silent about them in AA meetings. Juan continues to make progress with both his mental health and substance abuse disorders but with different therapeutic modalities for each.

An individual, who has not been coached by his counselor ahead of time to keep quiet about hallucinations during the AA meeting runs the risk of being ostracized by the group. Such incidents are unfortunate but avoidable with proper preparation for the AA group participation. Helping a recovering alcoholic, including one with schizophrenia, to stay in an AA group will allow that person to address the problem of alcoholism as well as to benefit from the curative factor that Yalom (in Corey, 2001) refers to as universality, even though the group itself does not address the schizophrenia. The schizophrenia issues can be dealt with in another format, such as individual therapy or in another group specifically geared to these issues.

It is also important for counselors to keep in mind that clients with COD often have cognitive limitations. Some of these limitations, including difficulty concentrating, may improve during the initial weeks of treatment but some may become more obvious as part of a specific disorder (e.g., schizophrenia, attention-deficit disorder).

COD TREATMENT MODELS

When teaching a class on substance abuse and treatment in counseling, Gillig (co-author) spends considerable time with students in addressing the question "Is addiction a disease?" While such a discussion is beyond the scope of this chapter, it does have considerable bearing on the type of model a new counselor will develop and what methods that counselor will choose to assist COD clients. If a counselor adheres to a "disease concept" model, then working in conjunction with 12-step groups that see addiction as a disease is a more natural fit. Such counselors would likely be more comfortable with a goal of abstinence for clients. On the other hand, if the disease concept does not fit with a particular counselor's world view, then an alternative model may represent a better fit. In our opinion, there is plenty of room for both models in the treatment of COD clients and either or both may be appropriate for a given client. For clients who meet DSM-IV-TR criteria for substance dependence, perhaps a disease concept model makes most sense; for clients who do not meet this criteria, or who meet DSM-IV-TR criteria for substance abuse but not for dependence, perhaps an alternative model would make more sense. In either case, there is no definitive answer and such a discussion is beyond the scope of this chapter.

Disease Concept Model

For those COD counselors who are comfortable working from a disease concept model with a given client, using 12-step groups as a treatment adjunct makes sense. In our experience, matching such clients to the proper community resources, including the location of nearby 12-step meetings is essential. Familiarity with the culture of the meetings is important, since some may have more of a religious focus and thus be more suited to some clients than others. Also, some meetings may be more supportive and provide a more healing environment for COD clients than others.

It is helpful for mental health counselors who work with COD clients on an outpatient basis to understand the culture and language of the 12-step recovery programs their clients may attend. A few of these programs are Alcoholics Anonymous, Cocaine Anonymous, Al-Anon, and Overeaters Anonymous. In some communities, alternatives to 12-step groups are available, such as Secular Organizations for Sobriety. It is especially important for the counselor to be aware of which 12-step groups are known for being accepting of, or specifically designed for, clients with COD.

A COD counselor can learn about AA by reading AA literature such as the Big Book or the Twelve Steps and Traditions, visiting groups, or discussing groups with colleagues. The counselor can also watch the movie "My Name is Bill W.," based on the true story of a thriving stockbroker whose life crumbled after the stock market crash in the 1920s and how he coped with alcoholism. Together with a fellow alcoholic, Bill W. formed a support group that would ultimately become Alcoholics Anonymous (Amador, 1989).

After the COD counselor and client eventually choose a group, the counselor should ensure that the client takes small steps that are self-reinforcing. These could include trying out several meetings before deciding which is the best, getting a phone number of someone from a meeting, calling that person, getting a temporary sponsor, or getting a sponsor. Helping the client find a sponsor that understands COD would be ideal but may be difficult. Knowing that he or she has a sponsor who understands the nature of two disorders may bring a certain sense of relief to the client.

When working with a COD client who is involved with a 12-step recovery program, it is important to prepare the client for participation in the group. The group process can be particularly stressful for clients with a high level of anxiety or serious mental illness. The counselor should be aware of the difficulties that a client may have participating in a group, and may need to help the client rehearse certain group activities like holding hands or reciting prayers. In some cases, the client may need additional help working out how he or she can actually attend the meeting. The counselor may need to write down very detailed instructions such as how to physically get to the meeting by noting the bus schedule and the walking route to the building (SAMHSA, 2005).

According to the SAMHSA (2005), the debriefing after the first 12-step meeting may be the turning point in recovery. The counselor must help the client overcome any initial obstacles after attending the first group. This may include a discussion of the client's reaction to the group and how he or she can prepare for future attendance. It may also include the importance of finding an appropriate sponsor.

CASE STUDY

The following describes how the counselor helps the client find a sponsor.

> Linda V. had attended her 12-Step group for about 3 months, and although she knew she should ask someone to sponsor her, she was shy and afraid of rejection. She had identified a few women who might be good sponsors, but each week in therapy she stated that she was afraid to reach out, and no one had approached her, although the group members seemed "friendly enough." The therapist suggested that Linda "share" at a meeting, simply stating that she'd like a sponsor but was feeling shy and didn't want to be rejected. The therapist and Linda role-played together in a session, and the therapist reminded her that it was okay to feel afraid and if she couldn't share at the next meeting, they would talk about what stopped her. After the next meeting, Linda related that she almost "shared" but got scared at the last minute, and was feeling bad that she had missed an opportunity. They talked about getting it over with, and Linda resolved to reach out, starting her sharing statement with, "It's hard for me to talk in public, but I want to work this program, so I'm going to tell you all that I know it's time to get a sponsor." This therapy work helped Linda to put her need out to the group, and the response from group members was helpful, with several women offering to meet with her to talk about sponsorship. This experience also helped Linda to become more attached to the group and to learn a new skill for seeking help. While she was helped by counseling strategies alone, others with "social phobia" may need antidepressant medications in addition to counseling (SAMHSA, 2005).

Alternative Models

Osborn (2001) argues against the disease concept model, stating that those with alcohol abuse and alcohol dependence can be best served by matching treatment to individual client needs; and that brief interventions that target specific symptoms are just as effective as more intensive and long-term treatment. Osborn (2001) also indicates that perhaps those with alcohol dependence should be treated differently than those who have problems with alcohol consumption but are not dependent.

An alternative model to the disease concept model is presented by Whittinghill, Whittinghill, and Loesch (2000) who suggest that substance abuse is not an all or nothing endeavor as some substance abuse counselors believe, but rather, that severity falls on a continuum, with sporadic detrimental use on one end and relentless addiction on the other. They see it as unfortunate that most users are forced into a one-size-fits-all approach that includes abstinence and the working of Alcoholics Anonymous' Twelve Steps even when the severity of their problem is minimal. They indicate that such an approach is doomed to failure with those who are abusing but not addicted.

Marlatt, Baer, and Quigley (1994) proposed a self-efficacy model that matches treatment focus with level of substance abuse problem severity that ranges from pre-use to severe addiction. The authors describe five types of self-efficacy that assist in substance abuse treatment. First, *resistance self-efficacy* is preventative and helps individuals learn to refuse pressure by others to begin using substances. Second, *harm reduction self-efficacy* is used to help substance abusers lessen problematic use by reducing frequency and amount of the substance used. Third, *action self-efficacy* is used to help addicted persons quit using by assisting them to see themselves as able to quit. Fourth, *coping self-efficacy* is used to help prevent relapse in those who are newly sober by learning and practicing refusal of a substance. Fifth, *recovery self-efficacy* helps addicts to interpret relapses as learning experiences, rather than failures, so they can return to abstinence.

Kim-Berg and Miller (1992) challenged domination of the disease concept and the components of the 12 steps in treatment of alcoholism. The authors confront what they perceive to be a circular argument by proponents of the traditional model of alcoholism that discredits positive outcomes to alternative treatments. Kim-Berg and Miller (1992) indicate that clients who respond favorably to briefer and alternative treatments are dismissed as not having been real alcoholics to begin with. In utilizing a solution-focused approach, Kim-Berg and Miller (1992) emphasize client successes, strengths, and resources rather than their illness or failures. They also stress the importance of accepting and working "within the client's frame of reference . . . assuming an atheoretical, nonnormative, client-determined posture toward alcohol problems . . ." (Kim-Berg & Miller, 1992, p. 7), keeping solutions simple rather than complex; paying attention to changes that happen naturally and using those changes to find a solution; focusing on the present and future; and collaborating and cooperating with clients in finding and implementing solutions.

"No single theory has been adequate to address the diversity of needs of individuals who are most accurately characterized as chemically dependent. No single theory has demonstrated a clear advantage in terms of efficacy over any other theoretical approach including the philosophy of Alcoholics Anonymous . . ." (Loos, 2002, p. 2). Loos's model of assisting chemically dependent clients is based on humanistic-existential theoretical models and includes other approaches, based on the needs of clients. After doing a client assessment including a thorough biopsychosocial history, clients are oriented to the therapeutic process and educated about the counselor's theoretical orientation. Clients are also educated about six basic feeling states: sad, happy, scared, hurt, angry, and embarrassed; about owning their thoughts and feelings; choosing behavior; expressing feeling behaviorally; making meaning through beliefs and values; attaching feelings to beliefs and values; and behaving morally and ethically. During counseling, cognitive-behavioral, cognitive-affective, and affective-behavioral interventions are used. This model borrows techniques from Ellis, Bandura, and Meichenbaum, such as confronting clients' thinking through guided imagery; changing maladaptive thinking, beliefs, and behaviors; role-play; assertiveness training; desensitization; homework assignments; and problem solving. Clients are also taught to recognize and scale their emotions on a 1–10 scale, with 1 being absence of the emotion, and 10 being the highest expression of the emotion (Loos, 2002).

OTHER TREATMENT ISSUES

When a substance abuse or COD client questions a particular counselor or staff member about whether he or she is in recovery from an addiction, especially in front of other clients, this has the potential to create a we-they situation if not handled effectively. Whether the counselor states that he or she is or is not in recovery, either response opens the door for the client to split staff. If the counselor answers in the affirmative, such a statement can create the perception that, as an addict in recovery, the counselor is better able to empathize with the client, making this counselor the "good guy" and those staff members not in recovery the "bad guys" (as they could not possibly possess the same level of empathy because they have not struggled with an addiction).

In the present authors' opinions, it is best to redirect such questioning by asking "How will knowing about my recovery be of help to you in your recovery?" or "How is your concern with my issues taking your focus off of your own recovery?" Other responses can be effective, such as "Staff have a policy to refrain from disclosing such information because we have found that such discussions do little to help clients focus on their own issues," or "Does a doctor have to have diabetes in order to treat a patient with diabetes? What is important is our ability to work together to accomplish your goals."

MULTIDISCIPLINARY TREATMENT TEAM

Multidisciplinary treatment teams are often beneficial to a client's recovery because each team member offers a unique perspective to diagnosis and treatment. Multidisciplinary teams typically include mental health counselors and substance abuse treatment counselors, case managers, nursing staff, and psychiatric consultants. While team members may play different roles, all are familiar with every client on the caseload, and all should be cross-trained in other disciplines. The team typically includes case managers who can provide useful assistance in life management (e.g., housing, income, and transportation) and some direct counseling or other forms of treatment. It is recommended that treatment programs serving COD clients have mental health specialists—such as mental health counselors with an understanding of substance abuse and mental disorders—on staff to assist with assessment and diagnosis. In addition to provision of direct client services, such professionals could function as consultants to the rest of the team on matters related to mental disorders.

Having an on-site prescribing psychiatrist is crucial to sustaining recovery and stable functioning for people with COD and has been shown to improve treatment retention and decrease substance abuse (SAMHSA, 2005). The on-site psychiatrist brings diagnostic, medication, and psychiatric services to clients for the major part of their treatment. Such use of an on-site psychiatrist can be an effective way to overcome impediments presented by off-site referral, such as distance and travel limitations, and the inconvenience and discomfort of starting services in an agency separate from the primary treatment unit. The psychiatrist should have expertise in working with substance abuse that can include certification by: the American Academy of Addiction Psychiatry, the American Society of Addiction Medicine, or the American Osteopathic Association (SAMHSA, 2005).

Each member of a COD treatment team should have extensive competency in both the substance abuse and mental health fields, including training in the following 10 areas:

1. Identifying and understanding the symptoms of the various mental disorders;
2. Comprehending the relationships among different mental symptoms, drugs of choice, and treatment history;
3. Specifying and altering approaches to meet the needs of particular clients and achieve treatment goals;

4. Obtaining services from multiple systems and collaborating on integrated treatment plans;
5. Understanding the differing perspectives regarding the characteristics of the person with COD;
6. Understanding the nature of addiction;
7. Becoming aware of the nature of mental disability;
8. Understanding impact of the conduct of treatment and staff roles in the treatment process;
9. Comprehending the interactive effects of both conditions on the person and his or her outcomes; and,
10. Dealing with staff burnout (SAMHSA, 2005).

A BRIEF DESCRIPTION OF THE COUNSELING PROCESS THAT LEADS TO TREATMENT PLANNING

Diagnosis and treatment with COD clients requires that helping professionals have the ability to diagnose and treat mental and emotional disorders, including substance abuse/dependence disorders. While counselor training is based on a wellness perspective, mental health counselors have additional training in assessment, diagnosis, and treatment of psychopathology. Such training gives mental health counselors a unique and ideal combination of capabilities. These counselors can look at clients through a wellness lens including their strengths and capabilities as well as examining clients for mental and emotional disorders, including substance disorders. Consequently, mental health counselors can examine from both a wellness and a psychopathology lens simultaneously.

A non-pathological method of assessment would involve helping clients identify their treatment issues as part of the diagnostic process. With a wellness lens, counselors can assess and render a diagnosis based on the identified issues alone, including asking clients about their strengths and resources, what has been working in their lives, and what they have used in the past to solve similar issues. At the same time, a wellness focus would not preclude mental health counselors from forming a well-thought-out DSM-IV-TR diagnosis based on evidence from the client. Having both an issues-based and a DSM-IV-TR–based diagnosis can be helpful in developing a collaborative treatment plan with COD clients.

However, before treatment planning can begin, counselors should help clients identify which of their treatment issues are behavioral and measurable. By being specific, behavioral, and measurable, an identified issue can serve as a baseline or pre-test, which will help in evaluating treatment progress. For instance, instead of saying that a client has a checking compulsion, it would be more beneficial to say that the client reports that she has a checking compulsion, as evidenced by stopping her car to check whether she hit someone for an average of 10 minutes a day, 5 days a week on the way to work, but not on the ride home. Of course, we would want to investigate the other situations in which the client does compulsive checking as well.

Setting measurable and meaningful objectives is the most difficult, but perhaps most important, part of the treatment planning process. Once we have identified a specific, behavioral, and measurable issue, we can set treatment objectives that are specific, behavioral, and measurable as well. In working with a client's issues, we could set lofty objectives (e.g., the elimination of checking behavior) or moderate objectives (e.g., reduction of stopping her car to check to see if she hit someone for an average of 2 minutes, 3 days a week) depending on whether the client is allowed to see the counselor for two sessions or ten sessions. In other words, the objectives need to be relevant and achievable given the setting and the client's resources.

Treatment planning is also the portion of the therapeutic process in which we help the client select specific counseling strategies and techniques, as well as setting timelines. Homework assignments can be used as steps to fulfilling the treatment objective(s). Once a treatment plan is created, in collaboration with the client, we can rather easily evaluate treatment "products" both formatively (during and after each session) and summatively (at termination of treatment and follow-up).

In addition to a balanced use of the nondirective counseling skills (i.e., attending, clarifying, supporting, and silence), use of formative evaluation during and after each session, and especially early in the counseling relationship, has the potential to facilitate the therapeutic alliance. Formative evaluation can be focused on both process (i.e., evaluating the counseling process) and product (i.e., evaluating the progress toward issue resolution and obtainment of treatment objectives). After a session, a counselor could inquire about how well the client thought the counselor understood the client's concerns. In doing so, the counselor would be using formative process evaluation. A counselor could also self-evaluate by asking herself the same question and comparing her answer to her client's answer. Following a session, a counselor could ask the client how much progress he or she has made toward identified treatment objectives, here using formative product evaluation. Once again, the counselor could compare her self-evaluation with that of the client.

Just as formative evaluation can involve both process and product, summative evaluation, occuring at the end of treatment and at follow-up can focus on process (i.e., by summarizing how much a counselor was empathic and caring toward a client throughout treatment) and product (i.e., with a client self-rating how strongly she agrees that she has better insight into and understanding of her concerns at termination and follow-up).

Counselors should be aware of how their role and the healing process are seen by persons of different cultures. Wherever appropriate, healing practices meaningful to these clients should be incorporated into treatment. An example would be the medically supervised use of traditional herbal tobacco with certain Native American tribes to establish rapport and promote emotional balance, or use of herbal tea to calm a Chinese client or help control cravings (SAMHSA, 2005).

CASE STUDY

A Case Study of William

For illustrative purposes, a case of a client with COD will be presented. This case will demonstrate assessment, diagnosis, and treatment planning with a client with COD. First, we will present an assessment of the client. Next, we will present both psychopathology-based and issues-based diagnostic summaries. Taken together, these diagnostic summaries will form the basis for development of the treatment plan.

Referral

William, a 16-year-old African American high school junior was referred for assessment and outpatient therapy by the family physician, due to a progression of school suspensions for fighting and drinking leading to his current expulsion from school. In the final incident, he pulled a knife on a female student in the classroom, before class. He denied this when later caught and confronted. From reports, it appears that he experienced a blackout during this incident that was witnessed by students and a teacher. In speaking with the high school principal, the evaluator was told that the client would be allowed to return to school after completing three counseling sessions. Several weeks after completing the sessions, William was permitted to return to school, only to be expelled again for giving alcohol to a classmate.

Assessment Methods Used

Assessment methods to evaluate William included: clinical interview and observation during which time both biopsychosocial history and mental status information were gathered (with and without mom present; other family members and extended family members were unable and/or unwilling to be present), MAST, DAST, MMPI-2, School Behavior Checklist, a review of school records including IQ scores on the WISC-III, review of court records, review of medical records, and phone conversations with both the school principal and the family doctor.

Records Review

According to school records, William has passed all grades thus far but his grade point average has dropped from 3.1 in junior high school to his current G.P.A. of 1.8. His best subjects are math and science, in which he usually gets Bs. He does poorly in English and spelling, typically getting Ds and Fs in these subjects. He has Wechsler Intelligence Scale for Children (WISC-3) verbal, performance, and full scale scores of 120, 115, and 118 respectively, which are above average, and a GPA of only 1.8 which is below average. From other school reports and observation, it appears the client has above average intelligence.

From court, hospital, and school records, the client was charged, 5 years ago, with assault and battery after badly beating another boy in a fight at school. The school filed and later dropped charges. He was charged with stealing and purse snatching prior to 5 years ago but these charges were dropped as well. Three years ago, the client was charged with assault with a weapon, convicted, and put on probation. Since he was drinking two to three beers weekly and smoking two marijuana cigarettes weekly when the incident occurred, his probation officer, along with his mother, had him admitted to Savanna Hospital for inpatient chemical dependency treatment. He is currently off probation. The school is considering filing charges for the latest knife-pulling incident. Also, during the course of counseling, the client was accused of raping a 17-year-old girl, which he denied; charges are pending.

Biopsychosocial History from Interview and Sessions

The client is an African American male currently expelled from a predominantly white, middle-class, rural high school. He does not feel that he fits in and holds different values from his classmates. He attended an inner-city grade school but his mother decided to move the family to a location where the client could have a chance not to be labeled and avoid following in his older brother's footsteps.

During the initial session, the client admitted to using both alcohol and marijuana in the past and admitted to current alcohol usage. According to his self-report, he drinks only two beers twice a week and has not used marijuana for more than a year. His mother, also in attendance, reported that her son "drinks a little now and then." She believed he currently drinks about a six-pack of beer a week and concurred that he has not smoked marijuana for more than a year. William denied other drug use/experimentation. The school principal stated that students and teachers reported smelling alcohol on William's breath a couple of times.

After several sessions, William admitted to drinking four to six beers on most nights. Sometimes he would skip a night or two if he knew in advance that his drinking would be questioned. In addition, he would drink up to a pint of vodka if available, which was the case about once a week. He also admitted to smoking four to five marijuana cigarettes weekly. While William reported that he began drinking at age 11 and smoking marijuana at age 13, he did so, at first, only occasionally and for "kicks." He admitted he became violent the first time he drank (he consumed approximately a pint of whiskey) and began throwing furniture around at a friend's house.

By mom's and the principal's report, the client becomes hostile, abusive, violent, and fights (using weapons) when intoxicated. The client reports that prior to beginning drinking, he had gotten into more than 100 fights. Even prior to his beginning drinking, school and court records indicate a history of stealing, running away from home on at least five occasions, constant truancy, starting fights, and purse-snatching. During the course of counseling, the client was accused of raping a 17-year-old girl, which he denied.

William reports himself to be single and unemployed. He held a job as a dishwasher in a local restaurant one-and-a-half years ago for three months. However, he was fired for drinking house wine with an older employee during his work time. He was a good junior high athlete in both track and football. After playing varsity football as a freshman, he was kicked off the team in his sophomore year for drinking at school.

The client has not formally dated but brags that he has had sex with as many as 10 girls, beginning at age 10. He does not currently have a girlfriend. He reports he picks his lovers up at parties and takes them out. According to his report, he strongly identifies with his father and feels that "women were put here to make me feel good."

During the course of treatment, when his mother's boyfriend offered to give him his car if he brought up his grades, the client maintained a 3.0 for one 6-week period. However, after getting the car, his grades slipped again. This gives evidence for his need for external, monetary rewards to do well in school. The fact that he has an above-average IQ, of 118, and a below-average GPA, of only 1.8, indicates that he is not working up to his potential scholastically.

Both mom and client report client to be in good health physically and medical records confirm this. He has a scar on the right forearm as a result of being stabbed there 2 years ago in a fight. He is currently not taking any prescription medications. He reports no known allergies (in addition to alcohol and possibly marijuana). Dad was a heavy drinker and the client's paternal grandfather and father's brother also had drinking problems, according to mom.

William was admitted as an inpatient to the adolescent unit at Savanna Hospital 3 years ago for 28-day treatment. He completed inpatient treatment for alcohol abuse but failed to attend aftercare as mom worked and could not bring him. He apparently attended several Alcoholics Anonymous meetings during treatment and after discharge but quit going 2 weeks after discharge. The client denies having received other mental health and/or drug/alcohol treatment.

Parents include: Esther, age 50, and Donald, age 53. They were married 22 years ago and have been divorced for the past 10 years. The client has not seen his father for 10 years and currently lives with mom. Client reports that his parents fought frequently when married and that dad was the disciplinarian. Mom would undermine dad's efforts to discipline the children. Mom currently has a 46-year-old boyfriend, Hal, whom the client dislikes.

Family functioning is typified by rigid boundaries and narrow definitions of what it is to be a man or a woman in society. Mom went to nursing school and got an LPN degree. She brought in a second (and sometimes primary) income for the last 5 years of the marriage. Dad was a heavy drinker and a womanizer according to mom. He received 2 DUI's during the marriage. Sister Kathy was a daddy's girl and his enabler.

Client is the youngest of three children. He has one brother, Andy, age 21, and one sister, Kathy, age 19. Kathy is a single parent with a 6-month-old baby. She works full time and lives alone with the baby in an apartment. Andy was the family scapegoat who was constantly in trouble. He was a gang member in California and has been in prison for armed robbery. The client identifies with his brother. The client served as the mascot and tried to lessen family tensions by being funny. Kathy was good at making the client and his brother look bad.

The client reports having been physically beaten by his father's fist and belt. He reports his brother was likewise beaten but denies that his sister was. Dad was verbally/emotionally abusive, often putting mom and the kids down. From observation in session, mom is subtly abusive and has labeled William a bad boy with no chance to redeem himself. The client and mom both denied sexual abuse within the family. Mom indicates that Children's Services investigated dad's abuse of the children years ago.

Mental Status Evaluation

This 16-year-old African American youth appeared about 2–3 years older than his stated age as evidence for early physical maturation. He appeared well nourished, was about 6 feet tall and weighed about 180 pounds. He had a very athletic physique. He was well groomed and neat. He maintained good eye contact throughout the session. The client was alert with no evidence of problems with psychomotor behavior. He did not appear to be intoxicated at the time of the initial session nor at subsequent sessions (with the exception of the last session). Neither did he smell of alcohol or marijuana. He later stated that he usually drank and/or smoked marijuana only at night and our sessions were during the daytime.

He was attentive and showed no evidence of speech or thinking disturbance. He was oriented to person, day of the week, day of the month, time, month, and year. While his long-term, remote memory appeared intact, when asked to recall what he had eaten for breakfast, he reported that he had eggs and toast. His mother reported that he had eaten only cereal that morning. He appeared to have confabulated to compensate for his problem with recent memory. This problem was later found to be just a motivational deficit as he could remember recent events when he wanted to. His short-term memory appeared intact as his ability to repeat digits forward and backward was within the normal range for his age.

The client had a flat affect as demonstrated by a monotone voice, lack of facial gestures while talking, and posture. While the client reported himself to be depressed, he denied almost all of the relevant symptoms reported in DSM-IV-TR for depression. Mom confirmed that he is usually quieter earlier in the day and his mood picks up when it is time to go out with friends.

No evidence was shown for delusions or hallucinations. He gave no hint of obsessions, compulsions, or anxiety. The client was neither depressed nor suicidal. He denied any intention to commit homicide but indicated that he was never one to walk away from a fight. He admitted a tendency to be impulsive and experienced little fear or autonomic nervous system arousal when confronted to fight. Neither did he experience guilt when he badly hurt classmates while fighting at school.

His insight into his drinking/smoking problems is limited as he denies that he has a real problem and states that he can quit at any time. He does admit, however, that he gets into more trouble and fights and that he feels invincible when drinking. He demonstrates poor judgment by his response to the question "What would you do if a younger, smaller boy tried to start a fight with you?" He responded, "I'd kick the hell out of him." He demonstrated good abstract thinking when asked about the meaning of proverbs.

Psychological Testing

Although William was given both the Michigan Alcohol Screening Test (MAST) and the Drug Abuse Screening Test (DAST) as a part of the initial interview, both failed to detect evidence of either alcohol or drug abuse/dependence. However, his high score on the MacAndrew Alcoholism Scale (MAC) of the Minnesota Multiphasic Personality Inventory (MMPI-2) is suggestive of alcohol or other substance abuse/dependence.

> In using the MacAndrew Alcoholism Scale-R of the MMPI-2, raw scores equal to or greater than 28 suggest substance abuse problems while raw scores less than 24 suggest unlikely substance abuse problems. Interpretation should be made with knowledge of the specific norm group representing the client (Graham, 1999).

The interviewer used caution in drawing definitive conclusions as it has been shown that African American adolescent non-abusers sometimes have high scores on the MAC, making them appear to be abusers when they are really not.

Alcohol Dependence

It appears as if William's primary substance is alcohol, on which he appears to be dependent (using DSM-IV-TR criteria). He continues to drink despite numerous blackouts and fighting while drinking, reports unsuccessful attempts to quit, drives while intoxicated, and has gotten kicked out of school and off the football team (which he enjoyed) for missing practice while drinking. He has demonstrated an increase in tolerance, reporting that he needs to drink at least a six-pack to get high. William admitted that at times when he plans not to drink or to have only one or two, he drinks until he is intoxicated. He has had failed attempts to control usage. He also stated that he has quit before on his own several times but always starts back up. He also admits to missing school repeatedly due to being hungover. He now states that when he doesn't drink, he becomes anxious and depressed.

Marijuana Abuse

While William did admit to smoking 4–5 marijuana cigarettes weekly, his current relationship to marijuana appears to be abusive (using DSM-IV-TR criteria). He admits he spends his dating money on marijuana and drives while getting high. One time he rode past a police car with his window open, smoking a joint. This has continued for more than a year. He does not feel bad when he runs out of marijuana, but merely increases his alcohol intake.

Conduct Disorder

Finally, using DSM-IV criteria, William was found to have a conduct disorder as evidenced by the following history which predated both his drinking and marijuana smoking: getting into more than 100 fights, stealing, running away from home on at least five occasions, constant truancy, fighting (using weapons), and purse-snatching. These occurred prior to the client's first drink and extended over at least 5 years' time. This type of behavior continued and intensified after he began drinking and smoking marijuana. During the course of counseling, the client was also accused of raping a 17-year-old girl, which he denied. Most of his acting out was done alone and is therefore, a solitary aggressive type and apparently severe.

ISSUES-BASED DIAGNOSTIC SUMMARY
CLIENT STRENGTHS
1. Above-average intelligence as evidenced by (AEB): having WISC-3 verbal, performance, and full scale scores of 120, 115, and 118, respectively, which are above average.
2. A history of doing well in math and science AEB: getting mostly Bs in these courses up to now.
3. Superior athletic ability in track and football AEB: client and mother's self-report.
4. Generally good physical health AEB: family physician's medical summary.

CLIENT ISSUES
1. Alcohol/marijuana issues AEB: increased tolerance, blackouts, continued use despite negative consequences (i.e., fighting, kicked out of school, threat of having probation restated, getting kicked off football team for drinking), failed attempts to control usage, frequent withdrawal such that he misses school, frequent intoxication, driving while drunk.
2. Conduct issues AEB: kicked off football team, school suspensions, pending rape charge, believes women were put here to make him feel good, fighting with and without weapons, stealing, running away, constant truancy, purse-snatching.
3. Decreased grades AEB: significant grade drop from 3.1 to 1.8 G.P.A. since junior high.
4. Family history of abuse AEB: client and brother beaten by dad's fist and belt, dad's verbal and emotional abuse, mom's verbal abuse.
5. Client lacks an effective male role model AEB: father had history of family violence, older brother is in prison for armed robbery and assault, client dislikes mom's current boyfriend.
6. As an African American, client reports he feels he is a misfit in his predominantly white, middle-class, rural high school.
7. Mom requests help with parenting skills AEB: observation during sessions and her self-report that she cannot control client.

TREATMENT PLAN: PRIORITY GOALS (OTHER GOALS ARE PUT ON THE BACK BURNER FOR THE TIME BEING)
1. Abstinence from mood-altering substances.
2. Elimination of antisocial behavior.

SPECIFIC ISSUES
1. Client drinks at least a six-pack of beer each night and a pint of vodka once a week at night, smokes 4–5 marijuana cigarettes a week. Three years ago, he drank 2–3 beers twice a week and smoked 2 marijuana cigarettes a week. He drinks and smokes marijuana with two friends usually at a local park between 10:00 P.M. and 1:00 A.M. nightly, and later on weekends.
2. The client gets into a fight once a week on average and every other fight is with a weapon. Approximately half the fights take place at school; the other half occur after school, usually on the way home.

TREATMENT OBJECTIVES
1. Short term (within 1 month): Reduce relapse into drinking every other day instead of every day and three instead of six beers with no vodka; marijuana to one cigarette twice a week.
2. Long term (within 3 months): Complete abstinence from all mood-altering chemicals.
3. Short term (within 1 month): Reduce fighting to once a week with no weapons.
4. Long term (within 3 months): Eliminate fighting.

TREATMENT STRATEGIES
1. Structural and strategic family therapy
2. Individual cognitive-behavioral therapy for client and mom
3. Brief solution-focused therapy

TREATMENT TECHNIQUES   (Give as assignments and use time lines here as well.)
1. Involve a school representative and probation officer in family sessions.
2. Help to empower mom to assume parental responsibility within the family.
3. Get client involved in a Big Brother program through which he is paired with an African American adult role model who can help him to work on feeling proud of his heritage and culture.
4. Get client involved in a sports activity every night after school.
5. Work with client on understanding the consequences of his use and how his life has been unmanageable.
6. Work with mom and client to get him in the house on school nights by 10:00 P.M., weekends by 11:00 P.M.
7. Reinforce client using token economy each week he refrains from fighting.
8. Have mom pay attention to client when he is behaving prosocially.
9. Find out what client does when he is successful in avoiding a fight.

Summary and Some Final Notations

In summary, it appears to be the rule rather than the exception that mental health disorders and substance abuse disorders co-occur. Because clients with co-occurring disorders have varied needs, their care requires flexible and integrated treatment methods and services. In assessing a client who presents with both an addictive disorder and a psychiatric disorder, counselors need to discover which came first, which is primary, and decide which one to begin treating first. Such discovery should be based on a thorough biopsychosocial history and records review. The culture of the client is also an important issue to address. Culturally effective counselors study the client's interpersonal interactions and familial expectations.

It appears that those with alcohol abuse and alcohol dependence can be best served by matching treatment to individual client needs and that both traditional and alternative interventions can be effective given specific client characteristics. It is advisable that interdisciplinary team members working with clients with co-occurring disorders be trained in both mental health and substance abuse disciplines. Both psychopathology-based and issues-based diagnostic summaries can be helpful in forming the basis for an effective, comprehensive, and collaborative treatment plan with objectives that are specific, behavioral, measurable, and meaningful.

Useful Web Sites

The following Web sites provide additional information relating to the chapter topics:

Addiction Treatment Forum
http://www.atforum.com/

Centers for Disease Control and Prevention: Information about intimate partner violence and treatment
http://www.cdc.gov/

National Institute on Alcohol Abuse and Alcoholism (NIAAA)
http://www.niaaa.nih.gov/

National Institute on Drug Abuse (NIDA)
http://www.nida.nih.gov/

National Institute on Drug Abuse (NIDA): Diagnosis and Treatment of Drug Abuse in Family Practice
http://www.nida.nih.gov/Diagnosis-Treatment/Diagnosis4 .html

RESOURCES FOR CO-OCCURRING ADDICTION AND PERSONALITY DISORDERS

Substance Abuse and Mental Health Services Administration (SAMHSA)
http://www.samhsa.gov/

Online group therapy
http://www.egetgoing.com

Substance Abuse and Mental Health Services Administration (SAMHSA) Fact Sheets
http://coce.samhsa.gov/searchresults .aspx?obj=85&key=fact%20sheet

http://coce.samhsa.gov/cod_resources/PDF/ AlcoholQuickFacts.pdf
http://coce.samhsa.gov/cod_resources/PDF/ ElderlyQuickFacts.pdf
http://coce.samhsa.gov/cod_resources/PDF/ GamblingQuickFacts.pdf
http://coce.samhsa.gov/cod_resources/PDF/ NicotineQuickFacts.pdf

Double Trouble in Recovery: A Recovery Group for the Dually Diagnosed
http://www.doubletroubleinrecovery.org/

References

American Psychiatric Association. (2000). Diagnostic and statistical manual of mental disorders, Text Revision (4th ed.). Washington, DC: American Psychiatric Association.

Amador, H. (1989). [Review of the movie *My Name Is Bill W.*] Earth's Biggest Movie Database on the Web. Retrieved November 9, 2006, from *http://www.imdb .com/title/tt0097939/plotsummary*

Armor-Garb, A. (2004). *Point of Entry Systems for Long-Term Care: State Case Studies,* prepared for the New York City Department of Aging.

Brems, C., & Namyniuk, L. L. (1999). Comorbidity and related factors among ethnically diverse substance using pregnant women. *Journal of Addictions & Offender Counseling, 19,* 2.

Chartas, N. D., & Culbreth, J. R. (2001). Counselor treatment of coexisting domestic violence and substance abuse: A qualitative study. *Journal of Addictions & Offender Counseling, 22,* 1.

Corey, G. (2001). *Theory and practice of counseling and psychotherapy. Sixth edition.* Belmont, CA: Brooks-Cole of Wadsworth/Thompson Learning.

Double trouble in recovery on the Web. Retrieved September 6, 2009, from *http://www.doubletroubleinrecovery.org/*

Duffy, M. (2004). Introduction: A global overview of the issues of and responses to teen gangs. In M. Duffy & S. E. Gillig (Eds.), *Teen gangs: A global view* (p. 6). Westport, CT: Greenwood Press.

Graham, J. (1999). *MMPI-2: Assessing personality and psychopathology: Second edition.* Oxford University Press, Inc: New York.

Grella, C. (2003). Contrasting the views of substance abuse and mental health treatment providers on treating the dually diagnosed. *Substance Use & Misuse, 38*(10), 1433–1446.

Johnson, M., Brems, C., Wells, R., Theno, S., & Fisher, D. (2003). Comorbidity and risk behaviors among drug users not in treatment. *Journal of Addictions & Offender Counseling, 23,* 108–118.

Juhnke, G., Vacc, N., Curtis, R., Coll, K., & Paredes, D. (2003). Assessment instruments used by addictions counselors. *Journal of Addictions & Offender Counseling, 23,* 66–72.

Kim-Berg, I., & Miller, S. (1992). *Working with the problem drinker.* New York: W.W. Norton & Company.

Loos, M. D. (2002). Counseling the chemically dependent: An integrative approach. *Journal of Addictions & Offender Counseling, 23,* 2–14.

Marlatt, G. A., Baer, J. S., & Quigley, L. A. (1994). Self-efficacy and addictive behavior. In A. Bandura (Ed.), *Self-efficacy in changing societies.* Marbach, Germany: Johann Jacobs Foundation.

Miller, W. R. & White, W. (2008). *Confrontation in addiction treatment.* on the Web. Retrieved November 9, 2006, from *http://www.addictioninfo.org/articles/ 2276/1/Confrontation-in-Addiction-Treatment/Page1 .html*

Osborn, C. (2001). Brief interventions in the treatment of alcohol use disorders: Definition and overview. *Journal of Addictions & Offender Counseling, 21*(2), 76–84.

Schneider, J. P. (2005). Coexisting disorders. In R. H. Coombs (Ed.), *Addiction counseling review: Preparing for comprehensive, certification and licensing examinations* (pp. 293–316). Mahway, NJ: Lawrence Erlbaum Associates.

Sciacca, K. (1997). Removing barriers: Dual diagnosis and motivational interviewing. *Professional Counselor 12*(1), 41–46.

Substance Abuse and Mental Health Services Administration (SAMHSA). (2005). *Substance abuse treatment for persons with co-occurring disorders. Treatment improvement protocol (TIP) Series 42* (DHHS Publication No. SMA 05-3992). Rockville, MD: Author.

Substance Abuse and Mental Health Services Administration (SAMHSA). (2009). *SAMHSA's Co-occurring Center for Excellence, fact sheets on the Web.* Retrieved September 6, 2009, from *http://coce.samhsa.gov/searchresults.aspx?obj=85&key =fact%20sheet*

Von Steen, P., Vacc, N., & Strickland, I. (2002). The treatment of substance-abusing clients in multiservice mental health agencies: A practice analysis. *Journal of Addictions & Offender Counseling, 22,* 61–71.

Whittinghill, D., Whittinghill, L., & Loesch, L. (2000). The benefits of a self-efficacy approach to substance abuse counseling in the era of managed care. *Journal of Addictions & Offender Counseling, 20*(2), 64–74.

Chapter 10

Group Therapy for Treatment of Addictions

Laura R. Simpson
Walden University
Donna S. Sheperis
Walden University

One very common treatment modality for substance use disorders is group counseling. According to Weiss, Jaffee, de Menil, and Cogley (2004), approximately 94% of treatment facilities within the United States utilize group counseling for treatment of substance abuse, and it has replaced individual counseling as the treatment approach of choice (Johnson, 2004). In addition to the low cost of group counseling, the popularity of this approach has evolved from peer-based self-help groups such as Alcoholics Anonymous (AA) and Narcotics Anonymous (NA) to include psycho-educational and psychotherapeutic approaches (Behavioral Health Treatment, 1997).

Groups have a number of important functions in substance abuse treatment including education, therapy, and support. This chapter will address the theory behind utilizing a group counseling approach as well as examining common types of groups employed for treatment of addictions. Additionally, ethical and legal issues, managing diversity in group settings, and group therapy with family members will be discussed.

THEORY BEHIND GROUP WORK

The research supporting the use of group work in the treatment of a variety of concerns is well established. Essentially, group counseling is an interpersonal treatment approach that emphasizes an expression of thoughts and feelings geared toward insight and behavioral change. Yalom and Lesczc (2005) proposed that groups offer a number of advantages over individual or other counseling methods including creating a sense of universality or the understanding that clients are not alone in their struggles. The empathy and support provided through group work creates the necessary atmosphere for the counseling process. Participants can explore relationship styles, try on new behaviors, and participate in rehearsal for change using the medium of the group (Corey, 2007). Ideally, through interpersonal learning and group cohesiveness, members develop a greater understanding of themselves and can capitalize on this insight by making necessary changes in the way they live their lives (Yalom & Lesczc, 2005).

Group counseling can be used for many purposes, both preventative and remedial in nature (Corey, 2007).

Preventative groups are those that members participate in to *avoid using substances*. They take place in schools, agencies, and communities. *Remedial groups* address *unhealthy behaviors that currently exist* and have resulted in negative consequences for the client. In addictions counseling, *aftercare groups* that offer treatment in an outpatient setting following an inpatient treatment stay would be considered remedial.

The content of the group may be preset or determined by the membership (Corey, 2007). Advantages of group counseling include using a collective mind-set to gain perspective on an individual counseling issue. Concepts related to interpersonal skills and trust are inherently worked through in a group environment. However, group counseling is not for everyone. The dynamics and interpersonal risks involved may prove to be too overwhelming for some clients, and some counseling issues are not best treated through the group process.

GROUP TREATMENT OF ADDICTION

When treating addiction there are specific dynamics that make group counseling the approach of choice. Although the design of a group may vary, there are certain benefits that contribute to the behavior change process. While many evidence-based practices are individualized, additions counselors disproportionately conduct treatment clients in groups (Sanders & Mayeda, 2009).

The influence of group members who have similar experiences is helpful in breaking down the denial frequently associated with addiction (Zweben, 1995). Because individuals who participate in long-term substance abuse typically exhibit poor communication skills and the inability to perpetuate healthy interpersonal relationships, group therapy affords an opportunity to: interact with others, promoting effective social skills and self-disclosure; explore new behaviors in a safe environment; and emotionally invest in others and in education about addiction (Campbell & Page, 1993; Johnson, 2004).

Joan has been a problem drinker for a number of years. She and her husband, Michael, have experienced a decline in their relationship over the last 5 years. Michael says he cannot talk to Joan, that she shuts him out, and that all she does is blame him for their troubles. How might group treatment for Joan's alcohol abuse facilitate a different style of communication in her marriage? Is Joan's behavior in group related to how she interacts with her husband, or are these unrelated concepts? What impact might feedback from other group members have on Joan? Is it possible she might be able to hear the observations of other group members or a group facilitator in spite of the fact that she rejects her husband's observations or perceptions about her relating style?

It offers an opportunity for positive interpersonal exchange to replace isolated self-involvement. Group members presented with an opportunity to identify and relay needs and emotions may result in their identifying and confronting maladaptive patterns of behavior (Weiss et al., 2004). According to Campbell and Page (1993), "Any effective therapeutic intervention must target not only drug use, but also a means by which meaningful communication can occur" (p. 34). Additionally, many individuals with addictions have blind spots for their own defenses but not necessarily those of others. Thus, the members may assist one another in confronting defense mechanisms and blind spots, resulting in accomplishment of treatment goals. Finally, group treatment uses peer influence and motivation to enhance individual commitment to recovery (Johnson, 2004).

AN OVERVIEW OF TYPES OF GROUPS

"The broad purposes of a therapeutic group are to increase members' knowledge of themselves and others, to help members clarify the changes they most want to make in their lives, and to provide members with the tools they need to make these changes" (Corey & Corey, 2006, p. 9). Essentially, members get an opportunity to "try on" new behaviors in a s setting that is safe and receive honest feedback from others concerning these behaviors. Often it is the first time individuals have an opportunity to learn how others perceive them.

The Association for Specialists in Group Work's (ASGW, 2000) developed a four-category system for classifying types of group work. ASGW standards identify standards of competence for the leaders and identifies particular areas of group work including (1) task groups, (2) psychoeducational groups, (3) counseling groups, and (4) psychotherapy groups. As counseling groups are not aimed at major personality changes and not concerned with the treatment of severe behavioral disorders, they are not frequently implemented for addictions work.

Psychoeducational Groups

A variety of issues common to recovery from addiction require specific planned treatment interventions. Because the focus of treatment combines educating members with fostering self-understanding through the dynamics of the group, these groups are sometimes referred to as psychoeducational treatment groups. Psychoeducational groups are an increasingly popular and important source of help for many clients. Perhaps their greatest asset is that they provide a planned framework that can be replicated, modified, and/or adapted to fit different types of client groups.

In structured psychoeducational groups it is not unusual for the agenda to be established before the group session. Compared to less structured, process-centered approaches, structured group approaches give the counselor greater responsibility for group goals and the way the group conducts its work. Although in psychotherapeutic approaches members are encouraged to take informal leadership roles and develop their own goals, agendas, and contracts, in psychoeducational groups the members' input is generally limited to modifying goals, agendas, and contracts the counselor has already developed. The interventions are planned and focus on specific learning outcomes. Integrating behavioral therapies with experiential learning is common practice. The group can aim to help members translate what they learn into specific action.

There are a variety of time-limited, structured groups that focus on transferring information about drugs and the consequences of use. Meetings usually contain a combination of educational material, exercises, role-play, and simulations to help members process discussion of the material and the problems they are experiencing outside the group.

It is not uncommon for school counselors to implement time-limited structured groups that are preventative in nature. For example, elementary school counselors might utilize programming which examines reasons kids use drugs and offer alternatives to drug use. Parents may also be included in the process through the use of homework.

In a series of studies on the efficacy of group work, members of groups with specific purposes, homogeneous concerns, clear agendas, and structured group meetings demonstrated greater success with treatment outcome than members of groups with less structure (Martin, Giannandrea, Rogers, & Johnson, 1996; Toseland & Rivas, 2001). Members report that they appreciate the leader providing specific information and effective strategies to help with their concerns. Thus, in a group program for individuals recovering from substance abuse, the leader can provide information about addiction, communication skills, assertiveness/social skills training, and other topics deemed appropriate. Studies have shown that even spiritual concerns can be successfully addressed within this format, allowing participants to examine beliefs and gain increased understanding of their feelings, problems, and questions within this domain (Phillips, Lakin, & Pargament, 2002). Psychoeducational designs also provide members with an opportunity to discuss specific concerns and learn stress reduction and other coping techniques.

Leaders of psychoeducational groups vary depending on the topics to be covered; they may be licensed professional counselors or paraprofessionals trained in the treatment of addictions.

Group leaders should keep in mind that members' concerns and needs are not always served by a time-limited, structured-group approach. A flexible structure maximizing member input has been found to be more effective in helping members to vent their concerns and give and receive help from fellow group members (Toseland & Rivas, 2001). Group counselors should be savvy enough to determine the goals and specific agendas that will best meet the needs of members.

There are also psychoeducational groups designed to assist in the *prevention* of addiction. Drug Abuse Resistance Education (D.A.R.E.) and similar programs are based on the theory that teaching children about the harmful effects of alcohol and drugs while helping them build self-esteem will deter the desire to abuse chemicals later in life (Doweiko, 2008). The D.A.R.E. program is typically conducted by local law enforcement and taught within a classroom setting. There is a great deal of testimonial support for these programs, but very little empirical evidence that they are effective in reducing substance abuse among children or adolescents (Doweiko, 2008; Gorman, 2003).

Psychotherapeutic Groups

Psychotherapeutic groups are commonly utilized in addictions treatment. Because group members have serious impairments in functioning as a result of their substance abuse, these types of groups explore the foundation of current behaviors, seeking to build insight and replace dysfunctional coping patterns with healthy ones.

Group psychotherapy offers a number of advantages over individual counseling. Group members can learn from and offer feedback to each other and provide behavioral models for each other; this is useful for clients who do not trust the counselor. The group format provides an opportunity for clients to work on many of the interpersonal deficits that contribute to their own addiction within the safety of the group setting.

Counselors sometimes utilize experiential activities with members. For example, genograms, or family maps, help counselors and clients see a family more clearly. A genogram is a visual representation of a person's family tree, created with lines, words, and geometric figures (Gladding, 2007). For addictions treatment, the genogram may reveal patterns of addiction, codependence, or other problem behaviors in the client's family system.

Finally, because of the nature of group therapy, each individual might find other members who provide a reflection of his or her family of origin, allowing him or her to work through problems from earlier stages of growth.

Individuals may participate in group counseling as part of an inpatient treatment regimen or as an adjunct to individual counseling in an outpatient setting. The majority of substance abuse rehabilitation programs use counseling groups as the primary method of working with clients (Doweiko, 2008; Weiss et al., 2004). For clients receiving inpatient treatment as a result of involuntary commitment, a common difficulty is resistance to group work. Many members begin with attitudes of resentment, blaming others, and operating under the conviction that they do not need counseling. Techniques and strategies must be employed to address resistance.

Individuals who experience chronic substance dependence or usage exhibit behavioral characteristics that can interfere with the ability to develop effective communication and to sustain healthy interpersonal relationships. As use of substances persists, social, personal, and work-related activities are negatively affected (Campbell & Page, 1993). Social and psychological problems develop or are exacerbated by the prominence of drugs in the user's lifestyle. Psychosocial aspects of the individual's life become so impaired that interpersonal interactions develop with maladaptive behavioral patterns (American Psychiatric Association, 2000). In attempting to treat these issues, a variety of methods may be employed including "techniques designed to induce regression to earlier experiences, methods to work with unconscious dynamics, and procedures aimed at helping members reexperience traumatic situations so that catharsis can occur" (Corey & Corey, 2006, p. 15).

While psychotherapeutic groups typically do not have specific agendas for each session, the group counselor may choose to offer specific topic areas for a session, encouraging the participants to explore pertinent life issues. "If topics reflect the life issues of the participants, they can be powerful catalysts" (Corey & Corey, 2006, p. 347). The topics chosen should reflect the purpose of the group. When working with participants suffering from addiction, topics could include identifying and dealing with family-of-origin issues, painful affective states that may contribute to the urge to use chemicals, and shame-based issues. Additionally, grief issues are a common focus of process groups as newly sober members attempt to cope with loss of friends, loss of coping mechanisms, and in general, loss of a way of life.

Inpatient treatment providers frequently encounter grief issues. Group members may struggle to say goodbye to a drug or behavior of choice, loss of power or money, or the social relationships associated with their addiction (Lawes, 2010). Group leaders may suggest writing letters to say goodbye, designing eulogies or even holding an actual funeral service for the issue.

It has been posited that up to 50% of individuals receiving treatment for addiction also have co-occurring disorders (James & Gilliland, 2005). Group counseling helps dually diagnosed clients develop the insight they need to sustain recovery from chemical dependence while maintaining psychiatric stability (*Addiction Letter*, 1995). The group process offers members the opportunity to share experiences involving addiction and mental illness in an atmosphere of acceptance and support while learning how their addictions influence their mental illness and how their mental illness affects their addiction. The group format allows clients to challenge one another in a climate that reinforces the reality and acceptance of both the addiction and the mental illness.

A skilled counselor knowledgeable in both addictions and group therapy treatment is rec-ommended to facilitate group psychotherapy of addicted clients. The counselor should be edu-cated about mental illness and well-versed in the jargon of self-help groups, such as AA, as clients may use self-help language as a defense to keep them from getting into deeper issues. A skilled group counselor will be able to balance the need to attend to substance abuse issues, while maintaining awareness about mental illness, resistance, and behavior destructive to the group therapy process. The group counselor must also be sensitive to the fact that not all addicted clients are compatible with group counseling. Individuals with severe pathology may not be capable of making the affective connection necessary to facilitate recovery (Behavioral Health Treatment, 1997).

Unfortunately, there is limited evidence that group psychotherapy approaches are effective in the treatment of substance disorders (Doweiko, 2008). However, treatment approaches that incorporate a larger proportion of group counseling to individual counseling are positively asso-ciated with increased likelihood of treatment success (Panas, Caspi, Fournier, & McCarty, 2003). Additionally, studies indicate that substance addicted clients participating in group counseling as part of a treatment regimen improved significantly on depression, suicide risk, and trauma symptoms (*Alcoholism and Drug Abuse Weekly*, 1997).

Self-Help Groups

Instead of seeking help from a mental health professional, many individuals seek assistance from self-help, or mutual-help, groups. These voluntary groups have members that share a common problem and meet for the purpose of exchanging social support. Most are self-governing, with members rather than experts or mental health professionals determining activities. They also tend to stress the importance of treating all members fairly and giving everyone an opportunity to express their viewpoints. The members face common problems so they benefit from the universality of the other members' concerns. These groups stress the importance of reciprocal helping, for members are expected to both give help to others and receive help from others. Self-help groups usually charge little in the way of fees. Alcoholics Anonymous (AA) is an example of a self-help or mutual-help group. AA is the "most frequently consulted source of help for drinking problems" (Doweiko, 2008, p. 446). In the years since its development, AA has grown to an association of 97,000 groups with approxi-mately 2 million people in 150 countries (Doweiko, 2008). There is an enormous variety of self-help groups.

Why are AA and NA *not* considered group therapy? The primary difference is the *role of the leader*. Recall that psychotherapeutic groups are led by counselors who facilitate the group. This person is trained in group roles and dynamics and typically has experience in providing group counseling. The group facilitator may or may not have personal experience in the topic under discussion. In other words, a psychotherapeutic group counselor facilitating an addiction recovery group may NOT be an addict themselves. Regardless of personal history, the group counselor in a psychotherapeutic group is not a participant but is exclusively a facilitator. AA and NA were developed as self-help or mutual-help groups. As such, they are led by individuals with history and experience in the topic under discussion. That is, *the leader of an AA or NA group is in addiction recovery* and functions in both a leadership and member role within the group.

TABLE 10.1 Comparison of Types of Groups Commonly Used in Addictions Counseling

Type	Basic Goal	Leader	Examples
Psychoeducational Group	Educating members on specific areas while providing emotional support	Both licensed mental health professionals and trained paraprofessionals	Addiction education group, anger management group, communication skills group
Psychotherapeutic Group	Improve psychological functioning and adjustment of individual members	Mental health professional, psychologist, clinical social worker, or certified alcohol and drug counselor	Interpersonal or cognitive-behavioral group counseling, psychodrama groups, interpersonal groups
Self-Help Group	Help members cope with or overcome specific problems while providing support to one another	Typically led by a volunteer participant and may not include a leadership position	Alcoholics Anonymous, Narcotics Anonymous, Al-Anon, SMART Recovery

Many groups based on the 12 steps of AA have emerged, including Narcotics Anonymous (NA) for the treatment of drug addiction, and Gamblers Anonymous (GA) for the treatment of compulsive gambling. Other groups based on the 12-step model have also emerged in response to the needs of family members requiring support, including Adult Children of Alcoholics (ACOA), Al-Anon, and Nar-Anon. These groups are covered in more detail in Chapter 12.

While the most prominent self-help groups are based on the 12-step model, SMART Recovery® is a group based on a cognitive behavioral model. It assists persons with substance or behavioral addictions through a four-point program. This four-point program includes enhancing and maintaining motivation to abstain, coping with urges, problem solving, and lifestyle balance (*http://www.smartrecovery.org*). SMART Recovery® states on its Web site that its purpose is offering assistance to persons choosing to abstain or considering abstinence from addictive behaviors by instruction in making changes in self-defeating cognitions, affect, or behaviors, and working toward satisfaction with life circumstances.

SMART Recovery® offers face-to-face meetings, online meetings, and an online message board for members to offer support to one another. Meetings are educational in nature and involve open discussions and treatment based on scientific knowledge, including the use of psychotropic medication and psychological treatment (*http://www.smartrecovery.org*).

When determining the most appropriate group treatment method for clients, consideration of the group format, general goals, and types of leadership is critical. The following table provides a comparison of typical group types and lists examples of each.

ETHICAL AND LEGAL ISSUES WITH GROUPS

The efficacy of group work within the field of addictions is well established. Addictions counselors face additional considerations when they undertake group treatment methods. The ethical and legal aspects of conducting group counseling are numerous. Counselors are best served by having a thorough understanding of how the Code of Ethics and Standards of Practice (American Counseling Association, 2005) as well as state and federal laws affect the services they provide. While many of the ethical and legal aspects of addictions work was covered in Chapter 4, the following section provides a view of group work in the field of addictions through the lens of the inherent legal and ethical components.

Competence of the Leader

Addictions groups may be facilitated by leaders who vary in formal training and personal experience with the recovery model. For example, addictions groups may be run by academically trained counselors in recovery, formally educated counselors with no personal history of addiction, or individuals in recovery with no formal academic training but much experience in the arena of recovery. For the purposes of this chapter, we will focus on counselors who have pursued formal academic training in counseling. Despite having a master's degree or higher, counselors may lead groups with limited training in the theory and techniques specific to group counseling (Gazda, Ginter, & Horne, 2001). Counselors who lead groups are called to practice within the scope of competence. The American Counseling Association (ACA) *Code of Ethics* (2005) states that counselors may only practice within areas in which they have received the necessary education, training, experience, and supervision. The ethical code further indicates a need for counselors to commit to ongoing education and training in any field of practice (ACA, 2005). While the code explicitly addresses competence, it remains somewhat vague and open to interpretation as to what constitutes necessary and sufficient education, training, experience, and supervision. Consequently, group counselors would do well to consult The Association for Specialists in Group Work (ASGW) *Professional Standards for the Training of Group Workers* (2000) for further clarification regarding leader competence.

The ASGW outlines the specific minimum training guidelines recommended leading psychoeducational and psychotherapeutic groups. In addition to one graduate course in group counseling and 10 or more hours of group experience, the ASGW recommends specific advanced coursework and 45–60 clock hours of supervised experience in order to specialize in group psychoeducation, counseling, or psychotherapy (ASGW, 1998). Demonstration and evaluation of core competencies are required and the ASGW (1998) recommends practica and internship experiences that correspond with the Council for Accreditation of Counseling and Related Educational Programs (CACREP). It is important to note that the competencies set forth by both ASGW and CACREP require the future group leader to participate in a personal group experience, the rationale being that such participation enhances the leader's understanding of the practical application of group theory.

Does meeting minimum standards ensure competence? Ethical group leaders do more than meet minimal requirements for training and experience. Being a competent and ethical group practitioner "[i]mplies functioning at a level of consciousness geared toward doing whatever it takes to function at the highest level, both personally and professionally" (Corey, Williams, & Moline, 1995, pp. 161–162). The group counselor is, after all, a human being prone to the same mishaps and errors of judgments as his or her clients. Group practitioners bring their personal lives to the profession of counseling, and their experiences, characteristics, and values play a part in the efficacy of their leadership style (Corey & Corey, 2006). Consistent and persistent evaluation of the effectiveness of counseling activities is the responsibility of all group leaders desirous of maintaining ethical standards and competence.

Screening of Participant

Group therapy is often the treatment of choice in addictions work. Whether agency structure, managed care influences, or treatment efficacy is behind the decision, many clients find themselves participating in groups. Group counselors are skilled at managing a diverse dynamic in a group setting and have an ethical responsibility to both the individual client and the group as a whole. In section A.8.a., the ACA Code of Ethics (2005) specifically calls counselors to screen members for compatibility with group goals and membership. Ultimately, it is the group counselor's responsibility to maximize treatment outcome and minimize any adverse effects on individual clients throughout group treatment while maintaining the integrity of the group process. Once properly screened and determined to be suitable for placement in a group, the client is entitled to the process of informed consent.

Informed Consent

Group leaders educate and engage clients through the use of informed consent, which communicates basic rights and responsibilities to the prospective group member. Because clients have the right to choose whether or not to enter into a particular counseling relationship (ACA, 2005), a thorough informed consent is part of the screening process to ensure that client and group-treatment method are a good fit. The informed consent should cover what the client should know before joining the group, as well as his or her rights and responsibilities during the group process (Corey & Corey, 2006). Ethically, group counselors inform prospective clients of the nature of the group process; benefits and limitations to such counseling; education training and credentials of the group counselor; expectations of the client within the group; the right to terminate the counseling relationship; and other concerns relevant to receiving services in a group environment (Corey & Corey, 2006). Finally, because of the nature of addiction, specifically illegal drug use, it is important for informed consent to address potential legal ramifications of disclosures made throughout the group counseling process.

Confidentiality

Confidentiality is of primary concern in the group treatment of addictions. Informed consent is critical in conveying information and expectations regarding confidentiality of the group counselor and the group members. The ACA *Code of Ethics* (2005) makes this clear, stating, "in group work, counselors clearly explain the importance and parameters of confidentiality for the specific group being entered" (p. 8). However, because only the counselor solicits consent from the client, confidentiality cannot be guaranteed as an absolute. That is, the group counselor cannot guarantee that breaches will not occur as this type of counseling includes, by its very nature, persons other than the client and the counselor. It has been the experience of these authors, as well as the reported experience of noted group experts Irwin Yalom (Yalom & Leszcz, 2005) and Gerald Corey (Corey, 2007) that breaches in group confidentiality are rare. Careful planning and presentation of expectations and limitations is paramount to creating the climate for confidentiality. After all, it is only within a climate of confidentiality that groups will enter into a productive, working stage.

Many group counselors find that involving the group in the process of establishing rules related to confidentiality is the most ethically responsible approach. As you might expect, members involved in establishing rules are often more responsive to those rules. Initial informed consent sets the stage for confidentiality expectations, but periodic reminders during group meetings are suggested to minimize risk (Corey, 2007). In addition to the right to confidentiality enjoyed by group members, group counselors must also explain the exceptions to confidentiality. Similar to exceptions to confidentiality in any counseling setting, the group counselor must discuss the ethical code that requires counselors to breach confidentiality when needed "to protect clients or identified others from serious and foreseeable harm or when legal requirements demand that confidential information must be revealed" (ACA, 2005, p. 7). Additionally, group counselors may need to breach confidentiality when a high risk of contracting a contagious, life-threatening disease exists (ACA, 2005).

Written agreements provide the clearest method of meeting the ethical and professional requirements related to confidentiality.

Voluntary Versus Involuntary Participation

Group counselors are often challenged with providing services to clients placed in the setting involuntarily. Examples include court-ordered treatment, groups conducted in correctional facilities, or even inpatient treatment facilities to which clients have been committed. Specific counseling and ethical concerns arise when faced with involuntary group participants. The counselor must work diligently to engage and encourage involuntary members to cooperate to avoid undermining the efficacy of the treatment (Corey, 2005). Because consequences are often built into the placement of clients in involuntary treatment, the counselor faces an enormous challenge to engage clients authentically. Clients may elect to attend, but not fully participate in the process, diminishing the treatment results.

In the experience of the authors, it is not uncommon practice in the rural Mississippi delta for area judges to refer individuals arrested for public intoxication to the local mental health center for addiction education classes. Members are court ordered and required to complete classes as a portion of their legal consequences. At the conclusion of classes, participants are provided evidence of completion, which they submit to the courts. Members that do not complete classes as ordered often face jail time. The classes are psychoeducational in nature and facilitators are often challenged to deal with a variety of issues including resistance, denial, minimizing, and even overt resentment. Thus, having leaders who are trained and prepared to deal with court ordered or involuntary group members is critical for the success of the group.

When involuntary clients are placed into a voluntary setting, the group counselor faces additional practical and ethical challenges. Because involuntary members might have different objectives for participating in the group than voluntary members (i.e., to remove or avoid a legal consequence), any behaviors that would undermine another member's ability to receive quality treatment would need to be assessed by the group counselor. The ethical code tells us that we must protect clients from any harm or trauma and must screen participants to ensure that the needs and goals of members are compatible with the group (ACA, 2005).

MANAGING DIVERSITY IN GROUP SETTINGS

Competent counselors understand the value of attending to diversity needs within all counseling environments, particularly within the group setting. Because no group is comprised of truly homogeneous members, the responsibility for attending to the diverse needs of the members lies with of the counselor who facilitates the group, whether it is psychoeducational or psychotherapeutic in nature. Research by Arredondo (1991) has proposed that groups are best addressed from a cultural perspective when three distinct dimensions are considered. The first includes classic issues of age, culture, ethnicity, gender, sexual orientation, and social class. Second, the counselor is challenged to address concepts such as educational background, geographic region, relationship status, and spiritual belief systems. Finally, the researchers propose that counseling is only truly culture sensitive when it accounts for the historical era and context of the current societal climate (Arredondo, 1991). Addiction treatment providers also suggest that the "best way to address racial and cross-cultural tension, as a group facilitator, is directly" (Sanders & Mayeda, 2009, p. 24). Talking about issues openly in group can minimize the effects they have on the group process. For purposes of this chapter, we will focus on the profound impact that issues of ethnicity, gender, sexuality, and type of addiction have on group counseling and its benefits.

Ethnicity

Counselors leading groups for clients who have addictions will naturally experience the impact and benefit that diverse ethnic backgrounds bring to the treatment approach. People of all ethnic backgrounds experience the ravages of addiction regardless of cultural approval or disapproval of the use of the substance (Frances & Miller, 1998). However, African American and Hispanic clients are three times as likely to seek treatment for substance abuse than Caucasian clients (Dowd & Rugle, 1999). As previously discussed, group counseling interventions are likely to be part of that treatment.

Arredondo (1991) indicates that all group counseling is cross-cultural, affected by societal biases and norms, and challenging to the leader regardless of the leader's ethnicity. Group counselors facilitate a balance of power or status among the members. Race carries inherent status cues which can alter the balance initially (Napier & Gershenfeld, 2003) requiring the counselor to continually assess the impact ethnicity has on the overall group alliance. The effective group counselor will be aware of personal values, the worldview of the client, and subsequently develop culturally appropriate interventions and group approaches (Arredondo, 1991).

Gender

Within residential treatment facilities, clients are routinely housed in all-male or all-female environments. The rationale behind this approach is to increase the safety of the clients as they work on extremely difficult life concerns. There are some drawbacks to this approach as heterogeneous group experiences afford participants the opportunity to work through family-of-origin and cross-gender relational issues while addressing addiction. However, distractions inherent in heterosexual relationships between men and women are minimized within gender-specific environments.

Gender plays a role in the group counseling process. Some men find the practice of group counseling unmasculine. The process of group therapy is a more stereotypically feminine method of dealing with interpersonal issues, with its heavy reliance on talking through conflicts and providing verbal supportive feedback (Gazda et al., 2001). As such, males often respond better to male-only groups where all are participating in what might be considered a feminine activity.

Men are typically conditioned to be independent and self-reflective. Group therapy by definition requires interdependence and a reliance on the thoughts and assistance of others. The "process" element of the group experience is frequently counterintuitive to the male experience, but the practicality and efficacy of that element often appeals to men and has become perhaps the most beneficial method in facilitating the therapeutic experience of men. Gazda et al. (2001) indicate that counselors leading men's groups "should be sensitive and do work around shame, guilt, abandonment, grief, fear, dependency, and anger, but not be afraid of any of these emotional states" (p. 71). Because these are often difficult emotions to address, counselors must be aware of their own fears about challenging men, resulting from some of the same gender stereotyping that challenges the group members. Men have the ability to create a nurturing and supportive environment and generally grow through the process of sharing their own stories (Gazda et al., 2001). The counselor sensitive to the needs and challenges of an all-male group experience can assist members in the creation of an environment where work on the addiction can occur.

In contrast, many groups dealing with varied counseling concerns are *de facto* women's groups because women are more naturally drawn to the sharing climate that defines the group experience. As with groups of any gender, working with women requires the counselor to facilitate interaction that encourages insight leading to behavioral change, and to maintain the sensitivity and range of clinical skills necessary to address concerns specific to this population. Women's groups led by women counselors may, in fact, be the most powerful, given that female counselors may be more in tune than their male counterparts with the underlying emotions that need to be addressed (Gazda et al., 2001). All-female groups are more likely to focus on feelings related to the effects the addiction has had on parenting, and on the guilt and shame that may be present as a result. An additional component that supports the efficacy of all-women groups is the increased likelihood of women survivors of sexual abuse participating in the treatment (NeSmith, Wilcoxon, & Satcher, 2000). This probability adds pressure to an already difficult dynamic as women struggle to overcome their addictions. However, other research has indicated that the negative elements predicted in male-led groups for women may not be a reality and that women respond favorably to male leadership in the group environment (NeSmith et al., 2000).

While there is strong research on the efficacy of the all-female group, some results indicate that a mixed-gender experience may be even more powerful for women clients. In fact, some evidence suggests that the mixed experience allows women the opportunity to participate in healthy relationships with men in a safe, controlled environment, which better prepares them for the realities of working in community-based 12-step groups and participating in a mixed-gender society overall (NeSmith et al., 2000). In spite of such benefits, the idea of mixed-gender treatment is helpful only when the sexes are equally represented in the group. Research indicates that women who are in the minority in groups tend to fall prey to exaggerated sex-role stereotypes and may lack the assertiveness needed to be honest and have their needs met within the group structure (Gazda et al., 2001). Women are often dominated by men in group experiences in general, which may reduce the efficacy of such an approach (NeSmith et al., 2000). The challenge again falls to the counselor, who must remain sensitive to both the needs of the group as an entity and the needs of each individual member. An understanding of gender from a developmental and cultural perspective, as well as an awareness of the implications inherent in that perspective is a critical attribute of the group counselor working with addictions.

Sexuality

Sexual minorities, such as gay, lesbian, and bisexual clients, are indicated to have two to three times the risk for addiction than their heterosexual counterparts (Cochran, Ackerman, Mays, & Ross, 2004). As such, group leaders may have the opportunity to run groups comprised of sexual minorities or may find themselves facilitating groups containing both heterosexual and Lesbian, Gay, Bisexual, Transgendered, and Questioning members.

Ben has been admitted to an inpatient facility for treatment of addiction to opioid pain medication. He reveals in group that when he is high, he engages in random sexual encounters. Although he considers himself heterosexual, he will go home with men or women when under the influence of narcotics. Group members insist he is bisexual, but he does not agree. Would the group process benefit from having Ben choose a label? How can this exchange be productive to the process and not a distraction?

Group counselors will then face the challenge of negotiating sexual identity stereotypes within the group environment, much like the gender stereotypes discussed previously.

Perhaps more than any other minority group, integrating sexual minorities into a largely heterosexual experience requires sensitivity and planning on the part of the group counselor to provide for member safety. Objective and unbiased treatment of sexual identity issues can challenge heterosexual facilitators and members, who may have a hard time setting aside their own beliefs for the greater good of the group experience. It falls upon the group counselor to both teach and model respect and to keep the focus on the recovery process. The skilled group counselor, aware of personal values and sensitive to the needs of the client as an individual and the group as a whole, is best suited to facilitating a climate for change.

Type of Addiction

There is an interesting phenomenon in the field of addictions, specifically alcohol and drug counseling, which may present a challenge to the group counselor. While group counseling is effective as a treatment intervention for a variety of substances, there are some dynamics between substance users that make group cohesion difficult.

Dre is a 21-year-old African American male with an addiction to crack cocaine. Harold is a 67-year-old Caucasian male with a fifth-a-day vodka habit. What impact might the cultural differences between these two members have on their willingness to participate? In spite of the obvious differences, what similarities might these members share?

Group counselors working in addictions find that differences in how members perceive the various types of substance use may create distance between members. These counselors find that individuals who have problems with alcohol may prefer treatment groups comprised of other alcoholics. Conversely, clients who are drug abusing or dependent are more open to treatment groups that address multiple substances.

In group settings, it is natural for defense mechanisms to emerge (James & Gilliland, 2005). The mindset of "well, alcohol is legal" and "at least I'm not a crackhead" creates challenges for the counselor working with a group comprised of members with diverse types of addictions. While Narcotics Anonymous acknowledges alcohol as a drug (World Service Office, 1993), the reverse is not true for Alcoholics Anonymous (AA Services, 1985). Drug abusing or dependent clients may experience this division in local AA meetings and this way of thinking may carry over into the psychoeducational or psychotherapeutic group realm. Experienced group counselors often have to navigate some tricky waters integrating these members into a working group setting.

GROUP COUNSELING FOR FAMILY MEMBERS OF ADDICTS

Because the spouses and children of addicts experience their own personal problems arising from the addiction, it is not difficult to understand the need for treatment opportunities to offer these family members. Additionally, the "attitudes, structure and function of the family system have been shown to be perhaps the most important variables in the outcome of treatment" for addicts (James & Gilliland, 2005). Thus, if the family system changes, it may assist the addict in sustaining progress and change.

The rationale for the treatment of the family member is clear. While the client receives treatment for addiction, the family members may require opportunities to learn new ways of coping and assistance in modifying stereotyped, repetitive, and maladaptive attitudes and responses to their family member's behavior. For example, family members often fail to recognize and admit that the symptoms of addiction have been present for some time; or they tolerate chronic addictive behavior, then reject the addict for displaying the behavior. Just as the addict rationalizes and makes excuses for using substances, addicts' family members often make excuses to themselves and to friends for the behavior instead of accepting that the individual is ill and needs treatment.

To aid an addict in recovery, family members must identify their own thoughts and attitudes, modify reactive behavior, and be educated about addiction and recovery (Anderson, 1981). This assists the family in learning how to stop centering their lives around the addict and detach from the substance abuse while learning to allow the addict to solve his or her own problem and to start to live life fully.

Many groups exist exclusively to offer support to family members of addicts. One such self-help group is Al-Anon. The book *Al-Anon's Twelve Steps and Twelve Traditions* (AA Services, 1985) offers a short history of its inception. According to this account, the wives of alcoholics attending AA began talking amongst themselves about the problems associated with living with an addict. Eventually, the wives designed their own set of 12 steps based on the AA steps, and Al-Anon became an official group. Many groups now exist, including Alateen for teenage family members of alcoholics, Nar-Anon for family members of drug addicts, and Adult Children of Alcoholics (ACOA) for adults realizing they have problems as a result of growing up in an alcoholic family system.

Regardless of the group format, family members of addicts should be provided an opportunity to come together to share their experiences, discuss problems, provide encouragement to each other, and learn to cope more effectively with various concerns. Through these groups, family members are afforded an opportunity to detach emotionally from the alcoholic's behavior while still loving the individual. Group therapy can also assist family members in understanding they did not cause the alcoholic to drink and to realize they can build a rewarding life in spite of the continued substance abuse or dependence.

CASE STUDIES

The following case studies illustrate two examples of group therapy for the treatment of substance abuse. One is psychoeducational in nature and the second is an open focus approach. Each contains examples of topics that are frequently included in substance abuse treatment.

Case Study I: Development of a Six-Session Alcohol and Drug Education Group

Group Dynamics

David, a substance abuse counselor, is organizing a psychoeducational group to offer addiction education to both addicts and families of addicts. The group members will be both self-referred and court ordered. Some members will be seeking information on addiction; some will be fulfilling the requirements of a judgment following DUI, or management referrals after a positive drug screen at work. Still others will be seeking to educate themselves about the behavior of a family member. The group will be ongoing and cyclical in nature so members may begin at any time and simply continue until they have completed all six sessions. Each session will have a specific agenda and cover subject matter pertinent to gaining general understanding of the process of addiction and related topics. Attendance will vary from week to week and the sessions are scheduled to meet for 60 minutes.

Questions for Consideration

1. How might the combination of both addicts and family members of addicts as group members affect the topic selection?
2. What potential diversity issues might result from having involuntary members as part of the group?
3. What legal and ethical issues are pertinent to this group?
4. What special considerations must be made to accommodate the proposed cyclical nature of the group?

David's Response

After consideration of the types of members making up the groups, David designs the following model.

Session I: Addiction: What Is It?

This session will explore the biological, psychological, and sociological aspects of addiction. It will examine the chemicals and behaviors associated with addiction, as well as co-occurring disorders. It will examine causes of addiction including genetics, brain chemistry, and societal influence. It will offer perspective on addiction including the disease model and addiction as a complex maladaptive behavior.

Session II: Codependency and Enabling

This session will explore the reciprocal and complementary nature of dependency based on the chemical dependent's need for care to survive and the caretaker's need to control the addict's behavior. It examines the differences between the behavior toward an addict (enabling) and one's relationship with an addict (codependency).

Session III: Life Skills Enhancement

During this session, members will learn stress-management techniques, examine problem-solving skills, and practice assertiveness training. It will emphasize the importance of communication and utilizing positive leisure and recreation alternatives. It will teach tools and techniques for self-directed change and promote recovery and the importance of living a satisfying life. It will offer suggestions on maintaining motivation and thinking rationally.

Session IV: Recovering Lifestyle

Group members will explore the various components and benefits of therapeutic intervention for the treatment of addiction including individual therapy, group therapy, and self-help programs. The session will address the concept of addiction as a complex maladaptive behavior with possible physiological factors and examine approaches to relapse prevention. This may include advocating the use of prescribed medications and psychological treatments.

Session V: What to Do and What Not to Do After Achieving Sobriety

This session includes review of important aspects of maintaining sobriety, including removing alcohol and/or drugs from the environment, buying over-the-counter medications, and promoting positive mind states and attitudes. This may include teaching HALT (hungry, angry, lonely, tired) as stress-producing states to avoid. Emphasis will be placed on coping with cravings and leading a balanced lifestyle.

Session VI: Self-Awareness/Spirituality

This session is devoted to endorsing the mind-body-spirit connection. It will focus on the importance of self-acceptance and spiritual cultivation to promote a sense of connectedness with self, others, and the universe. This session reiterates the link between negative emotions and thoughts and self-medicating with substances.

Discussion

Obviously, David must be well versed in addictions and addictions treatment. Maintaining structure in the group will help ensure that the limited time is used most effectively. Yet, the structure must be malleable, as processing of information may be necessary to ensure it is being received and understood. Structure through activities might offer concrete examples that will allow members to understand the implications for their own lives. David should be prepared to answer questions, provide additional information or resources, and make referrals.

David will have a number of diversity issues to address. As previously discussed, gender and socioeconomic differences present inherent challenges. Specific to the needs of this group membership, David will need to be sensitive to the different perspectives of the identified addict and the family members present. Family members may resent being placed in a group setting with addicts and may lash out at their family member who is the impetus for their being in the group, or may displace that anger onto other clients.

Because this is a revolving, open group, David will have additional challenges. Informed consent becomes critical in this type of environment. Membership in the group implies that the client has an addiction or that the group client is a family member of someone with an addiction. Because confidentiality is impossible for David to guarantee, as he can only control his own disclosures, he will need to conduct a thorough prescreening of members and carefully explain the limits of confidentiality at each meeting. Continually revisiting informed consent will assist David as he manages group members who are each at a different place in the group cycle of topics.

Case Study II: Psychotherapeutic Group, Open Focus

Group Dynamics

Nikki is a counselor for an inpatient alcohol and drug treatment facility. The treatment approach is based on the 12-step model of recovery. Each day, she facilitates a process-oriented therapy group for clients receiving treatment for addiction. The group is made up of adult males and females of various racial, ethnic, and socioeconomic backgrounds. Some members were voluntarily admitted to treatment and others were involuntarily committed to treatment. The group members have a variety of issues including chemical and behavioral addictions. Members will begin participation in the group upon admission to the program and continue until discharge. The size of the group could vary daily, but is typically between 8 and 16 members. Additionally, some members may be diagnosed with a co-occurring disorder.

Questions for Consideration

1. What are common issues for clients seeking treatment for addiction?
2. How might the variation of gender affect the interpersonal dynamics of the groups? Race? Socioeconomic status? Number of treatment attempts? Voluntary versus involuntary participation?
3. How should the facilitator address the issue of having a group made up of members at varying stages of recovery?
4. What legal and ethical considerations are pertinent to this group?

Nikki's Response

After consultation, Nikki realizes there are many issues for consideration. She recognizes the need to be educated and prepared to process the following issues:

Assertiveness Training

The group therapy format facilitates learning the difference between aggressive behavior and assertive behavior by offering ample opportunity for verbal exchange about sensitive subjects. Members learn to interact with one another and the leader in an honest, open way. Members are taught that aggression can take place passively, with remarks such as, "You're right, I wouldn't know about hangovers, I only smoke marijuana" or overtly, with remarks such as, "You're a whore that traded her body for drugs."

Character Defects

There are many characteristics of dysfunctional coping styles that show up through inappropriate interpersonal communication. Working with group members on self-pity, arrogance, lack of humility, overconfidence, and grandiosity are typical. The addict's defenses are "primitive and regressive" and may "personify the addict as self-centered and dependent" (James & Gilliland, 2005, p. 279). Such comments as "Why should I listen to you when your brain is fried?" facilitates members learning to recognize that grandiose behavior is overcompensation for feeling low. This lays the groundwork for successfully interacting with humility and teaches clients to respect others and avoid making generalizations.

Denial

A persistent and pervasive personal defense system, denial is the emotional refusal to acknowledge a person, situation, condition, or event the way it actually is (James & Gilliland, 2005). It is commonplace for substance abusers to deny they are "addicted" to their chemical or behavior of choice. While denial is a normal adaptive process for self-protection, within the addict it becomes an ongoing form of self-deception. Many addicts begin the process of recovery with remarks such as, "I can stop any time I want to."

Grief

The process of recovery often promotes an overwhelming sense of grief. Group members express sentiments such as, "I feel like I have lost my best friend." Group leaders may elect to teach members symptoms of grief, utilizing such resources as the Kubler-Ross Model (1969) of the cycle of grief to explain that the myriad of feelings being experienced is typical, and emphasize the importance of learning healthy coping alternatives.

Minimization

Statements such as "I only drink beer" or "I didn't inhale" are commonplace among chemically dependent individuals. "Clients often minimize the extent of their use in an attempt to convince themselves and others that they can continue to use" (Johnson, 2004, p. 116). In fact, minimization is so prevalent that many substance abuse professionals routinely assume that the amount of alcohol or drug use reported is only a small percentage of what is actually used. Family members of clients may also minimize reports of use as part of their own denial of the extent of the problem.

Modeling of New and Healthier Coping Strategies

Many inpatient treatment facilities allow their clients to gain privileges through the course of treatment, allowing the client to leave the facility to go home or visit friends and family. Upon returning, clients are afforded an opportunity to process their thoughts and feelings about being in the community, encountering friends or situations that challenge them, and reviewing what has and has not been working to cope with these circumstances.

Rationalization

Considered a characteristic of denial, rationalization is the chronic use of excuses to support both addiction and the feelings of inadequacy that lead to destructive acting and behaving. Addressing these excuses may be difficult for group leaders and family members because there may be elements of truth included in the "reasons" for using. For example, some addicts did have abusive childhoods or are involved in dysfunctional relationships. Even such comments as "After the accident I couldn't sleep at night" are not uncommon. However, the goal of rationalizing is to convince others that the user is justified and should not be confronted (Johnson, 2004).

Relapse and Aftercare Concerns

Exploration of the concepts of triggers and coping mechanisms for dealing with triggers including how to handle craving are common topics for group members. There is a great deal of fear involved in considering what the future holds, including the ability to cope with high-risk situations and the motivation to change behavior or return to past behavior. Research suggests a strong association between negative affective states and relapse, so the exploration of negative feelings is critical (Doweiko, 2008).

Resentment/Blame

It is not unusual for some clients to be resentful of being in treatment. Some may demonstrate hostility toward a family or staff member. A client might make statements such as, "My wife is such a nag, she makes me drink." Exploration of the displacement of these feelings and attempts to move clients toward personal responsibility are primary themes for building a foundation of sobriety.

Spiritual Cultivation

A major component of many chemical dependency programs is the careful analysis of clients' spiritual resources (James & Gilliland, 2005). This investigation has little to do with religion and instead focuses on the despair and hopelessness addicts feel and the emptiness in their lives they attempt to fill through their addiction. Being prepared to explore these feelings is critical.

Testing Behaviors

Clients often test the limits to determine consistency in the counselor's treatment approach by disobeying rules. As a result, breaking the ground rules should immediately be confronted by the group counselor. For example, if a member is late for a group and makes an excuse such as, "I forgot the time," the group leader may use this as an opportunity to address the excuse and explore whether the client has used this excuse to perpetuate the use of substances.

Discussion

In addition to addressing the issues outlined above, Nikki will have a number of diversity challenges in her setting. Issues of gender play out in inpatient facilities which, as previously indicated, often results in same-sex group meetings. Since Nikki will be managing a group whose composition will fluctuate regularly, she will need to manage any power differentials inherent in gender bias. Additionally, ethnic diversity carries its own set of social and cultural biases and Nikki will need to continuously evaluate that impact on the dynamic of the group to generate a climate most conducive to change. Because some clients will be there under an involuntary order, or after multiple treatment attempts, Nikki will be challenged with the impact resistance, anger, denial, and rationalization have on the group process. The stage set for the group in this case study is especially dynamic given its ongoing structural changes and challenges, creating a rich opportunity for the skilled group counselor to actively facilitate a multifaceted treatment approach.

Because the group is set within a larger treatment model provided by the institution, legal and ethical concerns may be first addressed within the overarching structure of the treatment facility. Informed consent for all components of treatment, including this group approach, will initially be addressed upon admission with a thorough informed consent. As previously indicated, confidentiality cannot be guaranteed when in a group setting but federal law protects clients in inpatient alcohol and drug treatment from having information shared outside of the facility by the employees of that facility. Following her own code of ethics as a counselor, it will be important for her to address confidentiality in the screening of group members, as well as with the overall group each session. Nikki's code of ethics as a counselor guide her to provide for the welfare of the client first and foremost. Because some members may be diagnosed with a co-occurring disorder, the impact this would have on the group dynamic would need to be evaluated. She will have to make decisions about group inclusion that may require her to offer alternative treatment to clients who would not benefit from—or might even be detrimental to—the group setting.

Nikki must learn, understand, and know how to use the group process to involve clients in positive change (Johnson, 2004). It takes skill and practice to engage members in talking to others while promoting safety to talk about self. Knowledge of a number of theories and models is recommended. Nikki must remember that essentially, in entering the program, members have admitted they have been unable to change on their own. As such, she must utilize the strongest interpersonal skills she possesses to help them change. She must always be cognizant that the alliance that evolves between herself and clients is one important factor in a positive outcome of the treatment process. Research indicates that empathy combined with a "supportive-reflective" style of therapy seems to be most effective (Doweiko, 2008).

STRATEGIES FOR EFFECTIVE GROUP TREATMENT

Clearly one very important factor for addiction treatment providers is retaining clients in treatment. Studies indicate that clients who complete treatment have higher recovery rates than those who drop out (Sanders & Mayeda, 2009). Thus, consideration of factors that can minimize conflict and prevent dropout are of critical significance. Sanders and Mayeda (2009) suggest the following strategies to increase group cohesion and address group conflict:

- Address outbursts directly and quickly to promote members feeling safe.
- Encourage members to maintain a normal tone of voice and avoid loud voices or yelling.
- Create contracts with members to address behaviors that require practice. For example, if a member has a tendency to lash out verbally when faced with conflict, when the group member demonstrates distress, address this history and request permission to address the issue in group in an effort to find appropriate ways to express feelings.
- If group members demonstrate emotions that seem linked to resentment related to giving up alcohol or drugs, address the issue openly to facilitate an opportunity to discuss this anger.
- Ask members to repeat back what they hear other members say when tension creates interference with hearing one another.
- If members seem to be relating strongly to another member, consider that members often have conflict with other members that are much like them. Ask those who are at odds to identify similarities between themselves.
- Facilitators must pay attention to and promptly take apart subgroups.
- Deal with members that monopolize group time in a straightforward and open manner.
- Allowing opportunities to shift between emotion and thoughts can be calming and allow room for growth.

Summary and Some Final Notations

This chapter reviewed group therapy, one of the primary treatment models for addiction within the United States. Psychotherapeutic, psychoeducational, and self-help groups were examined in detail, including proposed topic areas, considerations for facilitators, and diversity issues. Various legal and ethical issues related to the use of group therapy with addicted populations were examined. A review of the potential effectiveness of group therapy with family members of addicts was also provided. Comprehensive case studies were presented to assist students in understanding issues that must be considered when designing and facilitating a therapy group to treat addiction.

Useful Web Sites

The following Web sites provide additional information relating to the chapter topics:

The Addiction Recovery Guide
http://www.addictionrecoveryguide.org/treatment/online.html
Offers a variety of online treatment resources for alcohol and drug treatment by trained experts via the Internet.

American Counseling Association Code of Ethics
http://www.counseling.org/Resources/CodeOfEthics/TP/
    Home/CT2.aspx
Allows counselors to access the ACA Code of Ethics pertaining to group counseling.

Association for Specialists in Group Work
http://www.asgw.org/
A division of ACA founded to promote quality in group work, training practice, and research.

National Institute on Drug Abuse: Drug Counseling for Cocaine Addicts
http://www.nida.nih.gov/TXManuals/DCCA/DCCA5.html
Provides an overview of group treatment for cocaine addiction including outlines for psychoeducational and problem-solving groups.

SMART Recovery®

http://smartrecovery.org

SMART Recovery® is a nationwide, nonprofit organization that offers free support groups to individuals who desire to gain independence from any type of addictive behavior. SMART Recovery® also offers a free Internet message board discussion group, and sells publications related to recovery from addictive behavior.

Sober Recovery

http://www.soberrecovery.com/

Online resource guide to 12-step and 12-step-alternative programs. Includes information about addiction and recovery and provides support information for families and friends, with lists of, and links to, inpatient and outpatient recovery programs for adults and teens.

References

AA Services. (1985). *Al-Anon's twelve steps and twelve traditions.* New York: Al-Anon Family Group Headquarters, Inc.

AA Services. (2004). *Alcoholics Anonymous Big Book* (4th Ed.). New York: Alcoholics Anonymous World Services, Inc.

Addiction Letter. (1995). Group therapy offers 12 ways to manage dual diagnosis [Electronic version], *11*(10), 1–3.

Alcoholism and Drug Abuse Weekly (1997). *Study: Group therapy helps addicted women with abuse history, 9*(33), 5–7.

American Counseling Association. (2005). *ACA code of ethics.* Alexandria, VA: Author.

American Psychiatric Association. (2000). *Diagnostic and statistical manual of mental disorders* (4th ed., text revision). Washington, DC: Author.

Anderson, D. J. (1981). *Perspectives on treatment: The Minnesota experience.* Center City, MN: Hazelden Foundation.

Arredondo, P. (1991). Multicultural counseling competencies as tools to address oppression and racism. *Journal of Counseling and Development, 77*(1), 102–109.

Association for Specialists in Group Work. (1998). Best practice guidelines. *Journal for Specialists in Group Work. 23*(3), 237–244.

Association for Specialists in Group Work. (2000). Professional standards for the training of group workers. *Journal for Specialists in Group Work. 29*(3), 1–10.

Behavioral Health Treatment. (1997). Group therapy works well for addiction [Electronic version]. Behavioral Health Treatment, *2*(1), 1–3.

Campbell, L., & Page, R. (1993). The therapeutic effects of group process on the behavioral patterns of a drug addicted group [Electronic version]. *Journal of Addictions & Offender Counseling, 13*(2), 34–46.

Cochran, S. D., Ackerman, D., Mays, V. M., & Ross, M. W. (2004). Prevalence of non-medical drug use and dependence among homosexually active men and women in the US population. *Addiction, 99*(8), 989–999.

Corey, G. (2005). *Theory and practice of counseling & psychotherapy* (7th ed). Pacific Grove, CA: Brooks/Cole.

Corey, G. (2007). *Theory and practice of group counseling* (7th ed.). Belmont, CA: Wadsworth/Thompson Learning.

Corey, G., Williams, G. T., & Moline, M. E. (1995). Ethical and legal issues in group counseling. *Ethics & Behavior, 5*(2), 161–183.

Corey, M. S., & Corey, G. (2006). *Groups: Process and practice* (7th ed.). Pacific Grove, CA: Brooks/Cole.

Dowd, E. T., & Rugle, L. (Eds.). (1999). *Comparative treatments of substance abuse.* New York: Springer.

Doweiko, H. E. (2008). *Concepts of chemical dependency* (7th ed.). Belmont, CA: Thomson Brooks/Cole.

Frances, R. J., & Miller, S. I. (1998). *Clinical textbook of addictive disorders* (2nd ed.). New York: Guilford Press.

Gazda, G. M., Ginter, E. J., & Horne, A. M. (2001). *Group counseling and group psychotherapy: Theory and application.* Boston: Allyn & Bacon.

Gladding, S.T. (2007). Family therapy: History, theory and practice (4th Ed.).Upper Saddle River, NJ: Pearson Education, Inc.

Gorman, D. (2003). The best of practices, the worst of practices: The making of science-based primary intervention programs. *Psychiatric Services, 54*, 1087–1089.

James, R. K., & Gilliland, B. E. (2005). *Crisis intervention strategies* (5th ed.). Belmont, CA: Thomson Brooks/Cole.

Johnson, J. L. (2004). *Fundamentals of substance abuse practice.* Belmont, CA: Brooks/Cole-Thomson Learning.

Kubler-Ross, E. (1969). *On death and dying.* New York: McMillan Publishing.

Martin, M. K., Giannandrea, P., Rogers, B., & Johnson, J. (1996). Beginning steps to recovery: A challenge to the "come back when you're ready" approach. *Alcoholism Treatment Quarterly, 13*(2), 45–58.

Napier, R. W., & Gershenfeld, M. K. (2003). *Groups: Theory and experience* (7th ed.). Boston: Houghton Mifflin.

NeSmith, C. L., Wilcoxon, S. A., & Satcher, J. F. (2000). Male leadership in an addicted women's group: An empirical approach. *Journal of Addictions and Offender Counseling, 20*(2), 75–84.

Panas, L., Caspi, Y., Fournier, E., & McCarty, D. (2003). Performance measures for outpatient substance abuse services: Group versus individual counseling. *Journal of Substance Abuse Treatment, 25*(4), 271–279.

Phillips, R. E., Lakin, R., & Pargament, K. I. (2002). Development and implementation of a spiritual issues psychoeducational group for those with serious mental illness. *Community Mental Health Journal, 38*(6), 487–496.

Sanders, M., & Mayeda, S. (November/December; 2009). Decrease conflicts in groups. *Addiction Professional,* 21–25.

SMART Recovery: Self Management and Recovery Training (n.d.). Retrieved November 25, 2006, from *http://www .smartrecovery.org/resources/pdfs/faq.pdf*

Toseland, R. W., & Rivas, R. F. (2001). *An introduction to group work* (4th ed.). Needham Heights, MA: Allyn & Bacon.

Weiss, R. D., Jaffee, W. B., de Menil, V. P., & Cogley, C. B. (2004). Group therapy for substance use disorders: What do we know? *Harvard Review of Psychiatry, 12*(6), 339–351.

World Service Office. (1993). *It Works: How and Why: The Twelve Steps and Twelve Traditions of Narcotics Anonymous.* Van Nuys, CA: World Service Office.

Yalom, I. D., & Leszcz, M. (2005). *The theory and practice of group psychotherapy* (5th ed). New York: Basic Books.

Zweben, J. E. (1995). Integrating psychotherapy and 12 step approaches. In M. A. Washton (Ed.), *Psychotherapy and substance abuse* (pp. 124–140). New York.

Chapter *11*

Addiction Pharmacotherapy

Cass Dykeman
Oregon State University

RATIONALE FOR A CHAPTER ON PHARMACOTHERAPY OF ADDICTION

Why should a professional counselor read a chapter on the pharmacotherapy of addiction? Isn't it strange to use a drug to defeat an addiction to another drug? Also, isn't pharmacotherapy the sole domain of physicians? In the course of this chapter, I hope to orient you to the increasing role of pharmacotherapy in addiction treatment. With this knowledge, you will be in the best position to help your clients take full advantage of the myriad of treatment options that exist.

The pharmacotherapy approaches discussed in this chapter are not without controversy in the addictions treatment community. Many subscribe to the adage "you can't treat a drug with a drug" (O'Brien, 2005). Others disparage medication as a "crutch" and press clients to remain "drug free" (O'Brien, 2005). Indeed, a government report listed the "antimedication" bias in the addiction treatment community as a critical barrier to the development of addiction pharmacotherapy in the United States (Goodman et al., 1997). As a professional counselor, you are under an ethical obligation to provide your clients treatment based not upon bias but upon scientific evidence of effectiveness. Thus, attention to addiction pharmacotherapy is an ethical mandate no matter what prejudices you encounter at your worksite.

This chapter has four parts. In the first, we will focus on the specialized terms and concepts used in pharmacotherapy. These can be intimidating to professional counselors without an extensive background in the biological sciences. Yet, understanding these terms and concepts is essential to understanding the specific pharmacotherapies used in the addiction field. In the second part, I will offer my explication of the biology of craving. Next, I will address the professional counselor's role in addiction pharmacotherapy. In the final part, I will present the specific pharmacotherapies used in the treatment of addiction.

TERMS AND CONCEPTS

Key Pharmacotherapy Terms

As with learning foreign languages and statistics, terms are the foundation to knowledge acquisition. What follows are the key pharmacotherapy terms any professional counselor should know because they will be encountered frequently in your professional practice and reading. Other pharmacotherapy-specific terms I will use appear in a glossary at the end of this chapter.

ADDICTION (FROM A PSYCHOPHARMACOLOGICAL PERSPECTIVE). A chemical or behavior used to produce pleasure and to reduce painful affects, employed in a pattern characterized by two key features: (1) recurrent failure to control the behavior; and (2) continuation of the behavior despite significant harmful consequences (Goodman, 2008). Several neurotransmitters (e.g., glutamate) and hormones (e.g., insulin) are core factors in this desire to produce pleasure and reduce painful affects (Leggio, 2009).

AGONIST. A ligand (i.e., molecule) that activates a receptor (Preston et al., 2008).

ANTAGONIST. A ligand that blocks other ligands from activating a receptor (Preston et al., 2008).

NEUROTRANSMITTER. Chemicals released by nerve cells at synapses that influence the activity of other cells. Neurotransmitters may excite, inhibit, or otherwise influence the activity of cells (National Institute of Neurological Disorders and Stroke, 2007). In reference to addiction pharmacotherapy, the main neurotransmitters of interest include: acetylcholine (ACH), glutamate (GLU), γ-aminobutyric acid (GABA), serotonin (5HT), norepinephrine (NA), and dopamine (DA).

RECEPTOR. The location at which ligands bind to the nervous system to exert their effects (i.e., chemical signaling between and within cells) (Julien, 2007; Neubig et al., 2003).

REUPTAKE. Reabsorption of a neurotransmitter by way of a reuptake transporter pump embedded in a cell membrane (Preston et al., 2008).

KEY CONCEPTS OF NEUROLOGY IN PHARMACOTHERAPY

While fascinating, a comprehensive examination of pharmacotherapy neurology lies beyond the scope and goals of this chapter. Thus, we will focus on one key part of this neurology—the neurology of the synapse. A synapse has three parts: (1) a minute space between, (2) a presynaptic membrane of one neuron, and (3) a postsynaptic membrane of a receiving neuron (Julien, 2007). This minute space is known as the synaptic cleft. The presynaptic membrane is located at the axon terminal of a neuron (i.e., terminal bouton). The postsynaptic membrane is located on a dendrite of a neuron. See Figure 11.1 for a graphical overview of this neurology.

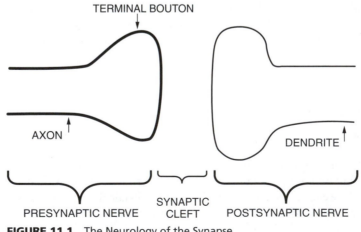

FIGURE 11.1 The Neurology of the Synapse

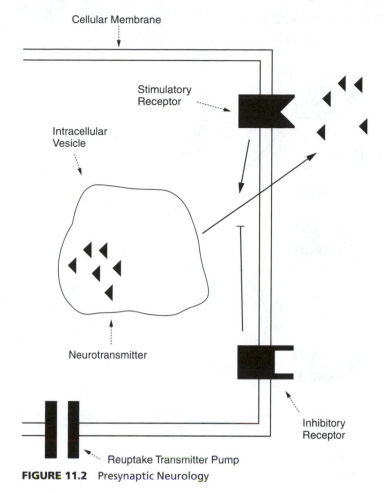

FIGURE 11.2 Presynaptic Neurology

The presynaptic side of this neurology controls neurotransmitter release (Shiloh et al., 2006). Generally, most neurons release only one transmitter (Shiloh et al., 2006). In the presynaptic axon terminal there are three parts to note: (1) reuptake transmitter pumps, (2) receptors, and (3) intracellular vesicles containing the neurotransmitter. Please note that there are receptors that can stimulate neurotransmitters and receptors that can inhibit such release. See Figure 11.2 for graphical representation of the presynaptic side.

The postsynaptic side of this neurology facilitates intracellular response (Shiloh et al., 2006). The postsynaptic nerve has three parts of note: (1) ion channels, (2) receptors, and (3) pumps. All three parts can either enhance or suppress the permeability of the postsynaptic membrane (Shiloh et al., 2006). See Figure 11.3 for graphical representation of the postsynaptic side.

In thinking about neurology of intracellular change, it may be helpful to employ the metaphor of "messengers" (Shiloh et al., 2006). Neurotransmitters can be thought of as "first messengers." These messengers interact with the postsynaptic nerve to induce consequent intracellular changes (Shiloh et al., 2006). Within the postsynaptic nerve, the first messengers set off a cascade of messenger changes including second, third, and fourth messengers. The nature and function of the final three messengers lies beyond the scope of this chapter.

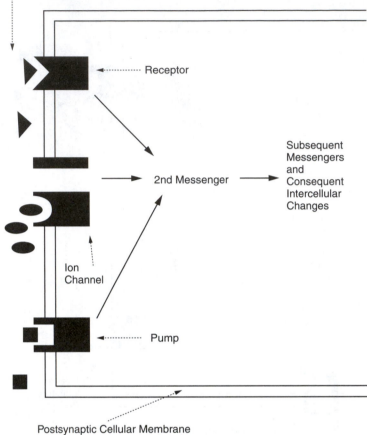

Neurotransmitters (1st Messenger)

Receptor

2nd Messenger

Subsequent Messengers and Consequent Intercellular Changes

Ion Channel

Pump

Postsynaptic Cellular Membrane

FIGURE 11.3 Postsynaptic Neurology

DIVERSITY AND PHARMACOTHERAPY

There are considerable cross-ethnic variations in drug effects (Lin & Poland, 2000). An example is drugs that impact pupil dilation. When the same amount of this type of medication was applied, Blacks were the least responsive, Asians in the middle, and Caucasians at the other extreme (Lin & Poland, 2000). In their major work in ethnic psychopharmacology, Lin and Poland (2000) concluded,

> Clinically, the importance of culture and ethnicity has been significantly intensi-fied because of the rapid and accelerating population shifts occurring in all metropolitan areas of the world. Furthermore, because of the rapid pace of inter-continental transportation and large-scale migration, most psychiatrists no longer have the luxury of practicing their trades in culturally or ethnically homo-geneous settings. Patients seeking help enter the clinic with divergent beliefs, expectations, dietary practices, and genetic constitution. These all have the potential of significantly affecting the outcome of psychopharmacotherapy and should not be ignored (p. 1017).

Another example concerns ethnic variations of the presence of an enzyme (CYP 2D6) that strongly impacts drug metabolism (*n.b.*, PM = Poor Metabolizer). Concerning CYP 2D6, Chaudhry et al. (2008) reported that:

> The frequency of CYP2D6 PMs ranges from >3% in the Cuna Amerindians, Middle Easterners, Mexican Americans and Asians to 10% in Caucasians in Europe and North America. . . . Among black Africans, there is a wide range of frequencies with 0–8% of Saharan Africans, 4% of Venda in South Africa, 1.9% of African-Americans and 19% of Sans Bushmen being classified as PMs . . . (p. 676).

Chaudhry et al. noted that these ethnic variations result from a complex interchange of genetic factors with ethnically based variables such as culture, diet, and societal attitudes. In Figure 11.4 I present a provisional causal chain based on the research reviews on ethnic psychopharmacology (Campinha-Bacote, 2007; Chaudhry et al. 2008; Chia-Hui, Chun-Yu, & Keh-Ming, 2008).

Given the existence of wide ethnic variations in the impact of medications, consideration of the interplay between ethnicity and pharmacotherapy represents best practice for the professional counselor. However, all the reviewers cautioned that *intra*-ethnic differences in psychopharmacology can be as large as *inter*-ethnic differences. As such, it is the wise clinician who avoids applying even well-researched ethnic distinctions indiscriminate of the history of each individual client.

Sex is another factor in the effects of a drug. In a major review of studies on sex differences in drug abuse, Lynch, Roth, and Carroll (2002) concluded,

> It is apparent that sex influences the behaviors induced by drugs, as well as pharmacological responses to drugs. Further research examining the factors that underlie sex differences may allow for the development of safe and effective sex-specific behavioral and pharmacological therapies for drug abuse (p. 133).

As with ethnicity, consideration of the interplay between sex and pharmacotherapy represents best practice for the professional counselor.

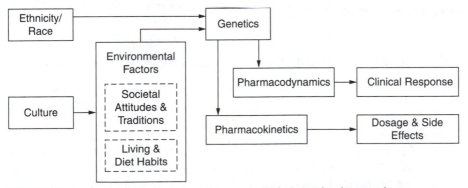

FIGURE 11.4 Provisional Causal Chain Concerning Ethnic Psychopharmacology
Source: n.b., this figure was inspired by a figure that appeared in Chia-Hui, Chun-Yu, and Keh-Ming (2008) and integrates the work of Campinha-Bacote (2007) and Chaudhry et al. (2008).

KEY CONCEPTS OF NEUROTRANSMITTERS IN PHARMACOTHERAPY

There are a number of endogenous chemicals that serve as neurotransmitters. The three with most relevance to addiction pharmacotherapy are serotonin (5HT), dopamine (DA), and norepinephrine (NA). Reiness (2009) describes the life cycle of neurotransmitters as follows:

> It is often convenient to divide up the "life cycle" of a neurotransmitter into particular stages. Usually these include: (1) synthesis of the transmitter; (2) packaging and storage in synaptic vesicles; (3) if necessary, transport from the site of synthesis to the site of release from the nerve terminal; (4) release in response to an action potential; (5) binding to postsynaptic receptor proteins; and (6) termination of action by diffusion, destruction, or reuptake into cells (p. 1).

Blocking reuptake is a major mechanism of the medications that we will discuss later in this chapter.

KEY CONCEPTS OF PHARMACOKINETICS IN PHARMACOTHERAPY

In discussing the four pharmacokinetic processes, Julien (2007) used a drug most readers of this chapter should be well familiar with: aspirin. In reference to aspirin, these processes can be described as follows:

1. *Absorption* of the aspirin into the body from the swallowed tablet.
2. *Distribution* of the aspirin throughout the body.
3. *Biotransformation* of the aspirin into by-products (i.e., metabolites).
4. *Elimination* of the waste by-products (Julien, 2007; Preston et al., 2008).

It is important to note that every drug will exhibit a unique kinetic profile (like a fingerprint) composed of these four processes (Preston et al., 2008).

The most important pharmacokinetic concept is half-life. The half-life of a drug is used to determine dosage amounts and time intervals (Preston et al., 2008). Knowledge of a drug's half-life is also important because it tells one how long a drug will remain in the body (Julien, 2007). For, instance it takes approximately 4 half-lives for 94% of a drug to clear the body (Julien, 2007). Significantly, even individual medications of the same type (i.e., benzodiazepines) can have very different half-lives.

KEY CONCEPTS OF PHARMACODYNAMICS IN PHARMACOTHERAPY

In the previous section we addressed how the body affects drugs. Now we turn our attention to how drugs affect the body. To produce an effect, a drug must bind to and interact with a receptor (Julien, 2007). Generally, it will do this in one of two ways: as an agonist or antagonist.

First, let us consider drugs as agonists. Once it binds to a receptor, an agonist activates or enhances cellular activity in a similar way to endogenous transmitters (Piascik, 2005; Shiloh, Nutt, & Weizman, 2005). This activity sets off the complex cascade of intracellular messengers mentioned earlier. See Figure 11.5 for a graphical representation of this process.

Now let us discuss drugs as antagonists. Antagonists bind to a receptor but do not activate the receptor (Piascik, 2005). However, its presence at a receptor blocks the binding of agonists or

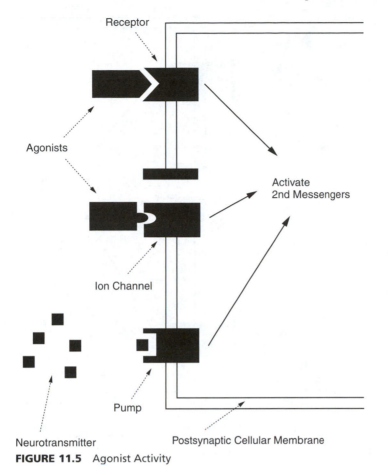

Receptor

Agonists

Activate
2nd Messengers

Ion Channel

Pump

Neurotransmitter   Postsynaptic Cellular Membrane
FIGURE 11.5   Agonist Activity

neurotransmitters to the receptor (Piascik, 2005). See Figure 11.6 for a graphical representation of this process.

Finally, let us consider receptors. The receptor is a membrane-spanning protein molecule (Julien, 2007). The life of a receptor is from 12 to 24 hours, after which time it wears out or is reabsorbed into the cell (Julien, 2007). The processes of downregulation and upregulation refer to the decrease or increase in the total number of receptors.

Good job, reader! You have made it through the basic science part of this chapter. We have examined the terms *neurology, diversity issues, pharmacokinetics,* and *pharmacodynamics*—terms necessary to understanding addiction pharmacotherapy. Before we examine treatment of specific addictions, let us turn our attention to the emerging biological theory of *craving* that underpins many pharmacotherapy strategies.

A BIOLOGICAL THEORY OF CRAVING

Why care about the biology of craving? The reason is that the development of craving plays a crucial role in (1) the transition from substance use to dependence, (2) the mechanisms underlying relapse, and (3) treatment (Verheul, Brink, & Geerlings, 1999). In addiction, there is not one type

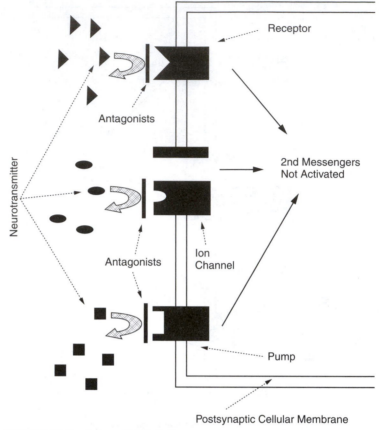

FIGURE 11.6 Antagonist Activity

of craving, but multiple types. These types are psychological readouts of dysregulation in different neurotransmitter systems.

As an illustration, let us examine these types in reference to alcohol addiction. Dutch addiction scholar Roel Verheul posited three types of craving for alcohol: (1) reward-sensitivity, (2) stress-reduction, and (3) disinhibition (Ooteman et al., 2009; Verheul & Brink, 2005). Verheul, Brink, and Geerlings (1999) described *reward-sensitivity*-based craving as the desire for the rewarding, stimulating, and enhancing effects of alcohol consumption. They presented evidence that such a craving is the result of dysregulation of the opioidergic/dopaminergic (OP/DA) neurotransmitter systems. Specifically, this form of craving arises out of a deficiency in the base levels of endogenous opioids and/or dopamine.

Verheul and Brink (2005) described *stress-reduction*-based craving as the desire for the reduction of tension or arousal. They presented evidence that such a craving is the result of dysregulation of the GABAergic/glutametergic (GABA/GLU) neurotransmitter systems. Specifically, this form of craving arises out of anxiety resultant from a deficiency in the base level of GABA (an inhibitory neurotransmitter) and an excess in the base level of GLU (an excitatory neurotransmitter).

Verheul, Brink, and Geerlings (1999) described *disinhibition*-based craving as the desire emerging from a lack of control. This lack can be either cognitive/attentional (i.e., obsessive) or behavioral, or both. They presented evidence that such a craving is the result of dysregulation of the serotonergic (5HT) neurotransmitter system. Specifically, this craving arises out of a deficiency in the base level of 5HT. The obsessive disinhibition form of craving can be defined as a loss of control in which obsessions flood in and overwhelm perception (Addolorato et al., 2005). This craving is similar to obsessive-compulsive disorder except that the obsession centers on alcohol (Anton, 2000). The behavioral disinhibition form of craving can be defined as a loss of control over impulsiveness, harm avoidance, and deviant behavior (Verheul & Brink, 2005).

A research team at the Catholic University of Rome has been focusing on the role of hormones in alcohol craving (Addolorato et al., 2009; Leggio, 2009). In particular, they have preliminary evidence that polymorphisms (DNA variations) within the following lead to deregulation in alcohol craving: (a) appetite stimulating hormones such as ghrelin, (b) appetite suppressing hormones such as leptin, and (c) volume-regulating hormones such as vasopressin. The team hopes to identify how these hormone polymorphisms can be modified in order to limit their effect on alcohol craving.

This research team described the addiction-treatment situation aptly:

> Before the discovery of anti-craving drugs, the administration of disulfiram and surveillance by relatives and/or therapeutic groups, waiting for spontaneous craving exhaustion, were the only treatment strategies to control craving (Addolorato et al., 2005, p. 59).

In the final part of this chapter, I will examine specific addiction pharmacotherapies, with an emphasis on current anticraving medications. I will start with chemical addictions (e.g., alcohol), moving on to behavioral addictions (e.g., gambling). However, before examining specific medications, let's first address the professional counselor's role in addiction pharmacotherapy.

THE PROFESSIONAL COUNSELOR'S ROLE IN ADDICTION PHARMACOTHERAPY

While you may find the information presented thus far interesting and even important, you may be wondering what role you, as a professional counselor, have to play in addiction pharmacotherapy. The answer is: a critical role. The prescribing physician works on a 15-minute billing cycle and unfortunately has little time for patient education. Also, many clients feel intimidated by physicians and do not voice their questions or concerns. This situation is problematic, because client attitudes toward the pharmacotherapy they are receiving predicts treatment adherence (Pettinati et al., 2005). For example, the questionnaire item "Sometimes, the medical profession makes me feel uncomfortable" was predictive of attendance in an alcohol dependence pharmacotherapy study (Pettinati et al., 2003). Indeed, research has shown that psychological interventions aimed at pharmacotherapy adherence improve addiction treatment outcomes (Reid et al., 2005).

Professional counselors differ from prescribing physicians in having more contact with their clients and more in-depth knowledge and training on how to form a strong working alliance. Thus, the professional counselor is in a better position to address the knowledge and attitudinal barriers to client-treatment adherence.

Addiction clients often balk at a physician's recommendation of pharmacotherapy. In a study of the mental illness treatment preferences of the lay public, less than 15% chose pharmacotherapy as the first treatment option (Riedel-Heller, Matschinger, & Angermeyer, 2005). Prominent reasons for psychiatric medication noncompliance include sexual dysfunction (Kennedy et al., 2006), weight gain (Kalinichev et al., 2005), and medication interfering with personal strategies for treatment (Deegan, 2005).

There has been some fear that the total abstinence philosophy of Alcoholics Anonymous may lead to noncompliance with addiction pharmacotherapy. However, in a study comparing AA participants and nonparticipants, no difference was found in attitudes toward the use of medication to treat alcoholism. Overall, 15% agreed it was all right, 29% disagreed that it was all right, and 56% stated that they did not know (Tonigan & Kelly, 2006). Interestingly, a large study of addictions counselors found that those clinicians who held a 12-step treatment philosophy were significantly less likely to support a pharmacotherapy intervention even when they had been provided evidence as to pharmacotherapy's effectiveness (Knudsen, Ducharme, Roman, & Link, 2005). At this point, the impact of counselor treatment prejudices on client noncompliance with addiction pharmacotherapy is unknown.

What can a clinician do to promote medication compliance in their clients? Weiden and Rao (2005) gave the following sage advice: (1) ask for—and listen to—the client's beliefs and attitudes about the prescribed medication, (2) work to understand the client's perspective rather than trying to contradict or correct this perspective, (3) understand that it is the client's subjective beliefs, rather than objective medical, reality that influences client compliance, (4) withhold responding until the client has discussed all major arguments for and against a medication, and (5) ground any discussion of compliance concerns within the client's point of view.

I would like to end with one recommendation in terms of client knowledge barriers to pharmacotherapy adherence. I think it is important for every professional counselor to have a psychopharmacological reference guide that they can pull out when the need for client education arises. Both Stahl (2008) and Preston et al. (2008) are clear and concise references and contain excellent suggestions for client education.

Now let's move on to specific addictions. First, we will examine the pharmacotherapies for addictions to chemicals such as nicotine, alcohol, cocaine, opiates, and methamphetamine. Second, we will review the pharmacotherapies for behavioral addictions (e.g., pathological gambling, Internet use, sex, exercise, and shopping).

SPECIFIC ADDICTION PHARMACOTHERAPIES

The Chemical Addictions

PHARMACOTHERAPY OF NICOTINE ADDICTION.   Addiction to nicotine is difficult to overcome. Roughly 90% of people who attempt to quit using nicotine relapse (National Institute of Drug Abuse, 2001). Fortunately, advances in pharmacotherapy have lowered this relapse rate. These advances include agonist substitution medications as well as antidepressants and anxiolytics. In this section I will examine the first- and second-line pharmacotherapies suggested by the U.S. Public Health Service (Fiore et al., 2000). I will then outline some promising experimental treatments.

First-Line: Nicotine Gum (Nicorette), Nicotine Nasal (Nicotrol) and Nicotine Oral Inhalation (Nicotrol), Nicotine Patch (Habitrol, Nicoderm), Nicotine Sublingual Tablets (Nicorette).   These medications belong to the agonist substitution class of pharmacotherapies. While it may seem counterintuitive, nicotine-based medication can be a useful tool for a client trying to overcome a nicotine addiction. The use of the nicotine-based medication noted above is called nicotine replacement therapy (NRT). The idea is that replacing the nicotine from cigarettes reduces withdrawal symptoms associated with smoking cessation, thus helping the client resist the urge to smoke (Silagy et al., 2001). In review of scientific literature on NRT from the respected and influential Cochrane Library, Stead et al. (2008) reported that,

> All of the commercially available forms of NRT (gum, transdermal patch, nasal spray, inhaler and sublingual tablets/lozenges) can help people who make a quit attempt to increase their chances of successfully stopping smoking. NRTs increase the rate of quitting by 50–70%, regardless of setting (p. 1).

In a major review, Kortmann et al. (2010) reported that the non-nicotine based medication bupropion presented quit rates similar to NRT. Thus, we now turn our attention to that medication.

PHARMACOTHERAPY CASE STUDY #1

Nicotine Dependence (DSM VI-TR 305.10) and Major Depressive Disorder—Moderate (DSM VI-TR 296.32)

Roger Peeters is a 37-year-old White male resident of Atlanta who emigrated from Belgium when he was 20 years old. He has been married for 12 years and has 2 sons aged 10 and 8. Roger works as the sales manager at a local Ford dealership.

In the last 6 months Roger has lost pleasure in activities he previously enjoyed. He quit his recreational indoor soccer team and no longer goes to watch his sons play soccer. Roger's sleep is fitful and in the last two months he has averaged missing one work day out of every five since he "didn't have it in him." Since his marriage Roger has maintained a weight of 150 lbs and a BMI of 21.5. However, in the last six months his weight has dropped to 120 lbs and his BMI to 17.2. Also, his pack a week smoking habit has increased to a pack a day. At his children's request Roger tried to quit smoking two months ago but found he needed nicotine for a "lift" to "keep going during the day." Also, he didn't like the cravings he felt when he tried to give up smoking. During the past week Roger missed three out of five days at work. On those days he felt he didn't even have enough energy to get out of bed.

Roger's wife has become increasingly concerned about her husband's behavior. When he couldn't get out of bed for work for three straight days she made an appointment for Roger with their family doctor. On the day of the appointment Roger's wife drove him to the doctor's office and attended the consultation between Roger and the doctor. The doctor inquired about changes in Roger's activity level, weight, and smoking. The doctor found Roger listless and unable to provide precise details on either activity level or smoking. Roger's score on the Beck Depression Inventory (BDI), filled out prior to the appointment, was 24 (Moderate Depression). When Roger's wife reported her perceptions on changes in Roger's activity level and smoking Roger appeared visibly surprised. It was at this point that Roger broke into tears and stated that he needed help. Roger's doctor gave him a dual diagnosis of Major Depression and Nicotine dependence. Given the presence of this dual diagnosis he prescribed bupropion (Wellbutrin, Zyban) rather than a nicotine replacement therapy or varenicline (Chantix). The doctor had Roger and his wife schedule an appointment for six weeks later to check on his progress. At the 6-week check-in Roger's score was 10 on the BDI (Minimal Depression). He reported greater energy and a perfect work attendance over the previous three weeks.

First-Line: Bupropion (Wellbutrin, Zyban). This medication belongs to the antidepressant class of pharmacotherapies. Bupropion is a weak inhibitor of DA and NA reuptake. A wide body of literature reports it to be effective in smoking cessation (Kortmann et al., 2010). Like many psycho-pharmacological treatment agents, it remains unclear exactly how bupropion promotes smoking cessation (Warner & Shoaib, 2005). There is emerging research to suggest that bupropion is an antagonist for nicotinic ACH receptors (nACH) and thus blocks nicotine's psychoactive and addictive effects (Kortmann et al., 2010). Interestingly, Cox et al. (2004) found that the antidepressant bupropion was equally effective in relapse prevention in smokers with or without comorbid depression.

Second-Line: Clonidine (Catapres). This medication belongs to the antihypertension class of pharmacotherapies. Clonidine is an alpha-2-receptor agonist. Though developed as a hypertensive medication, it has more recently been employed as an anxiolytic (Stahl, 2008). A recent study published by the Cochrane Library reported that clonidine was effective in reducing nicotine withdrawal and lowering the chance of relapse (Gourlay, Stead, & Benowitz, 2004). However, the reviewers went on to point out that this medication has a high side-effects profile that limits it use.

Second Line: Nortriptyline (Aventyl, Pamelor). This medication belongs to the antidepressant class of pharmacotherapies. It is one of the tricyclic antidepressants. Nortriptyline is an NA reuptake inhibitor (Stahl, 2008). There is no conclusive evidence on why such reuptake helps with nicotine dependence. However, there is some suggestion that NA serves as a functional nicotine receptor antagonist in the brain (Benowitz & Wilson-Peng, 2000). A major review of the literature on nortriptyline as a nicotine dependence pharmacotherapy reported this medication equal in effectiveness to that of both bupropion and NRT (Hughes, Stead, & Lancaster, 2005).

Second-Line: Varenicline (Chantix). This medication belongs to the agonist substitution class of pharmacotherapy. It is a partial agonist for ACH receptors that are activated by nicotine (i.e., nACH). In a review of 10 high-quality studies, Cahill, Stead, and Lancaster (2009) of the Cochrane Library's Tobacco Addiction Group reported that varenicline doubled the chances of recovery over placebo. In addition, they reported that (over both NRT and bupropion) varenicline improved chances of quitting by 50%.

Promising Pharmacotherapies: Immunotherapy (NicVax, NicQb, TA-Nic). In the area of addiction immunotherapy, nicotine vaccinations are furthest along in development (Kinsey, Jackson, & Orson, 2009). These vaccines have been successful in reducing the reinforcing action of nicotine (Henningfield at al., 2009). However, like all addiction immunotherapies, researchers have encountered wide variation in antibody production; thus, wide-scale applications of this approach remain elusive (Kinsey et al.).

PHARMACOTHERAPY OF ALCOHOL ADDICTION. The norepinephrine (NA), γ-aminobutyric acid (GABA), glutamate (GLU), opioid (OP), dopaminergic (DA), cholinergic (ACH), and serotonergic (5HT) systems all play a role in the neurochemical basis of alcohol dependence (Mann, 2004). As such, a wide variety of medications impacting these various systems have been developed to help conquer this addiction. In fact, in the last 50 years more than 150 medications have been used to treat various aspects of alcohol dependence (Schik et al., 2005). The rest of this section will examine the three main alcohol addiction pharmacotherapy subareas. These subareas are: (a) aversion treatment, (b) alcohol withdrawal treatment, and (c) anticraving treatment.

Aversion Treatment, First-Line: Disulfiram (Antabuse). This medication was the first pharmacotherapy available for alcohol addiction. Upon use of alcohol, this medication creates a very unpleasant intoxication with the goal of developing an aversion to alcohol (Mann, 2004). In the professional addiction literature the reports of disulfiram efficacy are mixed (Mann, 2004). The effectiveness of this medicine seems to be limited to three client groups: (1) adherent clients, (2) specific high-risk clients, and (3) clients with whom administration can be supervised (Garbutt, 2009).

Alcohol Withdrawal Treatment.   Alcohol Withdrawal Syndrome is a common event in addiction treatment (McKeon, Frye, & Delanty, 2008). This syndrome has been described as follows:

> Symptoms of alcohol withdrawal result from the lack of opposition to sympathetic nervous system activity in the brain once the central nervous system (CNS) depressant (alcohol) is stopped. Symptoms of uncomplicated withdrawal include tremor, tachycardia, increased blood pressure, increased body temperature, diaphoresis, insomnia, anxiety, and gastrointestinal upset. . . . Ten percent of alcoholics experience severe symptoms such as seizures and delirium tremens. In delirium tremens, or alcohol withdrawal delirium, the patient suffers from confusion, disorientation, illusions, and visual, tactile, and auditory hallucinations (Prince & Turpin, 2008, p. 1039).

Now let us turn to an examination of the treatments for Alcohol Withdrawal Syndrome.

First-Line: Diazepam (Valium) and the Other Longer Half-Life Benzodiazepines.   These medications belong to the anxiolytic class of pharmacotherapies. There is a long-standing history on the use of benzodiazepines to alleviate alcohol withdrawal. A Cochrane Library review on such use of benzodiazepines reported this type of medication effective against alcohol withdrawal symptoms when compared to placebo (Ntais, Pakos, Kyzas, & Ioannidis, 2005). The American Society of Addiction Medicine's (2003) practice guideline for alcohol withdrawal suggests the use of longer half-life (hl) benzodiazepines such as lorazepam (Ativan, 12-hour hl), diazepam (Valium, 20-hour hl), and chlordiazepoxide (Librium, 30-hour hl). While effective, benzodiazepines increase sedation, memory deficits, respiratory depression, and addiction (Leggio et al., 2008). Thus, the importance of non-benzodiazepine treatments for alcohol withdrawal such as baclofen, carbamazepine, and gabapentin.

PHARMACOTHERAPY CASE STUDY #2

Generalized Anxiety Disorder (DSM VI-TR 300.02), Alcohol Dependence (DSM VI-TR 305.00) and Sedative, Hypnotic, or Anxiolytic Dependence (DSM VI-TR 304.10)

Joe Washington is a single, 32-year-old multiracial (African-American & Haitian) resident of Los Altos, CA. He is Chief Financial Officer of an Internet startup company. Joe has suffered from anxiety as long as he can remember. About 2 years ago, he started to hear rumors of his company's demise. Also, his father was diagnosed with prostate cancer. Joe found that he could not shut his mind off from thinking about potential disasters in all parts of his life.

To cope with both his high state and trait anxiety, Joe started to drink heavily. His drinking led both to a breakup with his long-time partner and to chronic insomnia. About a year ago, he was arrested for a DUI while driving home from a party. Joe has always had a strong self-image as a law-abiding person, so his arrest disturbed him greatly. Thus, Joe went to see his family doctor for help with both his drinking and anxiety.

Joe's family physician, Dr. Smith, diagnosed Joe with both Generalized Anxiety Disorder (DSM VI-TR 300.02) and Alcohol Dependence (DSM VI-TR 305.00) and suggested a trial with an SSRI for anxiety and oxazepam (Serax) to manage any alcohol withdrawal symptoms. Joe declined use of an SSRI because he had heard about the potential sexual side-effects of this class of medication. As an alternative, Dr. Smith referred Joe to a local cognitive-behavioral (CBT) counselor skilled in working with alcoholism and anxiety comorbidity. Joe did quit drinking; however, he continued his use of oxazepam beyond the 5-day outpatient alcohol detoxification protocol Dr. Smith was following (see Prater, Miller, & Zylstra, 1999). He found it easy to obtain ample amounts of oxazepam from friends and co-workers who had been prescribed the medication for anxiety. Over the next six months, Joe's use of oxazepam steadily increased due to tolerance.

At Joe's annual physical, Dr. Smith ran a Drug and Alcohol Screen as part of Joe's blood work. This screen revealed Joe's oxazepam use. Dr. Smith confronted Joe about his continuing oxazepam use, at which point, Joe broke down and admitted this use, as well as having not gone to counseling. Dr. Smith agreed to help Joe get off oxazepam if he agreed to (1) go to counseling, and (2) sign release of information agreements so that Dr. Smith and the counselor could communicate. Joe readily agreed.

After listening to Joe, Dr. Smith diagnosed him with Sedative, Hypnotic, or Anxiolytic Dependence (DSM VI-TR 304.10). To ease the withdrawal symptoms while quitting, Dr. Smith opted for a slow withdrawal substitution strategy — specifically, substituting the long half-life benzodiazepine diazepam (Valium) for oxazepam, and slowly lowering the dosage over 14 weeks (see Ashton, 2002 for an example schedule). At a 14-week check-in Joe reported that he had quit the diazepam at Week 13 without a problem. Also during this time period, he completed a 10-session course of CBT. At discharge from counseling, Joe's score of 10 on the Hamilton Anxiety Scale was well below the cut-off point for GAD. In addition, he happily reported that his long-time partner had reentered his life.

Second-Line: Baclofen (Lioresal).   This medication belongs to the anticonvulsant class of pharmacotherapies. Baclofen is a GABA agonist. Baclofen monotherapy was able to suppress alcohol withdrawal symptoms (Leggio, 2009). In addition, baclofen lowered alcohol intake, alcohol craving, and anxiety (Addolorato et al., 2009).

Second-Line: Carbamazepine (Tegretol).   This medication belongs to the anticonvulsant class of pharmacotherapies. It works by both blocking voltage-sensitive sodium ion channels and inhibiting GLU release (Stahl, 2008). It has some advantages over the traditional use of benzodiazepine for alcohol withdrawal, including lack of (a) addictive potential, (b) interaction with alcohol, (c) a greater than benzodiazepine side effect profile, and (d) sedatory effects (Leggio, 2009; Schik et al., 2005). A recent study found that oxcarbazepine (Trileptal), a second-generation analogue of carbamazepine, was equally effective with alcohol withdrawal (Schik et al., 2005), and had the advantage of possessing some anticraving properties as well (Schik et al., 2005).

Anticraving Treatment: Overview.   There are two first-line treatments of alcohol craving—acamprosate and naltrexone. Building on the work of Verheul, it has been hypothesized that the "relief drinker/craver" is associated with glutamatergic dysfunction and responds to acamprosate while the "reward drinker/craver" is associated dopaminergic and opioidergic dysfunction and responds to naltrexone (Mann et al., 2009). Now let's examine these two first-line treatments in detail.

Anticraving Treatment:First-Line: Acamprosate (Campral).   This medication belongs to the anticraving class of pharmacotherapies. Acamprosate is a GLU antagonist. It eases the excitotoxicity caused by alcohol withdrawal (De Witte et al., 2005). In addition, this medication can lessen the glutametergically driven reinforcing properties of alcohol consumption (Olive, 2005). The purpose of this medication is to maintain abstinence from alcohol (Verheul et al., 2005).

Comprehensive reviews of high-quality studies found that acamprosate effectively maintained complete abstinence in detoxified alcohol-dependent clients (Kranzler & Gage, 2008; Ross & Peselow, 2009). I do need to note that a major U.S. government study did *not* find acamprosate efficacious in the treatment of alcohol dependence (Donovan et al., 2008). Given the overwhelming research in support of acamprosate's efficacy, it is plausible to conclude that this study's design may have influenced the outcomes (Garbutt, 2009; Kranzler & Gage, 2008).

Anticraving Treatment: First-Line: Naltrexone (ReVia, Depade).   This medication belongs to the anticraving class of pharmacotherapies. Garbutt (2009)describes it as follows:

> Naltrexone, by blocking endogenous opioids, reduces the rewarding properties of alcohol . . . thereby counteracting this important component of the behavioral response to alcohol. In fact, in the initial human studies of naltrexone for alcohol dependence, it was reported that patients who consumed alcohol and who were taking naltrexone were significantly less likely to experience their usual "high" or level of intoxication. . . . In addition, naltrexone has been reported to reduce alcohol craving in a number of clinical trials (p. S17).

There exists excellent evidence of naltrexone's efficacy with alcohol dependence (Donovan et al., 2008, Ross & Peselow, 2009). Interestingly, a recent study reported naltrexone's efficacy with Type A alcoholics but not Type B (Bogenschutz, Scott Tonigan, & Pettinati, 2009). In contrast to a Type B alcoholic, a Type A can be described as having: (a) later onset of disease, (b) fewer childhood risk factors, (c) less severe symptoms of substance abuse disorders, (d) fewer alcohol-related social and physical consequences, (e) less psychopathology, (f) less stress, and (g) less chance of prior treatment (Leggio et al., 2009). The reason for these differences is unclear.

Anticraving Treatment: Second-Line: Lamotrigine (Lamictal).   This medication belongs to the anticonvulsant class of pharmacotherapies. It works by both blocking voltage-sensitive sodium ion channels and inhibiting the release of excitatory neurotransmitters (e.g., Glutamente-GLU) (Stahl, 2008). How can lowering GLU levels reduce craving? Gass and Olive (2008) reported that,

> Pharmacological agents that attenuate glutamatergic signaling, either by receptor antagonism, release inhibition, or enhancement of cellular uptake, tend to reduce the reinforcing and rewarding effects of most drugs of abuse, and can also attenuate the reinstatement of drug-seeking behavior. . . . Given that glutamate transmission is one of the primary neurochemical substrates of synaptic plasticity, and the overwhelming evidence reviewed here that all drugs of abuse interact with glutamate transmission, it is not surprising that drugs of abuse can cause long-lasting neuroadaptions of glutamate systems in the brain. These adaptations somehow lead to compulsive drug use, loss of volitional control over drug intake, and hypersalience of drug-associated environmental cues or contexts, all of which are characteristic of addiction (p. 240).

This medication has also been found to ameliorate refractory bipolar depression (Lin, Mok, & Yatham, 2006) and unipolar depression (Gutierrez et al., 2005). Lamotrigine is efficacious in reducing alcohol consumption and craving in treating schizophrenic clients with alcohol dependence (a common comorbidity) (Kalyoncu et al., 2005). Given the efficacy of lamotrigine with different types of mental illnesses, this medication may be a useful tool in the treatment of alcohol/mental illness comorbidity.

PHARMACOTHERAPY OF COCAINE ADDICTION.   The leading theory on the etiology of cocaine addiction is the "dopamine hypothesis." National Institutes of Health (U.S.) researchers Prisinzano et al., (2004) clearly describe this hypothesis:

> Chronic exposure to cocaine causes excessive stimulation of dopamine neurons thereby producing long-term dopamine depletion in critical reward circuits in the brain. Such drug-induced deficits in dopamine transmission are presumed to underlie . . . the psychological manifestations of cocaine withdrawal, that contribute to relapse. . . . Thus, there is a strong rationale for restoration of "normal" dopamine function via therapeutic intervention. The "dopamine hypothesis" considers the ability of stimulants to increase extracellular DA as being of primary importance in mediating the addictive effects of stimulants (p. 48).

Another potential target for cocaine pharmacotherapy is the GABA system, given its ability to attenuate dopamine release and block cocaine-conditioned place preferences (Sofuoglu & Kosten, 2005). Finally, Uys and LaLumiere (2008) have posited a GLU model of cocaine addiction since glutamate receptor activation is necessary for reinstatement of cocaine seeking.

At present, there are no medications approved in the United States for the treatment of cocaine addiction (Prisinzano et al., 2004). In this section, I will describe medications that work through the DA, GLU, and GABA systems, and finally, take a look at a promising immunotherapy.

Promising Pharmacotherapies: Disulfiram (Antabuse).   This medication is used for the treatment of alcohol addiction by creating an unpleasant intoxication with the goal of developing an aversion to this substance (Mann, 2004). Its mechanism in treating cocaine dependence is quite different. Disulfiram use leads to increased DA levels (Sofuoglu & Kosten, 2005). As such, the medication serves an agonist substitution pharmacotherapy with cocaine addiction (Sofuoglu & Kosten, 2005). In a recent high-quality study, Carroll et al. (2004) found that participants assigned to disulfiram treatment reduced their cocaine use significantly more than those assigned to the placebo condition. Clearly, disulfiram represents an exciting potential pharmacotherapy for this difficult addiction.

Promising Pharmacotherapies: Topiramate (Topamax).   This medication belongs to the anticonvulsant class of pharmacotherapies. It works by blocking voltage-sensitive sodium ion channels, inhibiting the release of GLU, and promoting the release of GABA (Stahl, 2008). Small but high-quality studies have shown that topiramate-treated subjects were more likely to be abstinent from cocaine compared to placebo-treated subjects (Kampman et al., 2004; Uys and LaLumiere, 2008).

Promising Pharmacotherapies: Lamotrigine (Lamictal).   This medication belongs to the anticonvulsant class of pharmacotherapies. It works by both blocking voltage-sensitive sodium ion channels and inhibiting the release of excitatory neurotransmitters (e.g., Glutamente-GLU) (Stahl, 2008). Lamotrigine is efficacious in reducing cocaine consumption in bipolar spectrum clients (a common comorbidity) (Uys & LaLumiere 2008).

Promising Pharmacotherapies: Tiagabine (Gabitril).   This medication belongs to the anticonvulsant class of pharmacotherapies. Tiagabine inhibits the reuptake of GABA (Dodds, 2003). In a recent experiment on humans, tiagabine pharmacology attenuated subjective ratings of "stimulated" and "crave cocaine" in response to cocaine administration (Sofuoglu et al., 2005). In a high-quality study of tiagabine pharmacotherapy for cocaine addiction, the researcher found: (1) cocaine-free urine increased significantly from baseline by 33% with high-dose tiagabine, by 14% with low-dose tiagabine, and by 10% with placebo; and (2) self-reported cocaine use also decreased significantly more with tiagabine than with placebo (Gonzalez et al., 2003).

Promising Pharmacotherapies: Immunotherapy (TA-CD). Cocaine addiction is another area in which immunotherapy is being studied. Human trials have found immunotherapy substantially decreased cocaine's intoxicating effects in those generating sufficient antibodies (Haney et al., 2010). However, like immunotherapy with other addictions, the large variability of antibodies produced by the vaccines remains a barrier to wide, efficacious clinical use (Haney et al.).

PHARMACOTHERAPY OF OPIATE ADDICTION. Successful pharmacotherapy in this area started with the opioid agonist substitute methadone in the 1960s (Ashworth, 2005). Since that time, a dizzying variety of medications from divergent classes have been tried. To date, only agonist substitutes have been found consistently efficacious. In this section, we will review the three most commonly used.

First-Line: Methadone (Dolophine). This medication belongs to the agonist substitution class of pharmacotherapies. It is a full OP agonist (Dodds, 2003). Treatment with methadone for opioid dependence is currently considered "best practice" (Craig & Olson, 2004). In a Cochrane Library review on methadone, Mattick, Breen, Kimber, and Davoli (2003) concluded that this treatment was an effective intervention for opioid dependence as it retains clients in treatment and decreases use better than treatments that do not utilize opioid agonist pharmacotherapy. While efficacious, the use of an opiate to fight opioid dependence is not without controversy. In the United States, six states do not allow this treatment (McCance-Katz, 2004). Because of the risk of illegal diversion, this medication can only be administered through controversial specialty clinics (McCance-Katz, 2004). Thus, methadone treatment has been "both a life-saving and stigmatizing experience for many opioid-addicted patients" (McCance-Katz, 2004, p. 323).

PHARMACOTHERAPY CASE STUDY #3

Opioid Dependence (DSM VI-TR 304.00) in a Pregnant Patient (ICD-9-CM 646.80)

Dr. Donna Jones is an obstetrician in private practice in Spokane, WA. Last December 12th she was the on-call obstetrician at Deaconess Medical Center in the same city. At 3 A.M., she was called to Deaconess' emergency room. The ER doctor on staff had given a pregnancy test to Ana Garcia, a 22-year-old third-generation Mexican-American patient complaining of intense abdominal pain. Much to Ana's surprise, the pregnancy test came back positive. When Dr. Jones arrived at the ER she met Ana and engaged in *plática* (a chat) to put Ana at ease and build rapport. Dr. Jones then took a complete medical history and learned that Ana is currently on a methadone (Dolophine) treatment regimen of 105 mg/d for heroin addiction. Dr. Jones reviewed with her the results of an ultrasound test that revealed she was 27 weeks pregnant. Ana reported being shocked by this news and stated she wanted immediately to stop taking methadone to prevent hurting her baby.

Dr. Jones commended Ana for her desire for a healthy baby, but cautioned her not to stop her methadone because abrupt discontinuation of this drug has been known to cause fetal demise. Dr. Jones then told Ana that she was sending her upstairs to the Labor and Delivery unit for blood work and fetal monitoring to rule out premature labor as the cause for her abdominal pain. Later that morning Dr. Jones was happy to report that the tests and monitoring ruled out premature labor. Dr. Jones told Ana that with her permission, she would like to call the Spokane Methadone Clinic and advise them that Ana was pregnant and that they should gradually decrease (5 mg every 6 days) to 80 mg/d as long as drug cravings don't come back. Dr. Jones also advised Ana that upon delivery, her baby would be taken to the Neonatology Unit for close monitoring for opioid withdrawal symptoms. Ana's eyes filled with tears, and Dr. Jones asked what was wrong. Ana reported that her mother was a member of the La Leche League and would be very disappointed that Ana couldn't breastfeed her baby. Dr. Jones encouraged Ana to breastfeed her baby noting that the small amount of methadone in the breast milk was not harmful and could actually ease her baby's withdrawal symptoms.

Ana made it to full term and gave birth to a 6 pound 4 ounce baby girl named Maria. Maria spent two weeks in the Neonatology Unit to detox from methadone. She was given a diluted tincture of opium and oral clonidine (Catapres) for 12 days before symptoms abated. At the four week post-delivery follow-up appointment, Dr. Jones encountered a healthy Maria and an Ana who was still successfully adhering to her methadone treatment.

First-Line: Buprenorphine (Temgesic, Suboxone).   This medication belongs to the agonist substitution class of pharmacotherapies. It works as a partial agonist at the mu (μ) type of OP receptor (Elkader & Sproule, 2005). McCance-Katz (2004) noted that buprenorphine's property as a partial agonist

> . . . contributes to its utility in the treatment of opioid dependence in that buprenorphine is effective in preventing the onset of the opioid-abstinence syndrome in opioid-dependent individuals, while with escalating doses, buprenorphine produces less effect than full mu agonists and exhibits a "ceiling" effect—at which further dose increases produce no additional effects (p. 322).

A Cochrane Library review of the efficacy of buprenorphine versus methadone reported that there appears to be no significant difference between the two in terms of completion of treatment, but that withdrawal symptoms may resolve more quickly with buprenorphine (Gowing, Ali, & White, 2004). In contrast to methadone, buprenorphine can also be provided by means of office-based treatment. This treatment is more flexible, accessible, and comprehensive than the specialty-clinic-based methadone treatment (McCance-Katz, 2004). One reason buprenorphine can be provided through office-based treatment is that it is most often provided in a form that also contains the full OP agonist naloxone. This combination (*n.b.*: the brand name is Suboxone) prevents the diversion of buprenorphine for illicit injection drug use (McCance-Katz, 2004).

Second-Line: Morphine: Slow Release Oral (Compensan, Vendal, Kapanol).   This medication belongs to the agonist substitution class of pharmacotherapies. Kraigher et al. (2005) reported on their study of the European practice of using slow-release oral morphine (SROM) as an agonist substitution intervention for opioid dependence. They found the use of SROM resulted in significant decreases in both somatic complaints and opioid cravings. They also noted the 94% retention rate, which is high when compared to the reported retention rates for buprenorphine and methadone. Kraigher et al. (2005) reported that their results matched the findings of another recent study. The authors of that study reported finding that:

> Compared to methadone, SROM was associated with improved social functioning, weight loss, fewer and less troublesome side-effects, greater drug liking, reduced heroin craving, an enhanced sense of feeling "normal" and similar outcomes for unsanctioned drug use, depression and health. The majority of subjects preferred SROM (78%) over methadone (22%) (Mitchell et al., 2004, p. 940).

Given the benefits of this pharmacotherapy, it represents a good alternative for opioid addicts intolerant to methadone or with inadequate withdrawal suppression (Kastelic, Dubajic, & Strbad, 2008).

Promising Pharmacotherapies: Naltrexone (ReVia, Depade).   This medication belongs to the anticraving class of pharmacotherapies. It is an OP antagonist and thus would block the reinforcing effects of any opioid drug. Ross and Peselow (2009) reported mixed evidence on the efficacy of naltrexone with opioid addictions. The two noted that nalrexone efficacy issues may be related to (a) client preference for opiate maintenance approaches, and/or (b) client treatment adherence issues. Reece (2007) reported greater success treating cocaine addiction using a naltrexone implant program: "88% of the Perth implant patients and 78% of the USA implant patients were opiate free at 12 months" (p. 35).

Promising Pharmacotherapies: Immunotherapy (M-TT).   Given the cultural and economic barriers to methadone treatment present in most of the world, the development of a vaccine for this addiction would make a huge contribution to public health (Kinsey et al., 2009). This vaccine has been shown to produce antibodies that can block the reinforcing effects of opioids in animals (Anton & Leff, 2006). As of yet, human clinical trials have not begun (Kinsey et al., 2009).

PHARMACOTHERAPY OF METHAMPHETAMINE ADDICTION.   Methamphetamine (METH) pharmacotherapy is in its infancy. The GABA, glutamate (GLU), cannabinoid (CBD), noradrenergic (NA), serotonergic (5HT), and dopaminergic (DA) systems all appear involved with this addiction. In the rest of this section, we will examine some pharmacotherapy approaches currently being examined. Unless stated otherwise, all findings reported in this section were based on studies using rodents as research subjects.

Promising Pharmacotherapy: Fluoxetine (Prozac).   Fluoxetine is a selective serotonin reuptake inhibitor (SSRI). A study involving pretreatment with Fluoxetine showed that it had inhibitory effects on Meth-induced locomotor sensitization and abolished Meth-conditioned place preference (Takamatsu et al., 2006).

Promising Pharmacotherapy: Bupropion (Wellbutrin, Zyban).   This medication belongs to the antidepressant class of pharmacotherapies. Bupropion is a weak inhibitor of DA and NA reuptake. In a study using human subjects, Newton et al. (2006) reported that bupropion reduced Meth craving.

Promising Pharmacotherapy: Valproate (Depakote).   Meth can increase GLU. Such an increase is problematic since glutamate can prime drug-seeking behavior (Sun et al., 2005). Given this priming, a research team recently conducted experiments using valproate as a means to inhibit GLU increase and its consequent drug sensitization. valproate appears to inhibit Meth-induced behavioral sensitization via involvement of GABAergic system (modulating DA and GLU activity) (Coccurello et al., 2007).

Promising Pharmacotherapy: Naltrexone (ReVia, Depade).   This medication belongs to the anticraving class of pharmacotherapies. Naltrexone is an OP receptor antagonist. Anggadiredja, Sakimura et al. (2004) reported finding that Naltrexone administered before re-exposure to Meth-associated cues attenuated reinstatement of drug-seeking behavior.

Promising Pharmacotherapy: Diclofenac (Voltaren).   Diclofenac is a cyclooxygenase (COX) inhibitor. A recent study found this medication significantly attenuated the reinstatement of Meth-seeking behavior (Anggadiredja, Nakamichi et al., 2004).

Promising Pharmacotherapy: Rimonabant (Acomplia, Zimulti).   This medication is a CBD receptor antagonist (Anggadiredja, Nakamichi et al., 2004). Rimonabant has been shown to attenuate Meth-seeking behavior (Fattore et al., 2007).

Promising Pharmacotherapies: Lobeline.   Lobeline is a nACH partial agonist. It appears to reduce Meth use by reducing by Meth-evoked endogenous DA release (Rahman et al., 2008).

Promising Pharmacotherapies: Immunotherapy.   Kosten and Owens (2005) reviewed the use of antimethamphetamine antibodies to treat methamphetamine addiction. They reported that results in both rat and pigeon studies suggest immunotherapy could lead to quicker reductions in drug use. In their comprehensive review of Meth immunotherapy Ivy, et al. (2009) report,

> Preclinical studies in rats show that systemic administration of anti-(+)-Meth mono-clonal antibodies (mAbs) can rapidly remove the drug from its sites of action in critical tissues like the brain and heart, suggesting that immunotherapy could provide an important new medical strategy for addressing (+)-Meth-induced adverse health effects in humans (p. 7301).

As of yet, human clinical trials have not begun (Kinsey et al., 2009).

SUPPLEMENTAL SECTION: ALTERNATIVE MEDICINE.   In additional to the medications discussed above, herbal medications, drawn from around the world are being investigated for use with chemical addictions. These medications are used for aversion, anticraving and withdrawal treatments (Lin et al., 2008; Lu et al., 2009; Mačiulaitis et al., 2008; Ross & Peselow, 2009; Shi et al., 2006). See Table 11.1 for the medications being investigated, and for which addictions.

TABLE 11.1 Addiction and Herbal Medications

Addiction/Herb	Nicotine	Alcohol	Cocaine	Opioid	Metham-phetamine
Asian Ginseng		C	C	C	C
American Ginseng				C	R
Kava	C				
Tabernanthe Iboga	A	A	C	A	A
Voacanga Africana			A	A	A
Kudzu		C			
Ashwagandha				C	
Acanthaceae		C			
Red Sage		C			
Ayahuasca		A			
Corydolis Yanhusou		C		C	
Tai-Kang-Ning				C	
Fuzi				C	
Yang Jinhua				C	
Shen Fu				C	

C = Some Pre-Clinical or Clinical Study Evidence

A = Predominately Anecdotal Evidence

Source: Lin et al., 2008; Lu et al., 2009; Mačiulaitis et al., 2008; Ross & Peselow, 2009; Shi et al., 2006.

PHARMACOTHERAPY OF BEHAVIORAL ADDICTIONS.   Addiction is not limited to chemicals. Behaviors such as gambling, eating, shopping, and sex can be addictive. Like chemical addictions, these addictions track the following maladaptive pattern: (a) continued engagement in a behavior despite negative consequences, (b) diminished self-control over engagement in the behavior, (c) compulsive engagement in the behavior, and (d) an appetitive urge or craving state prior to the engagement in the behavior (Potenza, 2008). There is evidence that the same neurotransmitter deregulations involved in the etiology of chemical addictions are involved within the etiology of behavioral addictions (Brewer & Potenza, 2008). The pharmacotherapy of behavioral addictions is in its infancy. In this subsection I will discuss a few of the most promising pharmacotherapies.

Promising Pharmacotherapy: Naltrexone (ReVia, Depade).   This medication belongs to the anticraving class of pharmacotherapies. Naltrexone is an OP receptor antagonist. There is excellent evidence of this medication's efficacy with pathological gambling, especially with clients who have a positive family history of alcoholism (Grant et al. 2008).

Promising Pharmacotherapy: Lithium (Eskalith).   This medication belongs to the mood stabilizer (i.e., anti-manic) class of pharmacotherapies. How it works is unknown (Stahl, 2008). It has been found effective with clients with pathological gambling and bipolar spectrum disorder comorbidity (Petry, 2009).

Second-Line: Nalmefene (Revex).   This medication belongs to the anticraving class of pharmacotherapies. Naltrexone is an OP receptor antagonist. There is excellent evidence of this medication's efficacy with pathological gambling, especially with clients who have a positive family history of alcoholism (Grant et al. 2008).

Promising Pharmacotherapies: Topiramate (Topamax).   This medication belongs to the anticonvulsant class of pharmacotherapies. It works by both blocking voltage-sensitive sodium ion channels and inhibiting the release of GLU and promoting the release of GABA (Stahl, 2008). McElroy et al. (2009) reported on a number of controlled studies where topiramate was effective in treating various eating addictions. Toporamate may work with this addiction by (a) decreasing appetite, (b) enhancing satiety, and/or (c) reducing forms of eating motivated by the rewarding or hedonic properties of food (McElroy et al.).

Promising Pharmacotherapies: Fluvoxamine (Luvox).   This medication belongs to the antidepressant class of pharmacotherapies. It works by blocking the reuptake of 5HT (Stahl, 2008). There exist a number of case reports and small studies that suggest this medication is effective with shopping addiction (Marcinko, Bolanca, & Rudan, 2006). The exact mechanisms of fluvoxamine's effectiveness with this disorder are unclear.

GLOSSARY OF PHARMACOTHERAPY TERMS

Acetylcholine   A neurotransmitter. In this chapter it will be referred to by the abbreviation: ACH. *Nota bene*: the adjective form is "cholinergic." There are two types of ACH receptors. The ones that respond to nicotine are known as nicotinic acetylcholine receptors (nACH).

Agonist Substitution Pharmacotherapy   The administration of a medication pharmacologically related to the one producing dependence. Agents suitable for this pharmacotherapy are those that have the capacity to prevent the emergence of withdrawal symptoms and reduce craving. In general, it is desirable for substitution medicines to have a longer duration of action than the drug they are replacing, so as to delay the emergence of withdrawal symptoms and reduce the frequency of administration. This results in less disruption of normal life activities by the need to obtain the abused substance. Equivalent terms: substitution therapy, agonist pharmacotherapy, agonist replacement therapy, substitution maintenance therapy, and agonist-assisted therapy (World Health Organization, 2004).

Alpha 2 Receptor   A receptor located on the NA presynaptic terminal that, when stimulated, inhibits the release of NA (Shiloh, Nutt, & Weizman, 2005).

Anticonvulsants   A class of medication used to treat seizures (Stahl, 2008).

Anxiolytics   A class of medication used to treat anxiety (Ingersoll & Rak, 2006).

Axon   Long nerve cell fibers that conduct electrical impulses. Axons contact other nerve, muscle, and gland cells at synapses and release neurotransmitters that influence those cells (National Institute of Neurological Disorders and Stroke, 2007).

Behavioral Addiction   An addiction to behaviors such as gambling, Internet use, sex, exercise, and shopping (Grant, 2008).

Behavioral Sensitization   A neuroadaptation (resulting from repeated exposure to an addictive drug) that leads to a progressive increase of behavioral responses to that drug (Faria et al., 2008). Put another way, an addictive drug usurps the normal learning mechanisms and thereby "cements" behavioral responses related to drug-seeking behavior; this can progress to a form of habit-based learning so strong that it persists even in the face of tremendous adverse personal consequences (Wolf, 2002).

Brand Name   Medicines may have one or more brand names. These names are chosen by the company that make them. Several companies may make the same medicine, each with its own brand name (Patient UK, 2006). In this chapter the generic name will be used first, followed in parentheses by the most common brand names.

Cannabinoids   Both (1) the bioactive constituents of the marijuana plant, and (2) endogenous lipids with cannabinoid-like activity (Begg et al., 2005). In this chapter cannabinoids will be referred to by the abbreviation: CB.

Chemical Addiction   An addiction to various chemicals such as alcohol (Grant, 2008).

Cyclooxygenase (COX)   An enzyme that is part of the inflammatory pathway (Silasi & Kolb, 2007).

Dendrites   The treelike branches from nerve cell bodies that receive signals from other nerve cells at synapses (National Institute of Neurological Disorders and Stroke, 2007).

Dopamine   A neurotransmitter. In this chapter it will be referred to by its common abbreviation, DA. *Nota bene*: the adjective form is "dopaminergic."

Downregulation   A decrease in the number of receptors, making the cells less sensitive to a drug (Ingersoll & Rak, 2006).

Endogenous   A term meaning "produced by the body."

Ethnic Psychopharmacology   The study of differences in drug response and disposition among ethnic groups (Mendoza et al., 1991).

Excitotoxicity   Neuronal damage as the result of excessive glutamate exposure (De Witte et al., 2005).

First-Line Agent   A proven medication typically given first to a patient.

GABA (γ-aminobutyric acid)   A neurotransmitter. In this chapter it will be referred to by the abbreviation, GABA. *Nota bene*: the adjective form is "GABAergic."

Generic Name   Each medicine has an approved name called the generic name (Patient UK, 2006). In this chapter the generic name will be used first, followed by the most common brand names in parentheses.

Glutamate   A neurotransmitter. In this chapter it will be referred to by the abbreviation, GLU. *Nota bene*: the adjective form is "glutametergic."

Half-Life   The time for the plasma level of a drug to fall by 50% (Julien, 2007). In this chapter it will be referred to by the abbreviation "hl."

Hormones   Extracellular signaling molecules secreted by specialized cells that are released into the blood to exert specific biochemical actions on target cells located at distant sites (Chedrese, 2009).

Immunotherapy   The use of drug antibodies to prevent drugs of abuse from entering the central nervous system. How does immunotherapy work? The leading expert in addiction immunotherapy describes this therapy as follows: "Drugs of abuse are small molecules that can readily cross the blood brain barrier, while antibodies are larger molecules that cannot get into the brain" (Kosten, 2005, p. 177). Thus, he notes that any drug bound to an antibody also cannot cross the blood–brain barrier and cannot enter the brain. The primary uses in addiction treatment are (1) overdose treatment, and (2) relapse prevention (Kosten & Owens, 2005).

Ion Channels   Ion channels are membrane proteins that form a pore to allow the passage of specific ions. The opening and closing of ion channels are controlled by various means, including voltage (Jentsch, Hübner, & Fuhrmann, 2004).

Monotherapy and Polytherapy   Monotherapy is the use of one medication in treatment. Polytherapy is the use of multiple medications in treatment.

Neuron   A type of cell that is the basic component of the central nervous system (Julien, 2007). *Nota bene*: the adjective form is "neuronal."

Nicotinic   A type of cholinergic receptor activated by the drug nicotine (Hiranita, et al., 2004).

N Methyl D Aspartate (NMDA)   One type of glutamate receptor. Antagonists to this type of receptor include the drugs of abuse ketamine and phencyclidine (PCP).

Norepinephrine   A neurotransmitter. In this chapter it will be referred to by the abbreviation, NA. *Nota bene*: the adjective form is "noradrenergic."

Opioid   Any agent that binds to opioid receptors. These agents include natural and synthetic narcotics as well as endogenous opioid peptides (National Institute of Drug Abuse, 2000). In this chapter it will be referred to by the abbreviation, OP. *Nota bene*: the adjective form is "opioidergic."

Partial Agonist   An agonist that produces a submaximal response as well as antagonizing full (i.e., system maximal) agonists (Nature, 2009).

Pharmacodynamics   A drug's impact on the body (Preston et al., 2008).

Pharmacokinetics   The body's impact upon a drug (Preston et al., 2008).

Second-Line Agent   A proven medication typically given to a patient when a first-line agent: (1) doesn't work, (2) has too many side-effects, or (3) stops working.

Sensitization   The repeated exposure to psychostimulants that results in increased behavioral responses to the same dose of drug (Torres-Reverón & Dow-Edwards, 2005). Cross-sensitization to other drugs is possible.

Serotonin   A neurotransmitter. In this chapter it will be referred to by the abbreviation, 5HT (Shiloh et al., 2006). *Nota bene*: the adjective form is "serotonergic."

Upregulation   An increase in the number of receptors making the cells more sensitive to a drug (Ingersoll & Rak, 2006).

Summary and Some Final Notations

In this chapter we first examined the scientific foundations of addiction pharmacotherapy. Next we explored the emerging biological theory of craving. Then we discussed the professional counselor's role in addiction pharmacotherapy. Finally, the specific addiction pharmacotherapies for both chemical and behavioral addictions were detailed.

Useful Web Sites

The following Web sites provide additional information relating to the chapter topics:

American College of Neuropsychopharmacology
www.acnp.org

American Association for the Treatment of Opioid Dependence
www.aatod.org

Society for Neuroscience
www.sfn.org

References

Addolorato, G., Abenavoli, L., Leggio, L., & Gasbarrini, G. (2005). How many cravings? Pharmacological aspects of craving treatment in alcohol addiction: A review. *Neuropsychobiology, 51,* 59–66.

Addolorato, G., Leggio, L., Hillemacher, T., Kraus, T., Jerlhag, E., & Bleich, S. (2009). Hormones and drinking behaviour: New findings on ghrelin, insulin, leptin and volume-regulating hormones. An ESBRA Symposium report. *Drug and Alcohol Review, 28,* 160–165.

American Society of Addiction Medicine. (2003). *Pharmacological management of alcohol withdrawal: A meta-analysis and evidence-based practice guideline.* Chevy Chase, MD: Author.

Anggadiredja, K., Nakamichi, M., Hiranita, T., Tanaka, H., Shoyama, Y., Watanabe, S., et al. (2004). Endocannabinoid system modulates relapse to methamphetamine seeking: Possible mediation by the arachidonic acid cascade. *Neuropsychopharmacology, 29,* 1470–1478.

Anggadiredja, K., Sakimura, K., Hiranita, T., & Yamamoto, T. (2004). Naltrexone attenuates cue- but not drug-induced methamphetamine seeking: A possible mechanism for the dissociation of primary and secondary reward. *Brain Research, 1021,* 272–276.

Anton, B., & Leff, P. (2006). A novel bivalent morphine/heroin vaccine that prevents relapse to heroin addiction in rodents. *Vaccine, 24,* 3232–3240.

Anton, R. F. (2000). Obsessive-compulsive aspects of craving: Development of the Obsessive Compulsive Drinking Scale. *Addiction, 95* (Suppl 2), S211–S217.

Ashton, H. (2002). *Benzodiazepines: How they work and how to withdraw.* Newcastle upon Tyne, UK: The Royal Victoria Infirmary.

Ashworth, O. (2005). Methadone maintenance treatment as an effective harm minimisation intervention. *Mental Health Practice, 8,* 24–27.

Begg, M., Pacher, P., Batkai. S., Osei-Hyiaman, D., Offertaler, L., Mo, F. M., et al. (2005). Evidence for novel cannabinoid receptors. *Pharmacological Therapeutics, 106,* 133–145.

Benowitz, N. L., & Wilson-Peng, M. (2000). Non-nicotine pharmacotherapy for smoking cessation: Mechanisms and prospects. *CNS Drugs, 13,* 265–285.

Bogenschutz, M., Scott Tonigan, J., & Pettinati, H. (2009). Effects of Alcoholism Typology on response to naltrexone in the COMBINE Study. *Alcoholism: Clinical & Experimental Research, 33,* 10–18.

Brewer, J. A., & Potenza, M. N. (2008). The neurobiology and genetics of impulse control disorders: Relationships to drug addictions. *Biochemical Pharmacology, 75,* 63–75.

Cahill, K., Stead, L., & Lancaster, T. (2009). A preliminary benefit-risk assessment of varenicline in smoking cessation. *Drug Safety: An International Journal of Medical Toxicology and Drug Experience, 32,* 119–135.

Campinha-Bacote, J. (2007). Becoming culturally competent in ethnic psychopharmacology. *Journal of Psychosocial Nursing and Mental Health Services, 45,* 27–33.

Carroll, K. M., Fenton, L. R., Ball, S. A., Nich, C., Frankforter, T. L., Shi, J., et al. (2004). Efficacy of disulfiram and cognitive behavior therapy in cocaine-dependent outpatients: A randomized placebo-controlled trial. *Archives of General Psychiatry, 61,* 264–272.

Chaudhry, C., Neelam, K., Duddu, V., & Husain, N. (2008). Ethnicity and psychopharmacology. *Journal of Psychopharmacology, 22,* 673–681.

Chedrese, P. J. (2009). *Reproductive endocrinology: A molecular approach.* NY: Springer.

Chia-Hui, C., Chun-Yu, C., & Keh-Ming, L. (2008). Ethnopsychopharmacology. *International Review of Psychiatry, 20,* 452–459.

Coccurello, R., Caprioli, A., Ghirardi, O., & Virmani, A. (2007). Valproate and acetyl-L-carnitine prevent methamphetamine-induced behavioral sensitization in mice. Annals of *The New York Academy of Sciences, 1122,* 260–275.

Cox, L. S., Patten, C. A., Niaura, R. S., Decker, P. A., Rigotti, N., Sachs, D. P. L., et al. (2004). Efficacy of bupropion for relapse prevention in smokers with and without a past history of major depression. *JGIM: Journal of General Internal Medicine, 19,* 828–834.

Craig, R. J., & Olson, R. E. (2004). Predicting methadone maintenance treatment outcomes using the addiction severity index and the MMPI-2 Content Scales (Negative Treatment Indicators and Cynism Scales). *The American Journal of Drug and Alcohol Abuse, 30,* 823–839.

Deegan, P. E. (2005). The importance of personal medicine: A qualitative study of resilience in people with psychiatric disabilities. *Scandinavian Journal of Public Health, 66,* 29–35.

De Witte, P., Littleton, J., Parot, P., & Koob, G. (2005). Neuroprotective and abstinence-promoting effects of acamprosate: Elucidating the mechanism of action. *CNS Drugs, 19,* 517–537.

Dodds, K. (2003). *Nurse's handbook of behavioral and mental health drugs.* San Francisco: Blanchard & Loeb.

Donovan, D., Anton, R., Miller, W., Longabaugh, R., Hosking, J., & Youngblood, M. (2008). Combined Pharmacotherapies and Behavioral Interventions for Alcohol Dependence (The COMBINE Study): Examination of Posttreatment Drinking Outcomes. *Journal of Studies on Alcohol & Drugs, 69,* 5–13.

Elkader, A., & Sproule, B. (2005). Buprenorphine: Clinical pharmacokinetics in the treatment of opioid dependence. *Clinical Pharmacokinetics, 44,* 661–680.

Fattore, L., Spano, M. S., Deiana, S., Melis, V., Cossu, G., Fadda, P., et al. (2007). An endocannabinoid mechanism in relapse to drug seeking: A review of animal studies and clinical perspectives. *Brain Research Reviews, 53,* 1–16.

Faria, R., Lima Rueda, A., Sayuri, C., Soares, S., Malta, M., Carrara-Nascimento, P., et al. (2008). Environmental modulation of ethanol-induced locomotor activity: Correlation with neuronal activity in distinct brain regions of adolescent and adult Swiss mice. *Brain Research, 1239,* 127–140.

Fiore, M. C., Bailey, W. C., Cohen, S. J., Dorman, S. F., Goldstein, M. G., Gritz, E. R., et al. (2000). *Treating tobacco use and dependence. Clinical practice guideline.* Rockville, MD: U.S. Department of Health and Human Services, Public Health Service.

Garbutt, J. (2009). The state of pharmacotherapy for the treatment of alcohol dependence. *Journal of Substance Abuse Treatment, 36,* S15–S23.

Gass, J., & Olive, M. (2008). Glutamatergic substrates of drug addiction and alcoholism. *Biochemical Pharmacology, 75,* 218–265.

Gonzalez, G., Sevarino, K., Sofuoglu, M., Poling, J., Oliveto, A., Gonsai, K., et al. (2003). Tiagabine increases cocaine-free urines in cocaine-dependent methadone-treated patients: Results of a randomized pilot study. *Addiction, 98,* 1625–1632.

Goodman, C., Ahn, R., Harwood, R., Ringel, D., Savage, K., Mendelson, D., et al. (1997). *Market barriers to the development of pharmacotherapies for the treatment of cocaine abuse and addiction: Final report.* Washington, DC: Department of Health and Human Services.

Goodman, A. (2008). Neurobiology of addiction: An integrative review. *Biochemical Pharmacology, 75,* 266–322.

Gourlay, S. G., Stead, L. F., & Benowitz, N. L. (2004). Clonidine for smoking cessation. *The Cochrane Database of Systematic Reviews, 3,* Art. No.: CD000058.

Gowing, L., Ali, R., & White, J. (2004). Buprenorphine for the management of opioid withdrawal. *The Cochrane Database of Systematic Reviews, 4.* Art. No.: CD002025.

Grant, J. (2008). *Impulse Control Disorders: A clinician's guide to understanding and treating behavioral addictions.* NY: W. W. Norton.

Grant, J., Kim, S., Hollander, E., & Potenza, M. (2008). Predicting response to opiate antagonists and placebo in the treatment of pathological gambling. *Psychopharmacology, 200,* 521–527.

Gutierrez, R. L., McKercher, R. M., Galea, J., & Jamison, K. L. (2005). Lamotrigine augmentation strategy for patients with treatment-resistant depression. *CNS Spectrum, 10,* 800–805.

Haney, M., Gunderson, E., Jiang, H., Collins, E., & Foltin, R. (2010). Cocaine-specific antibodies blunt the subjective effects of smoked cocaine in humans. *Biological Psychiatry, 67,* 59–65.

Henningfield, J., Shiffman, S., Ferguson, S., & Gritz, E. (2009). Tobacco dependence and withdrawal: Science base, challenges and opportunities for pharmacotherapy. *Pharmacology & Therapeutics, 123,* 1–16.

Hiranita, T., Anggadiredja, K., Fujisaki, C., Watanabe, S., & Yamamoto, T. (2004). Nicotine attenuates relapse to methamphetamine-seeking behavior (craving) in rats. *Annals of the New York Academy of Science, 1025,* 504–507.

Hughes, J. R., Stead, L. F., & Lancaster, T. (2005). Nortriptyline for smoking cessation: A review. *Nicotine and Tobacco Research, 7,* 491–499.

Ingersoll, R. E., & Rak, C. F. (2006). *Psychopharmacology for helping professionals.* Belmont, CA: Thompson.

Ivy, C., Philip, A., Paul K. G., Ramakrishna R. P., Bruce E. B., Yingni, C., et al. (2009). The synthesis of haptens and their use for the development of monoclonal antibodies for treating methamphetamine abuse. *Journal of Medicinal Chemistry, 52,* 7301–7309.

Jentsch, T. J., Hübner, C. A., & Fuhrmann, J. C. (2004). Ion channels: Function unravelled by dysfunction. *Nature Cell Biology, 6,* 1039–1047.

Julien, R. M. (2007). *A primer of drug action.* NY: Worth.

Kalinichev, M., Rourke, C., Daniels, A. J., Grizzle, M. K., Britt, C. S., Ignar, D. M. et al. (2005). Characterisation of olanzapine-induced weight gain and effect of aripiprazole vs olanzapine on body weight and prolactin secretion in female rats. *Psychopharmacology, 182,* 220–231.

Kalyoncu, A., Mirsal, H., Pektas, O., Unsalan, N., Tan, D., & Beyazyurek, M. (2005). Use of lamotrigine to augment clozapine in patients with resistant schizophrenia and comorbid alcohol dependence: A potent anti-craving effect? *Journal of Psychopharmacology, 19,* 301–305.

Kampman, K. M., Pettinati, H., Lynch, K. G., Dackis, C., Sparkman, T., Weigley, C. et al. (2004). A pilot trial of topiramate for the treatment of cocaine dependence. *Drug and Alcohol Dependence, 75,* 233–240.

Kastelic, A., Dubajic, G., & Strbad, E. (2008). Slow-release oral morphine for maintenance treatment of opioid addicts intolerant to methadone or with inadequate withdrawal suppression. *Addiction, 103,* 1837–1846.

Kennedy, S., Fulton, K., Bagby, R. M., Greene, A., Cohen, N., & Rafi-Tari, S. (2006). Sexual function during bupropion or paroxetine treatment of major depressive disorder. *Canadian Journal of Psychiatry, 51,* 234–242.

Kinsey, B., Jackson, D., & Orson, F. (2009). Anti-drug vaccines to treat substance abuse. *Immunology & Cell Biology, 87,* 309–314.

Knudsen, H. K., Ducharme, L. J., Roman, P. M., & Link, T. (2005). Buprenorphine diffusion: The attitudes of substance abuse treatment counselors. *Journal of Substance Abuse Treatment, 29,* 95–106.

Kosten, T., & Owens, S. M. (2005). Immunotherapy for the treatment of drug abuse. *Pharmacological Therapies, 108,* 76–85.

Kosten, T. R. (2005). Future of anti-addiction vaccines. *Studies in Health Technology and Informatics, 118,* 177–185.

Kortmann, G., Dobler, C., Bizarro, L., & Bau, C. (2010). Pharmacogenetics of smoking cessation therapy. *American Journal of Medical Genetics. Part B, Neuropsychiatric Genetics: The Official Publication of the International Society of Psychiatric Genetics, 153B,* 17–28.

Kraigher, D., Jagsch, R., Gombas, W., Ortner, R., Eder, H., Primorac A., et al. (2005). Use of slow-release oral morphine for the treatment of opioid dependence. *European Journal of Addiction Research, 11,* 145–151.

Kranzler, H., & Gage, A. (2008). Acamprosate efficacy in alcohol-dependent patients: Summary of results from three pivotal trials. *American Journal on Addictions, 17,* 70–76.

Leggio, L. (2009). Understanding and treating alcohol craving and dependence: Recent pharmacological and neuroendocrinological findings. *Alcohol and Alcoholism, 44,* 341–352.

Leggio, L., Kenna, G., Fenton, M., Bonenfant, E., & Swift, R. (2009). Typologies of alcohol dependence. From Jellinek to genetics and beyond. *Neuropsychology Review, 19,* 115–129.

Leggio, L., Ray, L., Kenna, G., & Swift, R. (2009). Blood glucose level, alcohol heavy drinking, and alcohol craving during treatment for alcohol dependence: Results from the Combined Pharmacotherapies and Behavioral Interventions for Alcohol Dependence (COMBINE) Study. *Alcoholism, Clinical and Experimental Research, 33,* 1539–544.

Lin, D., Mok, H., & Yatham, L. (2006). Polytherapy in bipolar disorder. *CNS Drugs, 20,* 29–42.

Lin, K. M., & Poland, R. E. (2000). Ethnicity, culture and psychopharmacology. *Psychopharmacology: The fourth generation of progress, 162,* 1907–1917.

Lin, K., Bing, L., Lei, G., Suxia, L., Dan, W., Min, H., et al. (2008). Tai-Kang-Ning, a Chinese herbal medicine formula, alleviates acute heroin withdrawal. *American Journal of Drug & Alcohol Abuse, 34,* 269–276.

Lu, L., Liu, Y., Zhu, W., Shi, J., Liu, Y., Ling, W., & Kosten, T. (2009). Traditional medicine in the treatment of drug addiction. *American Journal of Drug & Alcohol Abuse, 35,* 1–11.

Lynch, W. J., Roth, M. E., & Carroll, M. E. (2002). Biological basis of sex differences in drug abuse: preclinical and clinical studies. *Psychopharmacology, 164,* 121–137.

Mačiulaitis, R., Kontrimavičiūtė, V., Bressolle, F., & Briedis, V. (2008). Ibogaine, an anti-addictive drug: Pharmacology and time to go further in development. A narrative review. *Human & Experimental Toxicology, 27,* 181–194.

Mann, K. (2004). Pharmacotherapy of alcohol dependence: A review of the clinical data. *CNS Drugs, 18,* 485–504.

Mann, K., Kiefer, F., Smolka, M., Gann, H., Wellek, S., & Heinz, A. (2009). Searching for responders to acamprosate and naltrexone in alcoholism treatment: Rationale and design of the predict study. *Alcoholism: Clinical & Experimental Research, 33*(4), 674–683.

Marcinko, D., Bolanca, M., & Rudan, V. (2006). Compulsive buying and binge eating disorder—a case vignettes. *Progress In Neuro-Psychopharmacology & Biological Psychiatry, 30,* 1542–1544.

Mattick, R. P., Breen, C., Kimber, J., & Davoli, M. (2003). Methadone maintenance therapy versus no opioid replacement therapy for opioid dependence. *The Cochrane Database of Systematic Reviews, 2.* Art. No.: CD002209.

McCance-Katz, E. (2004). Office-based buprenorphine treatment for opioid-dependent patients. *Harvard Review of Psychiatry, 12,* 321–338.

McElroy, S., Guerdjikova, A., Martens, B., Keck, P., Pope, H., & Hudson, J. (2009). Role of antiepileptic drugs in the management of eating disorders. *CNS Drugs, 23,* 139–156.

McKeon, A., Frye, M. A., & Delanty, N. (2008). The alcohol withdrawal syndrome. *Journal of Neurology, Neurosurgery & Psychiatry, 79,* 854–862.

Mendoza, R., Smith, M. W., Poland, R. E., Lin, K. M., & Strickland, T. L. (1991). Ethnic psychopharmacology: The Hispanic and Native American perspective. *Psychopharmacological Bulletin, 27,* 449–461.

Mitchell, T. B., White, J. M., Somogyi, A. A., & Bochner, F. (2004). Slow-release oral morphine versus methadone: A crossover comparison of patient outcomes and acceptability as maintenance pharmacotherapies for opioid dependence. *Addiction, 99,* 940–945.

National Institute of Drug Abuse. (2000). *The brain: Understanding neurobiology through the study of addiction.* NIH Publication No. 00-4871. Washington, DC: National Institutes of Health.

National Institute of Drug Abuse. (2001). *Nicotine addiction.* NIDA Research Report—Nicotine Addiction: NIH Publication No. 01-4342. Washington, DC: National Institutes of Health.

National Institute of Neurological Disorders and Stroke. (2007). *Spinal cord injury: Emerging concepts.* Retrieved January 2, 2010, from *http://www.ninds.nih.gov/news_and_events/proceedings/sci_report.htm#Summary*

Nature. (2009). Glossary terms. *Nature Reviews Drug Discovery.* NY: NPG. Retrieved January 2, 2010, from *http://www.nature.com/nrd/journal/v6/n9/glossary/nrd2361.html*

Neubig, R. R., Spedding, M., Kenakin, T., & Christopoulos, A. (2003). International Union of Pharmacology Committee on Receptor Nomenclature and Drug Classification. XXXVIII. Update on Terms and Symbols in Quantitative Pharmacology. *Pharmacological Review, 55,* 597–606.

Newton, T. F., Roache, J. D., De La Garza, R., Fong, T., Wallace, C. L., Li, S. H., et al. (2006). Bupropion reduces methamphetamine-induced subjective effects and cue-induced craving. *Neuropsychopharmacology, 31,* 1537–1544.

Ntais, C., Pakos, E., Kyzas, P., & Ioannidis, J. P. A. (2005). Benzodiazepines for alcohol withdrawal. *The Cochrane Database of Systematic Reviews, 3.* Art. No.: CD005063.

O'Brien, C. P. (2005). Anticraving medications for relapse prevention: A possible new class of psychoactive medications. *American Journal of Psychiatry, 162,* 1423–1431.

Olive, M. F. (2005). mGlu5 receptors: Neuroanatomy, pharmacology, and role in drug addiction. *Current Psychiatry Reviews, 1,* 197–214.

Ooteman, W., Naassila, M., Koeter, M., Verheul, R., Schippers, G., Houchi, H., et al. (2009). Predicting the effect of naltrexone and acamprosate in alcohol-dependent patients using genetic indicators. *Addiction Biology, 14,* 328–337.

Patient UK. (2006). *Generic vs. brand names for medicines.* Retrieved January 2, 2010, from *http://www.patient.co.uk/showdoc/23069074/*

Petry, N. M. (2009). Disordered gambling and its treatment. Cognitive and Behavioral Practice, 16, 457–467.

Pettinati, H. M., Monterosso, J., Lipkin, C., & Volpicelli, J. R. (2003). Patient attitudes toward treatment predict attendance in clinical pharmacotherapy trials of alcohol and drug treatment. *The American Journal on Addictions, 12,* 324–335.

Pettinati, H. M., Weiss, R. D., Dundon, W., Miller, W. R., Donovan, D., Ernst, D. B., et al. (2005). A structured approach to medical management: A psychosocial intervention to support pharmacotherapy in the treatment of alcohol dependence. *Journal of Studies on Alcohol* (Supplement), *15,* 170–178.

Piascik, M. T. (2005). *Receptors.* Lexington, KY: University of Kentucky Chandler Medical Center. Retrieved January 3, 2010, from *http://www.mc.uky.edu/pharmacology/instruction/pha824mp/PHA824mp.html*

Potenza, M. (2008). Review. The neurobiology of pathological gambling and drug addiction: An overview and new findings. *Philosophical Transactions of the Royal Society of London. Series B, Biological Sciences, 363,* 3181–3189.

Prater, C., Miller, K., & Zylstra, R. (1999). Outpatient detoxification of the addicted or alcoholic patient. *American Family Physician, 60,* 1175–1183.

Preston, J. D., O'Neal, J. H., & Talaga, M. C. (2008). *Handbook of psychopharmacology for therapists.* Oakland, CA: New Harbinger.

Prince, V., & Turpin, K. (2008). Treatment of alcohol withdrawal syndrome with carbamazepine, gabapentin, and nitrous oxide. *American Journal of Health-System Pharmacy, 65,* 1039–1047.

Prisinzano, T., Rice, K. C., Baumann, M. H., & Rothman, R. B. (2004). Development of neurochemical normalization ("agonist substitution") therapeutics for stimulant abuse: Focus on the dopamine uptake inhibitor, GBR12909. *Current Medicinal Chemistry-Central Nervous System Agents, 4,* 47–59.

Rahman, S., López-Hernández, G., Corrigall, W., & Papke, R. (2008). Neuronal Nicotinic Receptors as Brain Targets for Pharmacotherapy of Drug Addiction. *CNS & Neurological Disorders—Drug Targets, 7,* 422–441.

Reece, A. (2007). Psychosocial and treatment correlates of opiate free success in a clinical review of a naltrexone implant program. *Substance Abuse Treatment, Prevention, and Policy, 2,* 35.

Reid, S., Teesson, M., Sannibale, C., Matsuda, M., & Haber, P. S. (2005). The efficacy of compliance therapy in pharmacotherapy for alcohol dependence: A randomized controlled trial. *Journal of Studies on Alcohol, 66,* 833–841.

Reiness, G. (2009). *Neurotransmitters.* Portland, OR: Lewis & Clark College. Retrieved January 3, 2010, from *http://legacy.lclark.edu/~reiness/neurobiology/Lectures/Neurotransmitters.pdf*

Riedel-Heller, S. G., Matschinger, H., & Angermeyer, M. C. (2005). Mental disorders—who and what might help? Help-seeking and treatment preferences of the lay public. *Social Psychiatry and Psychiatric Epidemiology, 40,* 167–174.

Ross, S., & Peselow, E. (2009). Pharmacotherapy of addictive disorders. *Clinical Neuropharmacology, 32,* 277–289.

Schik, G., Wedegaertner, F., Liersch, J., Hoy, L., Emrich, H., & Schneider, U. (2005). Oxcarbazepine versus carbamazepine in the treatment of alcohol withdrawal. *Addiction Biology, 10,* 283–288.

Shi, J., Liu, Y., Fang, Y., Xu, G., Zhai, H., & Lu, L. (2006). Traditional Chinese medicine in treatment of opiate addiction. *Acta Pharmacologica Sinica, 27,* 1303–1308.

Shiloh, R., Nutt, D., & Weizman, A. (2005). *Essentials in clinical psychiatric pharmacotherapy.* Oxford, UK: Taylor & Francis.

Shiloh, R., Nutt, D., & Weizman, A. (2006). *Atlas of psychiatric pharmacotherapy.* NY: Informa Healthcare.

Silagy, C., Lancaster, T., Stead, L., Mant, D., & Fowler, G. (2001). Nicotine replacement therapy for smoking cessation. *Cochrane Database System Review, 3,* Art. No.: CD000146.

Silasi, G., & Kolb, B. (2007). Chronic inhibition of cyclooxygenase-2 induces dendritic hypertrophy and limited functional improvement following motor cortex stroke. *Neuroscience, 144,* 1160–1168.

Sofuoglu, M., & Kosten, T. R. (2005). Novel approaches to the treatment of cocaine addiction. *CNS Drugs, 19,* 13–25.

Sofuoglu, M., Poling, J., Mitchell, E., & Kosten, T. R. (2005). Tiagabine affects the subjective responses to cocaine in humans. *Pharmacology, Biochemistry, and Behavior, 82,* 569–573.

Stahl, S. M. (2008). *Essential psychopharmacology.* Cambridge: Cambridge University Press.

Stead, L. F., Perera, R., Bullen, C., Mant, D., & Lancaster, T. (2008). Nicotine replacement therapy for smoking cessation. *Cochrane Database of Systematic Reviews, 1,* Art. No.: CD000146.

Sun, W., Akins, C. K., Mattingly, A. E., & Rebec, G. V. (2005). Ionotropic glutamate receptors in the ventral tegmental area regulate cocaine-seeking behavior in rats. *Neuropsychopharmacology, 30,* 2073–2081.

Takamatsu, Y., Yamamoto, H., Ogai, Y., Hagino, Y., Markou, A., & Ikeda K. (2006). Fluoxetine as a potential pharmacotherapy for methamphetamine dependence: Studies in mice. *Annals of the New York Academy of Science, 1074,* 295–302.

Tonigan, J. S., & Kelly, J. F. (2003). AA-exposure and attitudes of 12-step proscriptions about medications. Retrieved on December 29, 2009, from: *http://casaa.unm.edu/posters/AA-Exposure%20and%20Attitudes%20of%2012-Step%20Proscriptions%20About%20Medications.pdf*

Torres-Reverón, A., & Dow-Edwards, D. L. (2005). Repeated administration of methylphenidate in young, adolescent, and mature rats affects the response to cocaine later in adulthood. *Psychopharmacology, 181,* 38–47.

Uys, J., & LaLumiere, R. (2008). Glutamate: the new frontier in pharmacotherapy for cocaine addiction. *CNS & Neurological Disorders Drug Targets, 7,* 482–491.

Verheul, R., & Brink, W. V. D. (2005). Causal pathways between substance use disorders and personality pathology. *Australian Psychologist, 40,* 127–136.

Verheul, R., Brink, W. V. D., & Geerlings, P. (1999). A three-pathway psychobiological model of craving for alcohol. *Alcohol and Alcohol Dependence, 34,* 197–222.

Verheul, R., Lehert, P., Geerlings, P. J., Koeter, M. W. J., & Brink, V. D. W. (2005). Predictors of acamprosate efficacy: Results from a pooled analysis of seven European trials. *Psychopharmacology, 178,* 167–173.

Warner, C., & Shoaib, M. (2005). How does bupropion work as a smoking cessation aid? *Addiction Biology, 10,* 219–231.

Weiden, P. J., & Rao, N. (2005). Teaching medication compliance to psychiatric residents: Placing an orphan topic into a training curriculum. *Academic Psychiatry, 29,* 203–210.

Wolf, M. E. (2002). Addiction: Making the connection between behavioral changes and neuronal plasticity in specific pathways. *Molecular Interventions, 2,* 146–157.

World Health Organization. (2004). *Substitution maintenance therapy in the management of opioid dependence and HIV/AIDS prevention: Position paper.* Geneva: Author.

Chapter 12

12-Step Facilitation of Treatment

Adrianne L. Johnson
State University of New York at Oswego

As explored in the previous chapter, groups are a highly effective modality for the treatment of addictions, and have a long and successful history in the field of chemical dependency. Twelve-step groups may be more appropriately titled "self-help groups"(because not all self-help groups have exactly 12 steps). The terms will be used interchangeably throughout the chapter.

The primary focus of self-help groups is to provide emotional and practical support and an exchange of information. Such groups use participatory processes to allow people to share knowledge, common experiences, and problems. Through their participation, members help themselves and others by gaining knowledge and information, and by obtaining and providing emotional and practical support. Traditionally, self-help groups have been in-person meetings, but more recently, Internet self-help groups have become popular.

One of the most widely recognized groups for the treatment of addictions is Alcoholics Anonymous (AA). Miller and McCrady (1993) note that Alcoholics Anonymous is the "most frequently consulted source of help for drinking problems" (p. 3). In fact, approximately 1 in every 10 adults in the United States has attended an Alcoholics Anonymous meeting at least once (Doweiko, 1999; Miller & McCrady, 1993; Zweben, 1995). Concurrently, affiliation with 12-step groups has been consistently linked to the achievement of abstinence among persons experiencing alcohol and other drug problems (Laudet & White, 2005). It is highly recommended that counselors, even if they do not regularly incorporate these groups into their counseling practice, should at least be familiar with them. The goal of this chapter, then, is to help counselors meet the following objectives:

1. To have a basic understanding of the foundation, history, and development of the 12-step model of treatment for addictions;
2. To gain a basic knowledge of the advantages and disadvantages of these groups, and how to use this knowledge to make appropriate referrals; and
3. To understand how to incorporate 12-step groups into culturally sensitive and client-appropriate addiction treatment for the most effective outcome.

HISTORY: DEVELOPMENT OF 12-STEP GROUPS

Alcoholics Anonymous

As will be discussed later, Alcoholics Anonymous (AA) is one of the most widely recognized 12-step groups, and has been an instrumental force in the establishment of other groups using its model. Alcoholics Anonymous was founded on June 10, 1935, when Dr. Robert Holbrook Smith, an alcoholic physician, had his last drink (Doweiko, 1999). His cofounder, Bill Wilson, a failed Wall Street stockbroker, had previously been affiliated with the New York Oxford Group, a nondenominational group of Christians committed to overcoming a common drinking problem. The two men met coincidentally in Ohio while Wilson was seeking support to stay sober during a business trip (Miller, 2005). The plan for the group was devised by the two men, with a shared aim to spread the supportive message of sobriety to other alcoholics.

During its early years, AA worked to find a method that would support its members in their struggle to both achieve and maintain sobriety. Within three years of its founding, three AA groups were in existence, yet, "it was hard to find two score of sure recoveries" (*Twelve Steps and Twelve Traditions*, 1981, p. 17). The then-new organization was unable to establish exactly *how* and *why* the message of the group worked for some members, but not for all. Since then, several dynamics have been identified that will be discussed later in this chapter. The new organization continued to grow to approximately 100 members in isolated groups by its fourth year (Doweiko, 1999). The early members decided to write about their struggle to achieve sobriety in order to share their discoveries with others, leading to the principles of the now well-established foundation. In the half century since its founding, Alcoholics Anonymous has grown to a fellowship of 87,000 groups including chapters in 150 countries, with a total membership estimated at more than 2 million (Doweiko, 1999; Humphreys & Moos, 1996). The first edition of *Alcoholics Anonymous* was published in 1939, detailing the well-known Steps and Traditions that now serve as the established guide to addictions recovery and maintenance among group members. The organization took its name from the title of the book, which has since come to be known as the "Big Book" of AA (*Twelve Steps and Twelve Traditions*, 1981).

Twelve Steps

1. We admitted we were powerless over alcohol—that our lives had become unmanageable;
2. Came to believe that a Power greater than ourselves could restore us to sanity;
3. Made a decision to turn our will and our lives over to the care of God as we understood Him;
4. Made a searching and fearless moral inventory of ourselves;
5. Admitted to God, to ourselves and to another human being the exact nature of our wrongs;
6. Were entirely ready to have God remove all these defects of character;
7. Humbly asked Him to remove our shortcomings;
8. Made a list of all persons we had harmed, and became willing to make amends to them all;
9. Made direct amends to such people wherever possible, except when to do so would injure them or others;
10. Continued to take personal inventory and when we were wrong promptly admitted it;
11. Sought through prayer and meditation to improve our conscious contact with God, as we understood Him, praying only for knowledge of His will for us and the power to carry that out; and
12. Having had a spiritual awakening as the result of these steps, we tried to carry this message to alcoholics, and to practice these principles in all our affairs.

Twelve Traditions

1. Our common welfare should come first; personal recovery depends upon A.A. unity.
2. For our group purpose there is but one ultimate authority—a loving God as He may express Himself in our group conscience. Our leaders are but trusted servants; they do not govern.
3. The only requirement for A.A. membership is a desire to stop drinking.
4. Each group should be autonomous except in matters affecting other groups or A.A. as a whole.
5. Each group has but one primary purpose—to carry its message to the alcoholics who still suffers.
6. An A.A. group ought never endorse, finance, or lend the A.A. name to any related facility or outside enterprise, lest problems of money, property, and prestige divert us from our primary purpose.
7. Every A.A. group ought to be fully self-supporting, declining outside contributions.
8. Alcoholics Anonymous should remain forever non-professional, but our service centers may employ special works.
9. A.A., as such, ought never be organized; but we may create service boards or committees directly responsible to those they serve.
10. Alcoholics Anonymous has no opinion on outside issues; hence the A.A. name ought never be drawn into public controversy.
11. Our public relations policy is based on attraction rather than promotion; we need always maintain personal anonymity at the level of press, radio, and films.
12. Anonymity is the spiritual foundation of all our traditions, ever reminding us to place principles before personalities.

Al-Anon

According to *Al-Anon's Twelve Steps and Twelve Traditions* (1985), wives would often wait while their husbands were at the early Alcoholics Anonymous meetings. While they waited, they would talk about their problems and struggles. At some point, they decided to try applying the same 12 Steps that their husbands had found so helpful to their own lives, and the group known as Al-Anon was born (*Al-Anon's Twelve Steps and Twelve Traditions*, 1985; Doweiko, 1999). In the beginning, each isolated group made whatever changes it felt necessary in the Twelve Steps. By 1948, however, the wife of one of the cofounders of Alcoholics Anonymous became involved in the growing organization, and in time, a uniform family support program emerged. This program, known as the Al-Anon Family Group, borrowed and modified the Alcoholics Anonymous Twelve Steps and Twelve Traditions to make them applicable to the needs of families of alcoholics (Doweiko, 1999).

Co-Dependents Anonymous

Co-Dependents Anonymous (CoDA) was founded in 1986 in Phoenix, Arizona, and is a 12-step program that strives for healthy relationships, from a point of departure of codependence on someone with an addiction. CoDA adheres to 12 steps and traditions similar to those of AA. Each group is allowed to function autonomously to meet its own needs, as long as it has no other affiliation except CoDA, and does not affect other groups of CoDA as a whole (CoDA World Fellowship Website, 1998). There are approximately 1,200 CoDA groups in the United States, and it is active in more than 40 countries.

Narcotics Anonymous (NA)

In 1953, a self-help group patterned after AA was founded, and called itself Narcotics Anonymous (NA). Although this group honors its debt to AA, the members of NA feel that:

We follow the same path with only a single exception. Our identification as addicts is all-inclusive in respect to any mood-changing, mind-altering substance. "Alcoholism" is too limited a term for us; our problem is not a specific substance, it is a disease called "addiction." (Narcotics Anonymous, 1982, p. x).

To the members of NA, it is not the specific chemical that is the problem, but the common disease of addiction. There is an important distinction to be made between AA and NA: The language of AA speaks of alcoholism, whereas NA speaks of "addiction" or "chemicals." Each offers the same program, with minor variations, to help the addicted person achieve sobriety (Doweiko, 1999).

Alateen

By 1957, in response to the recognition that teenagers presented special needs and concerns, Alateen was established after modifications to Al-Anon. These members follow the same 12 Steps outlined in the Al-Anon program, but the goal of the program is to provide teenagers the opportunity to share experiences, discuss current problems, learn how to cope more effectively, and offer encouragement to each other (*Facts about Alateen*, 1969).

Other Support Groups

Rational Recovery (RR) was founded in 1986 by Jack Trimpey, a California licensed clinical social worker, and is a source of counseling, guidance, and direct instruction on self-recovery from addiction to alcohol and other drugs through planned, permanent abstinence. This concept is designed as an alternative to AA and other 12-step programs ("Groups Offer Self-Help," 1991). The program closely follows the cognitive-behavioral school of counseling, and views alcoholism as reflecting negative, self-defeating thought patterns (Ouimette, Finney, & Moos, 1997). While RR and AA promote abstinence, the programs use different strategies. There are approximately 600 RR groups in the United States (Doweiko, 1999; McCrady & Delaney, 1995).

Rational Recovery (RR) specifically adheres to the following tenets:

- RR does not regard alcoholism as a disease, but rather a voluntary behavior;
- RR discourages adoption of the forever "recovering" drunk persona;
- There are no RR recovery groups;
- Great emphasis is placed on self-efficacy;
- There are no discrete steps and no consideration of religious matters.

Secular Organizations of Sobriety (SOS) was also founded in 1986; Dorsman (1996) estimates that approximately 1,200 SOS groups meet each week in the United States. SOS emerged as a reaction to the heavy emphasis on spirituality found in AA and NA (Doweiko; 1999; "Groups Offer Self-Help," 1991); the guiding philosophy of SOS stresses personal responsibility and the role of critical thinking in recovery (Doweiko, 1999).

Women for Sobriety (WFS) was founded in 1975 ("Groups Offer Self-Help," 1991), and McCrady and Delaney (1995) estimate that approximately 325 WFS groups meet in the United States. Doweiko (1999) states that this organization is specifically designed for and comprised of women, and is founded on the theory that the AA program fails to address the very real differences between the meaning of alcoholism for men and women (p. 485). For this group, however, there are 13 statements, not 12.

Women for Sobriety (WFS) is specifically designed for and comprised of women, and is founded on the theory that the AA program fails to address the differences of the meaning of alcoholism between men and women (Lewis, 1994). Additionally, WFS focuses on negative thought patterns, tendencies of guilt, relationships, and spiritual and personal growth. These points are delineated in the Thirteen Statements of Acceptance (Kirkpatrick, 1990; Miller, 2005):

1. I have a life-threatening problem that once had me.
2. Negative thoughts destroy only myself.
3. Happiness is a habit I will develop.
4. Problems bother me only to the degree I permit them to.
5. I am what I think.
6. Life can be ordinary or it can be great.
7. Love can change the course of my world.
8. The fundamental object of life is emotional and spiritual growth.
9. The past is gone forever.
10. All love given returns.
11. Enthusiasm is my daily exercise.
12. I am a competent woman and have much to give life.
13. I am responsible for myself and my actions.

Alcoholics Anonymous for Atheists and Agnostics (Quad A) tends to draw heavily from the traditional Alcoholics Anonymous (Rand, 1995), but with one important distinction: Quad A tends to downplay the emphasis on religion inherent in the traditional AA foundation. In fact, this organization tends to remove the power given to a higher force than the members themselves, instead stressing the forces in the individual's life that support recovery (Doweiko, 1999).

Moderation Management (MM) was established in 1994 as a free-of-charge, nonprofit support group that welcomes anyone concerned about their drinking, regardless of level of consumption. The founder, Shirley Kishline, states that the goal of MM is to "provide a supportive environment in which people who have made the decision to reduce their drinking can come together and to help each other change" (Kishline, 1996, p. 55). MM is a controversial group because moderation is the goal, not abstinence (Kishline, 1996). MM emphasizes that individuals will be most successful at attaining their goals with alcohol when these goals are chosen by the individual, and proposes that individuals should be responsible for their behavior and can change lifetime habits with a program of support.

National Association for Children of Alcoholics (NACoA) was formed in February 1983 in California, after two groups of professionals from across the country met twice during 1982 to share their concerns, knowledge, and experiences regarding children of alcoholics. One group included clinicians concerned with the needs of adults whose mental health problems stemmed from a childhood in an alcoholic family. The other group included counselors and social workers who primarily worked with young children experiencing a broad range of problems in families with parental alcoholism. The 22 physicians, psychologists, social workers, and educators who attended these meetings concluded that a national membership organization was needed to identify and address the unique problems of children of alcoholics and to provide them with a means through which to voice their concerns (Wenger, 1997). NACOA provides support and information through their confidential telephone, letter and email helpline, and via their Web site.

THE GROUP PROCESS: HOW 12-STEP GROUPS WORK

Goals

As with other counseling groups, 12-step addictions groups have established goals for members to work toward, which help them in their main goal of achieving addiction recovery. In a survey of outpatient drug abuse programs (Mejta, Naylor, & Maslar, 1994; Price et al., 1991), the following treatment goals that share similarities with other treatment modalities were identified:

- Abstinence from alcohol and other drugs;
- Steady employment;
- Stable social relationships;
- Positive physical and emotional health;
- Improved spiritual strength; and
- Adherence to legal mandates/requirements as applicable.

It is reasonable to assume that most 12-step groups incorporate these general goals into their general treatment foundation (a noted exception being Moderation Management, as discussed in the previous section), although individual groups differ in membership composition, individual aims and goals, and foundational beliefs. For example, the primary purpose of AA is twofold. Members strive to "carry the message to the addict who still suffers" (The Group, 1976, p. 1) and the organization seeks to provide for its members a program for living without chemicals. Doweiko (1999) notes that this is accomplished by presenting the individual with a simple, truthful, realistic picture of the disease of addiction; and by sharing their life stories, public confession of lies, distortions, self-deceptions, and denial that supported his/her own chemical use (p. 477).

The Twelve Steps and Twelve Traditions

Alcoholics Anonymous pioneered the 12-step model from which most other 12-step groups now operate. Each group of Alcoholics Anonymous is self-supporting, not-for-profit, and is "in cooperation with but not affiliated with" with the professional community (Alcoholics Anonymous World Services, 1991). All Alcoholics Anonymous groups are guided by the Twelve Steps and Twelve Traditions, which serve as a basis for many other groups as well.

Alcoholics Anonymous is not officially associated with any particular religious denomination, political affiliation, or organization, and notes that it "does not discriminate against any prospective member" (Alcoholics Anonymous World Services, 1991, p. 1), including those with addictions other than alcohol; it therefore welcomes nonalcoholics to open meetings. Alcoholics Anonymous does explicitly state, however, that while some professionals refer to alcoholism and drug addiction more generally as substance abuse or chemical dependency, the group makes the clear distinction that only those with alcohol problems are allowed to attend closed meetings (Alcoholics Anonymous World Services, 1991). There are six noted types of 12-step meetings (Miller, 2005); the counselor should be familiar with all types, and should invest time in attending some to gain a better understanding of the powerful dynamics at work:

1. Open meetings generally involve one recovering person speaking to the group about his/her addiction and recovery story. Nonaddicts are invited to attend and listen, and these meetings are generally helpful for those who want to learn more about addiction.
2. Closed meetings involve addicted individuals only.

3. Discussion meetings typically focus on a topic discussed by those addicts in attendance. Note that these meetings are called "participation meetings" in California.
4. In speaker meetings, one addicted person speaks to the audience about his or her addiction and recovery story, and the meeting may be open or closed.
5. In step meetings, the topic for discussion is one of the 12 steps, and these meetings are typically for addicted individuals only.
6. In Big Book meetings, a chapter from *Alcoholics Anonymous* is read and discussed.

It is important to note that, while the aforementioned Steps and Traditions have been the foundation for many other self-help groups, other groups have diverged due to differences in individual needs or in the belief systems of group members. More attention will be given to this later in the chapter.

Group Dynamics as Applied to 12-Step Groups

There are many different types of groups, as well as many different theoretical approaches to groups. Among the many varieties of group counseling, there is an enormous diversity in format, goals, and roles of the leader (McKay & Paleg, 1992). There are also many ways to select the members of a group. For example, they may be homogeneous by type or by age. There are advantages and disadvantages to every combination (Lawson, Lawson, & Rivers, 2001), and those aspects of diversity, composition, theoretical orientation, base, and foundation all play enormous roles in the outcome of the groups' efficacy. In their exploration of why certain self-help groups are so effective, Roots and Aanes (1992) identified eight characteristics that seem to contribute to a group's success:

1. Members have shared experience, in this case their inability to control their drug/alcohol use;
2. Education is the primary goal of Alcoholics Anonymous membership;
3. Self-help groups are self-governing;
4. The group places emphasis on accepting responsibility for one's behavior;
5. There is but a single purpose to the group;
6. Membership is voluntary;
7. The individual member must make a commitment to personal change; and
8. The group places emphasis on anonymity and confidentiality.

As will be discussed later in this chapter, clinicians often choose to include groups as part of the treatment plan, and make that decision based on the assessed needs of the client and his or her fit with the potential group. Although most treatment programs include both group and individual counseling, Lawson et al. (2001) found that often, it is in a group that the client makes the most progress toward significant therapeutic movement and suggests that as social beings, we are influenced more by a group of people than by just one person for any number of contextual, environmental, or personal reasons.

Twelve-step groups such as Alcoholics Anonymous (AA), Cocaine Anonymous (CA), and Narcotics Anonymous (NA) consider that helping others makes recovery possible. This helping component relies on the exchange of dialogue, reinforcing behavior, and encouraging messages of recovery through efforts modeled by the leader, which then filter throughout the group, often resulting in a successful outcome. Some studies suggest that AA and similar groups help individuals recover through common process mechanisms associated with enhancing self-efficacy, coping skills, and motivation; and by facilitating adaptive social network changes (Kelly, Magill, & Stout, 2009).

THE ROLE OF SPONSORS IN RECOVERY

Sponsorship reflects the structure of AA and functions on two levels. A sponsor is a more experienced person in recovery who guides the less-experienced "sponsee" through the program (Alcoholics Anonymous World Services, 1991). Level I Sponsorship is concerned with sobriety; the sponsor helps the "sponsee" to become or to stay sober. With Level II Sponsorship, the sponsor counsels the sponsee through the Twelve Steps so that recovery can be achieved (Brown, 1995).

The personal nature of the behavioral issues that lead to seeking help in twelve-step fellowships results in a strong relationship between sponsee and sponsor. As the relationship is based on spiritual principles, it is unique and not generally characterized as a "friendship." Fundamentally, the sponsor has the single purpose of helping the sponsee recover from the behavioral problem that brought the sufferer into twelve-step work, which reflexively helps the sponsor recover (*Twelve Steps and Twelve Traditions*, 1981).

The focus of the relationship, for both sponsor and sponsee, is on the Twelve Steps, with the sponsor serving as a guide and facilitator of the recovery process. The AA model encourages a gradual transition from primary dependence on the sponsor to a focus on the process itself. This shift demonstrates increased confidence and courage in the recovering addict working through the Steps, and allows for progress to be qualitatively evaluated by both the sponsor and the sponsee (Brown, 1995; Knack, 2009).

DO 12-STEP PROGRAMS REALLY WORK?

As already stated, 12-step groups have a long and successful history in the field of chemical dependency treatment. Lawson (2003) found that participation in 12-step groups during and after formal treatment has been associated with positive outcomes among substance users, and Donovan and Wells (2007) found that involvement in 12-step self-help groups, through both attending meetings and engaging in 12-step activities, is associated with reduced substance use and improved outcomes among alcohol- and cocaine-dependent individuals. Not surprisingly, a higher intensity of involvement has been associated with better drinking outcomes (Emrick et al., 1993; Zemore et al., 2004). For example, individuals who are heavier substance users and have more substance-related problems are more likely to affiliate with 12-step self-help groups and less likely to drop out after treatment than less impaired clients (Connors et al., 2001; McKellar, Harris, & Moos, 2009; Tonigan, Bogenschutz, & Miller, 2006). Research also suggests that early 12-step attendance might help to maintain better long-term alcohol abstinence for adolescents aged 13–15 years. Sterling, Chi, Campbell, and Weisner (2009) found that adolescents who attended 10–20 meetings within a period of 6 months had alcohol and drug abstinence rates significantly higher than adolescents who attended fewer meetings.

Other findings have consistently concluded that 12-step participation can enhance treatment outcomes among problem drinkers (Emrick, Tonigan, Montgomery, & Little, 1993; McIntire 2000; Tonigan, Toscova, & Miller, 1996; Zemore, Zaskutas, & Ammon, 2004); and scientific reviews of available data indicate that AA and related 12-step treatments such as Narcotics Anonymous are at least as helpful as other intervention approaches. Likewise, research on Narcotics Anonymous typically supports the efficacy of this approach (Alford, Koehler, & Leonard, 1991; Christo & Franey 1995; Johnsen & Herringer 1993; Kelly, Magill, & Stout, 2009; Toumbourou, Hamilton, U'Ren, Steven-Jones, & Storey, 2002; Zemore et al., 2004).

If this is the case, why run any other type of group? While specific advantages and disadvantages will be discussed later, some of the challenges of self-help groups are addressed here. First, it is unclear just how many people respond to self-help groups. Laudet (2003) suggests that the effectiveness of 12-step groups may be limited by high attrition rates and low participation. It may be safe to assume that some members who attend one or more of these groups do not attend consistently, do not reach group or therapeutic goals, or do not maintain sobriety. By the same measure, it may also be safe to assume that some members of these groups are sober, yet not happy or fully functioning. It is also important to remember that self-help groups are self-selective; because of this, membership consists of people who want to be members and who are willing to follow the guidelines of the group. This may explain the high degree of success reported among members (Lawson et al., 2001).

Although AA has been a social force in the United States for more than half a century, there has been surprisingly little empirical research into what elements of this and other 12-step programs are effective (Emrick et al., 1993), or for what types of people the 12-step model might be most useful (Galanter, Castaneda, & Franco, 1991; George & Tucker, 1996; McCaul & Furst, 1994; Tonigan & Hiller-Sturmhofel, 1994). Laudet, Magura, Cleland, Vogel, and Knight (2003) found that the following characteristics among group members are associated with the greatest long-term group retention, often leading to successful recovery: Older age; more lifetime arrests; more psychiatric symptoms but not taking psychiatric medication; being more troubled by substance abuse than by mental health; having a greater level of self-efficacy for recovery; residing in supported housing; and being enrolled in outpatient treatment at follow-up. And while a study of sponsorship as practiced in Alcoholics Anonymous and Narcotics Anonymous found that providing direction and support to other alcoholics and addicts correlates with sustained abstinence for the sponsor, the study also found that there were few short-term benefits for the sponsee (Crape, Latkin, Laris, & Knownlton, 2002).

SPECIFIC ADVANTAGES AND DISADVANTAGES OF 12-STEP GROUPS

Advantages

There are many advantages to incorporating 12-step groups into treatment. First, as discussed earlier, certain dynamics that can facilitate personal growth are more likely to exist in groups than in individual counseling. Kelly, Magill, and Stout (2009) suggest that AA-related changes occur via intrapersonal, behavioral, and social processes. The group setting offers support for new interaction dynamics, and encourages experimentation and behavioral rehearsal which is useful in generalizing to the world beyond the group. Additionally, they suggest that participants are able to explore their style of relating to others and to learn more effective social skills (Corey & Corey, 1992). AA provides a social outlet for its members. The 12-step group offers a safe, predictable, chemical-free place in which members can learn or relearn important social skills while experiencing a shared sense of purpose and belonging.

Predictability, consistency, universality, the opportunity to build social skills without chemical dependence, and the learning of coping skills are all factors present in self-help groups that lead to effective outcomes. There is a re-creation of the everyday world in some groups, particularly if the membership is diverse (Corey & Corey, 1992). The 12-step group allows its members to recognize that their problems are not unique, and members have the opportunity to learn about themselves through the experience of others; to experience emotional closeness and caring that encourage meaningful disclosure of the self; and to identify with the struggles of other members. This universality normalizes the recovery experience.

Another primary strength may lie in a group's ability to provide free, long-term, easy access and exposure to recovery-related common therapeutic elements (Kelly, Magill, & Stout, 2009). Lawson et al. (2001) suggests that economically, groups are a logical choice because a counselor can see approximately three times the number of clients in groups than in individual counseling. For counselors, this is an important point; incorporating self-help groups into treatment helps clients build skill that would be fundamentally lacking in individual sessions, and counselors who engage themselves in the self-help group process as leaders (if the group allows this) have the opportunity to reach a greater number of clients in single sessions.

For many addicted clients, economic concerns far outweigh the potential benefits of treatment, especially among culturally diverse, minority, and marginalized populations. Self-help groups offer a free opportunity to achieve treatment goals; Tonigan et al. (1996) found that affiliation with 12-step groups such as AA and NA, both during and after treatment, was identified both as a cost-effective and useful approach to promoting abstinence among persons experiencing alcohol- and other drug-related problems. Additionally, meetings are often held at multiple locations and times in order to reach a wider client base, so clients have frequent, regular opportunities to attend meetings between individual counseling sessions.

Disadvantages

While there are numerous advantages to self-help groups, there are significant disadvantages as well. Laudet and White (2005) point counselors to the lack of consistent empirical support for their effectiveness, as well as a general lack of trained professionalism (e.g., groups that are not led by counselors); the risk that members may become overly dependent on the group; that members may, and sometimes do, get bad advice from other group members; and that the usefulness of these groups is limited in time (i.e., only needed in early recovery) or in scope (i.e., deals with only one substance while some clients have multiple issues). Certainly, the boundaries of any group are dependent upon the amount of structure present, and that structure is dependent upon the ability of members to provide the necessary motivation and commitment to keep the group operating. Without appropriate modeling from a trained professional, there is the risk that boundaries will be violated and structure will be lacking, and harm or attrition may result. Further, addictions are often superficial, albeit damaging, problems. Clients with addictions may engage in replacing one problem symptom for another, without ever confronting or challenging the real issue(s) beyond the group process.

Lawson et al. (2001) also note that there is often a subtle pressure to conform to group norms, values, and expectations. Participants sometimes unquestioningly substitute a groups' values and norms for those they had unquestioningly acquired in the first place. In other words, members may be susceptible to replacing detrimental values, norms, and even behaviors with equally detrimental ones exhibited and observed in the group. This is especially salient when referring clients with possible Axis II disorders; clients may choose to abandon the chemical for a similar dependence on an observed behavior, an adopted value, or even another individual.

Hence, not all people are suited to all groups. The screening process for self-help groups is limited, and in most cases, especially in open groups, non-existent. Some individuals are inappropriate for groups (e.g., too suspicious, too hostile, or too fragile) and do not benefit from a group experience. As a result, some individuals are psychologically damaged by attending certain groups. Inevitably, some make the group a place to ventilate their miseries and be rewarded for their engagement in the catharsis process. Others use groups as vehicles for expressing their woes, in the hope that they will be understood and totally accepted, and make no attempt to actually effect substantial change in their lives (Lawson et al., 2001). Before an individual is referred to a group, all these factors need to be carefully weighed by both the counselor and the client, to increase the likelihood that the person will benefit from the self-help group experience.

An even stronger point of resistance to the incorporation of self-help groups into treatment by counselors is based on the fact that many groups operate from a foundation of Christianity. 12-step literature explicitly encourages helping as part of the recovery process, a point reinforced dramatically by Alcoholics Anonymous' twelfth step: 'having had a spiritual awakening as a result of these steps, we tried to carry this message to other alcoholics, and to practice these principles in all our affairs' (Alcoholics Anonymous World Services (1991), as cited in Zemore, Zaskutas, and Ammon, 2004). Twelve-step groups have been historically controversial for this very reason, and several aspects of the recovery program have been identified as potential stumbling blocks for both substance users and clinicians (Chappel & DuPont, 1999; Laudet, 2000). This is due to a multiplicity of factors, and a main criticism includes the lack of cultural sensitivity inherent in the foundation of many groups. Further, Davis and Jansen (1998) suggest that the [twelve-step model's] emphasis on spirituality, surrender, and powerlessness contradicts contemporary dominant western cultural norms of self-reliance and widespread secularism.

It is important for counselors to be culturally sensitive and aware of the predominantly white, middle-strata, male-defined view of addictions upon which most 12-step programs are founded. Heyward (1992) suggests that for women in particular, it is difficult to listen to religious language which may be interpreted as sexist from a dominant cultural standpoint. Further, the reliance on external support, and particularly on spiritual support as one of the cornerstones of the 12-step program, has been identified as a potential point of resistance to these organizations from certain ethnic groups (Laudet, 2003; Peteet, 1993; Smith, Buxton, Bilal, & Seymour, 1993). Bell (1993) suggests that African-American clients, for example, as well as people in other nondominant cultures, tend to see addiction issues as secondary to such problems as illiteracy, racism, and poverty. The reliance on the spiritual component of the group, therefore, may not be as relevant—and not as helpful—when considering the hierarchy of immediate needs of nondominant groups.

However, it should be noted at this point that the spiritual component of the 12-step group must be addressed on an individual basis with the client. Many clients from minority backgrounds (e.g., African Americans) have values shaped by cultural factors, which must be taken into consideration by the counselor before deciding to incorporate group participation into treatment. For example, note that African Americans tend to be more group-centered and sensitive to interpersonal matters, to have strong kinship bonds, be work and education oriented, and to have a strong commitment to religious values and church participation (McCollum, 1997; Sue & Sue, 1999). Thus, a 12-step group may in fact be an advantageous tool for the counselor because of the group's focus and emphasis on spirituality.

CASE STUDY

Nick identifies himself as an atheist, and tells his counselor that after serving as a combat soldier in Iraq, he no longer believes in a higher power. He appears committed to recovery, but resistant to suggestions of attending a 12-step group because of his personal views toward religious issues. He tells the counselor that he has lost many friends due to his beliefs and his continued alcohol use, and drinks daily to forget his combat experiences and fight the loneliness. The counselor inquires about prior treatment history, and Nick confides, "My last counselor referred me to AA for support, but I never went." The counselor believes that a group referral may be beneficial in assisting Nick toward recovery. What considerations should the counselor include in the decision to make a referral?

USING THE 12-STEP GROUP AS PART OF TREATMENT

While disadvantages and notable challenges exist with the 12-step model of addictions treatment, self-help groups that follow this model are still frequently used in the treatment of chemical abuse because of the advantages already discussed. Currently, 12-step groups are combined with other treatment modalities to maximize the potential for a successful outcome. Del Toro, Thom, Beam, and Horst (1996) suggest that 12-step programs, in addition to supportive medical follow-up visits and appropriate use of medications if needed, may greatly increase the probability of success and sustained recovery for addicts. A large number of studies have examined community AA group participation in relation to long-term outcomes following a variety of treatment approaches. These studies have found AA attendance over follow-up to be associated with enhanced abstinence outcomes and remission rates among different patient subgroups, including women, youth, dually-diagnosed individuals, and various populations of diverse ethnic backgrounds (Kelly, Magill, & Stout, 2009).

Traditional intervention strategies used in chemical dependency programs frequently include a combination of individual and group counseling, educational lectures on drug abuse, 12-step assignments, and self-help groups (Mejta, Naylor, & Maslar, 1994). Roman and Blum (1998) found in a representative sample of 450 private substance-user treatment centers, 90% of the facilities based their treatment on 12-step principles or variations of this model, with nearly one-half of the remaining 10% incorporating 12-step principles in combination with other approaches, including encouraged attendance at 12-step meetings.

Each counseling approach to the treatment process provides its own rationale for using groups as a therapeutic technique (Lawson et al., 2001). The reason a counselor chooses to use 12-step groups as part of that treatment plan should be congruent with the type of group chosen, and on the motivation of the client. Generally, self-help groups may work well with addicted clients in providing support for recovery, reducing a sense of isolation, and helping the client develop a sense of self-regulation (Khantzian & Mack, 1994; Miller, 2005). In addition, these groups provide overall support to counseling itself (Bristow-Braitman, 1995; Johnson & Phelps, 1991; Miller, 2005; Riordan & Walsh, 1994).

Counselors have a uniquely important role in helping clients process and reflect on their group experiences in individual sessions, helping them to generalize the new skills and values to situations and contexts beyond both individual counseling and the group. Since participation in 12-step meetings is typically voluntary, especially post-treatment, the decision of whether or not to incorporate self-help groups into long-term treatment or maintenance of recovery rests with both counselor and client, but primarily with the client.

The Role of the Counselor

An effective addictions counselor has a willingness to work with clients who suffer from addiction, is able to make appropriate referrals for a diverse client population at any time, and has an intimate knowledge of the workings of 12-step groups and how these and similar groups may enhance the counseling process and potential outcome when used in conjunction with counseling (Miller, 2005). Because the role of the addictions counselor is comprehensive and multifaceted, counselors have long been recognized as having a key role in substance users' treatment outcomes (Najavits, 2002). Counselors not only have significant influence on clients' attitudes toward 12-step groups, but it may also be concluded that clinicians' practices are critical to client outcomes (e.g., Luborsky, McLellan, Diguer, Woody, & Seligman, 1997; Najavits,

Crits-Christoph, & Dierberger, 2000; Project MATCH Research Group, 1998). 12-step referral practices are likely to be particularly important for clients' post-treatment recovery as well (Laudet & White, 2005).

For example, Laudet and White (2005) found that referrals to 12-step groups were effective at increasing meeting attendance irrespective of clients' religious backgrounds, and all clients experienced significantly better substance abuse outcomes when they participated in these groups. In fact, McCaul and Furst (1994) suggest that many substance abuse rehabilitation counselors view AA as being the single most important component of a person's recovery program. At least one study found that Alcoholics Anonymous participation was the only significant predictor of long-term recovery (McCaul & First, 1994).

Norcross (2003) and Miller (2005) suggests that self-help groups can include client education, motivation, empowerment, reinforcement, and social support, and strongly encourages counselors to incorporate the concept of self-help groups from the beginning of counseling. Counselors have an important role in educating clients about self-help groups, including addressing their misconceptions and concerns, suggesting particular group meeting formats (e.g., meetings for newcomers or specialized meetings for women, GLBTQ, or veterans), and reviewing different 12-step fellowships (e.g., AA, NA, CA) and alternative recovery support structures (e.g., Women for Sobriety, Secular Organization for Sobriety, church-based recovery ministries) (Laudet & White, 2005).

Counselors should also have a comprehensive understanding of the types of addictions and their associated groups. For example, addictions are not limited to the use of alcohol and illegal drugs, but include process addictions as well. Similar to a substance addiction, in which an individual is dependent upon alcohol or a drug, a process addiction is a series of activities or interactions on which a person becomes dependent. Process addictions include but are not limited to: work, shopping, sex, money, exercising, eating, gambling, religion, and relationships (National Addictions Awareness Week, 2004). Groups which fall into the process addiction category include: Online Gamers Anonymous (OLGA); Overeaters Anonymous (OA); Gamblers Anonymous (GA); Marijuana Anonymous (MA); Pagans in Recovery (PIR); and Workaholics Anonymous (WA). And, similarly to the diagnostic process of substance addiction, diagnosis of a process addiction is based on five criteria (Asenjo, n.d.):

1. Loss of willpower;
2. Harmful consequences;
3. Unmanageable lifestyle;
4. Tolerance or escalation of use;
5. Withdrawal symptoms upon quitting.

As already discussed, it is difficult to assess clients' views of 12-step programs in the addictions services field, but available findings suggest that they are generally amenable to participating in 12-step groups (Freimuth, 1996; Laudet, 2003), especially if their clinician has made an informed referral. Literature suggests that clinicians refer most of their substance-using clients to 12-step groups, and Humphreys (1997) found that, in a large survey of treatment programs within the Veteran's Administration system, 79% of clients were referred to Alcoholics Anonymous, 45% to Narcotics Anonymous, and 24% to Cocaine Anonymous. Counselors making referrals to these groups should be aware of their role as perceived experts in this area, and make referrals appropriately after conducting a thorough assessment of the fit between the client and the group, engaging the client in the decision-making process if possible.

However, while clinicians are generally favorable toward the incorporation of 12-step groups into treatment plans for clients, Laudet (2003) found that they also frequently cited convenience and scheduling issues as possible obstacles to clients' attending 12-step groups. It is important for counselors to understand how powerful culture, gender, and ethnicity are as salient factors in service accessibility (Lewis, 1994). Further, Laudet (2003) asserts the importance of fostering motivation for change, the need to assess clients' beliefs about and experiences with 12-step groups on a case-by-case basis, and to find a good fit between clients' needs and inclinations on the one hand, and the tools and support available within 12-step groups on the other.

It is critical for counselors to incorporate diversity into their referrals to 12-step groups, and, in working with a diverse client population, to have an awareness of the dynamics of the cultural system in which a client functions, and how the comprehensive treatment plan will best meet his or her needs. When making referrals to self-help groups, then, counselors should be aware of a client's worldview, feelings of powerlessness, and history of oppression. Just like other treatment modalities, not all 12-step groups meet the needs of all clients. And just as counselors need to be aware of the individual needs of the client, they have an ethical obligation to be aware of all cultural components and competencies in counseling clients with chemical addictions, especially taking into account the specific circumstances which affect client worldview.

These differences in worldview can lead to mismatches between helping approaches and client expectations. As Sue, Arredondo, and McDavis (1992) point out, "helping styles and approaches may be culturally bound" (p. 483). As already stated, some of the methods used routinely in addictions treatment, including those in 12-step groups, are based on a worldview perceived as "mainstream" but that actually reflects the values of the dominant white, male, American culture.

Counselors need to make appropriate referrals to groups compatible for their clients, and to be especially sensitive to the impact of such factors as racism, gender socialization, inequality, discrimination, and victimization on their clients' ability to benefit from groups (Lewis, 1994). Women clients, specifically, need the opportunity to focus on the cultural context of their addictions, and should be actively encouraged to explore issues related to gender and oppression because their substance abuse is often rooted in the gender socialization process. In many cases, an appropriate, supportive group can be a safe place to learn and build social skills, and can provide the outlet needed to work through these issues with other members who share similar experiences.

CASE STUDY

Rochelle, a 39-year-old African American woman in an urban community, has sought the assistance of a counselor at the insistence of her husband for what he describes as 'excessive alcohol use.' She tells the counselor that she has been drinking daily for 3 years since the death of a close friend and that her family is concerned about her. She complains that she doesn't feel supported by the community, and that her husband, whom she identifies as Caucasian, doesn't understand her. She appears resistant to counseling and tells the counselor that she has tried it before and doesn't feel that the counselor "get what she's saying." The counselor is considering a referral to a group. What considerations should the counselor include in the decision to make a referral?

SUGGESTIONS FOR COUNSELORS PROVIDING CARE. Actively integrating 12-step approaches into the treatment process provides low- or no-cost options for members and increases the capacity for providing treatment (Donovan & Wells, 2007). When making a referral to a self-help group or determining whether to incorporate a group into treatment, the counselor needs a list of all available self-help groups in the client's community. This information should be shared and discussed with the client to assess how the client's needs may best be served by the group. It is important for counselor and client to consider all groups that fit within the scope of meeting the goals of the treatment plan, but to choose those in which the client will feel the most comfortable and accepted to maximize the potential of a successful outcome.

When evaluating which group is most appropriate for the needs of the client and whether the client is appropriate for a group, counselors should note the following information:

- Does the client have a desire to stop the addiction? What type of addiction is it, or does the problem fall into more than one category?
- What is the gender of the client? To what extent may the addiction be conceptualized in terms of gender-role socialization?
- What is the cultural background of the client? What is his or her ethnicity? What cultural/ethnic background does he or she most identify with?
- What is the client's belief system? Is the client spiritual? Does the client adhere to a rigid religious structure? Is the client affiliated with any particular religious denomination?
- What is the client's affect like? Is he or she: Angry? Proud? Tearful? Manipulative? Mistrustful? Defensive? Guilty? Full of shame?
- Does the client demonstrate any personality traits or features that may affect adjustment to the group, and vice versa?

As pointed out earlier, accessibility may be an issue for some clients. If clients are being treated in one location and live in another, it is important that they attend groups in an area convenient both during and after addictions treatment (Miller, 2005). However, the counselor should take note if the client objects to attending groups near his or her home for anonymity reasons, in which case it is the counselor's responsibility to provide alternative group options for that client. Additionally, counselors need to make clients aware that while members of self-help groups make a commitment to not divulge specific information about meetings or identities of members in attendance to encourage free sharing in the group, there is no guarantee of anonymity. Acquiring this and other information at the outset of counseling will help the counselor determine if the client is appropriate for a group, and which group(s) he or she is appropriate for. This information will serve as a guide for the counselor in forthcoming sessions while processing the content of the group toward the aims and goals of treatment.

HOW CAN I LEARN MORE ABOUT GROUPS?

Consult.   Colleagues are a valuable resource for addictions and process information, and can provide case conceptualizations; personal experiences; mistakes and errors as well as successful outcomes; additional community resources; and collaborative opportunities for training and advocacy. Counselors should also seek supervision while providing client care; consistent supervision for practitioners is essential for competent, ethical practice. As the addictions counselor provides guidance, support, and education on the addictions process to the client, so does the supervisor provide the same for the addictions counselor.

Research.   Staying current on relevant research in the areas of addictions and associated treatment groups broadens the counselor's conceptualization of methods, models, and approaches to the treatment of addictions. Journal articles, texts, and educational resources provide a broad spectrum of information that helps expand the counselor's skill and knowledge base in this area. Counselors are cautioned to approach Internet resources skeptically; the Internet has generated a seemingly unlimited amount of useful articles and resources on the treatment of addictions and on process groups. However, there is a high potential for false information which may be harmful to the client and the recovery process. Suggested Web sites with recent and accurate information about specific groups are provided at the end of this chapter.

Get involved.   The effective addictions counselor has an intimate working knowledge of how 12-step/self-help groups work and how to incorporate them into treatment. Counselors should contact organizations and request literature on groups, and should attend various groups to familiarize themselves with the tenets, the process, membership requirements (if any), and the aims/goals of various groups to help in the client referral process. Maintaining professional networks within the addiction counseling field is also strongly recommended to increase and maintain a current working knowledge of treatment trends, continued educational opportunities, and a collegial support system for the counselor.

Summary and Some Final Notations

Counselors can contribute to the Institute of Medicine's (1990) goal of broadening the base of treatment for substance-use-related problems within their community (Caldwell, 1999). 12-step groups are often incorporated into treatment and combined with other treatment modalities to maximize the potential for a successful outcome. Group assignments and tenets are increasingly being integrated into formal services; and the attitudes, beliefs, and knowledge base of counselors regarding the role of 12-step groups in addictions treatment are greatly influential in clients' decision to participate.

Prior to a referral or the inclusion of a group into treatment, counselors need to become thoroughly familiar with the different types of 12-step groups and with their processes and procedures; how to engage the client in selecting the best match between his or her needs and treatment goals, and the foundations, aims, and structure of the group; and any cultural factors that may play a part in the efficacy of the outcome. Further, counselors have an essential role in incorporating diversity into referrals to 12-step groups. The addictions counselor needs to be aware of the client's worldview and the cultural circumstances which affect the client's willingness to participate in a group. It is imperative that the

counselor closely consider the multicultural implications of the inclusion of a group into treatment, and all considerations should be made from a position of awareness, sensitivity, and advocacy.

A few of the 12-step and affiliated groups discussed in this chapter include Alcoholics Anonymous, Al-Anon, Narcotics Anonymous, Alateen, Rational Recovery, Secular Organizations of Sobriety, Women for Sobriety, Alcoholics Anonymous for Atheists and Agnostics, and Moderation Management. Many groups have been established to address the multitude of needs and differing belief systems of group members, and all groups have their own guidelines to which they adhere. Effective addictions counselors will have lists of, and information on, all self-help groups in the client's community, including descriptions, meeting times, education materials, literature, brochures, and videos if available. The referral process should be a collaborative one between counselor and client, and the counselor should make a thorough determination of whether the client will benefit from a group experience while working toward treatment goals, as not all clients are appropriate for all groups.

Benefits of groups include the power dynamics of universality, a supportive environment for the practicing of new behaviors and skills, and the opportunity for clients to learn about themselves through the sharing of experiences that serve to facilitate personal growth. Conversely, disadvantages include a foundation of spirituality which may not be inclusive of all cultures, members working issues out inappropriately in the group setting, and the lack of professional training among group leaders. 12-step/self-help groups are voluntary and nonprofit, but counselors often cite accessibility and cultural insensitivity as reasons for noninclusion in treatment.

The importance of counselor inclusion of 12-step/self-help groups into addictions treatment has been acknowledged by several professional organizations (Laudet, 2003). Laudet and White (2005) suggest that counselors are expressing a growing interest in the potential role of groups in addictions treatment, and are currently seeking further information about how to best incorporate them into their practice. They suggest that, because counselors play an important role in fostering 12-step participation, the insights they develop through their research and practice can greatly contribute to the field of addictions counseling (Laudet, 2003).

Useful Web Sites

The following Web sites provide additional information relating to the chapter topic:

Al-Anon
http://www.al-anon.org

Alateen
http://www.al-anon.alateen.org

Alcoholics Anonymous
http://www.aa.org

Cocaine Anonymous (CA)
http://www.ca.org/

Co-Dependents Anonymous (CoDA)
http://www.codependents.org/

Crystal Meth Anonymous (CMA)
http://www.crystalmeth.org/

Debtors Anonymous (DA)
http://www.debtorsanonymous.org/

Drug and Alcohol Registry of Treatment
http://www.dart.on.ca/

Drug Rehab and Drug Rehabilitation Treatment Centers
http://www.drug-rehab.com/index.htm

Emotional Health Anonymous (EHA)
http://www.emotionsanonymous.org/

Gamblers Anonymous (GA)
http://www.gamblersanonymous.org/

Marijuana Anonymous (MA)
http://www.marijuana-anonymous.org/

Moderation Management (MM)
http://moderation.org/

Nar-Anon
http://www.nar-anon.org/Nar-Anon/Nar-Anon_Home.html

Narcotics Anonymous
http://www.na.org

National Addictions Awareness Week
http://www.naaw.net/addictions-process.php

National Association for Children of Alcoholics (NACoA)
http://nacoa.org/

National Center on Addiction and Substance Abuse at Columbia University
http://www.casacolumbia.org

National Institute on Alcohol Abuse and Alcoholism
http://www.niaaa.nih.gov

Nicotine Anonymous (NicA)
http://www.nicotine-anonymous.org/

Online Gamers Anonymous (OLGA)
http://www.olganon.org/

Overeaters Anonymous (OA)
http://www.oa.org/

Pagans in Recovery (PIR)
http://pagansinrecovery.com/

Rational Recovery
http://www.rational.org/recovery

Secular Organizations for Sobriety
http://www.sossobriety.org

Sexaholics Anonymous (SA)
http://www.sa.org/

SMART Recovery
http://www.smartrecovery.org/

Substance Abuse and Mental Health Services Administration
http://www.health.org

Women for Sobriety, Inc.
http://www.womenforsobriety.org

Workaholics Anonymous (WA)
http://www.workaholics-anonymous.org/page.php?page=home

References

Alcoholics Anonymous World Services. (1991). New York: Alcoholics Anonymous World Services.

Al-Anon's Twelve Steps & Twelve Traditions. (1985). New York: Al-Anon Family Group Headquarters.

Alford, G. S., Koehler, R. A., & Leonard, J. (1991). Alcoholics Anonymous–Narcotics Anonymous model inpatient treatment of chemically dependent adolescents: a 2-year outcome study. *Journal of Studies on Alcohol, 52,* 118–126.

Bell, P. (1993, July). *Chemical dependency and the African-American.* Presentation to the annual conference of the National Association of Drug and Alcohol Counselors, Chicago.

Bristow-Braitman, A. (1995). Addiction recovery: 12-Step programs and cognitive behavioral psychology, *Journal of Counseling and Development, 73,* 414–418.

Brown, S. (1995). *Treating alcoholism.* San Francisco: Jossey-Bass.

Caldwell, P. E. (1999). Fostering client connections with Alcoholics Anonymous: a framework for social workers in various practice settings. *Social Work in Health Care, 28*(4), 45–61.

Chappel, J., & DuPont, R. (1999). Twelve-step and mutual-help programs for addictive disorders. *Addictive Disorders, 22*(2), 425–446.

Christo, G., & Franey, C. (1995). Drug user's spiritual beliefs, locus of control and the disease concept in relation to narcotics anonymous attendance and six-month outcomes. *Drug and Alcohol Dependence, 38,* 51–56.

Corey, G., & Corey, M. S. (1992). *Group process and practice.* (4th ed.). Pacific Grove, CA: Brooks/Cole Publishing Co.

Crape, B. L., Latkin, C. A., Laris, A. S., & Knowlton, A. R. (2002). The effects of sponsorship in 12-step treatment of injection drug users. *Drug and Alcohol Dependence 6*(3), 291–301.

Davis, D. R., & Jansen, G. G. (1998). Making meaning of Alcoholics Anonymous for social workers: Myths, metaphors, and realities. *Social Work, 43*(2), 169–182.

Del Toro, I. M., Thom, D. J., Beam, H. P., & Horst, T. (1996). Chemical dependent patients in recover: Roles for the family physician. *American Family Physician, 53*(5), 1667–1681.

Donovan, D. M., & Wells, E. A. (2007). Tweaking 12-Step: The potential role of 12-step self-help group involvement in methamphetamine recovery. *Addiction, 102,* 121–129.

Dorsman, J. (1996). Improving alcoholism treatment: An overview. *Behavioral Health Management, 16*(1), 26–29.

Doweiko, H. (1999). *Concepts of chemical dependency.* (4th ed.). Pacific Grove, CA: Brooks/Cole Publishing Company.

Emrick, C. D., Tonigan, J. S., Montgomery, H., & Little, L. (1993). Alcoholics Anonymous: what is currently known? In B. S. McCrady, & W. R. Miller, (Eds.), *Research on Alcoholics Anonymous: Opportunities and alternatives* (pp. 41–78). New Brunswick, NJ: Rutgers Center of Alcohol Studies.

Facts about Alateen. (1969). New York: Al-Anon Family Group Headquarters.

Freimuth, M. (1996). Psychotherapists' beliefs about the benefits of 12-step groups. *Alcoholism Treatment, 14,* 95–102.

Galanter, M., Castaneda, R., & Franco, H. (1991). Group therapy and self-help groups. In R. J. Frances & S. I. Miller (Eds.), *Clinical textbook of addictive disorders.* New York: Guilford Press.

George, A. A., & Tucker, J. A. (1996). Help-seeking for alcohol-related problems: Social contexts surrounding entry into alcoholism treatment or Alcoholics Anonymous. *Journal of Studies on Alcohol, 57,* 449–457.

Group, The. (1976). Narcotics Anonymous World Service Office, Inc.

Groups offer self-help: Alternatives to AA. (1991). *Alcoholism & Drug Abuse Week, 3*(37), 6.

Heyward, C. (1992). Healing addiction and homophobia: Reflections on empowerment and liberation. *Journal of Chemical Dependency Treatment, 5*(1), 5–18.

Humphreys, K. (1997). Clinicans' referral and matching of substance abuse patients to self-help groups after treatment. *Psychiatric Services, 48,* 1445–1449.

Humphreys, K., & Moos, R. H. (1996). Reduced substance-abuse-related health care costs among voluntary participants in Alcoholics Anonymous. *Psychiatric Services, 47,* 709–713.

Institute of Medicine. (1990). *Broadening the base of treatment for alcohol problems.* Washington, DC: National Academy Press.

Johnsen, E., & Herringer, L. G. (1993). A note on the utilization of common support activities and relapse following substance abuse treatment. *Journal of Psychology, 127,* 73–78.

Johnson, P. N., & Phelps, G. L. (1991). Effectiveness in self-help groups: Alcoholics Anonymous as a prototype. *Family and Community Health, 14,* 22–27.

Kelly, J. F., Magill, M., & Stout, R. L. (2009). How do people recover from alcohol dependence? A systematic review of the research on mechanisms of behavior change in Alcoholics Anonymous. *Addiction Research & Theory, 17*(3), 236–259.

Khantzian, E. J., & Mack, J. E. (1994). How AA works and why it's important for clinicans to understand. *Journal of Substance Abuse Treatment, 11,* 77–92.

Kirkpatric, J. (1990). *Stages of the "new life" program.* Quakertown, PA: Women for Sobriety.

Kishline, A. (1996). A toast to moderation. *Psychology Today, 29*(1), 53–56.

Knack, W. A. (2009). Psychotherapy and Alcoholics Anonymous: An integrated approach. *Journal of Psychotherapy Integration, 19*(1), 86–109.

Laudet, A. (2000). Substance abuse treatment providers' referral to self-help: review and future empirical directions. *International Journal of Self-Help & Self-care, 1*(3), 195–207.

Laudet, A. (2003). Attitudes and beliefs about 12-step groups among addiction treatment clients and clinicians: Toward identifying obstacles to participation. *Substance Use and Misuse, 38*(14), 2017–2047.

Laudet, A. B., Magura, S., Cleland, C. M., Vogel, H. S., & Knight, E. L. (2003). Predictors of retention in dual-focus self-help groups. *Community Mental Health Journal, 39*(4), 281–297.

Laudet, A. B., & White, W. L. (2005). An exploratory investigation of the association between clinicians' attitudes toward twelve-step groups and referral rates. *Alcoholism Treatment Quarterly, 23*(1), 31–45.

Lawson, S. (2003). Surrendering the night: The seduction of victim blaming in drug and alcohol facilitated sexual prevention strategies. *Women Against Violence, 13,* 33–38.

Lawson, G. W., Lawson, A. W., & Rivers, P. C. (2001). *Essentials of Chemical Dependency Counseling* (3rd ed.). Gaithersburg, MD: Aspen Publishers, Inc. (CHAPTER 5, pp. 174–214.)

Lewis, J. A. (1994). Issues of gender and culture in substance abuse treatment. In J. A. Lewis (Ed.), *Addictions: Concepts and strategies for treatment* (pp. 37–40). Gaithersburg, MD: Aspen Publishers, Inc.

Luborsky, L., McLellan, A. T., Diguer, L., Woody, G., & Seligman, D. (1997). The psychotherapist matters: Comparison of outcomes across twenty-two therapists and seven patient samples. *Clinical Psychology: Science and Practice, 4,* 53–65.

McCaul, M. D., & Furst, J. (1994). Alcoholism treatment in the United States. *Alcohol Health & Research World, 18,* 253–260.

McCollum, V. J. C. (1997). Evolution of the African American family personality: Considerations for family therapy. *Journal of Multicultural Counseling and Development, 25,* 219–229.

McCrady, B. S., & Delaney, S. I. (1995). Self-help groups. In R. K. Hester & W. R. Miller (Eds.), *Handbook of alcoholism treatment approaches* (end ed.). New York: Allyn & Bacon.

McIntire, D. (2000). How well does AA work? An analysis of published AA surveys (1968–96) and related analyses/comments. *Alcoholism Treatment Quarterly, 18,* 1–18.

McKay, M., & Paleg, K. (Eds.). (1992). *Focal group psychotherapy.* Oakland, CA: New Harbinger Publications.

Mejta C. L., Naylor, C. L., & Maslar, E. M. (1994). Drug abuse treatment: Approaches and effectiveness. In J. A. Lewis (Ed.), *Addictions: Concepts and strategies for treatment* (pp. 59–77). Gaithersburg, MD: Aspen Publishers, Inc.

Miller, G. (2005). *Learning the language of addiction counseling* (2nd ed.). Hoboken, NJ: John Wiley & Sons, Inc.

Miller, W. R., & McCrady, B. S. (1993). The importance of research on Alcoholics Anonymous. In B. S. McCrady & W. R. Miller (Eds.), *Research on Alcoholics Anonymous.* New Brunswick, NJ: Rutgers Center of Alcohol Studies.

Najavitz, L. M., Crits-Christoph, P., & Dierberger, A. (2000). Clinicians' impact on the quality of substance use disorder treatment. *Substance Use Misuse, 35* (12–14), 2161–2190.

Narcotics Anonymous. (1982). Van Nuys, CA: Narcotics Anonymous World Service Office.

Norcross, J. C. (2003, August). *Integrating self-help into psychotherapy: A revolution in mental health practice* [Invited address]. Rosalee G. Weiss lecture on psychotherapy at the American Psychological Association, Toronto, Ontario, Canada.

Ouimette, P. C., Finney, J. W., & Moos, R. H. (1997). Twelve-step and cognitive-behavioral treatment for substance abuse: A comparison of treatment effectiveness. *Journal of Consulting and Clinical Psychology, 65,* 230–240.

Peteet, J. (1993). A closer look at the role of a spiritual approach in addictions treatment. *Journal of Substance Abuse Treatment, 10*(3), 263–267.

Price, R. H., Burke, A. C., D'Aunno, T. A., Klingel, D. M., McCaughain, W. C., Rafferty, J. A., & Vaughn, T. E. (1991). Outpatient drug abuse treatment services, 1988. Results of a national survey. In R. Pickens, C. G. Leukefeld, & C. Schuster (Eds.), *Improving drug abuse treatment* (pp. 63–91). Rockville, MD: National Institute on Drug Abuse. [(ADM) 91–1754]

Project MATCH Research Group. (1998). Matching alcoholism treatments to client heterogeneity: Project MATCH three-year drinking outcomes. *Alcoholism: Clinical & Experimental Research, 22,* 1300–1311.

Rand, L. (1995). A different road. *Chicago Tribune, 148*(53), Tempo Sect., 1, 7.

Riordan, R. J., & Walsh, L. (1994). Guidelines for professionals. Referral to Alcoholics Anonymous and other twelve step groups. *Journal of Counseling and Development, 72,* 351–355.

Roman, P. M., Blum, T. C. (1998). National Treatment Center Study. *Summary Report (No. 3): Second Wave On-Site Results.* Unpublished Manuscript, University of Georgia.

Roots, L. E., & Aanes, D. L. (1992). A conceptual framework for understanding self help groups. *Hospital and Community Psychiatry, 43,* 379–381.

Smith, D., Buxton, M., Bilal, R., Seymour, R. (1993). Cultural points of resistance to the 12-step recovery process. *Journal of Psychoactive Drugs, 25*(1), 97–108.

Sterling, S., Chi, F., Campbell, C., & Weisner, C. (2009). Three-year chemical dependency and mental health treatment outcomes among adolescents: The role of continuing care. *Alcoholism: Clinical & Experimental Research, 33*(8), 1417–1429.

Sue, D. W., Arredondo, P., & McDavis, R. J. (1992). Multicultural counseling competencies and standards: A call to the profession. *Journal of Counseling & Development, 70,* 477–486.

Sue, D. W., & Sue, D. (1999). *Counseling the culturally different: Theory and practice.* (3rd ed.). New York: John Wiley & Sons, Inc.

Tonigan, J. S., & Hiller-Sturmhofel, S. (1994). Alcoholics Anonymous: Who benefits? *Alcohol Health & Research World, 18,* 308–310.

Tonigan, J. S., Bogenschutz, M. P., & Miller, W. R. (2006). Is alcoholism typology a predictor of both Alcoholics Anonymous affiliation and disaffiliation after treatment? *Journal of Substance Abuse Treatment, 30,* 323–330.

Tonigan, J. S., Toscova, R., & Miller, W. R. (1996). Meta-analysis of the literature on Alcoholics Anonymous: Sample and study characteristics moderate findings. *Journal of Studies on Alcohol, 57*(1), 65–72.

Toumbourou, J. W., Hamilton, M., U'Ren, A., Steven-Jones, P., & Storey, G. (2002). Narcotics Anonymous participation and changes in substance use and social support. *Journal of Substance Abuse Treatment, 23*(1), 61–67.

Twelve Steps and Twelve Traditions. (1981). New York: Alcoholics Anonymous World Services.

Wenger, S. (1997). National association for children of alcoholics. *Alcohol Health & Research World, 21*(3), 267–270.

Zemore, S. E., Zaskutas, L. A., & Ammon, L. N. (2004). In 12-step groups, helping helps the helper. *Addiction, 99*(8), 1015–1023.

Zweben, J. E. (1995). Integrating psychotherapy and 12-step approaches. In A. M. Washton (Ed.), *Psychotherapy and substance abuse.* New York: Guilford Press.

Chapter *13*

Maintenance and Relapse Prevention[1]

Rochelle Moss
Henderson State University
Christopher C. H. Cook
Durham University

INTRODUCTION

After the client has completed the initial stages of treatment, the focus of the counseling process should be on establishing a firm foundation in a maintenance program for the prevention of a relapse. Although client relapse often occurs, this setback can be reframed as a learning experience in the growing awareness of one's limitations and weaknesses. The initial portion of this chapter delves into relapse prevention for addictive behavior, identifies high-risk situations, and examines by case study how seemingly irrelevant decisions play a part in a relapse. We also discuss the abstinence violation effect. The latter portion describes relapse prevention with specific daily maintenance practices as applied within a case study. In conclusion, some of the most recent findings in the field of substance abuse will be summarized to help us better understand the dynamic, complex issues of relapse and maintenance.

RELAPSE PREVENTION FOR ADDICTIVE BEHAVIORS

A relapse is often defined as a return to drug use after a period of abstention. Attempting to determine rates of relapse can be challenging due to many variables. Relapse rates are different depending on the drug, severity of the addiction, length of treatment, and how relapse is defined. Several studies have indicated a relapse as high as 90% for alcoholics (Doweiko, 1990; Orford & Edwards, 1977). A recent government study compared the relapse rates of drug addiction to other chronic illnesses (National Institute on Drug Abuse, n.d.). This study estimated the percentage of people with drug addictions who relapsed as 40% to 60% compared to Type 1 diabetes at 30% to 50%, and both asthma and hypertension at 50% to 70%. Regardless of the many factors involved, both practitioners and researchers agree that most individuals who attempt any significant behavior change will experience lapses and/or relapses.

Alcoholism is a relapsing condition that is found to be no different than other addictive behaviors (Polich, Amour, & Braiker, 1981). What do we mean by "relapsing condition"? In the broader context of medicine, "relapse" might be defined as a return of disease after an apparently full or partial recovery. However, the term is used even more broadly, in everyday life, to refer to falling back into a pattern of habitual (usually negative) behavior. In addiction treatment it can be used in either or both

---

[1] We would like to acknowledge the contribution that Jeff Sandoz made to the first edition of this chapter.

of these senses, but it might best be understood here to refer specifically to a return to a pattern of addictive behavior that had (for a shorter or longer period of time) apparently abated.

Relapse can occur following apparently spontaneous cessation of addictive behavior, self-motivated and deliberate attempts to overcome an addiction, involvement with a self-help (or mutual-help) program of recovery, or following involvement with a formal medical or psychological treatment program. However, for present purposes, it is perhaps best to think of relapse as something that occurs following an intervention or treatment intended to control or eliminate the behavior in question. Thus, a single drink taken by an alcoholic who had been completely abstinent for some months, as a result of engagement in a program of recovery supported by attendance at Alcoholics Anonymous (AA) or Rational Recovery (RR), would count as a relapse. The basic philosophy of such groups is that a relapse is a normal part of the addiction process and it is *not* a part of recovery. Similarly, a return to heavy drinking, by a client seeing a substance abuse counselor who had been assisting her in moderating her alcohol use, would also be a relapse. But a single drink taken by the latter client might not be understood as a relapse at all, as it might have been well within the limits agreed to with her counselor. This distinction immediately raises a series of important considerations.

First, "relapse" can mean different things for different clients engaged in different thera-peutic programs. This is not only a question of degree. For example, most 12-step programs aim at abstinence from all mood-altering substances. Thus, consumption of one glass of wine might count as a relapse for a formerly opioid-dependent client attending Narcotics Anonymous, but considered quite immaterial by the counselor of the same client engaged in a purely psychological program of cognitive behavior therapy focused on illicit drug use. Similarly, an alcoholic client who remains completely abstinent from alcohol might begin using tranquilizers in an addictive fashion and thus have relapsed—even though the counselor neglected to tell the client not to use tranquillizers. Such action by the client is referred to within AA circles as the "trading of one addiction in for another."

Second, it will sometimes be necessary to distinguish a "lapse" from a "relapse" (Marlatt & George, 1984), as a single glass of wine has a different significance for the client enrolled in a con-trolled drinking program, as compared with a member of AA. Thus, a single glass of wine consumed by one aiming at complete abstinence (whatever program of treatment one is engaged in as a means of achieving that goal) might well constitute a relapse when it is denied, leads to further drinking, or constitutes a breach of terms of employment in a safety-sensitive workplace. However, for another client, where the same behavior leads immediately to a meeting with a sponsor or counselor and thus to a helpful discussion about how it could be avoided in the future, it might be referred to merely as a "lapse." A lapse is thus a technical or modest breach of agreed treatment goals, which allows for learning and therefore eventual achievement of the ultimate aims and objectives of treatment. A relapse is a more serious violation of treatment goals, or a more minor violation in which such learning is not evident.

Third, relapse prevention is an approach to treatment compatible with other treatment models of widely varying philosophy. Multimodal therapies in conjunction with a supportive 12-step program offer the greatest promise for long-term abstinence. But this in turn raises another important question. What is "relapse prevention" in its pure form?

Relapse prevention is difficult to define because it constitutes a range of therapeutic methods applicable to a range of very different addictive behaviors, as well as to habits or behaviors that might not normally be considered "addictive" at all. In each case the aim is to prevent relapse, but like "relapse" the word "prevention" can mean different things. Thus, for example, a program of relapse prevention might be considered successful in the short term if it results in a reduction of the severity or frequency of relapse, even if it does not result in complete elimination of addictive behavior. On the other hand, another program of treatment might achieve complete abstinence in a larger proportion of clients but no reduction at all in those who are not abstinent.

Relapse prevention usually involves training clients in techniques that they will find useful in preventing or eliminating relapse. It is thus, in a sense, a form of "self-help" or self-regulation. However, it is not limited specifically to the realm of addictive behavior. There is reason to believe that overall lifestyle has an important part to play in the maintenance or elimination of addictive behavior; and so relapse prevention can legitimately address itself to matters such as spirituality, diet, exercise, and recreation, as well as to specific issues narrowly concerned with the addictive behavior itself. Furthermore, relapse prevention might involve prescription of pharmacological agents such as acamprosate or naltrexone, which can play a role in supporting or augmenting psychological treatments by reducing the urge or craving to use.

Relapse prevention might, ideally, completely remove the underlying causes of addictive behavior. However, in practice it is focused specifically upon the addictive behavior itself. A good outcome is thus defined purely in terms of an observed change in addictive behavior, and not on the basis of hypothesized or actual underlying factors. This is not to say that such considerations are unimportant, but simply that they are not an essential or distinctive component of this approach to treatment. Relapse prevention is sometimes employed in treatment settings where attention to such factors is considered vital; in other cases it is employed as part of a purely behavioral approach, where observable behavior alone is the criterion of success.

While we are mindful of all these various meanings of the term "relapse prevention," we will use it here to refer primarily to approaches to the recovery from addictive disorders, which may be taught or learned, with the objective of reducing the frequency and/or severity of relapse. The best possible outcome, of course, is that relapse prevention leads to a total elimination of relapse. However, no treatment for addictive disorders results in a 100% improvement for all clients. Relapse prevention allows the possibility of a degree of success even where there is not total success. More importantly, it allows the possibility that at least some failures (notably "lapses") can be learning experiences that predict a better outcome in the longer term.

RELAPSE PREVENTION MODEL

The Relapse Prevention (RP) model (Marlatt and Gordon, 1985) is one of the most well-known models used to prevent or manage relapse. It is an approach based upon cognitive behavioral theory and includes aspects of social learning theory. This model has evolved over time, and its proponents describe the relapse process as a complex, multidimensional system (Witkiewitz & Marlatt, 2004).

Counselors using the RP model are interested in understanding the factors which influence an individual to remain abstinent or to relapse. These include both intrapersonal and interpersonal factors. Intrapersonal factors include self-efficacy, outcome expectancies, craving, level of motivation, coping ability, and emotional states. Interpersonal factors involve social support, or the amount of emotional support available to the individual in treatment (Witkiewitz and Marlatt, 2004).

Self-Efficacy

Self-efficacy is defined as the degree to which a person feels capable and competent of being successful in a specific situation (Bandura, 1977). This belief in one's ability is context-specific and often derived from past successes in a similar situation. Self-efficacy level and rate of relapse are strongly related. If clients experience a lapse, their self-efficacy begins to fluctuate, and they have an increased risk of a full-blown relapse (Shiffman et al., 2000). However, if individuals maintain abstinence (e.g. success in smoking cessation), their self-efficacy increases (Gwaltney, Metrik, Kahler, & Shiffman, 2009).

Melanie was beginning a smoking cessation program. This was her third attempt to quit smoking. She expressed a high level of self-efficacy when discussing her ability to abstain from smoking while she was at work. She knew strategies that helped her resist the urge to smoke on her job, and had successfully used these strategies during the first two attempts. However, she had not been successful in refraining from smoking while out with friends. In this circumstance, she expressed a low level of self-efficacy. What strategies could the counselor use to help Melanie increase self-efficacy for not smoking while out with friends?

Outcome Expectancies

Outcome expectancy refers to the client's beliefs or thoughts about what is going to happen after using a substance. A positive outcome expectancy is associated with increased relapse rates because the individual anticipates positive consequences from the drug use.

Tyler is a college freshman receiving counseling for anxiety and drug abuse. He believes that drinking a couple of six packs of beer will result in him being more popular at the fraternity party because he will have less anxiety. This positive outcome expectancy results in Tyler's lapse. The counselor is hoping to assist Tyler in developing a negative outcome expectancy to increase the likelihood of him remaining abstinent. How could the counselor use cognitive behavioral therapy in this process?

Have you experienced the urge to smoke while trying on a bathing suit? These two events have actually been linked! Because body dissatisfaction leads to negative feelings, young women have the urge to smoke. These women believe that they will lose weight if they smoke and therefore feel better about themselves in a bathing suit (a positive outcome expectancy), which increases the likelihood of relapse (Lopez, Drobes, Thompson & Brandon, 2008).

Craving

Cravings refer to physiological responses which prepare the individual for the effect of a substance. When an addict is deprived of the substance (during abstinence) and is subject to cue exposure (e.g., seeing a beer advertisement), the individual will experience a craving. If the person believes that the beer is readily available, this increases the craving (Wertz & Sayette, 2001). However, high self-efficacy and effective coping strategies can be the "braking mechanism" to prevent relapse (Niaura, 2000).

Coping

Coping skills refer to strategies that help individuals to effectively manage their behavior, especially in high-risk situations. Many types of coping strategies are used in the field of substance abuse counseling. Behavioral approaches, such as meditation and deep breathing exercises, and cognitive coping strategies, such as mindfulness and self-talk, have proven to be effective in lowering relapse rates for substance abuse.

One of your best coping strategies is your ability to self-regulate. But can your self-regulation "muscle" get tired (Baumeister, Heatherton, & Tice, 1994)? If you've been under a lot of stress, resulting in overuse of self-control resources, your self-regulation "muscle" may become exhausted. This fatigue leads to using more ineffective coping strategies, such as drinking more.

Motivation

The level of motivation a person has to change a behavior is one of the most important factors in the efficacy of treatment. The transtheoretical model of motivation (Prochaska & DiClemente, 1984) described five stages of readiness to change: precontemplation, contemplation, preparation, action, and maintenance. Each stage represents an increase in motivation and readiness to follow through with the change process. Although this model describes a linear progression, there are usually many backward slides as well as forward movement. Levels of motivation depend upon positive and negative reinforcement and can be influenced by situations, life events, moods, social pressure, and numerous other variables.

Think of a time when you've tried to change a behavior. Maybe you're attempting to eliminate junk food from your diet. Did you experience a linear movement from early motivation to reaching your goal? Probably not! Most of us are affected by daily moods, unexpected life events, and changes in our confidence level. So you may have carried out your plan and had no junk food for a few days; then you had a conflict with your boss. After a few days of chips and candy, you re-evaluate and go back to the planning stage!

Emotional States

Both positive and negative feelings have been identified as major reasons for drug use, but negative feelings are thought to be the primary motive. An individual's abstinence self-efficacy, or the confidence in oneself to remain sober, is lowest when the person is experiencing emotions such as sadness, anger, anxiety, or regret. Most clients will experience shame and remorse, which are triggers for relapse. Negative affect has been specifically linked with lapses in alcohol use (Witkiewitz & Villarroel, 2009).

It seems as though traumatic events and disasters are linked to early relapse rates. Following the September 11 tragedy, early relapse rates were reported among smokers attempting to quit. The use of other substances increased, also. Similar behaviors were found after the Oklahoma City bombing. The increased levels of smoking were associated to higher stress levels, worry about safety, and post-traumatic grief (Forman-Hoffman, Riley, & Pici, 2005).

Social Support

In substance abuse counseling, the importance of social support for abstinence cannot be down-played. Social support can be both positive and negative. Families, spouses, and friends can provide a positive, supportive system that can improve the client's level of self-efficacy and negative mood. However, it is often difficult for a client's family and friends to stay supportive through numerous relapses and subsequent pain and distress. When clients are successful in minimizing negative support, they are more likely to maintain sobriety (Lawhon, Humfleet, Hall, Reus, & Munoz, 2009).

The Value of One — It Can Go Either Way!

The importance of a supportive social network cannot be emphasized enough! Being involved with others and receiving high levels of support from even **one** person prior to treatment leads to better outcomes. But drinkers' social networks include many other drinkers, and having even **one** person in the social network who drinks increases the risk of relapse (Havassy, Hall, & Wasserman, 1991).

Substance abuse counselors have found that clients are more likely to lapse or relapse immediately following treatment. But over time the recovering individuals have a tendency to relapse less as they learn coping strategies and increase their self-efficacy. To help a client stabilize and maintain sobriety, counselors need to be familiar with some common issues. Three of these essential elements in the Relapse Prevention model are: (1) high-risk situations; (2) seemingly irrelevant decisions; and (3) the abstinence violation effect.

HIGH-RISK SITUATIONS

At the heart of relapse prevention therapy is the observation that for every addict certain identifiable sets of circumstances present a high risk of relapse. These high-risk situations (HRS) are key events in relapse, which may pose a threat to one's level of confidence about exercising self-control (Marlatt & Gordon, 1985). The better able a client is to identify his or her own HRSs and to prepare in advance a repertoire of coping strategies designed to manage them without relapse, the more likely he or she is to achieve a good outcome. Marlatt and Gordon (1980) report that most relapses were associated with three kinds of HRS: (1) frustration and anger, (2) interpersonal temptation, and (3) social pressure.

Clients often recognize that they are more likely to drink when feeling negative emotions—anxiety, depression, etc.—but often overlook the fact that emotional highs can also be a problem. One of the coauthors of this chapter (CCHC), engaged in a research follow-up of clients from a 12-step treatment program some years ago, encountered the case of an alcoholic who had been abstinent for a year or more but who died from acute alcoholic poisoning on the night of his first and only relapse of drinking. The relapse was precipitated by his desire to celebrate success in clinching an important business deal. This idea seems to echo the words of Dr. William Silkworth, author of "The Doctor's Opinion" in *Alcoholics Anonymous*. "I have had many men who had, for example, worked a period of months on some . . . business deal which was to be settled on a certain date, favorably to them. They took a drink a day or so prior to the date, and then the phenomenon of craving at once became paramount to all other interests so that the important appointment was not met. These men were not drinking to escape; they were drinking to overcome a craving beyond their mental control" (*Alcoholics Anonymous,* 2001, pp. xxvii–xxviii).

Counselors who work with teens may think that an increase in substance abuse is due to conflict with adults or peers, or strong negative emotions. However, a recent study has shown that over two-thirds of adolescents relapse when they are trying to enhance a positive emotional state. In other words, teens use drugs and alcohol in an attempt to increase an already elated mood (Ramo & Brown, 2008).

Interpersonal temptation due to conflict is often recognized as preceding relapse but is easily used by addicts as a way of blaming others for their plight. In relapse prevention therapy this is understood as being an HRS, in which the client is responsible for putting into effect previously planned coping strategies as ways to manage anger, rejection, or conflict without relapse.

Social pressures to drink are often subtle and are pervasive in Western society. However, within given subcultures there are countless pressures to use other drugs, to engage in gambling, overeating, spending beyond personal means, and a variety of other potentially addictive behaviors. Once these pressures are recognized for what they are, it is possible to plan in advance how they will be managed. Many relapses occur simply because addicts do not plan ahead but allow themselves to be caught unawares. As most of us are not able to think up a convincing alternative plan of action at a moment's notice, a long-reinforced and familiar pattern of addictive behavior becomes the inevitable outcome for anyone being pressured to conform to social pressure to drink or use drugs or to engage in other patterns of addictive behavior. This is especially true where friends, family, or respected authority figures exert the social pressure.

Rachel had successfully abstained from drinking for three months but was now dreading going home for the holidays. She explained to the counselor that alcohol was at the center of much of her family's celebration. During counseling sessions, she detailed all of the situations in which she might feel pressured to drink. She and the counselor brainstormed refusal skills and rehearsed behavioral strategies, such as always having a drink (soft drink) in her hand. What other behavioral strategies could the counselor use with Rachel to help her maintain sobriety?

Relapse prevention therapy begins by assisting a client to identify their own HRSs. Keeping a diary of emotional states, social interactions, cravings, and lapses/relapses can assist in this process. A variety of questionnaires are also available to help with this process, such as the Inventory of Drinking Situations (Annis, 1982). Having identified the HRSs that are most difficult for a particular individual to manage, it is then important to consider what the habitual coping strategies for handling these situations might be. Clearly, addictive behavior (drinking, drug use, etc.) is likely to be the predominant pretreatment response. However, other coping strategies a client has used may be ineffective and thus unlikely to help prevent relapse.

Specific coping strategies must then be considered, planned, and implemented. This process begins with brainstorming—either individually or as part of a group—about what kinds of strategies might be possible for each HRS. After generating a list of as many possible coping strategies as can be imagined, the counselor should assist clients in the process of refining, modifying, combining, and improving upon a selected number of coping strategies. Ideally, these are then rehearsed. For example, there is much to be gained from encouraging alcoholics to role-play drink-refusal skills. The benefit is even greater if the role-plays are videotaped and played back, with discussion of how the client managed the situation. Alcoholics also benefit from recognizing the ploys that have been used by others to persuade them to join in with "social" drinking. Helpful suggestions in preparing for HRS include the following:

1. Be aware of intrapersonal triggers (thought patterns and related emotions) that lead one to substance abuse (e.g., expectations, anger, fear, resentment, irritation, frustration, disappointment, shame, etc.).
2. Use mnemonic devices to remember countermeasures in a plan of action.
3. Acquire a system of markers (emotional barometers) that will engage the memory to prompt the recall of an action plan.

4. Develop a back-up plan to diffuse emotions, utilizing resources, people, and activities.
5. Use multiple methods of stress relief; specifically, nonaddictive, healthy alternatives such as developing hobbies, meditation, relaxation, and physical exercise.

Have you surfed recently? A group of college students interested in decreasing their smoking habits were encouraged to do some "urge-surfing." If you want to try this, first think of specific urges you experience for an unwanted habit or behavior. Then picture the urges as waves, and imagine riding these waves as they naturally ebb and flow, rather than fighting the urge or giving in to it (Bowen & Marlatt, 2009).

Annis and Davis (1991) offered one of the more comprehensive relapse prevention models. This model, which is designed to initiate and maintain changes in drinking behavior, focuses on building confidence in one's ability and promoting self-efficacy. Procedures for this model include:

1. Develop a hierarchy of substance-abuse risk situations.
2. Identify strengths and resources in the environment and cope with affective, behavioral, and cognitive issues.
3. Design homework assignments by which the client is able to: (a) monitor thoughts and feelings in specific situations, (b) anticipate problematic situations, (c) rehearse alternative responses to drinking, (d) practice new behaviors within the more difficult situations, and (e) reflect on personal progress and increased levels of competence.

Counselors need to keep in mind specific risk factors that can influence whether or not a person will be successful in maintaining sobriety in the face of high-risk situations. These factors include stressful life events, the loss of family/social support, acute psychological distress, situational threats to self-efficacy, and both positive and negative emotions. Also, some clients have a greater potential for relapse due to a family history of alcoholism or drug addiction, the nature and severity of the addiction, and comorbid psychiatric and substance abuse diagnoses (Donovan, 1996; Shiffman, 1989).

SEEMINGLY IRRELEVANT DECISIONS (SIDs)

High-risk situations are not simply circumstances imposed by other people or the social environment. Sometimes they are the result of an individual's thought processes. These thought processes are varied and diverse and a comprehensive account is not possible here. Where thinking errors and psychological "traps" appear to be a prominent cause of relapse, there may be benefit in gaining specialist help in the form of cognitive therapy. On the other hand, there is much wisdom as to how such processes operate within the world of 12-step groups such as AA. Research in maintenance and relapse prevention indicates that multimodal treatment, along with attendance in a 12-step program, offers the best chance for long-term recovery and abstinence (Inaba & Cohen, 2000). Quite often the 12-step groups will prove to be more accessible and, as they come with the voice of personal experience, advice given there will be listened to more seriously than that offered by the professional counselor with no personal experience.

"Seemingly irrelevant decisions," or SIDs (also known as "set-ups") are decisions an individual makes that may seem irrelevant at the time, but very often can lead to a relapse. SIDs are perhaps best illustrated by way of an example.

It was a fine day, and John had finished work early after receiving a highly positive annual appraisal from his boss. He decided to walk home from work. He varied his usual route so as to stroll through the local park, enjoying the warm sun, the trees in blossom, and the sounds of children playing ball. He felt good about life, and his days of alcoholic drinking seemed far away. As he walked out of the park he passed a bar where he used to drink. Knowing that he did not want to drink anymore, but remembering that his old friends would be wondering what had happened to him, he went in to see how they all were "just for old time's sake." Once there, they ignored his pleas that he no longer drank alcohol and bought him a "proper man's drink." Telling him they were angry he hadn't called on them for weeks they said that they'd let bygones be bygones if only he joined them for "just one drink." Telling himself that there was nothing else he could do under the circumstances, John gave in. Within only a few hours the barman refused to serve him any more on grounds of his obviously drunken behavior. When he got home his wife was also angry, so he knew that he had "no choice" but to go to the home of another of his drinking friends, where he spent the night consuming yet more alcohol.

Decisions to walk home rather than take a bus, or to choose one route rather than another, are "seemingly irrelevant" to the mental processes of alcoholism. However, with hindsight, such decisions can set in motion an inexorable process of movement toward a relapse due to environmental triggers. Such relapses are often later viewed as "unavoidable." After all, what could John do once he was back in the bar, with all his old friends insisting that he drank alcohol?

Much of what has been said above is relevant to this example. John could have been aware that his feelings of well-being and success were as much an HRS as any disappointment in life. Had he also rehearsed a range of realistic strategies with which to resist pressures from his drinking friends, he might have been more likely to emerge from the bar without having had a drink. More importantly, he might have recognized that simply going into the bar was an extremely bad idea in the first place. However, the overall problem here was that an unconscious chain of decisions was being forged which made relapse almost inevitable. Because the decisions were seemingly irrelevant, and because their true purpose was partly or completely unconscious, John was able to argue that events caught him off guard. However, having once recognized such patterns of decision making (and most addicts are readily able to think of examples), it becomes extremely difficult to continue engaging in them without making conscious decisions. Once the process has become conscious, SIDs lose much of their power and the client can bring relapse prevention strategies into play.

THE ABSTINENCE VIOLATION EFFECT

One more psychological trap is worthy of mention here, if only because of the controversy it engenders among counselors and clients alike. The basis of this trap is that once human beings have set themselves a rule there seems to be an irresistible temptation to break the rule. Quite apart from the spiritual implications of this, and the responses to it offered by the world's major faith traditions, this observation has important psychological implications for the addictive process. This process is known as the *abstinence violation effect* (Marlatt & George, 1984).

The trap can present itself in various ways. The most common, and simplest, is that minor infringements of the rule are taken as a justifiable basis for major infringements. Thus, if Jenny has decided to stick to a diet in which she will not eat cake or candy, and if she finds herself forgetfully accepting a slice of birthday cake at a friend's celebration, she will then decide to go home and binge on cake and candy, because she has already failed. The rule has been broken, so she may as well enjoy breaking it to the full. Of course, in reality, if this is the first piece of cake that Jenny has had for a month she has not failed at all—she is doing enormously well. But, psychologically, she feels as though she has failed and so there is no longer any point in trying to adhere to the rule.

There are many more subtle manifestations of this psychological trap, but the general feature seems to be the transition from seeing the rule as being set by oneself for one's own good, to seeing it as imposed externally in some way and for its own sake (or for someone else's benefit). Circumstances are thus engineered whereby breaking the rule appears to be permissible, or breaking the rule a lot is seen to be no worse than breaking it a little.

From the perspective of relapse prevention, the important consideration is that small violations of the rule ("lapses") need not inevitably progress to major violations ("relapses"). Coping strategies can be learned that prevent this progression and over a period of time, make the behavior manageable. But herein lies the problem: other approaches to addiction therapy emphasize the unmanageability of addictive behavior. Step 1 of the 12 steps of AA states: "We admitted we were powerless over alcohol—that our lives had become unmanageable." (Members of AA are often reminded that "one drink makes one drunk.") The reinforcement of this message of powerlessness is thus criticized by some counselors as making relapse after only a single drink an inevitability, for alcoholics no longer have any reason at all to control their behavior, or any grounds for believing that they might be able to control their drinking if they tried. Alcoholism is a lack of ability to control drinking and therefore one drink will lead immediately, inevitably, and inexorably back to alcoholic drinking.

It is not possible to review the merits and demerits of these two positions here in full detail. However, some observations are important. First, if clients are involved in relapse prevention therapy based on a model of the psychology of learned behavior, as well as being engaged in a self-help program of recovery, it is better to talk about these apparent conflicts rather than pretend they do not exist. Second, there is not necessarily as much of a conflict as might first appear. Many members of AA, having had a relatively minor "slip," have gone to an AA meeting, or have sought help from their sponsor, and have found help that has prevented the "inevitable" relapse. Equally, a "slip" or "lapse," perhaps following a series of SIDs, can itself present an HRS that was better avoided in the first place—even according to relapse prevention theory. There is much wisdom in both traditions. Third, and finally, when planning relapse prevention therapy counselors should remember that people are all different. What might be possible for one might not be possible for another. However, admitting the impossibility of a certain set of circumstances inevitably presents the risk that when those circumstances are encountered no effort will be made to overcome them.

LIFESTYLE CHANGE

A key issue for many people with addictive disorders is that of imbalance in lifestyle. The dependence syndrome is characterized by salience—a phenomenon which involves the object of addiction assuming greater significance, and occupying more time in life, than it should. This has sometimes devastating consequences. Relationships, work, ethical standards, leisure activities, diet, sleep, health, values, spirituality, and other aspects of life may suffer. However, one way or another, the use of time and energy become seriously distorted, with more attention being given to engaging in (and defending) addictive behavior and less time being given to other things and people than is conducive to well-being.

Sometimes the lifestyle imbalance may result from the addiction. Sometimes it may contribute to it. Unemployment, for example, may be a consequence of drinking at work, or of the impairment of ability to fulfill obligations at work as a consequence of drinking at other times. However, unemployment may also be one of the contributory stresses around which heavier drinking develops, or may simply allow more time for drinking. Teasing out these cause and effect relationships is rarely productive in practice. What is clear is that a more balanced lifestyle will require less time drinking and more time devoted to constructive activity (such as job seeking, or voluntary work if paid employment is not an option). Practical measures to evaluate and change use of time may therefore be very important as a part of an overall relapse prevention strategy.

A useful exercise can sometimes be the exploration of how an addicted person approaches the "shoulds" and "wants" of life. Often it will be found that much time is devoted to one at the expense of the other. Thus, obligations are prioritized, with relentless disregard for leisure time and personal well-being, until the point is reached at which a relapse is inevitable (because drinking is the only habitual coping strategy employed to deal with the stress that this imbalance generates). Or else, a self-indulgent lifestyle is pursued with equally relentless disregard for relationships or social obligations. Within such a lifestyle drinking (or other addictive behavior) usually features prominently. If it does not, it soon emerges as a consequence of the lack of structure and discipline that such a lifestyle entails.

A 60-year-old male, Stanley, sought counseling after he was forced to take early retirement from a powerful state position. He was currently spending his days idle, remembering the importance of his life only a short time ago. He described his life after retirement as lonely and boring, and he felt useless and depressed. He realized he had a drinking problem when he "washed down breakfast with a beer" soon after his wife left for work each morning and spent his time finding "creative hiding places" for his liquor. He began attending a 12-step program and did well in the beginning (the meetings gave him a new focus) but relapsed after six months of sobriety. What lifestyle changes may have affected Stanley's initial drinking and relapse? What changes do you think would benefit him?

Exploration of lifestyle issues usually gets to the heart of what matters to people. How they spend their time, and what they devote their energy to, is usually a reflection of important desires and priorities in life. Once identified, these can provide motivational levers to enable change. For example, a desire to maintain custody of a child may provide motivation to comply with a court-mandated addiction treatment program. However, they also point to core beliefs and priorities which, explicitly or implicitly, are spiritual and/or religious. Identification of these core beliefs and priorities can help in regaining perspective and in identifying a treatment approach which will address the spiritual, as well as the psychological, social, and physical aspects of the addictive disorder. This may entail a 12-step treatment program (see Chapter 12) or a religious program, or it may be a reconnection with religious roots which occurs alongside engagement with a secular treatment program of some kind (Cook, 2009). It is therefore important that counselors are able to facilitate discussion of spiritual and religious matters in an affirming manner, without either proselytizing or undermining healthy religious beliefs which may be different than their own. On the other hand, some kinds of "pathological" spirituality (e.g., associated with extreme cults or with an addictive pattern of religious behavior) may need gentle challenging (Crowley & Jenkinson, 2009). The balance requires wisdom and a nonjudgmental willingness to explore spirituality from the perspective of what may be in the client's best interests.

CASE STUDY OF RELAPSE PREVENTION

The latter section of this chapter presents a case study utilizing principles of maintenance and relapse prevention. Both the biopsychosocial model (disease model) and the cognitive-social learning model are used to provide interventions from a multimodal perspective. Although some strategies are associated to a larger extent with a particular model, the necessary strategies for relapse prevention are very similar. These models take into consideration the biological, psychological, and social aspects of substance abuse and use a wide range of counseling techniques to minimize the possibility of relapse. The interventions rely heavily on techniques from behavioral, cognitive, and social learning theories, as well as addressing the client's physical health and well-being (Chiauzzi, 1991).

The client for this case study is Thomas, a 27-year-old male currently employed as a salesman, who is married and the father of a 2-year-old daughter. Thomas enters counseling when he realizes his life is out of control. His wife has threatened to leave him, he cannot keep a job for longer than a few months, and his angry outbursts have become more frequent. He has had a couple of anxiety attacks in recent months and has begun to consider suicide, thinking that life is not worth living.

Thomas reports that he has been consuming alcohol since high school. He reports drinking approximately a case of beer daily, the amount depending on his stress level. He often switches to bourbon and spends many weekends with his friends in a drunken state. His dependency on alcohol consumption has become more self-evident as the consequences of his drinking have become increasingly serious.

Thomas's initial treatment to stabilize his condition included several visits to his physician to regulate antianxiety and antidepressant medications. During therapy, he is taught the importance of remaining on these medications and following the prescribed dosage. With Thomas's previous history of anxiety and depression, maintaining sobriety may be partially dependent upon his consistent use of these medications.

In the recovery phase, after withdrawal and stabilization, the relapse prevention counselor has several treatment goals. First of all, Thomas needs to be able to identify HRSs; he must then develop strategies to cope with these situations. Also, the counselor must help Thomas identify (and possibly establish) support systems. These may include positive social support networks such as AA, church, supportive friends, and family members. Additional goals include learning about the nature of addictions, and identifying and managing warning signs of relapse. Finally, goals must include exploration of multisystemic issues related to Thomas's life—his relationships, environment, health, recreation, and family—and an evaluation of where positive change is needed.

Self-Assessment of High-Risk Situations

Initially, Thomas is taught to self-monitor HRSs. He is instructed to keep track of when, where, and why he wants to use alcohol. Thomas is given a chart on which he can track the risky situations, his thoughts and feelings at the time he has urges, and the coping strategies he uses to avoid substance use or to limit the amount consumed. Because substance use becomes habitualized after years of use and seems to be an automatic response, the self-monitoring strategy forces him to be consciously aware of his actions (Marlatt & Gordon, 1985).

When Thomas meets with his counselor, they use the chart as both an assessment tool and an intervention strategy. After examining the chart together, the counselor helps Thomas to see that the cues are centered mostly on stressful events, such as pressure to meet a quota on his sales

Self-Monitoring Chart

Date	Time	Situation	Thought(s)	Feeling(s)	Action
June 1	8:30 AM	Late for work; boss seems agitated	I'm probably going to get fired; he always seems down on me. I need a drink.	Anxiety and disappoint-ment in self	Get prepared for first client.
June 1	5:30 PM	Driving for 1½ hours in traffic	I am so mad at those stupid drivers. I deserve a drink when I get home. What a day!	Anger, frustration	Listen to upbeat music.
June 6	7:30 PM	Confron-tation with wife	I don't know what I'll do if she leaves me. I won't be able to go on. If I could only have a drink, I would have more confidence to convince her to stay.	Sadness, desperation	Go outside, walk around, and prepare what to say.

job or a difficult argument with his wife. Thomas believes he deserves a reward (in the form of a drink) for making it through the situation, or that he must have a drink to relieve the stress. He is experiencing severe anxiety regarding his wife's threats to leave him and thinks a drink will help relieve his stress and give him more courage. His feelings often include nervousness, anger, or disappointment.

Coping Strategies

The self-monitoring chart also helps Thomas become aware of the critical times when he makes a decision to drink and the alternative responses that help him resist. Thomas and his counselor brainstorm alternative behaviors for different high-risk situations and together determine several effective coping strategies for each. During future sessions, the counselor sets up a variety of situations and has Thomas rehearse these strategies.

For example, Thomas becomes aware that the stress of driving in rush-hour traffic usually results in an overwhelming urge to have a drink. After brainstorming alternatives, Thomas real-izes that he could use this time to unwind after his work by listening to music that produces a good mood. In addition, his counselor helps him to recognize his dysfunctional thinking during this situation. He has a tendency to blame the other drivers ("He cut me off on purpose. These stupid drivers need to get out of my way"), which increases his stress. He is helped to change to a healthier, less stress-inducing way of thinking, such as "All the drivers are trying to get home just like me. They didn't single me out to cut off." Thomas practices these strategies during counseling sessions by visualizing driving in traffic, listening to upbeat music, and thinking the more rational thoughts. This process teaches him to recognize his triggers, develop coping strategies, and use cognitive-behavioral techniques to change his dysfunctional thinking to minimize relapse (Gorski, 1993).

Lapse and Relapse Prevention Techniques

Also during the initial stage, the counselor teaches Thomas about lapses (single episode of use) and relapses (return to uncontrolled use). Although told that lapses and relapses are common, he is encouraged to use the knowledge gained from lapses to identify precipitating events and better coping strategies. In this way, lapses are reframed as learning experiences that can help prevent relapses. This view reduces the guilt, anxiety, and doubt that are often felt after a lapse and eliminates any moral injunctions against the client (Lewis, Dana, & Blevins, 1994).

The reframing of lapses as a learning experience can also help Thomas to dispute the "all or nothing" belief. Many times people with addictive behaviors have the irrational belief that if they slip one time then their situation is hopeless and they might as well give up, which leads to a total relapse. This was referred to previously as the abstinence-violation effect (AVE) where the client believes that absolute abstinence and complete loss of control are their only options. When viewing lapses as a normal part of the recovery process from which he can learn, Thomas realizes that he can regain control. This sense of control then leads to self-efficacy, enabling him to believe that he can have control in similar future situations.

At this time, the counselor provides several strategies to help in reducing lapses. Thomas is given a therapeutic contract to sign, which states that he agrees to leave the situation when a lapse occurs (Marlatt, 1985). This gives him a "time out" and limits the extent of alcohol use at the time of the lapse. Also, the counselor and Thomas work together to construct reminder cards of specific steps to take, as well as a list of support people to call (including their phone numbers). The cards may also include positive statements, such as "Remember, you are in control," "This slip is not a catastrophe. You can stop now if you choose," and "Visualize yourself in control." Thomas commits to using these strategies immediately following a lapse.

A counseling session soon follows during which Thomas reports a lapse and describes the situation. He describes his week as being extremely difficult, with problems at work as well as a major argument with his wife. He leaves his house Saturday morning, still angry after the disagreement on Friday evening, and decides to visit one of his friends. Thomas admits knowing this was a dangerous thing to do as the friend was one of his "drinking buddies." He states that his feelings of anger and frustration were overwhelming and "it just didn't matter." After a few beers, while Thomas was alone in the restroom, he remembered the card. He read the positive reminders and remembered the long-term versus the short-term consequences of drinking. He thought about the consequence of possibly losing his wife if he continues to drink and remembered the contract he has signed to leave immediately after the lapse. Thomas then tells his friend one of his rehearsed excuses and makes a quick exit. At the end of the session, the counselor helps Thomas to explore what he learned from this event and encourages feelings of self-efficacy.

Afterward, the counselor examines the situation for treatment gaps. She realizes that Thomas needs more work in handling negative emotions. During subsequent sessions, they return to the brainstorming stage so that he can learn (or be reminded of) coping strategies to use when he is angry, agitated, or depressed. Also, his support system is re-examined to determine the best person or group to go to for help when he is experiencing intense emotions.

Support Systems and Lifestyle Changes

Thomas and his counselor further examine his support system. Thomas has attended a 12-step program for several months, and although these meetings have provided him with a way to meet nonusing people, it is essential that he have a system of support outside the meetings. With a system of nonusing friends and family, the possibility of relapse is much less likely.

Thomas's wife has been supportive of him since he entered treatment and has attended a family treatment program independent of Thomas's program. Although emotionally disengaged in the beginning, she has made gains in reconnecting with Thomas, as she sees him showing a commitment to maintaining sobriety. Also, because Thomas reported that communication was a major problem in his marriage, he and his counselor have worked on developing skills and role-playing communication between him and his wife.

(It is important to mention here that although the involvement of the family is critical in relapse prevention, the process is not simple. The principle of family homeostasis must be considered when working with close family members. Central to this principle is the idea that when one member of the family experiences change, the other members will be affected and adjust in some manner [Jackson, 1957]. Boundaries, roles, and rules will need to be reorganized to establish a new sense of balance.)

Thomas's wife had taken on the role of main provider and was seen as the strong person in the family. Emotional roles were present, also, with Thomas being the angry one and his wife being the sullen, stoic one. Rules revolved around communication and sexual activity. Since Thomas's wife had become emotionally disengaged, she limited both communication and sex with him so as to avoid any sense of intimacy. As Thomas practiced sobriety and the will to be committed to his program, his wife was able to gradually become somewhat more open to both communication and sexual activity. However, the fear of being hurt again continues to cause her to withhold herself to some extent.

The issue of having a system of nonusing friends is important to Thomas not only for support but for companionship in recreational activities. Because Thomas's drinking has taken precedence the past few years, his only friends have been his drinking friends, and he has cultivated little interest in any activities outside of work. The counselor helps Thomas to establish a list of activities he thinks he would enjoy and would like to pursue. At the top of his list is working out at the gym. Since he and his wife have a family membership, he is able to begin right away and finds that working out actually produces a feeling of accomplishment and well-being. He establishes a friendship with a trainer who works at the gym, as well a couple of men who attend the gym at the same time.

These friendships provide social modeling for Thomas, who sees their interest in health and fitness as something he wishes to emulate. Social modeling can often be a strong motivator in changing individual behavior. Thomas perceives these individuals as having positive traits he wishes to acquire, and their personal encouragement helps him to develop an improved self-concept.

Along with the need to acquire healthy relationships and activities is the need to change old friends and unhealthy environments. This becomes an important focus during treatment. Thomas has several friends he refers to as his "drinking buddies" who often call and attempt to persuade him to meet them at their favorite bar. After an outing to the bar results in a 2-month relapse, Thomas realizes that he can no longer keep these friends and stay sober. During counseling, refusal skills are rehearsed, and Thomas and his counselor role-play different situations that Thomas previously encountered with his friends.

In addition, the counselor helps him explore other environments in which external cues prompt cravings and urges. He learns that being exposed to these cues often leads to a feeling of deprivation and an urge to use. Thomas is instructed by his counselor to determine which cues he can avoid, as well as which ones are more difficult or impossible to avoid. Social outings where others are drinking prove to be a major trigger, or cue, for Thomas. He learns that taking care of himself and maintaining his sobriety is his current priority and that he can decline these invitations without feeling guilty. The counselor also instructs him to remove as many cues as possible from his daily environment to decrease the frequency of his urges and cravings. One such change was as simple as taking a different route home from work so that he did not have to pass his favorite bar.

For unavoidable situations, Thomas is taught other strategies, including body awareness cues and mnemonic devices. Through body awareness techniques, he is able to identify the onset of physical urges to drink. The counselor has Thomas visualize a time when he feels a craving to drink and to give a detailed description of what is occurring in his body. He reports that he first feels his heart rate increase, then his hands start trembling and his mind begins to race. The counselor instructs Thomas to use the onset of these physical signs as a cue to identify an HRS.

At that time, the counselor explains the use of a mnemonic device, or memory aid, to help Thomas recall what he needs to do. An acrostic is given, using the word STOP. His instructions are to use each letter to evoke a reminder of his plan. "S" stands for "situation"—be aware of the high-risk situation; "T" stands for "think"—think about what I need to do; "O" is for "options"—recall the different options or strategies I've rehearsed for this situation; "P" is for "plan"—proceed with plan.

Other Lifestyle Changes

All areas in a client's life that could possibly lead to relapse need to be approached eventually during therapy. From the beginning, Thomas indicates that his job as a salesman is a major stressor. The pressure of having to reach a quota is often a cue for him to have a drink, and he thinks of himself as unsuccessful and inadequate. He and his counselor explore his options, and Thomas decides he needs to find work where he experiences less pressure. He finds an assistant manager position with a different company and, though he takes a salary cut, is relieved that he does not have the stress of meeting a quota.

Because of his employment record and past spending habits, Thomas has financial problems, leading to a huge amount of stress. For once in his life he is attempting to be responsible and remain sober, but creditors are harassing him and he has no money to pay for a broken furnace. Without financial assistance, the likelihood of a relapse is high. Thomas seeks help from his local bank; by consolidating his debt and getting a small loan, he feels capable of getting out from under his financial difficulties.

THE REALITY OF RELAPSE PREVENTION

When reading about the multitude of strategies and interventions involved in treatment of substance abuse, maintaining and preventing relapse may appear to be an overwhelming task. This chapter condenses a case study so that the interventions appear to be introduced at a rapid pace, but in actuality the case extends over many months. Although the counselor had a long list of the lifestyle changes needed to prevent relapse, these changes were prioritized and broken down into small, achievable steps.

To prevent clients from feeling overwhelmed, counselors must present the interventions at a pace at which clients can experience success and build self-efficacy. Realistic goals must be established, and the counselor has to be aware of the danger of having too many "shoulds" on the client's plate (Fisher & Harrison, 2000). Starting out slowly and finding a balance is important. The stress of clients trying to build their lives too quickly and taking on too much can lead to relapse. The "shoulds" need to be balanced with fun and pleasure. Feelings of resentment and shame are slowly replaced with gratitude and forgiveness (C. Wildroot, personal communication, January 12, 2010).

Summary and Some Final Notations

Relapse prevention and maintenance are complex and dynamic processes. All clients have their own individual risk factors. Multiple influences contribute to high risk situations—years of dependence, family history, social support, comorbid psychopathology, and physiological states (physical withdrawal). Cognitive factors also affect the risk of relapse, including the abstinence violation effect, level of motivation, self-efficacy, and outcome expectancies. When a person relapses, there is probably not one single distinct cause but rather a multitude of internal and external factors (Marlatt & Gordon, 1985).

In the Relapse Prevention model, cognitive behavioral strategies are taught and practiced. Counselors help clients identify more effective coping strategies to use during high-risk situations. Relaxation skills and mindfulness meditation (Marlatt, 2002) are practiced, and lifestyle changes encouraged. A supportive social network is stressed.

When an individual relapses, the goal of relapse prevention is to lessen the length and severity of the relapse and to decrease the amount of time it takes for the client to stabilize and return to maintenance. An integrated, multifaceted approach (Knack, 2009) provides the tools for the most effective treatment in preventing relapse—including medication, 12-step programs, and cognitive behavioral models. Although there is a high rate of relapse, the good news is that the longer clients maintain sobriety, the less likely they are to relapse.

Useful Web Sites

The following Web sites provide additional information relating to chapter topics:

About.com: Alcoholism & Substance Abuse
*http://alcoholism.about.com/od/relapse/Relapse_*
    Prevention.htm

Addiction Alternatives
http://www.addictionalternatives.com/philosophy/
    relapseprevention.htm

Dual Recovery Anonymous
http://www.draonline.org/relapse.html

Information for Individuals and Families
http://www.addictionsandrecovery.org

References

Alcoholics Anonymous. (2001). New York: Alcoholics Anonymous World Services, Inc.

Annis, H. (1982). *Inventory of drinking situations (IDS-TOO).* Toronto: Addiction Research Foundation of Ontario.

Annis, H., & Davis, C. (1991). Relapse prevention. *Alcohol Health & Research World, 15*(3), 204–212.

Bandura, A. (1977). Self-efficacy: Toward a unifying theory of behavioral change. *Psychological Review, 84,* 191–215.

Baumeister, R. F., Heatherton, T. F., & Tice, D. M. (1994). *Losing control: How and why people fail at self-regulation.* San Diego, CA: Academic Press.

Bowen, S., & Marlatt, A. (2009). Surfing the urge: Brief mindfulness-based intervention for college student smokers. *Psychology of Addictive Behaviors, 23*(4), 666–671.

Chiauzzi, E. J. (1991). *Preventing relapse in the addictions: A biopsychosocial approach.* New York: Pergamon Press.

Cook, C. C. H. (2009). Substance Misuse. In Cook, C., Powell, A., & Sims, A. (Eds.), *Spirituality and Psychiatry.* London, Royal College of Psychiatrists Press, 139–168.

Crowley, N., & Jenkinson, G. (2009). Pathological Spirituality. In Cook, C., Powell, A., & Sims, A. (Eds.), *Spirituality & Psychiatry.* London, Royal College of Psychiatrists Press, 254–272.

Donovan, D. M. (1996). Marlatt's classification of relapse precipitants: Is the emperor still wearing clothes? *Addiction, 91,* (Suppl.) 131–137.

Doweiko, H. E. (1990). *Concepts of chemical dependency*. Pacific Grove, CA: Brooks/Cole.

Fisher, G. L., & Harrison, G. L. (2000). *Substance abuse: Information for school counselors, social workers, therapists, and counselors* (2nd ed.). Needham Heights, MA: Allyn & Bacon.

Forman-Hoffman, V., Riley, W., & Pici, M. (2005). Acute impact of the September 11 tragedy on smoking and early relapse rates among smokers attempting to quit. *Psychology of Addictive Behaviors, 19*(3), 277–283.

Gorski, T. T. (1993). Relapse prevention: A state of the art overview. *Addiction & Recovery*, March/April, 25–27.

Gwaltney, C. J., Metrik, J., Kahler, C. W., & Shiffman, S. (2009). Self-efficacy and smoking cessation: A meta-analysis. *Psychology of Addictive Behaviors, 23*(1), 56–66.

Havassy, B. E., Hall, S. M., & Wasserman, D. A. (1991). Social support and relapse: Commonalities among alcoholics, opiate users, and cigarette smokers. *Addictive Behaviors, 16*, 235–246.

Inaba, D., & Cohen, W. (2000). *Uppers, downers, all arounders*. Ashland, OR: CNS Publications.

Jackson, D. D. (1957). The question of family homeostasis. *Psychiatric Quarterly Supplement, 31*, 79–90.

Knack, W. A. (2009). Psychotherapy and Alcoholics Anonymous: An integrated approach. *Journal of Psychotherapy Integration, 19*(1), 86–109.

Lawhon, D., Humfleet, G. L., Hall, S. M., Reus, V. I., & Munoz, R. F. (2009). Longitudinal analysis of abstinence-specific social support and smoking cessation. *Health Psychology, 28*(4), 465–472.

Lewis, J. A., Dana, R. Q., & Blevins, G. A. (1994). *Substance abuse counseling: An individualized approach* (2nd ed.). Pacific Grove, CA: Brooks/Cole Publishing.

Lopez, E. N., Drobes, D. J., Thompson, J. K., & Brandon, T. H. (2008). Effects of a body image challenge on smoking motivation among college females. *Health Psychology, 27*(Suppl. 3), 243–251.

Marlatt, G. A. (1985). Relapse prevention: Theoretical rationale and overview of the model. In G. A. Marlatt & J. R. Gordon (Eds.), *Relapse prevention: Maintenance strategies in the treatment of addictive behaviors* (pp. 3–70). New York: Guilford Press.

Marlatt, G. A. (2002). Buddhist psychology and the treatment of addictive behavior. *Cognitive and Behavioral Practice, 9*, 44–49.

Marlatt, G., & George, W. (1984). Relapse prevention: Introduction and overview of the model. *British Journal of Addiction 79*, 261–275.

Marlatt, G., & Gordon, J. (1985). *Relapse prevention*. New York: Guilford Press.

Marlatt, G. A., & Gordon, J. R. (1980). Determinants of relapse: Implications of the maintenance of behavior change. In P. O. Davidson & S. M. Davidson (Eds.), *Behavioral medicine: Changing health lifestyle* (pp. 410–452). New York: Brunner/Mazel.

Niaura, R. (2000). Cognitive social learning and related perspectives on drug craving. *Addiction, 95*, 155–164.

National Institute on Drug Abuse. (n.d.). *Addiction science: From molecules to managed care* [Data file]. Available from National Institutes on Drug Abuse site, *http://www.drugabuse.gov/pubs/teaching/Teaching6/Teaching9.html*

Orford, J., & Edwards, G. (1977). *Alcoholism*. Oxford: Oxford University Press.

Polich, J. M., Amour, D. J., and Braiker, H. B. (1981). *The course of alcoholism: Four years after treatment*. Report prepared for the National Institute on Alcohol Abuse and Alcoholism, U.S. Department of Health, Education, and Welfare. Santa Monica, CA: Rand Corporation.

Prochaska, J. O., & DiClemente, C. C. (1984). *The transtheoretical approach: Crossing the traditional boundaries of therapy*. Malabar, FL: Krieger.

Ramo, D. E., & Brown, S. A. (2008). Classes of substance abuse relapse situations: A comparison of adolescents and adults. *Psychology of Addictive Behaviors, 22*(3), 372–379.

Shiffman, S. (1989). Conceptual issues in the study of relapse. In M. Gossop (Ed.), *Relapse and addictive behavior* (pp. 149–179). London: Routledge.

Shiffman, S., Balabanis, M., Paty, J., Engberg, J., Gwaltney, C., Liu, K., et al. (2000). Dynamic effects of self-efficacy on smoking lapse and relapse. *Health Psychology, 19*, 315–323.

Wertz, J. M., & Sayette, M. A. (2001). A review of the effects of perceived drug use opportunity on self-reported urge. *Experimental and Clinical Psychopharmacology, 9*, 3–13.

Witkiewitz, K., & Marlatt, G. (2004). Relapse prevention for alcohol and drug problems: That was Zen, This is TAO. *American Psychologist, 59*(4), 224–235.

Witkiewitz, K., & Villarroel, N. A. (2009). Dynamic association between negative affect and alcohol lapses following alcohol treatment. *Journal of Consulting and Clinical Psychology, 77*(4), 633–644.

Chapter 14

Alcohol Addiction and Families

Misty K. Hook

The United States has long had a love–hate relationship with alcohol and other types of drugs. Although the government has employed various efforts to eliminate or curtail drug and alcohol use (e.g., Prohibition, the War on Drugs), prescription drugs are used liberally, illicit drugs are easily obtained, and the presence of alcohol in our culture remains strong. Happy hours are a staple of corporate life and becoming of legal drinking age is something many young adults eagerly anticipate. However, despite the largely favorable role drugs and alcohol play in our culture, addiction can have serious consequences—and nowhere is this more evident than in families who have one or more addicted members. Addiction has a long-term and devastating effect on the family, disrupting healthy family dynamics, and increasing the likelihood that family members will suffer negative physical and psychological harm.

Although the impact of addiction may not be widely discussed, it is quite pervasive. In a 2008 report, the annual National Household Survey on Drug Use and Health revealed that approximately 23.1 million Americans aged 12 years or older were dependent on either alcohol or illicit drugs (Office of Applied Studies, Substance Abuse and Mental Health Statistics). On an even broader scale, McIntyre (2004) estimates that 11% of the U.S. population abuses or is addicted to substances. In addition, for every person who is addicted to drugs or alcohol, it is believed that there are at least four to six other people, especially parents, partners, and children, who are equally affected. Using these percentages, we estimate that the number of people affected by alcohol or illicit drug abuse increases to approximately 45% to 68% of the U.S. population. Addiction also affects future generations. Estimates from the National Pregnancy and Health Survey (National Institute on Drug Abuse, 1994) concluded that 5.5% of U.S. women giving birth used illicit drugs sometime during their pregnancy and 18.8% drank at some time during pregnancy.

When focusing just on alcohol, the number of children of alcoholics (COAs) appears to be rising. In 1995, Eigen and Rowden found that the number of COAs in the United States under the age of 18 was approximately 17.5 million. However, more recent estimates place this number at one in four, or approximately 19 million children exposed to parental alcohol dependence, alcohol abuse, or both (Grant, 2000). The numbers are most likely even higher given the tendency of families with alcoholic members to be closed systems that hide their "secret" of addiction (Edwards, 2003). Consequently, due to the frequency of alcohol and drug abuse in American society, counselors and other healthcare professionals will almost certainly encounter families suffering from addiction (Rotunda, Scherer, & Imm, 1995). In order to offer the best treatment possible, counselors need to know how addiction affects the family and how best to treat it.

Public schools are beginning to acknowledge the adverse impact of an alcoholic member in the family. School counselors are being advised that almost 40% of their students may be being raised by an alcoholic caregiver. Given the negative academic outcomes for these students, the vast majority of school counselors agree there is a strong need for counseling and preventative services. However, the accrediting bodies have yet to make substance abuse coursework and training mandatory.

Before delving into the literature on families and addictions, it is important to note that it contains some serious gaps. Most studies examining the conceptualization and treatment of addicted family systems deal almost exclusively with Caucasian, heterosexual, intact families in which the male partner is addicted to a single substance. Studies involving addictions in women, people of color, same-sex couples, divorced parents, or individuals with comorbid drug problems and/or psychopathology are virtually absent (Roberts & Linney, 2000). The lack of attention to psychological difficulties is particularly problematic, as a large number of addicted people exhibit comorbid psychopathology. One study found that close to 60% of substance abuse patients had a dual diagnosis personality disorder, usually from Cluster B (Antisocial, Borderline, Histrionic, or Narcissistic) (Rounsaville et al., 1998). It seems evident that people with dual disorders are suffering from immense psychic pain given their much higher rates of suicide and suicide attempts than the general population (Brooner, King, Kidorf, Schmidt, & Bigelow, 1997; Halikas, Crosby, Pearson, Nugent, & Carlson, 1994). Since understanding the motivations behind the substance abuse are an important part of treatment, more needs to be known about the role psychopathology plays in addiction.

It is also important to note the primary role of alcohol in the addictions literature. Although addiction to legal and illicit drugs, gambling, and sexual addictions have equally damaging effects on families as alcohol abuse, few studies focus solely on these other dependencies. Some of the reasons behind the almost singular emphasis on alcohol may include the fact that it is legal, widely available, and accepted; alcohol addiction plays a larger role in our culture than do other drug addictions; alcohol abuse affects larger numbers of people than gambling or sexual addictions; and sexual addiction is an emerging trend, particularly with the increasingly widespread use of the Internet (Schneider, 2002). Thus, though the effects on the family from any kind of addiction are similar, this chapter will focus primarily on alcohol addiction.

Although drug-based definitions of addiction are still predominant in the field, a growing number of professionals are looking at other behaviors that are potentially addictive. These behaviors include gambling, computer game playing, shopping, exercise, eating, sex, and Internet use. All of these activities can and are done in moderation. However, the difference between a fun activity and an addiction is that healthy excessive activities enhance life while addictions detract from it (Griffiths, 2005a).

ADDICTION AND THE FAMILY

Family Counseling

In the early days of addictions counseling, counselors used to work only with the addict and family members were excluded. However, it quickly became clear that family members were influential in motivating the addict to get sober or in preventing the addict from making serious changes (Steinberg, Epstein, McCrady, & Hirsch, 1997). Consequently, including family members in counseling sessions became an integral part of treatment. Systems theorists strongly believe in the concept of *homeostasis*, the tendency of systems like families to balance themselves in response to change. Whenever there is a disruption in one family member, other members react to return the overall family dynamics to something that resembles normal functioning. Family counselors pay close attention to several aspects of family dynamics, including the structure of the family (boundaries, roles), family rules, and generational interactions.

In terms of structure, the family is viewed as an organism surrounded by a semipermeable boundary, a set of rules determining how people interact with those both inside and outside the family. Within each family, members occupy one or more roles that determine how they act and how others react to them. A healthy family structure is one that requires clear boundaries and flexible roles. Family rules govern the range of behavior a family system can tolerate; Positive rules take into account the needs of everyone in the family. Finally, generational interactions are the ways in which communication is conducted between the various subsystems (e.g., parental, sibling, partner). Healthy generational interactions are ones in which there is a clear hierarchy, flexible roles, and open communication.

CASE STUDY

Joanna and Leroy Williams have been married for 15 years. They have two children, Shoshana, age 12, and James, age 9. While Leroy always drank, it has only been a problem for the last 6 years. He will come home from work and drink the rest of the evening. Leroy refuses to help with any of the household chores or childcare responsibilities. He is verbally and emotionally abusive to Joanna and the children when he's been drinking and avoidant and withdrawn during the weekend days when he is sober. Joanna and Leroy attempted counseling once and Leroy did attend rehab but quickly re-lapsed after 3–4 months. He refuses to return to counseling and does not want Joanna to go either.

Question: What are some of the roles and rules in the Williams family?

ADDICTED FAMILY DYNAMICS: HOMEOSTASIS. In addicted families, the substance abuse initially threatens family homeostasis. People who become addicted to substances start to demonstrate clear patterns of behavior: They socialize with other users, family or friends who don't use are excluded, denial is frequent, and family relationships become strained. Leroy's drinking definitely causes a strain on the family. He either goes out with his friends to drink or drinks alone at home. In both situations, he does not interact with other family members while he is drinking. He is asked to help out with the kids and do chores around the house but refuses, frequently leading to arguments with Joanna. Leroy also doesn't attend school or athletic functions for the kids. They are angry with him because of his absence in their lives but are afraid to say anything for fear he will start yelling. No one, especially Leroy, mentions that his refusal to participate in family life is because of his drinking.

Once homeostasis is broken, other family members adapt to the substance use behavior in an effort to return balance to the family. They deny the addiction, change their behavior to cover up the substance abuse, and often sacrifice their needs for the sake of protecting the addict and the family system. Family members start to hide their true feelings and distort real-ity (Kinney, 2003). As Leroy's drinking started becoming a regular nightly event, Joanna kept denying there was a problem. At first she repeatedly asked him to participate with the kids and the household routine but, eventually, she quit asking. She now does everything herself. On days when she cannot drive the kids where they need to go, she enlists the help of neighbors and other adults. In addition to holding down a full-time job and attending school part time, she takes care of everything around the house. She also has sex with Leroy whenever he wants, even if it's late and she's tired. She believes it's easier to give in than to risk a confrontation. Joanna ignores her own anger and exhaustion and seeks individual counseling to help her cope better. Shoshana and James also participate in household chores and try to ease Joanna's burden. They avoid Leroy whenever possible. Thus, in attempting to maintain homeostasis, the Williams' family dynamics maintain the substance use (Lawson & Lawson, 2005; Meyers, Apodaca, Flicker, & Slesnick, 2002). Leroy has no domestic responsibilities and other family members avoid upsetting him, so he is free to drink whenever he is home. He pays no overt price for his addiction. As such, his drinking is now so insidious that it is the primary organizing factor around which the Williams family preserves its structure and stability (Chamberlain & Jew, 2003).

ADDICTED FAMILY DYNAMICS: BOUNDARIES.   Boundaries delineate the ways in which people relate to each other. They govern the rules surrounding how close family members can get to one another, how the family connects with the larger society, and how conflict is tolerated. In general, addictive family systems tend to have rigid, disengaged boundaries. Family members exhibit poor communication, higher levels of negativity and conflict, inadequate problem-solving skills, low cohesion, and an overall lack of organization and consistency (Fals-Stewart, Kelley, Cooke, & Golden, 2003; Lorber, et al., 2007). Given the unpleasantness of interpersonal encounters, they eventually become isolated from one another. Moreover, due to the secrecy surrounding the addiction, they also become isolated from the community. Consequently, emotional intimacy tends to be low in addicted family systems. However, the alcohol itself can be used as a way for the family to gain artificial closeness or as a tool to defuse conflict (Lawson & Lawson, 2005). Some studies have found that positive family interactions (e.g., avoiding conflict, achieving closeness, fun times) tend to occur only when the addicted family member is intoxicated (Roberts & Linney, 2000). In this way, the addiction is even further maintained by the family system.

In the Williams family, conversation tends to be at a minimum. Joanna talks with Shoshana and James about their school and extracurricular activities but discussion about the family rarely, if ever, occurs. The kids don't ask about Leroy and Joanna doesn't mention him. Whenever Leroy gets upset, he yells and says hurtful things. There have been times when he has pushed or poked one of the children. Consequently, Joanna and the kids have learned to give Leroy what he wants or stay out of his way when he's upset. Joanna tries to negotiate household tasks with Leroy but quickly gives up when he decides he's not going to do them. Thus, Shoshana and James have no positive role models for how to negotiate relationship difficulties. When there's a problem between Joanna and one of the kids or between Shoshana and James, nothing gets solved. The kids also do not have the opportunity to see positive role models for relationships in the community. While they both attend school and play sports, they have minimal interaction with community members beyond these events. People are never invited over to the house for fear of what they will see.

Addicted family systems miss some key ingredients of healthy families. These include willingness to spend time together, effective communication patterns, the ability to deal positively with crises, encouragement of individuals, clear roles, and a growth-producing structure.

ADDICTED FAMILY DYNAMICS: ROLES.   In families, as in other systems, people like to know how they are supposed to act and how they should respond to others. As such, they tend to take on roles, or specific ways of behaving. Everyone then knows what they are supposed to do and how they are expected to respond to the roles others play. In healthy family systems, roles can range from general (e.g., youngest child) to specific (e.g., the funny one) but will ultimately differ based on gender, culture, and the individual family.

While there are role variations in addicted family systems, Wegscheider (1981) described the four main roles children occupy. The first is that of the family hero. These children are extremely successful, self-reliant, and responsible. They give self-worth and validation to the family through their achievements. They often take care of everyone in the family and are some-times labeled as parentified. As is befitting her gender and status as the oldest child, Shoshana is the Williams' family hero. She gets good grades, helps around the house, and is a star on her soccer team. Whenever Joanna's exhaustion is too much to handle, Shoshana steps in and takes care of cooking dinner and helping James with his homework. Joanna is relieved that Shoshana can take care of herself and is pleased that she is so responsible. She doesn't see that Shoshana's self-reliance is covering up her depression and anxiety.

The second role is the scapegoat. This child acts out and is blamed for all of the family's problems. By acting out, the scapegoat takes the focus off the family's problems. The third role is that of the lost child or the adjuster (Black, 1981). These children follow directions, adjust to family dynamics, and offer relief by not needing attention. The last role is the mascot. These children are funny and outgoing. Everyone in the family tends to like them as they provide dis-traction by entertaining everyone around them (Fields, 2004; van Wormer & Davis, 2003). In the Williams family, James occupies the role of mascot. He does acceptable academic work and his teachers talk about how funny and lively he is in class. At home, James makes Joanna, Shoshana, and even Leroy laugh with his funny stories and fantastic impressions. James is rarely serious and seems unable to identify or express emotions like anger, sadness, or fear.

In healthy families, roles remain flexible, but in addicted family systems, they become rigid, particularly during times of stress. Thus, in the Williams family, as Leroy's drinking becomes more disruptive, Shoshana becomes more serious and responsible and James becomes more playful. If the children do not receive help, they are likely to play these roles throughout their lives. However, while the roles described above are helpful in understanding family dynam-ics, it must be noted that they are generalizations. They should not be used to stereotype people nor are they exclusive to only families with addiction issues; families who don't have alcohol-abuse problems may display these roles as well (Alford, 1998; van Wormer & Davis, 2003).

ADDICTED FAMILY DYNAMICS: RULES.   All families have rules that help organize family life. Some rules are overt, such as the exact time of curfew or not talking with one's mouth full. Other rules are covert. These are the unspoken rules that govern interpersonal behavior. Examples of covert rules in healthy families include ignoring Grandma's memory problems or giving large displays of affection when people come and go. In healthy families, both overt and covert rules tend to be present, logical, consistent, and designed to promote growth. In contrast, rules in addicted family systems tend to be arbitrary, illogical, inconsistent, and/or punitive (Brooks & Rice, 1997). Family members may use shaming to enforce rules or there may be a lack of conse-quences for breaking rules. The children in the family may feel out of control or anxious because they do not know or understand what they are supposed to do.

Typical rules in alcoholic families involve how best to deal with the addict and how to keep the addiction secret in order to protect and preserve the family (Lawson & Lawson, 2005).

Wegscheider (1981) outlined the three major rules that characterize an addicted family system. The first and most important rule is that the addict's drug use is the most important thing in the family's life. The household routine, family outings, finances, holidays, and how family members interact with one another all depend on the substance abuse. For the Williams family, everyone has to work around Leroy. If he joins them for dinner, they are not to say anything that will upset him. Even when money is tight, great care is taken to make sure there is always beer available. No one wants Leroy to drive while intoxicated to get more beer. Extended family get-togethers are planned well in advance and sometimes have to be cancelled (without complaint by anyone else) if Leroy says he's not up to making the trip.

The second rule is that the addict is not responsible for her or his behavior and the drug is not the cause of the family's problems. Excuses are made for how the addicted person responds. Joanna explains that Leroy's tiredness after a long day at work or his difficulty dealing with stress are reasons why he drinks. However, it is not the alcohol that is the problem. Instead, their problems stem from never having enough money, the fact that Leroy's parents did not teach him how to handle adversity, or that his friends are bad influences.

The third rule is that the status quo must be maintained at all times. Family members are extremely careful not to upset the routine. The Williams family cannot expect anything from Leroy nor can they tell other people, even extended family members, about his drinking.

In addition to the above rules, Black (1981) listed three other rules for people living in an addicted family system: don't talk, don't trust, don't feel. Family members are not allowed to talk about the addiction. As talking does not promote emotional intimacy and frequently leads to conflict it is not encouraged. The reality of the addiction is distorted (Brooks & Rice, 1997) such that no one acknowledges the elephant in the room. As a result, children in particular learn that they cannot trust their inner experiences. They also learn that they cannot trust others. The addicted family system is one in which people are not there for each other; they often do not nurture one another. Consequently, trusting both self and others becomes dangerous and something to be avoided. Finally, addicted family systems do not honor the feelings of anyone other than the addict. Other family members are encouraged to hide their feelings in order to preserve the family system. Feelings that threaten the status quo will be discouraged and/or ignored.

Stages in Addicted Family Systems

Washousky, Levy-Stern, and Muchowski (1993) have delineated four stages in the family system of the addict. The first stage is denial. The family begins to hide the abuse from each other and everyone else, offering other explanations for the addict's behavior and isolating themselves from people who may suspect the addiction. The second stage involves home treatment—attempts by family members to get the addict to stop using, usually by controlling her or his behavior. Family roles may undergo significant shifts as children try to care for parents, coalitions are formed, and other members' problems are neglected in order to keep the emphasis on the addict.

The third stage is chaos. The addiction is now so out of control that it can no longer be hidden. Other family members spin out of control, conflicts and confrontations escalate without resolution, and consequences for family members become more pronounced. This is the stage in which partners and/or children may experience serious emotional or physical problems and threats of divorce or separation are made but not completed. The last stage is control. Other family members identify the problem as an addiction and control is often attempted through divorce, separation, or total emotional isolation. The family then becomes ensnared in a cycle of helplessness and futile attempts to control the addict's behavior.

In counseling, the success of the treatment is frequently dependent upon which stage the family is currently experiencing (DiClemente & Velasquez, 2002). Many families in treatment are still in the denial stage and are not ready to change. In these instances, all counselors can do is plant seeds of change in family members (McIntyre, 2004) and wait for the family to cycle to another stage. To help counselors know where they should concentrate their energy, Miller and Tonigan (1996) have created an assessment instrument—The Stages of Change Readiness and Treatment Eagerness Scales, or SOCRATES—that determines the level of motivation to change.

Parenting in an Addicted Family System

The role of parent is one that brings a lot of stress. This is especially true in the United States, where unrealistic expectations set standards that most parents cannot meet. American culture perpetuates the myths that one or two people at most can adequately parent a child and that all people, especially women, know instinctively how to care for their children (Barnett & Rivers, 2004). Without sufficient information, ample time, energy, and assistance, good parenting skills are hard to achieve. Given these difficulties, it is hardly surprising that, for both women and men, becoming a parent can lead to decreased enjoyment in other social roles and subsequent abuse of alcohol (Richman, Rospenda, & Kelley, 1994).

> While there are gender differences, research shows that gender is less important than we think it is. Women are not better at parenting than men simply by virtue of their gender. Instead, parenting behavior— good or bad—is determined more by the situation than by your sex.

Alcohol and other substance abuse make good parenting difficult, if not impossible. Alcoholic parents are less likely to display positive affect toward their children (Fitzgerald, Zucker, & Yang, 1995), be less satisfied with being a parent (Watkins, O'Farrell, Suvak, Murphy & Taft, 2009), experience higher stress related to parenting, frequently engage in more punitive behavior, and may be less responsive to their infants (Schuler & Nair, 2001). Moreover, substance-abusing mothers in particular are at high risk of experiencing multiple problems that weaken their capacity to care for their children, including depression, increased exposure to parental and partner violence, sexual abuse, psychiatric disorders, violent behavior, and criminal behavior (Anglin & Perrochet, 1998; Nair, Schuler, Black, Kettinger & Harrington, 2003).

However, parents, especially the nonabusing parent, can have a buffering effect on children living in an addicted family system. Research has demonstrated that when at least one parent (usually the mother) can provide consistency and stability, positive outcomes can be achieved (McCord, 1988). For example, in an oft-cited study, Wolin, Bennett, and Noonan (1979) found that families who were able to maintain family rituals did not transmit alcoholism to their offspring. In contrast, families whose rituals were disrupted were more likely to produce alcoholic children. The authors concluded that regular and daily rituals serve to structure family life, increase connection, and provide a stable family identity. Similarly, Berlin and Davis (1989) demonstrated the critical nature of the mother's support and nurturance as a factor leading to a nonalcoholic outcome in adulthood. Yet another study found that children of alcoholic fathers have more stable homes and are better cared for than those with two alcoholic parents or an alcoholic mother (Williams, 1987). Thus, having the mother as the nonaddicted parent was an important factor in positive outcomes. However, other studies have not reported a gender difference. Consequently, it seems clear that as long as one parent can provide this stability, children have a better chance of good psychological outcomes.

ADDICTION AND THE COUPLE

Although the couple relationship in addicted family systems is of great importance, it has often been overlooked. As Fals-Stewart, Birchler, and Ellis (1999) point out, almost all of the empirical family studies with drug-abusing patients have ignored the partner subsystem in order to concentrate on the family of origin. Thus, the ways in which the addiction affects partner interactions and serves as a tool for the relationship have been largely disregarded. Moreover, just like research on addicted family systems in general, research on relationship functioning among alcoholics has not been completed with varied populations. Instead, it has focused primarily on married, middle class, Caucasian male problem drinkers with no comorbid psychopathology (McCrady & Epstein, 1995). Consequently, our knowledge about how addiction affects partner relationships is limited at best.

The Impact of Alcohol on Couple Relationships

Research has demonstrated that alcohol abuse has a strong detrimental effect on romantic relationships. Alcohol abuse contributes to sexual inadequacy (O'Farrell, 1990); marital discord (O'Farrell, 1995); higher rates of psychological and physical problems among nondrinking spouses (Moos, Finney, & Gamble, 1985); as well as higher rates of marital aggression, separation, and divorce (Kantor & Strauss, 1990; Schumm, O'Farrell, Murphy, & Fals-Stewart, 2009). The quality of the partnership is also correlated with the presence of a drinking problem. Studies have shown that partners report more satisfying relationships during periods of abstinence (Homish, Leonard, Kozlowski, & Cornelius, 2009). When the addict is in recovery, couple functioning appears to improve (Moos, Finney, & Cronkite, 1990).

Alcohol also appears to play a major role in interpersonal violence (McKinney, Caetano, Harris, & Ebama, 2009; Wekerle & Wall, 2002). While the exact reasons for this are unclear, the presence of alcohol is a major risk factor for female partners in particular. In a nationally representative sample, Rennison and Welchans (2000) revealed that nearly one million men committed violent crimes against their intimate female partners. Similarly, an examination of thousands of male members of the Armed Forces found that an alcohol problem significantly increased the likelihood of both mild and severe forms of husband-to-wife aggression (Pan, Neidig, & O'Leary, 1994). The relationship between alcohol and violence remained strong even after controlling for sociodemographic and personality variables.

Studies of addiction treatment groups also yielded startlingly high numbers of domestic violence offenders. In two separate studies, O'Farrell and Fals-Stewart (2000) discovered that approximately 60% of alcoholics had been violent toward their female partner in the year prior to treatment. Other studies found that the prevalence of domestic violence was at least twice as high in addiction treatment groups than in the general population (Fals-Stewart, Kashdan, O'Farrell, & Birchler, 2002; Schumm, O'Farrell, Murphy, & Fals-Stewart, 2009). Moreover, male physical aggression toward their female partner was more than eight times higher on days when they drank. There also appears to be a link between violence and sexual functioning in alcoholic couples (Epstein & McCrady, 1998).

In addition to the human toll, domestic violence is quite expensive. The Centers for Disease Control and Prevention recently reported that batterers' abuse costs over $5.8 billion per year nationally for their victims' health care and lost productivity. This amount does not include money spent by law enforcement agencies or other branches of the civil and criminal legal system.

Alcohol can have a major influence on the dissolution of the relationship. Numerous studies have shown a connection between problem drinking and relationship divorce or disruption (e.g., Kessler, Walters, & Forthofer, 1998; Leonard & Rothbard, 1999). For heterosexual couples, there is some question about whether the gender of the addicted partner makes a difference in the termination of the romantic relationship. The evidence for the impact of gender is mixed. Some studies (Leonard & Roberts, 1998; Roberts & Linney, 1998) have found that the husband's drinking, but not the wife's, predicted instability while others (Grzywacz & Marks, 1999) revealed that problem drinking was linked to lower marital quality regardless of who was doing the drinking. Whatever the influence of gender, it is apparent that alcohol can significantly contribute to the end of a relationship.

CASE STUDY

Michelle and Billy met in a bar. Although Michelle is generally a shy person, the alcohol made her friendly and she responded to Billy's flirting. The two have been married now for 10 years. They have no children. While both of them enjoy drinking after work, Michelle has really struggled to avoid abusing alcohol. A few years ago, she attended AA at Billy's request but stopped after only a few months. Michelle accepts the limitations Billy puts on her drinking when he is at home but will occasionally drink until she is intoxicated. Her drinking is the source of many heated arguments and Billy periodically threatens to leave the marriage.

Question: How much of a role has alcohol played in Michelle and Billy's relationship?

THE IMPACT OF COUPLES ON ALCOHOL ABUSE.   While alcohol clearly affects the relationship, in true systemic fashion, some researchers are trying to determine if the relationship itself influences the drinking behavior. For example, O'Farrell (1993) found that problematic marital interactions can stimulate drinking or even bring about renewed drinking. Moreover, alcohol can have a short-term positive effect on interpersonal interactions (Roberts & Linney, 2000). When people have difficulty obtaining intimacy or want to avoid conflict, they frequently draw a third person or object into their interaction. In this way, they are no longer forced to deal only with each other and can instead concentrate on the additional person or object. In such cases, alcohol can serve as the third point in the triangle. Thus, when the alcohol is removed, relationships can suffer. Studies have demonstrated that drug-abusing couples have significant difficulties in multiple areas, including communication (Birchler, 1995); lack of emotional support (Lex, 1990); abusiveness, lack of problem-solving skills, and high attribution of blame (Fals-Stewart & Birchler, 1998). However, as causality has not been determined, it is difficult to know if these couples had these problems before the addiction or if the addiction instigated them.

Alcohol definitely served as a way to help Michelle and Billy interact. Michelle freely admits that she probably would have ignored Billy had she not been intoxicated when they first met. Moreover, given her high level of anxiety and low self-confidence, Michelle has used alcohol to enhance their sex life. Although Billy gets angry about Michelle's excessive drinking, he too uses alcohol to help the two of them feel closer to one another. They rarely have deep conversations without alcohol present. However, their communication in general is superficial and problems are rarely, if ever, truly solved. Instead, they both blame one another for any conflicts that arise and avoid talking about anything even remotely controversial.

ENABLING AND CODEPENDENCE. In the early days of addictions treatment, researchers and counselors alike began wondering why the partner, usually female, stayed with the alcohol abuser. One theory that arose was the codependent personality. Codependency is excessive dependence upon a loved one by a person who looks to external sources for fulfillment. It is exemplified by inadequate or lost identity, neglect of self, and low self-esteem. Codependent people rescue others at the expense of their own needs and use control as a way of distracting attention from these needs. They are obsessed with the loved person and often believe that survival, theirs or their partner's, depends on maintaining the relationship. Codependency quickly became a popular theory for why (primarily) women stayed in horrible relationships, especially those characterized by addiction. However, there has been severe criticism of this theory. Rotunda and colleagues (1995) pointed out that the construct of codependence has not been empirically defined. Zelvin (1999) argued that codependency is merely a way to pathologize society's socialization of women to connect in any way possible. Moreover, society's ideal of true love—a relationship in which two people are fused into one entity (the couple)—actually promotes codependency (Zelvin, 2004).

Like codependency, enabling is another theory that explains the actions of the nonaddicted partner. Enabling is the manner in which the partner inadvertently maintains the drug or alcohol use. For example, one type of enabling behavior is the attempt to control both the addicted person's behavior as well as the surrounding environment. This allows some partners to appear to be in control of their lives and to be labeled overresponsible (Krestan & Bepko, 1990) when, in reality, they are attempting to prevent their world from falling apart. Such controlling behavior can engender defiance in the substance abuser, allow her or him to project responsibility for the consequences onto the enabler, and reinforce the mistaken belief that the addiction can be controlled. Thus, it becomes quite easy to blame the enabler for her/his role in the addiction instead of looking at how enabling is the result of living with a loved one's addiction and other dysfunctional family behaviors (Zelvin, 2004). As is true with codependency, enabling has not been empirically validated as a pathological personality trait (Rotunda et al., 1995). Despite this, codependency support groups are still used widely for support around change.

While Billy does not exhibit codependent traits, he demonstrates enabling behavior. When Michelle was in AA, he would drink alcohol in front of her. When confronted with this, he stated that she needed to learn self-discipline. Billy also enables Michelle's drinking by keeping alcohol around the house and by trying to strictly regulate her alcoholic intake. He measures out the exact amount of alcohol he has deemed acceptable for Michelle to drink each night. If she goes over that amount, he gets very upset. For her part, Michelle gets angry with his attempts to control her drinking and, when he goes out of town, drinks more to spite him.

PARTNERS AS RESOURCES. Partners can serve as important motivators for their significant others to change their addictive behavior and can be of great assistance in counseling. Research has shown that improving partner relationships can be a major factor in getting addicted people to stop drinking (Noel & McCrady, 1993). For example, one study discovered that 53% of male alcoholics were motivated by their spouses or family to seek treatment (Steinberg et al., 1997). Similarly, partners can be valuable allies in counseling sessions. Nonalcoholic partners may provide essential information, give constructive feedback and support to the clients (Zweben & Barrett, 1993), and help the addicted partner identify high-risk situations (McCrady, 1993; Stanton, 2005). Moreover, treating the relationship problems of drug-abusing couples has been shown to result in improved relationship variables (O'Farrell, Murphy, Stephan, Fals-Stewart, & Murphy, 2004).

However, while partners can be indispensable in treatment, there may be challenges. Sobriety or even a reduction in substance use can increase tension in the couple's relationship after the honeymoon period ends (Stanton, 2005). One major reason for increased tension is the need for forgiveness. In order to restore trust to the relationship, the nonaddicted partner frequently wants the addicted partner to understand how painful their addiction was and to apologize for the hurt. Once the forgiveness process has been negotiated, couples work can begin. Targets of intervention for couples include power (the couple needs to negotiate a workable power structure and increase tolerance for conflict), intimacy (both partners need to allow themselves to be vulnerable and learn how to negotiate for getting their needs met), boundaries, and determining the function of the drug abuse (Winn, 1995).

Billy was of great assistance in the counseling sessions with Michelle. She admitted that she wanted to stop drinking because it was the only way to save her marriage. Michelle was much more willing to listen to Billy's suggestions for ways to engage in abstinence than she was her counselor's. When counseling first started and their relationship started to change, both initially questioned whether it was worth it to maintain the marriage. However, once they began to see the positive results of increased communication and intimacy, both agreed to continue with counseling.

ADDICTION AND THE CHILDREN

Although addiction significantly affects the entire family, children are most affected Despite this truth, early addictions literature focused almost solely on the addict and ignored the other people in the system. However, with the advent of the Adult Children of Alcoholics (ACOA) movement, attention shifted to include the outcomes of children living in an addicted family environment. While much of the literature base is focused on adult children living out of, but still affected by, the dysfunctional family system, it seems as though the outcomes for children both in and out of the family environment are roughly the same. Consequently, this chapter will use the terms COAs and ACOAs interchangeably.

The problems associated with living in an alcoholic family are much greater than we may realize. Research estimates that there are 26.8 million COAs in the U.S., with over 11 million under the age of 18. Moreover, 76 million Americans, roughly 43% of the adult population, have been exposed to alcoholism in the family.

Of all family members, children have the least control over what happens and rarely have the freedom to leave. Moreover, the ways addiction affects children can begin before birth. First, there seems to be a genetic component to alcoholism and other types of addictions. Family studies, twin studies, adoption studies, half-sibling studies, and animal studies have all shown a tendency for addiction to run in families (Erickson, 2007; Lawson & Lawson, 1998). Thus, children of alcoholics tend to have an elevated risk for developing alcoholism themselves (Brook, Brook, Rubenstone, Zhang, Singer, & Duke, 2003).

Second, children of addicted parents are at risk for prenatal exposure to drugs and alcohol (Streissguth, Bookstein, Sampson, & Barr, 1995) which can lead to a host of cognitive, physiological, and psychosocial difficulties (Fields, 2004). Children suffering from Fetal Alcohol Syndrome show effects in morphological anomalies, growth retardation, and central nervous system deficits (Sokol & Clarren, 1989). Other negative effects can occur with lower levels of prenatal alcohol exposure (Cornelius, Day, Richardson, & Taylor, 1999).

A third way children are affected by alcohol addiction is by growing up in an addicted family system characterized by chaos, uncertainty, and an ever-changing reality (Brown, 1988). There is an overall lack of structure (e.g., distorted hierarchies, triangulation, parentification, rigid or nonexistent boundaries) and there may be inconsistencies in parenting or a lack of parenting altogether (Lawson & Lawson, 2005). Inconsistencies in discipline make it hard for children to learn cause-and-effect connections. Family rules are often arbitrary, unclear, and contradictory (Krugman, 1987) and can change depending on whether the addict is in a wet (active intoxication) or dry cycle (Lawson & Lawson, 2005). Emotional and physical neglect, high levels of conflict, partner instability, disorganization, violence, and/or physical and sexual abuse are all common (Giglio & Kaufman, 1990). Instead of a place of safety and love, the family environment consists of tension, fear, and shame and a basic lack of safety, all of which play into the child's sense of self. Children in addicted family systems are forced to adapt to the ongoing trauma (Kinney, 2003) and are deprived of the opportunity to attend to their own development.

Violence is yet another way children can be affected by addiction. In fact, the presence and risk of violence in addicted family systems cannot be understated. The link between alcohol use and interpersonal violence has been widely documented (Nicholas, & Rasmussen, 2006; Roberts, Roberts, & Leonard, 1999). Parental substance abuse is a risk factor for child abuse (Wekerle & Wall, 2002). Children of drug abusers are at greater risk for abuse, neglect, and disruption in primary care giving (Johnson & Leff, 1999). This is especially true when the addict is the mother. Gustavsson (1991) found that maternal substance abuse increases the likelihood that children will be removed from the home.

Physical abuse is not the only type of violence that can occur to children in an addicted family system. Sexual abuse is also frequent, but for different reasons. While addicted parents can and do sexually abuse their children, research has found that sexual abuse among children of alcoholics was more likely to have been perpetrated by "friends" of the family (Miller, Downs, Gondoli, & Keil, 1987) rather than family members themselves. A main reason for this rests with the nonexistent boundaries found in some addicted family systems. While some families dealing with addiction rigidly control their children's access to the community (children are taught to view the world outside the family as dangerous and are punished for talking to people outside the home), others leave their children completely unattended. Consequently, friends of the parents and other adults can have unsupervised access to children and frequently molest them (Krugman, 1987; Steinglass, Bennett, Wolin, & Reiss, 1987; Windle & Tubman, 1999).

Although substance abuse has a significant and usually detrimental effect on the children of addicted family systems, they do not all demonstrate negative outcomes. Many research studies have shown that children of alcoholics do not have physical or psychological outcomes that differ significantly from those who have not lived in an addicted family system (Windle & Tubman, 1999). The diathesis-stress model may be one answer to the question of why many COAs go on to live relatively normal lives. According to this model, the variation between personality characteristics (e.g., coping styles) and stressful life events (Belsky & Pluess, 2009) can make a difference. More positive personality traits coupled with less stressful life events can lead some COAs toward resilience while others, with different personality/stress pairings, spiral downward. The presence of psychiatric disorders within the family may be another reason why some COAs have better outcomes than others. Zucker, Ellis, Bingham, and Fitzgerald (1996) found that psychosocial outcomes among COAs vary depending on the existence of paternal comorbid antisocial behavior. Consequently, it appears as though there are many factors other than the presence of substance abuse that impact COAs' lives.

Behavioral Outcomes

Although many COAs and ACOAs go on to lead normal lives, it is important to know about the negative outcomes that can appear in both groups. Children living in an addicted family system can experience significant damaging effects as a result of the dysfunction. Many studies have documented the severe physiological consequences of living in an addicted environment. These include lower cognitive performance (Fitzgerald et al., 1993; Streissguth et al., 1995), attentional deficits (Sheridan & Green, 1993), and poorer neurological functioning (Poon, Ellis, Fitzgerald, & Zucker, 2000).

The link between COAs and negative behavioral outcomes is also well established. Children of alcoholics have elevated rates of impulsivity, conduct disorders (Fitzgerald et al., 1993), alexithymia (Windle, 1990), depression, and anxiety (Chassin, Rogosch, & Barrera, 1991; Kessler et al., 1994). They also exhibit lower academic achievement (McGrath, Watson, & Chassin, 1999; Poon et al., 2000) and a more external locus of control (Mun, Fitzgerald, Puttler, Zucker, & Von Eye, 2000), which makes them further affected by a negative environment.

Finally, COAs are at elevated risk for alcoholism. Brook et al. (2003) found that COAs are between 1.5 to 9 times more likely to develop an alcohol disorder in adulthood. This is especially true if the addicted family is extremely enmeshed and reactive to the alcohol abuser. Research has demonstrated that the lower the levels of differentiation in the family (i.e., being able to separate oneself from others), the higher the chance of transmitting addictive behaviors from one generation to the next (Lawson & Lawson, 2005).

Psychosocial Outcomes

Psychosocial outcomes of COAs also are affected as a result of an addicted family environment. Children's development of self can be severely disrupted. Because the reality of life in an addicted family system is constantly distorted, children quickly learn that they cannot trust their internal emotions and, as such, cannot trust themselves (Brooks & Rice, 1997; Fields, 2004; Kinney, 2003). Moreover, their home environment is one in which they have no control. COAs may have no opportunity to develop and internalize feelings of mastery or power because of the chaos. Consequently, they try to gain some kind of control, often by believing that they are the cause of the problem and if they can work hard enough at fixing themselves, the family can be healed (Lawson & Lawson, 2005).

THE COA SELF.   Brown (1992) hypothesized that, in response to trauma, COAs develop a defensive self, one that decreases their vulnerability. A defensive self includes denial, perceptual and cognitive distortions, fear of losing control, black and white thinking, overresponsibility, and a negation of self. Unfortunately, while the creation of a defensive self can be an adaptive coping mechanism while in the addicted family system, it ultimately can lead to unremitting

TABLE 14.1 Functions and Characteristics of COAs	
Characteristic	**Function of the Characteristic**
Dependence	Child's own needs are less important than supporting the family system; independence is a threat to parental authority
Difficulty expressing emotions	Disclosure is unwelcome and would risk exposure of faults, thereby causing anger in adults
Difficulty relaxing	Fear of being thought lazy; evolved from lack of opportunity to relax and play independently
Excessive loyalty	Terrified of abandonment; loyalty ensures the child's belief as deserving of approval
Overly responsible	Method of maintaining control; may be their role in the system
Fear of losing control	If others do not need them, it conveys the feeling that they are incapable, incompetent, and have shortcomings
Fear of conflict	Try to avoid at all costs due to fear of painful interactions and a lack of problem-solving skills
Overly self-critical	Internalized messages from others that they cannot do anything right and are responsible for the family's problems
Sensation seeking	Evolved from the childhood abuse that robbed them of their natural impulsivity, playfulness, and creativity

distrust of others, inhibition of curiosity, distrust of one's own senses, and feelings of unreality. Other characteristics of COAs that are supported by the literature (Ficaro, 1999; Rubin, 2001) can be found in Table 14.1.

COAs' RELATIONSHIPS WITH OTHERS. Living in an addicted family system necessarily affects the COA's relationships with others. As discussed previously, the distortion of reality makes it difficult for COAs to trust either themselves or others (Ficaro, 1999). This is especially true when considering the issues surrounding attachment (Rubin, 2001). Alcoholic parents are unpredictable and often abusive. They frequently discourage normal processes of development, including autonomy, desire for affection, and creation of critical thinking skills. Instead, children are encouraged to be dependent and compliant and not ask for too much lest they be considered needy. Attachment to such a parent lends itself to "splitting" or black and white thinking. In an effort to accept their conflicted feelings about addicted caregivers, children blame themselves for the abusive behavior and see themselves as deficient and unworthy of respect and care. In this fashion, they can avoid placing the blame on the "good" caregiver. As a result of splitting behavior, other people tend to be seen as either good or bad, with nothing in between (Brooks & Rice, 1997). This way of looking at people generalizes to other relationships, including romantic partners (Olmstead, Crowell, & Waters, 2003) and to the COA's relationship with their own children (Rubin, 2001). Moreover, in an alcoholic environment, it becomes difficult to develop good relationship skills. Consequently, COAs often fail to develop appropriate prosocial skills and find it difficult to have positive friendships (Kearns-Bodkin & Leonard, 2008; Windle & Tubman, 1999). Similarly, COAs are at increased risk for maladaptive relationship outcomes, including partner conflict and dissatisfaction, disrupted family environments, and ineffective or inefficient parenting practices (Fields, 2004; Kinney, 2003).

CASE STUDY

Betty and Leo are both children of drug-addicted fathers. They have been married for 15 years, but are unable to have children. They have entered counseling due to Leo's extramarital affair and dependency on prescription drugs. Betty is clearly overresponsible, as she is the primary breadwinner and takes care of the household and the couple's relationships with others. Leo complains that she rarely has time for him. While both Betty and Leo are always busy, their activities vary. Betty is usually occupied with some household task while Leo constantly seeks excitement. Neither one appears able to discuss their emotions or handle conflict appropriately. Whenever problems arise, they either yell at each other or wait for the problem to go away. Leo mentions that Betty is very hard on herself while Betty complains that Leo has minimal self-discipline.

Question: How would you help this couple with their distortions of reality?

COUNSELING ADDICTED FAMILY SYSTEMS

Efficacy of Couples and Family Counseling

The emphasis in addictions treatment has shifted from an almost sole focus on the addict to at least minimal inclusion of other family members. Research has consistently found that couples and family counseling have among the best outcomes for recovery from addiction. In the early 1990s, the National Institute of Drug Abuse funded several treatment outcome studies to evaluate the usefulness of family counseling with adolescent substance abusers. Most found family counseling to be superior to other modalities (Friedman, Tomko, & Utada, 1991; Joanning, Quinn, Thomas, & Mullen, 1992; Liddle & Diamond, 1991). Meta-analyses have shown that couples and family therapies are among the top five treatments for substance abuse and were superior to individually oriented treatment modalities (Edwards & Steinglass, 1995), peer group counseling, and various forms of treatment as usual (Stanton & Shadish, 1997). Family counseling has been found to be particularly effective at engagement and retention of problem drinkers (O'Farrell & Fals-Stewart, 2003; Waldron, 1997) as well as adolescent substance abusers (Rowe & Liddle, 2003). In one study with heroin abusers, McClelland, Arndt, Metzger, Woody, and O'Brien (1993) discovered that adding a family intervention component to individual counseling and methadone maintenance led to improved outcomes.

One possible reason for the efficacy of couples and family counseling may be due to the lack of empirically validated treatments. By its very multidimensional nature, couples and family counseling cannot be manualized (there are too many variables present) and can thus provide the flexibility needed to increase therapeutic outcome (Liddle, 1995). Thus, the task of counselors is to conceptualize behavior problems within a multidimensional framework and direct intervention strategies toward the systems targeted for change (Henggeler & Borduin, 1995).

Assessment of Addicted Family Systems

In deciding whether family counseling is appropriate for a family in which substance abuse is present, some researchers have suggested examining the impact of alcohol in the family. Thus, counselors should determine whether the family is indeed an alcoholic family or a family with an alcoholic member (Steinglass et al., 1987). This assessment will assist in determining which subsystems should be targeted for interventions specific to alcoholic families (Walitzer, 1999). Counselors need to be aware that alcoholic families contain three diagnostic tracks: the environment, the family system, and the individual, all of which respond differently to the supremacy of the alcoholism (Brown & Schmid, 1999). For example, the cultural milieu (the environment) can often determine how someone will respond to the development of an addiction. In a study examining gender differences in role expectations, the authors found that men may consider the development of addictions to be a natural part of participating in male culture, while women frequently are both more remorseful and more aware of the harmful impact of their behavior on their relationships (Strassner & Zelvin, 1997). Counselors must therefore take care to include questions about each diagnostic track in their initial assessment.

Although many practitioners advocate the use of formal assessment instruments during initial sessions, others maintain that the structured clinical interview is best, as long as honest disclosure is obtained (Chamberlain & Jew, 2003). In addition to helping the family feel more comfortable, the clinical interview allows for development of a solid therapeutic alliance and the counselor's observance of the family's nonverbal interactions. One assessment technique that is quite useful is the genogram. A genogram is a graphic, symbolic representation of generational family relationships. Because of its breadth and complexity, it can be used to pinpoint patterns of behavior and the psychological factors that disrupt relationships. Thus, this is a good therapeutic tool allowing for a more systemic focus and providing counselors with vital information the family may attempt to hide. For example, a special emphasis on the health status of family members (i.e., prominent histories of heart disease and other cardiovascular problems, liver disease, depression, suicide, miscarriages, mental retardation, or learning disabilities that may be linked to Fetal Alcohol Syndrome) as well as close attention to legal problems frequently can signify a substance abuse problem the family denies.

Ideally, assessment should include all adult members and school-age children who live in the family system. Including as many family members as possible allows for the utilization of many different sources of information, and serves to minimize distortions and inaccuracies (Chamberlain & Jew, 2003). All members must come to the session sober and agree that the counseling emphasis will be on the addiction as a family problem. Moreover, everyone must consent to the exploration of basic safety considerations during every session, especially if there is a history of domestic violence or child abuse.

As with every assessment, counselors should conduct the session in a supportive, caring, and nonjudgmental manner. The supportive and nonjudgmental nature of the questions and interpersonal interactions is especially important for a family struggling with addiction, however, as they already feel guilty, responsible, and shamed by the situation (Stanton & Heath, 1995). The counselor's sensitivity and lack of blame will help encourage self-disclosure and motivate family members toward change. Specific assessment questions should focus on the function and severity of the addiction for each individual and the family as a whole; the presence of emotional and behavioral problems for each person; and the existence of strengths, capabilities, and resilience they've developed in response to chemical dependency (McIntyre, 2004). Counselors also should be alert to the social problems common in an addict's life, such as excessive job loss, drug arrests, domestic violence, break-up of important relationships, frequent moves, and lack of interest in activities that once were important to the person (Chamberlain & Jew, 2003). In addition to the necessary questions, assessment should include validation of family stories and a demonstration of how family problems are directly connected to the addiction (Hartel & Glantz, 1999). Counselors also need to assess for the psychological, attitudinal, and behavioral skills the family will need to develop in order to support their substance-free existence (McIntyre, 2004).

Treatment Strategies for Addicted Family Systems

Within the addictions treatment community, there is debate about how much attention counselors should pay to having the addicted person achieve full sobriety. While many counselors believe that little work can be done without abstinence (Hartel & Glantz, 1999; Stanton & Heath, 1995; Steinglass et al., 1987), others maintain that it is not the counselor's job to monitor the sobriety of an addicted individual (Pascoe, 1999; Rotunda et al., 1995). Instead, they should pay close attention to how family dynamics maintain the alcohol consumption and work to change those. In this way, abstinence is not the primary foundation upon which the effectiveness of the counseling rests. Some counselors operate from a harm-reduction model (i.e., accepting the person wherever she or he is in the stages of change and assisting her or him through the process) so that when relapse occurs (as it will, since recovery is a process), everything is not lost.

As with assessment, treatment should be conducted through the three areas of interest: the environment, the system, and the individual. While working on the environment and the family system can occur in two separate phases, individual work can be accomplished throughout. In treating the environment, counselors must accomplish two primary tasks (Chamberlain & Jew, 2003). First, the family must create safety from external threats and the internalized family, or the family of origin. Toward this end, counselors should be nonblaming and noncontrolling (Stanton & Heath, 1995) and use consistency and predictability in interacting with the family.

Second, each family member must tell the story of the trauma. This is an important part of treatment because it helps eliminate the compartmentalizing, denial, and repression characterized by alcoholic families (van der Kolk & Kadish, 1987) and allows everyone to hear each family member's perspective. To accomplish this huge task, counselors must strive to make the counseling session an extremely safe place. While not a primary task in this area of treatment, an analysis of social-relational changes and how best to help at-risk individuals manage these transitions can be helpful in preventing future relapses (Richman et al., 1994).

The family system is the arena in which most work will take place. Counselors must be extremely active during this period of work, repairing the distortions of reality by educating about alcoholism, inferring the family rules and the punishments for breaking them, and challenging the rationalizations that supported the rules (Chamberlain & Jew, 2003; Hartel & Glantz, 1999). During this period, families may experience what is known as the emotional desert. This is when family processes are upset and the members become uncomfortable. Many family members may feel depressed and detached, and may feel the desire to return to the "wet" patterns of behavior (Steinglass et al., 1987). Counselors can help them through this difficult time by normalizing and validating their experiences and working through the issues eroding their desire for change (Stanton & Heath, 1995).

McIntyre (2004) also suggests some experiential exercises to help the family regain their desire for healing. For example, he encourages families to remain distrustful of the change process as a way of respecting their fear and previous experiences. He recommends an intervention known as "distrust days." Family members are asked to actively distrust each other on certain specified days while building trust the rest of the time. They are then asked to decide which they like better. In this way, nonaddicted family members start becoming less reactive to the substance abuser and can begin working on their own emotional processes. Family members are also told that they are expected to only do a little bit right and are sure to make mistakes (McIntyre, 2004). This lowers expectations of treatment and allows for small successes.

Another strategy for crossing the emotional desert is to use a criticism journal, in which family members keep track of every critical and fearful thought they have about the addict and the process of recovery. Family members can keep the journal until the end of counseling, at which time they can look back and see what changed.

Another intervention is to have family members write heartfelt letters to each other (McIntyre, 2004). All of these experiential treatment strategies give family members things to do while validating their experiences.

This period of work can allow time to focus on the couple subsystem. In matching the treatment to fit the family, counselors may want to change strategies and focus more on behavioral interventions. These can be more technical, with counselors teaching the nonabusing partner how to terminate the reinforcement contingencies that promote drinking, and increase behaviors that support abstinence (Roberts & Linney, 2000). Other interventions can be more general, such as teaching problem solving and communication skills (McCrady & Epstein, 1995). Developing increased cooperation and empathic understanding through communication exercises also can be beneficial (Rotunda et al., 1995).

Once the majority of the recovery work is done, counseling needs to focus on restabilizing the family so that they develop more healthy patterns of relating (Steinglass et al., 1987). During this period, counselors must identify strengths, help families create alternate coping strategies, and develop interactions that do not focus on the substance abuse (Hartel & Glantz, 1999; Stanton & Heath, 1995). They should address relapse prevention and teach families how to positively manage the effects of conflict (Rotunda et al., 1995). Once families believe they are firmly in recovery, the process of termination can begin.

Summary and Some Final Notations

Addiction affects not only the addicted person. It affects whole families, particularly the partners and children of substance abusers. Family members respond as best they can to addiction but frequently end up maintaining, instead of eliminating, the addiction. Addicted family systems tend to be characterized by unhealthy interactions and can result in most family members experiencing negative physical and emotional outcomes. Consequently, in order to provide the most effective service delivery, counselors must include the entire family in addictions treatment. In sessions, family counselors focus on the role family dynamics play in maintaining the addiction and concentrate interventions toward changing the ways family members relate to one another.

Useful Web Sites

The following Web sites provide additional information relating to the chapter topics:

American Association for Marriage and Family Therapy
http://www.aamft.org/index_nm.asp

American Psychological Association's Division on Psychopharmacology and Substance Abuse
http://www.apa.org/divisions/div28/

American Psychological Association's Division on Family Psychology
http://www.apa.org/divisions/div43/

International Association of Addiction and Offender Counselors
http://www.iaaoc.org/

International Association of Marriage and Family Counselors
http://www.iamfc.com/

National Association of Alcoholism and Drug Abuse Counselors
http://naadac.org/

National Institute on Drug Abuse
http://www.nida.nih.gov/

References

Alford, K. M. (1998). Family roles, alcoholism, and family dysfunction. *Journal of Mental Health Counseling, 20,* 250–261.

Anglin, M. D., & Perrochet, B. (1998). Drug use and crime: A historical review of research conducted by the UCLA Drug Abuse Research Center. *Substance Use & Misuse, 33,* 1871–1914.

Barnett, R., & Rivers, C. (2004). *Same difference: How gender myths are hurting our relationships, our children, and our jobs.* New York: Basic Books.

Belsky, J., & Pluess, M. (2009). Beyond diathesis stress: Differential susceptibility to environmental influences. *Psychological Bulletin, 135,* 885–908.

Berlin, R., & Davis, R. B. (1989). Children from alcoholic families: Vulnerability and resilience. In T. F. Dugan & R. Coles (Eds.), *The child in our times* (pp. 107–123). New York: Brunner/Mazel.

Birchler, G. R. (1995). Clinical themes encountered with substance-abusing couples. In G. R. Birchler (Chair), *Therapy with drug-abusing couples.* Symposium conducted at the Annual Meeting of the American Psychological Association, New York, New York.

Black, C. (1981). *It will never happen to me.* Denver: M.A.C. Publishers.

Brook, D. W., Brook, J. S., Rubenstone, E., Zhang, C., Singer, M., & Duke, M. R. (2003). Alcohol use in adolescents whose fathers abuse drugs. *Journal of Addictive Disease, 2,* 11–43.

Brooks, C. S., & Rice, K. F. (1997). *Families in recovery: Coming full circle.* Baltimore, MD: Paul H Brookes Publishing Co.

Brooner, R. K., King, V. L., Kidorf, M., Schmidt, C. W., & Bigelow, G. E. (1997). Psychiatric and substance use comorbidity among treatment-seeking opioid users. *Archives of General Psychiatry, 54,* 71–80.

Brown, S. (1988). *Treating adult children of alcoholics: A developmental perspective.* New York: Wiley.

Brown, S. (1992). *Safe passage: Recovery for adult children of alcoholics.* New York: Wiley.

Brown, S., & Schmid, J. (1999). Adult children of alcoholics. In P. J. Ott, R. E. Tarter, & R. T. Ammerman, (Eds.), *Sourcebook on substance abuse: Etiology, epidemiology, assessment, and treatment* (pp. 416–429). Needham Heights, MA: Allyn & Bacon.

Chamberlain, L., & Jew, C. L. (2003). Family assessment of drug and alcohol problems. In K. Jordan (Ed.), *Handbook of couple and family assessment* (pp. 221–239). Hauppauge, NY: Nova Science Publishers.

Chassin, L., Rogosch, F., & Barrera, M., Jr. (1991). Substance use and symptomatology among adolescent children of alcoholics. *Journal of Abnormal Psychology, 100,* 449–463.

Cornelius, M. D., Day, N. L., Richardson, G. A., & Taylor, P. M. (1999). Epidemiology of substance use during pregnancy. In P. J. Ott, R. E. Tarter, & R. T. Ammerman, (Eds.), *Sourcebook on substance abuse: Etiology, epidemiology, assessment, and treatment* (pp. 1–13). Needham Heights, MA: Allyn & Bacon.

DiClemente, C. C., & Velasquez, M. M. (2002). Motivational interviewing and the stages of change. In W. R. Miller & S. Rollnick (Eds.), *Motivational interviewing* (2nd ed., pp. 201–216). New York: Guilford Press.

Edwards, J. T. (2003). *Working with families: Guidelines and techniques* (6th ed.). Durham, NC: Foundation Place Publishing.

Edwards, M. E., & Steinglass, P. (1995). Family therapy treatment outcomes for alcoholism. *Journal of Marital and Family Therapy, 21,* 475–509.

Eigen, L. D., & Rowden, D. (1995). A methodology and current estimate of the number of children of alcoholics in the United States. In H. Adger, C. Black, S. Brown, L. D. Eigen, D. W. Rowden, J. L. Johnson, J. Moe, E. R. Morehouse, S. Wolin, & S. Wolin (Eds.), *Children of alcoholics: Selected readings* (pp. 78–97). Rockville, MD: National Association for Children of Alcoholics.

Epstein, E. E., & McCrady, B. S. (1998). Behavioral couples treatment of alcohol and drug use disorders: Current status and innovations. *Clinical Psychology Review, 18,* 689–711.

Erickson, C. K. (2007). *The science of addiction.* New York: W. W. Norton & Company.

Fals-Stewart, W., & Birchler, G. R. (1998). Marital interactions of drug-abusing patients and their partners: Comparisons with distressed couples and relationship to drug-abusing behavior. *Psychology of Addictive Behaviors, 12,* 28–38.

Fals-Stewart, W., Birchler, G. R., & Ellis, L. (1999). Procedures for evaluating the dyadic adjustment of drug-abusing patients and their intimate partners. *Journal of Substance Abuse Treatment, 16,* 5–16.

Fals-Stewart, W., Kashdan, T. B., O'Farrell, T. J., & Birchler, G. R. (2002). Behavioral couples therapy for drug-abusing patients: Effects on partner violence. *Journal of Substance Abuse Treatment, 22,* 87–96.

Fals-Stewart, W., Kelley, M. L., Cooke, C. G., & Golden, J. C. (2003). Predictors of the psychosocial adjustment of children living in households of parents in which fathers abuse drugs: The effects of postnatal parental exposure. *Addictive Behavior, 28,* 1013–1031.

Ficaro, R. C. (1999). The many losses of children in substance-disordered families. In N. B. Webb (Ed.), *Play therapy with children in crisis: Individual, group and family treatment* (2nd ed., pp. 294–317). New York: Guilford.

Fields, R. (2004). *Drugs in perspective: A personalized look at substance use and abuse* (5th ed.). New York: McGraw-Hill.

Fitzgerald, H. E., Sullivan, L. A., Ham, H. P., Zucker, R. A., Bruckel, S., & Schneider, A. M. (1993). Predictors of behavioral problems in three-year-old sons of alcoholics: Early evidence for onset of risk. *Child Development, 64,* 110–123.

Fitzgerald, H. E., Zucker, R. A., & Yang, H. (1995). Developmental systems theory and alcoholism: Analyzing patterns of variation in high-risk families. *Psychology of Addictive Behaviors, 9*(1), 8–22.

Friedman, A. S., Tomko, I. A., & Utada, A. (1991). Client and family characteristics that predict better family therapy outcome for adolescent drug abusers. *Family Dynamics of Addiction Quarterly, 1*(1), 77–93.

Giglio, J. J., & Kaufman, E. (1990). The relationship between child and adult psychopathology in children of alcoholics. *International Journal of the Addictions, 25,* 263–290.

Grant, B. F. (2000). Estimates of US children exposed to alcohol abuse and dependence in the family. *American Journal of Public Health, 90,* 112–115.

Griffiths, M. D. (2005a). A "components" model of addiction within a biopsychosocial framework. *Journal of Substance Use, 10,* 191–197.

Grzywacz, J. G., & Marks, N. F. (1999). Family solidarity and health behaviors: Evidence from the National Survey of Midlife Development in the United States (MIDUS). *Journal of Family Issues, 20,* 243–268.

Gustavsson, N. (1991). Chemically-exposed children: The child welfare response. *Child and Adolescent Social Work Journal, 8,* 297–307.

Halikas, J. A., Crosby, R. D., Pearson, V. L., Nugent, S. M., & Carlson, G. A. (1994). Psychiatric comorbidity in treatment-seeking cocaine abusers. *American Journal on Addiction, 3,* 25–35.

Hartel, C. R., & Glantz, M. D. (1999). The treatment of drug abuse: Changing the paths. In M. D. Glantz & C. R. Hartel (Eds.), *Drug abuse: Origins and interventions* (pp. 243–284). Washington, DC: American Psychological Association.

Henggeler, S. W., & Borduin, C. M. (1995). Multisystemic treatment of serious juvenile offenders and their families. In I. M. Schwartz & P. AuClaire (Eds.), *Home-based services for troubled children* (pp. 113–130). Lincoln: University of Nebraska Press.

Homish, G. G., Leonard, K. E., Kozlowski, L. T., & Cornelius, J. R. (2009). The longitudinal association between multiple substance use discrepancies and marital satisfaction. *Addiction, 104,* 1201–1209.

Joanning, H., Quinn, W., Thomas, F., & Mullen, R. (1992). Treating adolescent drug use: A comparison of family systems therapy, group therapy, and family drug education. *Journal of Marital and Family Therapy, 18*(4), 345–356.

Johnson, J. L., & Leff, M. (1999). Children of substance abusers: Overview of research findings. *Pediatrics, 103,* 1085–1099.

Kantor, G. K., & Strauss, M. A. (1990). The "drunken bum" theory of wife beating. In M. A. Strauss & R. J. Gelles (Eds.), *Physical violence in American families* (pp. 203–224). New Brunswick, NJ: Transaction.

Kearns-Bodkin, J. N., & Leonard, K. E. (2008). Relationship functioning among adult children of alcoholics. *Journal of Studies on Alcohol & Drugs, 69,* 941–950.

Kessler, R. C., McGonagle, K. A., Zhao, S., Nelson, C. B., Hughes, M., Eshleman, S., Wittchen, H. U., et al. (1994). Lifetime and 12-month prevalence of DSM-III-R psychiatric disorders in the United States: Results from the National Comorbidity Study. *Archives of General Psychiatry, 51,* 8–19.

Kessler, R. C., Walters, E. E., & Forthofer, M. S. (1998). The social consequences of psychiatric disorders: III. Probability of marital stability. *The American Journal of Psychiatry, 155,* 1092–1096.

Kinney, J. (2003). *Loosening the grip: A handbook of alcohol information.* New York: McGraw-Hill.

Krestan, J., & Bepko, C. (1990). Codependency: The social reconstruction of female experience. *Smith College Studies in Social Work, 60,* 216–232.

Krugman, S. (1987). Trauma in the family: Perspectives on the intergenerational transmission of violence. In B. A. van der Kolk (Ed.), *Psychological trauma* (pp. 127–151). Washington, DC: American Psychiatric Press.

Lawson, A., & Lawson, G. (1998). *Alcoholism and the family: A guide to treatment and prevention.* Austin, TX: ProEd Publishers.

Lawson, A. W., & Lawson, G. W. (2005). Families and drugs. In R. H. Coombs (Ed.), *Addiction counseling review: Preparing for comprehensive, certification, and licensing examinations* (pp. 175–199). Mahwah, NJ: Lawrence Erlbaum Associates.

Leonard, K. E., & Roberts, L. J. (1998). Marital aggression, quality, and stability in the first year of marriage: Findings from the Buffalo Newlywed Study. In T. N. Bradbury (Ed.), *The developmental course of marital dysfunction* (pp. 44–73). New York: Cambridge University Press.

Leonard, K. E., & Rothbard, J. C. (1999). Alcohol and the marriage effect. *Journal of Studies on Alcohol, 13,* 139–146.

Lex, B. W. (1990). Male heroin addicts and their female mates: Impact on disorder and recovery. *Journal of Substance Abuse, 2,* 147–175.

Liddle, H. A. (1995). Conceptual and clinical dimensions of multidimensional, multisystems engagement. *Psychotherapy: Theory, Research, Practice, Training Special Issue: New Frontiers and New Dimensions, 32,* 39–58.

Liddle, H., & Diamond, G. (1991). Adolescent substance abusers in family therapy: The critical initial phase of treatment. *Family Dynamics of Addiction Quarterly, 1*(1), 55–68.

Lorber, W., Morgan, D. Y., Eisen, M. L., Barak, T., Perez, C., & Crosbie-Burnett, M. (2007). Patterns of cohesion in the families of offspring of addicted parents: Examining a nonclinical sample of college students. *Psychological Reports, 101*(3), 881–895.

McClelland, A., Arndt, I., Metzger, D., Woody, G., & O'Brien, C. (1993). The effects of psychosocial services in substance abuse treatment. *Journal of the American Medical Association, 269,* 1953–1959.

McCord, J. (1988). Identifying developmental paradigms leading to alcoholism. *Journal of Studies on Alcohol, 49,* 357–362.

McCrady, B. S. (1993). Relapse prevention: A couple-therapy perspective. In T. J. O'Farrell (Ed.), *Treating alcohol problems: Marital and family interventions* (pp. 327–350). New York: Guilford.

McCrady, B. S., & Epstein, E. E. (1995). Directions for research on alcoholic relationships: Marital and individual-based models of heterogeneity. *Psychology of Addictive Behaviors, 9,* 157–166.

McGrath, C., Watson, A., & Chassin, L. (1999). Academic achievement in adolescent children of alcoholics. *Journal of Studies on Alcohol, 60,* 18–26.

McIntyre, J. R. (2004). Family treatment of substance abuse. In S. L. A. Straussner (Ed.), *Clinical work with substance-abusing clients,* (2nd ed., pp. 237–263). New York: Guilford Press.

McKinney, C. M., Caetano, R., Harris, T. R., & Ebama, M. S. (2009). Alcohol availability and intimate partner violence among US couples. *Alcoholism: Clinical & Experimental Research, 33,* 169–176.

Meyers, R. J., Apodaca, T. R., Flicker, S. M., & Slesnick, N. (2002). Evidence-based approaches for the treatment of substance abusers by involving family members. *The Family Journal: Counseling and Therapy for Couples and Families, 10*(3), 281–288.

Miller, B. A., Downs, W. R., Gondoli, D. M., & Keil, A. (1987). The role of childhood sexual abuse in the development of alcoholism in women. *Violence and Victims, 2,* 157–172.

Miller, W. R., & Tonigan, J. S. (1996). Assessing drinkers' motivation for change: The stages of change readiness and treatment eagerness scales (SOCRATES). *Psychology of Addictive Behaviors, 10,* 81–89.

Moos, R. H., Finney, J. W., & Cronkite, R. C. (1990). Alcoholism treatment: Context, process and outcome. New York: Oxford University Press.

Moos, R. H., Finney, J. W., & Gamble, W. (1985). The process of recovery from alcoholism II: Comparing spouses of alcoholics and matched community controls. In E. M. Freeman (Ed.), *Social work practice with clients who have alcohol problems* (pp. 292–314). Springfield, IL: Charles C. Thomas.

Mun, E.-Y., Fitzgerald, H. E., Puttler, I. I., Zucker, R. A., & Von Eye, A. (2000). Temperamental characteristics as predictors of externalizing and internalizing behavior problems in the contexts of high and low parental psychopathology. *Infant Mental Health Journal, 22,* 393–415.

Nair, P., Schuler, M. E., Black, M. M., Kettinger, L., & Harrington, D. (2003). Cumulative environmental risk in substance abusing women: Early intervention, parenting stress, child abuse potential and child development. *Child Abuse & Neglect, 27,* 997–1017.

National Institute on Drug Abuse (NIDA). (1994). *National pregnancy and health survey* [Press release]. Rockville, MD: National Clearinghouse for Alcohol and Drug Information.

Nicholas, K., & Rasmussen, E. (2006). Childhood abusive and supportive experiences, inter-parental violence, and parental alcohol use: Prediction of young adult depressive symptoms and aggression. *Journal of Family Violence, 21,* 43–61.

Noel, M. E., & McCrady, B. S. (1993). Alcohol-focused spouse involvement with behavioral marital therapy. In T. J. O'Farrell (Ed.), *Treating alcohol problems: Marital and family interventions* (pp. 210–235). New York: Guilford Press.

O'Farrell, T. (1990). Sexual functioning of male alcoholics. In R. L. Collins, K. E. Leonard, B. H. Miller, & J. S. Searles (Eds.), *Alcohol and the family: Research and clinical perspectives* (pp. 244–271). New York: Guilford Press.

O'Farrell, T. J. (1993). A behavioral marital therapy couples group program for alcoholics and their spouses. In T. J. O'Farrell (Ed.), *Treating alcohol problems: Marital and family interventions* (pp. 170–209). New York: Guilford.

O'Farrell, T. J. (1995). Marital and family therapy. In R. K. Hester & W. R. Miller (Eds.), *Handbook of alcoholism treatment approaches: Effective alternatives* (pp. 195–220). Boston: Allyn & Bacon.

O'Farrell, T. J., & Fals-Stewart, W. (2000). Behavioral couples therapy for alcoholism and drug abuse. *Behavior Therapist, 23*(3), 49–54.

O'Farrell, T. J., & Fals-Stewart, W. (2003). Alcohol abuse. *Journal of Marital and Family Therapy, 29*(1), 121–146.

O'Farrell, T. J., Murphy, C. M., Stephan, S. H., Fals-Stewart, W., & Murphy, M. (2004). Partner violence before and after couples-based alcoholism treatment for male alcoholic patients: The role of treatment involvement and abstinence. *Journal of Consulting and Clinical Psychology, 72,* 202–217.

Office of Applied Studies, Substance Abuse and Mental Health Statistics. (2008). *Results from the 2008 National Survey on Drug Use and Health: National Findings.* Retrieved December 27, 2009, from *http://www.oas.samhsa.gov/nsduh/2k8nsduh/2k8Results.cfm#7.3.1*

Olmstead, M. E., Crowell, J. A., & Waters, E. (2003). Assortative mating among adult children of alcoholics and alcoholics. *Family Relations, 52*(1), 64–71.

Pan, H. D., Neidig, P. H., & O'Leary, K. D. (1994). Predicting mild and severe husband-to-wife physical aggression. *Journal of Consulting and Clinical Psychology, 62,* 975–981.

Pascoe, W. (1999). Enhancing the creative process in couple therapy. *Journal of Couples Therapy, 8*(1), 5–10.

Poon, E., Ellis, D. A., Fitzgerald, H. A., & Zucker, R. A. (2000). Intellectual, cognitive and academic performance among sons of alcoholics during the early elementary school years: Differences related to subtypes of familial alcoholism. *Alcoholism: Clinical and Experimental Research, 24,* 1020–1027.

Rennison, C. M., & Welchans, S. (2000). *Intimate partner violence.* Washington, DC: U.S. Department of Justice, Bureau of Justice Statistics, Special Report.

Richman, J. A., Rospenda, K. M., & Kelley, M. A. (1994). Gender roles and alcohol abuse across the transition to parenthood. *Journal of Studies on Alcohol, 56,* 553–557.

Roberts, L. J., & Linney, K. D. (1998, November). *Alcohol use, marital functioning and the family life cycle.* Paper presented at the Annual Meeting of the National Council on Family Relations, Milwaukee, WI.

Roberts, L. J., & Linney, K. D. (2000). Alcohol problems and couples: Drinking in an intimate relational context. In K. B. Schmaling & T. G. Sher (Eds.), *The psychology of couples and illness: Theory, research, & practice* (pp. 269–310). Washington, DC: American Psychological Association.

Roberts, L. J., Roberts, C. F., & Leonard, K. E. (1999). Alcohol, drugs, and interpersonal violence. In V. B. Van Hasselt & M. Hersen (Eds.), *Handbook of psychological approaches with violent criminal offenders: Contemporary strategies and issues* (pp. 493–519). New York: Plenum.

Rotunda, R. J., Scherer, D. G., & Imm, P. S. (1995). Family systems and alcohol misuse: Research on the effects of alcoholism on family functioning and effective family interventions. *Professional Psychology: Research and Practice, 26,* 95–104.

Rounsaville, B. J., Kranzler, H. R., Ball, S., Tennen, H., Poling, J., & Trifffleman, E. (1998). Personality disorders in substance abusers: Relation to substance abuse. *Journal of Nervous and Mental Diseases, 186,* 78–95.

Rowe, C. L., & Liddle, H. A. (2003). Substance abuse. *Journal of Marital and Family Therapy, 29*(1), 97–120.

Rubin, D. H. (2001). *Treating adult children of alcoholics: A behavioral approach.* New York: Academic Press.

Schneider, J. P. (2002). The new "elephant in the living room": Effects of compulsive cybersex behaviors on the spouse. In A. Cooper (Ed.), *Sex and the internet: A guide book for clinicians* (pp. 169–186). New York: Brunner-Routledge.

Schuler, M. E., & Nair, P. (2001). Witnessing violence among inner-city children of substance abusing and non-substance abusing women. *Archives of Pediatrics & Adolescent Medicine, 155,* 342–346.

Schumm, J. A., O'Farrell, T. J., Murphy, C. M., & Fals-Stewart, W. (2009). Partner violence before and after couples-based alcoholism treatment for female alcoholic patients. *Journal of Consulting and Clinical Psychology, 77,* 1136–1146.

Sheridan, M. J., & Green, R. G. (1993). Family dynamics and individual characteristics of adult children of alcoholics: An empirical analysis. *Journal of Social Service Research, 17,* 73–97.

Sokol, R., & Clarren, S. (1989). Guidelines for use of terminology describing the impact of prenatal alcohol on the offspring. *Alcoholism: Clinical & Experimental Research, 13,* 597–598.

Stanton, M. (2005). Couples and addiction. In M. Harway (Ed.), *Handbook of couples therapy* (pp. 313–336). Hoboken, NJ: John Wiley & Sons.

Stanton, M. D., & Heath, A. W. (1995). Family treatment of alcohol and drug abuse. In R. H. Mikesell, D.-D. Lusterman, & S. H. McDaniel (Eds.), *Integrating family therapy: Handbook of family psychology and systems theory* (pp. 529–541). Washington, DC: American Psychological Association.

Stanton, M. D., & Shadish, W. R. (1997). Outcome, attrition and family-couples treatment for drug abuse: A meta-analysis and review of the controlled, comparative studies. *Psychological Bulletin, 122,* 170–191.

Steinberg, M. L., Epstein, E. E., McCrady, B. S., & Hirsch, L. S. (1997). Sources of motivation in a couples outpatient alcoholism treatment program. *American Journal of Drug and Alcohol Abuse, 23,* 191–205.

Steinglass, P., Bennett, L. A., Wolin, S. J., & Reiss, D. (1987). *The alcoholic family.* New York: Basic Books.

Strassner, S. L. A., & Zelvin, E. (1997). *Gender and addictions: Men and women in treatment.* Northvale, NJ: Aronson.

Streissguth, A. P., Bookstein, F. L., Sampson, P. D., & Barr, H. M. (1995). Attention: Prenatal alcohol and continuities of vigilance and attentional problems from 4 through 14 years. Development *and Psychopathology, 7,* 419–446.

van der Kolk, B. A., & Kadish, W. (1987). Amnesia, dissociation, and the return of the repressed. In B. A. van der Kolk (Ed.), *Psychological trauma.* Washington, DC: American Psychiatric Press.

van Wormer, K., & Davis, D. R. (2003). *Addiction treatment: A strengths perspective.* Pacific Grove, CA: Brooks/Cole Thomson Learning.

Waldron, H. B. (1997). Adolescent substance abuse and family therapy outcomes: A review of randomized trials. In T. H. Ollendick & R. J. Prinz (Eds.), *Advances in clinical child psychology* (Vol. 19, pp. 199–234). New York: Plenum.

Walitzer, K. S. (1999). Family therapy. In P. J. Ott, R. E. Tarter, & R. T. Ammerman, (Eds.), *Sourcebook on substance abuse: Etiology, epidemiology, assessment, and treatment* (pp. 337–349). Needham Heights, MA: Allyn & Bacon.

Washousky, R., Levy-Stern, D., & Muchowski, P. (1993). The stages of family alcoholism. *EAP Digest,* 38–42.

Watkins, L. E., O'Farrell, T. J., Suvak, M. K., Murphy, C. M., & Taft, C. T. (2009). Parenting satisfaction among fathers with alcoholism. *Addictive Behaviors, 34,* 610–612.

Wegscheider, S. (1981). *Another chance: Hope and help for the alcoholic family.* Palo Alto, CA: Science & Behavior Books.

Wekerle, C., & Wall, A. (2002). Introduction: The overlap between relationship violence and substance abuse. In C. Wekerle and A. Wall (Eds.), *The violence and addiction equation: Theoretical and clinical issues in substance abuse and relationship violence* (pp. 1–21). NY: Brunner-Routledge.

Williams, C. (1987). Child care practices in alcoholic families: Findings from a neighborhood detoxification program. *Alcohol Health and Research World, 94,* 74–77.

Windle, M. (1990). Temperament and personality attributes of children of alcholics. In M. Windle & J. Searles (Eds.), *Children of alcoholics: Critical perspectives* (pp. 129–167). New York: Guildford Press.

Windle, M., & Tubman, J. G. (1999). Children of alcoholics. In W. K. Silverman & T. H. Ollendick (Eds.), *Developmental issues in the clinical treatment of children* (pp. 393–414). Boston: Allyn & Bacon.

Winn, M. E. (1995). Drawing upon the strengths of couples in the treatment of chronic drug addiction. *Journal of Family Psychotherapy, 63*(3), 33–54.

Wolin, S., Bennett, L., & Noonan, D. (1979). Family rituals and the recurrence of alcoholism over generations. *American Journal of Psychiatry, 136,* 589–593.

Zelvin, E. (1999). Applying relational theory to treatment of addicted women. *Affilia: Journal of Women in Social Work, 14*(1), 9–23.

Zelvin, E. (2004). Treating the partners of substance abusers. In S. L. A. Straussner (Ed.), *Clinical work with substance-abusing clients,* (2nd ed., pp. 264–283). New York: Guilford Press.

Zucker, R. A., Ellis, D. A., Bingham, C. R., & Fitzgerald, H. E. (1996). The development of alcoholic subtypes: Risk variation among alcoholic families during early childhood years. *Alcohol Health & Research World, 20,* 46–54.

Zweben, A., & Barrett, D. (1993). Brief couples treatment for alcohol problems. In T. J. O'Farrell (Ed.), *Treating alcohol problems: Marital and family interventions* (pp. 353–380). New York: Guilford.

Chapter 15

Persons with Disabilities and Addictions

Debra A. Harley
University of Kentucky
Malachy Bishop
University of Kentucky

Jennifer Burris
University of Kentucky

INTRODUCTION

Alcohol abuse and other drug addictions are significant national problems affecting people from all walks of life, leading to effects detrimental to the individual's physical, social, and psychological health, and the welfare of others. While difficult to determine the exact number of people who are substance abusers, an estimated 20 million individuals are classified as having a diagnosis of alcohol abuse or addiction (Office of Applied Studies [OAS], 2005). Many of these are individuals with coexisting disabilities. In the United States there are approximately 58 million people with disabilities (PWDs) *(www.vaboard.org/downloads/usdisabilitiesestimates.doc)*.

The prevalence of substance abuse disorders is thought to be almost twice as high in adults with disabilities as in the general population, and more than 20% of persons eligible for state Vocational Rehabilitation services experience substance abuse or dependence (Krahn, Deck, Gabriel, & Farrell, 2007). Among PWDs, younger adults are reported to use more illicit drugs and older adults more likely to abuse prescription medication (Bachman, Drainoni, & Tobias, 2004; Brucker, 2008). In addition, substance abuse disorders are the most frequently occurring comorbid disability among persons with mental health diagnoses. Research has documented a high rate of co-occurring substance abuse disorders among Supplemental Security Income (SSI) beneficiaries with mental health disorders (Bachman et al.). For individuals with mental disorders the relationship between the disorder and substance abuse is complex and potentially interactive, in that dependency can be masked by the symptoms of psychiatric disorders such as depression, anxiety, or bipolar disorder (Kinney, 2008).

A significant number of people currently seeking treatment for substance abuse disorders also have a physical, cognitive, sensory, or affective disability. Many PWDs are unable to access treatment they desperately need because of the double stigma of having a substance abuse disorder and a coexisting disability. In addition, persons with both disabilities and substance abuse disorders are less likely to enter or complete treatment because physical, attitudinal, or communication barriers limit their treatment options or else render their treatment experiences unsatisfactory (West, Graham, & Cifu, 2009a). Another possible factor attributed to low treatment participation of PWDs could be the failure of physicians to identity and refer these individuals to treatment (West, Luck, Capps, Cifu, Graham, & Hurley, 2009).

As one of the largest and most diverse minority groups in the United States PWDs are disproportionately represented among those with substance abuse disorders. As specified in the *Diagnostic and Statistical Manual of Mental Disorders* (DSM-V), substance abuse is a disability, and not a symptom of another disabling condition (American Psychiatric Association [APA], 2010). Although it is possible that a reciprocal causal relation exists between substance abuse and disability, most recent research supports the hypothesis that the presence of a disability significantly increases the risk for alcohol and illicit drug use and prescription abuse (Brucker, 2007). One of the major issues in diagnosis of substance abuse and addictions in persons with disabilities is that abuse and addiction are frequently either seen as occurring secondary to another disability, and thus receive limited clinical attention, or else they are not recognized at all (West, Luck, Capps, Cifu, Graham, & Hurley, 2009).

The purpose of this chapter is to discuss issues that affect persons with disabilities with regard to substance abuse and addictions. The chapter presents material on how issues of addiction can be specifically addressed in rehabilitation counseling settings. In addition to a case study, an overview of the characteristics and status of persons with disabilities and addictions is presented, including racial disparities in substance abuse and disability; risk factors for persons with disabilities; treatment utilization and outcomes; and intervention strategies in rehabilitation settings. Workers in a majority of inpatient rehabilitation training programs have expressed concern about alcohol and drug problems among their patients (Basford, Rohe, Barnes, & DePompolo, 2002; Goodwin, 2009). Rehabilitation counselors, other counselors, and human service providers need to understand addictions as it relates to persons with disabilities. Given recent developments in service provision and legislative mandates, rehabilitation counselors and other human service providers must also be aware of new trends regarding culturally diverse populations, veterans, domestic violence, and persons with AIDS among PWDs and substance abuse and addiction.

Before going further, several issues are presented as a framework for this chapter and to provide clarity to the reader. First, it should be noted that any type of substance abuse addiction or disorder is characterized by a pattern of continued pathological use of a substance or participation in a behavior, which results in repeated adverse personal and social consequences related to use or behavior (DSM-V, 2010). Second, although this chapter addresses substance abuse and addictions, other addictions—such as eating disorders, compulsive gambling, Internet addiction, workaholism, and sexual addictions—are becoming increasingly prevalent in society, with a common core of behaviors (Goodman, 2009). Third, increasingly individuals are polysubstance users or have multiple or cross addictions. This can enhance the effects of the drugs and help manage the side effects of coming down from one drug (Handbook of Disabilities, 2009). Finally, throughout this chapter we use the terms *substance abuse*, *alcohol dependence*, and *addiction* interchangeably. However, we acknowledge that the *Diagnostic and Statistical Manual of Mental Disorders* provides specific diagnostic criteria for alcohol and/or substance use disorders. The reader should refer to the *DMS-V* for additional information.

OVERVIEW OF THE CHARACTERISTICS AND STATUS OF PEOPLE WITH DISABILITIES AND ADDICTIONS

People with disabilities in the United States are often classified by categories (e.g., cognitive, mental physical, sensory) and by their need for assistance based on functional limitations (e.g., activities of daily living). In addition, an individual is categorized based on severity of his or her disability (Brault, 2008). Across these categories, PWDs' employment rate is also impacted, as well as a divergence in the employment rate trends across gender and ethnicity/race (Stapleton, Burkhauser, & Houtenville, 2004). According to Brault, of the 291.1 million people in the population, 35.0 million (12.0%) of people had a severe disability. Of those aged 21 to 64, 28.1 million had a disability and 45.6 percent of this group were employed. Additional examination of the data revealed that the employment rate was 30.7 percent for PWDs with severe disabilities, compared to 75.2 percent for people with a non-severe disability and 83.5 percent for people with no disability. Further examination of the data by gender and race/ethnicity reveal even more startling statistics for those with severe disabilities. That is, for all races and genders 12.0 percent of those with disabilities had severe disabilities, White non Hispanic accounted for 12.4 percent, African American (including Black) 14.4 percent, Asian 7.7 percent, and Hispanic (any race) 8.7 percent. As of 2005, the employment rate of PWDs has shown a consistently lower rate for those with severe disabilities and those of ethnic minority groups (Barnow, 2008; Brault). Additional information on employment and earnings of PWDs can be obtained from the U.S. Census Bureau on *Americans with Disabilities: 2005 Household Economic Studies* (Brault).

Employment rates and income earnings are only two of the indicators that describe the status of PWDs. Another distinguishing factor is the occurrence of substance abuse and addiction among this population. People with disabilities and substance abuse disorders have the lowest successful closure rates in vocational rehabilitation agencies (Hollar, McAweeney, & Moore, 2008). Interestingly, with the Contract with America Advancement Act of 1996 (P.L. 104-121), which mandated that individuals no longer qualify for SSI solely because they were disabled as a result of substance abuse, higher rates of drug use have been found among people receiving rehabilitation services for all major drug categories (Bachman et al., 2004). Other studies have shown substance abuse disorders affect PWDs more than other mental disorders. For example, Bombardier et al. (2004) found that persons with multiple sclerosis (MS) screened positive for possible alcohol abuse or dependence, and 7.4 percent reported misusing illicit drugs or prescription medications. The authors of this study reported that substance abuse may be present in up to 19 percent of the sample and contribute to high rates of depression. In addition, there may be greater risk of harm due to substance abuse in people with MS because of the potential magnification of motor and cognitive impairment. In a study of individuals with brain injury and spinal cord injury, Kolakowsky-Hayner et al. (2002) found that persons with spinal cord injury (SCI) were more likely to drink on a daily basis post-injury, and persons with traumatic brain injury (TBI) were more inclined to use illicit drugs post-injury. Both SCI and TBI had a higher rate of post-injury versus pre-injury drug use. Yet, other research has identified rates of pre- and post-injury substance abuse among TBI and SCI groups equating to substantial numbers of individuals in need of substance abuse treatment (Langlois, Rutland-Brown, & Thomas, 2004; National Spinal Cord Injury [SCI] Statistical Center, 2008). Basford et al (2002) found that individuals with nervous system injuries are more likely to report substance abuse. Brucker (2008) reported that persons with developmental disabilities are significantly less likely to use prescription drugs and opiates than others in treatment. Other studies suggest that among persons with developmental disabilities, such as mental retardation and autism, rates of abuse have been estimated to be as high as 14% (Burgard, Donohue, Azrin, & Teichner, 2000; McGillicuddy, 2006).

PWDs and Substance Abuse

- PWDs tend to abuse substances at a higher rate than people without disabilities.
- PWDs have a higher rate of isolation and reduced socialization, increasing risk for AOD abuse.
- PWDs with specific types of disabilities abuse substances at a higher rate.
- Attitudes about substance abuse for PWDs are more negative than for people without disabilities.
- Similar among women without disabilities, gender bias exists about AOD for women with disabilities who abuse substances.

The 2004 National Survey on Drug Use and Health: National Findings (NSDUH) (OAS, 2005) reported that 19.1 million Americans, or 7.9% of the population aged 12 or older, were current illicit drug users (i.e., used an illicit drug during the month prior to the survey interview). In addition, 121 million (50.3%) Americans aged 12 or older were current drinkers of alcohol; 55 million (22.8%) participated in binge drinking; and 16.7 million (6.9%) were heavy drinkers. These numbers are all similar to the corresponding estimates for 2002 and 2003. Tobacco use among Americans was 70.3 million (29.2%) of the population. The NSDUH shows that the illicit drug category with the largest number of new users was nonmedical use of pain relievers (2.4 million, with the average age at first use 23.3 years). Of the 22.5 million Americans classified with substance dependence or abuse, 3.4 million were classified with dependence on or abuse of both alcohol and illicit drugs, 3.9 million were dependent on or abused illicit drugs but not alcohol, and 15.2 million were dependent on or abused alcohol but not illicit drugs. The number of persons needing treatment for an illicit drug use problem in 2004 (8.1 million) was higher than the number needing treatment in 2003 (7.3 million).

A look at PWDs by race/ethnicity who abuse substances reveals that Hispanics have the lowest rates of polydrug use disorder and Whites have the highest rates of lifetime alcohol and anxiety disorders (Perron et al., 2009). Perron et al. also found that for those who had at least one lifetime drug use disorder, Whites exhibited the highest rate of abuse, followed by African Americans/Blacks, and Latinos/Hispanics. In an update to the report on mental health problems among minorities, following the Surgeon General's Report on Mental Health of 2002, Sherer (2009) indicated that the overall prevalence of mental health problems among Asian Americans and Pacific Islanders (AA/PIs) does not significantly differ from that of other Americans, but AA/PIs have the lowest utilization rates of mental health services among ethnic groups. Mexican Americans (MAs) born outside the United States have lower prevalence rates of lifetime disorders than MAs born in the United States, and 25 percent of Mexican-born immigrants show signs of mental illness or substance abuse, compared with 48 percent of U.S.-born MAs. African Americans are twice as likely to have somatic symptoms than White Americans (WAs). American Indians (AIs) are five times more likely to die of alcohol-related causes than WAs.

Taken together, the evidence suggest that ethnic minorities are overrepresented among the nation's vulnerable and have, relative to Whites, disproportionately higher disabilities resulting from unmet mental health needs. However, one must be aware that wide differences exist within minority groups and lumping them together in statistical analyses do not distinguish between the 561 tribes and some 200 languages of AIs; diverse cultures of Hispanic groups; the 43 separate ethnic groups of AA/PI groups from countries ranging from India to Indonesia; and geographical diversity of African Americans (Sherer, 2009). Harley (2005) reported that while African Americans' alcohol use is less than that of Whites, they tend to use more in response to stressors, their use rests in historical patterns and influences, and alcohol and other drug use frequently results in more adverse outcomes with regard to severity and devastation in their lives, families, and communities. It is important to note that high rates of abstinence also occur among American Indians (OAS, 2005). This is often overlooked because a gross examination of drinking prevalence appears to support the idea that these populations have a higher alcohol consumption rate than other ethnic groups or subgroups in the United States (Fisher & Harrison, 2008). The National Household Survey on Drug Abuse (NHSDA) (Substance Abuse and Mental Health Services Administration [SAMHSA], 2009) further delineates sociodemographic differences in substance use among and within racial/ethnic subgroups (see following sidebar).

Sociodemographic Differences in Substance Use Among Ethic Subgroups

- Households with low family income have a high prevalence of use of any illicit drug use.
- Regardless of racial/ethnic subgroup, relatively high prevalences of illicit drug use are found among individuals who reside in the West; reside in metropolitan areas with populations greater than 1 million.
- High prelevances of illicit drug use among those who use English.
- High prevalences of illicit drug use among those who lack insurance coverage.
- High prevalaences among those unemployed.
- High prevalences among those with less than a high school education.
- High prevalences among those who have never been married.

CASE STUDY

The Case of Beverly

We present this case study here because it highlights a number of important considerations that will be revisited and discussed in the remainder of the chapter. You are invited to review the information in this case study as a counselor, and to consider the concept of addiction in light of the potential risk factors, intervention strategies, and treatment recommendations that will enhance Beverly's ability to gain and maintain sobriety. Particular attention should be given to sociocultural issues, age, gender, sexual orientation, military status, occupation, and the existence of multiple addictions.

Beverly is a 26-year-old African American female who just returned from Iraq after serving two terms of duty. She was engaged in active combat. After receiving injuries resulting in polytrauma she received an honorable discharge. Subsequently, she was diagnosed with posttraumatic stress disorder (PTSD), substance abuse, and chronic pain. She was discharged from the hospital after six months. She is a single mother of one. Beverly attended six months of technical college with a major in mechanical studies. After dropping out of college she enlisted in the army. Otherwise, she has no employment history. Most of her friends are veterans and their primary recreational activities are focused on drinking, gambling, and hanging out together. Beverly spends little time with her daughter or her family of origin. Her mother has given her the ultimatum of going into treatment or she will file for custody of her child. She acquiesces and enters treatment because she does not want to lose her daughter. Her mother also has agreed to attend family counseling.

During Beverly's last few days in treatment, she reveals during the family session that she is a lesbian. Her mother is upset by the news and tells Beverly that if she does not change her ways she will burn in hell because she is sinning against God. Over the next several counseling sessions, Beverly and her mother have several heated debates. In addition to family counseling Beverly attends a support group for veterans. Her friends have decided to give her a party to celebrate her completion of treatment.

Beverly has not yet made up her mind about attending the party and does not tell her mother about it. Upon leaving the treatment center, Beverly and her counselor make arrangements for her to live with another veteran new to recovery. The transition causes her to experience anxiety. That evening Beverly is preoccupied and has difficulty sleeping. Two weeks posttreatment, the day of the party arrives. When Beverly gets there, she has a smoke and several drinks to calm her nerves. She tells her friends about the problems with her mother and the stress of coming out. Beverly leaves with several of her friends to go to a bar, where they have drinks and talk about being "screwed" by the government after risking their lives in Iraq.

The next day, she has some remorse about her behavior, but feels that life without her child and the betrayal of her mother is not worth living. She rationalizes that drinking makes her feel more confident about handling her problems.

Beverly continues to drink and party for several months at her prior rate. She has not been able to find work and her mother refuses to let her see her daughter. One night while driving, Beverly is arrested for DUI and disorderly conduct. The judge gives her the option of going into treatment or being sentenced to jail. Beverly chooses treatment.

RISK FACTORS FOR PERSONS WITH DISABILITIES

Risk factors are those issues which can contribute to the person engaging in alcohol and other drug use and abuse (AOD). People with disabilities abuse substances for many of the same reasons as people without disabilities, Other reasons include, but are not limited to, isolation, depression, employment and financial issues, and as a coping mechanism for adjustment to disability. Moreover, alcohol and substance abuse disorders co-occur with mental disorders at very high rates (Yalisove, 2004). Substance dependence or abuse is more prevalent among persons with major depressive episodes (MDE) than those without (22.0% vs. 8.6%, respectively) (OAS, 2005). In addition, persons with serious psychological distress (SPD) (21.4 million)—a term describing persons with a high level of distress due to any type of mental problem—is highly correlated with substance dependence or abuse (4.6 million, or 21.3%), while the rate among adults without SPD is 7.9%. In 2004, 27.5 million adults (12.8%) received treatment for mental health problems. This estimate is similar to estimates in 2002 and 2003 (OAS, 2005). Additional research confirm that PWDs have more frequent interactions with the medical community than nondisabled persons and may receive more prescriptions, especially for opiates, stimulants and depressants, thus increasing the opportunity for abuse (Brucker, 2008).

Another risk factor for PWDs is societal and attitudinal. Attitudes about disability influence the ways nondisabled people react to persons with disabilities, which can affect the latter's treatment outcomes. In addition, stereotypes and expectations of others influence the ways people think about their own disabilities. Some examples of attitudinal and societal risks/barriers are beliefs that:

1. PWDs do not abuse substances.
2. PWDs should receive exactly the same treatment protocol as everyone else, so that they are not singled out as being different. Being mainstreamed into society means that you should do exactly the same things as everyone else.
3. Serving people with disabilities requires going to extremes.
4. People with cognitive disabilities are not capable of learning how to stay sober.
5. PWDs deserve pity, so they should be allowed more latitude to indulge in substance use (Bachman et al., 2004; Brucker, 2007).

Many of these attitudes include the perception that PWDs are not normal, or are helpless, fragile, and sick. Many of these beliefs are common among counselors and other professionals. Counselors (and other helping professionals) who hold these beliefs may screen out those who would benefit from their programs, deny a client appropriate accommodation for his or her disability, or unwittingly enable clients to use their disabilities to avoid treatment (West, Graham, & Cifu, 2009a). Persons with disabilities often end up with labels of social deviance, which render them as double outcasts when identified as having AOD abuse (Kinney, 2008). Clearly, counselor perception may be a significant barrier to overcome for persons with disabilities in accessing treatment for addictions.

There are a number of reasons directly related to the disability which might contribute to the increased risk of AOD abuse among persons with disabilities. These risk factors can be divided into five categories: health and medical, psychological, social, economic and employment, and access (Brucker, 2007; West, Graham, & Cifu, 2009b). Each is discussed below.

Health and Medical Risk Factors

People with disabilities often use medications over extended periods of time. Some disability-related conditions require multiple concurrently prescribed medications. Individuals using prescribed medications require specific information on how these drugs influence behavior or interact with other drugs such as alcohol and over-the-counter medication. Disabilities such as arthritis, bipolar disorder, diabetes, epilepsy, and cystic fibrosis may place a person at risk for problems related to medication use. For example, in the case of William, who has polytrauma and a diagnosis of PTSD and bipolar disorder, for which he takes medication, he knowingly or unknowingly uses alcohol. William's use of alcohol may interact dangerously with his medication.

Other medical conditions (e.g., hypoglycemia, HIV/AIDS, ulcers, hematological diseases, cardiovascular diseases) (Kinney, 2008) associated with some disabilities can decrease a person's tolerance for AOD. This decreased tolerance can lead to dangerous levels of intoxication, especially when medications are combined with alcohol. In addition, individuals who experience chronic pain or discomfort can become dependent on prescribed medications or use other drugs such as alcohol to attempt to achieve temporary relief (U.S. Department of Health and Human Services, 2003). Awareness of such considerations is critical for counselors. It is also important that counselors help their clients to be aware that the presence of a disability or chronic illness may create an increased risk of accidents from AOD misuse due to balance, mobility, or vision impairments.

Psychological Risk Factors

Psychological risk factors include enabling behavior, increased stress on family life, and the stress associated with adjustment to disability. Frequently, family, friends, and professionals may inadvertently encourage individuals with disabilities to use AOD inappropriately. Enabling behavior (making it easy for someone to engage in a behavior) may be motivated by misplaced feelings of sympathy, guilt, frustration, or camaraderie. Clearly, in Beverly's case, her friends encourage her to use alcohol as a way of coping with problems and as a way to express her feelings.

With the onset of a disability, a family may experience additional expenses, difficult adjustments to daily routines, and reduced income due to loss of a job. Such factors significantly increase the stress that can lead to unhealthy AOD-related behaviors. Initial reactions to the onset of a disability or illness can include shock, denial, anger, depression, resentment, guilt, and embarrassment (Olney, Kennedy, Brockelman, & Newsom, 2004). An unhealthy coping strategy for any of these reactions could be AOD use or abuse.

Social Risk Factors

Social factors include peer group differences, reduced levels of social support, and isolation. Individuals with disabilities, especially those who acquired the disability before adulthood, may have less opportunity for association with peer groups (West, Graham, & Cifu, 2009b). These social limitations can result in gravitation to peer groups that tolerate abuse of alcohol and other drugs. In addition, this could mean that persons with disabilities may be vulnerable to AOD abuse through peer pressure due to a lack of social experience or a need for acceptance. Beverly returns to her prior socialization patterns after treatmen; her friends provide her with the social opportunity to engage in alcohol use. In addition, her friends are themselves veterans, who may not have effective coping skills and therefore reinforce her use of alcohol.

Individuals with disabilities tend to have fewer social outlets and have related problems with excess free time. Both of these situations contribute to risk of AOD abuse. A person with fewer social options can have difficulty finding new friends in order to avoid negative influences. Isolation further exacerbates this problem. Individuals with disabilities are frequently isolated due to a lack of transportation, recreational, or social opportunities. This can lead to depression and low self-esteem, both of which can contribute to substance abuse and addiction (Moore, 1998; Resource Center on Substance Abuse and Disability, 1992). In addition, persons with disabilities experience negative outcomes that include the increased likelihood of being the victims of crime (Burgard et al., 2000).

Economic and Employment Risk Factors

Individuals with disabilities have a disproportionate amount of bills associated with medical treatment, assistive technology, transportation, and related costs, which create financial anxieties and stress. Likewise, as a group, they experience higher rates of underemployment or unemployment (Potts, 2005). Unemployment is one of the most profound issues facing the disability community (Barnow, 2008; Brault, 2008; Stapleton et al., 2004). Only 45% of Americans with disabilities aged 21 to 64 are working (Brault). In 2004 only 35% of persons with severe disabilities were employed (Harris Survey, 2004) and 30.7 percent in 2005 (Brault). In 2004, an estimated 19.9% of unemployed adults were classified with dependence or abuse, while 10.5% of full-time employed adults and 11.9% of those employed part-time were classified as such. Of the 20.3 million adults classified with dependence or abuse, 15.7 million (77.6%) were employed (OAS, 2005).

Access Risk Factors

Individuals with disabilities frequently encounter limited access to substance abuse materials or programs. This has been found to be especially true among those who experienced traumatic injuries, SCI, and mobility limitations (West, Graham, & Cifu, 2009b). Many of the issues of access to treatment programs are due to physical accessibility of the facility. For individuals with disabilities whose primary language is other than English, communication barriers may also be a factor. For a number of reasons, therefore, the individual with a disability should, when possible, be referred to an AOD agency or program in his or her community. Consideration must also be given to different learning styles and cognitive or sensory limitations. If local treatment in the community is not possible, steps should be taken to ensure that access to programs is appropriate and equitable.

Specialized treatment is often necessary for people with certain types of disabilities. For example, many members of the deaf community benefit from specialized services, which are better equipped to handle specific cultural, language, and community issues that may arise. Many individuals who are deaf will prefer to be served by programs that specifically address their needs and whose staff is fluent in sign language. Unlike many other people with disabilities, people who are deaf often do not identify with a medical model of disability and instead embrace a cultural model that emphasizes their abilities within the deaf community and their own language and values (Bryan, 2007). Realistically, most programs are unable to provide such specialized and/or segregated services for clients who are deaf. A reasonable alternative may therefore be the arrangement of an accommodation, such as a sign language interpreter or the use of pencil and paper for communication. Accommodation does not mean giving special preferences; it does mean reducing barriers to equal participation in the program. It is likely that, on occasion, there will be only one deaf client in a program.

AOD Abuse Among the Deaf

- People who are deaf are disproportionately affected by AOD abuse.
- People who are deaf experience greater levels of isolation than other groups with disabilities.
- AOD use is cited as one of the major coping strategies employed by people who are deaf.
- Accessibility to treatment programs is more difficult for people who are deaf.
- The use of sign language in treatment programs is highly preferred by people who are deaf.

For ethnic minority groups, four cultural perspectives—sociocultural, physiological, psychological, and developmental—need to be defined. *Sociocultural* risk factors refer to the ways a person perceives who he or she is within larger social and cultural contexts (Sue & Sue, 2008). For example, American Indians use substances to cope with mourning, and as a result of modeling (Marlatt & VandenBos, 1997; May, 1995). *Physiological* risk factors predispose a group to a particular condition or disorder because of medical or health situations (e.g., metabolic disorders). Research examining the physiological theory of substance dependence and addiction is inconclusive. *Psychological* risk factors refer to one's locus of control (internal vs. external). Latinos, for example, have the lowest ratings of internal locus of control when compared to other ethnic minorities (Caetano, 1995). According to Fisher and Harrison (2008), language deficiencies can severely limit one's sense of personal autonomy and perceived control, reinforcing how one sees opportunities for economic, social, or educational improvement. The shame associated with such deprivation can exacerbate lowered feelings of self-worth and put Latino individuals at psychological risk for substance abuse and addiction. *Developmental* risk factors are related to attaining satisfactory life and work aspirations. Failure to achieve one's goals can frequently be expressed in depression and dependency. For example, high unemployment among African American men has a deleterious effect upon drinking behavior and is correlated with increased risk of alcohol problems (Bonhomme, Stephens, & Braithwaite, 2006). Substance abuse and addiction among ethnic minorities is also a function of rate of acculturation and assimilation. Thus, in working with clients who are members of racial and ethnic minority groups, gaining a sense of their cultural orientation and becoming familiar with their values, practices, and worldview is important. Each of these cultural factors and risk factors has implications for the treatment process.

TREATMENT UTILIZATION AND OUTCOMES

Given that AOD addiction has numerous dimensions and disrupts many aspects of an individual's life, treatment is not simple and is even more complicated for PWDs (National Institute on Drug Abuse [NIDA], 2009). Treatment processes differ according to treatment program; counselors typically help guide persons with substance abuse problems or addictions through stages of care: detoxification, rehabilitation, and aftercare (Parran, 2009). At times, medical intervention may be required, depending on an individual's general health, either before or concurrently with treatment. For example, an individual may need vitamin treatment, dental care, and other basic health care due to malnutrition and poor hygiene. Substance abuse and addictions treatment is provided in a number of venues, including through inpatient, outpatient, or partial hospitalization (i.e., day care) (Nugent & Jones, 2009; Parran), and through an array of techniques and modalities: medical intervention (e.g., antabuse, chemotherapy); individual counseling; group work; working with families; self-help; pharmacotherapy; spiritual counseling; meditation; activity therapy; self-help programs; or behavioral approaches (Kinney, 2008). Treatment programs should be integrated and inclusive. Most people with disabilities do not want or need separate programs, which often limit opportunities and perpetuate segregation and the misperception of what it means to be different. However, service components can and should be individualized. Since the 1970s, scientific research has shown that treatment can help individuals addicted to AOD stop using, avoid relapse, and successfully recover their lives. Based on this research, key principles have emerged that should form the basis for any effective treatment program (NIDA, 2009) (see Table 15.1).

Inpatient treatment usually lasts about 4 weeks but can last as long as 6 months; partial hospitalization often runs 5 or more hours a day, 5 days a week, for 4 to 6 weeks; and outpatient treatment for an unspecified period of time (Nugent & Jones, 2009). Residential treatment programs can be extremely effective, especially for those with more severe problems. For example, therapeutic communities (TCs) are highly structured programs in which clients remain at a residence, typically for 6 to 12 months. The focus of the TC is on the resocialization of the client to a substance-free lifestyle (NIDA, 2009). The type of setting selected for treatment depends on the needs of the client. For example, a client with medical complications may benefit from inpatient or partial hospitalization, whereas a client who is employed and needs to continue working

TABLE 15.1 Key Principles of Effective Treatment Programs

- Addiction is a complex and treatable disease affecting physiological, brain function, and behavior.
- There is no single or one-size-fits-all treatment approach which is appropriate for everyone.
- Treatment needs to be readily available, easily accessible, and provide accommodations.
- Effective treatment attends to multiple needs of the individual across cultural, psychosocial, positionality, and disability, not merely to AOD abuse.
- Remaining in treatment for an adequate period of time is important.
- Individual and/or group counseling and other behavioral therapies are the most commonly used forms of AOD treatment.
- Medications are an important element of treatment for many clients, especially when combined with counseling and other behavioral therapies.
- An individual's treatment and services plan must be assessed continually and modified as necessary to ensure that it meets his or her changing needs.
- Many AOD addicted individuals also have other mental disorders.
- Medically assisted detoxification is only the first stage of addiction treatment and by itself does little to change long-term substance abuse.
- Treatment does not need to be voluntary to be effective.
- Drug use during treatment must be monitored continuously, as lapses during treatment do occur.
- Treatment programs should assess clients for the presence of infectious diseases as well as provide targeted risk-reduction counseling.

may find outpatient care more feasible. However, there are specific guidelines for determining type of treatment an individual may require. The American Society of Addiction Medicine (ASAM) (2001) has developed patient placement criteria to guide decisions about the appropriate treatment setting. Six dimensions have been identified as germane to determining the type of treatment required. These dimensions are presented below.

1. Dimension 1: Acute intoxication and/or likelihood of withdrawal syndromes.
2. Dimension 2: Biomedical conditions and complications.
3. Dimension 3: Emotional-behavioral conditions.
4. Dimension 4: Acceptance of need for treatment.
5. Dimension 5: Relapse or likelihood of continued use.
6. Dimension 6: Recovery environment.

Taking into account assessment results in these domains, five levels of client care have been identified. These specify the kind of care required, given the client's status. These levels of care are as follows:

1. Level 0.5: Early intervention. (This level of care was added when the criteria were reviewed and subsequently revised. So as not to introduce confusion by renumbering the existing levels, it was numbered 0.5 [one-half], to place it before Level I.)
2. Level I: Outpatient services
3. Level II: Intensive outpatient and partial hospitalization services
4. Level III: Inpatient/residential services
5. Level IV: Medically managed intensive inpatient services (ASAM, 2001)

For persons with physical and psychiatric disabilities, these criteria for treatment services are crucial, because such persons may have multiple medical problems and chronic conditions which further complicate treatment. To better facilitate positive outcome rates in treatment, clients with disabilities must be assessed in a more culturally specific, flexible, and holistic way (West et al., 2009b). However, matching studies suggest that little improvement in outcomes has resulted from matching (Ouimette, Finney, Gima, & Moos, 1999a, 1999b). In fact, "the least restrictive environment for treatment should be used unless the severity of the substance use disorder and related medical, psychiatric, and social problems is such that structured or medically monitored treatment is needed" (Daley & Marlatt, 2006, p. 39). The advantages and disadvantages of types of treatment programs are presented in Table 15.2. Specific intervention strategies in rehabilitation settings are discussed below.

TABLE 15.2 Advantages and Disadvantages of Treatment Programs

	Inpatient	Outpatient	Self-help
Advantages	Intensive education	Cost	Free
	Intensive counseling	Continue to work	Convenient
	New friends	Life with support	Open to everyone
	Protected setting		History of success
Disadvantages	Cost	Lack of Insurance	Biases
	Protected from real life	Limited spaces available	May not be for everyone
		Less structured	
		Increased relapse	

INTERVENTION STRATEGIES IN REHABILITATION SETTINGS

Rehabilitation settings for substance abuse treatment and recovery include such settings as halfway or transition houses, VA hospitals, general hospitals and clinical settings, programs for the homeless, and substance abuse programs. Counselors working in substance abuse or rehabilitation settings are likely to face complex clinical decisions when determining eligibility for services; for example, deciding whether treatment will commence despite continued use of substances, or whether abstinence from all drugs (i.e., medications) should be required for services (Toriello & Leierer, 2005). Counselors can deliver intervention from a traditional (i.e., medical/disease) model, a contemporary clinical orientation (i.e., client-centered approaches), or somewhere along the continuum (Goodwin, 2009).

Treatment and intervention for persons with disabilities in rehabilitation settings must include a continuum of care, starting with assessment, moving to individualized intervention, and ending with aftercare (or continuing care) services. Given the chronic nature of addictions, before proceeding further several statements about rehabilitation expectations should be made. First, recovery takes time because addictions encroach upon every aspect of one's life and thus, must be diffused systematically. Second, progress is not constant in the recovery process. There is occasional backsliding and plateaus are common. Third, as is possible in any chronic illness, relapse is part of recovery. McLellan, Lewis, O'Brien, and Kleber (2000) found that substance disorder relapse and noncompliance rates are similar to other chronic conditions. Regardless of the drug of choice and population, research studies consistently find that "lots of people who receive treatment for AOD problems use again after leaving treatment" (Fisher & Harrison, 2008, p. 156).

People with both a substance abuse disorder and a coexisting disability have life problems (previously discussed in this chapter) that make treatment more complex and heighten the possibility of relapse. These individuals may need assistance and individualized accommodations in order to:

1. Learn activities of daily living (ADL) such as basic grooming, dressing appropriately, using public transportation, and cooking.
2. Develop prevocational skills.
3. Learn social skills that may be lacking because of both substance use disorders and disability-related problems.
4. Learn to engage in healthy recreation.
5. Obtain financial benefits for which they are eligible.
6. Parenting and childcare skills.
7. Simplifying language for those with developmental disabilities or translating 12-steps into sign language for the deaf.
8. Build new peer networks (Zubenko, 2006).

In addition, research indicated that persons with AOD problems and disabilities encounter procedural and other obstacles when they attempt to rectify such problems. For example, if a client has been sober for 6 months or more (even though such a requirement is counterproductive and can act to maintain a vicious cycle between a lack of vocational skills and substance-use disorders) he or she may be declared ineligible for some vocational rehabilitation programs (Bachman et al., 2004; Brucker, 2008; Krahn et al., 2007).

In counseling persons with addiction problems and disabilities, counselors must have a clear understanding of the client's psychosocial history and presenting problems. This should include an individual's work history; educational background; family; marital history; employment status; military history; mental health history; functional limitations; criminal history; history of substance use and treatment; involvement in vocational, physical, or social rehabilitation; and past history of abuse (since many people with disabilities have been victims of physical, emotional, and/or sexual abuse) (Goodwin, 2009).

Let us take the case of Beverly (presented earlier in this chapter) for illustrative purposes. The counselor should ask her some basic questions, such as:

1. Do you feel you have a disability, or has anyone ever told you that you have one?
2. Have you ever had to stay in a hospital overnight, or gone to an emergency room for any reason?
3. Have you ever seen a doctor for a long period of time, more frequently than just one visit or for routine check-ups?
4. Do you take any kind of medication (prescription and over-the-counter)? (Expand with questions regarding compliance with medications.)
5. Were you ever diagnosed with a disability? (Consider asking this question in regard to specific types of disabilities.)
6. Have you ever incurred any type of injury? If so, what type? What were the outcomes?
7. How many jobs have you had in the past three years? What was the longest job that you held?
8. What hobbies do you have?
9. What is your family life like? (Ask a series of questions about family life and relationships.)

Other questions should focus on cultural needs, cross-addictions, and medical needs. The result of these questions and the interview is to help identify areas in which Beverly may have disabilities, impairments, and functional limitations. Assessment of her responses will help the counselor determine how these limitations will affect her participation in the program, and identify additional information needed to make sure she can get the maximum benefit from treatment. Given her status as a female veteran, gender specific questions should also be asked. A broad range of interconnected services that address problems related to trauma, mental health, and substance abuse should be implemented.

Gender Specific Focus in Addressing Sexual Assault

1. Offer trauma-specific and trauma-informed services.
2. Integrate mental health, substance abuse, and trauma services.
3. Provide a comprehensive range of core services.
4. Involve PWDs in central roles.
5. Sensitivity to issues of gender, sexuality, and culture.
6. Provide additional needed services and integration.
7. Provide services related to HIV needs.

For treatment to succeed, counselors should consider clients' strengths as well as their limitations or challenges. In addition, clients must understand the particular strengths they can bring to the recovery process; these may include those positive attributes of an individual which he or she uses to promote self-esteem, well being, and empowerment. For example,

Beverly's strengths include her desire to maintain custody of her child, to work on identity issues, and to participate in family counseling. The challenges for her are her inability to complete projects (e.g., education) and to obtain and maintain employment (e.g., she has not been employed since her discharge from the army), and to learn how to generalize her educational and vocational (military experience) successes to her social and psychological processes. She has the additional challenge of being an Iraq veteran with PTSD and polytrauma, requiring treatment that is individualized and specific to her circumstances, as well as the need for long-term treatment alternatives (Harley, 2009). Issues of Beverly's sexuality and her treatment as a woman in a combat zone must also be addressed within the context of her substance abuse and as separate counseling issues. "Many military—especially soldiers—have little opportunity to socialize other than in bars" (Craig, 2004, p. 208). Curry (2007) suggested that the key to aiding veterans in adjusting to post-deployment environments is seamless transitions. Three critical areas to address include (a) general considerations in care (i.e., connect veterans with each other, offer practical help with specific problems, attend to board needs of the person), (b) methods of care (i.e., education about posttraumatic stress reactions, training in coping skills, exposure therapy, cognitive restructuring, family counseling), and (c) pharmacotherapy (i.e., pharamacologic treatment of acute stress reaction) (Ruzek et al., 2004).

In general, people have a number of skills that strengthen their ability to cope with the stresses and transitions that occur throughout their lifetime, and learning these skills is a critical part of human development (Kail & Cavanaugh, 2010). A strength-based approach to treatment is especially important for people with disabilities because they have so frequently been viewed in terms of what they cannot or should not attempt. As a result, PWDs have learned to define themselves in terms of their limitations and inabilities. According to Koppelman and Goodhart (2008), PWDs are often viewed as incapable of possessing certain skills of self-determination. However, this is not to say that persons with disabilities should not understand their functional limitations, especially in relation to their risk for relapse (Fisher & Harrison, 2008). Over 15 years ago, Glenn (1994) recommended using a strength-based approach, through which counselors in rehabilitation settings could help clients learn skills to succeed in treatment and maintain sobriety. More recent research is consistent with Glenn's suggestions as a basis for continuity of care for PWDs:

1. Incorporate opportunities to strengthen resiliency skills as part of the rehabilitation program. Address those factors that place a person at risk for problems related to substance abuse and addictions; assist clients by providing for their development in all areas: psychosocial, emotional, mental, and physical (Center for Substance Abuse Treatment [CSAT], 2005).
2. Locate or establish peer-support prevention counseling programs. Positive role models are important for people with disabilities who are confronting life challenges. Too often, establishing effective peer support programs for PWDs is a challenge, especially for those with hidden disabilities and for ethnic minorities (Perron et al., 2009; Velez, Campos-Holland, & Arndt, 2008).
3. Promote healthy lifestyle changes and skills training through multidisciplinary and interdisciplinary support groups (Fallot & Harris, 2004).
4. Establish educational and decision-making sessions on coping, assertiveness training, stress management, healthy living, modification skills, and substance abuse (Zubenko, 2006).

5. Organize 12-step meetings in independent living centers and other disability service agencies that are accessible to and used by people with disabilities; and encourage the development of accessible recovery support groups in other 12-step programs for the individual and family members (Krahn et al., 2007).

In addition, Galanter and Kleber (2008) recommended that counselors in substance abuse treatment and recovery programs who are not skilled in disability-related issues should refer clients to Independent Living Centers (ILC). Unavailability of, or limited access to, specialized substance abuse and addictions programs for persons with disabilities may necessitate collaborative and coordinated efforts across agencies and programs, or creating alternatives. Alternatives are typically required because neither the mental health nor substance abuse treatment systems provides sufficient resources for treatment of co-occurring addictions and disabilities (i.e., clients are treated for their disabilities in one facility and their addictions in another) (Yalisove, 2004). Other treatment programs promote sequential treatment in which one condition (usually a psychiatric disorder) is treated before the addiction disorder. The belief is that the client must be mentally stable to benefit from substance abuse treatment. Yet, some programs offer parallel treatment in which the client is simultaneously involved in addiction and mental health treatment. For persons with disabilities, an integrated treatment approach in which both mental health and addiction treatment are combined into a unified and comprehensive program involving counselors and clinicians cross-trained in both approaches is best (Galanter & Kleber; Kinney, 2008).

Access to Treatment

- PWDs should be screened for alcoholism, substance abuse, and related mental health issues
- A transition program should be part of treatment
- Attention should be given to reintegration with family and to employment settings
- A major part of treatment is individualized prevention interventions to protect against recidivism

Treatment programs in rehabilitation settings should follow modified guidelines prescribed by Kleber (1994), including the following:

- *Assessment*, to include a medical examination, drug use history, psychosocial evaluation, and, when warranted, a psychiatric evaluation and a review of socioeconomic factors; and eligibility for public health, public assistance, employment, and educational and vocational assistance programs.
- *Same-day intake*, to retain the client's involvement and interest in treatment.
- *Documenting findings and treatment*, to enhance clinical case supervision.
- *Preventive and primary medical care*, provided on site if possible.
- *Testing for infectious diseases*, at intake and at intervals throughout treatment, for infectious diseases such as hepatitis, retrovirus, tuberculosis, HIV and AIDS, syphilis, gonorrhea, and other STDs.
- *Weekly random drug testing*, to ensure abstinence and compliance with treatment.
- *Pharamacotherapeutic interventions*, by qualified medical practitioners, as appropriate for those patients having mental health disorders, those addicted to opiates, and HIV-positive individuals and AIDS patients.

- *Group counseling interventions,* to address unique emotional, physical, and social problems.
- *Basic substance abuse counseling,* including individual, family, or collateral counseling, trained and certified when possible. Staff training and education are integral to successful treatment.
- *Practical life skills counseling,* including vocational and educational counseling and training. These can be provided through linkages with community programs.
- *General health education,* including nutrition, sex, and family planning, with an emphasis on contraception counseling for adolescents and women.
- *Peer support groups,* particularly useful for those with disabilities to provide role models.
- *Liaison services,* with immigration, legal aid, and criminal justice system authorities.
- *Social activities,* to establish or restore clients' perceptions of social interaction.
- *Alternative housing,* for homeless clients or for those whose living situations are conducive to maintaining the addict lifestyle.
- *Relapse prevention,* which combines aftercare and support programs such as 12-step programs within an individualized plan to identify, stabilize, and control the stressors that trigger and promote relapse to substance abuse.
- *Outcome evaluation,* to enable refinement and improvement of service delivery.

Counselors in rehabilitation settings will need to select appropriate and effective strategies from various models to apply to persons with disabilities. Most importantly, intervention must match the client's clinical severity, biopsychosocial, cultural, and social needs. Uniform client placement criteria to determine appropriate levels of care may not be possible for persons with disabilities and addictions. Nevertheless, counselors will need to rely on multiple program resources and on multidimensional and integrated program planning and service delivery to meet the needs of persons with disabilities and addictions. The counselor should work with the client to set up incremental goals, rather than expecting major changes all at once (SAMSHA, 2009; Stevens & Smith, 2009).

Summary and Some Final Notations

Persons with disabilities are more likely to have substance abuse problems and addictions and less likely to get effective treatment for these problems than those without a coexisting disability. Too often, people with disabilities are enabled by family members and professionals to use substances because of misperceptions and stereotypes. In addition to having the same risk factors as those without disabilities, persons with disabilities are at risk because of societal attitudes; for social and economic reasons; and due to higher rates of depression or anxiety, health and medical issues, and greater isolation. The presence of a disability increases the risk for substance abuse.

People with disabilities come to rehabilitation settings with issues that require a great deal of understanding on the part of counselors and other service providers. These clients need a thorough psychosocial and cultural assessment, and individualized treatment plans to meet their needs. Treatment programs must address not only the substance abuse problem but the disability and any medical conditions as well. Any effort to address addictions without addressing disabilities usually yields limited outcomes for the client.

Clients bring assets to the treatment process, which must be incorporated into the treatment process. Clients with addictions and disabilities may benefit from an integrated, multidisciplinary approach to treatment. Counselors should select an intervention approach that meets the individualized needs of clients.

Summary of Key Points About PWDs

- Are disproportionately affected by substance abuse
- Have higher rates of isolation and unemployment
- Usually have multiple interrelated issues leading to substance abuse
- In addition to substance abuse, treatment programs must address the disability and medical problems
- Clients bring assets to their treatment

Useful Web Sites

The following Web sites provide additional information relating to the chapter topic, substance abuse, and addictions for people with disabilities:

American Academy of Addiction Psychiatry (AAAP)
http://www.aaap.org

American Medical Association (AMA)
http://www.ama-assn.org

Center for Substance Abuse Prevention (CSAP)
http://www.prevention.samhsa.gov

Center for Research on Women with Disabilities (CROWD)
http://www.bcm.edu/crowd.?pmid=1422

DisabilityInfo.gov: Health: Substance Abuse
www.disabilityinfo.gov

DRM Webwatcher: Substance Abuse and People with Disabilities
www.disabilitiyresources.org/SUBSTANCE-ABUSE.html

National Guideline Clearinghouse
http://www.guideline.gov/browse/gaupdated.aspx

Office of Disability
www.hhs.gov/od/about/fact_sheet/substanceabuse

Substance Abuse and Mental Health Services Administration (SAMHSA)
http://ncadi.samhsa.gov

Substance Abuse Resources and Disability Issues (SARDI)
http://www.med.wright.edu/citar/sardi/

My Helping Lab
http://www.myhelpinglab.com

References

American Psychiatric Association. (2010). *Diagnostic and statistical manual of mental disorders* (4th ed.). Washington, DC: Author.

American Society of Addiction Medicine (ASAM). (2001). *ASAM PPC-2R: ASAM patient placement criteria for the treatment of substance-related disorders* (2nd ed.— revised). Chevy Chase, MD: Author.

Bachman, S. S., Drainoni, M., & Tobias, C. (2004). Medicaid managed care, substance abuse treatment, and people with disabilities: Review of the literature. *Health and Social Work, 29,* 189–196.

Barnow, B. S. (2008, November). The employment rate of people with disabilities. *Monthly Labor Review,* 44–50.

Basford, J. R., Rohe, D. E., Barnes, C. P., & DePompolo, R. W. (2002). Substance abuse attitudes and policies in U. S. rehabilitation training programs: A comparison of 1985 and 2000. *Archives of Physical Medicine and Rehabilitation, 83,* 517–522.

Bombardier, C. H., Blake, K. D., Ehde, D. M., Gibbons, L. E., Moore, D., & Kraft, G. H. (2004). Alcohol and drug abuse among persons with multiple sclerosis. *Multiple Sclerosis, 10,* 35–40.

Bonhomme, J., Stephens, T., & Braithwaite, R. (2006). African-American males in the United States prison system: Impact on family and community. *The Journal of Men's Health & Gender, 3*, 223–226.

Brault, M. W. (2008, December). *Americans with disabilities: 2005 Household economic studies.* Washington, DC: U.S. Department of Commerce.

Brucker, D. (2007). Estimating the prevalence of substance use, abuse, and dependence among social security disability benefit recipients. *Journal of Disability Policy Studies, 18*, 148–159.

Brucker, D. L. (2008). Prescription drug abuse among persons with disabilities. *Journal of Vocational Rehabilitation, 29*, 105–115.

Bryan, W. V. (2007). *Multicultural aspects of disabilities: A guide to understanding and assisting minorities in the rehabilitation process* (2nd ed.). Springfield, IL: Thomas.

Burgard, J. F., Donohue, B., Azrin, N. H., & Teichner, G. (2000). Prevalence and treatment of substance abuse in the mentally retarded population: An empirical review. *Journal of Psychoactive Drugs, 32*, 293–298.

Caetano, R. (1995). The prevention of alcohol-related problems among United States Hispanics: A review. In P. A. Langton, L. G. Epstein, & M. A. Orlani (Eds.), *The challenge of participatory research: Preventing alcohol-related problems in ethnic communities* (pp. 279–303). (DHHS Publication No. [SMA] 95–3042). Washington, DC: U.S. Department of Health and Human Services.

Center for Substance Abuse Treatment. (2005). *A strength-based approach toward addiction treatment for women.* Rockville, MD: U.S. Department of Health and Human Services.

Craig, R. J. (2004). *Counseling the alcohol and drug dependent client.* Boston: Pearson.

Curry, R. (2007). PTSD in today's war veterans: The road to recovery. *Social Work Today, 7*, 13–16.

Daley, D. C., & Marlatt, G. A. (2006). *Overcoming your alcohol or drug problem: Effective recovery strategies. Therapist guide* (2nd ed.). New York: Oxford University Press.

Fallot, R. D., & Harris, M. (2004). Integrated trauma services team for women survivors with alcohol and other drug problems and co-occurring mental disorders. In B. W. Veysey & C. Clark (Eds.), *Responding to physical and sexual abuse in women with alcohol and other drug and mental disorders: Program building* (181–199). Binghamton: Haworth Press.

Fisher, G. L., & Harrison, T. C. (2008). *Substance abuse: Information for school counselors, social workers, therapists, and counselors* (4th ed.). Boston: Pearson.

Galanter, M., & Kleber, H. D. (Eds.). (2008). *The American psychiatric publishing textbook of substance abuse treatment* (4th ed.). Arlington, VA: American Psychiatric Publishing.

Glenn, M. K. (1994). Preparing rehabilitation specialists to address the prevention of substance abuse problems. *Rehabilitation Counseling Bulletin, 38*, 164–179.

Goodman, A. C. (2009). Economic analyses of multiple addictions for men and women. The *Journal of Mental Health Policy and Economics, 12*, 139–156.

Goodwin, L. R. (2009). Treatment for substance use disorders. In I. Marini & M. A. Stebnicki (Eds.), *The professional counselor's desk reference* (pp. 703–723). New York: Springer.

Handbook of Disabilities. (2009, August 18). Substance abuse. Retrieved December 19, 2008 from *http://www .rcep7.org/projects/handbook/handbkdir.html*

Harley, D. A. (2005). African Americans and substance abuse. In D. A. Harley & J. M. Dillard (Eds.), *Contemporary mental health issues among African Americans* (pp. 119–131). Alexandria, VA: American Counseling Association.

Harley, D. A. (2009). Services for PTSD and polytrauma service members and veterans. In I. Marini & M. A. Stebnicki (Eds.), *The professional counselor's desk reference* (767–776). New York: Springer.

Harris Survey of Americans with Disabilities. (2004). Commissioned by National Organization on Disabilities. New York: Harris Interactive, Inc.

Hollar, D., McAweeney, M., & Moore, D. (2008). The relationship between substance use disorders and unsuccessful case closures in vocational rehabilitation agencies. *Journal of Applied Rehabilitation Counseling, 39*, 48–52.

Kail. R. V., & Cavanaugh, J. C. (2010). *Human development: A lifespan view* (5th ed.). Belmont, CA: Wadsworth.

Kinney, J. (2008). *Loosening the grip: A handbook of alcohol information* (9th ed.). Boston: McGrawHill.

Kleber, H. D. (1994). *Assessment and treatment of cocaine-abusing methadone-maintained patients.* Treatment Improvement Protocol Series (No. 10, NIH Pub. No. 94–3003). Rockville, MD: I.S. Department of Health and Human Services.

Kolakowsky-Hayner, S. A., Gourley, E. V., Kreutzer, J. S., Marwitz, J. H., Meade, M. A., & Cifu, D. X. (2002). Post-injury substance abuse among persons with brain injury and persons with spinal cord injury. *Brain Injury, 16*, 583–592.

Koppelman, K. L., & Goodhart, R. L. (2008). *Understanding human differences: Multicultural education for diverse America.* Boston: Pearson.

Krahn, G., Deck, D., Gabriel, R., & Farrell, N. (2007). A population-based study on substance abuse treatment for adults with disabilities: Access, utilization, and treatment outcomes. *The American Journal of Drug and Alcohol Abuse, 33*, 791–798.

Langlois, J. A., Rutland-Brown, W., & Thomas, K. E. (2004). *Traumatic brain injury in the United States: Emergency department visits, hospitalizations, and deaths.* Atlanta, GA: Centers for Disease Control and Prevention, National Center for Injury Prevention and Control.

Marlatt, G. A., & VandenBos, G. R. (Eds.), (1997*). Addictive behaviors.* Washington, DC: American Psychological Association.

May, P. A. (1995). The prevention of alcohol and other drug abuse among American Indians: A review and analysis of the literature. In P. A. Langton, L. G. Epstein, & M. A. Orlandi (Eds.), *The challenge of participatory research: Preventing alcohol-related problems in ethnic communities* (pp. 183–243). (DHHS Publication No. [SMA] 95–3042). Washington, DC: U.S. Department of Health and Human Services.

McGillicuddy, N. B. (2006). A review of substance use research among those with mental retardation. *Mental Retardation and Developmental Disabilities Research Reviews, 12,* 41–47.

McLellan, A. T., Lewis, D. C., O'Brien, C. P., & Kleber, H. D. (2000). Drug dependence, a chronic medical illness: Implications for treatment, insurance, and outcome evaluation. *Journal of the American Medical Association, 284,* 1689–1695.

National Institute on Drug Abuse. (2009). NIDA infofacts: Treatment approaches for drug addiction. Retrieved December 31, 2009 from *http://www.nida.nih.gov/ Infofacts/TreatMeth.html*

National Spinal Cord Injury Statistical Center (2008). Spinal cord injury facts and figures at a glance, January 2008. Washington, DC: National Institute on Disability and Rehabilitation Research. Retrieved December 16, 2009 from *http://www.spinalcord.uab.edu*

Nugent, F. A., & Jones, K. D. (2009). *Introduction to the profession of counseling* (5th ed.). Upper Saddle River, NJ: Pearson.

Office of Applied Studies (OAS). (2005). 2004 *National survey on drug use & health: National findings.* Retrieved November 17, 2009 from *http://www.oas .samsha.gov/nsduh/2k4nsduh/2k4overview/2k4overview .htm#ch9*

Olney, M. F., Kennedy, J., Brockelman, K. F., & Newsom, M. A. (2004). Do you have a disability? A population-based test of acceptance, denial, and adjustment among adults with disabilities in the U.S. *Journal of Rehabilitation, 70,* 4–9.

Ouimette, P. C., Finney, J. W., Gima, K., & Moos, R. H. (1999a). A comparative evaluation of substance abuse treatment III. Examining mechanisms underlying patient-treatment matching hypotheses for 12-step and cognitive-behavioral treatments for substance abuse. *Alcoholism: Clinical and Experimental Research, 23,* 545–551.

Ouimette, P. C., Finney, J. W., Gima, K., & Moos, R. H. (1999b). A comparative evaluation of substance abuse treatment IV. The effect of comorbid psychiatric diagnoses on amount of treatment, continuing care, and 1-year outcomes. *Alcoholism: Clinical and Experimental Research, 23,* 552–557.

Parran, T. (2009). Addiction and substance abuse. Retrieved December 31, 2009 from *http://www.netwellness.org/ healthtopics/substanceabuse/faq2.cfm*

Perron, B. E., Mowbray, O. P., Glass, J. E., Delva, J., Vaughn, M. G., & Howard, M. O. (2009). Differences in service utilization and barriers among Blacks, Hispanics, and Whites with drug use disorders. *Substance Abuse Treatment, Prevention, and Policy, 4.* Available online at *http://www.substanceabusepolicy.com/content/4/1/3*

Potts, B. (2005). Disability and employment: Considering the importance of social capital. *Journal of Rehabilitation, 71,* 20–25.

Ruzek, J. I., Curran, E., Friedmann, M. J., Gusman, F. D., Southwick, S. M., Swales, P., et al. (2004). Treatment of the returning Iraq war veteran. The Iraq war clinician guide (2nd ed.). Retrieved November 25, 2009 from *http://www.ncptsd.va.gov*

Sherer, R. A. (2009). Mental health problems among minorities. Retrieved December 31, 2009 from *http://www .healthyplace.com/anxiety-panic/main/mental-health-pr*

Stapleton, D. C., Burkhauser, R. V., & Houtenville, A. J. (2004, December). *Has employment rate of people with disabilities declined? Policy brief.* Ithaca, NY: Cornell University.

Stevens, P., & Smith, R. L. (2009). *Substance abuse counseling: Theory and practice* (4th ed.). Upper Saddle River, NJ: Merrill.

Substance Abuse and Mental Health Services Administration (SAMHSA). (2009). Depression in racial/ethnic minorities. Retrieved December 31, 2009 from *http://www.oas .samhsa.gov/NHSDA/ethnic/ethn1006.htm*

Sue, D. W., & Sue, D. (2008). *Counseling the culturally diverse: Theory and practice* (5th ed.). Hoboken, NJ: Wiley & Sons.

Toriello, P. J., & Leierer, S. J. (2005). The relationship between the clinical orientation of substance abuse professionals and their clinical decisions. *Rehabilitation Counseling Bulletin, 48,* 75–88.

U.S. Department of Health and Human Services. (2003). *2001 National Household Survey on Drug Abuse* (NHSDA). Washington, DC: Author.

Velez, M. B., Campos-Holland, A. L., & Arndt, S. (2008). City's racial composition shapes treatment center characteristics and services. *Journal Ethnic Substance Abuse, 7,* 188–199.

West, S. L., Graham, C. W., & Cifu, D. X. (2009a). Rates of alcohol/other drug treatment denials to persons with physical disabilities: Accessibility concerns. *Alcoholism Treatment Quarterly, 27,* 305–316.

West, S. L., Graham, C. W., & Cifu, D. X. (2009b). Prevalence of persons with disabilities in alcohol/other drug treatment in the United States. *Alcoholism Treatment Quarterly, 27,* 242–252.

West, S. L., Luck, R. S., Capps, C. F., Cifu, D. X., Graham, C. W., & Hurley, J. E. (2009). Alcohol/other drug problems screening and intervention by rehabilitation physicians.. *Alcoholism Treatment Quarterly, 27,* 280–293.

Yalisove, D. (2004). *Introduction to alcohol research: Implications for treatment, prevention, and policy.* Boston: Pearson.

Zubenko, N. (2006). Substance abuse treatment for disabled persons. *Counselor, 7,* 62–67.

Chapter 16

Substance Abuse Prevention Programs for Children, Adolescents, and College Students

Abbé Finn
Florida Gulf Coast University

THE NEED FOR PREVENTION PROGRAMS FOR CHILDREN, ADOLESCENTS, AND COLLEGE STUDENTS

The National Center for Chronic Disease Prevention and Health Promotion (NCCDPHP) has identified alcohol, tobacco, and drug abuse as leading causes of serious health problems, disability, and premature death (2002). Approximately 9.1% of people in the United States aged 12 years or older are dependent on some type of psychoactive substance (Substance Abuse and Mental Health Administration [SAMSHA], 2004). Substance abusers usually initiate use during childhood or adolescence, negatively impacting the rest of their lives. The peak ages for alcohol abuse are between 18 and 29 years old (Grant et al., 2004). College students show higher rates of alcohol use and abuse than their non-college peers (Dawson, Grant, Stinson, & Chou, 2004; Johnston, O'Malley, & Bachman, 2003; Slutske et al., 2004; Slutske, 2005). Twenty percent of college students meet the diagnostic criteria for alcohol abuse—twice the rate of the average population (National Center on Addiction and Substance Abuse at Columbia University [CASA], 2007; Dawson et al., 2004; Knight et al., 2002; Slutske, 2005). College members of fraternities and sororities have the highest rate of binge alcohol abuse and are most likely to be diagnosed with alcohol addiction (Knight et al., 2002). During a 10-year period, the proportion of students abusing controlled prescription drugs has increased exponentially. For example, the abuse of pain killers (Percocet, Vicodin, and OxyContin) has increased by more than 300%; stimulants (Ritalin and Adderall) by 90%; and daily marijuana use by 110% (The National Center on Addiction and Substance Abuse at Columbia University [CASA], 2007). The CASA (2007) report concluded that the rate of combined alcohol and substance abuse by American college students threatens the well-being of the current generation and the capacity of the United States to maintain its lead in a global economy.

> Approximately 20% of college students meet the diagnostic criteria for alcohol abuse—twice the rate of the average population. Alcohol and drug abuse are also predictive of high-risk sexual behaviors, which may lead to HIV. Almost 80% of juveniles in the American criminal justice system were under the influence of a psychoactive substance when they committed their first crime.

In addition, alcohol and drug abuse are also predictive of high-risk sexual behaviors, which may lead to HIV, a major killer of young adults (NCCDPHP, 2002; CASA, 2007). However, effective drug-prevention programs can reduce the risk for all three behaviors (McCoy, Lai, Metsch,

Messiah, & Zhao, 2004) and increase the health, productivity, and life expectancy of adolescents and young adults.

The variety of abused substances is increasing as new drugs are invented. Some young people abuse chemicals, not drugs, that were never intended for human consumption. Some of these chemicals are intentionally inhaled for the purpose of intoxication. In 1998, 25% of adolescents admitted that they had used inhalants (Kurtzman, Otsuka, & Wahl, 2001). In the vernacular, this is a process known as "huffing." These substances are potentially lethal, carcinogenic, and liver-toxic. There can be irreversible brain damage or death from a single use. It is difficult to monitor the use of these substances, since many are found in products available in every home, market, or school.

In the United States, the problem of substance abuse is enormous, with dire consequences for the quality of life of millions of people. For example, almost 80% of juveniles in the American criminal justice system were under the influence of a psychoactive substance when they committed their crime (The National Center on Addiction and Substance Abuse at Columbia University [CASA], 2004).

The composite estimated cost for industry, social service organizations, the criminal justice system, and the healthcare industry from substance abuse in the United States is in the billions of dollars. These figures are computed by estimating the cost to industry due to the loss of productivity caused by on-the-job injuries, accidents, and increased health benefit costs of substance abusing employees; expenses caused by absenteeism; and damages caused by impaired workers on the job. Healthcare cost estimates include the expense of treating patients suffering physical consequences of substance abuse, such as increased rates of liver disease, or medical treatment of traumatic injury incurred while under the influence of intoxicants.

As expensive as these numbers appear, the greatest toll cannot be assigned a monetary value. It is the cost borne by those who love and depend on the substance abuser. Long before drugs take the life of the addict, they damage lives and destroy the addict's relationships with others (van Wormer & Davis, 2003). These consequences include partner violence, sexual violence, property crimes, child abuse and neglect, loss of life (Executive Office of the President, 2001), and destruction of relationships with employers, family, and friends.

In addition, the younger the onset of drug abuse, the greater the negative consequences to the person's cognitive, interpersonal, and educational development. There is evidence that children and adolescents are particularly vulnerable to physical problems associated with exposure to alcohol, drugs, and tobacco products. There is additional evidence that drug and alcohol use during adolescence, when the brain is continuing to develop, causes irreversible damage to the brain's higher-order cortical function (Volkow & Li, 2005; Wuetrich, 2001). The incomplete development of the prefrontal cortex increases susceptibility to high-risk behavior because this part of the brain is responsible for judgment, decision-making, and emotional control (Gogtay et al., 2004).

The younger the onset of drug abuse, the greater the negative consequences to the person's cognitive, interpersonal, and educational development. In 10 years, the number of emergency room admissions due to complications from recreational use of prescription narcotics (oxycodone or hydrocodone) increased by 352%. In 12 years, the rate of opioid and benzodiazepines prescription drug abuse has risen 344% and 450%, respectively.

While use of some illicit substances by young people has recently been declining, the illegal use of prescription drugs, such as benzodiazepines and narcotic pain killers, and the use of medical and nonmedical inhalants have shown a sharp increase (Johnston, O'Malley, Bachman, & Schulenberg, 2005; Sung, Richter, Vaughan, Johnson, & Thom, 2005). The rates of illicit drug and alcohol use by adolescents and young adults are on the rise, with the percentage increasing from 27% in 1992 to 40% in 1996 (Johnston, O'Malley, & Bachman, 1996). Specifically, use of opioids has risen to 9.4% of high school seniors illegally using narcotics during the past year (Johnston, O'Malley, & Bachman, 2003). In 10 years the number of emergency room admissions due to complications from recreational use of prescription narcotics (oxycodone or hydrocodone) increased by 352%. Sung et al. (2005) describe typical adolescent opioid abusers as poor Black females with drug-abusing environmental role models. On the other hand, McCabe, Boyd, and Teter (2005) describe typical adolescent opioid abusers as White male cigarette and marijuana smokers who drink alcohol. The accurate profile of young opioid users is hazy, but it is clear that opioid abuse by adolescents is becoming a new epidemic in need of effective prevention programs (Compton & Volkow, 2006; McCabe et al., 2005; Sung et al., 2005). A new media campaign warns parents and grandparents of the increased risk of prescription drug abuse by their children or grandchildren, through theft of their prescription medications (Compton & Volkow, 2006; McCabe et al., 2005; Office of National Drug Control Policy, 2002; Sung, et al., 2005).

On college campuses the rate of substance use and abuse has been growing at an alarming rate. For example, between 1995 and 2007 the abuse of prescription opioid pain medications increased by 344%. During that same period there was a 450% increase in abuse of a class of depressants known as benzodiazepines, including drugs commonly known as Valium and Ativan. There is an increased health risk because college students are combining these medications with alcohol, leading to rapid intoxication and overdoses, some of which lead to premature death (CASA, 2007).

In addition to the risks of addiction due to substance abuse, half of newly diagnosed HIV patients are under the age of 25, indicating that they contracted the virus while adolescents or young adults. One-third of people infected with HIV contracted the disease through intravenous drug use (IDU) (CDC, 2005). Drug users who do not use intravenous drugs also show a much higher rate of HIV infection than nondrug users (McCoy et al., 2004), because substance use increases the likelihood of other high-risk behaviors such as unsafe sexual practices with multiple partners, while inhibiting the likelihood of protected sex (CDC, 2005). Therefore, preventing drug use has the added value of decreasing the risk of contracting HIV/AIDS, other sexually transmitted infections, unplanned pregnancies (CASA, 2007), and reducing the likelihood of fetal drug and alcohol exposure.

PUBLIC HEALTH PREVENTION PROGRAM MODEL

According to the public health model of disease prevention, substance abuse prevention programs fall into three general types: primary, secondary, and tertiary. Some programs are designed to include all youth; others are designed to focus on targeted vulnerable groups (James & Gilliland, 2001).

Primary prevention programs target problem behaviors before symptoms occur. Participants are selected because they fall into an at-risk category. The purpose of these programs is to stop the problem before it begins. An example of this type of prevention program would be one that targets elementary school children for education regarding the risks involved with tobacco use. This is a reasonable target group because research shows that most people who become addicted to tobacco began use during middle or high school; and because tobacco products are so highly addictive, experimentation can easily lead to addiction (McDonald, Roberts & Descheemaeker, 2000).

Primary prevention programs target problem behaviors before symptoms occur. Secondary prevention programs are designed for people who have already demonstrated problematic behaviors. The goal of a tertiary prevention program is to reduce the risk of further harm.

Secondary prevention programs are designed for people who have already demonstrated problematic behaviors. The goal is to stop the behavior before it escalates to a serious problem with dangerous consequences. Some secondary prevention programs can be described as a harm-reduction model. For example, when it comes to alcohol, some programs focus on responsible drinking rather than abstinence (Marlatt & Witkiewitz, 2002; van Wormer & Davis, 2003).

"Juvenile Drug Court" (JDC) diversionary programs are an example of tertiary prevention programs. Their goal is to divert drug offenders to treatment and recovery programs rather than jail, thus breaking the cycle of addiction and recidivism within the criminal justice system. Other examples include the mandated counseling programs for students convicted of violating alcohol and drug use policies on campus (Carey, Henson, Carey, & Maisto, 2009); and the relapse-prevention program that is part of most drug-abuse recovery programs (Compton et al., 2005).

DRUG ABUSE RISK FACTORS FOR ADOLESCENTS

In researching drug addiction, some common characteristics have emerged and been identified as risk factors. These characteristics precede the onset of substance use (Hser, Grella, Collins, & Teruya, 2003). These cluster into five categories. The first consists of individual characteristics such as mental illness, school failure, antisocial behavior, drug experimentation at a young age, and criminal activity. The second cluster includes attitudes such as distrust of authority figures, anger toward adults, and a fascination with deviant behaviors. The third cluster includes psychosocial characteristics such as low self-esteem, poor social skills, desire to fit in with peers, poor peer-pressure refusal skills, and lack of self-advocacy skills. The fourth cluster consists of family characteristics such as family history of drug use or dependence, family antisocial behavior, and parents with ineffective behavior-management skills. The fifth and final category includes environmental characteristics such as poverty; lack of support services; community tolerance of drug use, violence, and criminal behavior; easy access to drugs and alcohol; and family and friends who use drugs (Goldberg, 2006). The presence of the risk factor does not presume a cause–effect relationship. All people presenting with these characteristics will not automatically become substance abusers. It is assumed that the greater number of factors present, the more vulnerable the young person is to the threat of addiction (Callas, Flynn, & Worden, 2004).

Program administrators utilize the risk factor approach in several ways. Some use the information to profile students and identify which ones should be included in the primary prevention program (Bousman et al., 2005; Ellickson & Morton, 1999; Griffin, Botvin, Nichols, & Doyle, 2003; Vanyukov et al., 2003). Others utilize risk factors so that, when a risk factor is identified, addiction prevention can be included with intervention for the other identified problem; for example, Post Traumatic Stress Disorder (Beiderman, Faraone, Wozniak, & Monteaux, 2000; Zeitlin, 1999). Vulnerabilities and other factors are further explored in Chapter 19.

ALCOHOL AND DRUG ABUSE RISK FACTORS FOR COLLEGE STUDENTS

College students have two major tasks when they leave home: to assimilate into a new culture, and to achieve academically. These tasks are, paradoxically, at cross purposes because, when students spend too much time making new friends their grades suffer; and when they focus solely on studying, they are often socially isolated. Many freshman use alcohol and drugs to reduce their social anxiety, fit in socially, and as a major part of their recreational activities (Vaughan, Corbin, & Fromme, 2009). When college students enter the Greek system of fraternities and sororities, their rate of alcohol abuse increases dramatically (Capone, Wood, Borsari, & Laird, 2007; Park, Sher, Wood, & Krull, 2009). College and university health centers provide counseling services and implement programs to combat these and other psychological problems (Cooper 1999; Gallagher, 2009; Minami et al., 2009), and 93.4% report an increase of students with severe psychological problems (Gallagher, 2009).

In order for a prevention program to be effective, it must be designed especially to address the community needs. It is better to prevent people from becoming addicted than to try to treat them after the problem has emerged. In order to stop drug abuse in adults, it is important to prevent the experimentation and use by adolescents of identified gateway drugs.

PROGRAM NEEDS ASSESSMENT

In order for a prevention program to be effective, it must be designed especially to address community needs. These assessments identify the types of drugs being abused or likely to be abused in the future; community services that are already in place or need to be developed; community and institutional goals; and resources necessary for the implementation of a proposed substance abuse prevention program. The four types of needs indicators are: "drug use indicators, problem-behavior indicators, psychological or developmental characteristics, and social or economical conditions" (Sales, 2004, p. 82). Drug use indicators identify the types of drugs, prevalence rate of use, and the number of people secondarily impacted. Drug use indicators are comprised of arrest records, survey responses, incarceration rates, school disciplinary actions, and treatment data. Problem-behavior indicators are behaviors associated with and caused by addictions. These could include children in foster care due to parental substance abuse, neglect, or parental drug-related incarceration; school dropout rates; and positive HIV secondary to drug use. Psychological and developmental vulnerabilities also contribute to the risk factors. These include many correlated factors such as age-related developmental factors; family structures and interaction styles; and individual characteristics such as a history of physical and/or sexual abuse, low self-esteem, homelessness, and/or mental or psychiatric disorders. Social, economic, and environmental factors include poverty, high crime rates, community tolerance for violence and drug distribution and use, substandard housing, blighted communities resources, and disadvantages associated with discrimination (Sales, 2004).

Some of this data is available through community and governmental agencies, or can be collected from surveys and/or interviews. The National Association on Substance Abuse has several instruments that can be modified or used in their original forms for needs assessment.

The most effective substance abuse treatment programs target previously identified problems through needs assessments; apply scientifically proven intervention methods for reducing substance abuse risk actors; enhance resistance and resiliency factors; and monitor the impact of the programs (Arthur & Blitz, 2000).

TYPES OF SUBSTANCE ABUSE PREVENTION PROGRAMS

Clearly, preventing people from becoming addicted in the first place is better than trying to treat them after the problem has emerged. The question is: What programs are best at preventing addictions? Many types of programs have been tried. These programs have used scare tactics, social skills and peer pressure resistance training, education regarding drug abuse facts, and parent and family training regarding behavior management and communication skills (Catalano & Hawkins, 1996; Dwyer, Nicholson, Battistutta, & Oldenburg, 2005; Hawkins, Catalano, & Arthur, 2002).

Prevention programs can be categorized along nine different strategies. Each will be reviewed. They are:

1. School/college based prevention programs focusing on education, peer mediation, and reduction of negative peer pressure
2. Mass media campaigns reporting risks and consequences of drug use, and restriction of media campaigns that glamorize the use of harmful substances
3. Early diagnosis and treatment of emotional problems
4. Improvement of personal and interpersonal skills
5. Harm-reduction programs
6. Campaigns to reduce the access to drugs
7. Juvenile Drug Court, drug court, and other diversionary programs
8. Approaches focusing on improving the family, improving parenting skills, and reduction of child abuse
9. Multimodal programs using some features from all of the above

School/College-Based Prevention Programs

High schools and colleges are ideal platforms for launching drug abuse prevention programs because they provide convenient access to target populations, and offer opportunities to administer program curriculum, practice the activities, and evaluate the outcome. The earliest school/college based programs focused on providing the facts regarding the dangers of drug use, and encouraging healthy alternatives and healthy expression of emotions (Botvin, 2000). Other programs have taught students the social skills thought to be necessary for drug avoidance. Because the temptation to use drugs is omnipresent, social skills, such as the ability to refuse drugs, are considered essential if adolescents and young adults are to successfully avoid the consequences of drug abuse (Botvin et al., 2000).

SCHOOL-BASED ADOLESCENT SUBSTANCE ABUSE/USE PREVENTION PROGRAMS. Most adolescent drug abuse prevention programs focus on keeping students from experimenting with tobacco, alcohol, and marijuana, which have been identified as "gateway drugs." When surveyed, most substance abusers in treatment identify these as the first drugs they experimented with and used. These drugs were viewed as landmarks for the port of entry into drug abuse. That is why so many of the early prevention programs focused on abstinence. Any use of substances was understood to be the first step on a slippery slope leading to drug abuse and addictions. According to this assumption, in order to stop drug abuse in adults, it is important to prevent the experimentation and use by adolescents of these identified gateway drugs. However, there is controversy regarding the assumption of inevitable progression from the experimental use of a drug such as tobacco to addiction or abuse of the most dangerous drugs (Golub & Johnson, 2002).

The most well-known school-based drug abuse prevention program is Drug Abuse Awareness and Resistance Education (DARE). It is the most widely implemented and well-funded alcohol and drug abuse prevention program to date, with $750 million in funding in 1991 (Clayton, Cattarello, & Johnstone, 1996); 80% of school districts in America used some form of the program in 2001 (Birkeland, Murphy-Graham, & Weiss, 2005). Developed in 1983 by the Los Angeles Unified School District in cooperation with the Los Angeles Police Department, it originally targeted children making the transition from elementary to middle school, an age thought to be most vulnerable to poor decisions due to the stress encountered at developmental turning points, and to consequences from bad choices. However, in some school districts, DARE was expanded to include children from kindergarten to third grade, middle school, and high school.

DARE's core curriculum advocates strict abstinence from any drug use. It provides information about the effects of drugs and promotes skills and techniques that help students refuse drugs; resist peer pressure; avoid drug use related to gang involvement; and enhance self-esteem and self-advocacy. The program calls for 1 hour of education and training each week for 17 consecutive weeks, using a copyrighted curriculum taught by uniformed police officers. (The officers take 80 hours of classes covering instruction techniques and information regarding the dangers of drug use.) The program is delivered in lecture and interactive format. In 1991 the DARE program was touted as the cure for the child and adolescent drug abuse epidemic (United States Department of Justice, 1991).

Initial efficacy studies showed some positive impact from the DARE program. For example, a study of seventh grade students indicated that program participants were better at refusing drugs and used at a lower rate than the comparison group of nonparticipants (DeJong, 1987). Other outcome studies demonstrated changes in students' attitudes toward drug use, finding them to have a more negative attitude toward drugs and finding their use to be less attractive (Harmon, 1993; Ringwalt, Ennett, & Holt, 1991). In research evaluating the long-term impact of DARE on the drug use patterns of high school seniors, utilizing qualitative and quantitative methods of enquiry, researchers found that the DARE training had a minimal effect on the prevention of drug use in adolescents, and its initial positive effects decayed over time (Botvin, Nichols, & Doyle 2003; Clayton et al., 1996; Lynam et al., 1999; Rosenbaum & Hanson, 1998; Wysong & Wright, 1995). After a seven-year follow-up study utilizing quantitative and qualitative methods, Wysong and Wright (1995) concluded that there was no positive long-term impact from the DARE curriculum. Focus groups conducted with graduates who had been student role models for the younger participants revealed their doubts at having made any substantial impact on the lives of the participants. In a 7-year follow-up study with at-risk students, the findings were even more pessimistic. Study subjects recalled the DARE experience in negative terms stating that the curriculum was "boring" and the situations were "phony" (Wysong & Wright, 1995, p. 296).

Researchers found that the DARE training had minimal effect on the prevention of drug use in adolescents and the initial positive effects following the training decayed over time.

In spite of the lack of evidence demonstrating the effectiveness of DARE, many school districts continue to utilize the program. Administrators continue the program for many reasons. Some say they disbelieve the evidence, in light of anecdotal data that they have collected. Others ignore the data because the program evaluators only measured the outcome of the officially stated goals. For example, some educators continue to value DARE because of the improved relationship between law enforcement officers and the school community. In a community in which this relationship is historically strained, this is a highly valued, but unmeasured, outcome. In addition, community stakeholders may have very different reasons for valuing the DARE curriculum. For example, they may perceive an increased rate of community involvement in education as a result of the DARE community outreach (Birkeland et al., 2005).

There may be a high rate of measurement error with these program evaluations. For example, Fendrich and Rosenbaum (2003) did follow-up surveys with high school students who had participated in DARE during the seventh grade. They found that over the course of their middle through high school years, from 41% to 81% of survey respondents recanted their stories regarding the amount and variety of their substance use. The highest level of recanting occurred regarding the use of cocaine and methamphetamines. It is hypothesized that since the DARE program uses uniformed officers to communicate the curriculum and collect the data, as students mature they may distrust whether the information is truly confidential. It cannot be overlooked that this high rate of inconsistency among survey responses over time decreases the reliability of the research findings.

DARE is not the only prevention program showing little or no long term impact. To test the efficacy of a social skills training drug prevention program, Botvin et al. (2000) randomly assigned students to a treatment or a control group. During the seventh grade, the treatment group received training and education regarding peer pressure resistance, the influence of advertising on behavior, and the influence of modeling by parents, friends, and media personalities on behavior (Botvin, 2000). The students had reinforcing education in the eighth and ninth grades. Six and a half years later, both groups of students were surveyed again to measure the efficacy of the prevention program. The data indicated that students who had received the life skills training were significantly less likely to use illicit drugs during their high school years (Botvin et al., 2000).

Another school drug prevention program, Early Action Against Teen Drug Use: Teens as Communicators to Their Peers, is designed for high school students. It combines drug awareness education, problem solving skills training, interactive role plays, communication skills training, critical thinking skills language arts, and recognition of positive peer influences. The product of a collaboration between the Office of National Drug Policy and the New York Times in Education Program (*New York Times* Knowledge Network, 2003), this program is an integrated curriculum designed to meet national educational content standards in language arts, health, life skills, visual arts, mathematics, and behavioral studies. An integrated curriculum is very important in order to justify the classroom time spent on prevention programs, because educators are encouraged to demonstrate that they are meeting their state educational standards while teaching these programs. In the era of high-stakes testing, administrators will not approve lessons that do not reinforce the state grade standards. Counselors and educators are driven by the pressure to demonstrate that their activities improve student learning. These programs have the longer-range goal of preventing drug use in the future while meeting state educational standards.

The lesson plans for Early Action Against Teen Drug Use: Teens as Communicators to their Peers are available on the Web free of charge to educators: *http://www.nytimes.com/learning/teachers/NIE/earlyaction/*. There are 14 learning modules available integrating newspaper articles, current research findings, and resources that guide students and teachers in the fight against substance abuse. The lesson plans include activities such as lists of topics for role plays of drug resistance strategies, and an imaginary letter from a friend describing his or her new friends who are encouraging her to smoke cigarettes. The students must respond to the friend's request for help, developing strategies to avoid exposure to marijuana use. In addition, the *New York Times* links current articles that cover timely topics about the risks of substance use to classes registered with them online. At this time, there are no evaluations of this program.

IN-SCHOOL DRUG TESTING. Some school-based programs attempt to limit drug use by identifying drug users through drug testing (Naylor, Gardner, & Zaichkowsky, 2001). Those who test positive are either sanctioned in some way, or required to enter treatment programs. Schools justify drug testing because of the belief that it will reduce drug use among students and increase student learning and school performance. The test sample can come from sweat, saliva, hair, breath, or urine.

Schools that use drug testing must develop the testing protocols in a scientific and systematic manner so that reliability, validity, and confidentiality are guaranteed. Also, before initiating a drug testing policy, the school must get legal advice and make certain that there is informed consent from the parents, faculty, and students. Without community support, the program is doomed to failure (Office of National Drug Control Policy, 2002). When parents challenged the right of school personnel to drug test students, the United States Supreme Court (*Vermonia School District 47* v. *Acton*, 1995) supported the constitutionality of these procedures for students participating in competitive extracurricular sports.

When people think of drug testing they often think of screenings for performance-enhancing drugs. Anabolic steroid abuse is not a problem confined to adults. Approximately half of male and female high school students participate in some type of organized sports. There is a tremendous amount of pressure for these young people to excel in their sports. The external pressure and internal desire to win can drive many athletes to resort to unhealthy, extreme measures. These can play out in the form of eating disorders and use of performance-enhancing drugs (Mayo Clinic, 2007). Unfortunately, most high school athletes are not deterred from drug use by random drug screens because most are not tested for drugs (Naylor, et al., 2001). In an effort to address these concerns, Elliott, Goldberg, Moe, DeFrancesco, and Durham, from the Department of Medicine at Oregon Health & Science University, designed and developed a program targeting female athletes, known as ATHENA (Athletes Targeting Healthy Exercise and Nutrition Alternatives). The ATHENA program utilizes a team-centered approach capitalizing on the potential for positive peer influences. The ATHENA program requires team members to participate in eight 45-minute classroom sessions during the season. Each team is divided into squads consisting of six members, with one identified as the squad leader. A coach supervises the squads and a squad leader and a member of the coaching staff lead the sessions. Each squad leader participates in a 90-minute video training session and follows a script during the sessions; participants follow workbook activities. The sessions focus on providing accurate nutritional information, information about the dangers of amphetamines and other performance-enhancing drugs; social skills training, including drug-refusal skills; and information regarding the influence of media campaigns on the perpetuation of unrealistic physical standards of beauty. The squads become a support group encouraging healthy eating habits and maintenance of healthy exercise and dietary norms. The participants have nutritional guides as resources and complete journals recording nutritional intake, physical activities, and emotions. These activities were included because female athletes, compared with their age mates, are at an increased risk for eating disorders (Elliot et al., 2004).

The ATHENA program utilizes a team-centered approach capitalizing on the potential for positive peer influences. The responsibility for preventing drug abuse on campus is shared by all members of the academic community.

In another study, known as SATURN (Student Testing Using Random Notification), drug-use patterns of students from two different schools were compared. In the drug testing school (DT), athletes were tested during the preseason. In the control school (C), they were not tested. Students at both schools completed confidential drug-use questionnaires. In the DT school, if students tested positive to substances, their parents were notified and the student was referred to counseling. However, no disciplinary actions were taken. At the end of the school year, evaluation of the data indicated that this was a highly successful program. The drug-tested athletes had significantly lower rates of illicit drug use (including steroids) while the untested group increased their use. In the DT group, 75% fewer athletes used illicit drugs than the C group (Goldberg et al., 2003).

INSTITUTIONS OF HIGHER EDUCATION (IHE) SUBSTANCE ABUSE INTERVENTION PROGRAMS. It is estimated that 20% of students on college campuses meet the *DSM IV-TR* criteria for alcohol substance abuse, and 8.2% of students had abused prescription drugs in the past month (CASA 2007). Beyond the ethical imperative to address substance abuse problems on campus, there are also compelling financial reasons, since IHEs are open to liability for failing to prevent foreseeable threats to students' health and safety. For example, Massachusetts Institute of Technology and the University of Miami paid court-ordered awards of 6 million and 14 million dollars respectively for substance-related student deaths (CASA, 2007).

The responsibility for preventing drug abuse on campus is shared by all members of the academic community. It is recommended that IHEs develop comprehensive programs focusing on a culture change in collaboration with alumni, student organizations, community members, NCAA, faculty, parents, and students.

CASA (2007) made some specific recommendations for administrators. For example, IHEs should have clear policies banning drug use on campus and in dormitories. In addition, CASA suggests banning smoking on campus. There should also be comprehensive health and counseling/psychological services on campus, with no negative consequences for utilizing these resources. Recreational activities, including sporting events, should be alcohol- and drug-free. Offers for endorsements from alcohol and tobacco companies should be refused. Further, the CASA Report (2007) recommends scheduling classes and examinations on Fridays and Saturdays to counteract the increasing trend of beginning the weekend on Thursday evenings. Where appropriate, substance abuse prevention information should be included in the curriculum.

Administrators are asked to commit the appropriate financial resources to combat substance abuse on campus. These include sufficient funding to support student health and psychological/counseling services. In addition, student health and wellness programs should be implemented, focusing on changing campus attitudes towards drug use, identifying students at highest risk for abuse, and providing assessments and intervention services when appropriate (CASA, 2007). There will be many students whose level of addiction and other mental health issues require interventions beyond the scope of the university health and wellness programs. Therefore, students' health insurance policies should provide mental health and addiction coverage.

Harm-Reduction Programs

Proponents of harm-reduction programs characterize their philosophy as more realistic and pragmatic (Marlatt & Witkiewitz, 2002). They recognize that the thrill-seeking adolescent and college student view prohibitions as a challenge, resulting in their doing the opposite of what they are told. In addition, when society reserves the use of alcohol solely for adults, it becomes forbidden fruit. As a result of this prohibition, it has become a cultural expectation that some young adults drink to intoxication on their twenty-first birthday, flaunting their new legal status. Because of the rise in deaths due to alcohol poisoning, bars in some places are forbidding birthday celebrants from having "twenty-one in twenty-one" parties, where the person celebrating his birthday drinks twenty-one shots of distilled spirits within twenty-one minutes (MSNBC, 2005).

Promoters of the harm-reduction model believe that fewer people would die from alcohol poisoning if responsible drinking were publicly promoted, rather than the unrealistic demand of abstinence until 21 years of age (Toumbourou, et al., 2007).

The proponents of harm-reduction programs characterize their philosophy as more realistic and pragmatic recognizing that the thrill-seeking adolescents and college students view prohibitions as a challenge, resulting in their doing the opposite of what they are told. An example of a harm-reduction program is the media campaign: "*Friends don't let friends drive drunk.*"

There is international support for this approach. The World Health Organization (WHO) recommends the utilization of a wide range of programs, including harm-reduction approaches. They suggest exposing all citizens to accurate information about, for example, moderate use of alcohol, as a primary prevention, with early identification and intervention for people who show signs of abuse (WHO, 2001). The WHO suggests focusing on informing young people about the dangers of binge drinking, which is viewed as an international problem (Marlatt & Witkiewitz, 2002). Binge drinking is defined as six or more drinks by a man or five or more drinks by a woman in one sitting within five hours (Wechsler, Lee, Kuo, & Lee, 2000).

Another example is the campaign, "Friends Don't Let Friends Drive Drunk." This campaign was funded by the liquor industry to improve its public image and to reduce the number of casualties caused by drunk driving.

Mass Media Campaigns

Mass media is an effective means for transmitting information to the public. Specific groups can be effectively reached through targeting print journalism, television, and other programs watched by teens. Targeted media includes magazines such as *Sports Illustrated*, sports programs, MTV, and other network programming. The goals of using mass media are to communicate information to enable young people to refuse drug use, to prevent young people from experimentation, and to encourage occasional users to stop (National Institute on Drug Abuse, 2003). In the past, government-funded advertising campaigns attempted to protect young people from the ravages of drug abuse through scare tactics and exaggerations regarding the risks of drug use. One infamous commercial showed an egg frying in a very hot pan. The voice over said, "This is your brain on drugs." The simplistic message became material for comedy routines but did little to educate youths regarding the real risks of experimentation, use, and abuse of substances. Though scare tactics may frighten some people away from use, they are not effective with the most vulnerable individuals, who tend to be both thrill seeking and impulsive. There is evidence that the frightening messages attract rather than deter them from experimentation (van Wormer & Davis, 2003).

More recently, antidrug media messages have focused on refusal skills, and on the power of parents as "the antidrug." The purpose of the message is to empower parents to intervene in their children's lives and to get involved. The sophisticated public service commercials give direct information to parents and offer Web addresses for more information and advice (*http://www.theantidrug.com*). Unfortunately, these messages may be less than effective. When asked, adolescents report having been exposed to the commercials and remembering the message, but said they had little impact on their behavior. However, there is evidence to show that the commercials are very effective with parents. Research indicates that parents experience a change in attitudes regarding the dangers of drugs such as marijuana. Research also shows that, as a result of the media campaign, more parents are having substantive discussions with their children regarding the dangers of substance use and increasing their monitoring of their children's activities (Hornik et al., 2003). Media campaigns are an important part of comprehensive drug abuse prevention programs (Sanders, 2000).

Early Diagnosis and Treatment of Emotional Problems

Practitioners working in psychiatric treatment facilities have long noticed a co-occurrence of substance abuse and psychiatric problems (Falls-Stewart, & Lucente, 1994). These include depression, suicidal behavior, conduct disorder, attention-deficit hyperactivity disorder, eating disorders, psychosis (Zeitlin, 1999), and post-traumatic stress disorder. Seventy-five percent of adolescents in treatment for substance abuse have a co-occurring psychiatric disorder (Biederman et al., 2000; Hser, et al., 2003). Usually the symptoms of the psychiatric disorders are present before the emergence of experimentation and use of intoxicating and addictive substances. Therefore, it is recommended that adolescents in treatment for psychiatric disorders should receive drug abuse prevention as part of their psychiatric treatment plan (Hser et al., 2003; Zeitlin, 1999).

Seventy-five percent of adolescents in treatment for substance abuse have a co-occurring psychiatric disorder.

Restriction of Drug Access

Amid a great deal of political fanfare, in 1971 President Nixon declared a "war on drugs." Congress pledged that the country would be drug free by 1995. Obviously, that pledge has not been fulfilled. There has been an attempt to control the recreational and nonmedical use of prescription drugs and to restrict the flow of drugs into the country. However, 13–18 metric tons of heroin is consumed yearly in the United States (Department of Health and Human Services [DHHS], 2004). In 2005, the U.S. government budgeted $6.63 billion for U.S. government agencies directly concerned with restricting illicit drug use. The U.S. government has attempted to restrict importation by strengthening the borders and interdicting illegal substances before they enter the United States and has also attempted to reduce importation from the supply side; it also uses foreign aid to pressure drug-producing countries to stop cultivating, producing, and processing illegal substances. Some of the foreign aid is tied to judicial reforms, antidrug programs, and agricultural subsidies to grow legal produce (DHHS, 2004).

In an attempt to reduce drug supplies, the government has incarcerated drug suppliers. Legislators have mandated strict enforcement of mandatory sentences resulting in a great increase in prison populations. As a result, the arrest rate of juveniles for drug-related crimes has doubled in the past 10 years, while arrest rates for other crimes have declined by 13%. A small minority of these offenders (2 out of every 1,000) will be offered JDC diversionary programs as an option to prison sentences (National Center on Addictions and Substance Abuse at Columbia University [CASA], 2004).

The arrest rate of juveniles for drug-related crimes has doubled in the past 10 years while arrest rates for other crimes have declined by 13%. Eighty percent of adjudicated youth are in jail due to drug crimes. JDC programs are cost beneficial: incarceration for each of the 122,696 drug-offending juveniles in prison costs $43,000 per year.

Juvenile Drug Court Diversionary Programs

Once a young person enters the juvenile court system, it is very likely that they have fallen into the abyss of a lifetime within the prison system (National Institute of Justice [NIJ], 2000). Juvenile Drug Court (JDC) diversionary programs provide supervision through weekly or bi-weekly hearings. The JDC team may consist of a judge, prosecutor, defense attorney, probation officer, substance abuse treatment provider, law enforcement officials, the juvenile and his or her family, social workers, counselors and vocational counselors, and educators (CASA, 2004). The team decides on a case-by-case basis which drug offending juveniles are most likely to benefit from the program. Participants are selected from a pool of convicted, drug abusing juvenile delinquents. The first JCD began in Las Vegas, Nevada in 1994. As of November 2003, there were 294 JCDs in 46 states with 4,500 participants and 4,000 completers (CASA, 2004).

Juveniles in the JCD program receive close supervision by a parole officer, and periodic drug testing. If they fail to follow all the provisions of the treatment plan or test positive for substances during the designated period of supervision, they are rearrested and sent to jail, to serve out their sentence.

Eighty percent of adjudicated youth are in jail due to drug crimes. These include possession of illegal substances; driving while under the influence; crimes committed to acquire substances or support the expensive drug habit; and crimes such as assaults and murder committed to control their competitors and maintain the drug business (NIJ, 2000).

Of the 80% of youth incarcerated for crimes involving drugs and alcohol, 44% meet the clinical diagnosis for substance abuse or dependence. Once in jail, however, only 1.6% receive any treatment for addictions (McAuliffe, Woodwarth, Zhang, & Dunn, 2002; CASA, 2004). JDC diversionary programs have the added benefit of providing an opportunity for diagnosis and treatment of coexisting psychiatric disorders among juvenile offenders. It is estimated that 64% to 71% of adjudicated youth have a diagnosable mental disorder, with 20% having conditions in the serious range (Teplin, Abram, McClelland, Dulcan, & Mericle, 2002).

In addition to being more humane than incarceration, JDC programs are also cost beneficial. For example, the cost of incarceration for each of the 122,696 drug-offending juveniles in prison is $43,000 per year; JDC diversionary programs cost $5,000 per year—saving federal, state, and local governments $4,662,448,000 (CASA, 2004). Even if many failed the treatment, there would still be very large savings, even without computing the cost benefit of children maturing to lead productive lives rather than lives of crime, incarceration, addiction, and premature disability or death (CASA, 2004).

Risk Reduction and Protective Programs

The public health model of epidemiology assumes that the natural history of diseases can be studied to gain a better understanding of contributing factors so that disease can be prevented or controlled. Risks as well as risk-reduction factors are analyzed and isolated. The more risk factors present, the greater the likelihood that the disease will emerge (Ellickson & Morton, 1999). In theory, if risk/ precursor factors are controlled and resiliency/protective factors increased, the risk for developing the disease will decline (Hawkins et al., 2002). Risk and protective factors vary among communities. Therefore, after a disease or disorder has been identified, the risk and protective factors should be isolated for that population, and targeted for intervention (Dishion, Capaldi, & Yoerger, 1999).

When risk factors are controlled and resiliency factors increased, the rate of disease declines.

Risk and protective factors fall into the following categories: personal, family, community, school, peer groups, and demographic. They often interact in an additive way, creating a synergistic effect. Many substance abuse prevention programs begin by assessing the presence of risk factors, then targeting groups in which they are highest. Personal risk factors include: a history of mental illness, thrill seeking behavior, and impulsivity. Family risk factors include: heightened levels of family discord, dysfunctional communication styles, parent and family drug use, lack of parental supervision (Kilpatrick et al., 2000), and divorce (Morgan, 2005). Some programs focus on strengthening family interactions and parenting skills. For example, in the addiction recovery program for addicted mothers, all participants received traditional treatment for addiction but half of the participants additionally received child development training, attachment and parenting skills education (Suchman et al., 2004). Others focus on the behavior of adolescents to improve healthy decision making (Poulin & Nicholson, 2005).

Multimodal Programs

Multimodal programs address addictions prevention from several perspectives simultaneously. Some are launched in schools or higher education institutions, providing services to students, families, and educators. Others focus on changing the community and the environment. This type of program is based upon the Ecological Systems Theory (Santrock, 2009) which posits that behavior is influenced by socioeconomic, environmental, and cultural factors; family relations; parental behaviors; and parenting competency. Epidemiological research on addiction and abuse has supported these findings. These characteristics can have a protective or compromising influence on a young person's ability to avoid drug, alcohol, or tobacco use (Volkow & Li, 2005). Therefore, it is logical to train a wide range of influential members in the adolescent's environment—parents, classmates, and educators—on ways to improve communication, teach effective behavior management skills, and increase knowledge regarding the impact of family dynamics on adolescent drug abuse (Dishion & Kavanagh, 2000). Parents participate because, although their children push them away in their quest for freedom and self-actualization, they continue to exert a powerful influence on their children. Peers and classmates participate because, during this developmental period, teens increasingly turn to friends for information and look to them as role models for normative behavior. Teachers also participate because, since most adolescents are in school, they have opportunities to observe them and provide immediate feedback on their behavior.

Ecological Systems Theory posits that behavior is influenced by socioeconomic, environmental, and cultural factors.

The Adolescent Transition Program (ATP) is an example of this type of program. The project was funded by a grant by the National Institute on Drug Abuse and run by the staff and administration of the schools. The program calls for a Family Resource Room that contains a library and counseling offices. ATP provides prevention services and counseling to middle school students, their families, teachers, and classmates. Counseling services are available to students and their families in the school and in home visits. Parents are given access to parenting and family management training, and education regarding drug use and abuse (Dishion & Kavanagh, 2000). These services are available throughout the school year, with home visits during the summer.

Another example of a school-centered multimodal approach is the SHAPe Curriculum (Success, Health, and Peace), a 6-week health education training during which students are given homework assignments to complete with their parents. The goals of these assignments are to improve the parent and child relationship, increase school success, healthy choices, self advocacy, self respect, emotional maturity, and peaceful problem solving skills (Dishion & Kavanagh, 2000). Weekly newsletters and programs on public access television provide additional information.

SUBSTANCE ABUSE PREVENTION OUTCOMES

Determining the effectiveness of prevention programs is difficult because the successful ones either reduce or keep something from happening. It is much easier to measure what happens, rather than what doesn't happen. Further, in the rush to reduce the terrible impact of substance abuse, many programs are instituted without valid evaluation measures in place, or that lack evaluation as part of the design. For example, many are implemented without constructing a comparison/control group.

With this in mind, there is evidence to show that school-based programs are effective in preventing some students from experimentation and drug use. The effective programs have several components in common. They include social-skills training, parental involvement, peers as educators and mediators, and partnerships with community members (Goldberg, 2006).

Prevention programs that attempt to solve the global problems of addictions by focusing on single factors or by teaching a few specific skills are ineffective. Single-episode exposure methods, such as 20 minutes of drug education regarding the health risks of tobacco, increased students' knowledge regarding the health risks of drug use, but failed to deter students from experimenting with drugs (Tobler, 1996).

For most participants in prevention programs, several methods with a series of contacts over time are required. Because many factors result in drug abuse, effective prevention programs must first identify the risk factors, decide who will participate in the program, and create a multimodal approach with several contacts over time. The process should address the most important factors associated with addiction because they work together to transition people from sobriety to addiction (Ellickson & Morton, 1999; Hawkins et al., 2002).

Shin (2001) reviewed effective programs and discovered five essential components: (1) adequate contact hours in the program, with exposure lasting at least 3 years; (2) the involvement of peers; (3) an emphasis on refusal skills, social skills, and decision making skills; (4) changes in students' expectations and definitions of "normal behavior"; and (5) cooperation and involvement of parents, peers, and community members.

Five essential components of effective prevention programs are: (1) contact hours; (2) peers; (3) skills; (4) change in "normal behavior"; and (5) cooperative involvement. Effective intervention programs are valuable because the later the onset of substance abuse, the later people begin using substances, the less time they use, and the less amounts they use, and the greater the impact on prevention of serious and pervasive negative consequences.

It is essential that outcome data be used for evaluation of program effectiveness because some programs have been found to increase rather than decrease targeted behaviors. For example, programs that attempt to normalize drug use so that students will be more open about discussing their problems, may result in increased use by increasing participants' belief that "everyone is doing it." Programs utilizing scare tactics may have the opposite effect by inadvertently piquing the interest of thrill seekers (Carter, Stewart, Dunn, & Fairburn, 1997).

Skara and Sussman (2003) performed a meta-analysis of the long-term results of 25 adolescent substance abuse prevention programs. Analysis of this data was difficult because the programs vary widely from each other. For example, the programs ranged from 5 sessions to 384 sessions over 3 months to 3 years. Most studies indicated that the treatment programs were effective in preventing some participants from smoking cigarettes. These effects (9% to 14% reduction rate) lasted up to 15 years in some cases. Out of nine programs that assessed use of alcohol and marijuana, the five that had booster sessions the next year or two following initial training had a positive long-term impact on the participants. These studies showed that approximately 71% of the participants used less alcohol than the control group, findings which indicate that comprehensive programs with more intervention sessions, as well as booster follow-up sessions, had greater long-term impact on the substance use reduction. None of these programs are as effective as inoculations against addictions. However, given the dire consequences from the experimentation, use, and abuse of tobacco, alcohol, and other intoxicating substances, any delay or reduction in use is worth the effort. This is because the earlier people begin using substances, the longer they use, and the larger amounts they use, the more serious and pervasive the negative consequences (Skara & Sussman, 2003).

Summary and Some Final Notations

Abuse of tobacco, alcohol, and other substances are a major public health hazard, contributing to crime (CASA, 2004) poverty, child abuse, neglect (The Executive Office of the President, 2001), mental and physical disability, and premature death (NCCDPHP, 2002; Volkow & Li, 2005; Wuetrich, 2001). Most people who abuse substances began as children or adolescents. The rate of substance abuse among children, adolescents, and young adults has risen to epidemic proportions. In response to this public health nightmare, educators, lawmakers, and public health and mental health professionals rushed to develop prevention programs. Most were initiated without the inclusion of an evaluation component. Some promised miraculous results which could not be realized. Some of these programs target the most vulnerable youth (Callas, Flynn, & Worden, 2004), others are inclusive of individuals and their families.

Many different types of abuse prevention programs exist (Biederman et al., 2000; CASA, 2007; Dishion & Kavanagh, 2000; Hser et al., 2003; Marlatt & Witkiewitz, 2002; National Center on Addiction and Substance Abuse at Columbia University, 2004). Some focus on educating people about the risks of drug abuse; others train participants to refuse peer pressure to experiment with substances; still others use a multimodal approach training parents (to improve communication and behavior management), school personnel, peers, and students (to improve refusal skills, self-esteem, problem-solving skills, and stress reduction). The programs demonstrating the greatest impact are multimodal in their approach, working with the student, family, school/institution of higher education, and community. Some of these multimodal programs demonstrated lasting results during 15 years of follow-up study (Skara & Sussman, 2003). Given the severity and lifelong negative consequences of substance use, any positive outcome from these prevention programs is welcomed. However, more rigorous research is needed to develop prevention programs that are most effective and efficient in delivery of their information with the greatest outcomes.

Useful Web Sites

The following Web sites provide additional information relating to the chapter topics:

American College Counseling Association
http://www.collegecounseling.org/

American Counseling Association
http://www.counseling.org/

American Psychological Association
http://www.apa.org/topics/topicaddict.html

American School Counseling Association
http://www.schoolcounselor.org/

Drug Abuse Prevention Program
http://www.drugfree.org/Parent/Resources/resources.aspx?
  ResourceType= Pamphlets&gclid= CLiH5OTN94sNIgod
  XsgXg

Drug Prevention Media Campaign
http://www.mediaprograms.samhsa.gov/

Effective Drug Prevention Programs for Every Community
http://modelprograms.samhsa.gov

NIDA for Teens
http://www.backtoschool.drugabuse.gov/

Preventing Drug Abuse Among Children and Adolescents
http://www.drugabuse.gov/prevention/examples.html

SAMHSA's Center for Substance Abuse Prevention
http://prevention.samhsa.gov

Steroid Prevention Program Scores with High School Athletes
http://www.nida.nih.gov?NIDA_Notes/NNVol12N4/
  steroid.html

Stopping Tobacco Sales to Minors
http://prevention.samhsa.gov/tobacco/default.gov/

Stop Underage Drinking
http://www.stopalcoholabuse.gov/

References

Arthur, M., & Blitz, C. (2000). Bridging the gap between science and practice in drug abuse prevention through needs assessment and strategic community planning. *Journal of Community Psychology, 28*(3), 241–255.

Biederman, J., Faraone, S., Wozniak, J., & Monteaux, M. (2000). Parsing the association between bipolar, conduct, and substance use disorders: A familial risk analysis. *Biological Psychiatry, 48*, 1037–1044.

Birkeland, S., Murphy-Graham, E., & Weiss, C. (2005). Good reasons for ignoring good evaluation: The case of the drug abuse resistance education (DARE) program. *Evaluation and Program Planning, 28*, 247–256.

Botvin, G. (2000). Preventing drug abuse in schools: Social and competence enhanced approaches targeting individual-level etiological factors. *Addictive Behaviors, 25*(6), 887–897.

Botvin, G., Griffin, K., Diaz, T., Scheier, L., Williams, C., & Epstein, J. (2000). Preventing illicit drug use in adolescents: Long-term follow-up data from a randomized control trial of school population. *Addictive Behaviors, 24*(5), 769–774.

Bousman, C., Blumberg, E., Shillington, A., Hovell, M., Lehman, S., & Clapp, J. (2005). Predictors of substance use among homeless youth in San Diego. *Addictive Behaviors, 30*, 1100–1110.

Callas, P., Flynn, B., & Worden, J. (2004). Potentially modifiable psychosocial factors associated with alcohol use during early adolescence. *Addictive Behaviors, 29*, 1503–1515.

Capone, C., Wood, M. D., Borsari, B., & Laird, R. D. (2007). A prospective examination of relations between fraternity/sorority involvement, social influences and alcohol use among college students: Evidence for reciprocal influences. *Psychology of Addictive Behaviors, 21*, 316–327.

Carey, K., Henson, J., Carey, M., & Maisto, S. (2009). Computer versus in-person intervention for students violating campus alcohol policy. *Journal of Consulting and Clinical Psychology, 77*, 1, 74–87.

Carter, J., Stewart, D., Dunn, V., & Fairburn, C. (1997). Primary prevention of eating disorders: Might it do more harm than good? *International Journal of Eating Disorders, 22*, 167–172.

Catalano, R. F., & Hawkins, J. D. (1996). The social development model: A theory of antisocial behavior. In J. D. Hawkins (Ed.), *Delinquency, crime: Current theories* (pp. 149–219). New York: Cambridge University Press.

Centers for Disease Control and Prevention (CDC). (2005). *HIV prevention strategic plan through 2005. Atlanta, GA*: Division of HIV/AIDS Prevention, National Center for HIV, STD, and TB Prevention, Center for Disease Control and Prevention.

Clayton, R., Cattarello, A., Johnstone, B. (1996). The effectiveness of drug resistance education (Project DARE): 5-year follow-up results. *Preventive Medicine, 25,* 307–318.

Compton, W., & Volkow, N. (2006). Major increases in opioid analgesic abuse in the United States: Concerns and strategies. *Drug and Alcohol Dependence, 81*(2), 103–107.

Compton, W., Stein, J., Robertson, E., Pintello, D., Pringle, B., Volkow, N. (2005). Charting a course for health services research at the National Institute on Drug Abuse. *Journal of Substance Abuse Treatment, (29),* 167–172.

Cooper, S. (1999). Changing the campus drinking culture: An initiator—catalyst consultation approach. *Consulting Psychology Journal: Practice and Research, 51,* 3, 160–169.

Dawson, D. A., Grant, B. F., Stinson, F. S., & Chou, P. S. (2004). Another look at heavy episodic drinking and alcohol use disorders among college and noncollege youth. *Journal of Studies on Alcohol, 65,* 477–488.

DeJong, W. (1987). A short term evaluation of project DARE (drug abuse resistance education). *Journal of Drug Education, 17,* 279–294.

Department of Health and Human Services (DHHS). (2004). National Drug Control Strategy. Washington, DC: Government Printing Office.

Dishion, T., & Kavanagh, K. (2000). A multilevel approach to family-centered prevention in schools: Process and outcome. Addictive Behaviors, *25*(6), 899–911.

Dishion, T., Capaldi, D., & Yoerger, K. (1999). Middle childhood antecedents to progression in male adolescent substance use: An ecological analysis of risk protection. *Journal of Adolescent Research, 14,* 175–206.

Dwyer, S., Nicholson, J., Battistutta, D., & Oldenburg, B. (2005). Teacher's knowledge of children's exposure to family risk factors: Accuracy and usefulness. *Journal of School Psychology, 43,* 23–38.

Ellickson, P., & Morton, S. (1999). Identifying adolescents at risk for hard drug use: Racial/ethnic variations. *Journal of Adolescent Health, 25,* 382–395.

Elliot, D., Goldberg, L., Moe, E., DeFrancesco, C., Durham, M., & Hix-Small, H. (2004). Preventing substance use and disordered eating. *Archives of Pediatric Adolescent Medicine, 158,* 1043–1049.

Executive Office of the President: Office of Drug Control Policy. (2001). *Economic costs of drug abuse in the United States 1992–1998.* Washington, D.C.: Author.

Falls-Stewart, W., & Lucente, S. (1994). Treating obsessive-compulsive disorder among substance abusers: A guide. *Psychology of Addictive Behaviors, 8,* 14–23.

Fendrich, M., & Rosenbaum, D. (2003). Recanting of substance use reports in a longitudinal prevention study. *Drug and Alcohol Dependence, 70,* 241–253.

Gallaghar, R. (2009). National Survey of Counseling Center Directors 2009. Retrieved February, 13, 2010 from *http://www.collegecounseling.org/pdf/nsccd_final_v1.pdf*

Gogtay, N., Giedd, J., Lusk, L., Hayashi, K., Greenstein, D., Vaituzis, A., et al. (2004). Dynamic mapping of the human cortical development during childhood through early adulthood. *Proceedings of the National Academy of Science, USA 101*(21), 8174–8179.

Goldberg, R. (2006). Drugs and the law. In *Drugs across the spectrum* (5th ed., pp. 71–89). Belmont, CA: Thompson, Wadsworth.

Goldberg, L., Elliot, D., MacKinnon, D., Moe, E., Kuehl, K., Nohre, L., et al. (2003). Drug testing athletes to prevent substance abuse: Background and pilot study results of the SATURN (Student Athlete Testing Using Random Notification) study. *Journal of Adolescent Health, 32*(16), 116–125.

Golub, A., & Johnson, B. (2002). The misuse of the 'Gateway Theory' in US policy on drug abuse control: A secondary analysis of the muddled deduction. *International Journal of Drug Policy, 13,* 5–19.

Grant, B. F., Dawson, D. A., Stinson, F. S., Chou, S., Dufour, M. C., & Pickering, R. P. (2004). The 12-month prevalence and trends in DSM-IV alcohol abuse and dependence: United States, 1991–1992 and 2001–2002. *Drug & Alcohol Dependence, 74,* 223–234.

Griffin, K., Botvin, G., Nichols, T., & Doyle, M. (2003). Effectiveness of a Universal Drug Abuse Prevention Approach for youth at high risk for substance use initiation. *Preventive Medicine, 36*(1), 1–7.

Harmon, M. (1993). Reducing the risk of drug involvement among early adolescents: An evaluation of drug abuse resistance education (DARE). *Evaluation Review, 17,* 221–239.

Hawkins, J., Catalano, R., & Arthur, M. (2002). Promoting science-based prevention in communities. *Addictive Behaviors, 27,* 951–976.

Hornik, R., Maklan, D., Cadell, D., Barmada, C., Jacobsohn, L. et al. (2003). *Evaluation of the national youth anti-drug media campaign-executive summary.* Rockville, MD: National Institute on Drug Abuse.

Retrieved November 3, 2005, from *http://www.nida.nih.gov/PDF/DESPR/1203ExSummary.PDF*

Hser, Y., Grella, C., Collins, C., & Teruya, C. (2003). Drug-use initiation and conduct disorder among adolescents in drug treatment. *Journal of Adolescence, 26,* 331–345.

James, R., & Gilliland, B. (2001). Off the couch and into the streets. In *Crisis intervention strategies* (4th ed., pp. 649–680). Belmont, CA: Brooks/Cole.

Johnston, L. D., O'Malley, P. M., & Bachman, J. G. (1996). *National survey results on drug use from the Monitoring the Future study, 1975–1995. Volume I: Secondary school students* (NIH Pub. No. 97–4139). Rockville, MD: National Institute on Drug Abuse.

Johnston, L. D., O'Malley, P. M., & Bachman, J. G. (2003). *National survey results on drug use from the Monitoring the Future Study, 1975–2002. Volume I: Secondary school students* (NIH Pub. No. 03–5375). Rockville, MD: National Institute on Drug Abuse.

Johnston, L. D., O'Malley, P. M., Bachman, J. G., & Schulenberg, J. E. (2005). *Monitoring the Future national results on adolescent drug use: Overview of key findings, 2004* (NIH Publication No. 05–5726). Bethesda, MD: National Institute on Drug Abuse.

Kilpatrick, D. G., Acierno, R., Saunders, B., Resnick, H., Best, C., & Schnurr, P. (2000). Risk factors for adolescent substance abuse and dependence: Data from a national sample. *Journal of Consulting and Clinical Psychology, 68,* 19–30.

Knight, J. R., Wechsler, H., Kuo, M., Seibring, M., Weitzman, E. R., & Schuckit, M. A. (2002). Alcohol abuse and dependence among U.S. college students. *Journal of Studies on Alcohol, 63,* 263–270.

Kurtzman, K., Otsuka, K., & Wahl, R. (2001). Inhalant abuse by adolescents. *Journal of Adolescent Health, 28,* 170–180.

Lynam, D., Milich, R., Zimmerman, R., Novak, S., Logan, T., Leukefield, C., et al. (1999). Project DARE: No effects at 10-year follow-up. *Journal of Consulting and Clinical Psychology, 67*(4), 590–593.

Marlatt, G., & Witkiewitz, K. (2002). Harm reduction approaches to alcohol use: Health promotion, prevention, and treatment. *Addictive Behaviors, 27,* 267–287.

Mayo Clinic. (2007). Performance-enhancing drugs and your teen athletes. Retrieved May 2, 2007, from *www.mayoclinic.com/health/perfarmance-enhancing-drugs/sm00045*

McAuliffe, W., Woodworth, R., Zhang, C., & Dunn, R. (2002). Identifying substance abuse treatment gaps in substate areas. *Journal of Substance Abuse Treatment, 23*(3), 199–208.

McCabe, S., Boyd, C., & Teter, C. (2005). Illicit use of opioid analgesics by high school seniors. *Journal of Substance Abuse Treatment, 28,* 225–230.

McCoy, C. B., Lai, S., Metsch, S., Messiah, S., & Zhao, W. (2004). Injection drug use and crack cocaine smoking: Independent and dual risk behaviors for HIV infection. *Annals of Epidemiology, 14*(8), 535–542.

McDonald, C., Roberts, S., & Descheemaeker, N. (2000). Intentions to quit in substance-abusing teens exposed to a tobacco program. *Journal of Substance Abuse Treatment, 18,* 291–308.

Minami, T., Davies, D. R., Tierney, S. C., Bettmann, J., McAward, S., et al. (2009). Preliminary evidence on the effectiveness of psychological treatments delivered at a university counseling center. *Journal of Counseling Psychology, 56,* 2, 309–320.

Morgan, O. (2005). Prevention. In P. Stevens & R. Smith (Eds.), *Substance abuse counseling: Theory and practice* (3rd ed., pp. 314–338). Upper Saddle River, NJ: Pearson, Merrill Prentice Hall.

MSNBC. (2005). Binge drinking reaches deep across America. Retrieved May 4, 2007, from *http://www.msnbc.com/id/7179876/*

National Center on Addiction and Substance Abuse at Columbia University (CASA). (2004). *Criminal neglect: Substance abuse, juvenile justice and the children left behind.* New York: Author.

National Center on Addiction and Substance Abuse at Columbia University (CASA). (2007). *Wasting the Best and the Brightest: Substance Abuse at America's Colleges and Universities.* New York: Author.

National Center for Chronic Disease Prevention and Health Promotion. (2002). *Adolescent and school health: Injury.* Retrieved October 10, 2005, from *http://www.cdc.gov/nccdphp/dash/injury.htm*

National Institute of Justice (NIJ). (2000). *1999 Annual Report on drug use among adult and juvenile arrests. Publication No. NCJ 181426.*

National Institute on Drug Abuse. (2003). Evaluation of the National Youth Anti-drug Media Campaign—Executive summary. Retrieved November 4, 2005, from *http://www.nida.gov/DESPR/Westat/exec_summ.html*

Naylor, A., Gardner, D., & Zaichkowsky, L. (2001). Drug use patterns among high school athletes and non athletes. *Adolescence, 36,* 627–639.

New York Times Knowledge Network. (2003). Early action against teen drug use: Teens as communicators to their peers. Retrieved November 1, 2005, from *www.nytimes.com/learning*

Office of National Drug Control Policy. (2002). *What you need to know about drug testing in schools.* Washington,

DC: Report NO NCJ-195522. *http://www.whitehouse drugpolicy.gov/index.html*

Park, A., Sher, K., Wood, P., & Krull, J. (2009). Dual mechanisms underlying accentuation of risky drinking via fraternity/sorority affiliation: The role of personality, peer norms, and alcohol availability. *Journal of Abnormal Psychology, 118,* 2, 241–255.

Poulin, C., & Nicholson, J. (2005). Should harm minimization as an approach to adolescent substance use be embraced by junior and senior high schools? *International Journal of Drug Policy, 16*(6), 403–414.

Ringwalt, C., Ennett, S., & Holt, K. (1991). An outcome evaluation of Project DARE, (drug abuse resistance education). *Health Education Research, 6,* 327–337.

Rosenbaum, D., & Hanson, G. (1998). Assessing the effects of school based drug education: A six year multilevel analysis of Project DARE. *Journal of Research in Crime and Delinquency, 35*(4), 381–412.

Sales, A. (2004). *Preventing abuse: A guide for school counselors.* Washington, DC: Office of Educational Research and Improvement.

Sanders, M. (2000). Community-based parenting and family support interventions and the prevention of drug abuse. *Addictive Behaviors, 25*(6), 929–942.

Santrock, J. (2009). The science of life-span development. *Life-Span Development* (12th Ed., 38–73). New York: McGraw Hill.

Shin, H. (2001). A review of school-based drug prevention program evaluations in 1990's. *American Journal of Health Education, 32,* 139–147.

Skara, S., & Sussman, S. (2003). A review of 25 long-term adolescent tobacco and other drug use prevention program evaluations. *Preventive Medicine, 37,* 451–474.

Slutske, W. S. (2005). Alcohol use disorders among US college students and their non-college-attending peers. *Archives of General Psychiatry, 62,* 321–327.

Slutske, W. S., Hunt-Carter, E. E., Nabors-Oberg, R. E., Sher, K. J., Bucholz, K. K., Madden, P. A., et al. (2004). Do college students drink more than their non-college-attending peers? Evidence from a population-based longitudinal female twin study. *Journal of Abnormal Psychology, 113,* 530–540.

Substance Abuse and Mental Health Services Administration (SAMHSA). (2004). *Results from 2003 National Survey on Drug Use and Health. (NDSUH Series H-25).* Rockville, MD: Office of Applied Studies, Substance Abuse and Mental Health Services Administration.

Suchman, N., Mayes, L., Conti, J., Slade, A., & Runsaville, B. (2004). Rethinking parenting interventions for drug-dependent mothers: From behavior management to fostering emotional bonds. *Journal of Substance Abuse Treatment, 27*(3), 176–189.

Sung, H., Richter, L., Vaughan, R., Johnson, P., & Thom, B. (2005). Nonmedical use of prescription opioids among teenagers in the United States: Trends and correlates. *Journal of Adolescent Health, 37,* 44–51.

Teplin, L., Abram, K., McClelland, G., Dulcan, M., & Mericle, A. (2002). Psychiatric disorders in youth in juvenile detention. *Archives of General Psychiatry, 59*(12), 1133–1143.

Tobler, N. (1996). Meta-analysis of 143 adolescent drug prevention programs: Quantitative outcome results of program participants compared to a control or comparison group. *Journal of Drug Issues, 16,* 537–567.

Toumbourou, J., Stockwell, T., Neighbor, C., Marlott, G., Sturge, J., & Rehm, J. (2007). Interventions to reduce harm associated with adolescent substance use. *Lancet, 9570,* (369), 1391–1401.

United States Department of Justice, Bureau of Justice Assistance. (1991). *Program brief: An introduction to DARE: Drug Abuse Resistance Education,* 2nd ed. Washington, DC: Bureau of Justice Assistance.

van Wormer, K., & Davis, D. (2003). *Addiction treatment: A strength perspective.* Pacific Grove, CA: Brooks/Cole.

Vaughan, E., Corbin, W., & Fromme, K. (2009). Academic and Social Motives and Drinking Behavior. *Psychology of Addictive Behaviors, 23,* 4, 564–576.

Vermonia School District 47 v. *Acton,* 15 S Ct 2386 (1995).

Volkow, N., & Li, T. (2005). Drugs and alcohol: Treating and preventing abuse, addiction, and their medical consequences. *Pharmacology & Therapeutics, 108,* 3–17.

Wechsler, H., Lee, J., Kuo, M., & Lee, H. (2000). College binge drinking in the 1990s: A continuing problem: Results of the Harvard School of Public Health 1999 College alcohol study. *Journal of American College Health, 48,* 199–210.

World Health Organization (WHO). (2001). *The World Health Organization Report, 2001—Mental Health: New understanding, new hope.* Geneva, Switzerland: Author.

Wuetrich, B. (2001). Getting stupid. *Discover, 22*(3), 56–63.

Wysong, E., & Wright, D. (1995). A decade of DARE: Efficacy politics and drug education. *Sociological Focus, 28*(3), 283–311.

Zeitlin, H. (1999). Psychiatric comorbidity with substance misuse in children and teenagers. *Drug and Alcohol Dependence, 55,* 225–234.

Chapter *17*

Cross-Cultural Counseling: Engaging Ethnic Diversity

Jane E. Rheineck
Northern Illinois University
Vanessa Alleyne
Montclair State University

The substance abuse treatment field has begun more, and increasingly sophisticated, discussions of multicultural issues in recent years. As research into the etiology and consequences of addiction has expanded, so too has understanding of significant differences in use and abuse by, and treatment of chemical dependency for, diverse cultural, racial, and ethnic groups in the United States. This chapter will discuss current perspectives on substance abuse and treatment for people of color, as well as the use of culturally competent practices when providing services.

An examination of who is using drugs and alcohol, becoming addicted, and being treated reveals startling differences among cultural, racial, and ethnic groups. Until recently, little has been written about this in the research and treatment literature. What is more often emphasized in mainstream news media is the active role of non-Whites in illegal sale, distribution, and incarceration for—and addiction to—drugs in the United States, contributing to the development of stereotyped perceptions (Chideya, 1995). Figure 17.1 illustrates the stratification of both illicit drug and alcohol dependence among the different races over the course of the previous month (ages 12 years and up). Clearly, there are disproportionate numbers compared to the overall population of each group. Native Americans have the highest rate of dependence on both illicit drugs (12.6%) and heavy use alcohol (11.6%). Binge drinking for Native Americans was .02% behind Whites. Following Native Americans in illicit drug use are Black/African Americans at 9.5%, Whites at 8.2%, Latinos at 6.6% and Asians at 4.2%. In regards to alcohol binge drinking, Latinos report the highest incident at 17.9% followed by Whites at 16.8%, Native Americans at 16.6%, Blacks/African Americans at 15% and Asians at 10%. Native Americans report the highest incident of heavy use at 11.6 followed by Whites at 7.8%, Latinos at 5.5%, Blacks/African Americans at 4.1% and Asians at 2.6% (SAMHSA, 2007).

WHY DOES CULTURE MATTER IN SUBSTANCE ABUSE TREATMENT?

Contrary to popular belief, substance use and abuse is not an equal opportunity phenomenon. Persons use, abuse, and become addicted to substances in significantly different ways. Research has established that patterns and perceptions of substance use vary widely by gender and cultural group, adversely affecting some groups while largely overlooking others (Beckett et al., 2005; National Institute on Drug Abuse [NIDA], 2003). Differences in cultural norms, practices, and beliefs have been shown to affect rates of use (NIDA, 2003), as well as perceptions about each group. As a result, significantly different consequences of drug and alcohol use exist for persons from each cultural group in this country. Some groups are highlighted more publicly, incarcerated more often, and have less access to sources of

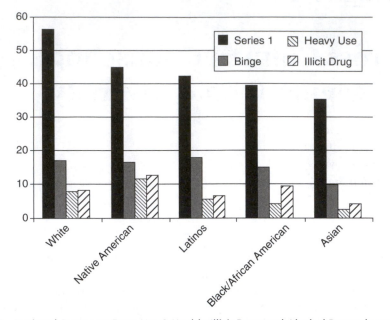

FIGURE 17.1 National Survey on Drug Use & Health: Illicit Drug and Alcohol Dependence in 2006
Source: Substance Abuse and Mental Health Services Administration (2007).

assistance (Beckett et al., 2005; Field et al., 2009). Understanding the reasons behind these differences, and working to erase these disparities is an important thrust of current research activity.

The "drug wars," as they have come to be known in federal policy parlance, are being fought at various levels, and with varying degrees of commitment. Government policy and action on this critical health issue is racially, culturally, and politically driven, and shifts in accord with the beliefs of those who seek election to public office. Interdiction, longer prison sentences, and occasionally treatment are interchangeably discussed and promoted as short-term solutions to this long-term problem that has social and economic, not political, roots.

An examination of who is providing and receiving treatment reveals racial stratification that is reflective of American society as a whole (Marger, 1994). Treatment providers—those who work "in the trenches" of recovery in hospitals, treatment centers, and therapeutic communities—are largely divided along race and class lines. Professional staff members—counselors, social workers, psychologists, psychiatrists, physicians, nurses, treatment center directors—are overwhelmingly White. Paraprofessional staff members, many of whom are recovering addicts, serve as addiction counselors and as intake and aftercare assistants, and are largely non-White. Drug abuse researchers and academicians, reporting on the field's phenomena, are predominantly White.

Each cultural, racial, and ethnic group has its own history, experience, and cultural perspective on the use of alcohol and illicit substances. Because of the breadth and depth of this topic and the importance of understanding the context of each group, we recommend additional sources to provide a more comprehensive understanding of addiction in people of color. This chapter will provide an overview and discuss the substance-related experiences of African

Americans, Latinos, Asian Americans, and Native Americans, and will place that information into the context of substance abuse counseling and treatment today.

DEFINITIONS

This chapter will adhere to definitions of these terms used in the American Counseling Association's Multicultural Counseling Competencies as operationalized (Arredondo et al., 1996; Sue, Arredondo, & McDavis, 1992). In this context, cultural groupings in the United States refer to persons with similar historic and geographic origins as well as racial heritage. The United States, as the reference point for this chapter, is considered a multicultural society consisting of members of five major cultural groups: African/Black, Asian, Caucasian/European, Hispanic/Latino, and Native American or indigenous groups.

As perspectives on these concepts have matured, research in substance abuse has begun to appreciate the need to treat ethnicity, race, and culture as multidimensional constructs. In the past, these concepts have been treated as dichotomous, descriptive categories, which obscure relevant information; e.g., different races exist within an ethnic group, and psychological identification with racial or ethnic groups can vary significantly.

How Did We Get to This Point?

Consistent with other areas of counseling, racial and ethnic issues in substance abuse treatment were largely absent from research and clinical perspectives until the 1970s. Despite significant differences in substance and treatment utilization, neither race nor ethnicity was included in characterizations of substance abusers until the 1970s. Tucker (1985) discussed the negation of these issues, indicating that, "In 1963 the field displayed shockingly little concern for ethnic [racial] issues, and existing work was often embedded in the context of the 'White middle-class' values that characterized social and biomedical science at the time" (p. 1038).

Consistent with the mental health model and major psychological theorists, race and culture, as salient aspects of personality, were largely ignored in the addiction community. Under the nonracial paradigm, it was argued that the emphasis in addiction treatment must single-mindedly focus on sobriety in order to devote full attention to the arduous process of preventing relapse into drug or alcohol abuse.

A passive negation of culture and race in the treatment literature evolved into the use of a colorblind doctrine in clinical practice. Racial and cultural issues, if acknowledged at all, were often seen as diversionary matters, subsumed under the larger issue of staying sober. One of the longest-lasting forms of nonprofessional treatment in the addiction field, the 12-step program of Alcoholics Anonymous, espoused this nonracial paradigm. Under the umbrella of anonymity, demographic and personal characteristics were sublimated to the overarching concern of maintaining another day's sobriety.

Early researchers (Brisbane & Womble, 1985; Gary & Gary, 1985) argued against the colorblind paradigm, citing its ineffectiveness with African American alcoholic clients. Colorblindness, it was believed, worked against the interests of African American clients because it assumed that race and skin color were not relevant aspects of the self brought into treatment.

As awareness of racial, ethnic, and cultural group differences in drug and alcohol use and treatment were documented, culturally sensitive or racially focused treatment issues and outcomes began to infuse the treatment literature (Barr, Farrell, Barnes, & Welte, 1993; Boyd, Blow, & Orgain, 1993; D'Avanzo, 1997; Harris-Offit, 1992; Ja & Aoki, 1993; Rowe & Grills, 1993;

Wallace, 1993). Often the rationale for incorporating race and culture into treatment was based on a growing recognition that members of differing groups entered treatment with distinctly different perspectives due to their sociopolitical status as members of historically denigrated groups in this society. Thus, treatment interventions were developed to recognize and build on cultural differences in order to improve treatment outcomes.

Typically, attempts were made to modify existing treatment approaches by incorporating the belief systems, cultural values, and practices of a particular racial group. For example, Pena and Koss-Chioino (1992) advocated modifying family systems approaches in drug treatment to incorporate the "bicultural" nature of the African American experience, utilizing modifications based on Boyd-Franklin's approach; for example, incorporating the extended kinship networks, spiritual values, and appreciating role flexibility in the African American family (Boyd-Franklin, 2003).

Other approaches have since advocated the development of new treatment models altogether, arguing that existing practices, based on Eurocentric ideas, are incompatible with, or dismissive of, other cultural perspectives (Harris-Offit, 1992; Longshore, Grills, Annon, & Grady, 1998; Rowe & Grills, 1993). African-centered, Muslim-based, Asian- or Native-American-centered cultural perspectives that emphasize acquisition of power (e.g., spiritual, communal, personal) instead of notions of powerlessness espoused in traditional 12-step approaches, have been created. Programs in which emphasis is placed on group and communal healing; interdependence instead of individualized treatment plans; and use of reciprocity and relational respect instead of confrontational, unequal positions between staff and client have been suggested (Rowe & Grills, 1993; Moore, Madison-Colmore, & Moore, 2003).

Unfortunately, consistent with other work in drug treatment at the time, many culturally based treatment approaches have suffered from a lack of empirical support (Hanson, 1985; Heath, 1991; Tucker, 1985). Thus, there does not appear to be consensus regarding whether or not such efforts are more effective than modes that do not consider culture as a treatment variable. Lowery (1998) has argued that successful recovery for Native American substance abusers must encompass cultural teachings that are spiritual, relational, and intergenerational; Washington and Moxley (2001) have successfully integrated prayer into recovery efforts with African American women; while Lewis (2004) applied a Womanist theory approach that proved successful. In addition, culturally specific programs have successfully been implemented for Southern Asian immigrants in New York (Sachs, 1999) and Asian American adolescents in San Francisco (Yuen & Nakano-Matsumoto, 1998). The result has been the creation of a body of work that appears to be relevant and useful for clients, but which needs a stronger research foundation upon which to build (Beauvais, 1998).

TREATMENT NEEDS AND ISSUES FOR PEOPLE OF COLOR

As efforts to diversify and professionalize substance abuse treatment services continue to expand, there is growing recognition of the need to incorporate cultural knowledge into an understanding of all clients, but particularly clients of color. While there are many reasons to broaden our understanding of clients of color, what is known about the efficacy of drug treatment for various cultural, racial, and ethnic groups today is sufficient to suggest that new paradigms are needed. Although Whites are more likely to use drugs and alcohol, racial and ethnic groups are overrepresented in the addiction and treatment population (Adlaf, Smart, & Tan, 1989; Chideya, 1995). Some groups, most notably African Americans, have more alcohol-related problems than Whites (e.g., health, criminality), even though research indicates that African Americans do not drink more than Whites (especially at younger ages), and have a higher proportion of alcohol abstainers (Barr et al., 1993; Lee, Mavis, and Stoffelmayr, 1991). This would suggest that addiction treatment plans for visible racial and ethnic groups ought to be more specific and focused in order to address the increased level of severity of addiction and its related difficulties.

Improving the relationship between clients and counselors is at the core of improving treatment outcomes. Relationship formation is critical to the psychotherapeutic process (Rogers, 1951). Current clinical research concurs with this view, and also contends that racial, cultural, and ethnic issues are not just demographic facts, but are in fact psychological phenomena that influence the therapeutic interaction between client and counselor (Carter, 1995; Constantine & Sue, 2005; Helms, 1990, 1995, 1999; Sue & Sue, 2003). Several clinicians and researchers suggest that, instead of marginalizing or ignoring cultural/race issues in the therapeutic dyad, therapy can and should alter those assumptions by assuming that culture and race is always present and operating in the lives of both client and counselor. Within this paradigm, the emphasis then shifts to building the relationship, rather than addressing racial issues, in order to be culturally sensitive. Cultural, ethnic, and racial issues may or may not be salient for clients, depending on a variety of factors. Assessing for cultural factors should therefore be incorporated into counseling practices in order to determine salience while building the relationship.

DISPARITIES IN USE AND ACCESS TO TREATMENT

Every large cultural group in the United States consists of different racial/ethnic subgroups, each with their own customs and values pertaining to substance use and abuse. The variations within each group are such that generalizations about any specific culture would lead to erroneous beliefs negatively affecting judgment, perception, and action. The following information about substance use and treatment access will present a brief summary of information about persons of color and substance use in this country in order to provide a base of knowledge for the counselor in training.

People of Color

NATIVE AMERICANS AND ALASKAN NATIVES.   As of July 2008, the Native American population was estimated at just over 3 million people (U.S. Census Bureau, 2009). Today nearly two-thirds of Native Americans live away from traditional native communities, also known as reservations (Robbins, 1994). The experience of life on reservations has historically contributed to significant health disparities experienced by many Native Americans. The long-term impact of forced relocations, lack of economic opportunity on many reservations, and family division brought about by the U.S. government's boarding-school policies for Native children (phased out in the mid 1900s) has generated conditions of grinding poverty and limited access to health care. Access to and use of illegal drugs and alcohol is reinforced by these difficult conditions, as well as by the limited availability of prevention and treatment services to stem the tide of use (Szlemko, Wood, & Thurman, 2006).

As of 2008 there were just over 3 million Native American/Alaska natives living in the United States (U.S. Census Bureau, 2009), a figure that has increased tenfold since the beginning of the 20th century. These individuals, representing more than 550 federally recognized tribes including Alaskan Natives, share a common cultural heritage but are extremely diverse in the ethnic and racial manifestations of that culture.

Alcohol, drug, and tobacco usage patterns and related illness and death rates are collectively higher for many Native Americans than for other population groups. In fact, "Native Americans as a group have the highest rates of alcohol-related deaths of all ethnicities in the United States" (Ehlers, 2007). Even so, promising community based interventions have been described in treatment literature in recent years (Szlemko, et al., 2006). Cultural belief systems in many Native American tribes may incorporate values that differ significantly from broader American patterns. The following are some attributes and skills counselors need to be aware of when working with Native Americans (Cliff, 2005; Szlemko et al., 2006).

Attributes:

- Cultural stereotypes and generalizations.
- Chronic, historical trauma that has built up through generations and as a result, distrust of the White, dominant culture.
- Institutional racism; treatment programs often do not meet cultural needs.
- Spiritual differences different from the dominant culture.
- Perspectives on collectivism.
- Views of human interrelatedness with nature.
- Respect for spiritual and elder wisdom that may differ sharply from American values of individualism.
- Emphasis on youth.

Skills:

- Include extended kin for support of identity formation, a sense of belonging and a shared history of survival of the group.
- Integration of spirituality.
- Integrate traditional ceremonial and healing customs.
- Understand communalism and its importance in recovery (Cliff, 2005; Szlemko et al., 2006).

Thus, behavior change for Native Americans confronting substance abuse may emerge more naturally from collaboration, ceremony, and spiritual renewal rather than confrontation, as is often practiced in more traditional substance abuse treatment programs.

What emerges clearly from studies of Native American substance use and treatment patterns is the understanding that, despite the significant impact of substance use among indigenous communities in the United States, a variety of culturally congruent interventions are in place and available for treatment providers to draw upon.

ASIAN AMERICANS/PACIFIC ISLANDERS.   According to the U.S. Census Bureau (2009), the growth rate of Asian/Pacific Islanders was second only to Latinos in growth rate, with a population of just over 14 million in 2008. Information about alcohol and drug abuse by Asian/Pacific Islanders has been fairly sparse until recently, when broader national surveys have been able to capture larger sample sizes. Until that time, Asians were often relegated to the Census category of "other," which contributed to the underreporting of clear information.

The picture that has emerged of Asian/Pacific Islanders today is of significantly different substance use patterns among subgroups. As an entire group, the estimate of illicit drug use is 2.7%, yet the estimate for some Asian subgroups is 6.9%, higher than the average for all persons in the United States (NIDA, 2003).

Persons having origins in the Far East, Southeast Asia, the Indian subcontinent, or Hawaii, Guam, Samoa, or other Pacific Islands constitute the incredibly diverse cultural/racial group known broadly as Asian American/Pacific Islanders. More than 30 Asian and 21 Pacific Islander ethnic groups are included, suggesting that sweeping generalizations about Asian American practices and behaviors have little value. The U.S. Census Bureau (2009) reported over 14 million persons of Asian/Pacific Islanders living in the United States in 2008.

Alcohol consumption patterns among Asian/Pacific Islanders may also be affected by physiological factors. An often-reported finding is that the effects of alcohol ingestion may be felt more strongly and cause facial flushing, nausea, and headache among some Asian subgroups (Luczak, Elvine-Kreis, Shea, Carr, & Wall, 2002; van Wormer & Davis, 2003). This physiological reaction, caused by the absence of aldehyde dehydrogenase, an enzyme needed to metabolize alcohol and safely remove it from the body, is estimated to occur in 47% to 85% of Asians, as opposed to some 3% to 29% of Whites (Chan, 1986).

Religious affiliations of Asian/Pacific Islanders are broad (e.g., Buddhism, Hinduism, Christianity, Muslim), and may incorporate beliefs that restrict or prohibit the use of alcohol or other mind-altering substances (Franklin & Markarian, 2005).

Finally, as with all other cultural groups, acculturation and length of exposure to American cultural patterns can have a significant impact on substance use patterns among Asian/Pacific Islanders. Greater degrees of acculturation are generally associated with increased use of illicit substances in many groups, and Asian/Pacific Islanders are no exception. Some attributes and counseling skills counselors need to be aware of when working with Asian/Pacific Islanders (Hosley, Gensheimer, & Yang, 2003; Shea & Yeh, 2008) include:

Attributes:

- Language barriers.
- The stigma attached to seeking professional help.
- Treatment is a form of acculturation.
- Acculturation in treatment can be coercive.
- Some Asian Americans believe in genetic etiology while others believe in psychosocial etiology.
- Asian cultures often emphasize family hierarchy, emotional restraint, and avoidance of shame (Zane & Yeh, 2002).
- Eastern philosophical influences may contradict with traditional western approaches; not focusing on personal issues to preserve social harmony (Yeh, 2000).

Skills:

- Initiate outreach and collaboration with ethnic churches and ethnic organizations' health services.
- Provide explanations for symptoms and possible treatment.
- Psychoeducational groups.
- Provide avenues for anonymity (online discussion groups), especially for Asian males, who have more negative attitudes toward treatment (Chang, Yeh, & Krumboltz, 2001).

LATINOS. The Latino population has become the fastest-growing ethnic minority in the United States, increasing from 10% of the population in 2000 to an expected 24% by 2050 (NIDA, 2003). Currently, this group has recently surpassed African Americans to become the largest minority population within the United States (U.S. Census Bureau, 2009).

Although the encompassing term *Latino* is used, it is important to recognize the heterogeneity of this population, distinguishing various subculture heritages such as Cuban, Mexican, Puerto Rican, or other countries from South and Central America.

As with any identified minority group, differences within the group are far more diverse than those between groups. For example, one study conducted by Katz and Ulbrich (as cited in NIDA, 2003) reported no relationship between family structure and drug and alcohol use among Cubans, while persons of Mexican and Puerto Rican descent had more drug and alcohol use in homes headed by women. A previous study by Nielsen (as cited in NIDA, 2003) also indicated that Mexican American men and women may be more likely than their other Latino counterparts to engage in alcohol use.

> Latinos currently account for 46.9 million people in the United States. The NIDA also reported that the Latino population comprises the largest segment of the adolescent population, with a median age of 26.6 years, compared with the overall median age of 35.9 years.

The NIDA also reported that young Latinos had a higher prevalence of drug use (other than alcohol) compared to their non-Latino peers. Mexican American men and women may be more likely than their other Latino counterparts to engage in alcohol use. Delgado (as cited in NIDA, 2003) postulated that "stresses associated with what often are more constrained economic conditions, combined with lower educational attainment, generally a higher degree of drug availability, and the possible impact of racism on self-esteem are believed to make Latinos particularly vulnerable to alcohol and other drug use and associated problems" (p. 12).

Selected attributes of and counseling skills directed to Latino-Americans (Substance Abuse and Mental Health Services Administration, n.d.; Torres-Rivera, Wilbur, Phan, et al., 2004) include:

Attributes:

- Potential language barriers.
- Understand the "power" of the Latino family.
- Substance abuse problems for Latinos are multidimensional and complex (Torres-Rivera, et al., 2004).
- The sociopolitical history of racism and discrimination of the Latino culture.
- Awareness of important survival skills (i.e., distrust of the white culture).
- Most Latinos are social-centric; self-esteem and self-definition are a result of family influence (Arredondo, 1995).
- The hierarchy of gender.

Skills:

- Collaboration with the whole family.
- Group and psychoeducational interventions.
- Avoid helping Latinos adjust to the dominant culture. Rather, investigate the system of values, beliefs, and attitudes of those that are "using."
- Integrate spiritual, cultural, and family values of the client. This may include indigenous healing practices.

- Supportive confrontation.
- Provide explanations for symptoms and possible treatment.
- Encourage honesty and expression of emotion which are highly valued in the Latino culture.

AFRICAN AMERICANS. African Americans, who constitute approximately 39,058,834 of the U.S. population, claim ancestry from Africa and the Caribbean as well as many parts of Central and South America. Persons born and raised in the United States and persons born in South America or the Caribbean before emigrating here share common racial and cultural characteristics but may differ widely in their perspectives on other factors (U.S. Census Bureau, 2009).

The arrival of Africans onto the shores of America stands apart from all other cultural, ethnic, and racial groups who began new lives in this country. While every other group arrived voluntarily, Africans were uprooted and brought to America involuntarily as slaves. This cultural upheaval has had profound sociocultural, economic, and psychological effects on the experience of African Americans ever since, resulting in traumatic cultural losses and significant disparities in access to education, employment, health care, and financial services. The racism inherent in the practice of slavery has, hundreds of years later, continued to subtly shape policies and practices while limiting access to the ladder of success.

As of 2008 there were over 39 million African Americans living in the United States Rates of poverty, family dissolution, unemployment, incarceration, ill health, and shortened life span are much greater for African Americans than their White counterparts (U.S. Department of Health and Human Services [DHHS], 2001). Substance use and abuse among African Americans must be considered within this historical and contemporary context.

Today, substance use in African American communities continues to contribute to disproportionate rates of violence and health difficulties (Luchansky et al., 2006). An additional contextual factor is the extent to which African American urban communities are targeted for liquor and tobacco advertising. The private sector has contributed to alcohol and tobacco addiction in many non-White communities of this country. These companies and their advertisers have historically targeted African American and Latino communities, boldly seeking to encourage and promote the use of liquor and tobacco. Visits to any urban community of visible racial/ethnic group members will reveal billboards; bodega advertisements; sponsorship of community events; free lighters, T-shirts, and caps; and financial and other donations to neighborhood initiatives, all provided by alcohol and tobacco companies. These same items are simply not found in middle- and upper-middle-class White neighborhoods. The public health community's promotional efforts, drawn from the one-third of the federal drug budget directed toward prevention and treatment, are no match for the millions of dollars annually poured into these neighborhoods in an effort to encourage use and addiction (Alaniz, 1998; Yancey et al., 2009).

Selected attributes and counseling skills to be aware of within the African-American community (Lewis, 2004; Roberts, Jackson, and Carlton-LaNey, 2000) include:

Attributes:

- Awareness of the racist historical background that still shapes policy today.
- Negative experiences with society (white dominant culture) have made African Americans resistant to treatment that is typically provided by the dominant culture (U.S. Department of Health and Human Services, 2001).

- May have different beliefs, attitudes, and behaviors toward health (Campbell & Alexander, 2002).
- May have more external stressors that impede treatment (socioeconomic status, family influences).
- Disproportionate rates of poverty, family dissolution, unemployment, incarceration, ill health, and shortened life span.
- African American women are more affected by negative images of themselves (compared to other racial groups) and tend to internalize these images (hooks, 1984; Taylor, 1999).
- Communally based; therefore, look to community or religious leaders when seeking help.

Skills:

- For African American women in particular, integrating the impact of race, gender, and sexual orientation (Womanist/Feminist theory) and how these factors can create material consequences in the lives of African American women (Collins, 2000).
- Life-skills training.
- Integrating religion and/or spirituality.
- Fellowship; family, friends, religious leaders.
- Having treatment programs with counselors and staff of color.
- Provide an ethic of caring; the sharing of one's (counselor) own experiences. In particular, counselors who have had their own success in recovery (Collins, 2000).

THEORETICAL FRAMEWORKS

Racial and Cultural Identity Models

Theories of racial identity development (Cross, 1971, 1978; Helms, 1990) have been in existence for approximately the last 30 years. Racial and cultural identity theories view race as a psychological, not demographic, variable, which exists in a race-based culture. Like ego identity, racial identity formation is also seen as a dynamic, lifelong developmental process of racial self-actualization (Thompson & Carter, 1997). Rather than accounting for behavior on the basis of sweeping, racially based group generalizations, racial identity theories view race as a within-group variable, thereby allowing for the examination of an individuals' identification with his or her racial group. For people of color, the development of racial identity involves a transformative process that reflects attitudes and behaviors of internalized racism. For Whites, the process involves recognition and psychic movement away from identification with racism at individual, institutional, and cultural levels (Helms, 1995).

In its earlier conception (Cross, 1971, 1978) racial identity was seen as a staged developmental process of psychological movement from less developed to healthier stages of identification with and internalization of one's racial group membership. Helms (1990) has since described each stage as representing a "worldview," through which racial information about self, other, and institutions is organized. The theory views racial identity as an aspect of ego status, and includes thoughts, feelings, and behaviors exhibited toward oneself as a member of a racial group, as well as toward other groups. Such a view includes specific cognitive, affective, and behavioral expressions organized into schemata, which govern one's outlook and interaction with others.

Helm's Racial Identity (1984, 1986, 1990)

Pre-encounter: identification with Whites is a source of approval.
Encounter: recognition of one's ability to attain success in White society.
Immersion-Emersion: To immerse oneself in all aspects of learning about African-American culture.
Internalization: When aspects of Black identity are merged; individuals feel comfortable with their own race and also respect and interact comfortably with Whites.

Racial identity theory has been empirically investigated in numerous studies that have identified relationships between racial identity status and affective, personality, and counseling variables (Austin, Carter, & Vaux, 1990; Goodstein & Ponterotto, 1997; Martin & Nagayama Hall, 1992; Munford, 1994; Nghe & Mahalik, 2001; Parham and Helms, 1985a, 1985b; Pyant & Yanico, 1991; Richardson & Helms, 1994). Studies of Black racial identity development and its relationship to other aspects of psychological functioning have identified several consistent findings in college and employment settings. To date, racial identity theory has had more limited use in clinical settings. Pena, Bland, Shervington, Rice, and Foulks (2000) conducted a factor analytic study of the use of the Black racial identity attitude scale with a sample of 294 African American men in treatment for cocaine dependence. This study, utilizing a four-factor solution, provided structural validity for the use of this instrument in this sample of substance abusers. More recently, Alleyne (2004), in her study of treatment motivation and racial identity in African Americans seeking substance abuse treatment, found that racial identity statuses were related to type of treatment motivation and treatment retention. Persons with internalized racial identity were more likely to feel confident about their choice of substance abuse treatment, and were engaged in treatment for longer periods. Externally motivated persons who were immersed in their racial identity tended to leave treatment earlier than other groups.

Association of Multicultural Counseling and Development (AMCD) Multicultural Counseling Competencies

In working with people of color, it is imperative to understand that all people are culture bound and that effective counseling must reflect the client's culture (Torres-Rivera, Wilbur, Phan, Maddux, & Roberts-Wilbur, 2004; Torres-Rivera, Wilbur, & Roberts-Wilbur, 1998). The Multicultural Counseling Competencies (MCC) provides such a framework for best practices when working with people of color. The MCC consists of three domains: (a) Counselor Awareness of Own Cultural Values and Biases, (b) Counselor Awareness of Client's Worldview, and (c) Culturally Appropriate Intervention Strategies. Within each domain, there are three sub-skills: (a) Beliefs and Attitudes, (b) Knowledge, and (c) Skills (Arredondo, Toporek, Brown, Jones, Locke, & Sanchez, et al., 1996). This framework is comprehensive and provides appropriate structure to work with various clients in substance abuse counseling. The following will focus on the three domains and their application in treatment of people of color.

COUNSELOR AWARENESS OF OWN CULTURAL VALUES AND BIASES.   Effective counseling with people of color mandates that counselors develop the specific awareness, knowledge, and skills associated with a particular racial or ethnic minority, but also requires awareness of one's own cultural attitudes and beliefs. In a study conducted by Hoare, as cited in Baruth and

Manning (1999), "a well grounded, mature psychosocial identity is necessary for the acceptance of culturally different persons and clients who may have different perceptions of reality. Identity is a complex and multifaceted entity which can be perceived in terms of culture, development, and gender, and directly influences how counselors perceive situations, as well as their counseling effectiveness" (p. 30). In addition, counselors who increase their multicultural competence will better understand how their own personal dimensions affect their perception and understanding of the personal dimension of their client, which will translate to culturally appropriate treatment (Arredondo et al., 1996). Self-awareness improves the delivery of services, the continuity of treatment, and ultimately the success rate of the culturally diverse client (Richardson & Molinaro, 1996).

Arredondo et al. (1996) identified "counselor awareness of own cultural values and biases" as an important focus in their discussion of the American Counseling Association's Multicultural Competencies. The culturally skilled counselor believes, understands, and integrates their self-awareness as well as awareness of racism, sexism, and poverty. They value individual differences as well as collective cultures, and understand that diversity goes beyond race and ethnicity. Arredondo et al. (1996) identified the following as crucial steps for the competent multicultural counselor to take in regard to awareness of culture and sensitivity to cultural heritage:

- Identify culture(s) to which they belong.
- Identify specific cultural groups from which they derived fundamental culture heritage and significant beliefs and attitudes.
- Recognize the impact of their beliefs on their ability to respect others.
- Identify specific attitudes, beliefs, and values from their own cultural heritage that support behaviors demonstrating respect and valuing.
- Engage in an ongoing process of challenging their beliefs and attitudes that do not support respecting and valuing differences.
- Appreciate and articulate positive aspects of their heritage that provide them with strengths and understanding of differences.
- Recognize the influence of other personal dimensions of identity and their role in self-awareness.

To establish the awareness, knowledge, and skills pertaining to cultures different from one's own, it makes sense that understanding one's self is critical. Sue et al. (1992) stated that counselors must be able to identify their specific cultural group and the beliefs and attitudes derived from it. They must recognize the impact these beliefs, attitudes, and, consequently, assumptions have on their ability to interact, communicate, and ultimately provide interventions to persons who are culturally different. Counselors must actively challenge the beliefs, attitudes, and assumptions that may hinder effective treatment for culturally different clients, but also recognize the culturally specific attributes of self that provide empathy toward and understanding of cultural differences. This emphasis on awareness and individual change promotes effective counseling techniques, interventions, and treatment modalities.

COUNSELOR AWARENESS OF CLIENT'S WORLDVIEW AND CULTURALLY APPROPRIATE INTERVENTION STRATEGIES.   The final two domains of the MCC examine the worldview of the client, and interventions suitable for ethnically diverse clients. Counselors should be aware of their own emotional reactions to a cross-cultural counseling experience and gain knowledge of the particular group or groups they are working with. Going beyond the counseling session in obtaining that knowledge and information is an integral component of multicultural competence, as well as understanding those cultural and institutional barriers that may hinder access to treatment. Finally, culturally competent counselors educate their clients, as well as the community at large, in an attempt to eliminate the biases, prejudices, and discrimination perpetuated in our culture (Arredondo et al., 1996).

Association for Multicultural Counseling and Development (MCC's)

1. Counselor awareness of own cultural values and biases.
2. Counselor awareness of client's worldview.
3. Culturally appropriate intervention strategies.

CASE SCENARIOS

Lawrence

Lawrence is a 46-year-old African American male who has been addicted to cocaine for 16 years. He has supported his drug addiction with crimes including burglary, theft, and pimping. He has two children—Jamar, 19, and DaNelle, 24. He has minimal contact with his children and has been in and out of their lives for the past 15 years. Though he has been involved in 10 different treatment programs (all court mandated), none has been successful. Currently, Lawrence is living with a female associate and has convinced her to engage in prostitution to support their substance abuse addiction. Lawrence has reported for treatment (court mandated). How would you approach treatment using the MCC model?

Jorgé

Jorgé is a 25-year-old Latino male. He is currently a college student; however, his grades have slipped because of his addiction to alcohol and marijuana. He smokes daily and drinks heavily on the weekends. Jorgé has been using since he was 16 years old. His marijuana and alcohol use began as a "rite of passage" to fit in with the older kids in the neighborhood. He has a girlfriend who is currently pregnant with their first child. His substance use has increased since he found out about the pregnancy. Since his family has a strong Latin cultural foundation, he feels he is being pressured to "do the right thing" and marry his girlfriend. His addiction has caused him to lose his employment and he was recently issued his third violation for drinking under the influence. The court has ordered counseling as part of his restitution.

LaDonna

LaDonna is a 20-year-old Native American female. Although she did not grow up on the reservation, her parents participated in and practiced many of the ancient rituals. She has had strong ties to Navajo people through her grandparents and other extended kin. She is the oldest daughter and has four younger siblings. After high school, she went away to college to get a "well-rounded experience." LaDonna was the first in her family to attend college and has become a role model of sorts to her younger siblings as well as many of the other Navajo children. After arriving on campus approximately two years ago, she has had a difficult time adjusting to life away from her family. To "fit in" and make new friends, she began to "party" as soon as she arrived. LaDonna now drinks almost daily and never passes up a "good" party. In fact, she admits that alcohol helps her cope and alleviates the stress and frustration of not knowing what direction to take her life. Her grades over the last year have declined and she's now concerned that her undergraduate grade point average may not be good enough to attend graduate school. LaDonna has come to the university counseling center to help her get life "back on track." Utilizing the MCC, how would you approach your counseling sessions with LaDonna?

Carl

Carl Zhang was born and raised in Beijing, China. He is a 30-year-old single male now living in Atlanta, Georgia. He came to the United States to attend college on the West Coast. He did well in school; earning good grades and becoming involved with the Asian-American community on campus. He had many friends and enjoyed the university culture. He also adopted his "American" name to "fit in." After receiving his graduate degree from the same university, he took a position with a firm in Atlanta (approximately 6 years ago). Since graduating and relocating, Carl has been lonely, reports feeling isolated and like "he just doesn't fit in." He is an only child and feels a tremendous amount of pressure to be successful and to "honor" his family back in Beijing. As a result, he reports that he drinks alcohol to "calm" him. He recently overdosed on prescription medication and alcohol, which prompted him to see a professional counselor. He reports feeling "hopeless," and "out of control" and reluctantly shares with you that he thinks he might be gay. Utilizing the MCC, how would you establish a counseling relationship with Carl?

Table 17.1 will assist you in the decision-making and problem-solving process when working with the four identified multicultural groups. The authors have provided some examples for Lawrence's case. Now go through the cases of Jorgé, LaDonna, and Carl using the MCC model.

TABLE 17.1 Culturally Appropriate Intervention Strategies

Attitudes and Beliefs	Lawrence	Jorgé	LaDonna	Carl
Culturally skilled counselors are aware of their negative and positive reactions toward other racial and ethnic groups that may prove detrimental to the counseling relationship.	What kind of thoughts and emotions come when you realize Lawrence is breaking the law? Has little to no relationship with his children? How do you feel about him "pimping" and encouraging women to prostitute?	What are positive and negative reactions you have toward Jorgé?	What are some positive and negative reactions you have toward LaDonna?	What are some positive and negative reactions you have toward Carl?
Culturally skilled counselors are aware of stereotypes and preconceived notions they may hold toward other racial and ethnic groups.	Do you think that all African Americans are criminals?	What stereotypes do you have about the Latino culture?	Do you have any preconceived notions regarding the Native American population?	Do you hold the "model minority" belief that Asian Americans have been successful, function well, and have few cultural adjustments?

TABLE 17.1 Culturally Appropriate Intervention Strategies

Attitudes and Beliefs	Lawrence	Jorgé	LaDonna	Carl
Knowledge				
Possess specific knowledge and information about the particular group with which they are working. They are aware of life experiences, cultural heritage, and historical background. This particular competency is linked to "minority identity development models."	African Americans have been oppressed and discriminated against since the days of slavery. Overall, African Americans have a lower socioeconomic status than White Americans. At what stage is Lawrence in the Helms Racial Identity model?	What is the historical and cultural background of Latinos? Do you know the differences between Latino subgroups?	How is LaDonna's background different than that of her non-Native American peers? What might be her adjustment issues to college?	What are the attributes of Chinese Americans? Why was Carl's adjustment to college relatively uneventful compared to his relocation to Atlanta?
Culturally skilled counselors understand how race, culture, and ethnicity may affect personality formation, vocational choices, manifestation of psychological disorders, help-seeking behavior, and beliefs in appropriateness or inappropriateness of counseling.	Poverty, illiteracy, lack of education, limited job opportunities, and urban stressors are prevalent in the African American community. African Americans have a high incident of mental health misdiagnosis (Baker & Bell, 1999).	How might Jorgé feel about counseling and why?	How might LaDonna feel about counseling and why?	How might Carl feel about counseling and why?
Culturally skilled counselors understand and have knowledge of the sociopolitical influences that impinge upon the lives of minorities. Immigration issues, poverty, racism, stereotyping, and powerlessness may impact self-esteem and self-concept in the counseling process.	40% of the nation's prison population is African American males (Becker, 2003). African American women in particular struggle with lower self-esteem than any other racial group. Per capita income for African Americans is less than any other group (U.S. Department of Health and Human Services, 2001).	Does Jorgé have immigration issues? What about poverty and racism?	What would you estimate LaDonna's self-esteem to be? What impact does her culture and the transition away from her family have on that?	How might being gay impact his cultural background and beliefs? How does family "pressure" affect his self-esteem? His autonomy?

(Continued)

TABLE 17.1 Culturally Appropriate Intervention Strategies

Attitudes and Beliefs	Lawrence	Jorgé	LaDonna	Carl
Skills				
Culturally skilled counselors should familiarize themselves with relevant research and the latest findings on mental health that affect various ethnic and racial groups. They should actively seek out educational experiences that enrich their knowledge, understanding, and cross-cultural skills for more effective counseling behavior.	Read professional journals and scholarly books. Attend workshops and conferences. Do course work related to the topic. Consult with experts.	Read professional journals and scholarly books. Attend workshops and conferences. Do course work related to the topic. Consult with experts.	Read professional journals and scholarly books. Attend workshops and conferences. Do course work related to the topic. Consult with experts.	Read professional journals and scholarly books. Attend workshops and conferences. Do course work related to the topic. Consult with experts.
Become actively involved with minority individuals outside the counseling setting so that the perspective of minorities is seen as more than an academic helping exercise.	Church, sporting events, community benefits, political functions, social functions.			
Beliefs and Attitudes				
	Respect for religious and/or spiritual beliefs because they affect worldview and psychosocial functioning. Respect for indigenous helping practices. Value bilingualism and do not view another language as an impediment.			
Knowledge				
	Have clear knowledge and understanding of the generic characteristics of counseling and therapy (culture bound, class bound, monolingual) and how they may clash with other cultures. Are aware of institutional barriers that prevent minorities from using mental health services. Have knowledge of potential biases in assessment instruments. Have knowledge of family structures, hierarchies, values, and beliefs from various cultures. Are aware of discriminatory practices at the social service and community level that may affect the psychological welfare of the population being served.			

TABLE 17.1 Culturally Appropriate Intervention Strategies

Attitudes and Beliefs	Lawrence	Jorgé	LaDonna	Carl
Skills				

Engage in verbal and nonverbal helping responses. Counselors should not be tied down to just one modality but should have the ability to modify their approach.

Exercise institutional intervention skills on behalf of their clients.

Seek consultation with traditional healers or religious and spiritual healers.

Interact in the language requested or find appropriate referrals.

Have training and expertise in assessment and understand the cultural limitations and adjust accordingly.

Attend to, as well as work to eliminate, biases, prejudices, and discriminatory contexts in conducting evaluations and providing interventions. Should develop sensitivity to issues of oppression, sexism, heterosexism, elitism, and racism.

Summary and Some Final Notations

The success of intervention with any population is understanding that it is culture-bound. The formula for success begins with culture-appropriate awareness, knowledge and skills, as a result of which trust and rapport (essential components to therapeutic success) will develop. The paradigms for effective and operational counseling will also evolve as the populations we serve change. Counselors must remain open and aware as treatment modalities also grow and change. These paradigms explore domains such as worldviews, cultural values, belief systems, and racial identities. The prerequisite to developing multicultural competencies is counselor self-awareness, and a counselor who understands his or her racial identity can then provide a positive influence on the counseling process and its outcome (Richardson & Molinaro, 1996).

Understanding the developmental process and cultural attributes of specific racial and ethnic minorities (as well as their subgroups) is essential to understanding the treatment needs of these populations. Developmental models such as Helms's Black Racial Identity Model provide structure and assistance for skill development, which can promote effective treatment when working with people of color. As awareness, knowledge, and skills increase, multicultural competencies will also increase. The counselor's own self-awareness of their culture cannot be neglected. It is an important component of the successful treatment equation. Without this self-awareness and understanding of one's own culture, the counseling relationship is incomplete and effective treatment will be elusive.

Useful Web Sites

The following Web sites provide additional information relating to the chapter topics:

Motivational Interviewing–Resources for Clinicians, Researchers, and Trainers
www.motivationalinterviewing.org

The National Center on Addiction and Substance Abuse at Columbia University
www.casacolumbia.org

Boston College, Lynch School of Education
http://www.bc.edu/bc_org/avp/soe/isprc/default.html

Association for Multicultural Counseling and Development
www.amcdaca.org

References

Adlaf, E. M., Smart, R. G., & Tan, S. H. (1989). Ethnicity and drug use: A critical look. *International Journal of the Addictions, 24*(1), 1–18.

Alaniz, M. (1998). Alcohol availability and targeted advertising in racial/ethnic minority communities. *Alcohol Health & Research World, 22*(4), 286–289. Retrieved June 6, 2007, from PsychInfo database.

Alleyne, V. (2004). The relationship between Black racial identity, motivation, and retention in substance abuse treatment. Dissertation Abstracts International: Section B: *Sciences and Engineering, 64*(10-B), 5204.

Arredondo, P. (1995). MTC theory and Latina(o)-American population. In D. W. Sue, A. E. Ivey, & P. B. Pedersen (Eds.), *A theory of multicultural counseling and therapy* (pp. 217–235). Pacific Grove, CA: Brooks/Cole.

Arredondo, P., Toporek, R., Brown, S. P., Jones, J., Locke, D. C., Sanchez, J. et al. (1996). Operationalization of the multicultural counseling competencies. *Journal of Multicultural Counseling and Development, 24*(1), 42–78.

Austin, N. L., Carter, R. T., & Vaux, A. (1990). The role of racial identity in Black students' attitudes toward counseling and counseling centers. *Journal of College Student Development, 31*, 237–244.

Barr, K. E. M., Farrell, M. P., Barnes, G. M., & Welte, J. W. (1993). Race, class and gender differences in substance abuse: Evidence of middle class/underclass polarization among Black males. *Social Problems, 40*(3), 314–326.

Baruth, L. G., & Manning, M. L. (1999). Multicultural counseling and psychotherapy: A lifespan *perspective* (2nd ed.). Upper Saddle River, NJ: Merrill.

Beauvais, F. (1998). American Indians and alcohol. *Alcohol Health Research World, 22*(4), 253–259.

Beckett, K., Nyrop, K., Pfingst, L., & Bowen, M. (2005). Drug use, drug possession arrests, and the question of race: Lessons from Seattle. *Social Problems, 52*(3).

Boyd, C. J., Blow, F., & Orgain, L. S. (1993). Gender differences among African-American substance abusers. *Journal of Psychoactive Drugs, 25*(4), 301–305.

Boyd-Franklin, N. (2003). *Black families in therapy: Understanding the African American experience.* New York: Guilford Press.

Brisbane, F. L., & Womble, M. (1985). Afterthoughts and recommendations. *Alcoholism Treatment Quarterly, 2*(3/4), 249–258.

Campbell, C. I., & Alexander, J. A. (2002). Culturally competent treatment practices and ancillary service use in outpatient substance abuse treatment. *Journal of Substance Abuse Treatment, 11,* 325–337.

Carter, R. T. (1995). *The influence of race and racial identity in psychotherapy.* New York: John Wiley & Sons.

Chan, A. W. (1986). Racial differences in alcohol sensitivity. *Alcohol and Alcoholism, 21*(1), 93–104.

Chang, T., Yeh, C. J., & Krumboltz, J. D. (2001). Processes and outcome evaluation of an online support group for Asian American male college students. *Journal of Counseling Psychology, 48*, 319–329.

Chideya, F. (1995). *Don't believe the hype: Fighting cultural misinformation about African Americans.* New York: Penguin Books.

Cliff, S. (2005). Culturally sensitive substance abuse treatment for Native Americans. Retrieved from *http://www.wellbriety-nci.org/Publications/CulturallySensitive SubAbuseTX.doc.*

Collins, P. H. (2000). *Black feminist thought: Knowledge, consciousness, and the politics of empowerment* (2nd ed.). New York: Routledge.

Constantine, M. G., & Sue, D. W. (2005). *Strategies for building multicultural competence in mental health and educational settings.* Hoboken, NJ: John Wiley & Sons.

Cross, W. E. (1971). The Negro-to-Black conversion experience: Toward a psychology of Black liberation. *Black World, 20*(9), 13–27.

Cross, W. E. (1978). Models of psychological nigrescence: A literature review. *Journal of Black Psychology, 5*(1), 13–31.

D'Avanzo, C. E. (1997). Southeast Asians: Asian-Pacific Americans at risk for substance misuse. *Substance Use and Misuse, 32*(7), 829–848.

Ehlers, C. L. (2007). Variations in ADH and ALDH in southwest California Indians. *Alcohol Research and Health, 30,* 14–17.

Field, C. A., Caetano, R., Harris, T. R., Frankowski, R., & Roudsari, B. (2009). Ethnic differences in drinking outcomes following a brief alcohol intervention in the trauma care setting. *Society for the Study of Addiction, 105,* 62–73. doi: 10.1111/j.1360-0443.2009.02737

Franklin, J., & Markarian, M. (2005). Substance abuse in minority populations. In R. J. Frances, S. I. Miller, & A. H. Mack (Eds.), *Clinical textbook of addictive disorders* (pp. 321–339). New York, NY: The Guilford Press.

Gary, L. E., & Gary, R. B. (1985). Treatment needs of Black alcoholic women. *Alcoholism Treatment Quarterly, 2*(3/4), 97–113.

Goodstein, R., & Ponterotto, J. G. (1997). Racial and ethnic identity: Their relationship and their contribution to self-esteem. *Journal of Black Psychology, 23*(3), 275–292.

Hanson, B. (1985). Drug treatment effectiveness: The case of racial and ethnic minorities in America—Some research questions and proposals. *The International Journal of the Addictions, 20*(1), 99–137.

Harris-Offitt, R. (1992). Cultural factors in the assessment and treatment of African-American addicts: Afrocentric considerations. In B. C. Wallace (Ed.), *The chemically dependent: Phases of treatment and recovery* (pp. 289–297). New York: Brunner/Mazel.

Heath, D. B. (1991). Uses and misuses of the concept of ethnicity in alcohol studies: An essay in deconstruction. *The International Journal of the Addictions, 25*(5A & 6A), 607–628.

Helms, J. E. (1990). *Black and White racial identity: Theory, research, and practice.* New York: Greenwood Press.

Helms, J. E. (1995). An update of Helm's White and people of color racial identity models. In J. G. Ponterotto & J. M. Casas (Eds.), *Handbook of multicultural counseling* (pp. 181–198). Thousand Oaks, CA: Sage.

Helms, J. E. (1999). Another meta-analysis of the White Racial Identity Attitude Scale's Cronbach alphas: Implications for validity. *Measurement & Evaluation in Counseling & Development, 32*(3), 122–137.

Hooks, B. (1984). *Feminist theory: From margin to center.* Boston: South End Press.

Hosley, C. A., Gensheimer, L., & Yang, M. (2003). Building effective working relationships across culturally and ethnically diverse communities. 82 *Child Welfare,* 157–168.

Ja, D. Y., & Aoki, B. (1993). Substance abuse treatment: Cultural barriers in the Asian-American community. *Journal of Psychoactive Drugs, 25*(1), 61–71.

Lee, J. A., Mavis, B. E., & Stoffelmayr, B. E. (1991). A comparison of problems-of-life for Blacks and Whites entering substance abuse treatment programs. *Journal of Psychoactive Drugs, 23*(3), 233–239.

Lewis, L. E. (2004). Culturally appropriate substance abuse treatment for parenting African American women. *Issues in Mental Health Nursing, 25,* 451–472. doi: 10.1080/0161284049443437

Longshore, D. G., Grills, C., Annon, K., & Grady, R. (1998). Promoting recovery from drug abuse: An Africentric intervention. *Journal of Black Studies, 28*(3), 319–333.

Lowery, C. T. (1998). American Indian perspectives on addiction and recovery. *Health and Social Work, 23*(2), 127–135.

Luchansky, B., Nordlund, D., Estes, S., Lund, P., Krupski, A., & Stark, K. (2006). Sustance abuse treatment and criminal justice involvement for SSI recipients: Results from Washington State. *American Journal on Addictions, 15,* 370–379.

Luczak, S. E., Elvine-Kreis, B., Shea, S. H., Carr, L. G., & Wall, T. L. (2002). Genetic risk for alcoholism relates to level of response to alcohol in Asian-American men and women. Journal of Studies in Alcohol, 63, 74–83.

Marger, M. H. (1994). *Race and ethnic relations: American and global perspectives* (3rd ed.). Belmont, CA: Wadsworth Publishing.

Martin, J. K., & Nagayama Hall, G. C. (1992). Thinking black, thinking internal, thinking feminist. *Journal of Counseling Psychology, 39,* 509–514.

Moore, S. E., Madison-Colmore, O., & Moore, J. L. (2003). An Afrocentric approach to substance abuse treatment with adolescent African American males: Two case examples. *The Western Journal of Black Studies, 27*(4), 219–230.

Munford, M. B. (1994). Relationship of gender, self-esteem, social class, and racial identity to depression in Blacks. *Journal of Black Psychology, 20*(2), 157–174.

National Institute of Drug Abuse (NIDA). (2003). *Drug use among racial/ethnic minorities: Revised* (DHHS Publication No. 03-3888). Washington, DC: U.S. Government Printing Office.

Nghe, L. T., & Mahalik, J. R. (2001). Examining racial identity statuses as predictors of psychological defenses in African American college students. *Journal of Counseling Psychology, 48,* 10–16.

Parham, T. A., & Helms, J. E. (1985a). Attitudes of racial identity and self-esteem of Black students: An exploratory investigation. *Journal of College Student Personnel, 26*(2), 143–147.

Parham, T. A., & Helms, J. E. (1985b). Relation of racial identity attitudes to self-actualization and affective states of Black students. *Journal of Counseling Psychology, 32*(3), 431–440.

Pena, J. M., & Koss-Chioino, J. D. (1992). Cultural sensitivity in drug treatment research with African American males. *Drugs & Society, 6,* (1–2), 157–179.

Pena, J. M., Bland, I. J., Shervington, D., Rice, J. C., & Foulks, E. F. (2000). Racial identity and its assessment in a sample of African American men in treatment for cocaine dependence. *American Journal of Drug and Alcohol Abuse, 26,* 97–112.

Pyant, C. T., & Yanico, B. J. (1991). Relationship of racial identity and gender-role attitudes to Black women's psychological well-being. *Journal of Counseling Psychology, 38*(3), 315–322.

Richardson, T. Q., & Helms, J. E. (1994). The relationship of racial identity attitudes of black men to perceptions of "parallel" counseling dyads. *Journal of Counseling and Development, 73*(2), 172–178.

Richardson, T. Q., & Molinaro, K. L. (1996). White counselor self-awareness: A prerequisite for developing multicultural competence. *Journal of Counseling and Development, 74,* 238–242.

Robbins, M. L. (1994). Native American perspective. In J. U. Gordon (Ed.), *Managing multiculturalism in substance abuse services.* Thousand Oaks, CA: Sage Publications.

Roberts, A., Jackson, M., & Carlton-LaNey, I. (2000). Revisting the need for feminism and afrocentric theory when treating African-American female substance abusers. *Journal of Drug Issues, 30*(4), 901–917.

Rogers, C. R. (1951). *Client-centered therapy: Its practice, implications and theory.* Boston: Houghton Mifflin.

Rowe, D., & Grills, C. (1993). African-centered drug treatment: An alternative conceptual paradigm for drug counseling with African-American clients. *Journal of Psychoactive Drugs, 25*(1), 21–33.

Sachs, S. (1999, June 16). Tying drug and alcohol programs to immigrants' backgrounds. *New York Times,* late edition (East Coast), 1–2.

Shea, M., & Yeh, C. J. (2008). Asian American students' cultural values, stigma, and relational self-construal: Correlates of attitudes toward professional help seeking. *Journal of Mental Health Counseling, 30,* 157–172.

Sue, D. W., & Sue, D. (2003). *Counseling the culturally diverse: Theory and practice* (4th ed.). Hoboken, NJ: John Wiley and Sons.

Sue, D. W., Arredondo, P., & McDavis, R. J. (1992). Multicultural counseling and standards: A call to the profession. *Journal of Multicultural Counseling and Development, 20*(2), 64–89.

Szlemko, W. J., Wood, J. W., & Thurman, P. J. (2006). Native Americans and alcohol: Past, present and future. *The Journal of General Psychology, 133*(4), 435–451.

Taylor, J. Y. (1999). Colonizing images and diagnostic labels: Oppresive mechanisms for African American women's health. *Advances in Nursing Science, 21*(3), 32–45.

Thompson, C. E., & Carter, R. T. (Eds.). (1997). *Racial identity theory: Applications to individual, group and organizational interventions.* Mahwah, NJ: Lawrence Erlbaum Associates.

Torres-Rivera, E., Wilbur, M., Phan, L., Maddux, C., & Roberts-Wilbur, J. (2004). Counseling Latinos with substance abuse problems. *Journal of Addictions & Offender Counseling, 25,* (26–42).

Torres-Rivera, E., Wilbur, M. P., & Roberts-Wilbur, J. (1998). The Puerto Rican prison experience: A multicultural understanding of values, beliefs, and attitudes. *Journal of Addictions & Offender Counseling, 18,* 63–77.

Tucker, M. B. (1985). U.S. Ethnic minorities and drug abuse: An assessment of the science and practice. *The International Journal of the Addictions, 20*(6 & 7), 1021–1047.

Substance Abuse and Mental Health Services Administration (SAMHSA)-Department of Health and Human Services, (2007). Retrieved October 31, 2010 from *http://www.oas.samhsa.gov/nsduh/2k7nsduh/2k7results.cfm#2.7*

U.S. Census Bureau. (2009). Retrieved December 28, 2009 from *http://factfinder.census.gov/servlet/QTTable?-ds_name=PEP_2008_EST&-qr_name=PEP_2008_EST _DP1-geo_id=01000US*

U.S. Department of Health and Human Services (2001). *Mental health: Culture, race, & ethnicity—A supplement to mental health: A report of the Surgeon General.* Rockville, MD: U.S. Department of Health and Human Services, Substance Abuse and Mental Health Services Administration, Center for Mental Health Services.

van Wormer, K., & Davis, D. (2003). *Addiction treatment: A strengths perspective.* Pacific Grove, CA: Brooks/Cole.

Wallace, B. C. (1993). Cross cultural counseling with the chemically dependent: Preparing for service delivery within our culture of violence. *Journal of Psychoactive Drugs, 24*(3), 9–20.

Washington, O. G. M., & Moxley, D. P. (2001). The use of prayer in group work with African American women recovering from chemical dependency. *Families and Society, 82,* 49–59.

Yancey, A. K., Cole, B. L., Brown, R., Williams, J. D., Hillier, A., Kline, R. S., Ashe, M., Grier, S. A., Backman, D., & McCarthy, W. J. (2009). A cross-sectional prevalence study of ethnically targeted and general audience outdoor obesity-related advertising. *The Milbank Quarterly, 87,* 155–184.

Yeh, C. J. (2000). Depathologizing Asian-American perspectives of health and healing. *Asian American and Pacific Islander Journal of Health, 8,* 138–149.

Yuen, F., & Nakano-Matsumoto, N. (1998). Effective substance abuse treatment for Asian American adolescents. *Early Child Development and Care, 147,* 43–54.

Zane, N., & Yeh, M. (2002). Asian American mental health: Assessment theories and methods. In K. Kurasaki, S. Okazaki, & S. Stanley (Eds.). In *The use of culturally-based variables in assessment* (pp. 123–138). Kluwer Academic/Plenum: New York.

Chapter *18*

Gender and Addictions

Cynthia A. Briggs
Winona State University, Walden University

INTRODUCTION

Understanding addiction is no easy task. Addiction confounds, confuses, and challenges the most skilled counselors because it affects women and men, young and old, of all races, ethnicities, and sexual orientations. No one method of treatment has proven effective for all clients. Counseling professionals and counselor educators strive to better understand addicted clients, introducing new therapies and ideas in research and practice. In this chapter, gender influences on addictive behavior and treatment outcomes are examined. First, an historical overview of the complex relationship between gender and addiction is presented. Second, the biological, psychological, and social impacts of alcohol and drug dependence are viewed through a gendered lens. Finally, historical trends and new treatment paradigms are discussed.

The reader will note that more attention is placed on women's issues with regard to addiction. This emphasis is not meant to minimize the experience of men. Rather, because the vast majority of research and theory included all-male samples, women's needs have been largely neglected in the literature. Thus, women's issues are given a bit more attention here to compensate for this gap.

GENDER, ALCOHOL, AND DRUG USE AND ABUSE IN THE UNITED STATES

Women and men throughout history experienced different societal norms and stereotypes with regard to alcohol and drug use. For example, alcohol use in colonial times was "pervasive,"—a part of almost every aspect of daily life—and was consumed by men, women, and children alike (Straussner & Attia, 2002). Alcohol has long been used in the United States as a part of ritual, as a social rite, as medicine, and as a coping mechanism. However, though it was socially acceptable for men to imbibe, the use of alcohol by women began to draw criticism in the 1830s when author Harriet Martineau identified only four reasons why women might drink: cultural oppression, vacuousness, self-medication, and prescribed medication (Straussner & Attia, 2002). Thus, the notion of women as social drinkers was culturally discouraged. Alcohol was seen as a man's means to inebriation, and unladylike for women to consume. Women who became addicted to alcohol were subject to societal distain, imprisonment, and, in extreme cases, sterilization as "treatment" (Straussner & Attia, 2002).

An increase of moral and religious influence in government led to the temperance movement in the late 1800s and early 1900s. The plight of women abused by drunken husbands became a social concern, while women who themselves consumed alcohol continued to be stigmatized, often portrayed as prostitutes (Straussner & Attia, 2002). The moralization of alcohol use became ingrained in societal thinking: women were whores, saints, or helpless victims, depending on the apparent role alcohol played in their lives (NCASA, 2006), while alcoholic men were stereotyped as drunken abusers (Straussner & Attia, 2002). The relationship between gender and alcohol became increasingly complex and difficult to navigate.

To understand the pervasive nature of societal gender norms, try this experiment: close your eyes, and imagine a typical bar scene. Men and women are gathered around the bar, chatting with the bartender, playing pool, talking and laughing in crowded booths. Perhaps there's smoke in the air. Now, imagine a typical man in this scene. Imagine him holding a brown beer bottle, taking a big swig. He orders several shots of whiskey for him and his male friends, and on the count of three they all down the shots together, laughing loudly and following the shots with beer chasers. Our man orders another round for his friends, and they have a noisy toast before again downing whiskey shots followed by more beer.

Imagining this, what feelings come up for you? What perceptions do you have of this group of men? What words would you use to describe them?

Now imagine the exact same scene, except with a group of women downing shots and guzzling beer straight from the bottle. What changes about your perceptions? What words would you (or others) use to define them? Are there any judgments that come up for you? What are they?

The complicated relationship between gender and drinking behaviors continues today. There remain subtle messages about a woman's virtue or a man's masculinity based on drinking behaviors. However, in birth cohorts since World War II, statistics demonstrate a shrinking demographic difference between male and female drinking behaviors (Keyes, Grant, & Hasin, 2007). One disturbing trend in modern times is the emergence of binge drinking as a pastime for young men and women, particularly during the college years. Consuming five to six drinks in rapid succession becomes a competitive act, as women try to "keep up with the boys" by drinking as heavily and rapidly as their male counterparts. This is dangerous practice, as women suffer the negative effects of excessive alcohol use more quickly and severely than men (Briggs & Pepperell, 2009).

Counseling research literature has long considered problem drinking worthy of study. However, only 29 studies on women alcoholics appeared in the English language research literature between 1929 and 1970. Male-only population samples were used, as alcoholism was perceived to be a "man's problem" (Bride, 2001; Greenfield, 2002; Lynch, Roth, & Carroll, 2002). This changed during the 1970s and 1980s, when government and societal attention to problem drinking for women reached a peak, and the number of research studies increased rapidly. In recent years, interest in this subject has waned, replaced by concern about illicit drug use, reflecting government funding preferences (Straussner & Attia, 2002).

The relationship between gender and drug use is similarly complex, driven by cultural impressions and moral thinking. In the 1800s, prescription medications often contained addictive substances including opium, cocaine, or cannabis (Gordon, 2002; Straussner & Attia, 2002). Laudanum, liquid opium dissolved in alcohol, was often prescribed, particularly to women, to treat a variety of vague symptoms (Straussner & Attia, 2002). Ultimately, women were among the primary consumers of opiates and cocaine in the 19th century as these drugs were added to pain medications and remedies specifically targeted toward them (Gordon, 2002). At that time, lawmakers and prophets assumed that the "numberless dope fiends" in the United States were men, laid low by drug use. However, the typical opium addict was a middle-aged, southern, White woman taking medication prescribed by her doctor (Gray, 1998). When women taking prescription medication began displaying signs of addiction, they were often given new medications to help alleviate symptoms (Gordon, 2002). Thus, their addictive problems were minimized or ignored, and men were considered the primary consumers and abusers of illicit drugs.

Into the modern age, men and women continued to use drugs, often in very different ways. For women, drugs of abuse and dependence were more often prescribed (Nelson-Zlupko, Kauffman, & Dore, 1995). In the 1950s, barbiturate abuse became prevalent as these drugs were prescribed for sleep, while amphetamines were prescribed for weight loss. Tranquilizers and sedatives such as Valium were prescribed to women to reduce anxiety (Straussner & Attia, 2002). The use of cocaine increased in the 1980s as women sought its appetite-suppressing effects. The less-expensive derivative, crack cocaine, became prevalent in poorer, African American and Hispanic communities. The social backlash against mothers who used crack cocaine, especially while pregnant, resulted in legal action against many women, rather than treatment (Straussner & Attia, 2002).

Time for another perception check: imagine you're a drug addiction counselor, and a new female client comes to your office. She describes regular crack cocaine use, alcohol use, and abuse of prescription medication. She also smokes marijuana occasionally. What perceptions would you hold of this woman? What assumptions might you make? Now imagine she is a mother, with small children at home while she uses. How does your perception of her change? Are there different or new assumptions you'd make about her?

And finally, if this client was a man, a father, would your assumptions about him be the same or different?

Today, women's use of drugs and alcohol continues to be quite pervasive. Nationwide, it is estimated that 5% of women, about 3 million, abuse illicit drugs. About 4.5 million abuse alcohol, and 3.5 million abuse prescription drugs (Gordon, 2002). Women's abuse of prescription drugs, including pain medication, tranquilizers, and stimulants, is equal to or exceeds that of men (Gordon, 2002; Nelson-Zlupko et al., 1995).

During the past 30 years, alcohol use disorders rose for women: in the early 1980s, surveys showed a lifetime prevalence of 5.17 men experiencing alcohol-use disorders to each woman. By the early 1990s, that gap had closed to 2.45 men to each woman (Greenfield, 2002). Similarly, in the 1950s, the age of initiation to alcohol for adolescent girls and boys aged 10–14 showed a male-to-female ratio of 4:1. In other words, for every girl who took her first drink between the ages of 10 and 14, four boys took their first drinks. By the early 1990s, this ratio was 1:1 (Greenfield, 2002): Girls and boys are now equivalent in their early drinking behaviors. The gender difference in alcohol use behaviors among adults is also shrinking (Keyes, Grant & Hasin, 2007).

However, in the United States, men continue to be the primary consumers and abusers of alcohol and other drugs. The 2008 U.S. National Survey on Drug Use and Health (USNSDUH) determined that 11.5% of men 12 and older had a substance abuse or dependence problem, compared to only 6.4% of women ("Addiction in Women," 2010). Just over 53% of alcohol users are men, compared to only 40% of women (Lynch et al., 2002), and 20% of men abuse alcohol, compared to 7% to 12% of women ("Addiction in Women"). Nationwide, it is estimated that 7.7% of men abuse illicit drugs, compared to 5% of women (Gordon, 2002). Specifically, men are approximately three times more likely than women to report daily marijuana use, while men and women are tied in their use of stimulants such as cocaine or amphetamines. And women are more likely than men to receive prescriptions for opioids, and thus more likely to abuse or become addicted to them ("Addiction in Women"). Men are more likely to have used a psychedelic drug and to have developed an addiction to alcohol or marijuana than women (Gordon, 2002). Also unlike women, men are more likely to abuse illicit (street) drugs, while women tend to abuse licit (prescription or over-the-counter) drugs (Nelson-Zlupko et al., 1995). With regard to nicotine, 35% of men and 23% of women 12 and older reported tobacco use (most often cigarettes) in 2008 ("Addiction in Women"). Men tend to outnumber women in treatment programs, often at a rate of three or four to one (Greenfield, 2002; Veach, Remley, Kippers, & Sorg, 2000).

Clearly, the relationship between gender, alcohol, and drug addiction is complex, affected by moral climate, legal precedence, and gender roles. To more fully understand the experience of addiction, it is necessary to explore addiction from multiple perspectives: biological, psychological, and social. In the following sections, each will be discussed from a gendered perspective.

WOMEN AND ADDICTION

Until recently, the complex experience of addicted women remained largely unexamined from both a scientific and cultural perspective. Though women have long struggled with addiction to drugs and alcohol, the counseling community largely ignored their unique needs and experiences. Scientifically speaking, most research studies on addiction featured all-male samples (Friedman, 2003). Subsequently, most treatment strategies and milieus targeted the needs of men (Cook, Epperson, & Gariti, 2005; Gordon, 2002). The following sections will examine the specific biological, psychological, and social needs of women addicts.

Biological Considerations

Women metabolize alcohol and drugs differently than men. For example, with regard to alcohol, women are intoxicated after consuming only half as much as men, metabolize alcohol differently (Angove & Fothergill, 2003), develop cirrhosis of the liver more quickly, and are at greater risk of death due to alcohol-related violence or accidents (Greenfield, 2002). Also, women begin problem drinking later than men, drink smaller quantities, and are less frequent drinkers. However, the time between onset of problem drinking and physical problems is shorter than that of men (Gordon, 2002; Greenfield, 2002). This phenomenon is commonly referred to as *telescoping* (Parks et al., 2003). Telescoping occurs in part because women's bodies have a higher fat-to-water ratio than men's (Angove & Fothergill, 2003); therefore, alcohol becomes more concentrated in the female system and ethanol becomes concentrated in all body parts, including the liver and brain (Greenfield, 2002). Additionally, alcohol dependence in women increases the risk of death five times (compared to non-alcohol-dependent women) versus three times for alcohol-dependent men (Greenfield, 2002). Alcohol-dependent women are also more susceptible than men to liver damage, heart problems (Angove & Fothergill, 2003; Haseltine, 2000), osteoporosis, cardiovascular disease, and breast cancer (Gordon, 2002).

With regard to drug use, again, women tend to use more heavily and become addicted more quickly than their male counterparts (Nelson-Zlupko et al., 1995). While drug use carries the risk of damage to health for all abusers, there are problems specific to women that are important to consider. These include malnourishment, hypertension, and sexually transmitted diseases, to which women are particularly susceptible (Gordon, 2002). There are also health risks for female substance abusers related to age. For example, younger women are most at risk of accidental death or injury, suicide, and overdose related to their drug use; middle-aged women are more likely to develop breast cancer or osteoporosis; and older women who abuse substances are prone to bone fractures, such as the hip, due to accidents or falls (Gordon, 2002). Additionally, the death rate for female addicts is higher than that of male addicts (Cook et al., 2005).

Hormones appear to play a significant role in the development of addiction for women, particularly with regard to the menstrual cycle. For example, during pre-ovulation, when estrogen is high, addicted women experience stronger effects from stimulants such as cocaine or amphetamines. However, during post-ovulation, when estrogen is lower and progesterone is higher, women addicted to alcohol or nicotine experience enhanced effects from those drugs. Helping women understand the relapse risks related to the menstrual cycle is an important psychoeducational element of addictions counseling (Briggs & Pepperell, 2009; Lynch, Roth, & Carroll, 2002).

Unfortunately, addicted women are more likely to contract sexually transmitted diseases than their male counterparts, especially HIV. Specifically, addicted women are less likely to use condoms during sex, thus increasing their vulnerability to STDs (Dudish & Hatsukami, 1996). Studies on incarcerated, addicted women also show a greater likelihood of sexually risky behaviors and HIV infection (Guyon, Brochu, Parent, & Desjardins, 1999). Women using intravenous drugs are more likely to acquire HIV as well (Lynch et al., 2002), as they are more likely than men to share needles with their partners.

CASE STUDY

Introducing Sandra

Case studies for this chapter are based on the author's experiences as an addictions counselor. Identifying information and names have been altered to protect clients' anonymity.

Sandra is a 33-year-old woman who identifies herself as Caucasian and lesbian. She is court-ordered to treatment after an arrest for possession of crack cocaine. Sandra began using crack about three years ago when she began dating a woman who also used the drug. Sandra reports that "within just a few weeks" her use went from casual to compulsive, and she now feels the drugs "own" her and "make me do terrible things." She is deeply ashamed about her behavior and states that "my parents and God are so disappointed in me."

If you were Sandra's counselor, how would you apply the biological concepts presented in this section to her case? How would you use this information to educate her about the etiology and risks of her drug use?

Psychological Considerations

Psychological problems go hand-in-hand with addiction. In fact, every diagnosis found in the *DSM-IV-TR* is more likely to be found in an addicted woman than in a nonaddicted woman (Gordon, 2002). For example, 78% of men and 86% of women with alcohol dependence also meet the criteria for at least one other psychiatric diagnosis (Sonne, Back, Zuniga, Randall, & Brady, 2003). In particular, addicted women are most likely to suffer from affective disorders such as depression and anxiety. In this regard, women differ from men: specifically, they appear more likely to develop an affective disorder prior to the addiction, while men are more likely to experience the dependency first (Bride, 2001; Gordon, 2002). In general, it appears that individuals who have difficulty "expressing, tolerating, or modulating" strong emotions are more vulnerable to developing addiction disorders (McKechnie & Hill, 2009, p. 109). Often, women begin abusing alcohol or drugs following a traumatic event (Nelson-Zlupko et al., 1995) including childhood sexual abuse (Bride, 2001; McKechnie & Hill, 2009). Thus, alcohol treatment alone may be enough to remit an alcohol-dependent man's affective disorder, while women may require ongoing treatment to alleviate their co-occurring psychiatric condition.

Depression that occurs with alcohol dependence can lead to suicidal ideation. For example, alcoholic women are five times more likely to attempt suicide than nonalcoholic women. In fact, the rate of alcoholic women who die from a suicide attempt is equal to that of alcoholic men who attempt suicide (Gordon, 2002). To understand how significant this is, compare it with the fact that among nonalcoholics, men successfully commit suicide at a rate of four times that of women (National Institute of Mental Health [NIMH], n.d.). Women addicted to crack cocaine also experienced higher rates of suicidal ideation (Dudish & Hatsukami, 1996). "Suicide thoughts, attempts, and completions are highly related to substance abuse, particularly with co-morbid depression. Substance abuse has been related to a greater frequency of suicide attempts, repeat suicide attempts, and more serious ideation" (Wilke, 2004, p. 232).

In addition to affective disorders such as anxiety and suicidality, women experience other gender-specific psychological phenomena with regard to substance abuse. Specifically, they are more likely than men to use drugs to cope with negative moods, to internalize childhood problems, and to self-medicate with drugs or alcohol as a coping mechanism (Haseltine, 2000; Hegamin, Anglin, & Farabee, 2001). Addicted women are also more likely than men to experience sexual dysfunction, bulimia, and low self-esteem (Angove & Fothergill, 2003; Gordon, 2002).

CASE STUDY

Sandra

Sandra experiences intense shame and guilt about her behavior. As a result, she avoids her parents, whom she describes as "loving and supportive." Some days, her depression is debilitating and she struggles to get out of bed. By the weekend, though, her desire for crack overwhelms her, and she finds herself binging with her friends and her girlfriend. She also admits to you that while attending college in her early twenties, she was raped at a party. "I was so drunk, I had no idea what was going on. I should have known better." After the rape she dropped out of college and moved home, lapsing into a long depressive phase. She admits she has suicidal thoughts, and sees few alternatives to "getting out" of this situation.

How would you apply the psychological concepts presented in this section to her case? How would you use this information to educate her about the etiology and risks of her drug use?

Social Considerations

As described in the historical overview that began this chapter, women are affected by social norms around alcohol and drug use. Social factors may influence how women seek treatment for addiction and also affect their likelihood of becoming addicted in the first place. According to Angove and Fothergill, "Society is responsible for pushing some women into chemical solutions" (2003, p. 215). For example, women's development of problem drinking appears inextricably linked to relationships. Women with a family history of alcoholism or drug dependence are at greater risk of becoming dependent themselves (Gordon, 2002; Kaskutas, Zhang, French, & Witbrodt, 2005; Nelson-Zlupko et al., 1995). Also, addicted women experience over-responsibility within their families of origin, experience high levels of familial strife, and are often discouraged from seeking treatment by their family members (Nelson-Zlupko et al., 1995). Women seem more susceptible than men to social pressure to drink or use drugs, and are more likely to have a substance-abusing partner (Gordon, 2002). For example, women heroin addicts are more likely to be introduced to the drug by a male friend, while men are more likely to be introduced to heroin by other men. Also, these women are more likely to buy heroin from their male partners, to support their drug habits with their partners, and to share needles with their partners, than men are with their female partners (Cook et al., 2005; Gordon, 2002).

On a broader cultural level, society tends to judge women's problem drinking and drug use more harshly than men's (Angove & Fothergill, 2003; Haseltine, 2000; Lynch et al., 2002; Kaskutas et al., 2005; Matthews & Lorah, 2005). Thus, women often feel compelled to hide their drinking from family and social supports out of a sense of guilt and shame (Angove & Fothergill, 2003), and may hesitate to seek treatment (Roeloffs, Fink, Unutzer, Tang, & Wells, 2001). Women entering treatment for addiction are less likely than men to have family support, and are more likely to have a lower socioeconomic status, less education, and to be unemployed (Gordon, 2002; Haseltine, 2000; McCance-Katz, Carroll, & Rounsaville, 1999).

Special Considerations for Addicted Women

WOMEN WHO PARENT.   Women have particular concerns with regard to their children, both during and after pregnancy. Pregnant women who abuse alcohol put their babies at risk of developing fetal alcohol syndrome (FAS), the most preventable form of mental retardation. In fact, as many as one third of women who drink six drinks a day or more may give birth to a child with FAS (Gordon, 2002). Children born with this syndrome suffer developmental delays, behavioral problems, and facial and neurological abnormalities (Gordon, 2002). Other birth defects that can occur include heart problems, growth delays, and mental and behavioral abnormalities (March of Dimes, n.d.). Addicted pregnant women might also deliver prematurely, experience vaginal infections, or suffer miscarriages (Nelson-Zlupko et al., 1995).

Women with children might also perceive barriers to addiction treatment. They may be hesitant to enter treatment for fear of retribution or investigation by social services (Gordon, 2002). Addicted women already in the criminal justice system often internalize shame, perceiving themselves as "bad mothers" (Hegamin et al., 2001). For example, women who are single parents and are referred to treatment through the court system may internalize complex feelings of inadequacy if parenting young children. Additionally, they may fear losing their children if they seek treatment for dependence (Greenfield, 2002). In other words, addicted women may perceive the court system and treatment community as punitive rather than restorative.

Finally, for women who are the sole or primary parent, a lack of child care can be a barrier to treatment. Research has shown that women are more likely to be successful in addictions treatment if ancillary services are available to specifically address their social and gender-related needs, such as child care. Unfortunately, most service providers seem to lack the awareness or resources necessary to provide gender-specific care, including services for women with infants and young children (Fendrich, Hubbell, & Lurigio, 2006). In fact, only 41% of U.S. treatment facilities that accept women clients offer special programs or groups for women; of these, only 18% offer child care (Drug and Alcohol Services Information System [DASIS], 2005). Addicted women thus perceive treatment as hostile or unsupportive of their needs, and are unable to receive the care necessary for recovery (Fendrich et al., 2006).

WOMEN, ADDICTION, AND VIOLENCE.   Women suffer unique social consequences for their drinking and drug use behaviors. For example, they may believe that drinking improves sexual performance. In fact, the opposite is true: sexual appetites are generally decreased by alcohol use (Gordon, 2002). The cultural stereotype that women who drink are more likely to have sex may be part of the reason that women are often the victims of sexual assault while under the influence

(Gordon, 2002). Men who are sexually aggressive toward women impaired by substances may justify their attacks by implying that the victim "wanted" to have sex (Gordon, 2002). With regard to physical violence, it appears excessive alcohol use also contributes to women's likelihood of attack, as an intoxicated woman may appear vulnerable to an attacker, or may herself behave aggressively, initiating a violent exchange (Wells et al., 2007).

Increasingly, practitioners and researchers alike are becoming aware of the dangerous intersection of addiction and violence against women. This relationship appears to be bidirectional: women who experience violence are more likely to become addicted, and addicted women are more likely to experience violence (Gordon, 2002; Matthews & Lorah, 2005). The numbers of women addicted to alcohol or drugs who are also victims of violence are shocking: as many as 90% of women with drug abuse and dependence problems report being sexually abused at least once in their lifetime, and 40% to 74% of alcoholic women have been victimized by sexual assault, incest, or rape (Gordon, 2002). Women who were violated during childhood are particularly vulnerable to developing mental health problems, personality disorders, suicidality, and addiction (Schafer, Verthein, Oechsler, Deneke, Riedel-Heller, & Martens, 2009). These numbers are far higher than the general population, where it is estimated that one in six women has been the victim of rape or attempted rape (Rape, Abuse & Incest National Network [RAINN], n.d.).

Women who have experienced the repeated violence of sexual assault appear to be at higher risk for abusing drugs and/or alcohol than their peers (Cook et al., 2005; Gordon, 2002). In addition, they are more likely to develop mental health problems and to have contracted HIV/AIDS than women who have not experienced chronic violence. With regard to childhood abuse, approximately 23% of female alcoholics report a history of childhood sexual abuse, compared to 11% in the general population. Similarly, women who are alcohol or drug dependent are also more likely to be victimized by their partners (Cook et al., 2005; Gordon, 2002).

WOMEN AND TOBACCO USE.   The negative impact of nicotine on the lives of Americans is often eclipsed by our focus on other drug and alcohol dependence. In fact, while about 25,000 Americans die each year from causes related to drug abuse, and about 100,000 die from alcohol-related problems, about 430,000 die each year from tobacco use (Reconsider, n.d.). Though men made up the majority of smokers until World War II, since the 1950s the number of women using nicotine has increased to rates higher than those of men (Gordon, 2002). Also, it appears more difficult for women to stop smoking than it is for men, as cravings are linked to a woman's menstrual cycle, and they receive less partner support for quitting smoking than men (Gordon, 2002).

For all people, smoking increases rates of lung cancer, heart disease, and cancer of the larynx, oral cavity, and esophagus. Specifically for women, smoking increases the likelihood of contracting cancer of the cervix as well as heart disease, especially when paired with an oral contraceptive. With regard to pregnancy, nicotine has been linked to increased rates of spontaneous abortion, perinatal mortality, premature birth, low birth weight, and to behavioral problems in infants (Gordon, 2002).

CASE STUDY

Sandra

Sandra describes her relationship with her crack-cocaine-using girlfriend as "on again, off again." "There is so much drama," she reports to you with a sigh. She describes frequent, verbal arguments that occasionally become physical, followed by tearful apologies and reconciliation. Sandra says she knows this pattern is destructive, and the relationship is hindering her recovery, but can't seem to break away from her girlfriend. "She loves me so much. I worry if I stop using with her, she'll leave me for good."

If you were Sandra's counselor, how would you apply the social concepts presented in this section to her case? How would you use this information to educate her about the etiology and risks of her drug use?

MEN AND ADDICTION

Women are not alone in suffering due to the impact of addiction to drugs or alcohol. Men also experience gender-specific consequences from substance abuse and dependence. In the following section, the biological, psychological, and social impacts of addiction on men are examined.

Biological Considerations

Men continue to be the primary consumers of alcohol and drugs, with the exception of prescription medication (Substance Abuse and Mental Health Services Administration [SAMHSA], 2002; U.S. Department of Health and Human Services [USDHHS], n.d.). Bearing this in mind, it becomes particularly important to understand the physical effects of alcohol and drug abuse on men. In the case of alcohol, while recent studies have shown that light-to-moderate alcohol consumption can benefit heart health, heavy or chronic drinking can lead to increased heart problems for men (Haseltine, 2000), and can also lead to stroke and high blood pressure (USDHHS, n.d.). Men with a family history of alcoholism may be particularly susceptible to developing the disease, as some studies demonstrate a genetic link for alcoholism, particularly for sons of alcoholic fathers (Nelson-Zlupko et al., 1995; Straussner, 1997). Young men aged 18–29, are most at risk for developing alcohol dependence, and young to middle-aged men who drink heavily or develop alcoholism have an elevated chance of mortality compared to their nondrinking counterparts (Banks, Pandiani, Schacht, & Gauvin, 2000). Older men, however, experience a decrease in risk of mortality due to alcohol abuse compared to their younger counterparts, but still elevated compared to their nondrinking peers (Banks et al., 2000).

While many studies explore gender differences in patterns of alcohol abuse, fewer studies closely examine gendered drug abuse and dependence. Though empirical data is limited, some interesting statistics have emerged from research. For example, men are three times more likely to abuse marijuana on a weekly basis than women. Men are also more likely to smoke cigarettes, use non-prescription opiates (particularly heroin), abuse inhalants, and suffer more severe complications from cocaine use than women (Straussner, 1997). Biologically speaking, some studies have shown that aggressive boys, who may have an imbalance of testosterone, are more likely to abuse substances than their nonaggressive peers (Straussner, 1997). Also, men who abuse cocaine are more likely to be diagnosed with attention-deficit/hyperactivity disorder (McCance-Katz et al., 1999).

CASE STUDY

Tom

Tom is a 53-year-old African American heterosexual male. He is court-ordered to treatment following his second Driving While Intoxicated (DWI) charge. As a result, his driver's license has been revoked for one year and his current forms of transportation are city bus and moped. He is currently separated from his second wife. "She left me because of my drinking," he admits, "because she's afraid it's going to kill me." Diagnosed with hypertension, Tom's doctor has advised him to cut down on his drinking if he wants to avoid future heart problems and early mortality. "I've been drinking beer every day since I was 15. What am I supposed to do about it? Plus my buddies tell me alcohol is good for your heart."

If you were Tom's counselor, how would you apply the biological concepts presented in this section to his case? How would you use this information to educate him about the etiology and risks of his drug use?

Psychological Considerations

Psychological needs and reinforcement contribute to addictive behavior for both men and women. However, there are significant gender differences worth exploration. While women often abuse drugs and alcohol for relational reasons or as a result of negative emotions, men tend to abuse drugs and alcohol in an effort to stimulate or suppress feelings (Haseltine, 2000; Hegamin et al., 2001). For example, men might use to get high, to feel more relaxed in social situations, to stimulate emotion, or to experience a feeling of adventure (Haseltine, 2000; Straussner, 1997). Paradoxically, men may also abuse substances to suppress feelings, such as using marijuana or heroin to control feelings of anger or violence (Straussner, 1997). Finally, they may abuse substances, such as alcohol or cocaine, to increase their perception of personal power in their lives (Straussner, 1997; Wade, 1994). Thus, while women use in reaction to emotions (such as depression or anxiety), men use to manipulate emotions: either to heighten positive feelings, or suppress negative ones (McKechnie & Hill, 2009; Wade, 1994).

While addicted women tend to present with affective disorders such as depression, men are more likely to exhibit sociopathology (Haseltine, 2000; Landheim, Bakken, & Vaglum, 2003), engage in criminal behavior (Nelson-Zlupko et al., 1995), and engage in violent behavior (Dudish & Hatsukami, 1996; Hoaken & Pihl, 2000; McKechnie & Hill, 2009) more often than their sober peers. They are also more likely to express overconfidence and rationalization with regard to their addiction treatment (Haseltine, 2000), and to be in denial about the extent of their substance abuse problems (Nelson-Zlupko et al., 1995). Additionally, while women tend to internalize or self-blame for their problems with alcohol and drugs, men tend to externalize, or blame others (Straussner, 1997). All of these factors need to be taken into consideration when counseling addicted men. On a lighter note, addicted men tend to have a more positive outlook on their lives and future potential than addicted women (Nelson-Zlupko et al., 1995).

CASE STUDY

Tom

Tom admits he drinks to feel good. "I just love it. My buddies and I, we sit around the garage, or in the basement, watch football, and down a couple of cases of beer. What am I supposed to do if I stop drinking?" He readily acknowledges that alcohol elevates his mood and makes him feel in control of life. "I guess it came from watching my dad, you know? He was a big guy, a strong guy, and I always wanted to be just like him. He always had a beer in his hand, his whole life . . . he died of a heart attack when he was about my age."

How would you apply the psychological concepts presented in this section to his case? How would you use this information to educate Tom about the etiology and risks of his drug use?

Social Considerations

Socially speaking, men and women abuse and become addicted to substances for different reasons. For example, drug-dependent men are more likely to use alcohol or drugs to socialize, often in bars or other social settings (Nelson-Zlupko et al., 1995) and in conjunction with positive emotional experiences (Gordon, 2002). Thus, men appear to use substances in an effort to create community and to feel connected. Heavy drinking may be considered a way of building camaraderie among men (Straussner, 1997; Wade, 1994). Developmentally speaking, while adolescent girls and boys tend to abuse substances at similar rates through experimentation, young men tend to demonstrate problem drinking and drug use behaviors earlier than young women (Palmer, Young, Hopfer, Corley, Stallings, Crowley, & Hewitt, 2009). Thus what appears "typical" adolescent experimentation for boys ("boys will be boys") may actually be a precursor to dangerous and health-compromising addiction by the early twenties.

Unlike women, men also tend to have social support from their family members once they decide to seek treatment for their substance abuse problems (Nelson-Zlupko et al., 1995). Men also receive more social support from the court system to receive treatment, as they are more likely to be mandated to treatment (Parks et al., 2003). Subsequently, men tended to report more legal problems due to their alcohol use than women (Banks et al., 2000; Brown, Alterman, Rutherford, Cacciola, & Zaballero, 1993).

Like women, men are more likely to be the victims of violent attacks while under the influence of alcohol. Men who are under the influence and who have been drinking heavily may be targeted as vulnerable by an attacking party, or may themselves incite aggression through violent behaviors. The likelihood of physical assault (not sexual) may be more significant for men than women as evidenced by emergency room data on reported injuries (Wells, Thompson, Cherpitel, MacDonald, Marais, & Borges, 2007). However, study results have been mixed.

Finally, men suffering from unemployment experience shame similar to that of addicted mothers, as described in the previous section. Conventional social roles identify men as the primary breadwinner within a family structure. Thus, those who find themselves unemployed may possess a deep-seated sense of guilt and self-loathing as they are unable to financially support their loved ones. These men may turn to drugs and alcohol as a means of suppressing their shameful feelings (Straussner, 1997; Wade, 1994).

CASE STUDY

Tom

Tom's motivation to seek counseling treatment lies both in his desire to regain his license and clear his legal record, and in his hope of saving his marriage. "She stood with me after the first DWI," Tom reports. "She's a good woman. She said she'd take me back if I stop drinking." Tom also states that he has lost his job as a delivery driver because he lost his license. Not having employment has been tough on him, and he has few educational or vocational resources to draw on. "What am I supposed to do? I've got no money, no job, no wife, and no license. What kind of man is that?"

If you were Tom's counselor, how would you apply the social concepts presented in this section to his case? How would you use this information to educate him about the etiology and risks of his drug use?

TREATMENT CONSIDERATIONS

The purpose of this section is to evaluate treatment strategies from the perspective of gender. A brief review of commonly used treatment paradigms is provided. Also, general treatment conditions are identified as effective components of treatment for men and women. Specific treatment concerns, treatment outcomes, and relapse prevention for women and men are reviewed. Finally, case studies and sample treatment interventions are presented.

Treatment Overview and History

Since the 1940s, the Minnesota model of treatment provided the backbone for addictions counseling. Currently about 95% of treatment programs in the United States are based on this model, which incorporates residential treatment with education about the disease model of addiction and attendance at 12-step meetings (Veach et al., 2000). In this age of managed care, inpatient treatment lacks cost effectiveness, so outpatient treatment has become the treatment of choice (Pagliaro & Pagliaro, 2000). However, most treatment centers continue to use the Minnesota model modified for outpatient treatment, paying particular attention to the character and spirituality of clients (Matthews & Lorah, 2005).

Despite the fact that the this model has a long history of use by addictions counselors, it is not necessarily the best treatment for all clients, particularly women. It is important to remember that Caucasian men developed both the Minnesota model and Alcoholics Anonymous (AA) (Matthews & Lorah, 2005). Because these models reflect middle-class, male, Caucasian values, they may fail to take into account the unique needs of women (Matthews & Lorah, 2005).

In this section, treatment qualities that address gender difference will be described. One such quality is the counselor/client relationship: regardless of theoretical orientation, the relationship between counselor and client is the single greatest predictor of treatment success (Fiorentine & Hillhouse, 1999). If clients do not feel empathy from and connection with their counselors, the likelihood that they will leave treatment before completion is high. The same holds true for clients seeking addictions counseling. One way to improve the odds of a successful counseling relationship is to pair clients and counselors on cultural features such as gender (Fiorentine & Hillhouse, 1999). Also, regardless of clients' gender, addictions counselors can increase the odds of client success by:

- Addressing gender issues as integral to the counseling process
- Examining client problems in a societal context
- Acting as an advocate for clients experiencing gender oppression
- Engaging in collaborative counseling
- Facilitating clients' freedom to choose success (Straussner, 1997)

The following sections describe additional gender-specific treatment needs for women and men.

Gender-Specific Treatment Needs: Women

Though the Minnesota model is the current benchmark for addictions treatment, it does not necessarily meet the needs of all clients, particularly women. For example, confrontation, a hallmark of this treatment philosophy, has been shown to be less effective for women clients, who prefer a more collaborative treatment modality (Beckerman & Fontana, 2001). Also, the Minnesota model places clinical focus on individual pathology. Thus, societal conditions such as discrimination, oppression, abuse, and sexism are not taken into account as factors in women clients' battle with addiction (Matthews & Lorah, 2005). Finally, the structure of the Minnesota model is hierarchical and non-mutual. Women may find this type of system alienating, preferring collective models of treatment (Matthews & Lorah, 2005).

Often, treatment centers pair the Minnesota model with 12-step practices. In the 12-step progression, clients are encouraged to acknowledge their personal powerlessness (Cocaine Anonymous, n.d.). Recall that two men began the 12-step movement. Dr. Bob and Bill W. enjoyed privileged lifestyles, and as a result found their personal power and ego kept them from sobriety. For these two men, giving up power facilitated their recovery (Matthews & Lorah, 2005). However, for women, personal power is often in short supply. Thus, the 12 steps may actually further minimize women who are in a position of powerlessness prior to entering treatment (Matthews & Lorah, 2005). In other words, women may perceive the treatment system as perpetuating a culture that is already oppressive.

It appears that the most prevalent treatment modalities in use today are not as effective for women as they are for men. However, as the research literature has focused almost exclusively on men, identifying more effective treatment modalities is difficult. For example, since 1984, only one randomized study has been published in which mixed-gender versus single-sex (female) groups are compared for treatment outcomes and success (Kaskutas et al., 2005). Furthermore, because most addictions studies have been conducted with all-male participants, misperceptions about substance abuse for women flourish: for example, that women are less likely to suffer from alcohol and drug problems, that researching women is significantly more complicated than studying men, and that no gender difference exists for women with alcohol disorders (Greenfield, 2002; Roeloffs et al., 2001).

In reality, women are less frequently studied than men as they experience greater reluctance to seek addiction-specific treatment (Bride, 2001; McCance-Katz et al., 1999). Women are more likely to seek the advice of a physician, counselor, or OB/GYN for substance abuse problems (Greenfield, 2002), perhaps out of shame (Cook et al., 2005). In these settings, they are more likely to be misdiagnosed and less likely to be referred to counseling for treatment (Greenfield, 2002). In a compelling qualitative study, Shaughney (2009) describes a process of "hailing," or repeated calls from concerned others, that ultimately compel an addicted woman into treatment. Hailing might originate from authority figures, friends, family members, co-workers, medical professionals, counselors, or concerned others, and repeated hailing over time may facilitate women's readiness to enter treatment. Shaughney asserts that coming to grips with the term "addict" is not a one-time event, but a progression over time, as addicted women come to internalize addiction as a part of their identity.

Once they are referred to a counselor for addictions treatment, women may experience additional barriers: lack of child care, mistrust of social services, sexism, financial limitations, and cultural stigma around women's addiction, which all play a role in attrition rates for addicted women (Roeloffs et al., 2001; Nelson-Zlupko et al., 1995). Also, low numbers of female addictions counselors means women clients lack role models through the treatment process (Nelson-Zlupko et al., 1995). Finally, women are more likely to present with psychiatric symptoms than men, further complicating the course of counseling treatment (Parks et al., 2003).

In order to attract and retain addicted women clients in treatment, some have suggested offering alternatives to traditional modes of therapy, which often include mixed-gender group treatment. Mixed-gender groups offer the following potential barriers to women: first, male group members tend to dominate the group discussion; second, women are more reluctant to discuss deeply personal issues in a mixed group; and third, women are more likely to acquiesce to the topical preferences of male group members (NeSmith, Wilcoxon, & Satcher, 2000). Also, they may be less likely to discuss aspects of their personal lives, including sex, with men (Kaskutas et al., 2005). It appears that women in a mixed-gender group may comply with societal gender roles rather than feeling empowered to assert their wishes and needs for the group. However, positive outcomes may emerge from mixed-gender groups as well. For example, for many women it may be their first opportunity to relate to men in a healthy, safe environment. Also, being in a mixed-gender group is more realistic with regard to the socialization issues women will face upon leaving the group (NeSmith et al., 2000).

However, women-only groups offer benefits as well. Particularly when working with women who have been sexually abused, or have struggled with an eating disorder, female-only groups provide a safe place for women to attempt recovery (Nelson-Zlupko et al., 1995; NeSmith et al., 2000). Additionally, women who have been sexually or violently assaulted may be reluctant to seek assistance in mixed-gender facilities (Greenfield, 2002) and may experience greater difficulties with relapse and treatment completion (Schafer et al., 2009). Women choosing female-only treatment programs were more likely to have dependent children, identify as lesbian, to have a family history of substance abuse problems, and to have suffered sexual abuse (Greenfield, 2002). One reason women may be more likely to attend a women-only treatment facility or program is that these programs appear more likely to offer ancillary services specifically for them, including case management, child care, and other health services (Fendrich et al., 2006).

CASE STUDIES

Sandra and Tom

Review the case study details for Sandra and Tom. Based on what you've learned in this section about mixed-gender vs. single-gender treatment, which do you feel would be best for Sandra? Why? Which would be best for Tom? Why? Imagine them attending the same addiction treatment group. How would they fare? What obstacles or supports would they offer to one another?

Working with same-sex counselors also appears to be important, as women state a preference for women counselors (Hegamin et al., 2001). Though limited information exists about the efficacy of women-oriented addictions treatment, it does appear that women who might otherwise avoid treatment may feel drawn to a program that is designed for women only (Gordon, 2002; Weisner, 2005) and that some studies demonstrate current treatment modalities (including mixed-gender groups) are less effective for women (Bride, 2001). Regardless of treatment paradigm or gender makeup of treatment groups, counselors should increase their awareness of and sensitivity to women-specific considerations. For example, focusing on overcoming personal disadvantage, understanding oppression, and strength building appears more important for women than for men (Nelson-Zlupko et al., 1995). Other elements of treatment for women should include:

- Addressing complications from incest, sexual assault, or sexual abuse
- Collaborative counseling rather than hierarchy
- Attention to general and reproductive health
- Available child care during treatment
- Parenting classes
- Access to individual counseling
- Access to female counselors (Bride, 2001; Nelson-Zlupko et al., 1995)

Finally, counselors should be open to exploring alternative, cutting edge therapies, including holistic healing methods such as yoga, meditation, and mindfulness training; expressive arts including music or art therapy; and acupuncture as a supplemental treatment. While little empirical research to date exists on the effectiveness of these therapies, they show promise when integrated into a comprehensive counseling program (Briggs & Pepperell, 2009).

Gender-Specific Treatment Needs: Men

Men tend to outnumber women in addictions treatment at a rate of 4:1, to acknowledge problem alcohol use earlier than women; and to benefit more from addictions counseling than women clients (Nelson-Zlupko et al., 1995; Parks et al., 2003). Thus, counselors entering the field of addictions must be ready to meet the needs of male clients. Just as the Minnesota and 12-step models may not meet the complex needs of women, men require special consideration when designing counseling interventions. For example, traditional counseling, which often focuses on expression of feelings, may not be an entirely appropriate intervention for men, particularly in the early stages of treatment (Wade, 1994). As men often use drugs and alcohol to suppress their emotions (Straussner, 1997), they may find it difficult, threatening, or impossible to divulge emotions from the outset of treatment (Straussner, 1997; Wade, 1994). In fact, if men in the early stages of addictions counseling experience pressure to share emotions before they are ready to do so, counselors may find clients' resistance to treatment increasing, making headway difficult (DiClemente, 2003). Instead, interventions such as goal setting, creating lists and contracts, and homework assignments may be more beneficial in drawing men into the counseling process (Wade, 1994). These techniques help men to draw boundaries around the counseling process, making it feel safer for them to eventually delve into deeper emotional issues. Similarly, openly addressing how counseling may seem "unmasculine" to male clients is also important. Men may perceive a loss of manhood as they seek help, and talking about this issue assists them in overcoming their fears (Wade, 1994). One goal of addictions counseling is to assist men in building effective coping and communication skills (Cook et al., 2005).

For both men and women, addictions counseling must address the whole client, as opposed to just the addicted behaviors. For men specifically, focusing early on concrete concerns around employment, health, and family issues acknowledges their needs outside of the addiction. By addressing these issues early on, the counselor demonstrates awareness of the client's needs, and offers evidence that counseling will be effective for the client in the long run (Wade, 1994). Other factors specific to men that may contribute to a positive treatment outcome include:

- Health education
- Anger management skill training
- Social-skills training
- Recreational and leisure opportunity development (Wade, 1994)

Finally, it is important for addictions counselors to be aware that men are more likely than women to be mandated to treatment by the legal system (Parks et al., 2003). As drug laws become increasingly stringent, counselors will increasingly receive clients from this source (Beckerman & Fontana, 2001; Gray, 1998). Court-ordered clients present particular challenges to counseling professionals. It has been demonstrated that court-ordered clients with low socioeconomic status, prior convictions, and a history of heroin use are less likely to succeed in mandated treatment (Rempel et al., 2003). Also, clients mandated to treatment, as opposed to those entering voluntarily, do not possess the same levels of self-motivation to complete treatment. It is thus the responsibility of the counselor to assess clients' strengths and barriers, and to determine their level of motivation for change (DiClemente, 2003).

Treatment for court-ordered clients is worthy of examination also. Most court-ordered treatment occurs in large, heterogeneous groups. Clients of all ages, genders, races, and addictions are combined, and generally group meetings are conducted in a psychoeducational format (Beckerman & Fontana, 2001). In this type of setting, it is easy for individual counseling needs to be overlooked, and for clients to feel lost in the system. Beckerman and Fontana (2001) describe a gender-specific model in which clients were separated into all-male or all-female groups, where individual member needs (as described above) were acknowledged. Group members were offered case management services, free child care during treatment sessions, individual contact with counselors, and support-services needs assessment. Overall, both groups demonstrated greater success in abstaining from alcohol and drugs, as evidenced by urinalysis test results (Beckerman & Fontana, 2001). Thus single-sex groups that focus on gender-specific client needs may benefit both male and female clients.

It is important to note that both men and women suffer from the stereotyped gender roles that pervade U.S. cultural values. With regard to identity development, it was long assumed that men and women developed gender identity in similar ways. Feminist research has determined that while men develop male identity features based on cultural norms such as autonomy and independence, women tend to establish their identities in connection with others, through community. Thus, group counseling may feel like "coming home" for women as it allows them to connect with others in meaningful ways. For men, group counseling may feel threatening or foreign, as they are less acculturated to sharing feelings with others. Counselors must be sensitive to both genders, understanding the cultural supports and barriers that may enhance or hinder progress in treatment (Briggs & Pepperell, 2009; Gilligan, Ward, & Taylor, 1988).

Treatment Outcomes and Relapse Prevention

Gender differences also exist with regard to treatment outcomes. In one study, among patients who completed a 30-day treatment program, women were more likely to relapse than men (Greenfield, 2002). They were also more likely to drop out of outpatient treatment after the first session than men (Greenfield, 2002). Possible predictors for the attrition of women in treatment are history of sexual abuse or physical assault, co-occurring affective disorders such as depression or anxiety, and self-referral, as they are more likely to self-refer to treatment (Greenfield, 2002; Haseltine, 2000; Shäfer et al., 2009), while men are more likely to enter treatment because of family opposition to use or court order (Haseltine, 2000; Parks et al., 2003). With regard to re-entry to treatment following attrition or relapse, men were more likely to return to treatment following pressure from social institutions including place of employment, the criminal justice system, or family, while women were more likely to re-enter at the encouragement of a social worker or counselor (Haseltine, 2000).

Summary and Some Final Notations

Addiction affects women and men very differently. In order to be truly effective, counselors must understand the biological, psychological, and social impact of addiction on all their clients, both male and female. Gender-sensitive treatment is essential to client success.

Useful Web Sites

The following Web sites provide additional information relating to the chapter topics:

March of Dimes

www.marchofdimes.com

The March of Dimes provides information about women, alcohol, and drug use, and pregnancy.

National Institute on Drug Abuse (NIDA)

www.drugabuse.gov/infofacts/treatwomen.html

Infofact sheets, provided by the National Institute on Drug Abuse (NIDA) gives information specific to women's issues.

Office of Applied Studies

http://www.oas.samhsa.gov

SAMHSA, a division of the USDHHS, is the government's primary agency for providing addition information to counseling professionals and the general public. Gender-specific counseling information and research publications can be found here.

Stephanie Covington

http://www.stephaniecovington.com/

Dr. Covington is a pioneer and leader in women's issues and addiction in counseling. Her integrative, holistic treatment approaches epitomize effective gender-sensitive counseling practices. Many books, workshops, and materials available through her site.

U.S. Department of Health and Human Services (USDHHS)

http://womenshealth.gov/

This Web site, supported by the United States Department of Health and Human Services (USDHHS), provides addiction and health information for both men and women.

Women for Sobriety

http://www.womenforsobriety.org/

Women for Sobriety offers a gender-sensitive alternative to the 12-step program for women suffering from addiction. The organization is strength-based, community focused, and positive. Groups are only open to women addicts and alcoholics.

Women, Girls, and Addiction: Celebrating the Feminine in Counseling Treatment and Recovery

http://www.routledge.com/books/Women-Girls-and-Addiction-isbn9780415993524

This landmark text presents a feminist perspective on addiction treatment for women and girls, and explores with depth the developmental, psychological, sociological, and biological components of the addiction process. Holistic and comprehensive treatment options are discussed.

References

Addiction in women. (2010, January). *Harvard Mental Health Letter, 26*(7), 1–3.

Angove, R., & Fothergill, A. (2003). Women and alcohol: Misrepresented and misunderstood. *Journal of Psychiatric and Mental Health Nursing, 10,* 213–219.

Banks, S. M., Pandiani, J. A., Schacht, L. M., & Gauvin, L. M. (2000). Age and mortality among white male problem drinkers. *Addiction, 95,* 1249–1254.

Beckerman, A., & Fontana, L. (2001). Issues of race and gender in court-ordered substance abuse treatment. In J. J. Hennessy & N. J. Pallone (Eds.), *Drug courts in operation: Current research* (pp. 45–61). New York: Haworth Press.

Bride, B. E. (2001). Single-gender treatment of substance abuse: Effect on treatment retention and completion. *Social Work Research, 25,* 223–232.

Briggs, C. A., & Pepperell, J. P. (2009). *Women, girls and addiction: Celebrating the feminine in counseling treatment and recovery.* New York: Routledge.

Brown, L. S., Alterman, A. I., Rutherford, M. J., Cacciola, J. S., & Zaballero, A. R. (1993). Addiction severity index scores of four racial/ethnic and gender groups of methadone maintenance patients. *Journal of Substance Abuse, 5,* 269–279.

Cocaine Anonymous. (n.d.). The twelve steps. Retrieved November 5, 2005, from: *http://www.ca.org/12and12.html*

Cook, L. S., Epperson, L., & Gariti, P. (2005). Determining the need for gender-specific chemical dependence treatment: Assessment of treatment variables. *The American Journal on Addictions, 14,* 328–338.

DiClemente, C. C. (2003). *Addiction and change: How addictions develop and addicted people recover.* New York: The Guilford Press.

Drug and Alcohol Services Information System (DASIS). (2005). Report. Retrieved November 17, 2006, from *http://oas.samhsa.gov/2k6/womenTx/womenTX.htm*

Dudish, S. A., & Hatsukami, D. K. (1996). Gender differences in crack users who are research volunteers. *Drug & Alcohol Treatment, 42,* 55–63.

Fendrich, M., Hubbell, A., & Lurigio, A. J. (2006). Providers' perceptions of gender-specific drug treatment. *Journal of Drug Issues, 36,* 667–686.

Fiorentine, R., & Hillhouse, M. P. (1999). Drug treatment effectiveness and client-counselor empathy: Exploring the effects of gender and ethnic congruency. *Journal of Drug Issues, 29,* 59–74.

Friedman, S. R. (2003). Harm reduction among post-treatment men: Some reflections. *Addiction Research and Theory, 11,* 163–165.

Gilligan, C., Ward, J. V., & Taylor, J. M. (1988). *Mapping the moral domain.* Boston: Harvard University Press.

Gordon, S. M. (2002). *Women & addiction: Gender issues in abuse and treatment* (Report No. CG031857). Wernersville, PA: Caron Foundation. (ERIC Document Reproduction Service No. ED466897)

Gray, M. (1998). *Drug crazy.* New York: Random House, Inc.

Greenfield, S. F. (2002). Women and alcohol use disorders. *Harvard Review of Psychiatry, 10,* 76–85.

Guyon, L., Brochu, S., Parent, I., & Desjardins, L. (1999). At-risk behaviors with regard to HIV and addiction among women in prison. *Women & Health, 29,* 49–66.

Haseltine, F. P. (2000). Gender differences in addiction and recovery. *Journal of Women's Health & Gender-Based Medicine, 9,* 579–583.

Hegamin, A., Anglin, G., & Farabee, D. (2001). Gender differences in the perception of drug user treatment: Assessing drug user treatment for youthful offenders. *Substance Use & Misuse, 36,* 2159–2170.

Hoaken, P. N. S., & Pihl, R. O. (2000). The effects of alcohol intoxication on aggressive responses in men and women. *Alcohol and Alcoholism, 35,* 471–477.

Kaskutas, L. A., Zhang, L., French, M. T., & Witbrodt, J. (2005). Women's programs versus mixed-gender day treatment: Results from a randomized study. *Addiction, 100,* 60–69.

Keyes, K. M., Grant, B. F., & Hasin, D. S. (2007). Evidence for a closing gender gap in alcohol use, abuse, and dependence in the United States population. *Drug and Alcohol Dependence, 93,* 21–29.

Landheim, A. S., Bakken, K., & Vaglum, P. (2003). Gender differences in the prevalence of symptom disorders and personality disorders among poly-substance abusers and pure alcoholics. *European Addiction Research, 9,* 8–17.

Lynch, W. J., Roth, M. E., & Carroll, M. E. (2002). Biological basis of sex differences in drug abuse: Preclinical and clinical studies. *Psychopharmacology, 164,* 121–137.

March of Dimes. (n.d.). *Drinking alcohol during pregnancy.* Retrieved January 8, 2006, from *http://www.marchofdimes.com/professionals/681_1170.asp*

Matthews, C. R., & Lorah, P. (2005). An examination of addiction treatment completion by gender and ethnicity. *Journal of Addictions & Offender Counseling, 25,* 114–125.

McCance-Katz, E. F., Carroll, K. M., & Rounsaville, B. J. (1999). Gender differences in treatment-seeking cocaine abusers: Implications for treatment and prognosis. *The American Journal on Addictions, 8,* 300–311.

McKechnie, J., & Hill, E. M. (2009). Alcoholism in older women religious. *Substance Abuse, 30,* 107–117.

National Institute of Mental Health (NIMH). (n.d.). *In harm's way: Suicide in America.* Retrieved January 15, 2006, from *http://www.nimh.nih.gov/publicat/harmaway.cfm#readNow*

NCASA. (2006). *Women under the influence.* Baltimore, MD: The Johns Hopkins University Press.

Nelson-Zlupko, L., Kauffman, E., & Dore, M. M. (1995). Gender differences in drug addiction and treatment: Implications for social work intervention with substance-abusing women. *Social Work, 40,* 45–54.

NeSmith, C. L., Wilcoxon, S. A., & Satcher, J. F. (2000). Male leadership in an addicted women's group: An empirical approach. *Journal of Addictions & Offender Counseling, 20,* 75–83.

Pagliaro, A. M., & Pagliaro, L. S. (2000). *Substance use among women: A reference and resource guide.* Philadelphia: Brunner/Mazel.

Palmer, R. H. C., Young, S. E., Hopfer, C. J., Corley, R. P., Stallings, M. C., Crowley, T. J., & Hewitt, J. K. (2009). Developmental epidemiology of drug use and abuse in adolescent and young adulthood: Evidence of generalized risk. *Drug and Alcohol Dependence, 102,* 78–87.

Parks, C. A., Hesselbrock, M. N., Hesselbrock, V. M., & Segal, B. (2003). Factors affecting entry into substance abuse treatment: Gender differences among alcohol-dependent Alaska Natives. *Social Work Research, 27,* 151–161.

Rape, Abuse & Incest National Network (RAINN). (n.d.). *Statistics.* Retrieved January 15, 2006, from *http://www.rainn.org/statistics/index.html?PHPSESSID=66c026241c7d0b099bb208a4406a9363*

Reconsider: Forum on Drug Policy. (n.d.). Annual causes of deaths in the U.S. Retrieved November 28, 2005, from *http://www.reconsider.org/issues/public_health/estimated_deaths_.htm*

Rempel, M., Fox-Kralstein, D., Cissner, A., Cohen, R., Labriola, M., Farole, D., et al. (2003). *The New York state adult drug court evaluation: Policies, participants, and impacts.* New York: Center for Court Innovation.

Roeloffs, C. A., Fink, A., Unutzer, J., Tang, L., & Wells, K. B. (2001). Problematic substance use, depressive symptoms, and gender in primary care. *Psychiatric Services, 52,* 1251–1253.

Schäfer, I., Verthein, U., Oechsler, H., Deneke, C., Riedel-Heller, S., & Martens, M. (2009). What are the needs of alcohol dependent patients with a history of sexual violence? A case-register study in a metropolitan region. *Drug and Alcohol Dependence, 105,* 118–125.

Shaughney, A. (2009). Identities under construction: Women hailed as addicts. *Health, 13*(6), 611–628.

Sonne, S. C., Back, S. E., Zuniga, C. D., Randall, C. L., & Brady, K. T. (2003). Gender differences in individuals with comorbid alcohol dependence and post-traumatic stress disorder. *The American Journal on Addictions, 12,* 412–423.

Straussner, S. L. A. (1997). Gender and substance abuse. In S. L. A. Straussner & E. Zelvin (Eds.), *Gender and addictions* (pp. 3–27). Northvale, NJ: Jason Aronson Inc.

Straussner, S. L. A., & Attia, P. R. (2002). Women's addiction and treatment through a historical lens. In S. L. A. Straussner & S. Brown (Eds.), *The handbook of addiction treatment for women* (pp. 3–25). San Francisco: Jossey-Bass.

Substance Abuse and Mental Health Services Administration (SAMHSA). (2002). *Results from the 2001 Household Survey on Drug Abuse.* Retrieved January 8, 2006, from *http://www.oas.samhsa.gov/nhsda/2k1nhsda/vol1/toc.htm#v1*

U.S. Department of Health and Human Services (USDHHS). (n.d.). *Alcohol and drug abuse in men.* Retrieved January 8, 2006, from *http://womenshealth.gov/mens/ men.cfm?page=110&mtitle=alcohol#4*

Veach, L. J., Remley, T. P., Kippers, S. M., & Sorg, J. D. (2000). Retention predictors related to intensive outpatient programs for substance use disorders. *American Journal of Drug & Alcohol Abuse, 26,* 417–428.

Wade, J. C. (1994). Substance abuse: Implications for counseling African American men. *Journal of Mental Health Counseling, 16,* 415–433.

Weisner, C. (2005). Substance misuse: What place for women-only treatment programs? *Addictions, 100,* 7–8.

Wells, S. W., Thompson, J. M., Cherpitel, C., MacDonald, S., Marais, S., & Borges, G. (2007). Gender differences in the relationship between alcohol and violent injury: An analysis of cross-national emergency department data. *Journal of Studies on Alcohol and Drugs, 68,* 824–833.

Wilke, D. J. (2004). Predicting suicide ideation for substance abusers: The role of self-esteem, abstinence, and attendance at 12-step meetings. *Addiction Research and Theory, 12*(3), 231–240.

Chapter 19

Lesbian, Gay, Bisexual, and Transgender Affirmative Addictions Treatment

Anneliese A. Singh
The University of Georgia
Pamela S. Lassiter
The University of North Carolina at Charlotte

Sexual orientation, gender identity, and gender expression are critical issues to consider in addictions counseling. Though closely interrelated constructs, there are some important distinctions of which counselors should be aware. Sexual orientation is typically defined in the counseling literature as one's same-sex attractions. People who have same-sex attractions may self-define as lesbian, gay, bisexual, queer, questioning, or other self-generated labels. Gender identity refers to one's sense of being masculine or feminine (or both), while gender expression refers to how one expresses their gender to others (Singh, Boyd, & Whitman, 2010). "Transgender" is an umbrella term that may include people who identify as transsexual, genderqueer, gender-bending, or other terms that define one's gender variance or non-conforming identity and expression. For a more in-depth discussion of language and terminology appropriate to use with LGBT people, we refer readers to the glossary in *Bending the mold* (Lambda Legal, 2008). In this chapter, we attempt to address LGBT issues in addictions counseling in their entirety; however, while not unimportant to address, our discussion of issues related to transgender people and substance abuse will necessarily be limited, because of the sparse literature available on this topic. Prevalence rates of addiction in the LGBT community are difficult to approximate (Matthews, Selvidge, & Fisher, 2005). While estimating the percentage of the general population who identify as LGBT is complex, understanding rates of substance abuse and addiction among the LGBT population is even more difficult. Some researchers have reported rates of alcohol abuse as high as 33% (Saghir, Robins, Walbran, & Gentry, 1970; Weinburg & Williams, 1974), while others have found no significant difference in rates of use when comparing heterosexual women with lesbian or bisexual women (McKirnan & Peterson, 1989). A meta-analysis of adolescent substance abuse research suggested sexual orientation becomes a serious risk factor, with LGB youth more likely to abuse substances (e.g., alcohol, tobacco) than their heterosexual peers (Marshal et al., 2008). Historically, there have been few studies concerning the rates of alcoholism in the LGBT population (Cabaj, 1997; Hughes & Wilsnack, 1997). In those studies, frequencies may be inflated due to sampling issues (Cabaj, 1997; Friedman & Downey, 1994; Drabble, Midanik, & Trocki, 2005). Many studies that reported higher rates of substance abuse problems for the LGBT community relied on recruiting participants from gay bars. Those potential participants who are more hidden within society are not adequately included in the data, while those who would be more likely to abuse chemicals might be more likely to attend gay bars. To further complicate estimates of abuse, many studies extrapolate lesbian substance use based on studies conducted with gay men.

Despite these methodology issues, it is estimated that 28% to 35% of gay men and lesbians have engaged in some form of recreational drug use, compared to 10% to 12% of the heterosexual population (Ungvarski & Grossman, 1999; Drabble, Midanik, & Trocki, 2005). The importance of bars as social gathering places for sexual minorities may contribute to increased levels of substance abuse (Trocki, Drabble, & Midanik, 2005). Based on these estimates, it is critical for counselors to develop culturally competent treatment skills for this population.

In order to gain competence in this area, counselors must not only be familiar with addictions issues in general, but they also must examine the systems of heterosexism and homoprejudice that affect the lives of LGBT individuals. *Heterosexism* has been defined as an ideological system that assumes that all individuals are heterosexual and that heterosexuality is a "normal" model of sexual identity (Chernin & Johnson, 2002). Using heterosexuality as normative in this manner is problematic for LGBT individuals because heterosexism is also used to devalue, or legitimize ignorance of, LGBT issues. Because heterosexism is insidious and permeates every part of society, it will certainly appear in addictions treatment settings. For instance, heterosexist assumptions about addictions work would include recovery relapse interventions that do not recognize and include LGBT individuals' support systems as important, or ignore and pathologize LGBT identities while leading addictions groups.

While heterosexism is defined as the invisibility or devaluation of LGBT people, *homoprejudice* is the irrational hatred and fear of LGB individuals (Bobbe, 2002). Logan (1996) asserted that the word "homoprejudice" implies a fear of LGB people and does not adequately encapsulate the active prejudice and discrimination that LGB people experience. Instead, she encourages counselors to use the word "homoprejudice." *Transprejudice* is often forgotten about in the LGB community, so it is critically important for addictions counselors to also recognize that transprejudice (hatred and fear of individuals with nontraditional gender expression) exists, and that transgender people may feel rejected by both LGB and heterosexual communities (Singh, Boyd, & Whitman, 2010).

Heterosexism, homoprejudice, and transprejudice are systems of oppression that have negative consequences for LGBT people and provide significant stressors in their lives. Because a major role of the addictions counselor is to assess stress and coping factors in the lives of people struggling with addiction, it is important to develop attitudes, knowledge, and skills with LGBT issues. For instance, a gay man may have begun using alcohol as a teenager to cope with his sexual identity and the feeling that he would be ostracized from his family for being gay. On the other hand, a transgender woman may have used drugs to numb the pain of feeling the disconnection between the sex she was assigned at birth (male) and her gender identity as a woman.

Counselors should understand that homoprejudice and transprejudice can be internalized, causing LGBT clients to hold negative attitudes about their own sexual identity (Szymanski, Kashubeck-West, & Meyer, 2008) and/or gender identity (Carroll & Gilroy, 2002). This internalization can appear in the form of guilt, shame, and negative self-concept about one's gender or sexual identity. These negative feelings can greatly affect addiction treatment, as LGBT individuals may be vulnerable to alcohol and drug use and relapse when attempting to cope with their sexual orientation, gender identity, and/or expression.

Because of the damaging impact heterosexism, homoprejudice, and transprejudice have on the mental health of LGBT individuals, LGBT-affirmative treatment has become the standard of care for counselors to provide to this population (Association for Lesbian, Gay, Bisexual, and Transgender Issues in Counseling, 2004). These competencies are currently under revision to become specific to LGB, intersex, and ally competencies. In addition, specific counseling competencies for those working with transgender clients also exist and have been endorsed by the American Counseling Association (Association for Lesbian, Gay, Bisexual, and Transgender Issues in Counseling, 2009). Chernin and Johnson (2002) assert that LGBT-affirmative therapies seek to explore and validate how LGBT people experience and understand universal issues, such as family and social systems, religion and spirituality, career and life planning, and thoughts and feelings about oneself. The purpose of this chapter is to provide the reader with culturally relevant and helpful information that counselors may incorporate in the assessment and treatment of LGBT individuals living with addiction.

COMMON TERMS FOR AND MYTHS ABOUT LGBT PEOPLE

The field of counseling and mental health has a long history of viewing "homosexuality" and non-traditional gender expression as a disorder (Bobbe, 2002). In fact, homosexuality was categorized as a mental disorder as recently as 1973 in the *Diagnostic and Statistical Manual of Mental Disorders* (American Psychiatric Association, 1973). Because of its history of pathology, it is no longer best practice to use this word to refer to LGB people. Furthermore, although an LGB identity is no longer considered pathological, transgender people continue to face the stigma of diagnosis because Gender Identity Disorder (GID) remains a classification in the current edition of this same manual (American Psychiatric Association, 2000). Transgender activists, scholars, and practitioners continue to advocate that the GID label be removed because of their view that transgender identity is a medical condition rather than a psychological one (Carroll & Gilroy, 2002; Lev, 2007).

Because of the evolving terminology used by individuals in the LGBT community, becoming competent with treatment of this population requires knowledge of current and past uses of terms, along with their definitions. Addictions counselors should be curious and have knowledge about how these terms are used differently within specific ethnic/racial groups in order to understand how LGBT individuals define themselves ethnically or racially. For the purposes of this chapter, common terms are listed in the following sidebar.

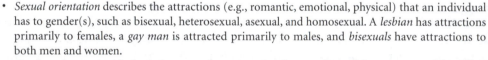

- *Sexual orientation* describes the attractions (e.g., romantic, emotional, physical) that an individual has to gender(s), such as bisexual, heterosexual, asexual, and homosexual. A *lesbian* has attractions primarily to females, a *gay man* is attracted primarily to males, and *bisexuals* have attractions to both men and women.
- *Gender* refers to the ideological system that categorizes humans into a binary system of "male" or "female," and *gender identity* describes how a person self-identifies their gender (e.g., transgender, woman, man). *Transgender* is an umbrella term used to describe people who have nontraditional gender expression (e.g., transsexual, transman, drag queen).
- *Queer* is a term that is being reclaimed by the LGBT community to refer to people who challenge the restrictive system of heterosexuality and traditional gender norms. This word was once used to denigrate LGBT people; therefore, some people find the term problematic. However, the trend in the LGBT community is to use the word with a sense of pride and inclusion of all LGBT people.

In addition to having a strong grasp of the appropriate terms and definitions used to describe the LGBT community, it is also important to be aware of the myths that surround this population. Similar to other populations who hold marginalized identities, the energy that LGBT individuals use to counter or ignore pervasive myths about being LGBT is time-consuming and stressful. For instance, bisexual people are often targeted with the myth that they are "confused" and "want to have their cake and eat it too" (Horowitz & Newcomb, 1999). These myths, such as the myth that bisexual individuals are "over-sexed," can be pervasive as they may be held by members of both the straight *and* queer community. Gay men are similarly targeted as being overly sexual, and along with this may come the myth that all gay men live with HIV/AIDS or are sexual predators. These myths are problematic because gay men have to struggle to be seen as people who want to engage in long-term partnerships and/or raise children. On the other hand, lesbians face the myths that they are "trying to be men," not interested in sex, and are more interested in pursuing stereotypically male jobs. In addition to myths bound specifically to each group, there are widely held stereotypes about all of the groups. These include stereotypes that LGBT people want to "recruit" heterosexuals into being homosexual and that being LGBT is a mental disorder or is not "normal."

The most important myth for addictions counselors to be aware of in treatment is that LGBT people can "choose" their gender or sexual identity. This stereotype is especially concerning because it has historical roots in the counseling and psychological professions and is practiced by some counselors as *reparative* or *conversion therapy*. In these therapies, counselors attempt to convert LGB people to being heterosexual. It is important to know that these therapies have been deemed unethical, because LGB identity is no longer defined as an abnormal sexual identity (Chernin & Johnson, 2002). However, because survey research suggests counselors continue to hold negative and/or stereotypic beliefs about LGBT individuals (Brown, 1996), addictions counselors may work with clients who have suffered harm in reparative therapy programs or been in treatment programs in which heterosexism and homoprejudice were endorsed. In these cases, counselors need to educate clients about the ethical guidelines and standards of care in the counseling profession that demand affirmative practice with LGBT individuals, in addition to intentionally creating an LGBT-affirmative environment in addictions treatment.

COMING OUT, CULTURAL DIFFERENCES, AND ADDICTION

Coming out is a term used to describe the process of sexual identity development for lesbian, gay, and bisexual people. Although transgender individuals are not typically included when counselors and academics discuss the coming-out process, research has shown that there is a process of gender identity development that exists for transgender people as well (Singh, Hays, & Watson, in press). There are numerous coming out models for LGB clients (Cass, 1984; Coleman, 1989; Troiden, 1989). Because the stages of coming out may stress significant relationships that LGBT people have with their family, friends, and community (Caitlin & Futterman, 1997), it is important that addictions counselors assess what stage of sexual identity development the client is in to provide culturally competent addiction treatment. This treatment must recognize and assess the extensive energy that LGB people expend on the coming-out process in their personal and professional lives. Trujillo (1997) asserts that LGB people must manage a "triple consciousness" about their sexual identity: how they think about themselves, how the world thinks about them, and the discrepancy between the two (Trujillo, 1997).

Counselors should also know that there are many sexual identity models to draw from in working with LGBT clients (Cass, 1979; Cox & Gallois, 1996; Troiden, 1998). Kus and Latcovich's (1994) coming-out model delineates four stages that counselors may easily use to assess sexual identity stage for a client seeking treatment. The four stages include *identification* (using terms such as lesbian, gay, and bisexual and identifying one's attraction to the same sex), *cognitive changes* (accessing community resources and activities in the LGB community), *acceptance* (giving oneself permission to be LGB), and *action* (sharing about one's LGB identity with family, friends, and others, and embracing one's sexual identity). Because bars are often viewed by the LGBT community as the only safe places for them to explore and validate their sexual identity, assessment of a client's coming-out stage is important historically and currently to understand their social support systems. For instance, if a gay man living with alcohol addiction is recently identifying his attraction to men in the identification stage of coming out, he may increase his use of alcohol to manage internalized homoprejudice and/or explore his sexual identity in the LGBT bar scene. A culturally competent counselor working with this client should be adept and normalizing and affirming of his sexual identity, as well as identifying LGBT-affirmative addiction recovery systems in the community.

However, when assessing the coming-out process as it relates to addiction (see Assessment section for more specific information), it is also critical to understand that different cultural groups (e.g., race/ethnicity, religious/spiritual affiliation) may have coming-out processes that are very different. For instance, research has shown that Asian Americans' coming-out process typically occurs in predominantly White LGBT communities and they often experience racism and discrimination in these spaces (Chung, 2002; Singh, Chung, & Dean, 2006). Additionally, African American, Native American, and Latin American LGBT people must also manage societal racism (Bridges, Selvidge, & Matthews, 2003) in addition to heterosexism as they move through the addiction and recovery process. Therefore, counselors must be adept in assessing not only LGBT-community support for people of color in addictions treatment, but also the safety level of their connections to their families and community. Chernin and Johnson (2002) recommend that counselors raise questions with LGBT clients of color in order to clarify support networks, and assist in clarifying how clients think and feel about their sexual and ethnic/racial identity, through the following questions: "With which groups do I identify most clearly? What role does sexual orientation play in my life? How open am I willing to be?" (p. 35).

Advice to Addictions Counselors About Clients' "Coming-Out" Processes

- Do not assume every client is straight or gender-conforming. This can place pressure on LGBT people to self-disclose about their sexual orientation and/or gender identity.
- Create an environment in all counseling modalities (e.g., individual, partners, group) where at the beginning of each intake session, an affirmative stance is stated about all multicultural identities (e.g., race/ethnicity, gender identity and expression, sexual orientation, socioeconomic status, disability).
- If and when LGBT clients come out about their sexual orientation and/or gender identity, respond in an affirmative manner about this disclosure. Explore how this (or these) identities might shape counseling goals or needs.
- Do not "out" clients to others involved in treatment (e.g., family, friends, employers, co-workers) unless there is specific permission granted from the client. Because of the extensive heterosexism, homoprejudice, and transprejudice that exists in society, the consequences for outing an LGBT client can place them in harm's way.
- Do not highlight a client's sexual orientation and/or gender identity and expression in client conceptualization, case supervision, and consultation unless this is a significant aspect of their treatment. With heterosexual and non-transgender clients, be sure to explore their gender identity and/or sexual orientation as well in case consultation and client conceptualization.

CASE SCENARIO

Coming Out and Cultural Issues in Addictions Treatment

Asim is a 36-year-old Muslim male of South Asian heritage who presents for individual counseling and who reports abusing alcohol and marijuana. When you ask about precipitants to his drinking behavior, Asim shares that he began abusing substances after the end of a difficult relationship three years ago. When you ask for more information about this relationship, Asim hesitates and you notice that Asim is not using any identifying pronouns about this individual. Asim suddenly changes the subject and asks whether it is possible to be attracted to people of both genders.

1. How will you answer Asim's question in a manner that honors both his cultural and sexual identities?
2. What are interventions you could utilize that would invite Asim to share more about his past relationship and sexual orientation?
3. What are cultural issues that may bring strengths and challenges to Asim's treatment in addiction counseling?

LGBT-AFFIRMATIVE ADDICTION TREATMENT AND ASSESSMENT

Culturally relevant assessment and interventions with LGBT people living with addiction issues must recognize the unique context in which they live. Called the "hidden minority" (Fassinger, 1991) due to the pervasiveness of heterosexism, and the resulting assumption of a hetero-normative standard in society, this same invisibility is present when attempting to understand the unique addictions concerns of this population. Therefore, it is not surprising that rates of alcohol and drug abuse for this population are difficult to estimate (Holmes & Hodge, 1997). Counselors should be aware that the LGBT community is often divided in its social networks along gender lines (Fassinger, 1991). Therefore, the types of drugs abused, location of abuse, and potential triggers for relapse can look quite different depending on the population. Below is an abbreviated list of the ways alcohol and drug addiction may vary across LGBT communities:

- *Transgender* people may face challenges in being underemployed (Carroll et al., 2002), or over-represented in entertainment environments such as drag shows, or as sex workers (Bockting, Robinson, & Rosser, 1998). These environments may be dangerous, and research has shown that it is particularly important to provide transgender individuals working in these settings psychoeducation about HIV/AIDS prevention, safer sex, and sexual assault due to lack of knowledge about these risks (Bockting et al., 1998). Transgender people show high rates of substance abuse and face treatment issues that include external and internal transprejudice, hate crimes, job and career loss, family estrangement, isolation, lack of medical care, and low self-esteem. They also may distrust counselors due to previous bad experiences with health-care providers. Further, transgender people may choose hormone therapy, which may affect mood and serve as relapse triggers, including self-injection requirements simulating illicit drug use (Substance Abuse and Mental Health Services Administration [SAMHSA], 2003).
- *Gay men* may abuse anabolic steroids due to the body image pressure that exists particularly within White gay male cultures; use of which may also be associated with higher risk for contracting HIV/AIDS (Bolding, Sherr, Maguire, & Elford, 1999). In urban areas, gay men may attend all-night circuit parties or dance venues where "party" or designer drugs, such as crystal methamphetamine, Ecstasy (methylenedioxymethamphetamine), special K (ketamine hydrochloride), and GHB (gamma-hydroxybutyrate), are taken to "last through the night." Gay men also demonstrate high rates of addiction to the Internet, which researchers believe is linked to the homoprejudice and invisibility they face in society, and the increasing access to a gay male community online (Chaney & Chang, 2005). Gay men have also been shown to potentially rely on gay bars and parties for social and sexual connections; may or may not connect sex and intimacy; face HIV/AIDS as a daily reality, with rates of contraction rising again for men of color and young men; and may experience additional shame and targeting for being "too effeminate" (SAMHSA, 2003).

- *Lesbian women* have been shown to abuse alcohol at higher rates than their heterosexual counterparts (Jaffe, Clance, Nichols, & Emshoff, 2000), and research has shown that alcohol abuse may begin as a way to cope with their emerging sexual identity (McNally & Finnegan, 1992). In addition, survey data shows lesbians abuse marijuana more than other illicit drugs (Skinner & Otis, 1992). SAMHSA (2003) has also shown that lesbians have higher rates of alcoholism than heterosexual women and that their use of alcohol tends to show less decline with age; may attend LGB bars, which provide safe space for them to socialize and find support; and manage stress related to possible trauma history, coming-out issues, and "passing" as heterosexual.
- *Bisexual* people are typically underrepresented in studies examining queer populations (Horowitz & Newcomb, 1999), which suggests that we have little information on their addiction patterns. Others may view bisexual identity as a behavior rather than as a sexual orientation, and bisexuals may face identity and self-acceptance issues that could complicate addictions treatment. They may also be labeled by some providers as immature, living with borderline personality disorder, or as "acting out" with their sexual behavior (SAMHSA, 2003).
- *Queer or Questioning Youth* may use substances for the same reasons as non-gay youth, but may also use to soothe effects of shame and social isolation, to help deny feelings of same-sex attractions, and/or to cope with ridicule. They may also face challenging sexual development issues in isolation. Many experience first sexual attractions at age 10, have first sexual experiences between 13 and 15, and begin to identify orientation from 15 to 16 years. Transgender and queer youth of color are at highest risk for violence (SAMHSA, 2003).

LGBT-Specific Assessment of Addiction

Every sound clinical assessment process begins with relationship building. This is particularly important when working with LGBT clients. Without a strong therapeutic alliance, individuals will not want to begin the journey toward recovery and will not be motivated to stay engaged in treatment through more challenging times. Trust is particularly important with groups who experience discrimination and oppression as a daily part of living. Assessment procedures with people who abuse substances typically involve clinical interviews with the client and with people who may be in their family-of-origin or members of their support group in combination with objective assessment instruments. Potential barriers to a strong therapeutic alliance include interviews that assume heterosexuality, and assessment tools laden with heterosexist bias. Counselors should ask about family and other relationships in a manner that communicates acceptance to people of all sexual identities. Each client, regardless of cultural context, should be asked about sexual orientation in a relaxed, matter-of-fact manner as a normal part of the assessment procedure (Finnegan & McNally, 1987). Additionally, inclusion of partners in the assessment process is crucial.

Affirmative Assessment with LGBT Clients

It is important to use open-ended questions when assessing clients' sexual orientation and/or gender identity. For instance, rather than asking if a client is married (since not all LGBT people have access to marriage rights in the United States and globally), a counselor could ask the following" "Tell me about your relationship history?" and "Share about the partners you have had in your life?"

- What other open-ended questions typically used in addictions assessment should be changed to demonstrate respect and a welcoming environment for LGBT clients?

AFFIRMATIVE USE OF LANGUAGE WITH LGBT CLIENTS.   A basic consideration when assessing and treating sexual and gender minorities who are struggling with substance abuse and with their families is the counselor's use of language. It is important for the counselor to be knowledgeable and aware of relevant terms for this culture in order to facilitate trust and credibility with sexual minority clients. For example, the term *homosexual* suggests that this community is just about sex when, in fact, sexuality plays the same role in all of our lives regardless of sexual orientation. Gay men and lesbians are no more sexual than non-gay people. The words *gay* and *lesbian* suggest these are the only two groups within the larger community of sexual minorities, but bisexual and transgendered people are also represented in the gay community. Although they exist in smaller numbers, the kind of discrimination and oppression they experience is like that of gay men and lesbians.

The term *sexual preference,* commonly used by uninformed people, is considered to be offensive by many LGB people and their allies. A more correct term is s*exual orientation,* as "preference" suggests that LGB people have a choice about their sexual identity. Gay people, like non-gay people, discover their sexual orientation in terms of their attractions to the same gender. Gay men and lesbians *come out* as a statement of integrity. They are simply being who they are. The only choice they make is how to integrate this part of their being into their lives. The term *coming out* infers an event or a single action that one performs, when in reality this is a complex process that occurs repeatedly over a lifetime and can actually be required many times within a single day. Because people are generally assumed to be heterosexual, LGB people have to decide when, where, and with whom they disclose their sexual orientation on an ongoing basis with varying consequences (e.g., acceptance, rejection, or physical harm) for this disclosure. This management of sexual identity can be extremely difficult to negotiate while also attempting to become clean and sober. Often the client seeking recovery is "young" in his or her sexual identity development and new to a recovery identity. Managing both identities can be complicated and overwhelming. With regard to working with transgender clients, it is most appropriate to use the terms that transgender people use to describe themselves—from use of pronouns, names, and other gender identity and expression markers. Do not use words like "the name she prefers" or use the pronouns related to the sex a transgender client was assigned at birth. See the American Counseling Association (2009) *Competencies for Counseling with Transgender Clients* for further information on best practices with transgender clients.

In addition to assessing substance abuse issues, counselors will need to be well-versed in different models of sexual identity development, in order to better understand the interplay between recovery identity development and sexual identity development (Cass, 1979; Cox & Gallois, 1996; Troiden, 1989). Just as a person from a sexual minority group evolves into self-acceptance of their sexual orientation, a client will need to move from an identity as an addict to identity as a recovering person. Often multiple levels of identity development will intersect in terms of race, age, gender, ability status, socioeconomic status, religious/spiritual affiliation, and recovery. It will take a skilled and aware counselor to assist clients in managing these multiple identities.

PSYCHOSOCIAL HISTORY.   A complete psychosocial history should be gathered about relevant information in multiple areas in order to get a complete picture of an LGBT individual's life. The counselor should gather this information from both the client and significant others about patterns of alcohol and other drug (AOD) use, including frequency, acute dose, duration, tolerance, and co-occurring physical signs and symptoms of addiction. Patterns of use should include contextual information about where, when, and with whom the client uses most often. If this history indicates the client uses more frequently at bars, the treatment goals will need to reflect alternative social outlets within the LGBT community. The history should also include information about the client's family history of addiction, degree of outness, family support for sexual orientation, family addiction history, dating and relationship history (including history of partners with substance abuse issues), and a detailed account of how substance use has affected the client's significant relationships. Information should be gathered concerning communicable disease (e.g., HIV/STD, Hepatitis C) status, safer-sex practice issues especially related to substance use, and patterns of drug administration (e.g., needle-sharing). For some LGBT clients, as with heterosexual counterparts, use of mood altering chemicals may lead to unprotected sexual activity. In addition, counselors should be prepared to gather information concerning employment history (paying special attention to the impact of sexual orientation and gender identity and expression on career issues), legal history, history of mental illness, sexual and physical abuse history, and mental status information. Higher rates of suicide and eating disorders (van Wormer, 1995) are other factors to assess when working with LGBT clients.

Spirituality may also be a vital part of the recovery process for a LGBT person, and therefore may be an important part of the assessment. Counselors should explore the client's concepts of spirituality, including religious history and the intersections between faith and sexual identity particular to the client. The client's openness to spiritually-focused 12-step ancillary programs will be greatly affected by past experiences with organized religion, especially around sexual identity. Religiously sanctioned prejudice and condemnation toward sexual minorities may obstruct the client's willingness to find spiritual fellowship with other recovering people. In order to set an open tone around spirituality during the assessment process, counselors may want to use the phrase "spiritual community center" instead of "church." Assessment questions centered around life purpose or meaning may help the clinician to access spiritual dimensions, without creating defensiveness related to past experiences with religious condemnation.

Often psychometric instruments are used in assessing substance abuse and dependence. Counselors should scrutinize assessment instruments for heterosexist bias and gender bias. It is recommended that all assessment tools use gender-neutral language. This helps set a positive tone for future therapeutic work. Many can be modified to use inclusive language without affecting their validity and reliability. Additionally, counselors will need to be familiar with psychometric instruments that assess internalized homonegativity, especially considering the importance of guilt and shame in the recovery process for addicts. Intersecting identities may necessitate additional dimensions for the assessment process. The coming-out process may be different for people of color, people living in poverty, and people of varying ages, ability status, and socioeconomic levels. Every unique identity will bring different stressors and joys in each stage.

CASE SCENARIO

Lesbian Client Coming Out in a Support Group

Sharon is a 23-year-old woman who identifies as a lesbian and reports abusing alcohol for the past 8 years. She has been in both individual and group addictions counseling for the past month, and has been attending Alcoholics Anonymous (AA) meetings. Traditional Christian prayers have been used to close many of the AA meetings she has attended. Sharon describes "being out" in other areas of her life (e.g., family, friends, work), but says she feels uncomfortable disclosing her sexual orientation to her sponsor and in other friendships she is developing in the support group. She asks you what she should do and if she should disclose her sexual orientation to the group.

1. What would you say to Sharon that would be affirmative of her sexual orientation and validate her concerns?
2. How will you explore challenges that Sharon may face if she does decide to disclose her sexual orientation to the group?

LGBT-Specific Treatment of Addiction

Sexual and gender identity issues should be integrated into the substance abuse client's treatment plan as appropriate. Counselors should focus on those problems most important to the client, and treatment plans should be created collaboratively. According to Cabaj (1997), each of the following factors should be considered when developing a treatment plan with a sexual or gender minority client: life stage; coming-out process; support available; current and past relationships; degree of comfort with sexual identity; and issues related to career, finances, and health. In nurturing a therapeutic relationship, SAMHSA (2003) recommends counselors become aware of certain underlying assumptions regarding sexual or gender minority groups. These assumptions include:

- Each person's unique life story, including their circumstances and experiences, may affect recovery and should be explored by the counselor.
- Legal prohibitions against LGB behavior limits social outlets to settings such as LGBT bars, homes, or clubs where AODs may be central.
- LGBT people may have experienced discrimination as a result of their gender or sexual identity, and may have internalized homonegativity as a result.
- LGBT people may have been victims of antigay violence or hate crimes.
- Increasing numbers of LGBT individuals are becoming parents.
- LGBT-sensitive and affirmative treatments are more likely to have successful outcomes with this population.

Modality Issues

Substance abuse treatment modalities include individual therapy, couples and family counseling, group counseling, and a variety of therapeutic community milieus. Higher treatment success rates have been associated with family involvement, and group therapy is often the modality of choice in treatment settings (Capuzzi & Gross, 1992; Feldstein & Miller, 2006; Hogue, Dauber, Samuolis, & Liddle, 2006; Kinney, 2003). However, special considerations need to be taken when working with a LGBT client in these settings.

Partners should be invited to attend treatment along with the client, but it is also important to consider that they may not feel comfortable or want to openly discuss sexual orientation and/or gender identity and expression concerns in a group setting with primarily heterosexual and/or gender-conforming members. Many LGBT clients will have "chosen" families comprised of close friends; it may be appropriate to include them in the treatment process. It may also be appropriate to begin with single unit family therapy and psychoeducational experiences before referring them to a family group environment. Likewise, a LGBT individual may not feel comfortable disclosing his or her orientation in a heterosexual group. These issues should be discussed with the client prior to prescribing any treatment modality.

In group and community treatment settings, clients need guidance and support when deciding where and when to "come out." This is especially true if the client is early in the sexual and/or gender identity development process *and* is early in recovery. Often, LGBT clients early in their sexual identity experience "pink cloud" altruism, disclosing their sexual and/or gender identity in settings in which they are unprepared to manage the potential consequences and are then unable to cope with potential negative consequences. Most residential or inpatient treatment communities set up living quarters based on binary gender models which may complicate daily life for LGBT clients seeking recovery. For example, many substance abuse treatment centers struggle deciding which dormitory (male or female) would be most appropriate for a transgender person. For some, the client's treatment stay may range from awkward to dangerous. LGBT stigma management is also an important coping skill for LGBT clients to develop when they are early in their sexual identity and/or gender identity and recovery. Counselors need to prepare clients for potential rejection and discrimination they will experience as a result of living a more open life as a LGBT person.

Counselors may also need to educate non-LGBT clients in treatment about treating every community or group member with respect, including setting ground rules that discrimination and disrespect of members will not be tolerated. It can be healing for LGBT clients to obtain acceptance and support from heterosexual and gender-conforming group members, and this acceptance may be the first time they experience safety sharing their LGBT identity in a group setting. Regardless of the treatment modality, LGBT clients need to be treated with respect and dignity.

LGBT people who abuse substances also need assistance identifying social and recovery support communities that are both safe and affirmative of their identity. This may be difficult in rural settings, where sexual minorities are even more hidden. Some urban areas may offer LGBT-specific 12-step meetings. Counselors should know the details about these resources, including the relative "health" of the LGBT groups in the community. Clients should learn how to identify healthy, safe recovery meetings and sponsors. It will also be valuable to help LGBT clients view 12-step meetings as support for recovery, and not an avenue for dating. Sponsorship should be with someone of differing sexual and/or gender identities from the client, especially initially. For example, a gay man may choose a lesbian sponsor. Just as a heterosexual man would not sponsor a woman, this helps eliminate the dual role attraction might create. If LGBT-specific 12-step groups do not exist in the client's community, the counselor will need to prepare the client for possible prejudice and discrimination in traditional self-help settings. Finally, counselors should be aware that some LGBT clients show reluctance to become involved in 12-step fellowships due to experiences of discrimination from organized religion. Assisting clients to explore the wounds inflicted by some of these experiences may help formulate or identify a chosen, more autonomous spirituality. Finding and learning to nurture a healthy spiritual life can be crucial to recovery for LGBT people.

Despite warnings to stay away from social settings where alcohol and other drugs are present, many LGBT clients will continue to socialize in bars and at LGBT parties in order to connect with the LGBT community. Counselors need to help clients address this concern openly and strategize about how to handle this situation without relapse. Recovery skills such as sponsorship, relaxation, visualization, meditation, and journaling may all be valuable coping strategies in helping the client maintain sobriety. Role-playing various social settings that are potential triggers for relapse while in the counseling office may also help prepare the client to guard against it.

Relapse Prevention

Relapse prevention is an important part of any recovery treatment plan. Unique triggers exist for LGBT clients, which require unique strategies. Counselors should help clients identify triggers that may cause relapse, as well as ways to counteract those triggers based on the individual's situation. Some common relapse precursors for LGBT clients are: coming-out issues, experience of shame, low self-esteem, internalized homonegativity and/or transnegativity, verbal and physical attacks, grief and loss due to HIV/AIDS, learning about HIV status, and social situations where AODs are present. Treatment and prevention plans should provide clients with the skills and strategies to overcome these potential triggers, as well as empower the client to become more resilient in the face of unique challenges to long-term recovery.

CASE SCENARIO

A Gay Transgender Man with a Relapse Crisis

Kasey is an African American man (who was assigned the sex of female at birth but who identifies as a male) in his early thirties. While in inpatient treatment for his alcoholism he learned he is HIV positive. Now that he has returned home, he is afraid he will never have another relationship and is unsure of how to negotiate his HIV status with potential partners. Kasey feels he should tell his close-knit family about his health status in order to get the support he needs, but has never disclosed his sexual orientation or his gender identity to them. It was hard enough to admit his alcoholism. Although he left treatment feeling a great deal of hope for his life, he has begun to doubt his self-worth and whether his sobriety is worth all the effort. He is overwhelmed with thoughts of using and has begun to connect with old drinking buddies.

1. As Kasey's counselor, how would you help him sort out the disclosure issues he is struggling with?
2. How would you help him find the support he needs to avert this relapse? What recovery skills would you help him develop to cope with this crisis?
3. How would you help Kasey utilize this crisis to enhance his overall recovery? What competencies can you identify that might contribute to his personal resiliency?
4. How would you address the intersections of Kasey's gender identity and sexual orientation in counseling? How would you discuss this intersections of identity in addition to his diagnosis of HIV?

Resilience strategies might be particularly helpful with a population that experiences multiple levels of societal oppression (e.g., substance abuser, sexual minority, gender difference, race diversity). Ten strategies to build resilience, adapted from the Discovery Health Channel and the American Psychological Association (as cited in Miller, 2005), are:

1. Make connections.
2. Avoid seeing crises as insurmountable problems.
3. Accept that change is a part of living.
4. Move toward one's goals.
5. Take decisive actions.
6. Look for opportunities for self-discovery.
7. Nurture a positive view of self.
8. Keep things in perspective.
9. Maintain a hopeful outlook.
10. Take care of one's self.

Helping LGBT clients discover their own resiliency, often born out of adversity, survival, and adaptation, can be one of the most fulfilling aspects of recovery. Claiming this source of inner strength can help establish a foundation on which to build a healthy life.

Role of Addictions Counselors Working with LGBT Clients

Regardless of the treatment setting, counselors will work with LGBT clients, and have a unique opportunity to powerfully impact the lives of LGBT clients seeking help with substance abuse issues. It is the counselor's responsibility to follow best-practice guidelines and to become competent when working with this population. The following list highlights some important principles for culturally competent treatment provision:

- Remember every client has the right to be treated with sensitivity and respect.
- Become knowledgeable and competently trained to work with LGBT issues.
- Be aware of the myths and realities regarding LGBT people.
- Display LGBT cultural symbols such as the rainbow flag and LGBT 12-step literature in your office as a sign of affirmation.
- Become knowledgeable and aware of the Stages of Change Model (Prochaska & Norcross, 2002) and how these stages might be affected by the client's stage of sexual identity development.
- Do not confront sexual and/or gender identity and expression identity—explore, work collaboratively, and use empowerment strategies.
- Challenge agency discrimination and prejudice against this population, including exclusionary language in treatment-team processes and agency policies.
- Remember that LGBT clients live in a heterosexual and gender-conforming world and are not afforded the same legal protections and privileges (e.g., marriage) as their heterosexual counterparts.
- Clients should not be required to discuss sexual and/or gender identity or relationship issues in mixed groups if they are uncomfortable doing so.
- If a counselor is uncomfortable working with LGBT clients, they should acknowledge this lack of competence and refer to counselors who are LGBT-friendly.
- Do not try to change the sexual orientation and/or gender identity of the client.
- Self-monitor countertransference issues. Examine your own biases and reactions with a counselor, colleague, or a supervisor.
- Be diligent in exploring your own heterosexist assumptions and language.
- Remain flexible and individualize treatment strategies based on the unique contexts of the client.

Creating a Safe Environment for LGBT People

Because LGBT individuals have extensive, and often daily, experiences with prejudice due to their sexual orientation or gender identity and expression, it is important for counselors to ensure that their counseling office and the organization in which they work send a clear message that the environment is safe for them to disclose their struggles. Keeping LGBT magazines (e.g., *The Advocate, Curve, Girlfriends*) and LGBT books (e.g., *My Gender Workbook* by Kate Bornstein) in the waiting room and in counseling offices is one way to send this affirmative message. Another, more significant way to send a welcoming message to LGBT people is to display a "Safe Zone" or rainbow sticker on the front door of the building, reception desk, and/or counseling office, as these symbols can be a universal message of welcome and safety that LGBT people recognize. It is important, however, to seriously assess the safety of the counseling environment before deciding to display such a symbol. Counselors may want to consider organizing a "Safe Zone" committee to assess not only LGBT attitudes within the workplace, but also to consider offering LGBT trainings. In addition, counselors should have brochures on hand for organizations that are affirmative of LGBT clients and their families and friends, should they need additional support outside of addictions counseling.

The Pride Institute: An Example of LGBT-Focused Addiction Treatment

"How can you recover when you can't be yourself? Begin your recovery where you can be yourself" (Pride Institute, 2006). This is the basis of the philosophy of the Pride Institute, an organization dedicated to providing culturally relevant and appropriate addictions treatment for LGBT people. Individuals seeking treatment first call a central office; they receive a phone assessment and a referral to a treatment center (located in Minneapolis, Dallas, Fort Lauderdale, Chicago, and New York City). The Pride Institute offers individual and group counseling modalities and also provides treatment for issues comorbid with addiction (e.g., depression, anxiety).

The Pride Institute appears to achieve positive recovery outcomes with its LGBT clients due to: assumptions of its safety and freedom from homoprejudice and heterosexism; encouragement to discuss how coming out and other issues that affect LGBT people (e.g., HIV/AIDS, domestic partnership) can influence the addiction process; LGBT-friendly staff; creation of a LGBT community of treatment and recovery; and counseling modalities specifically geared toward LGBT people. Addictions counselors may use any of the above strategies to enhance their cultural competence with LGBT individuals, which may entail moving from valuing the client's cultural identity to actually doing LGBT social advocacy.

How to Be an Advocate for LGBT-Affirmative Treatment

Social advocacy on behalf of LGBT people is one of the most important roles that addictions counselors may hold when working with clients who struggle with addictions issues. With social justice named as the fifth force in counseling (Ratts, D'Andrea, & Arredondo, 2004) and the endorsement of the Advocacy Competencies by the American Counseling Association (Counselors for Social Justice, 2004), best practices for counselors working with this population include a careful assessment of how they incorporate affirmative counseling in their work with LGBT people living with addiction. In addition, the movement for social justice in counseling urges counselors to recognize how systems of privilege and oppression affect the mental well-being of clients. For counselors working with LGBT people living with addictions issues, this translates to moving beyond the traditional counseling role to advocating on behalf of the LGBT population for culturally relevant addiction treatment. In order to support addictions counselors in their advocacy efforts, we suggest five major ways in which they can intervene on behalf of LGBT clients seeking addiction treatment:

1. *Create a "zero" tolerance policy about heterosexist behaviors and language.* Counselors may enlist their fellow staff members to create a policy directing agency personnel to deliver LGBT-affirmative and LGBT-inclusive addiction treatment. Including LGBT staff and clients in this process may provide additional insight into the effectiveness of the resulting policy, as well as ensure that it is enforceable and meaningful and accounts for overt (e.g., LGBT-demeaning jokes) and covert (e.g., excluding LGBT clients and/or staff from access to resources) prejudicial acts. Counselors can advocate for sexual orientation, and gender identity and expression, to become part of a larger non-discrimination clause the organization may have, to address its mission of serving diverse clients. In addition, counselors may access materials from The National Gay and Lesbian Task Force (*http://www.ngltf.org*) and the Human Rights Campaign (*http://www.hrc.org/*), both of whom have guidelines on how to create LGBT-positive work environments.

2. *Create a team to conduct an assessment of how LGBT-friendly the addiction setting appears to others.* Sending a clear message that LGBT people are valued and understood is critical to establishing a LGBT-affirmative environment. How many LGBT magazines are in the reception area? What types of LGBT books and pride symbols are on the bookshelves of counselor offices and group-treatment rooms? Having a team assess and answer these questions will ensure a more welcoming environment for this population, as well as sending a clear message to other clients and staff that heterosexism, homoprejudice, and transprejudice are not acceptable.

3. *Hold focus groups and workshops in the LGBT community.* Although the bar scene may feel like the safest place for LGBT people to interact and socialize within the queer community, counselors may play a significant role in education about the importance of alcohol- and drug-free spaces and support networks in the community. Holding focus groups in the LGBT community may also enhance understanding of the local queer culture. In addition, providing LGBT-centered addiction and recovery is a way to outreach in a nonthreatening manner to LGBT people who distrust counseling and psychological professionals.

4. *Write letters to representatives and local straight and queer newspapers about LGBT issues in addiction.* Counselors witness first-hand how heterosexism, homoprejudice, and transprejudice feed the addictive cycle, in addition to how these systems are internalized by clients in the form of negative attitudes. Writing letters to demand equitable treatment of LGBT people in the mental health system, as well as asking representatives and local newspapers to highlight LGBT issues are advocacy activities that directly challenge and counter heterosexism in the fields of mental health and substance abuse.

5. *Use your knowledge of local addiction, mental health, and LGBT community resources to raise awareness about LGBT issues in addiction.* Counselors may seek out local resources to ensure their addiction work utilizes the most current information on LGBT-friendly 12-step programs, treatment centers, and other community organizations. Counselors may take their advocacy one step further by compiling and distributing a LGBT addiction resource guide that includes this information as a service to the community. In compiling this guide, a team of local counselors, LGBT allies, and LGBT community leaders could be convened to lead this effort collaboratively.

Top 10 Ways Addictions Counselors Can Advocate for LGBT People

1. Include LGBT magazines (e.g., *The Advocate, Curve, Girlfriends*) in the reception area.
2. Post a list of LGBT-friendly 12-step meetings in the local, regional, and national area.
3. Develop a statement that heterosexism, homoprejudice, and transprejudice will not be tolerated while in treatment.
4. Ensure that all paperwork is LGBT-inclusive and free of heterosexist language (use gender-neutral language, such as "partner" rather than "spouse") and includes "transgender" as a gender box.
5. Train fellow counselors and staff on LGBT culture (e.g., media, language, resources) to ensure a LGBT-friendly environment at all levels of treatment.
6. Hire openly LGBT staff to serve so that others may see them as role models.
7. Write letters to representatives at the local, state, and national level to advocate on behalf of issues important to LGBT people.

8. Be aware that the LGBT community is more heterogeneous than homogeneous (e.g., political awareness, coming-out stages, language, gender, race/ethnicity, disability status, socioeconomic status, religious/spiritual affiliation).
9. Provide psychoeducation on LGBT people and addictions issues in the LGBT community (e.g., bars, parks, pride festivals, social organizations, nonprofits, Internet).
10. Constantly monitor one's level of awareness, knowledge, and skills in working with LGBT people living with addiction in order to increase one's competence with these issues.

CASE STUDY

The Story of Sonali

This story weaves together the complex intersection of race/ethnicity, gender identity and expression, socioeconomic status, disability, and religious/spiritual affiliation. As you read through this case study, think about the opportunities for culturally competent treatment with Sonali, as well as the ways that you may engage in advocacy efforts both within the treatment center and outside of the office. Questions about the case study follow this short description:

What Would You Do?

Sonali, a first-generation student of South Asian heritage who is struggling with alcohol addiction, presents in your office and asks you "to help save her." She reports that she found your addiction treatment center's information on the Internet, and that she has been court-ordered to a 90-day treatment program for alcohol addiction due to a DUI she received 2 weeks ago. She is tearful in her presentation and reports many depressive symptoms (e.g., loss of weight, insomnia, anhedonia, isolation from others, hopelessness). She repeats over and over how scared she is that her parents "will find out" about her drinking habits, and doesn't know how she will pay for treatment because she is living on financial aid. She also shares with you that she has "secrets that cannot be told" to her family about who she loves, and reports relationship difficulties with her best friend. She shares that she needs to do a "puja" at her temple as soon as possible in order to "get better."

  You assess Sonali's consumption of alcohol; she has recently increased her drinking to a six-pack of beer nightly for the past month. When you ask about the escalation of her alcohol abuse, she shares that she is not ready to face her parents over the winter holiday break and that she and her best friend will be in two different cities. She reports that she first began drinking about 2 years ago, when she started sneaking into a local bar to "hang out with good friends." When you ask about the nature of her relationship with her best friend, she gets fidgety and has minimal eye contact. She repeatedly asks you to help her "solve her problems" and "make the pain go away."

Questions

1. What additional information do you need to gather about Sonali in order to provide culturally competent addictions treatment?
2. How will you assess Sonali's stage of sexual identity development? What questions would be important to ask, and what questions might be inappropriate?
3. What are the subtle messages that Sonali will receive about her multiple identities (e.g., sexual identity, gender identity and expression, class identity, racial/ethnic identity) as

she enters the addiction treatment center's lobby and your personal office? How can you structure an inviting and nonheterosexist environment?

4. As you read Sonali's intake before she comes to your office, what information will you use to begin building good rapport?

5. How will you ensure that you deliver culturally competent assessment and treatment to Sonali in regard to her sexual identity? How will you explore the intersection between her sexual identity and her racial/ethnic identity?

6. What are the opportunities for advocacy prior, during, and after treatment with Sonali? How might you engage your fellow counselors in these advocacy efforts? Are there ways that you could bring these advocacy efforts to the local, regional, national, and international counseling organizations of which you are a member?

Summary and Some Final Notations

Counselors must address issues of heterosexism, homoprejudice, and transprejudice in order to work effectively with LGBT people seeking recovery from alcohol and drug abuse. Because they must constantly make decisions about coming out in their family, friend, and work relationships, counselors must recognize that the same hesitancy to come out may exist in an addictions treatment setting. Accurate assessment and treatment interventions with alcohol and drug abuse that include acknowledgement of society's devaluation of LGBT identities by counselors allows a more accurate and honest rapport to build between counselor and the client in recovery. Because counselors are privy to the intimate ways that LGBT mental health is shaped by heterosexism, homoprejudice, and transprejudice, it is important to use this knowledge in advocacy and social justice efforts on behalf of LGBT people both within and outside the counseling office.

Regardless of the complexity of issues, abstinence and sobriety should be a priority in assisting the LGBT substance abuser. Establishing a safe, affirmative environment will help in developing a strong therapeutic alliance. Collateral issues may include alienation from family, multiple identity management issues, trauma history, HIV/AIDS, suicide potential, domestic violence, trust issues, and parenting issues. Alienation from family and friends due to a combination of social damage from addictive behavior and sexual orientation stigma create complex barriers for the LGBT substance abuser to overcome. Culturally competent treatment strategies provide the best opportunity for sexual minority clients to overcome addiction and lead fulfilling, healthy lives.

Useful Web Sites

The following Web sites provide additional information relating to the chapter topics:

Association for LGBT Issues in Counseling (ALGBTIC)
http://www.algbtic.org

Amigas Latinas
http://www.amigaslatinas.og

Children of Lesbians and Gays Everywhere
http://www.colage.org

Communities United Against Violence
http://cuav.org

Deaf Queer Resource Center
http://www.deafqueer.org

Gay and Lesbian Alliance Against Defamation
http://glaad.org

Gay and Lesbian Medical Association
http://glma.org

Gay Parent Magazine Online
http://www.gayparentmag.com

Human Rights Campaign
http://www.hrc.org

Lambda Legal Defense and Education Fun
http://www.lambdalegal.org

National Gay and Lesbian Task Force
http://www.thetaskforce.org

National Minority AIDS Council
http://www.nmac.org

National Native American AIDS Prevention Center
http://www.nnaapc.org

Parents, Families and Friends of Lesbians and Gays (PFLAG)
http://www.pflag.org

People of Color Against AIDS Network
http://www.pocaan.org

Pride Institute
http://www.pride-institute.com

Religious Tolerance
http://www.religioustolerance.org

Soulforce
http://www.soulforce.org

Substance Abuse and Mental Health Services Administration (SAMHSA)
http://www.samhsa.gov

Transgender Forum's Resource Guide
http://www.3dcom.com/tgfr.html

Trikone: Lesbian, Gay, Bisexual and Transgender South Asians
http://www.trikone.org

Zuna Institute (African American lesbians)
http://www.zunainstitute.org

References

American Psychiatric Association. (1973). *Diagnostic and statistical manual of mental disorders* (3rd ed.). Washington, DC: Author.

American Psychiatric Association. (2000). *Diagnostic and statistical manual of mental disorders* (5th ed.). Washington, DC: APA.

American Counseling Association. (2009). *Competencies for counseling with transgender clients*. Retrieved February 7, 2010 from *http://www.algbtic.org*.

Association for Gay, Lesbian, and Bisexual Issues in Counseling. (2004). Competencies for counseling gay, lesbian, bisexual, and transgendered (LGBT) clients. Retrieved February 7, 2010 from *http://www.algbtic.org/resources/competencies.html*

Bobbe, J. (2002). Treatment with lesbian alcoholics: Healing shame and internalized homophobia for ongoing sobriety. *Health and Social Work, 27*, 218–223.

Bockting, W. O., Robinson, B. E., & Rosser, B. R. S. (1998). Transgender HIV prevention: A qualitative needs assessment. *AIDS Care, 10*, 505–526.

Bolding, G., Sherr, L., Maguire, M., & Elford, J. (1999). HIV risk behaviours among gay men who use anabolic steroids. *Addiction, 94*, 1829–1835.

Bridges, S. K., Selvidge, M. D., & Matthews, C. R. (2003). Lesbian women of color: Therapeutic issues and challenges. *Multicultural Counseling & Development, 31*, 113–131.

Brown, L. S. (1996). Ethical concerns with sexual minority patients. In R. P. Cabaj & T. S. Stein (Eds.), *Textbook of homosexuality and mental health* (pp. 897–916). Washington, DC: American Psychiatric Press.

Cabaj, R. J. (1997). Gays, lesbians, & bisexuals. In J. H. Lowinson, P. Ruiz, R. B. Millman, & J. G. Langrod (Eds.), *Substance abuse: A comprehensive textbook* (3rd ed., pp. 725–733). Baltimore: Williams & Wilkins.

Caitlin, R., & Futterman, D., (1997). *Lesbian and gay youth: Care and counseling*. Philadelphia: Hanley & Belfus.

Capuzzi, D., Gross, D., & Stauffer, M. D. (Eds.) (2010). *Introduction to groupwork* (5th ed). Boulder, CO: Love Publishing.

Carroll, L., & Gilroy, P. (2002). Transgender issues in counselor preparation. *Counselor Education and Supervision, 41*, 233–242.

Carroll, L., Gilroy, P. J., & Ryan, J. (2002). Counseling transgendered, transsexual, and gender-variant clients. *Journal of Counseling and Development, 80*, 131–140.

Cass, V. C. (1979). Homosexual identity formation: A theoretical model. *Journal of Homosexuality, 4*, 219–235.

Chaney, M. P., & Chang, C. Y. (2005). A trio of turmoil for Internet sexually addicted men who have sex with men: Boredom proneness, social connectedness, and dissociation. *Sexual Addiction and Compulsivity, 12*, 3–18.

Chernin, J. N., & Johnson, M. R. (2002). *Affirmative psychotherapy and counseling for lesbians and gay men.* Thousand Oaks, CA: Sage.

Chung, Y. B. (2002). *Theory and research on Asian American sexual minorities.* Paper presented at the American Psychological Association Annual Convention, Chicago.

Counselors for Social Justice (2004). *Advocacy competencies.* Retrieved November 5, 2005, from *http://www .counselorsforsocialjustice.org/advocacycompetencies.html*

Cox, S., & Gallois, C. (1996). Gay and lesbian development: A social identity perspective. *Journal of Homosexuality, 30*, 1–30.

Drabble, L., Midanik, L., Trocki, K. (2005). Reports of alcohol consumption and alcohol-related problems among homosexual, bisexual, and heterosexual respondents: Results from the 2000 National Alcohol Survey. *Journal of Studies on Alcohol, 66*(1), 111–120.

Fassinger, R. E. (1991). The hidden minority: Issues and challenges in working with lesbian women and gay men. *The Counseling Psychologist, 19*, 157–176.

Feldstein S., & Miller W. (2006). Substance use and risk-taking among adolescents. *Journal of Mental Health, 15*, 633–643.

Finnegan, D. G., & McNally, E. B. (1987). *Dual identities: Counseling chemically dependent gay men and lesbians.* Center City, MN: Hazelden.

Friedman, R. C., & Downey, J. I. (1994). Homosexuality. *The New England Journal of Medicine, 331*, 923–930.

Hogue, A., Dauber, S., Samuolis, J., & Liddle, H. (2006). Treatment Techniques and Outcomes in Multidimensional Family Therapy for Adolescent Behavior Problems. *Journal of Family Psychology, 20*, 535–543.

Holmes, K. A., & Hodge, R. H. (1997). Gay and lesbian people. In J. Philleo & F. L. Brisbane (Eds.), *Cultural competence in substance abuse prevention* (pp. 153–176). Washington, DC: National Association of Social Workers.

Horowitz, J. L., & Newcomb, M. D. (1999). Bisexuality, not homosexuality: Counseling issues and treatment approaches. *Journal of College Counseling, 2*, 148–164.

Hughes, T. L., & Wilsnack, S. C. (1997). Use of alcohol among lesbians: Research and clinical implications. *American Journal of Orthopsychiatry, 67*, 20–36.

Jaffe, C., Clance, P. R., Nichols, M., & Emshoff, J. (2000). The prevalence of alcoholism and feelings of alienation in homosexual and heterosexual women. *Journal of Gay and Lesbian Psychotherapy, 3/4*, 25–35.

Kinney, J. (2003). *Loosening the grip.* Boston: McGraw-Hill.

Kus, R. J., & Latcovich, M. A. (1994). Special interest groups in Alcoholics Anonymous: A focus on gay men's groups. *Journal of Gay and Lesbian Social Services, 2*, 67–82.

Lambda Legal. (2008). *Bending the mold: An action kit for transgender youth.* Retrieved February 7, 2010, from *http://www.lambdalegal.org*

Lev, A. (2007). Transgender communities: Developing identity through connection. In K. Bieschke, R. Perez, & K. DeBord (Eds.), *Handbook of counseling and psychotherapy with lesbian, gay, bisexual, and transgender clients* (2nd ed., pp. 147–175). Washington, DC: American Psychological Association.

Marshal, M. P., Friedman, M. S., Stall, R., King, K. M., Miles, J., Gold, M. A., et al. (2008). Sexual orientation and adolescent substance use: A meta-analysis and methodological review. *Addiction,103*, 546–556.

Matthews, C. R., Selvidge, M. M. D., & Fisher, K. (2005). Addictions counselors' attitudes and behaviors towards gay, lesbian, and bisexual clients. *Journal of Counseling and Development, 83*, 57–65.

McKirnan, D. J., and Peterson, P. L. (1989). Alcohol and drug use among homosexual men and women: epidemiology and population characteristics. *Addictive Behaviors, 14*, 545.

McNally, E. B., & Finnegan, D. G. (1992). Lesbian recovering alcoholics: A qualitative study of identity transformation—a report on research and applications to treatment. In D. L. Weinstein (Ed.), *Lesbian and gay men: Chemical dependence and treatment issues* (pp. 93–104). New York: The Haworth Press.

Miller, G. (2005). *Learning the language of addiction counseling.* Hoboken, NJ: Wiley.

Pride Institute (2006). *The Pride Institute.* Retrieved on November 30, 2006, from *http://www.pride-institute .com*

Prochaska, J. O., & Norcross, J. C. (2002). Stages of change. In J. C. Norcross (Ed.), *Psychotherapy relationships that work: Therapist contributions and responsiveness to patients* (pp. 303–313). New York: Oxford University Press.

Ratts, M., D'Andrea, M., & Arredondo, P. (2004, July). Social justice counseling: Fifth force in counseling. *Counseling Today*, 28–30.

Saghir, M. T., Robins, E., Walbran, B., & Gentry, K. A. (1970). Psychiatric disorders and disability in the female homosexual. *American Journal of Psychiatry*, 127, 147–154.

Singh, A. A., Boyd, C. J., & Whitman, J. S. (in press). Counseling competency with transgender and intersex individuals. In J. Cornish, L. Nadkarni, B. Schreier, & E. Rodolfa (Eds.), *Handbook of multicultural competencies* (pp. 415–442). New York, NY: Wiley & Sons.

Singh, A. A., Chung, Y. B., & Dean, J. K. (2006). Acculturation and internalized homoprejudice of Asian American lesbian and bisexual women. *The Journal of LGBT Issues in Counseling, 1,* 3–20.

Singh, A. A., Hays, D. G., & Watson, L. (2010). The resilience experiences of transgender individuals. *Journal of Counseling and Development.*

Skinner, W. F., & Otis, M. D. (1992). *Drug and alcohol use in the lesbian and gay community: Findings of the Trilogy Project.* Paper presented at The Lesbian and Gay Alcohol and Other Drug Research Symposium for the California State Department of Alcohol and Drug Programs, Los Angeles.

Substance Abuse and Mental Health Services Administration (SAMHSA). (2003). *A provider's introduction to substance abuse treatment for lesbian, gay, bisexual, and transgender individuals* (DHHS Publication No. SMA 03-3819). Rockville, MD: Author.

Szymanski, D. M., Kashubeck-West, S., & Meyer, J. (2008). Internalized heterosexim: A historical and theoretical overview. *The Counseling Psychologist, 36*(4), 510–524.

Trocki, K. F., Drabble, L., & Midanik, L. (2005). Use of heavier drinking contexts among heterosexuals, homosexuals and bisexuals: Results from a national household probability survey. *Journal of Studies on Alcohol, 66,* 105–110.

Troiden, R. R. (1998). *Gay and lesbian identity: A sociological analysis.* New York: General Hall.

Trujillo, C. M. (1997). Sexual identity and the discontents of difference. In B. Greene (Ed.), *Ethnic and cultural diversity among lesbians and gay men* (pp. 266–278). Newbury Park, CA: Sage.

Ungvarski, P. J., & Grossman, A. H. (1999). *Health problems of gay and bisexual men. Nursing Clinics of North America, 34,* 313–326.

van Wormer, K. (1995). *Alcoholism treatment: A social work perspective.* Chicago: Nelson-Hall.

Weinburg, M. S., & Williams, C. J. (1974). *Male homosexuals: Their problems and adaptations.* New York: Oxford University Press.

INDEX